WORDSWORTH CLASSICS
OF WORLD LITERATURE

General Editor: Tom Griffith

THE GREAT COMEDIES AND TRAGEDIES

William Shakespeare

The Great Comedies and Tragedies

A Midsummer Night's Dream
Much Ado About Nothing
As You Like It, Twelfth Night

Romeo and Juliet, Hamlet, Othello,
King Lear, Macbeth

With Introductions by Judith Buchanan
and Emma Smith

WORDSWORTH CLASSICS
OF WORLD LITERATURE

For my husband
ANTHONY JOHN RANSON
with love from your wife, the publisher
Eternally grateful for your
unconditional love

Readers who are interested in other titles from Wordsworth Editions are invited to visit our website at www.wordsworth-editions.com

First published 2005 by Wordsworth Editions Limited
8B East Street, Ware, Hertfordshire SG12 9HJ

ISBN 978 1 84022 145 9

Wordsworth Editions is
the company founded in 1987 by
MICHAEL TRAYLER

Typeset in Great Britain by Antony Gray
Printed and bound by Clays Ltd, St Ives plc

CONTENTS

NOTE ON THE TEXT

None of Shakespeare's plays exists in an original manuscript. Ever since the earliest sixteenth- and seventeenth-century editions, therefore, the plays have been shaped, in small but significant ways, by publication. There is no 'original' – except a printed one – to revert to. Different editors see their role in different ways, but most modern editions try to balance authenticity with accessibility. Thus, most modern editions, like this one, have modernised spelling and punctuation, *dramatis personae*, and additional stage directions. Where two early texts of a play exist, the editor must adjudicate between their competing claims in order to draw up his or her own text.

This edition is derived from the New Shakespeare series produced under the general editorship of Sir Arthur Quiller-Couch and John Dover Wilson. In it the following typographical conventions have been adopted to indicate editorial intervention:

Original stage directions are indicated between two single quotation marks; all other stage directions are editorial.

Where two differing versions of the play exist, passages which are not found in both are enclosed in square brackets.

Readers who would like to find out more about the early texts of Shakespeare's plays and the issues involved in editing are referred to Stanley Wells and Gary Taylor, *William Shakespeare: A Textual Companion* (Oxford, 1987).

INTRODUCTION TO THE FOUR COMEDIES

The Name of the Rose, a novel by Umberto Eco and now also a film starring Sean Connery, is based upon the speculation that Aristotle wrote a second book of the *Poetics*, 'the book everyone . . . believed lost or never written'. Aristotle's first book of *Poetics* famously dealt with tragedy. Eco's fictional hypothesis about a lost sequel to this work, in line with scholarly debate on the subject, is that it would have considered comedy and the causes of laughter. Eco speculates that in this later book Aristotle would have revoked his disparaging asides about the debasing effects of comedy, and offered instead a more fully expounded vision of comedy that was life-affirming, showing how laughter may be both instructive and regenerative. But in *The Name of the Rose* the only copy of the hypothetical work is destroyed by a fire started by an elderly monk who believes laughter is a corrupting influence, and who fears the subversive effects of such a treatise. The world of Eco's story is thus left, as indeed our own has been, with no Aristotelian blue-print for what comedy is, or what social and psychological functions it fulfils.

In the absence of a developed Aristotelian pattern, Renaissance theorists produced their own. In particular, defences were offered to the specific charges thrown at comedy that it was an immoral influence on individuals and a destabilising influence on society; that it fostered a derisive cruelty and a social subversiveness. As comic theorists parried the blows struck by the moralists, definitions became skewed by the need to identify the form as actively fulfilling some social good. The point of greatest consistency across Renaissance defences of comedy, therefore, was an insistence upon its function as morally corrective of the ills of society. Sir Philip Sidney in his *Defence of Poetry* (*c.*1580), Ben Jonson in the prologue to *Every Man in His Humour* (1598), and Thomas Heywood in *An Apology for Actors* (1612), all made comedy's capacity to act as a model for instruction the bedrock of their argument: comedy, it was claimed, was improving. Sidney's argument is representative:

> Comedy is an imitation of the common errors of our life, which he [the comic writer] representeth in the most ridiculous and scornful sort that may be, so as it is impossible that any beholder can be content to be such a one . . . So . . . the right use of comedy will (I think) by nobody be blamed.

There were occasional forays into acknowledging some other role for comedy. Thomas Heywood, for example, allowed himself momentarily to outline a more frivolous function. The morally corrective lessons of comedy, he wrote, may be:

> mingled with sportful accidents . . . to refresh such weary spirits as are tired with labour or study, to moderate the cares and heaviness of the mind, that they may return to their trades and faculties with more zeal and earnestness, after some small soft and pleasant retirement.

In similar vein, Sidney suggested that a 'delightful laughter' might be possible which did not spring simply from mean-mindedness. Asserting the value of pleasant distraction in this way was not, however, the norm.

Renaissance defences of comedy sound nervous. They spring from the belief that comedy – a theatrical form either so frivolous as to be unworthy of serious critical attention, or so anarchic as to be worthy of the severest sort of moral censure – is the poor and disreputable relation of tragedy. It is to counter this cultural attitude that Renaissance defences of comedy are so over-insistent about its moral worth, and hence so misleading in their descriptions of what comic drama in reality is and does.

In the Induction to Shakespeare's comedy *The Taming of the Shrew*, a messenger is sent to inform Christopher Sly that the players are ready to perform 'a pleasant comedy'. He interrogates the messenger about the nature of the play: 'A Christmas gambol or a tumbling trick?' His suspicion is that comedies are either the frolics on offer during seasonal festivals ('A Christmas gambol') or a spectacle in clowning ('a tumbling trick'). The page gravely contradicts him. The promised play, he intimates, is neither of these things but rather something more weighty: 'a kind of history', a story with a design. Their bandying of definitions provides a useful starting point for a consideration of Shakespeare's comedies.

Christopher Sly's first guess, 'A Christmas gambol', highlights one significant facet of Shakespeare's comedies: their close association with the conventions of Elizabethan holiday festivals. When in *As You Like It* Rosalind says: 'Come, woo me, woo me; for now I am in a holiday humour and like enough to consent' (4.1.61–2), the implication is that being 'in a holiday humour' makes possible things that would not be so throughout the rest of the year. She may be inclined to consent to being wooed when 'in a holiday humour' although she might not have done when in her 'working-day world' (1.3.12). Shakespeare's festive comedies catch their characters in a moment of holiday humour, or they generate the circumstances to put them in one. Holiday festivals in Shakespeare create a sense of possibility and release. Such a sense is the driving force of all four of the comedies in this collection and springs directly from the high spirits of 'a holiday humour'. Typically, the plots of these plays offer a temporary escape from the usual run of life. Things which might not have been possible before suddenly become so in the new-found liberty of a festive moment.

The titles of the first and last plays in this volume – *A Midsummer Night's Dream* and *Twelfth Night* – are specifically derived from Elizabethan holiday festivals, and the celebration of both these festivals involved, to different degrees and with differing festive expressions, the joyous overturning of the norms of behaviour that usually regulated life. The holiday moment was known to be temporary, and with that limitation, it was accepted that liberties would be taken, hierarchies challenged, the usual ordering systems abandoned, and a taste for revelry indulged. All this was licensed on the understanding that life would be returned to its sober, ordered self the following day. Shakespeare's comedies trade upon this sense of a 'holiday humour' in order to explore what happens to characters when they are removed from their usual context, or released by some other means from the restrictions that normally govern their social interactions.

Thus the Athenian lovers in *A Midsummer Night's Dream* find themselves running around in a wood at night away from parents, home and the law of Athens. In *As You Like It* Rosalind disguises herself as a boy, Celia as a peasant girl, and the two friends go into temporary exile in the forest of Arden; here they enjoy their new identities in the freedom and unfamiliarity of a new context. In *Twelfth Night* Viola finds herself shipwrecked in an unknown land, disguises herself as a boy and tries out her new identity upon the inhabitants of the new land. Even in *Much Ado About Nothing*, in which no characters go away and some characters actually come home, there is nevertheless a sense that life has been jostled out of its ordinary routine into a moment of heightened festivity by the safe return of the men from the wars. Characters in Shakespeare's comedies therefore find themselves in a world that is less contained and regulated than the working-day world to which they are accustomed. In the liberty of the new context a playful inventiveness may be indulged, and discoveries made about how the world may be renewed.

The festive moment, the 'getting-away-from-it-all' experience, provides the opportunity for characters to experiment with alternative social forms from those which structure the rest of life. For example, the absolute nature of divisions of class, gender and sexuality may be challenged in the fluidity of the new context, and off-beat relationships may be formed with carefree abandon. Women may become men, men may consciously or otherwise woo men, women may woo women, a shepherdess may fall for a noble woman, a fairy queen sleep with an ass, a gentlewoman marry a knight, a beggar be convinced that he is a lord. These plays create the space in which such subversive attitudes to social organisation may be entertained. Their willingness to flirt with the notion that people and structures may be coaxed out of rigid positions into riskier ways of relating might quite reasonably be seen as threatening to any who had an interest in protecting the tight social hierarchies of the *status quo*. The moralist critics of comic form in the Renaissance, therefore, had a point: comedy *can* challenge the stability of things by suggesting that people may cross socially imposed boundaries. Its view of the world as adaptable and protean may even be frightening to those who wish to ensure that it remain anchored in a safely traditional place.

A fluid view of character may, however, be read more positively:

not as a threat, but as an expression of optimism about the world. In tragedy characters tend to be identifiable by consistent character traits and patterns of mind. Through the course of the action they are seen to live out something fundamental about themselves, and their refusal, or inability, to adjust leads them inexorably towards catastrophe. This is an uncompromising and brittle view of character. Comedy's more cheerful and pragmatic view, by contrast – that people can change, be transformed – means that a resolution to problems may be found. Potential catastrophes may be brought back from the brink. Whatever scrapes the world may get itself into, the optimistic implication of the comedies is that it will ultimately always be redeemable.

The page's assertion in *The Taming of the Shrew* that the 'pleasant comedy' to be played for Christopher Sly is to be 'a kind of history' intimates that it will be the unfolding of a story with form and design. It is not, that is, to be merely 'a tumbling trick', a spectacle of clowning. There may be some comic buffoonery within it, but this will be contained within a larger narrative framework with shape and purpose. This is the case for all of Shakespeare's comedies, and the particular narrative shape follows a similar general pattern across the comedies. Each plot emerges from a problem situation. In the course of each play, the opening problem is then intensified and complicated to a point of maximum confusion and potential upset. The liberation of being away from home, or in a moment set apart from the humdrum mainstream of life, then enables the component elements of the initial problem to come to rest in a different, and less problematic, configuration. In the closing stages of the play, the chaos is resolved, however improbably, into a general good-will, and a peaceful return to normal life is made possible. Typically, this resolution is defined and sealed by a spate of marriages, while any 'left-over' characters either offer benedictions upon the marriages, or comment ironically on proceedings, or are socially marginalised. The movement is therefore through chaos and pain, often via some process of displacement, to a point of marital union and the re-establishment of normal social conventions.

The most crucially defining feature of a comedy is its ending. The phrase 'comic ending' does not mean that it need be funny, but rather that the drama's problems and tensions are brought to a point of harmonious resolution in it. This may be achieved by the most improbable of circumstances and, in Shakespeare's comedies, it often is. The harmonious ending is part of the comic formula. It need not be realistic. In fact, there is often something ludicrously neat about the resolution achieved – far too neat to have much in common with real life. The comedies themselves are sometimes delightfully aware, even at the height of their confusion, of their ultimate comic narrative destination. In Act III of *A Midsummer Night's Dream*, for example, Puck offers a blithe prophecy about how all the muddles will end:

> Jack shall have Jill,
> Nought shall go ill;
> . . . and all shall be well. (3.2.461–63)

His lack of concern for which particular Jack shall have which particular Jill acknowledges that the drama is adhering to a formula, that the neat pattern of the ending is ultimately more important than anything specific about characters:

> Yet but three? Come one more;
> Two of both kinds makes up four. (3.2.437–38)

At the end of *As You Like It* Hymen feels a similar responsibility to count the lovers:

> Peace ho! I bar confusion.
> 'Tis I must make conclusion
> Of these most strange events.
> Here's eight that must take hands
> To join in Hymen's bands . . . (5.4.116–120)

Where the nature of characters is important in the tragedies, in the comedies it is the overall narrative pattern they make that matters most. The neat choreography of a comic ending determines that as many 'Jacks' as are available marry as many 'Jills' as can be found.

This standard process of pairing off at the end of the comedies represents in part a formulaic abdication from the more daring or experimental issues explored earlier in each play. After a joyous flirtation with alternative forms of social interaction in the course of the play, a ringing endorsement of conservative structures is then offered in its closing moments. Yet even in the midst of this adherence to the comic convention, moments of self-parody may be found. In *As You Like It*, for example, the central characters are beset by a host of problems that need to be cleared away in order to make room for a comic ending. Some of these problems are solved organically by the unfolding action. Others, however, seem destined to haunt the ending with points of unresolved tension. These outstanding problems, however, are then dramatically solved by a sudden and extravagant explanation for which we are totally unprepared. Even in the context of a comedy, it seems excessive. In the final stages of the drama the wicked Duke Frederick is bearing down upon the central characters with an army in order to exact vengeance. Jaques de Boys narrates the story in all its delightful improbability:

> And to the skirts of this wild wood he came,
> Where, meeting with an old religious man,
> After some question with him, was converted
> Both from his enterprise and from the world,
> His crown bequeathing to his banish'd brother,
> And all their lands restor'd to them again
> That were with him exil'd. (5.4.150–56)

No reason or excuse is offered in order to make this sudden conversion seem more probable. It arrives out of the blue and has no pretensions to psychological credibility. Its only logic is that it is a structural necessity to make possible the happy ending. It is offered as a self-conscious joke about the ludicrous neatness required for a comic ending. Shakespeare therefore provides the requisite tidy comic resolution while at the same time poking fun at the necessarily plastic nature of the resolution achieved. As the end of *As You Like It* powerfully illustrates, comic form is about finding a narrative patterning that may characterise a hearty optimism about life.

However, the four plays collected here do not all take an identical attitude to the comic resolution. Written between 1595 and 1602, and reproduced here in order of composition, they usefully demonstrate an evolution in Shakespeare's comic form. Most particularly, the development from *A Midsummer Night's Dream* to *Twelfth Night* testifies to an increasingly problematic view of comic endings. As Shakespeare was moving into his main tragic writing phase (1601–6), he seems to have become less convinced that any drama may be brought to a fully harmonious resolution. In this period he became increasingly interested in the elements in his dramas that militate *against* harmony. The more mature comedies do not, therefore, reach a point of absolute closure in the way the earlier ones did. The comic pattern is not as neat as it once was. In the later comedies, not every 'Jack' finds a compliant 'Jill', nor does every threatening Duke undergo a dramatic, eleventh hour conversion. *Twelfth Night*, the last play in this collection, marks a watershed in Shakespeare's comic writing: it exposes the fracture lines appearing in his vision of what comedy is and what it can do. It is an appreciably darker play than its predecessors and does not allow itself the consolation of banishing all problems in the encompassing warmth of a romantic haze. Instead, some key characters are painfully excluded from the final resolution and are left understandably embittered by the experience of watching others fall happily into couples.

In general, however, Shakespeare's comedies follow more the patterns of fantasy or wish-fulfilment than the uneven, and not entirely satisfying, patterns of real life. Typically, they present a world in which virtue is finally rewarded, wickedness either punished or converted, and love gloriously requited. With a few exceptions, they present a moral universal. Characters are taken where an audience's unconscious wish might want them taken. Whereas in *Romeo and Juliet* we might secretly will Juliet to wake up in time in order to avert catastrophe, or in *Othello* we might feel frustrated that Desdemona is unable to launch a more convincing defence and so save herself, in the comedies a characteristic response to the formulaic happy ending is a satisfied sigh. It is a sigh, however, made by a slightly distanced observing audience, not by one caught up crucially in an act of identification with any one of the protagonists. We are very rarely expected to feel *with* a character in the comedies. Laughter frequently operates as an alienating device, and more often than not we are able to enjoy the follies and the misunderstandings from a position of superior information. In this way we are spared the potential trauma of identification. Characters within the comedies themselves undergo traumas, but we are mostly held aloof from them. Our concentration, like Puck's, is more on the narrative pattern of events than on the mini-fates of individuals within it.

And then, just when we feel secure in our distance, and in our ability to laugh *at* the characters rather than feel *with* them, these plays have a tendency to pull the rug from under our feet and challenge the security of our distanced position. In *A Midsummer Night's Dream*, Puck attempts to persuade us that it is a very small leap from being 'an auditor' to being 'an actor' (3.1.70–71). We are manœuvred in stages into acknowledging our own agency, our own unwitting involvement in events. Puck concludes his argument with a flourish when, in the Epilogue, he persuades us that the whole action has emerged from *our* dream life, that whatever is capable of offending in it is the product of *our* fantasy world. In *As You Like It*, Rosalind is equally aware that the line between observation and participation may be a thin one. When asked if she would like to *see* a pageant, she replies, 'I'll prove a busy actor in their play' (3.4.55). The title of *As You Like It*, which denies us the luxury of believing ourselves unconnected with the action, perhaps suggests that we might even unconsciously be a 'busy actor' in hers: the play, that is, may be unfolding as *we* like it. In *Twelfth Night* we are made to feel keenly our responsibility in the gulling of Malvolio. The crucial role of an appreciative audience in the life of a joke is made explicit early in the play:

> unless you laugh and minister occasion to him, he is gagged.
> (1.5.80–81)

The joke played upon Malvolio becomes increasingly sadistic. Having found it funny in its early, tame stages, it is we, the audience, who have been 'laugh[ing] and minister[ing] occasion' to this particular joke, and so inadvertently driving it to the extremes that then make us feel uncomfortable. Shakespeare thus toys with audience sympathy, pulling us into a complicity with the mischief-makers in order then to make us feel guilty at the way our sympathy has tended. One of the features of Shakespeare's comedies, therefore, is the complex play of alienation and disconcerting involvement that they typically encourage in their audience. In amongst the delight afforded by seeing these plays in performance, an audience can also intermittently be disorientated as its spectating position is pulled around by the sophisticated wiles of the play.

The four Shakespeare comedies in this volume incorporate

elements of all three definitions offered by Christopher Sly and the page: 'a Christmas gambol' (a festive piece of holiday entertainment), 'a tumbling trick' (a spectacle in clowning) and a 'kind of history' (a shaped and meaningful narrative). The plays are irreducibly individual in character and frustrate efforts to produce any one definition that might apply equally to them all. Nevertheless, some general characteristics apply. They are all, for example, playfully self-conscious about their own theatricality and wise to their manipulations of audience involvement. The comedies, more, perhaps, than any other generic group of Shakespeare plays, pay repeated and conscious tribute to the role of an audience in imaginatively colluding to bring the theatrical event to life.

The collective triumph of these plays lies in mingling delightfully humorous stage business and dexterous word-play with a more serious consideration of issues of identity, gender, dreaming, the meaning of love and of the theatre itself. Phrases from them have infiltrated our language and culture ('All the world's a stage', 'The course of true love never did run smooth', 'Lord, what fools these mortals be!', 'If music be the food of love, play on', 'O mistress mine, where are you roaming?', 'I will be horribly in love with her', 'I was adored once too') and several of their characters – Bottom, Dogberry, Jaques, Malvolio, Sir Toby Belch – have passed into our communal affection. A small percentage of the humour is dependent on knowing something of the time in which they were written. Much of it, however, is timeless, dependent only on an awareness of the persistent idiosyncracies and cycles of human folly, aspiration and desire.

Judith Buchanan
Worcester College, Oxford

A MIDSUMMER NIGHT'S DREAM

INTRODUCTION

When Bottom the Weaver awakes in Act 4 of *A Midsummer Night's Dream*, he is awed and bemused at the half-recollection of the dream he has had:

> I have had a most rare vision. I have had a dream – past the wit of man to say what dream it was. Man is but an ass, if he go about to expound this dream. (4.1.203–6)

Bottom thinks that he would sound silly if he tried to explain his dream. Despite his fear of sounding like an ass, however, he then *does* make efforts to describe it. He has a compelling sense of the importance of what he has experienced. He cannot, however, tease that feeling into words: his stumbling efforts to do so are comically inadequate. His instinct to fight shy of expounding is thus proved sound: it is easy to slip into idiotic commentary in attempting to make sense of a dream that, by definition, defies the logic of the waking world.

As the play's Epilogue suggests, *A Midsummer Night's Dream* itself, like Bottom's 'most rare vision' within it, has a dream-like quality that resists rational analysis. Like Bottom's experience of *his* dream, the experience of watching or reading the play leaves one both with a sense of having been exposed to something profound and with a sense of frustration as one recognises the tantalisingly elusive character of that something. Those intending 'to expound this dream' should therefore be alert to Bottom's warning. Nevertheless, significantly more may be ventured by way of analysis of the play than Bottom is prepared to risk in relation to his private dream.

History

Written *c.*1595, *A Midsummer Night's Dream* lacks a single literary source. Instead it draws loosely upon a wide range of earlier poems and plays, both classical and English, including works by Ovid, Apuleius, Seneca, Plutarch, Chaucer, Lyly and Spenser. These partial literary debts are woven together with a few subtly encoded topical references and a healthy dose of fantasy to produce a play genuinely from Shakespeare's own imagination. Although there is no conclusive proof, there is a certain amount of evidence within the play itself to suggest that it was first performed as part of a noble couple's wedding celebration. The entire movement of the play is given direction by the preparations for Duke Theseus' marriage to Hippolyta, and the fairies' formal marriage blessings at the end are succeeded by an entirely gratuitous blessing upon the owner of 'this palace'. The play may well have been first performed in a private house, whose owner is therefore being formally recompensed for his hospitality by a brief tribute in the closing moments of the play.

The occasion which is most likely to have been its inspiration was Elizabeth Carey's marriage to Thomas, son of Henry Lord Berkeley, on 19 February 1596 at the Carey family mansion, property of Sir George Carey, in Blackfriars. Queen Elizabeth I herself may well have been present at these celebrations and so could have been in the audience for the first performance of the play, to receive in person the tributes paid to her in it. This performance context is even parodied within the play itself: some honest workmen earnestly desire to produce a play, as part of a marriage celebration, that will please their ruler and be performed in his presence. Thus the play-within-the-play represents a comically exaggerated burlesque of the project of *A Midsummer Night's Dream* as a whole. Queen Elizabeth I made a public and political virtue of her virginity, and in Elizabethan England an artistic trend evolved in which the virgin queen was respectfully represented in various allegorical ways. Because the Roman goddess Diana was goddess of both chastity and the moon, these two things came to be associated with each other. Thus it was that the cult of Elizabeth often courteously chose to represent her as a lunar presence, casting her chaste and benevolent beams upon the world. The prevalence of references to the moon and moonshine in the play may be read as part of this culture in which the influence of the chaste monarch is universally felt. Oberon's description of a 'fair vestal' and, more particularly, an 'imperial votaress' (2.1.158,163), entirely superfluous to the plot, are also among the play's passing tributes to Elizabeth. The play, however, opens on a more problematic note in relation to the moon. Theseus is complaining about the amount of time that must elapse before he may marry Hippolyta, and he does so by reference to the cycles of the moon:

> . . . but O, methinks, how slow
> This old moon wanes! She lingers my desires . . . (1.1.3–4)

Performed in the mid-1590s, quite possibly in the presence of a chaste and elderly queen who was often represented by lunar imagery and who showed little sign of dying, this complaint against the 'old moon' for refusing to wane is, perhaps, an opening of no little daring.

If A *Midsummer Night's Dream* started life as part of a private festivity, as seems probable, it would have been transferred to the public playhouses soon afterwards. There is no record of it in the Stationer's Register as a publicly performed play until 7 September 1598, but it was almost certainly performed on the public stage considerably earlier than that.

Plot summary

Set in ancient Athens, the play refers to Greek mythology for some of its characters and action. We discover at its opening that Duke Theseus has first forcibly subdued, and then wooed, the Amazon Hippolyta, whom he is now preparing to marry. Egeus bursts in upon these preparations with a serious matter for Theseus' consideration. Hermia, Egeus' daughter, will not consent to marry Demetrius, her father's choice of husband for her, and instead stubbornly asserts her love for Lysander. Theseus pronounces judgment by invoking the ancient law of Athens. The disobedient daughter in such a case has three options: she must either consent to her father's wishes, or live out the rest of her life as a virgin in a closed convent, or be put to death. In response to this ultimatum, Lysander and Hermia resolve to flee together that night through the wood to Lysander's aunt, some seven leagues away, where they may then safely be married. This plan they confide to Helena, Hermia's long-time friend. Helena is herself desperately in love with Demetrius and perversely decides that she may find some favour with him by telling him that the woman he loves, Hermia, will be fleeing the town under cover of darkness. Demetrius resolves to follow Hermia, and in turn Helena resolves to follow Demetrius. Meanwhile Theseus has commissioned the people of Athens to prepare entertainments for his forthcoming wedding celebrations. In response to this commission, some simple-minded working men, later referred to as 'rude mechanicals', are rehearsing a version of 'Pyramus and Thisbe' under the direction of Peter Quince, in the hope of being chosen to perform for the royal nuptials. Bottom the Weaver, a particular enthusiast for the play, is cast in the role of Pyramus. These mechanicals arrange to reconvene later in the wood outside the town, where they will be able to rehearse in greater privacy.

The play's action then removes to the less civilised, and less regulated, environment of the same wood near Athens which, we discover, is inhabited by fairies and ruled over by Oberon, the Fairy King. Here, three different plot threads are pursued – the mechanicals' play rehearsals, the amorous tangles of the fleeing (and chasing) lovers, and the events in fairy world. It quickly transpires that the fairy world is in turmoil. Their Queen, Titania, is in fierce dispute with her lover, Oberon. Tremors are being felt in the natural world as a result. Out of spite towards Titania, Oberon instructs a mischievous spirit, Puck, to go in search of a 'little Western flower', the juice of which, when administered to a sleeper's eyes, magically makes that sleeper fall in love with whatever s/he sees first upon awakening. Puck fetches the flower and Oberon drops the juice into the eyes of the sleeping Titania.

Meanwhile, for his own amusement, Puck disrupts the mechanicals' play rehearsal by magically converting Bottom's head into the head of an ass. To Puck's intense satisfaction, the rest of the acting troupe all flee in terror at the sight of their friend thus transformed. As it happens, it is Bottom's ass's head that Titania then sees first upon awakening. She duly falls in love with the hybrid monster, offering him fairy hospitality that is both gracious and amorously demanding. The Fairy Queen and the man-turned-ass fall asleep in each other's arms. Partly mistaking Oberon's instructions, Puck drops the same magical juice into the eyes of first Lysander and then Demetrius, each of whom sees Helena upon awakening. As a consequence, each forswears his previous love for Hermia and vehemently asserts his undying love for Helena. Helena herself is convinced that the men are cruelly mocking her by their sudden and excessive declarations of love, and that Hermia must be complicit in this mockery. Hermia, by contrast, becomes convinced that Lysander's sudden and inexplicable rejection of her is part of some dreadful scheme of Helena's making. The four become embroiled in hot dispute, but through Puck's intervention lose each other in a frantic chase through the wood before any real harm can be done. Exhausted, each of the four lovers then falls asleep and Puck drops the magical antidote into Lysander's eyes so that his former affection for Hermia will be restored to him when he awakes.

Meanwhile Oberon has similarly undone the effects of the juice on Titania, with whom he is then immediately reconciled, and Puck has returned the still sleeping Bottom to his human form. Theseus and Hippolyta, out on a dawn hunt, are surprised to discover the sleeping bodies of the four lovers in the wood. The sound of the hunting horn awakens the young people who, in some bemusement, try to account for their dream-like experiences of the night just passed. Theseus, seeing that they have now resolved themselves into two happy couples, overrules Egeus' wishes, and decrees instead that they shall all four be married as part of the same ceremony which will solemnise his own union with Hippolyta. Bottom awakes to find himself alone but with an odd memory of an extraordinary dream. He decides he shall ask Peter Quince to compose a ballad about this momentous dream and that it shall be called Bottom's Dream 'because it hath no bottom'.

The action shifts back to Athens where Theseus chooses 'Pyramus and Thisbe' as the entertainment for the collective nuptial celebrations. It is performed with charming ineptitude in front of the royal party, and the performance is punctuated throughout by ludicrous reassurances from the actors that their play is not real and by sarcastic comments from the floor. The newly wedded lovers go to bed and the fairies appear in the Duke's palace to bestow blessings upon the three marriages. Puck delivers the epilogue in which he reasserts the dream quality of the whole performance.

The wood near Athens

A temporary displacement from a familiar urban setting to an unfamiliar rural one is the structuring principle of several Shakespeare comedies. The intensity of a problem encountered in the town provides the momentum for a hasty removal to the country. In the apparent freedom of this new setting, the conventions and constraints that governed the old life naturally fall away. This liberation provides the space and opportunity for the component elements of the initial problem to be cast into the air and so to come to rest in a different, and less problematic, configuration. A peaceful return to the town is thus made possible. Through the temporary disruption of being away from home, therefore, characters gain not only a refreshed vision but, crucially, a material improvement in their circumstances. By the end of each play, the town has ceased to function as the oppressive citadel from which one must escape, and has been reconfigured as the centre of civilised courtesy and familial belonging to which one may gladly return.

This pattern of escape from a (problem-ridden) urban to a (problem-solving) rural environment implies a starkly value-laden contrast between the two settings. It is easy to imagine the urban setting as a place of overbearing authority and cramping regulations pitted against a pastoral ideal or Arcadian retreat, a place of innocence, virtue and wholesome simplicity. Although this notion of the rural retreat is helpful in relation to that on offer in a play such as *As You Like It*, it is not at all appropriate in *A Midsummer Night's Dream*. Romantics in the nineteenth century consistently found a delicate beauty and poetic sweetness in the wood near Athens, and in the action of the play as a whole. The play was read most frequently as a celebration of the redemptive power of the imagination. Without denying the beauty and delicacy of the poetry, it is also appropriate, however, to attend to those elements in the wood, and in the play more generally, that are far from sweet and that testify not only to the redemptive power of imagination but also, on occasion, to its murky depths.

The wood in which the majority of the play's action takes place is, the text tells us, 'A wood *near* Athens' (2.1 – my italics). Its proximity to everything that is familiar to the Athenians is repeatedly emphasised. As Lysander reminds Hermia, it is but 'a league without the town' (1.1.165) and Peter Quince is similarly insistent, locating it only 'a mile without the town' (1.2.93). Lysander remembers meeting Hermia and Helena there once to do observance to a May morning, and Hermia reminds Helena of the many times they have lain out upon banks of primroses in that wood and shared confidences. Because it is both local and apparently familiar, there is no expectation that this wood should be out of the ordinary. As things turn out, however, it proves to be thoroughly disconcerting. It is its seeming familiarity that makes this enchanted wood constantly bemusing for the mortals, since it stubbornly refuses to be what they expect of it. Athens was threatening and oppressive for Hermia and Lysander, but the hostility encountered there was a known quantity. The strangenesses and hostilities encountered in the wood are both unexpected and incomprehensible. The mortals are therefore constantly disconcerted by the wood's refusal either to be the comfortable and knowable place they would like to believe it, or to be an honest and identifiable enemy. It feels as if it *should* be familiar because it is close to home, but it proves very far from homely.

The hasty escape from the barbaric and patriarchal law of Athens does not, therefore, lead *A Midsummer Night's Dream*'s characters into a soothing pastoral ideal. The lullaby with which Titania's fairy retinue sings her to sleep implicitly acknowledges that any moment of peace in the wood, even for the Fairy Queen herself, has to be earned by the active suppression of some of the opposing forces at large:

> You spotted snakes with double tongue,
> Thorny hedgehogs, be not seen;
> Newts and blind-worms, do no wrong,
> Come not near our fairy queen. (2.2.9–12)

Hermia's sleep at the end of the same scene is troubled by just such a snake as has been banished by the fairies from Titania's sleeping presence. In Hermia's dream, a 'crawling serpent' (2.2.154) appears on her breast and eats her heart away while Lysander sits smiling at this predatory act done upon his lover. Clearly there is some point to the fairies' lullaby of banishment: women sleeping in this wood *are* vulnerable to predatory snakes, real or imaginary. Seeking the comfort of the waking world,

Hermia awakes in panic from the nightmare of seeing her lover condoning the violence being done to her. However, she discovers very little comfort in the waking world. Lysander has disappeared leaving her alone in the wood, and when she finally does find him, he treats her with summary disdain. The waking world does not precisely duplicate the dreamworld with which she has to contend, but it imitates its tone. In both she feels frighteningly alone in a world of predators.

Helena too encounters a potential aggressor in the wood. Demetrius is anxious to shake her off to enable him to pursue Hermia the more easily. His contempt for her leads him at one point to threaten that if she does not return to Athens, he may 'do [her] mischief in the wood' (2.1.237). The specifically sexual nature of the threatened 'mischief' he has already made clear to her:

> You do impeach your modesty too much
> To leave the city and commit yourself
> Into the hands of one that loves you not,
> To trust the opportunity of night
> And the ill counsel of a desert place
> With the rich worth of your virginity. (2.1.214–19)

Rather than being fearful for her virginity, however, Helena has in fact already implored him to abuse her in some fashion:

> I am your spaniel; and, Demetrius,
> The more you beat me, I will fawn on you.
> Use me but as your spaniel, spurn me, strike me,
> Neglect me, lose me; only give me leave,
> Unworthy as I am, to follow you.
> What worser place can I beg in your love -
> And yet a place of high respect with me -
> Than to be used as you use your dog? (2.1.203–10)

Thus Demetrius' sexual threat, if not exactly what Helena might have wished, is arguably the logical extension of the exploitative treatment she has explicitly sought. Helena, accustomed to habitual neglect, seems to have developed a fantasy life that has taken a disturbing, and specifically masochistic, turn. The less controlled environment of the wood removes the constraints that have prevented these otherwise civilised Athenians from revealing their more primitive and instinctive selves. In the frightening absence of civilised checks and balances, both Helena and Demetrius find themselves exposing their basest impulses. He, it seems, would rape her as an act of contempt. She, it seems, would almost have him do so.

Titania's fantasies also become disturbing – she lusts after an ass – but in her case this happens directly through Oberon's magical intervention. Once in possession of the magical flower, he exults in the destructive power he wields over her:

> And with the juice of this I'll streak her eyes,
> And make her full of hateful fantasies. (2.1.257–58)

His particular choice of the word 'streak', rather than some more innocuous verb (dab, sprinkle, anoint, wet, treat), suggests an act of violence upon the tenderness and fragility of an eyeball, as if something is to be scraped across its vulnerable surface. As a result of this physical interference, he looks forward too to warping her inner life. No fairy lullaby of banishment can, it seems, rescue Titania from Oberon's venomous influence. Like the complicitly smiling Lysander in Hermia's nightmare, Oberon will take pleasure in observing his lover become a prey to 'hateful fantasies'. When in the next act Hermia calls Demetrius 'thou serpent' (3.2.73), the implied elision between predatory, sexually intrusive serpents and predatory, sexually aggressive men finally becomes explicit.

Although most of the acts, or threatened acts, of aggression in the play are committed by men on women (Theseus' wooing of Hippolyta with his sword, Egeus' insistent call for the death of his own daughter, Oberon's desire to exact physical and psychological revenge on Titania, Demetrius' rape threat to Helena), there is one occasion when an aggressive female sexuality impresses itself insistently upon a man – or a man of sorts at least. When Bottom-turned-ass is entertained by Titania and her retinue, he initially expresses his keen desire to find his way out of the wood. The Queen of the Fairies replies:

> Out of this wood do not desire to go:
> Thou shalt remain here, whether thou wilt or no.
> (3.1.138–9)

Since he has been forbidden to leave, Bottom nobly makes small talk instead with four of Titania's fairies. Titania then imperiously instructs these same fairies about the exact nature of the hospitality their guest-prisoner is to receive:

> Come, wait upon him; lead him to my bower.
> The moon, methinks, looks with a watery eye,
> And when she weeps, weeps every little flower,
> Lamenting some enforced chastity.
> Tie up my love's tongue, bring him silently. (3.1.182–6)

Bottom is to be gagged and led to her bower, whether he will or not. Titania's momentary digression about the weeping moon and the corresponding weeping of 'every little flower' is scarcely a digression at all. It will be recalled that the moon was associated with chastity through the figure of the goddess Diana. Besides contributing to the play's tapestry of allusions to the chastity of Elizabeth I, Titania's lines also reveal her own plans in relation to Bottom. 'Enforced' has changed its meaning over time. Here it means not 'insisted upon' but rather 'forced' or 'violated'. The moon, and with her the flowers, are therefore weeping in sorrow for the forcing of someone's virginity. 'Tie up my love's tongue, bring him silently', Titania says immediately afterwards. He is led like a lamb to the slaughter. Little wonder the moon and the flowers are weeping.

There is a pervasive brutality and a violent sexuality in the play that simmers below the surface of many of its interactions. This violent potential is just about contained for much of the action, but it erupts intermittently as an indicator of the ugly depths only partially disguised by the shimmeringly poetic surfaces. Puck intimates at one point that the mechanicals are shedding their clothes in the wood:

> For briars and thorns at their apparel snatch; (3.2.29)

There is a sense in which the wood reduces all characters to the most naked and basic version of themselves. Just as literally it strips the mechanicals of their clothes, so emotionally it pares away decorum and the veneer of civilisation and exposes the raw, unrefined essence of *all* the characters caught within its spell. Their threats, desires, fantasies, fears and dreams are frequently found to be of a troubling character. The removed context of Oberon's enchanted wood therefore acts as a catalyst, bringing to the surface those darker human impulses which might well have remained more decorously suppressed in a more civilised environment. Being in a context of unchecked psychological and sexual expression, the play suggests, may bring to light some truths about humanity which are far from pretty. The wood's 'musk-rose bud' may look beautiful at a first glance, but, as its flower is opened up, it is found to be inhabited by 'cankers', destructive worms eating it from within (2.2.3). The unmasking of hidden ugliness is, it seems, integral to the processes of the wood.

The ending

Having confronted the depths of human ugliness, however, the play then negotiates a dramatic change of tone in its ending. Everything that has tended towards violence, brutality or a dark sexuality is wilfully fought down, and Puck's blithe prophecy is fulfilled:

> Jack shall have Jill,
> Nought shall go ill;
> . . . and all shall be well. (3.2.461–63)

The Athenians emerge from a dark night of exploring the confused and confusing world of their own inner selves into the literal and moral light of the morning where more wholesome truths may be, and perhaps need to be, asserted. Hermia and Lysander are restored to each other, she wisely deciding to forget her fantasy fears about him and he his aggression to her. Demetrius, still under the influence of Oberon's magical juice, now reciprocates Helena's love for him, each of them choosing not to remember the dangerous sexual edge of their conversation of the night before. Oberon abandons his campaign to brutalise and humiliate Titania, and she stares in horror at the ass with whom she has spent the night. The resulting reconciliation between the Fairy King and Queen restores the cycle of the seasons and the balance of the natural world, both of which had been disturbed by the ferocity of the earlier dissension between them. Theseus' relationship with Hippolyta is no longer to be dictated by his sword, but rather he is to wed her, as he promised, 'in another key' (1.1.18). The harmony of the end is therefore won by the active overcoming of some of the dominant forces of confusion and perversion that have held sway in the play.

In Act 1 Lysander had lamented how swiftly 'quick bright things' may 'come to confusion' (1.1.149). The end of the play reverses this process, showing the equally swift rescue of these particular 'quick bright things' from the confusion into which they had indeed speedily tumbled. The pervasive 'hateful fantasies' are diffused, transformed into a harmonious resolution through the agency of magic and, more schematically, through the exigencies of comic form. Puck's formulation that 'Jack shall have Jill' suggests that the lovers' individual identities are not crucially relevant. *They* vehemently insist upon their distinction from each other and upon the specific appeal of one over another. Puck, however, mistakes one Athenian youth for another, Helena claims that she and Hermia are 'like to a double cherry' (3.2.209), and we tend to find all four of them more generically definable than individually knowable. They are young, headstrong, humourless, hyperbolic lovers, and as such they are types far more than personalities. As Puck's lack of concern for their specific names indicates, they are more interesting for the entertaining patterns they form as affiliations between them are made, broken, exchanged, broken and remade than for anything inherent in them as individuals. Puck's hearty confidence that 'all shall be well' is finally justified, but which specific Jack has which specific Jill has been fairly arbitrarily determined simply to ensure a satisfying pattern at the end.

One of the slightly barbed jokes of the play is, therefore, to point out how highly specific lovers feel to each other and how simultaneously interchangeable they can seem to an onlooker. For a play which may well have been first performed as part of the celebrations for a real marriage, it is peculiarly cynical both about the processes of falling in love and about the nature and reliability of the bonds that then hold couples together. Puck's scathing 'Lord, what fools these mortals be!' (3.2.115) is entirely apt in the terms of the play, but might well have had a slightly odd resonance in the context of a real wedding.

The mechanicals and humour

What, ironically, might have been *more* appropriate for the festivities of a wedding celebration would have been the energetic good humour generated by the scenes that do not feature lovers directly at all – the mechanicals' scenes. Henri Bergson's theory of laughter suggests that humour is often derived from a sense of 'le méchanique plaqué sur le vivant', the automated superimposed upon the living. In other words, it is from the encounter between an entirely consistent, unchanging thing and a world of living fluctuation that comedy emerges. The world of *A Midsummer Night's Dream* is dramatically in flux. Not only do lovers fall in and out of love with each other and a fairy princess dote upon and then abhor an ass, but nature is in drastic upheaval, the seasons are in disorder, and all things are feeling the concomitant tremors. In the midst of all this, the mechanicals are a point of astonishing consistency. Surprisingly for players (who might have been expected to be more versatile in their identities), they are the most fixed characters in the play, and are most obviously themselves no matter where they are, what they are wearing or what role they are endeavouring to fulfil. Despite their fixity, they are touchingly concerned lest the quality of their performances dupe their audience into believing the presentation to be real. Their fear is that the audience will fail to discriminate between the dramatic fiction of 'Pyramus and Thisbe' on the one hand and actuality on the other, and so become convinced that the tragic and disturbing events in the play are *really* taking place. Such is their anxiety on the matter that they incorporate into their presentation over-insistent disclaimers about the reality of the event, as a means of reassuring their audience that no harm is really being done and that, for example, no real lion is about to savage them:

> Fair ladies . . . I would entreat you, not to fear, not to tremble: my life for yours! If you think I come hither as a lion, it were pity of my life. No, I am no such thing; I am a man, as other men are. (3.1.34–38)

This naive belief in the transcendent power of their own illusions is all the funnier since it is abundantly clear (most obviously, of course, in their literal embodiments of Wall and Moonshine) that their illusions are crude and *un*convincing. While firmly believing themselves to be protean, then, these artisan players are remarkably unchanging and personally uncompromised through an impressive range of encounters – with fairies, with royalty and with the possibilities of stage production.

Of all the mechanicals, Bottom is the most dramatic illustration of Bergson's notion of the comic clash between consistency and change. Even as an ass, Bottom remains gloriously himself, an entirely consistent 'mechanical' point in a world of vacillation. Confronted with a fairy, and one, moreover, 'of no common rate', Bottom is polite with his usual robust good humour, but he is not overawed. Told that she loves him, he says she can have little reason for that, but then again, he continues, reason and love do not always go together, so perhaps she does after all. Even with long hairy ears and calling for 'good dry oats' (4.1.32), he is still entirely recognisable as a good-hearted, literal-minded, enthusiastic artisan with a slight tendency to smugness about his own (pedestrian) wit: he is, that is, unchanged from the Bottom to whom we were introduced at the mechanicals' first rehearsal in Athens. In the flurry of other restorations at the end of the play, therefore, Bottom does not fundamentally need to be restored to a self he has lost – for he never lost it. In fact, it is Bottom's fate not to be able to lose himself or to transform himself into something else, even when, for dramatic purposes, he might need to. Thus, when trying to play Pyramus, he keeps breaking in as himself, Bottom the Weaver, to answer comments from the floor about how the action is proceeding. It is the combination of the mechanicals' inflexibility with their contrary conviction that they will be believed to have become everything they play, that makes them such endearing figures of fun, both for us and for their on-stage audience.

The most vigorous humour of the play, then, is provided by the mechanicals. But other areas of the action are funny as well. The murky depths and troubling undertones of the lovers' and the fairies' stories do not disable the comic humour which can, despite simmering darknesses around and beneath and within it, be genuinely hilarious. The unnerving nature of some aspects of the play may even make the relief at being able to laugh at it the greater. Discussing the comedies in over-sombre terms, as if they were tracts rather than pieces of dramatic entertainment, is a critical tendency that misrepresents what the plays are. They undeniably deal with subjects of some seriousness, but they do not do so in a sombre way: they are funny plays. There is, for example, both a poetic lightness of touch and a highly energetic comic will in *A Midsummer Night's Dream* that ensures that the seriousness, and the poignancy, of some of its material is contained within a wider framework of delight.

Offending shadows

Interpretations of *A Midsummer Night's Dream*, on both page and stage, have undergone a shift over this century. The play has moved from being a delicate ballet of tripping fairies and momentarily wayward lovers frolicking entertainingly in an Arcadian retreat to being a more tonally mixed exploration of the power of the imagination. Imagination as explored in the play is now understood to have the power not only to liberate but also to ensnare, as the brutality and perversity of its own darkest repressions surface. It may redeem, but it may also degrade. Productions have become darker. Accordingly, an understanding of the significance of the play's ending has also shifted. No longer may it be considered merely the natural outworking of the action that precedes it. Rather the comic ending has to be earned, to be won by the active suppression of those powerful forces and influences that tend away from harmony and away from comedy. In the early stages of the play Helena, musing on the processes of love, has offered an optimistic assessment of its transforming power:

> Things base and vile, holding no quantity,
> Love can transpose to form and dignity. (1.1.232–33)

In *A Midsummer Night's Dream* those emotions and impulses which are 'base and vile' *are* finally 'transpose[d] to form and dignity' in the graceful pairings of the noble lovers. It is not 'Love', however, as Helena had supposed, which effects this transposition. Love had merely enhanced the agony and the confusion. Rather it is the play's internal dramatist, the destiny-deciding figure of Oberon, who intervenes to right the situational and emotional muddles of the night. Demetrius is, necessarily, still under the influence of the magical aphrodisiac at the end of the play. That this is integral to the harmony of the ending serves to illustrate the constructed nature of the resolution achieved. The solution found is not organic, but imposed.

In the Epilogue, Puck delivers a conventional, and tongue-in-cheek, apology on behalf of the actors for any offence that may have been caused by the performance:

> If we shadows have offended,
> Think but this and all is mended,
> That you have but slumber'd here
> While these visions did appear.
> And this weak and idle theme,
> No more yielding but a dream . . . (5.1.407–12)

His courteous plea is that, if anything controversial be found in it, the play should be dismissed as a dream. This seemingly converts it into a thing of nought, something ephemeral and insubstantial. Yet it has another effect too. Redefining the play as something that has emerged from the audience's dream offloads the responsibility for it onto us, the audience, since we are asked to believe that we have conjured the details of the drama from our *own* dreamworld imaginations. If the dream has moments of nightmare about it, claims the Epilogue, it is *our* designing fantasy that is leading it into those dark realms.

Earlier, when Puck stumbled upon the rehearsals for the play-within-the-play, he had become excited at the prospective role he saw for himself:

> What a play towards? I'll be an auditor;
> An actor too perhaps, if I see cause. (3.1.70–71)

Now, in the Epilogue, Puck implicitly encourages his audience to realise that not he alone, but *all* 'auditors' are 'actor[s] too perhaps'. The implication of depicting the play as the audience's dream is that the audience is involved in making it happen, that the movement of the drama needs to be seen as following the dictates of some communal imaginative will. We are not merely 'auditors', with the luxury of remaining at a neutral, observing distance from the action, but 'actor[s] too perhaps', with an active, determining involvement in it. The audience's own agency, or active involvement, is hinted at again, and more disturbingly, in the last few lines of the Epilogue:

> Now to 'scape the serpent's tongue,
> We will make amends ere long;
> Else the Puck a liar call.
> So, goodnight unto you all.
> Give me your hands, if we be friends,
> And Robin shall restore amends. (5.1.417–22)

In seeking to 'scape the serpent's tongue' Puck is, literally, hoping that the performance will be applauded by the audience rather than hissed. The mention of a serpent cannot, however, fail to trigger other associations in the context of a play that has been crawling with serpents of one sort or another. The recurring serpent imagery thoughout the play makes this cumulative association inevitable. The snake and blind-worms in the fairies' lullaby are banished from Titania's sleeping presence lest they disrupt her peace. Lysander's persistently expressed desire to sleep with Hermia is quickly followed by a predatory and aggressive serpent invading her dreamlife and eating her heart away. The canker-worms inside the musk-rose bud are destroying its beauty from within. Hermia wonders if a worm or an adder might have killed her love while he slept, and then accuses Demetrius of being himself a serpent. The serpent is a pervasive image of threat in the play. It represents the tug downwards of the imagination, the tug away from harmony and health towards the perverse and the destructive. In the play's final moments, we the audience are then asked to refrain from using *our* 'serpent's tongue'. The play's cumulative serpent imagery thus comes to rest by casually casting its audience in the association-laden role of the serpent.

A Midsummer Night's Dream, like many Shakespeare comedies, denies its audience the space to sit back and enjoy the spectacle from a consistently detached perspective. And, like Titania's double-edged entertainment of Bottom, it makes its demands with disarming delicacy and charm. We are manœuvred into acknowledging that we are somehow implicated in the drama unfolding before us, as we discover that we are being held accountable for having ourselves dreamt it. If we see perversity and brutality in the wood, and identify it as emerging from the ugly depths of liberated imaginations, we are asked to consider whether those troubling imaginations might not in fact be our own. In the very act of expressing the hope that the play has not offended, therefore, the Epilogue is potentially, although very gracefully, the moment of greatest offence in the play. We are courteously asked to acknowledge our own capacity to be the destructive, hissing serpent of the dream, and, yet more fundamentally, to recognise that anything we find offensive in *The Dream* may have emerged from our own murky fantasy world.

Scene: Athens, and a wood hard by

CHARACTERS IN THE PLAY

THESEUS, *Duke of Athens*
HIPPOLYTA, *Queen of the Amazons, betrothed to Theseus*
EGEUS, *an old man, father to Hermia*
LYSANDER, DEMETRIUS } *young gentlemen, in love with Hermia*
PHILOSTRATE, *master of the revels to Theseus*
HERMIA *(short and dark), daughter to Egeus, in love with Lysander*
HELENA *(tall and fair), in love with Demetrius*

PETER QUINCE, *a carpenter*
NICK BOTTOM, *a weaver*
FRANCIS FLUTE, *a bellows-mender*
TOM SNOUT, *a tinker*
ROBIN STARVELING, *a tailor*
SNUG, *a joiner*

OBERON, *King of the Fairies*
TITANIA, *Queen of the Fairies*
ROBIN GOODFELLOW, THE PUCK
PEASEBLOSSOM, COBWEB, MOTH, MUSTARDSEED } *fairies*

Other fairies attending their King and Queen

Attendants on Theseus and Hippolyta

A MIDSUMMER NIGHT'S DREAM

ACT I SCENE I

The hall in the palace of Duke Theseus. On one side a small platform with two chairs of state; on the other side a hearth; at the back doors to right and left, the wall between them opening out into a lobby

THESEUS *and* HIPPOLYTA *enter and take their seats, followed by* PHILOSTRATE *and attendants*

THESEUS Now, fair Hippolyta, our nuptial hour
Draws on apace: four happy days bring in
Another moon: but O, methinks how slow
This old moon wanes! She lingers my desires,
Like to a step-dame, or a dowager,
Long withering out a young man's revenue.

HIPPOLYTA Four days will quickly steep themselves in night:
Four nights will quickly dream away the time:
And then the moon, like to a silver bow
New-bent in heaven, shall behold the night
Of our solemnities.

THESEUS Go, Philostrate,
Stir up the Athenian youth to merriments,
Awake the pert and nimble spirit of mirth,
Turn melancholy forth to funerals:
The pale companion is not for our pomp.
[*Philostrate bows and departs*
Hippolyta, I wooed thee with my sword,
And won thy love doing thee injuries:
But I will wed thee in another key,
With pomp, with triumph, and with revelling.

EGEUS *enters, haling along his daughter* HERMIA *by the arm, followed by* LYSANDER *and* DEMETRIUS

EGEUS [*bows*] Happy be Theseus, our renownéd duke

THESEUS Thanks, good Egeus. What's the news with thee?

EGEUS Full of vexation come I, with complaint
Against my child, my daughter Hermia.

Stand forth, Demetrius. My noble lord,
This man hath my consent to marry her.
Stand forth, Lysander. And, my gracious duke,
This man hath witched the bosom of my child.
Thou, thou, Lysander, thou hast given her rhymes,
And interchanged love-tokens with my child:
Thou hast by moonlight at her window sung,
With feigning voice, verses of feigning love:
And stol'n the impression of her fantasy
With bracelets of thy hair, rings, gauds, conceits,
Knacks, trifles, nosegays, sweetmeats – messengers
Of strong prevailment in unhardened youth.
With cunning hast thou filched my daughter's heart,
Turned her obedience, which is due to me,
To stubborn harshness. And, my gracious duke,
Be it so she will not here before your grace
Consent to marry with Demetrius,
I beg the ancient privilege of Athens:
As she is mine, I may dispose of her:
Which shall be either to this gentleman,
Or to her death; according to our law
Immediately provided in that case.

THESEUS What say you, Hermia? Be advised, fair maid.
To you your father should be as a god;
One that composed your beauties; yea and one
To whom you are but as a form in wax
By him imprinted, and within his power
To leave the figure or disfigure it.
Demetrius is a worthy gentleman.

HERMIA So is Lysander.

THESEUS In himself he is:
But in this kind, wanting your father's voice,
The other must be held the worthier.

HERMIA I would my father looked but with my eyes.

THESEUS Rather your eyes must with his judgment look.

HERMIA I do entreat your grace to pardon me.
I know not by what power I am made bold;
Nor how it may concern my modesty
In such a presence here to plead my thoughts:

But I beseech your grace that I may know
The worst that may befall me in this case
If I refuse to wed Demetrius.

THESEUS Either to die the death, or to abjure
For ever the society of men.
Therefore, fair Hermia, question your desires,
Know of your youth, examine well your blood,
Whether, if you yield not to your father's choice,
You can endure the livery of a nun,
For aye to be in shady cloister mewed,
To live a barren sister all your life,
Chanting faint hymns to the cold fruitless moon.
Thrice blesséd they that master so their blood,
To undergo such maiden pilgrimage:
But earthlier happy is the rose distilled,
Than that which withering on the virgin thorn
Grows, lives and dies in single blessedness.

HERMIA So will I grow, so live, so die, my lord,
Ere I will yield my virgin patent up
Unto his lordship, whose unwishéd yoke
My soul consents not to give sovereignty.

THESEUS Take time to pause, and by the next new moon –
The sealing-day betwixt my love and me
For everlasting bond of fellowship –
Upon that day either prepare to die
For disobedience to your father's will,
Or else to wed Demetrius as he would,
Or on Diana's altar to protest
For aye austerity and single life.

DEMETR. Relent, sweet Hermia – and, Lysander, yield
Thy crazéd title to my certain right.

LYSANDER You have her father's love, Demetrius;
Let me have Hermia's: do you marry him.

EGEUS Scornful Lysander! True, he hath my love;
And what is mine my love shall render him.
And she is mine, and all my right of her
I do estate unto Demetrius.

LYSANDER I am, my lord, as well derived as he,
As well possessed: my love is more than his

My fortunes every way as fairly ranked –
If not with vantage – as Demetrius':
And, which is more than all these boasts can be,
I am beloved of beauteous Hermia.
Why should not I then prosecute my right?
Demetrius, I'll avouch it to his head,
Made love to Nedar's daughter, Helena,
And won her soul; and she, sweet lady, dotes,
Devoutly dotes, dotes in idolatry,
Upon this spotted and inconstant man.

THESEUS I must confess that I have heard so much:
And with Demetrius thought to have spoke thereof;
But, being over-full of self-affairs,
My mind did lose it. [*he rises*] But Demetrius come,
And come Egeus, you shall go with me:
I have some private schooling for you both.
For you, fair Hermia, look you arm yourself
To fit your fancies to your father's will;
Or else the law of Athens yields you up
(Which by no means we may extenuate)
To death, or to a vow of single life.
Come, my Hippolyta: what cheer, my love?
Demetrius and Egeus, go along:
I must employ you in some business
Against our nuptial, and confer with you
Of something nearly that concerns yourselves.

EGEUS With duty and desire we follow you.
[*all depart save Hermia and Lysander*

LYSANDER How now, my love? Why is your cheek so pale?
How chance the roses there do fade so fast?

HERMIA Belike for want of rain, which I could well
Beteem them from the tempest of my eyes.

LYSANDER Ay me! [*he comforts her*]
For aught that I could ever read,
Could ever hear by tale or history,
The course of true love never did run smooth;
But, either it was different in blood –

HERMIA O cross! Too high to be enthralled to low.

LYSANDER Or else misgraffèd in respect of years –

HERMIA O spite! Too old to be engaged to young.
LYSANDER Or else it stood upon the choice of friends –
HERMIA O hell! To choose love by another's eyes!
LYSANDER Or, if there were a sympathy in choice,
War, death, or sickness did lay siege to it –
Making it momentany as a sound,
Swift as a shadow, short as any dream,
Brief as the lightning in the collied night
That, in a spleen, unfolds both heaven and earth;
And ere a man hath power to say 'Behold!'
The jaws of darkness do devour it up:
So quick bright things come to confusion.
HERMIA If then true lovers have been ever crossed,
It stands as an edict in destiny:
Then let us teach our trial patience,
Because it is a customary cross,
As due to love as thoughts and dreams and sighs,
Wishes and tears, poor Fancy's followers.
LYSANDER A good persuasion: therefore hear me, Hermia:
I have a widow aunt, a dowager
Of great revénue, and she hath no child:
From Athens is her house remote seven leagues:
And she respects me as her only son.
There, gentle Hermia, may I marry thee:
And to that place the sharp Athenian law
Cannot pursue us. If thou lovest me then,
Steal forth thy father's house tomorrow night;
And in the wood, a league without the town,
Where I did meet thee once with Helena,
To do observance to a morn of May,
There will I stay for thee.
HERMIA My good Lysander,
I swear to thee by Cupid's strongest bow,
By his best arrow with the golden head,
By the simplicity of Venus' doves,
By that which knitteth souls and prospers loves,
And by that fire which burned the Carthage queen,
When the false Troyan under sail was seen,
By all the vows that ever men have broke –

In number more than ever women spoke –
In that same place thou hast appointed me,
Tomorrow truly will I meet with thee.

LYSANDER Keep promise, love. Look, here comes Helena.

HELENA *is seen passing through the lobby*

HERMIA God speed, fair Helena: whither away?

HELENA [*coming forward into the hall*]
Call you me fair? That 'fair' again unsay.
Demetrius loves your fair: O happy fair!
Your eyes are lode-stars, and your tongue's sweet air
More tuneable than lark to shepherd's ear,
When wheat is green, when hawthorn buds appear.
Sickness is catching: O, were favour so,
Yours would I catch, fair Hermia, ere I go!
My ear should catch your voice, my eye your eye,
My tongue should catch your tongue's sweet melody.
Were the world mine, Demetrius being bated,
The rest I'ld give to be to you translated.
O, teach me how you look, and with what art
You sway the motion of Demetrius' heart.

HERMIA I frown upon him; yet he loves me still.

HELENA O that your frowns would teach my smiles such skill.

HERMIA I give him curses; yet he gives me love.

HELENA O that my prayers could such affection move.

HERMIA The more I hate, the more he follows me.

HELENA The more I love, the more he hateth me.

HERMIA His folly, Helena, is no fault of mine.

HELENA None, but your beauty; would that fault were mine.

HERMIA Take comfort: he no more shall see my face:
Lysander and myself will fly this place.
Before the time I did Lysander see,
Seemed Athens as a paradise to me:
O then, what graces in my love do dwell,
That he hath turned a heaven unto a hell!

LYSANDER Helen, to you our minds we will unfold:
Tomorrow night, when Phoebe doth behold
Her silver visage in the wat'ry glass,
Decking with liquid pearl the bladed grass –
A time that lovers' flights doth still conceal –

Through Athens' gates have we devised to steal.
HERMIA And in the wood, where often you and I
Upon faint primrose beds were wont to lie,
Emptying our bosoms of their counsel sweet,
There my Lysander and myself shall meet,
And thence from Athens turn away our eyes,
To seek new friends and stranger companies.
Farewell, sweet playfellow: pray thou for us
And good luck grant thee thy Demetrius!
Keep word, Lysander: we must starve our sight
From lovers' food till morrow deep midnight. [*she goes*
LYSANDER I will, my Hermia. Helena, adieu:
As you on him, Demetrius dote on you! [*he goes*
HELENA How happy some o'er other some can be!
Through Athens I am thought as fair as she,
But what of that? Demetrius thinks not so:
He will not know what all but he do know.
And as he errs, doting on Hermia's eyes,
So I, admiring of his qualities.
Things base and vile, holding no quantity,
Love can transpose to form and dignity.
Love looks not with the eyes, but with the mind:
And therefore is winged Cupid painted blind.
Nor hath Love's mind of any judgment taste:
Wings and no eyes figure unheedy haste.
And therefore is Love said to be a child,
Because in choice he is so oft beguiled.
As waggish boys in game themselves forswear,
So the boy Love is perjured every where.
For ere Demetrius looked on Hermia's eyne,
He hailed down oaths that he was only mine.
And when this hail some heat from Hermia felt,
So he dissolved, and show'rs of oaths did melt.
I will go tell him of fair Hermia's flight:
Then to the wood will he tomorrow night
Pursue her: and for this intelligence
If I have thanks, it is a dear expense:
But herein mean I to enrich my pain,
To have his sight thither and back again. [*she goes*

SCENE 2

A room in the cottage of Peter Quince

QUINCE, BOTTOM, SNUG, FLUTE, SNOUT, *and* STARVELING

QUINCE Is all our company here?

BOTTOM You were best to call them generally, man by man, according to the scrip.

QUINCE Here is the scroll of every man's name, which is thought fit, through all Athens, to play in our interlude before the duke and the duchess, on his wedding-day at night.

BOTTOM First, good Peter Quince, say what the play treats on: then read the names of the actors: and so grow to a point.

QUINCE Marry, our play is 'The most lamentable comedy, and most cruel death, of Pyramus and Thisby.'

BOTTOM A very good piece of work, I assure you, and a merry. Now, good Peter Quince, call forth your actors by the scroll. Masters, spread yourselves.

QUINCE Answer, as I call you. Nick Bottom, the weaver.

BOTTOM Ready: name what part I am for, and proceed.

QUINCE You, Nick Bottom, are set down for Pyramus.

BOTTOM What is Pyramus? A lover, or a tyrant?

QUINCE A lover that kills himself, most gallant for love.

BOTTOM That will ask some tears in the true performing of it. If I do it, let the audience look to their eyes: I will move storms: I will condole in some measure. To the rest – yet my chief humour is for a tyrant. I could play Ercles rarely, or a part to tear a cat in, to make all split.

'The raging rocks
And shivering shocks
Shall break the locks
Of prison-gates,
And Phibbus' car
Shall shine from far
And make and mar
The foolish Fates.'

This was lofty. Now name the rest of the players. This

is Ercles' vein, a tyrant's vein: a lover is more condoling.

QUINCE Francis Flute, the bellows-mender.

FLUTE Here, Peter Quince.

QUINCE Flute, you must take Thisby on you.

FLUTE What is Thisby? A wand'ring knight?

QUINCE It is the lady that Pyramus must love.

FLUTE Nay, faith: let not me play a woman: I have a beard coming.

quince That's all one: you shall play it in a mask: and you may speak as small as you will.

BOTTOM An I may hide my face, let me play Thisby too: I'll speak in a monstrous little voice. 'Thisne? Thisne?' – 'Ah, Pyramus, my lover dear, thy Thisby dear, and lady dear.'

QUINCE No, no, you must play Pyramus: and Flute, you Thisby.

BOTTOM Well, proceed.

QUINCE Robin Starveling, the tailor.

STARV'LING Here, Peter Quince.

QUINCE Robin Starveling, you must play Thisby's mother. Tom Snout, the tinker.

SNOUT Here, Peter Quince.

QUINCE You, Pyramus' father; myself, Thisby's father; Snug, the joiner, you the lion's part: and I hope here is a play fitted.

SNUG Have you the lion's part written? pray you, if it be, give it me: for I am slow of study.

QUINCE You may do it extempore: for it is nothing but roaring.

BOTTOM Let me play the lion too. I will roar that I will do any man's heart good to hear me. I will roar that I will make the duke say, 'Let him roar again: let him roar again.'

QUINCE An you should do it too terribly, you would fright the duchess and the ladies, that they would shriek: and that were enough to hang us all.

ALL That would hang us, every mother's son.

BOTTOM I grant you, friends, if you should fright the ladies out of their wits, they would have no more discretion but to hang us: but I will aggravate my voice so, that I will roar you as gently as any sucking dove: I will roar you an 'twere any nightingale.

QUINCE You can play no part but Pyramus: for Pyramus is a sweet-faced man; a proper man as one shall see in a summer's day; a most lovely, gentleman-like man: therefore you must needs play Pyramus.

BOTTOM Well, I will undertake it. What beard were I best to play it in?

QUINCE Why, what you will.

BOTTOM I will discharge it in either your straw-colour beard, your orange-tawny beard, your purple-in-grain beard, or your French-crown-colour beard, your perfect yellow.

QUINCE Some of your French crowns have no hair at all; and then you will play barefaced. [*he distributes strips of paper among them*] But, masters, here are your parts, and I am to entreat you, request you, and desire you, to con them by tomorrow night: and meet me in the palace wood, a mile without the town, by moon-light; there will we rehearse: for if we meet in the city, we shall be dogged with company, and our devices known. In the meantime, I will draw a bill of properties, such as our play wants. I pray you, fail me not.

BOTTOM We will meet, and there we may rehease most obscenely and courageously. Take pains, be perfect: adieu.

QUINCE At the duke's oak we meet.

BOTTOM Enough: hold, or cut bow-strings. [*they go*

ACT 2 SCENE 1

The palace wood, a league from Athens. A mossy stretch of broken ground, cleared of trees by wood-cutters and surrounded by thickets. Moonlight.

PUCK *and a* FAIRY, *meeting*

PUCK How now, spirit! Whither wander you?

FAIRY Over hill, over dale,
Thorough bush, thorough briar,
Over park, over pale,
Thorough flood, thorough fire,
I do wander everywhere,
Swifter than the moonës sphere:
And I serve the Fairy Queen,
To dew her orbs upon the green.
The cowslips tall her pensioners be,
In their gold coats spots you see:
Those be rubies, fairy favours:
In those freckles live their savours.
I must go seek some dewdrops here,
And hang a pearl in every cowslip's ear.
Farewell, thou lob of spirits: I'll be gone –
Our queen and all her elves come here anon.

PUCK The king doth keep his revels here tonight.
Take heed the queen come not within his sight.
For Oberon is passing fell and wrath,
Because that she as her attendant hath
A lovely boy, stol'n from an Indian king:
She never had so sweet a changeling.
And jealous Oberon would have the child
Knight of his train, to trace the forests wild.
But she, perforce, withholds the lovéd boy,
Crowns him with flowers, and makes him all her joy.
And now they never meet in grove, or green,
By fountain clear, or spangled starlight sheen,
But they do square – that all their elves, for fear,

Creep into acorn cups and hide them there.

FAIRY Either I mistake your shape and making quite,
Or else you are that shrewd and knavish sprite
Called Robin Goodfellow. Are not you he
That frights the maidens of the villagery,
Skim milk, and sometimes labour in the quern,
And bootless make the breathless housewife churn,
And sometime make the drink to bear no barm,
Mislead night-wanderers, laughing at their harm?
Those that Hobgoblin call you and sweet Puck,
You do their work, and they shall have good luck
Are not you he?

PUCK Thou speak'st aright;
I am that merry wanderer of the night.
I jest to Oberon, and make him smile
When I a fat and bean-fed horse beguile,
Neighing in likeness of a filly foal;
And sometime lurk I in a gossip's bowl,
In very likeness of a roasted crab,
And, when she drinks, against her lips I bob,
And on her withered dewlap pour the ale.
The wisest aunt, telling the saddest tale,
Sometime for three-foot stool mistaketh me:
Then slip I from her bum, down topples she,
And 'tailor' cries, and falls into a cough:
And then the whole choir hold their hips and laugh,
And waxen in their mirth, and neeze, and swear
A merrier hour was never wasted there.
But room, faëry: here comes Oberon.

FAIRY And here my mistress. Would that he were gone.

The clearing is suddenly thronged with fairies:
OBERON *and* TITANIA *confront each other*

OBERON Ill met by moonlight, proud Titania.

TITANIA What, jealous Oberon! Fairies, skip hence –
I have forsworn his bed and company.

OBERON Tarry, rash wanton. Am not I thy lord?

TITANIA Then I must be thy lady: but I know
When thou hast stol'n away from fairy land,

And in the shape of Corin sat all day,
Playing on pipes of corn, and versing love,
To amorous Phillida. Why art thou here,
Come from the farthest steep of India?
But that, forsooth, the bouncing Amazon,
Your buskined mistress and your warrior love,
To Theseus must be wedded; and you come
To give their bed joy and prosperity.

OBERON How canst thou thus for shame, Titania,
Glance at my credit with Hippolyta,
Knowing I know thy love to Theseus?
Didst thou not lead him through the glimmering night
From Perigouna, whom he ravishéd?
And make him with fair Aegles break his faith,
With Ariadne, and Antiopa?

TITANIA These are the forgeries of jealousy:
And never, since the middle summer's spring,
Met we on hill, in dale, forest, or mead,
By pavéd fountain, or by rushy brook,
Or in the beachéd margent of the sea,
To dance our ringlets to the whistling wind,
But with thy brawls thou hast disturbed our sport.
Therefore the winds, piping to us in vain,
As in revenge, have sucked up from the sea
Contagious fogs: which falling in the land,
Hath every pelting river made so proud
That they have overborne their continents.
The ox hath therefore stretched his yoke in vain,
The ploughman lost his sweat, and the green corn
Hath rotted ere his youth attained a beard;
The fold stands empty in the drownéd field,
And crows are fatted with the murrion flock;
The nine men's morris is filled up with mud,
And the quaint mazes in the wanton green
For lack of tread are indistinguishable.
The human mortals want their winter cheer;
No night is now with hymn or carol blest;
Therefore the moon, the governess of floods,

Pale in her anger, washes all the air,
That rheumatic diseases do abound.
And thorough this distemperature we see
The seasons alter: hoary-headed frosts
Fall in the fresh lap of the crimson rose,
And on old Hiems' thin and icy crown
An odorous chaplet of sweet summer buds
Is, as in mockery, set. The spring, the summer,
The childing autumn, angry winter, change
Their wonted liveries; and the mazéd world,
By their increase, now knows not which is which.
And this same progeny of evils comes
From our debate, from our dissension:
We are their parents and original.

OBERON Do you amend it then: it lies in you.
Why should Titania cross her Oberon?
I do but beg a little changeling boy,
To be my henchman.

TITANIA Set your heart at rest,
The fairy land buys not the child of me.
His mother was a vot'ress of my order;
And in the spicéd Indian air, by night,
Full often hath she gossiped by my side;
And sat with me on Neptune's yellow sands,
Marking th' embarkéd traders on the flood;
When we have laughed to see the sails conceive
And grow big-bellied with the wanton wind;
Which she, with pretty and with swimming gait
Following – her womb then rich with my young squire –
Would imitate, and sail upon the land,
To fetch me trifles, and return again,
As from a voyage, rich with merchandise.
But she, being mortal, of that boy did die;
And for her sake do I rear up her boy;
And for her sake I will not part with him.

OBERON How long within this wood intend you stay?

TITANIA Perchance till after Theseus' wedding-day.

If you will patiently dance in our round,
And see our moonlight revels, go with us:
If not, shun me, and I will spare your haunts.

OBERON Give me that boy, and I will go with thee.

TITANIA Not for thy fairy kingdom. Fairies, away!
We shall chide downright, if I longer stay.
[*Titania departs in anger with her train*

OBERON Well, go thy way. Thou shalt not from this grove,
Till I torment thee for this injury.
My gentle Puck, come hither. Thou rememb'rest
Since once I sat upon a promontory,
And heard a mermaid, on a dolphin's back,
Uttering such dulcet and harmonious breath
That the rude sea grew civil at her song,
And certain stars shot madly from their spheres
To hear the sea-maid's music.

PUCK I remember.

OBERON That very time I saw – but thou couldst not –
Flying between the cold moon and the earth,
Cupid all armed: a certain aim he took
At a fair Vestal, thronéd by the west,
And loosed his love-shaft smartly from his bow,
As it should pierce a hundred thousand hearts
But I might see young Cupid's fiery shaft
Quenched in the chaste beams of the wat'ry moon:
And the imperial Vot'ress passéd on,
In maiden meditation, fancy-free.
Yet marked I where the bolt of Cupid fell.
It fell upon a little western flower;
Before, milk-white; now purple with love's wound –
And maidens call it Love-in-idleness.
Fetch me that flower, the herb I showed thee once.
The juice of it, on sleeping eyelids laid,
Will make or man or woman madly dote
Upon the next live creature that it sees.
Fetch me this herb, and be thou here again
Ere the leviathan can swim a league.

PUCK I'll put a girdle round about the earth

In forty minutes. [*he vanishes*

OBERON Having once this juice,
I'll watch Titania when she is asleep,
And drop the liquor of it in her eyes:
The next thing then she waking looks upon –
Be it on lion, bear, or wolf, or bull,
On meddling monkey, or on busy ape –
She shall pursue it with the soul of love.
And ere I take this charm from off her sight –
As I can take it with another herb –
I'll make her render up her page to me.
But who comes here? I am invisible,
And I will overhear their conference.

DEMETRIUS *enters the clearing,* 'HELENA *following him*'

DEMETR. I love thee not. Therefore pursue me not.
Where is Lysander and fair Hermia?
The one I'll slay. The other slayeth me.
Thou told'st me they were stol'n unto this wood:
And here am I, and wood within this wood,
Because I cannot meet my Hermia:
Hence, get thee gone, and follow me no more.

HELENA You draw me, you hard-hearted adamant;
But yet you draw not iron, for my heart
Is true as steel. Leave you your power to draw,
And I shall have no power to follow you.

DEMETR. Do I entice you? Do I speak you fair?
Or rather do I not in plainest truth
Tell you I do not nor I cannot love you?

HELENA And even for that do I love you the more:
I am your spaniel; and, Demetrius,
The more you beat me, I will fawn on you.
Use me but as your spaniel: spurn me, strike me,
Neglect me, lose me: only give me leave,
Unworthy as I am, to follow you.
What worser place can I beg in your love –
And yet a place of high respect with me –
Than to be uséd as you use your dog?

DEMETR. Tempt not too much the hatred of my spirit,
For I am sick when I do look on thee.

HELENA And I am sick when I look not on you.
DEMETR. You do impeach your modesty too much
To leave the city and commit yourself
Into the hands of one that loves you not,
To trust the opportunity of night
And the ill counsel of a desert place
With the rich worth of your virginity.
HELENA Your virtue is my privilege for that
It is not night when I do see your face,
Therefore I think I am not in the night –
Nor doth this wood lack worlds of company,
For you in my respect are all the world.
Then how can it be said I am alone
When all the world is here to look on me?
DEMETR. I'll run from thee and hide me in the brakes,
And leave thee to the mercy of wild beasts.
HELENA The wildest hath not such a heart as you.
Run when you will; the story shall be changed.
Apollo flies, and Daphne holds the chase;
The dove pursues the griffin; the mild hind
Makes speed to catch the tiger. Bootless speed,
When cowardice pursues and valour flies.
DEMETR. I will not stay thy questions – let me go:
Or, if thou follow me, do not believe
But I shall do thee mischief in the wood.
HELENA Ay, in the temple, in the town, the field,
You do me mischief. Fie, Demetrius!
Your wrongs do set a scandal on my sex
We cannot fight for love, as men may do;
We should be wooed and were not made to woo.
[*he goes*
I'll follow thee and make a heaven of hell,
To die upon the hand I love so well. [*she follows after*
OBERON Fare thee well, nymph. Ere he do leave this grove,
Thou shalt fly him, and he shall seek thy love.

PUCK *reappears*

Welcome, wanderer. Hast thou the flower there?
PUCK Ay, there it is.
OBERON I pray thee, give it me.

I know a bank where the wild thyme blows,
Where oxlips and the nodding violet grows,
Quite over-canopied with luscious woodbine,
With sweet musk-roses, and with eglantine:
There sleeps Titania sometime of the night,
Lulled in these flowers with dances and delight;
And there the snake throws her enamelled skin,
Weed wide enough to wrap a fairy in.
And with the juice of this I'll streak her eyes,
And make her full of hateful fantasies.
Take thou some of it, and seek through this grove:
A sweet Athenian lady is in love
With a disdainful youth; anoint his eyes –
But do it when the next thing he espies
May be the lady. Thou shalt know the man
By the Athenian garments he hath on.
Effect it with some care, that he may prove
More fond on her than she upon her love.
And look thou meet me ere the first cock crow.

PUCK Fear not, my lord: your servant shall do so.

[*they depart*

SCENE 2

Another part of the wood. A grassy plot before a great oak-tree, behind the tree a high bank overhung with creepers, and at one side a thorn-bush. The air is heavy with the scent of blossom

TITANIA *lies couched in her bower beneath the bank; her fairies attending her*

TITANIA Come now, a roundel and a fairy song:
Then, for the third part of a minute, hence –
Some to kill cankers in the musk-rose buds,
Some war with rere-mice for their leathern wings,
To make my small elves coats, and some keep back
The clamorous owl that nightly hoots and wonders
At our quaint spirits. Sing me now asleep;
Then to your offices, and let me rest.

'Fairies sing'

You spotted snakes, with double tongue,
Thorny hedgehogs, be not seen;
Newts and blind-worms do no wrong,
Come not near our Fairy Queen.

Philomele, with melody,
Sing in our sweet lullaby,
Lulla, lulla, lullaby,
Lulla, lulla, lullaby,
Never harm,
Nor spell, nor charm,
Come our lovely lady nigh.
So good night, with lullaby.

1 FAIRY Weaving spiders come not here:
Hence you long-legged spinners, hence:
Beetles black approach not near:
Worm nor snail do no offence.

Philomele, with melody,
Sing in our sweet lullaby,
Lulla, lulla, lullaby,
Lulla, lulla, lullaby,
Never harm,
Nor spell, nor charm
Come our lovely lady nigh.
So good night, with lullaby. [*Titania sleeps*

2 FAIRY Hence, away: now all is well:
One aloof stand sentinel. [*the fairies steal away*

OBERON *appears, hovering above the bank; he alights and anoints the eyes of Titania with the juice of the flower*

OBERON What thou see'st when thou dost wake,
Do it for thy true-love take;
Love and languish for his sake.
Be it ounce, or cat, or bear,
Pard, or boar with bristled hair,
In thy eye that shall appear
When thou wak'st, it is thy dear:
Wake when some vile thing is near. [*he vanishes*

LYSANDER *approaches with* HERMIA *leaning upon his arm*

LYSANDER Fair love, you faint with wand'ring in the wood;
And to speak troth I have forgot our way.
We'll rest us, Hermia, if you think it good,
And tarry for the comfort of the day.

HERMIA Be't so, Lysander: find you out a bed:
For I upon this bank will rest my head.

LYSANDER One turf shall serve as pillow for us both,
One heart, one bed, two bosoms, and one troth.

HERMIA Nay, good Lysander: for my sake, my dear,
Lie further off yet; do not lie so near.

LYSANDER O take the sense, sweet, of my innocence!
Love takes the meaning in love's conference.
I mean that my heart unto yours is knit,
So that but one heart we can make of it:
Two bosoms interchainéd with an oath,
So then two bosoms and a single troth.
Then by your side no bed-room me deny,
For lying so, Hermia, I do not lie.

HERMIA Lysander riddles very prettily.
Now much beshrew my manners and my pride,
If Hermia meant to say Lysander lied.
But, gentle friend, for love and courtesy
Lie further off – in human modesty:
Such separation as may well be said
Becomes a virtuous bachelor and a maid.
So far be distant – and good night, sweet friend:
Thy love ne'er alter till thy sweet life end!

LYSANDER Amen, amen, to that fair prayer, say I –
And then end life when I end loyalty!
Here is my bed: sleep give thee all his rest.

HERMIA With half that wish the wisher's eyes be pressed.
['*they sleep*'

PUCK *appears*

PUCK Through the forest have I gone,
But Athenian found I none
On whose eyes I might approve
This flower's force in stirring love.

Night and silence – who is here?
Weeds of Athens he doth wear:
This is he, my master said,
Despiséd the Athenian maid:
And here the maiden, sleeping sound,
On the dank and dirty ground.
Pretty soul, she durst not lie
Near this lack-love, this kill-courtesy.
[he anoints the eyelids of Lysander
Churl, upon thy eyes I throw
All the power this charm doth owe:
When thou wak'st, let love forbid
Sleep his seat on thy eyelid.
So awake when I am gone;
For I must now to Oberon. *[he vanishes*

'Enter DEMETRIUS *and* HELENA, *running'*

HELENA Stay; though thou kill me, sweet Demetrius.
DEMETR. I charge thee, hence, and do not haunt me thus.
HELENA O, wilt thou darkling leave me? Do not so.
DEMETR. Stay, on thy peril; I alone will go.
[he breaks from her and disappears into the wood
HELENA O, I am out of breath in this fond chase!
The more my prayer, the lesser is my grace.
Happy is Hermia, wheresoe'er she lies;
For she hath blesséd and attractive eyes.
How came her eyes so bright? Not with salt tears –
If so, my eyes are oft'ner washed than hers.
No, no: I am as ugly as a bear,
For beasts that meet me run away for fear.
Therefore no marvel though Demetrius
Do, as a monster, fly my presence thus.
What wicked and dissembling glass of mine
Made me compare with Hermia's sphery eyne?
But who is here? Lysander! On the ground!
Dead? Or asleep? I see no blood, no wound.
Lysander, if you live, good sir, awake.
LYSANDER [*leaps up*]
And run through fire I will, for thy sweet sake.
Transparent Helena! Nature shows her art,

That through thy bosom makes me see thy heart.
Where is Demetrius? O, how fit a word
Is that vile name to perish on my sword!

HELENA Do not say so, Lysander, say not so.
What though he love your Hermia? Lord! what though?
Yet Hermia still loves you: then be content.

LYSANDER Content with Hermia? No: I do repent
The tedious minutes I with her have spent.
Not Hermia, but Helena I love –
Who will not change a raven for a dove?
The will of man is by his reason swayed;
And reason says you are the worthier maid.
Things growing are not ripe until their season:
So I, being young, till now ripe not to reason –
And touching now the point of human skill,
Reason becomes the marshal to my will,
And leads me to your eyes; where I o'erlook
Love's stories, written in Love's richest book.

HELENA Wherefore was I to this keen mockery born?
When at your hands did I deserve this scorn?
Is't not enough, is't not enough, young man,
That I did never, no, nor never can,
Deserve a sweet look from Demetrius' eye,
But you must flout my insufficiency?
Good troth, you do me wrong, good sooth, you do,
In such disdainful manner me to woo.
But fare you well: perforce I must confess
I thought you lord of more true gentleness.
O, that a lady, of one man refused,
Should of another therefore be abused! [*she goes*

LYSANDER She sees not Hermia. Hermia, sleep thou there,
And never mayst thou come Lysander near.
For, as a surfeit of the sweetest things
The deepest loathing to the stomach brings,
Or as the heresies that men do leave
Are hated most of those they did deceive,
So thou, my surfeit and my heresy,
Of all be hated, but the most of me!

And all my powers, address your love and might
To honour Helen, and to be her knight.
[*he follows Helena*

HERMIA [*awaking*] Help me, Lysander, help me; do thy best
To pluck this crawling serpent from my breast.
Ay me, for pity! What a dream was here?
Lysander, look how I do quake with fear.
Methought a serpent eat my heart away,
And you sat smiling at his cruel prey.
Lysander! What, removed? Lysander! Lord!
What, out of hearing gone? No sound, no word?
Alack, where are you? Speak, an if you hear;
Speak, of all loves! I swoon almost with fear.
No? Then I will perceive you are not nigh.
Either death or you I'll find immediately. [*she goes*

ACT 3 SCENE I

QUINCE *(carrying a bag)*, SNUG, BOTTOM, FLUTE, SNOUT, *and* STARVELING *come up severally or in pairs and gather beneath the oak-tree*

BOTTOM Are we all met?

QUINCE Pat, pat: and here's a marvellous convenient place for our rehearsal. This green plot shall be our stage, this hawthorn-brake our tiring-house – and we will do it in action as we will do it before the duke.

BOTTOM Peter Quince!

QUINCE What say'st thou, bully Bottom?

BOTTOM There are things in this comedy of Pyramus and Thisby that will never please. First, Pyramus must draw a sword to kill himself; which the ladies cannot abide. How answer you that?

SNOUT By'r lakin, a parlous fear.

STARV'LING I believe we must leave the killing out, when all is done.

BOTTOM Not a whit: I have a device to make all well. Write me a prologue, and let the prologue seem to say we will do no harm with our swords, and that Pyramus is not killed indeed: and, for the more better assurance, tell them that I, Pyramus, am not Pyramus but Bottom the weaver: this will put them out of fear.

QUINCE Well, we will have such a prologue, and it shall be written in eight and six.

BOTTOM No, make it two more: let it be written in eight and eight.

SNOUT Will not the ladies be afeard of the lion?

STARV'LING I fear it, I promise you.

BOTTOM Masters, you ought to consider with yourselves – to bring in (God shield us!) a lion among ladies is a most dreadful thing. For there is not a more fearful wild-fowl than your lion living; and we ought to look to't.

SNOUT Therefore, another prologue must tell he is not a lion.

BOTTOM Nay, you must name his name, and half his face must be seen through the lion's neck, and he himself must speak through, saying thus, or to the same defect: 'Ladies', or 'Fair ladies – I would wish you', or 'I would request you', or 'I would entreat you, not to fear, not to tremble: my life for yours. If you think I come hither as a lion, it were pity of my life. No: I am no such thing: I am a man as other men are.' And there indeed let him name his name, and tell them plainly he is Snug the joiner.

QUINCE Well, it shall be so. But there is two hard things: that is, to bring the moonlight into a chamber: for you know, Pyramus and Thisby meet by moonlight.

SNOUT Doth the moon shine that night we play our play?

BOTTOM A calendar, a calendar! Look in the almanac; find out moonshine, find out moonshine.

QUINCE *takes an almanac from his bag and searches therein*

QUINCE Yes, it doth shine that night.

BOTTOM Why, then may you leave a casement of the great chamber window, where we play, open; and the moon may shine in at the casement.

QUINCE Ay, or else one must come in with a bush of thorns and a lantern, and say he comes to disfigure or to present the person of Moonshine. Then, there is another thing: we must have a wall in the great chamber; for Pyramus and Thisby, says the story, did talk through the chink of a wall.

SNOUT You can never bring in a wall. What say you, Bottom?

BOTTOM Some man or other must present wall; and let him have some plaster, or some loam, or some rough-cast about him, to signify wall; and let him hold his fingers thus [*he stretches out his fingers*], and through that cranny shall Pyramus and Thisby whisper.

QUINCE If that may be, then all is well. [*takes out a book and opens it*] Come, sit down, every mother's son, and rehearse your parts. Pyramus, you begin: when you have spoken your speech, enter into that brake – and so every one according to his cue.

PUCK *appears behind the oak*

PUCK What hempen home-spuns have we swagg'ring here,
So near the cradle of the Fairy Queen?
What, a play toward? I'll be an auditor,
An actor too perhaps, if I see cause.

QUINCE Speak, Pyramus. Thisby, stand forth.

BOTTOM 'Thisby, the flowers ha' odious savours sweet' –

QUINCE [*prompts*] 'Odious' – odorous!

BOTTOM – 'odours savours sweet,
So hath thy breath, my dearest Thisby dear.
But hark, a voice! Stay thou but here awhile,
And by and by I will to thee appear.' [*exit into the brake*

PUCK A stranger Pyramus than e'er played here!
[*he follows Bottom*

FLUTE Must I speak now?

QUINCE Ay, marry, must you. For you must understand he goes but to see a noise that he heard, and is to come again.

FLUTE 'Most radiant Pyramus, most lily-white of hue,
Of colour like the red rose on triumphant briar,
Most brisky juvenal, and eke most lovely Jew,
As true as truest horse that yet would never tire,
I'll meet thee, Pyramus, at Ninny's tomb.'

QUINCE 'Ninus' tomb', man! Why, you must not speak that yet! That you answer to Pyramus. You speak all your part at once, cues and all. Pyramus enter; your cue is past; it is, 'never tire'.

FLUTE O – 'As true as truest horse that yet would never tire.'

Enter from the brake BOTTOM *with an ass's head;* PUCK *following*

BOTTOM 'If I were fair, Thisby, I were only thine.'

QUINCE O monstrous! O strange! We are haunted.
Pray, masters! Fly, masters! Help!
[*they all run away and hide them in the bushes*

PUCK I'll follow you: I'll lead you about a round,
Through bog, through bush, through brake, through briar;
Sometime a horse I'll be, sometime a hound,
A hog, a headless bear, sometime a fire,
And neigh, and bark, and grunt, and roar, and burn,

Like horse, hound, hog, bear, fire, at every turn.

[*he pursues them*

BOTTOM Why do they run away? This is a knavery of them to make me afeard.

SNOUT *peers from behind a bush*

SNOUT O Bottom, thou art changed! What do I see on thee?

BOTTOM What do you see? You see an ass-head of your own, do you? [*Snout disappears*

QUINCE *stealthily returns*

QUINCE Bless thee Bottom, bless thee! Thou art translated.

[*he turns and flees*

BOTTOM I see their knavery. This is to make an ass of me, to fright me if they could: but I will not stir from this place, do what they can. I will walk up and down here, and will sing that they shall hear I am not afraid.

[*he sings through his nose, braying at whiles*

The ousel cock, so black of hue,
With orange-tawny bill,
The throstle with his note so true,
The wren with little quill . . .

TITANIA [*comes from the bower*]
What angel wakes me from my flow'ry bed?

BOTTOM The finch, the sparrow, and the lark,
The plain-song cuckoo gray,
Whose note full many a man doth mark,
And dares not answer, nay . . .
For indeed, who would set his wit to so foolish a bird? Who would give a bird the lie, though he cry 'cuckoo' never so?

TITANIA I pray thee, gentle mortal, sing again!
Mine ear is much enamoured of thy note;
So is mine eye enthrallèd to thy shape,
And thy fair virtue's force – perforce – doth move me,
On the first view, to say, to swear, I love thee.

BOTTOM Methinks, mistress, you should have little reason for that. And yet, to say the truth, reason and love keep little company together now-a-days. The more the pity, that some honest neighbours will not make them friends. Nay, I can gleek upon occasion.

TITANIA Thou art as wise as thou art beautiful.

BOTTOM Not so, neither: but if I had wit enough to get out of this wood, I have enough to serve mine own turn.

TITANIA Out of this wood do not desire to go:
Thou shalt remain here, whether thou wilt or no.
I am a spirit of no common rate:
The summer still doth tend upon my state,
And I do love thee: therefore go with me.
I'll give thee fairies to attend on thee:
And they shall fetch thee jewels from the deep,
And sing, while thou on presséd flowers dost sleep:
And I will purge thy mortal grossness so,
That thou shalt like an airy spirit go. [*she calls*
Peaseblossom, Cobweb, Moth, and Mustardseed!
[*as she utters each name a fairy alights before her and replies*

PEASE. Ready!

COBWEB And I –

MOTH And I –

MUSTARD. And I –

ALL [*bowing*] Where shall we go?

TITANIA Be kind and courteous to this gentleman;
Hop in his walks and gambol in his eyes,
Feed him with apricocks and dewberries,
With purple grapes, green figs, and mulberries;
The honey-bags steal from the humble-bees,
And for night-tapers crop their waxen thighs,
And light them at the fiery glow-worm's eyes,
To have my love to bed and to arise;
And pluck the wings from painted butterflies,
To fan the moonbeams from his sleeping eyes.
Nod to him, elves, and do him courtesies.

PEASE. Hail, mortal!

COBWEB Hail!

MOTH Hail!

MUSTARD. Hail!

BOTTOM I cry your worships mercy, heartily. I beseech your worship's name.

COBWEB [*bows*] Cobweb.

BOTTOM I shall desire you of more acquaintance, good Master Cobweb: if I cut my finger, I shall make bold with you. Your name, honest gentleman?

PEASE. [*bows*] Peaseblossom.

BOTTOM I pray you, commend me to Mistress Squash, your mother, and to Master Peascod, your father. Good Master Peaseblossom, I shall desire you of more acquaintance too. Your name, I beseech you sir?

MUSTARD. [*bows*] Mustardseed.

BOTTOM Good Master Mustardseed, I know your patience well. That same cowardly, giant-like, Oxbeef hath devoured many a gentleman of your house. I promise you your kindred hath made my eyes water ere now. I desire you of more acquaintance, good Master Mustardseed.

TITANIA Come, wait upon him; lead him to my bower.
The moon, methinks, looks with a wat'ry eye:
And when she weeps, weeps every little flower,
Lamenting some enforcéd chastity.
Tie up my love's tongue, bring him silently.
[*they move towards the bower*

SCENE 2

The clearing with the mossy slopes

OBERON *appears*

OBERON I wonder if Titania be awaked;
Then, what it was that next came in her eye,
Which she must dote on in extremity.

PUCK *enters the clearing*

Here comes my messenger. How now, mad spirit?
What night-rule now about this haunted grove?

PUCK My mistress with a monster is in love.
Near to her close and consecrated bower,
While she was in her dull and sleeping hour,
A crew of patches, rude mechanicals
That work for bread upon Athenian stalls,

Were met together to rehearse a play
Intended for great Theseus' nuptial-day.
The shallowest thick-skin of that barren sort,
Who Pyramus presented, in their sport
Forsook his scene and ent'red in a brake;
When I did him at this advantage take,
An ass's noll I fixéd on his head.
Anon his Thisbe must be answeréd,
And forth my mimic comes. When they him spy,
As wild geese that the creeping fowler eye,
Or russet-pated choughs, many in sort,
Rising and cawing at the gun's report,
Sever themselves and madly sweep the sky,
So, at his sight, away his fellows fly;
And at a stump here o'er and o'er one falls –
He 'murder' cries, and help from Athens calls.
Their sense thus weak, lost with their fears thus strong,
Made senseless things begin to do them wrong.
For briars and thorns at their apparel snatch:
Some sleeves, some hats; from yielders all things catch.
I led them on in this distracted fear,
And left sweet Pyramus translated there:
When in that moment (so it came to pass)
Titania waked and straightway loved an ass.

OBERON This falls out better than I could devise.
But hast thou yet latched the Athenian's eyes
With the love-juice, as I did bid thee do?

PUCK I took him sleeping – that is finished too –
And the Athenian woman by his side;
That, when he waked, of force she must be eyed.

DEMETRIUS *and* HERMIA *approach*

OBERON Stand close; this is the same Athenian.

PUCK This is the woman: but not this the man.

DEMETR. O, why rebuke you him that loves you so?
Lay breath so bitter on your bitter foe.

HERMIA Now I but chide: but I should use thee worse,
For thou, I fear, hast given me cause to curse.
If thou hast slain Lysander in his sleep,

Being o'er-shoes in blood, plunge in the deep,
And kill me too.
The sun was not so true unto the day
As he to me. Would he have stolen away
From sleeping Hermia? I'll believe as soon
This whole earth may be bored, and that the moon
May through the centre creep and so displease
Her brother's noontide with th' Antipodes.
It cannot be but thou hast murd'red him –
So should a murderer look; so dead, so grim.

DEMETR. So should the murdered look, and so should I,
Pierced through the heart with your stern cruelty.
Yet you, the murderer, look as bright, as clear,
As yonder Venus in her glimmering sphere.

HERMIA What's this to my Lysander? Where is he?
Ah, good Demetrius, wilt thou give him me?

DEMETR. I had rather give his carcase to my hounds.

HERMIA Out, dog! Out, cur! Thou driv'st me past the bounds
Of maiden's patience. Hast thou slain him then?
Henceforth be never numb'red among men!
O, once tell true: tell true, even for my sake:
Durst thou have looked upon him being awake?
And hast thou killed him, sleeping? O brave touch!
Could not a worm, an adder, do so much?
An adder did it; for with doubler tongue
Than thine, thou serpent, never adder stung.

DEMETR. You spend your passion on a misprised mood:
I am not guilty of Lysander's blood;
Nor is he dead, for aught that I can tell.

HERMIA I pray thee, tell me then that he is well.

DEMETR. An if I could, what should I get therefore?

HERMIA A privilege never to see me more,
And from thy hated presence part I so
See me no more, whether he be dead or no.
[*she hurries away*

DEMETR. There is no following her in this fierce vein.
Here therefore for a while I will remain.
So sorrow's heaviness doth heavier grow
For debt that bankrupt sleep doth sorrow owe;

Which now in some slight measure it will pay,
If for his tender here I make some stay. [*he lies down*

OBERON What hast thou done? Thou hast mistaken quite,
And laid the love-juice on some true-love's sight.
Of thy misprision must perforce ensue
Some true love turned, and not a false turned true.

PUCK Then fate o'er-rules, that, one man holding troth,
A million fail, confounding oath on oath.

OBERON About the wood go swifter than the wind,
And Helena of Athens look thou find.
All fancy-sick she is, and pale of cheer
With sighs of love that costs the fresh blood dear.
By some illusion see thou bring her here:
I'll charm his eyes against she do appear.

PUCK I go, I go – look how I go –
Swifter than arrow from the Tartar's bow. [*he vanishes*

OBERON *bends over the sleeping* DEMETRIUS

OBERON Flower of this purple dye,
Hit with Cupid's archery,
Sink in apple of his eye.
When his love he doth espy,
Let her shine as gloriously
As the Venus of the sky.
When thou wak'st, if she be by,
Beg of her for remedy.

PUCK *reappears*

PUCK Captain of our fairy band,
Helena is here at hand,
And the youth, mistook by me,
Pleading for a lover's fee.
Shall we their fond pageant see?
Lord, what fools these mortals be!

OBERON Stand aside. The noise they make
Will cause Demetrius to awake.

PUCK Then will two at once woo one;
That must needs be sport alone.
And those things do best please me
That befall prepost'rously. [*they stand aside*

HELENA *comes up, followed by* LYSANDER

LYSANDER Why should you think that I should woo in scorn?
Scorn and derision never come in tears.
Look when I vow, I weep; and vows so born
In their nativity all truth appears.
How can these things in me seem scorn to you,
Bearing the badge of faith to prove them true?

HELENA You do advance your cunning more and more.
When truth kills truth, O devilish-holy fray!
These vows are Hermia's – will you give her o'er?
Weigh oath with oath, and you will nothing weigh:
Your vows, to her and me, put in two scales,
Will even weigh; and both as light as tales.

LYSANDER I had no judgment when to her I swore.

HELENA Nor none, in my mind, now you give her o'er.

LYSANDER Demetrius loves her: and he loves not you.

DEMETR. [*awaking*] O Helen, goddess, nymph, perfect, divine!
To what, my love, shall I compare thine eyne?
Crystal is muddy. O, how ripe in show
Thy lips, those kissing cherries, tempting grow!
That pure congealéd white, high Taurus' snow,
Fanned with the eastern wind, turns to a crow,
When thou hold'st up thy hand. O let me kiss
This princess of pure white, this seal of bliss!

HELENA O spite! O hell! I see you all are bent
To set against me for your merriment.
If you were civil and knew courtesy,
You would not do me thus much injury.
Can you not hate me, as I know you do,
But you must join in souls to mock me too?
If you were men, as men you are in show,
You would not use a gentle lady so:
To vow, and swear, and superpraise my parts,
When I am sure you hate me with your hearts.
You both are rivals, and love Hermia;
And now both rivals, to mock Helena.
A trim exploit, a manly enterprise,
To conjure tears up in a poor maid's eyes
With your derision! None of noble sort

Would so offend a virgin, and extort
A poor soul's patience, all to make you sport.

LYSANDER You are unkind, Demetrius; be not so –
For you love Hermia; this you know I know;
And here, with all good will, with all my heart,
In Hermia's love I yield you up my part:
And yours of Helena to me bequeath,
Whom I do love, and will do till my death.

HELENA Never did mockers waste more idle breath.

DEMETR. Lysander, keep thy Hermia: I will none.
If e'er I loved her, all that love is gone.
My heart to her but as guest-wise sojourned,
And now to Helen is it home returned,
There to remain.

LYSANDER Helen, it is not so.

DEMETR. Disparage not the faith thou dost not know,
Lest to thy peril thou aby it dear.

HERMIA *is seen approaching*

Look where thy love comes: yonder is thy dear.

HERMIA *spies* LYSANDER *and runs towards him*

HERMIA Dark night, that from the eye his function takes,
The ear more quick of apprehension makes.
Wherein it doth impair the seeing sense,
It pays the hearing double recompense.
Thou art not by mine eye, Lysander, found;
Mine ear, I thank it, brought me to thy sound.
But why unkindly didst thou leave me so?

LYSANDER [*turning away*]
Why should he stay whom love doth press to go?

HERMIA What love could press Lysander from my side?

LYSANDER Lysander's love, that would not let him bide –
Fair Helena! Who more engilds the night
Than all yon fiery oes and eyes of light.
Why seek'st thou me? Could not this make thee know
The hate I bear thee made me leave thee so?

HERMIA You speak not as you think: it cannot be.

HELENA Lo! She is one of this confederacy.
Now I perceive they have conjoined all three

To fashion this false sport in spite of me.
Injurious Hermia, most ungrateful maid,
Have you conspired, have you with these contrived,
To bait me with this foul derision?
Is all the counsel that we two have shared,
The sisters' vows, the hours that we have spent,
When we have chid the hasty-footed time
For parting us – O! Is all forgot?
All school-days' friendship, childhood innocence?
We, Hermia, like two artificial gods,
Have with our needles created both one flower,
Both on one sampler, sitting on one cushion,
Both warbling of one song, both in one key;
As if our hands, our sides, voices, and minds,
Had been incorporate. So we grew together,
Like to a double cherry, seeming parted,
But yet an union in partition,
Two lovely berries moulded on one stem:
So, with two seeming bodies, but one heart,
Two of the first, like coats in heraldry,
Due but to one, and crownéd with one crest.
And will you rend our ancient love asunder,
To join with men in scorning your poor friend?
It is not friendly, 'tis not maidenly –
Our sex, as well as I, may chide you for it;
Though I alone do feel the injury.

HERMIA Helen, I am amazéd at your words.
I scorn you not – it seems that you scorn me.

HELENA Have you not set Lysander, as in scorn,
To follow me and praise my eyes and face?
And made your other love, Demetrius
(Who even but now did spurn me with his foot!)
To call me goddess, nymph, divine and rare
Precious, celestial? Wherefore speaks he this
To her he hates? And wherefore doth Lysander
Deny your love (so rich within his soul)
And tender me (forsooth!) affection,
But by your setting on, by your consent?
What though I be not so in grace as you,

So hung upon with love, so fortunate,
But miserable most, to love unloved?
This you should pity rather than despise.

HERMIA I understand not what you mean by this.

HELENA Ay, do! Persévcr, counterfeit sad looks,
Make mouths upon me when I turn my back,
Wink at each other, hold the sweet jest up.
This sport, well carried, shall be chronicled.
If you have any pity, grace, or manners,
You would not make me such an argument.
But, fare ye well: 'tis partly my own fault:
Which death or absence soon shall remedy.

LYSANDER Stay, gentle Helena; hear my excuse,
My love, my life, my soul, fair Helena!

HELENA O excellent!

HERMIA Sweet, do not scorn her so.

DEMETR. If she cannot entreat, I can compel.

LYSANDER Thou canst compel no more than she entreat.
Thy threats have no more strength than her weak prayers.
Helen, I love thee – by my life I do;
I swear by that which I will lose for thee,
To prove him false that says I love thee not.

DEMETR. I say I love thee more than he can do.

LYSANDER If thou say so, withdraw, and prove it too.

DEMETR. Quick, come –

HERMIA [*staying him*] Lysander, whereto tends all this?

LYSANDER Away, you Ethiop!

HERMIA No, no!

DEMETR. [*scoffs*] Ye will
Seem to break loose! Take on as you would follow!
But yet come not. You are a tame man, go!

LYSANDER Hang off, thou cat, thou burr! Vile thing, let loose;
Or I will shake thee from me like a serpent.

HERMIA Why are you grown so rude? What change is this,
Sweet love? [*she keeps her hold upon him*

LYSANDER Thy love! out, tawny Tartar, out!
Out, loathéd med'cine! O hated potion, hence!

HERMIA Do you not jest?

HELENA Yes, sooth: and so do you.
LYSANDER Demetrius, I will keep my word with thee.
DEMETR. I would I had your bond, for I perceive
A weak bond holds you. I'll not trust your word.
LYSANDER What? Should I hurt her, strike her, kill her dead?
Although I hate her, I'll not harm her so.
HERMIA What? Can you do me greater harm than hate?
Hate me! Wherefore? O me, what news, my love!
Am not I Hermia? Are not you Lysander?
I am as fair now as I was erewhile.
Since night you loved me; yet since night you left me.
Why then, you left me – O, the gods forbid! –
In earnest, shall I say?
LYSANDER Ay, by my life!
And never did desire to see thee more.
Therefore be out of hope, of question or doubt:
Be certain: nothing truer: 'tis no jest
That I do hate thee and love Helena.
HERMIA [*to Helena*] O me, you juggler, you canker-blossom.
You thief of love! What! Have you come by night
And stol'n my love's heart from him?
HELENA Fine, i'faith!
Have you no modesty, no maiden shame,
No touch of bashfulness? What! Will you tear
Impatient answers from my gentle tongue?
Fie, fie, you counterfeit, you puppet you!
HERMIA 'Puppet?' Why, so – ay, that way goes the game!
Now I perceive that she hath made compare
Between our statures; she hath urged her height;
And with her personage, her tall personage,
Her height, forsooth, she hath prevailed with him.
And are you grown so high in his esteem
Because I am so dwarfish and so low?
How low am I, thou painted maypole? Speak;
How low am I? I am not yet so low,
But that my nails can reach unto thine eyes.
[*she makes towards her*
HELENA I pray you, though you mock me, gentlemen,
Let her not hurt me. I was never curst

I have no gift at all in shrewishness:
I am a right maid for my cowardice:
Let her not strike me. You perhaps may think,
Because she is something lower than myself,
That I can match her.

HERMIA Lower! Hark, again.

HELENA Good Hermia, do not be so bitter with me.
I evermore did love you, Hermia,
Did ever keep your counsels, never wronged you;
Save that, in love unto Demetrius,
I told him of your stealth unto this wood.
He followed you; for love I followed him.
But he hath chid me hence, and threat'ned me
To strike me, spurn me; nay, to kill me too.
And now, so you will let me quiet go,
To Athens will I bear my folly back,
And follow you no further. Let me go.
You see how simple and how fond I am.

HERMIA Why, get you gone. Who is't that hinders you?

HELENA A foolish heart that I leave here behind.

HERMIA What! With Lysander?

HELENA With Demetrius.

LYSANDER Be not afraid: she shall not harm thee, Helena.

DEMETR. No, sir; she shall not, though you take her part.

HELENA When she is angry, she is keen and shrewd.
She was a vixen when she went to school;
And though she be but little, she is fierce.

HERMIA 'Little' again? Nothing but 'low' and 'little'!
Why will you suffer her to flout me thus?
Let me come to her.

LYSANDER Get you gone, you dwarf;
You minimus, of hind'ring knot-grass made;
You bead, you acorn.

DEMETR. You are too officious
In her behalf that scorns your services.
Let her alone; speak not of Helena;
Take not her part; [*he draws his sword*]
for if thou dost intend
Never so little show of love to her,

Thou shalt aby it.

LYSANDER [*also draws*] Now she holds me not;
Now follow, if thou dar'st, to try whose right,
Of thine or mine, is most in Helena.
[*he turns into the wood*

DEMETR. Follow! Nay, I'll go with thee, cheek by jowl.
[*he hastens after*

HERMIA You, mistress, all this coil is 'long of you:
Nay: go not back.

HELENA I will not trust you, I,
Nor longer stay in your curst company.
Your hands than mine are quicker for a fray;
My legs are longer though to run away. [*she runs off*

HERMIA I am amazed, and know not what to say.
[*she follows slowly*

OBERON [*to Puck*] This is thy negligence. Still thou mistak'st,
Or else commit'st thy knaveries wilfully.

PUCK Believe me, king of shadows, I mistook.
Did not you tell me I should know the man
By the Athenian garments he had on?
And so far blameless proves my enterprise
That I have 'nointed an Athenian's eyes:
And so far am I glad it so did sort,
As this their jangling I esteem a sport.

OBERON Thou see'st these lovers seek a place to fight:
Hie therefore, Robin, overcast the night,
The starry welkin cover thou anon
With drooping fog as black as Acheron,
And lead these testy rivals so astray,
As one come not within another's way.
Like to Lysander sometime frame thy tongue;
Then stir Demetrius up with bitter wrong;
And sometime rail thou like Demetrius:
And from each other look thou lead them thus;
Till o'er their brows death-counterfeiting sleep
With leaden legs and batty wings doth creep:
Then crush this herb into Lysander's eye;
Whose liquor hath this virtuous property,
To take from thence all error with his might,

And make his eyeballs roll with wonted sight.
When they next wake, all this derision
Shall seem a dream and fruitless vision,
And back to Athens shall the lovers wend
With league whose date till death shall never end.
Whiles I in this affair do thee employ,
I'll to my queen and beg her Indian boy;
And then I will her charméd eye release
From monster's view, and all things shall be peace.

PUCK My fairy lord, this must be done with haste,
For night's swift dragons cut the clouds full fast;
And yonder shines Aurora's harbinger,
At whose approach ghosts wand'ring here and there,
Troop home to churchyards. Damnéd spirits all,
That in crossways and floods have burial,
Already to their wormy beds are gone;
For fear lest day should look their shames upon,
They wilfully themselves exile from light,
And must for aye consort with black-browed night.

OBERON But we are spirits of another sort.
I with the morning's love have oft made sport,
And like a forester the groves may tread,
Even till the eastern gate, all fiery-red,
Opening on Neptune with fair blesséd beams,
Turns into yellow gold his salt green streams.
But, notwithstanding, haste – make no delay:
We may effect this business yet ere day. *[he goes*

A fog descends

PUCK Up and down, up and down,
I will lead them up and down.
I am feared in field and town.
Goblin, lead them up and down.
Here comes one. *[he vanishes*

LYSANDER *returns, groping in the dark*

LYSANDER Where art thou, proud Demetrius? Speak thou now.

PUCK Here, villain! Drawn and ready. Where art thou?

LYSANDER I will be with thee straight.

PUCK Follow me then

To plainer ground. [*Lysander follows the voice*

DEMETRIUS *approaches, groping likewise*

DEMETR. Lysander! Speak again.
Thou runaway, thou coward, art thou fled?
Speak! In some bush? Where dost thou hide thy head?

PUCK Thou coward, art thou bragging to the stars,
Telling the bushes that thou look'st for wars,
And wilt not come? Come recreant, come thou child,
I'll whip thee with a rod. He is defiled
That draws a sword on thee.

DEMETR. Yea, art thou there?

PUCK Follow my voice: we'll try no manhood here.
[*Demetrius follows the voice*

LYSANDER *returns*

LYSANDER He goes before me and still dares me on:
When I come where he calls, then he is gone.
The villain is much lighter-heeled than I:
I followed fast; but faster he did fly;
That fallen am I in dark uneven way,
And here will rest me. [*he lies down upon a bank*]
Come, thou gentle day,
For if but once thou show me thy grey light,
I'll find Demetrius and revenge this spite. [*he sleeps*

DEMETRIUS *returns, running*

PUCK Ho, ho, ho! Coward, why com'st thou not?

DEMETR. Abide me if thou dar'st, for well I wot
Thou runn'st before me, shifting every place,
And dar'st not stand, nor look me in the face.
Where art thou now?

PUCK Come hither; I am here.

DEMETR. Nay, then thou mock'st me. Thou shalt buy this dear,
If ever I thy face by daylight see.
Now, go thy way. Faintness constraineth me
To measure out my length on this cold bed.
By day's approach look to be visited.
[*he lies down upon another bank and sleeps*

HELENA *enters the clearing*

HELENA O weary night, O long and tedious night,
Abate thy hours! Shine comforts from the east,
That I may back to Athens by daylight,
From these that my poor company detest.
And sleep, that sometimes shuts up sorrow's eye,
Steal me awhile from mine own company.
[*she gropes her way to the bank where Demetrius lies and falls asleep thereon*

PUCK *reappears*

PUCK Yet but three? Come one more.
Two of both kinds makes up four.
Here she comes, curst and sad.
Cupid is a knavish lad,
Thus to make poor females mad.

HERMIA *returns, dejected*

HERMIA Never so weary, never so in woe;
Bedabbled with the dew and torn with briars;
I can no further crawl, no further go;
My legs can keep no pace with my desires.
Here will I rest me till the break of day.
Heavens shield Lysander, if they mean a fray!
[*she gropes her way to the bank on which Lysander lies and falls asleep*

PUCK On the ground
Sleep sound:
I'll apply
To your eye,
Gentle lover, remedy.
[*he anoints Lysander's eyes with the love-juice*
When thou wak'st,
Thou tak'st
True delight
In the sight
Of thy former lady's eye:
And the country proverb known,
That every man should take his own,

In your waking shall be shown.
Jack shall have Jill;
Nought shall go ill;
The man shall have his mare again, and all shall be well.
[*he vanishes; the fog disperses*

ACT 4 SCENE 1

TITANIA *approaches with* BOTTOM, *his ass's head garlanded with flowers; fairies follow in their train;* OBERON *behind all, unseen*

TITANIA Come, sit thee down upon this flow'ry bed,
While I thy amiable cheeks do coy,
And stick musk-roses in thy sleek smooth head,
And kiss thy fair large ears, my gentle joy.
[*they sit; she embraces him*

BOTTOM Where's Peaseblossom?

PEASE. Ready.

BOTTOM Scratch my head, Peaseblossom. Where's Monsieur Cobweb?

COBWEB Ready.

BOTTOM Monsieur Cobweb, good monsieur, get you your weapons in your hand and kill me a red-hipped humble-bee on the top of a thistle; and, good monsieur, bring me the honey-bag. Do not fret yourself too much in the action, monsieur; and, good monsieur, have a care the honey-bag break not – I would be loath to have you overflown with a honey bag, signior. Where's Monsieur Mustardseed?

MUSTARD. Ready.

BOTTOM Give me your neaf, Monsieur Mustardseed. Pray you, leave your curtsy, good monsieur.

MUSTARD. What's your will?

BOTTOM Nothing, good monsieur, but to help Cavalery Cobweb to scratch. I must to the barber's, monsieur; for methinks I am marvellous hairy about the face – and I am such a tender ass, if my hair do but tickle me I must scratch.

TITANIA What, wilt thou hear some music, my sweet love?

BOTTOM I have a reasonable good ear in music. Let's have the tongs and the bones.

TITANIA Or say, sweet love, what thou desir'st to eat.

BOTTOM Truly, a peck of provender. I could munch your good dry oats. Methinks I have a great desire to a bottle of hay. Good hay, sweet hay, hath no fellow.

TITANIA I have a venturous fairy, that shall seek
The squirrel's hoard, and fetch thee thence new nuts.

BOTTOM I had rather have a handful or two of dried peas. But, I pray you, let none of your people stir me; I have an exposition of sleep come upon me.

TITANIA Sleep thou, and I will wind thee in my arms.
Fairies, be gone, and be all ways away.
[the fairies leave them
So doth the woodbine the sweet honeysuckle
Gently entwist: the female ivy so
Enrings the barky fingers of the elm.
O, how I love thee! How I dote on thee! *[they sleep*

OBERON *draws nigh and looks upon them;* PUCK *appears*

OBERON Welcome, good Robin. See'st thou this sweet sight?
Her dotage now I do begin to pity.
For meeting her of late behind the wood,
Seeking sweet favours for this hateful fool,
I did upbraid her and fall out with her.
For she his hairy temples then had rounded
With coronet of fresh and fragrant flowers;
And that same dew which sometime on the buds
Was wont to swell like round and orient pearls
Stood now within the pretty flowerets' eyes
Like tears that did their own disgrace bewail.
When I had at my pleasure taunted her,
And she in mild terms begged my patience,
I then did ask of her her changeling child;
Which straight she gave me, and her fairy sent
To bear him to my bower in Fairyland.
And now I have the boy, I will undo
This hateful imperfection of her eyes.
And, gentle Puck, take this transformèd scalp
From off the head of this Athenian swain;
That he, awaking when the other do,
May all to Athens back again repair,
And think no more of this night's accidents
But as the fierce vexation of a dream.

But first I will release the Fairy Queen.
Be as thou wast wont to be: [*he anoints her eyes*
See as thou wast wont to see.
Dian's bud o'er Cupid's flower
Hath such force and blesséd power.
Now, my Titania! Wake you, my sweet queen.

TITANIA My Oberon! What visions have I seen!
Methought I was enamoured of an ass.

OBERON There lies your love.

TITANIA How came these things to pass?
O, how mine eyes do loathe his visage now!

OBERON Silence, awhile. Robin, take off this head.
Titania, music call; and strike more dead
Than common sleep of all these five the sense.

TITANIA Music, ho! Music! Such as charmeth sleep. [*soft music*

PUCK Now, when thou wak'st, with thine own fool's eyes peep.
[*he plucks the ass's head from him*

OBERON Sound, music. [*the music waxes loud*]
Come, my queen, take hands with me,
And rock the ground whereon these sleepers be.
[*they dance*
Now thou and I are new in amity,
And will tomorrow midnight solemnly
Dance in Duke Theseus' house triumphantly,
And bless it to all fair prosperity.
There shall the pairs of faithful lovers be
Wedded, with Theseus, all in jollity.

PUCK Fairy King, attend, and mark:
I do hear the morning lark.

OBERON Then, my queen, in silence sad,
Trip we after the night's shade:
We the globe can compass soon,
Swifter than the wand'ring moon.

TITANIA Come my lord, and in our flight,
Tell me how it came this night
That I sleeping here was found
With these mortals on the ground. [*they vanish*

There is a sound of horns; THESEUS, HIPPOLYTA, EGEUS *and others are seen approaching, arrayed for the hunt*

THESEUS Go, one of you, find out the forester;
For now our observation is performed,
And since we have the vaward of the day,
My love shall hear the music of my hounds.
Uncouple in the western valley, let them go:
Dispatch, I say, and find the forester.
[a servant bows and departs
We will, fair queen, up to the mountain's top,
And mark the musical confusion
Of hounds and echo in conjunction.

HIPPOLYTA I was with Hercules and Cadmus once,
When in a wood of Crete they bayed the bear
With hounds of Sparta: never did I hear
Such gallant chiding; for, besides the groves,
The skies, the fountains, every region near
Seemed all one mutual cry. I never heard
So musical a discord, such sweet thunder.

THESEUS My hounds are bred out of the Spartan kind:
So flewed, so sanded; and their heads are hung
With ears that sweep away the morning dew –
Crook-kneed, and dewlapped like Thessalian bulls;
Slow in pursuit; but matched in mouth like bells,
Each under each. A cry more tuneable
Was never hollaed to, nor cheered with horn,
In Crete, in Sparta, nor in Thessaly.
Judge when you hear. But, soft, what nymphs are these?

EGEUS My lord, this is my daughter here asleep –
And this Lysander – this Demetrius is –
This Helena, old Nedar's Helena.
I wonder of their being here together.

THESEUS No doubt they rose up early to observe
The rite of May; and, hearing our intent,
Came here in grace of our solemnity.
But, speak, Egeus; is not this the day
That Hermia should give answer of her choice?

EGEUS It is, my lord.

THESEUS Go, bid the huntsmen wake them with their horns.

[horns, and a shout; the lovers awake and 'start up'
Good morrow, friends. Saint Valentine is past;
Begin these wood-birds but to couple now?

LYSANDER Pardon, my lord. *[they kneel to Theseus*

THESEUS I pray you all, stand up.
I know you two are rival enemies:
How comes this gentle concord in the world,
That hatred is so far from jealousy
To sleep by hate, and fear no enmity?

LYSANDER My lord, I shall reply amazedly,
Half sleep, half waking. But as yet, I swear,
I cannot truly say how I came here.
But, as I think – for truly would I speak,
And now I do bethink me, so it is –
I came with Hermia hither. Our intent
Was to be gone from Athens, where we might,
Without the peril of the Athenian law –

EGEUS Enough, enough, my lord; you have enough.
I beg the law, the law, upon his head.
They would have stol'n away, they would, Demetrius,
Thereby to have defeated you and me:
You of your wife, and me of my consent –
Of my consent that she should be your wife.

DEMETR. My lord, fair Helen told me of their stealth,
Of this their purpose hither to this wood,
And I in fury hither followed them;
Fair Helena in fancy following me.
But, my good lord, I wot not by what power –
But by some power it is – my love to Hermia,
Melted as melts the snow, seems to me now
As the remembrance of an idle gaud
Which in my childhood I did dote upon:
And all the faith, the virtue of my heart,
The object and the pleasure of mine eye,
Is only Helena. To her, my lord,
Was I betrothed ere I saw Hermia:
But, like in sickness did I loathe this food,
So, as in health, come to my natural taste,
Now I do wish it, love it, long for it,

And will for evermore be true to it.

THESEUS Fair lovers, you are fortunately met.
Of this discourse we more will hear anon.
Egeus, I will overbear your will;
For in the temple, by and by, with us,
These couples shall eternally be knit.
And, for the morning now is something worn,
Our purposed hunting shall be set aside.
Away with us, to Athens! Three and three,
We'll hold a feast in great solemnity.
Come, Hippolyta.

[*Theseus, Hippolyta, Egeus and their train depart*

DEMETR. These things seem small and undistinguishable,
Like far-off mountains turnéd into clouds.

HERMIA Methinks I see these things with parted eye,
When everything seems double.

HELENA So methinks:
And I have found Demetrius like a jewel,
Mine own, and not mine own.

DEMETR. Are you sure
That we are well awake? It seems to me,
That yet we sleep, we dream. Do not you think
The duke was here, and bid us follow him?

HERMIA Yea, and my father.

HELENA And Hippolyta.

LYSANDER And he did bid us follow to the temple.

DEMETR. Why then, we are awake; let's follow him;
And by the way let us recount our dreams.

[*they follow* THESEUS

BOTTOM [*awaking*] When my cue comes, call me, and I will answer. My next is, 'Most fair Pyramus'. Heigh-ho! [*he yawns, and looks about him*] Peter Quince! Flute, the bellows-mender! Snout, the tinker! Starveling! God's my life! Stol'n hence, and left me asleep! I have had a most rare vision. I have had a dream – past the wit of man to say what dream it was. Man is but an ass, if he go about to expound this dream. [*he rises*] Methought I was – there is no man can tell what . . . [*he passes his hand across his head, touching his ears*] Methought I was, and methought I had . . . but man is but a patched fool, if he will offer to say what methought I had. The eye of man hath not heard, the ear of man hath not seen, man's hand is not able to taste, his tongue to conceive, nor his heart to report, what my dream was. I will get Peter Quince to write a ballad of this dream: it shall be called Bottom's Dream, because it hath no bottom: and I will sing it in the latter end of our play, before the duke. Peradventure, to make it the more gracious, I shall sing it at her death. [*he goes*

SCENE 2

The room in Peter Quince's cottage

QUINCE, FLUTE, SNOUT *and* STARVELING

QUINCE Have you sent to Bottom's house? Is he come home yet?

STARV'LING He cannot be heard of. Out of doubt he is transported.

FLUTE If he come not, then the play is marred. It goes not forward, doth it?

QUINCE It is not possible. You have not a man in all Athens able to discharge Pyramus but he.

FLUTE No, he hath simply the best wit of any handicraft man in Athens.

QUINCE Yea, and the best person too – and he is a very paramour for a sweet voice.

FLUTE You must say 'paragon'. A paramour is, God bless us, a thing of naught.

SNUG *enters*

SNUG Masters, the duke is coming from the temple, and there is two or three lords and ladies more married – if our sport had gone forward, we had all been made men.

FLUTE O sweet bully Bottom! Thus hath he lost sixpence a day during his life: he could not have 'scaped sixpence a day. An the duke had not given him sixpence a day for playing Pyramus, I'll be hanged. He would have deserved it: sixpence a day in Pyramus, or nothing.

BOTTOM *enters*

BOTTOM Where are these lads? Where are these hearts?

QUINCE Bottom! O most courageous day! O most happy hour!

[*they all crowd about him*

BOTTOM Masters, I am to discourse wonders: but ask me not what; for if I tell you, I am not true Athenian. I will tell you everything, right as it fell out.

QUINCE Let us hear, sweet Bottom.

BOTTOM Not a word of me. All that I will tell you is, that the duke hath dined. Get your apparel together – good strings to your beards, new ribbons to your pumps – meet presently at the palace, every man look o'er his part; for the short and the long is, our play is preferred. In any case, let Thisby have clean linen; and let not him that plays the lion pare his nails; for they shall hang out for the lion's claws. And, most dear actors, eat no onions nor garlic; for we are to utter sweet breath; and I do not doubt but to hear them say, it is a sweet comedy. No more words. Away, go away!

[*they hurry forth*

ACT 5 SCENE 1

The hall in the palace of Duke Theseus. A curtain conceals the entrance to the lobby at the back. A fire burns upon the hearth. Lights and torches

THESEUS *and* HIPPOLYTA *enter, followed by* PHILOSTRATE, *lords and attendants. The Duke and Duchess take their seats*

HIPPOLYTA 'Tis strange, my Theseus, that these lovers speak of.

THESEUS More strange than true. I never may believe
These antic fables, nor these fairy toys.
Lovers and madmen have such seething brains,
Such shaping fantasies, that apprehend
More than cool reason ever comprehends.
The lunatic, the lover, and the poet,
Are of imagination all compact.
One sees more devils than vast hell can hold;
That is, the madman. The lover, all as frantic,
Sees Helen's beauty in a brow of Egypt.
The poet's eye, in a fine frenzy rolling,
Doth glance from heaven to earth, from earth to heaven;
And as imagination bodies forth
The forms of things unknown, the poet's pen
Turns them to shapes, and gives to airy nothing
A local habitation and a name.
Such tricks hath strong imagination
That, if it would but apprehend some joy,
It comprehends some bringer of that joy;
Or in the night, imagining some fear,
How easy is a bush supposed a bear!

HIPPOLYTA But all the story of the night told over,
And all their minds transfigured so together,
More witnesseth than fancy's images,
And grows to something of great constancy –
But howsoever strange and admirable.

THESEUS Here come the lovers, full of joy and mirth.

LYSANDER *and* HERMIA, DEMETRIUS *and* HELENA *enter, laughing and talking together*

Joy, gentle friends! Joy and fresh days of love
Accompany your hearts!

LYSANDER More than to us
Wait in your royal walks, your board, your bed!

THESEUS Come now; what masques, what dances shall we have,
To wear away this long age of three hours
Between our after-supper and bed-time?
Where is our usual manager of mirth?
What revels are in hand? Is there no play
To ease the anguish of a torturing hour?
Call Philostrate.

PHILOSTR. Here, mighty Theseus.

THESEUS Say, what abridgment have you for this evening?
What masque? What music? How shall we beguile
The lazy time, if not with some delight?

PHILOSTR. There is a brief how many sports are ripe;
Make choice of which your highness will see first.
[*he presents a paper*

THESEUS 'The battle with the Centaurs, to be sung
By an Athenian eunuch to the harp.'
We'll none of that: that have I told my love,
In glory of my kinsman Hercules.
'The riot of the tipsy Bacchanals,
Tearing the Thracian singer in their rage.'
That is an old device; and it was played
When I from Thebes came last a conqueror.
'The thrice three Muses mourning for the death
Of Learning, late deceased in beggary.'
That is some satire, keen and critical,
Not sorting with a nuptial ceremony.
'A tedious brief scene of young Pyramus
And his love Thisby; very tragical mirth.'
Merry and tragical! Tedious and brief!
That is hot ice and wondrous strange snow.
How shall we find the concord of this discord?

PHILOSTR. A play there is, my lord, some ten words long;
Which is as brief as I have known a play;

But by ten words, my lord, it is too long;
Which makes it tedious: for in all the play
There is not one word apt, one player fitted.
And tragical, my noble lord, it is;
For Pyramus therein doth kill himself.
Which when I saw rehearsed, I must confess,
Made mine eyes water; but more merry tears
The passion of loud laughter never shed.

THESEUS What are they that do play it?

PHILOSTR. Hard-handed men that work in Athens here,
Which never laboured in their minds till now;
And now have toiled their unbreathed memories
With this same play against your nuptial.

THESEUS And we will hear it.

PHILOSTR. No, my noble lord,
It is not for you: I have heard it over,
And it is nothing, nothing in the world;
Unless you can find sport in their intents,
Extremely stretched and conned with cruel pain,
To do you service.

THESEUS I will hear that play:
For never anything can be amiss,
When simpleness and duty tender it.
Go bring them in; and take your places, ladies.
[*Philostrate departs; the rest of the court make ready to hear the play*

HIPPOLYTA I love not to see wretchedness o'ercharged,
And duty in his service perishing.

THESEUS Why, gentle sweet, you shall see no such thing.

HIPPOLYTA He says they can do nothing in this kind.

THESEUS The kinder we, to give them thanks for nothing.
Our sport shall be to take what they mistake
And what poor duty cannot do, noble respect
Takes it in might not merit.
Where I have come, great clerks have purposéd
To greet me with premeditated welcomes;
Where I have seen them shiver and look pale,
Make periods in the midst of sentences,
Throttle their practised accent in their fears,

And in conclusion dumbly have broke off,
Not paying me a welcome. Trust me, sweet,
Out of this silence yet I picked a welcome;
And in the modesty of fearful duty
I read as much as from the rattling tongue
Of saucy and audacious eloquence.
Love, therefore, and tongue-tied simplicity
In least speak most, to my capacity.

PHILOSTRATE *returns*

PHILOSTR. So please your grace, the Prologue is addressed.

THESEUS Let him approach.

Enter before the curtain QUINCE *for the Prologue*

QUINCE If we offend, it is with our good will.
  That you should think, we come not to offend,
But with good will. To show our simple skill,
  That is the true beginning of our end.
Consider then, we come but in despite.
  We do not come, as minding to content you,
Our true intent is. All for your delight
  We are not here. That you should here repent you,
The actors are at hand: and, by their show,
  You shall know all, that you are like to know.,

[*he whips behind the curtains*

THESEUS This fellow doth not stand upon points.

LYSANDER He hath rid his prologue like a rough colt: he knows not the stop. A good moral, my lord – it is not enough to speak; but to speak true.

HIPPOLYTA Indeed he hath played on his prologue like a child on a recorder – a sound, but not in government.

THESEUS His speech was like a tangled chain; nothing impaired, but all disordered. Who is next?

Enter before the curtain PYRAMUS *and* THISBY, WALL, MOONSHINE, *and* LION, *as in dumb-show, with* QUINCE *for the Presenter*

QUINCE Gentles, perchance you wonder at this show,
  But wonder on, till truth make all things plain.
This man is Pyramus, if you would know:
  This beauteous lady Thisby is certain.

This man, with lime and rough-cast, doth present
  Wall, that vile Wall which did these lovers sunder:
And through Wall's chink, poor souls, they are content
  To whisper. At the which let no man wonder.
This man, with lantern, dog, and bush of thorn,
  Presenteth Moonshine. For, if you will know,
By moonshine did these lovers think no scorn
  To meet at Ninus' tomb, there, there to woo:
This grisly beast (which Lion hight by name)
The trusty Thisby, coming first by night,
Did scare away, or rather did affright
And, as she fled, her mantle she did fall:
  Which Lion vile with bloody mouth did stain.
Anon comes Pyramus, sweet youth, and tall,
  And finds his trusty Thisby's mantle slain:
Whereat, with blade, with bloody blameful blade,
  He bravely broached his boiling bloody breast.
And Thisby, tarrying in mulberry shade,
  His dagger drew, and died. For all the rest,
Let Lion, Moonshine, Wall, and lovers twain
At large discourse, while here they do remain.

THESEUS I wonder if the lion be to speak.

DEMETR. No wonder, my lord:
One lion may, when many asses do.

[*exeunt all save Wall and Pyramus*

WALL *steps forward*

WALL In this same interlude it doth befall
That I, one Snout by name, present a wall:
And such a wall, as I would have you think,
That had in it a crannied hole or chink:
Through which the lovers, Pyramus and Thisby,
Did whisper often very secretly.
This loam, this rough-cast, and this stone, doth show
That I am that same wall; the truth is so.
And this the cranny is, right and sinister,

[*he stretches forth his fingers*

Through which the fearful lovers are to whisper.

THESEUS Would you desire lime and hair to speak better?

DEMETR. It is the wittiest partition that ever I heard discourse, my lord.

PYRAMUS *steps forward*

THESEUS Pyramus draws near the wall: silence!

PYRAMUS O grim-looked night! O night with hue so black!
O night, which ever art when day is not
O night, O night, alack, alack, alack,
I fear my Thisby's promise is forgot!
And thou, O wall! O sweet, O lovely wall!
That stand'st between her father's ground and mine,
Thou wall, O wall! O sweet and lovely wall!
Show me thy chink to blink through with mine eyne.
[*Wall obeys*
Thanks, courteous wall. Jove shield thee well for this!
But what see I? No Thisby do I see.
O wicked wall, through whom I see no bliss,
Cursed be thy stones for thus deceiving me!

THESEUS The wall, methinks, being sensible, should curse again.

PYRAMUS No, in truth, sir, he should not. 'Deceiving me' is Thisby's cue: she is to enter now, and I am to spy her through the wall. You shall see, it will fall pat as I told you. Yonder she comes.

Enter THISBY

THISBY O wall! Full often hast thou heard my moans,
For parting my fair Pyramus and me.
My cherry lips have often kissed thy stones;
Thy stones with lime and hair knit up in thee.

PYRAMUS I see a voice: now will I to the chink
To spy an I can hear my Thisby's face.
Thisby!

THISBY My love! thou art my love, I think.

PYRAMUS Think what thou wilt, I am thy lover's grace;
And, like Limander, am I trusty still.

THISBY And I like Helen, till the Fates me kill.

PYRAMUS Not Shafalus to Procrus was so true.

THISBY As Shafalus to Procrus, I to you.

PYRAMUS O! Kiss me through the hole of this vile wall.

THISBY I kiss the wall's hole, not your lips at all.

PYRAMUS Wilt thou at Ninny's tomb meet me straightway?
THISBY 'Tide life, 'tide death, I come without delay.
[*exeunt Pyramus and Thisby*
WALL Thus have I, Wall, my part dischargéd so;
And being done, thus Wall away doth go. [*exit Wall*
THESEUS Now is the mural down between the two neighbours.

DEMETR. No remedy, my lord, when walls are so wilful to hear without warning.

HIPPOLYTA This is the silliest stuff that ever I heard.

THESEUS The best in this kind are but shadows: and the worst are no worse, if imagination amend them.

HIPPOLYTA It must be your imagination then; and not theirs.

THESEUS If we imagine no worse of them than they of themselves, they may pass for excellent men. Here come two noble beasts, in a moon and a lion.

Enter LION *and* MOONSHINE

LION You ladies, you, whose gentle hearts do fear
The smallest monstrous mouse that creeps on floor,
May now perchance both quake and tremble here,
When lion rough in wildest rage doth roar.
Then know that I as Snug the joiner am
A lion fell, nor else no lion's dam.
For if I should as lion come in strife
Into this place, 'twere pity on my life.

THESEUS A very gentle beast, and of a good conscience.

DEMETR. The very best at a beast, my lord, that e'er I saw.

LYSANDER This lion is a very fox for his valour.

THESEUS True: and a goose for his discretion.

DEMETR. Not so, my lord, for his valour cannot carry his discretion; and the fox carries the goose.

THESEUS His discretion, I am sure, cannot carry his valour, for the goose carries not the fox. It is well: leave it to his discretion, and let us listen to the moon.

MOON. This lanthorn doth the hornéd moon present –

DEMETR. He should have worn the horns on his head.

THESEUS He is no crescent, and his horns are invisible within the circumference.

MOON. This lanthorn doth the hornéd moon present,

Myself the man i'th' moon do seem to be.

THESEUS This is the greatest error of all the rest: the man should be put into the lantern. How is it else the man i'th' moon?

DEMETR. He dares not come there for the candle – for, you see, it is already in snuff.

HIPPOLYTA I am aweary of this moon. Would he would change!

THESEUS It appears, by his small light of discretion, that he is in the wane: but yet, in courtesy, in all reason, we must stay the time.

LYSANDER Proceed, Moon.

MOON. All that I have to say, is to tell you that the lanthorn is the moon, I the man i'th' moon, this thorn-bush my thorn-bush, and this dog my dog.

DEMETR. Why, all these should be in the lantern; for all these are in the moon. But, silence; here comes Thisby.

Enter THISBY; LION *and* MOONSHINE *draw back the curtain before the lobby, discovering a placard within inscribed* NINUS' TOMB

THISBY This is old Ninny's tomb. Where is my love?

LION [*roars*] Oh –

[*Thisby casts her mantle from her and runs away*

DEMETR. Well roared, Lion.

THESEUS Well run, Thisby.

HIPPOLYTA Well shone, Moon. Truly, the moon shines with a good grace. [*Lion paws Thisby's mantle*

THESEUS Well moused, Lion.

DEMETR. And then came Pyramus.

Enter PYRAMUS; *exit* LION

LYSANDER And so the lion vanished.

PYRAMUS Sweet moon, I thank thee for thy sunny beams.
I thank thee, moon, for shining now so bright.
For, by thy gracious, golden, glittering gleams,
I trust to take of truest Thisby sight.
But stay. O spite!
But mark, poor knight,
What dreadful dole is here!
Eyes, do you see?
How can it be?

O dainty duck, O dear!
Thy mantle good,
What, stained with blood?
Approach, ye Furies fell!
O Fates, come, come,
Cut thread and thrum,
Quail, crush, conclude, and quell!

THESEUS This passion – and the death of a dear friend – would go near to make a man look sad.

HIPPOLYTA Beshrew my heart, but I pity the man.

PYRAMUS O wherefore, Nature, didst thou lions frame?
Since lion vile hath here deflowered my dear.
Which is – no, no – which was the fairest dame
That lived, that loved, that liked, that looked with cheer.
Come, tears, confound;
Out, sword, and wound
The pap of Pyramus:
Ay, that left pap,
Where heart doth hop. *[he stabs himself*
Thus die I, thus, thus, thus.
[he drops the sword and staggers across the floor to fall within the tomb
Now am I dead,
Now am I fled,
My soul is in the sky.
Tongue, lose thy light!
Moon, take thy flight! *[exit Moonshine*
Now die, die, die, die, die.' *[he muffles his face*

DEMETR. No die, but an ace, for him – for he is but one.

LYSANDER Less than an ace, man – for he is dead, he is nothing.

THESEUS With the help of a surgeon, he might yet recover, and prove an ass.

HIPPOLYTA How chance Moonshine is gone before Thisby comes back and finds her lover?

THESEUS She will find him by starlight. Here she comes, and her passion ends the play.

Enter THISBY

HIPPOLYTA Methinks she should not use a long one for such a Pyramus: I hope she will be brief.

DEMETR. A mote will turn the balance, which Pyramus, which Thisby, is the better: he for a man, God warr'nt us; she for a woman, God bless us.

LYSANDER She hath spied him already with those sweet eyes.

[THISBY *discovers* PYRAMUS *in the tomb*

DEMETR. And thus she moans, videlicet –

THISBY
Asleep, my love?
What, dead, my dove?
O Pyramus, arise,
Speak, speak. Quite dumb?

[*she uncovers his face*

Dead, dead? A tomb
Must cover thy sweet eyes.
These lily lips,
This cherry nose,
These yellow cowslip cheeks,
Are gone, are gone:
Lovers, make moan:
His eyes were green as leeks.
O Sisters Three,
Come, come to me,
With hands as pale as milk;
Lay them in gore,
Since you have shore
With shears his thread of silk.
Tongue, not a word:
Come, trusty sword,
Come, blade, my breast imbrue.

[*she searches Pyramus for the sword and not finding it stabs herself perforce with the scabbard*

And farewell, friends:
Thus Thisby ends:
Adieu, adieu, adieu.

[*she falls heavily across the body*

Enter LION, MOONSHINE *and* WALL; *they close the curtain before "Ninny's tomb"*

THESEUS Moonshine and Lion are left to bury the dead.

DEMETR. Ay and Wall too.

LION No, I assure you, the wall is down that parted their fathers. [*he plucks a paper from his bosom*] Will it please you to see the Epilogue, or to hear a Bergomask dance between two of our company?

THESEUS No Epilogue, I pray you – for your play needs no excuse. Never excuse; for when the players are all dead, there need none to be blamed. Marry, if he that writ it had played Pyramus and hanged himself in Thisby's garter, it would have been a fine tragedy: and so it is truly, and very notably discharged. But come, your Bergomask: let your Epilogue alone.

MOONSHINE *and* WALL *dance the Bergomask and go out;* THESEUS *rises*

The iron tongue of midnight hath told twelve!
Lovers, to bed – 'tis almost fairy time.
I fear we shall out-sleep the coming morn,
As much as we this night have overwatched.
This palpable-gross play hath well beguiled
The heavy gait of night. Sweet friends, to bed.
A fortnight hold we this solemnity,
In nightly revels, and new jollity.

The Duke leads HIPPOLYTA *forth, followed by the lovers, hand in hand, and the rest of the court; the lights are extinguished and all is dark, save for the dying embers on the hearth*

PUCK *appears broom in hand*

PUCK Now the hungry lion roars,
And the wolf behowls the moon;
Whilst the heavy ploughman snores,
All with weary task fordone.
Now the wasted brands do glow,
Whilst the screech-owl, screeching loud,
Puts the wretch that lies in woe
In remembrance of a shroud.
Now it is the time of night,
That the graves, all gaping wide,

Every one lets forth his sprite,
 In the church-way paths to glide.
And we fairies, that do run
 By the triple Hecate's team
From the presence of the sun,
 Following darkness like a dream,
Now are frolic. Not a mouse
Shall disturb this hallowed house.
I am sent with broom before,
To sweep the dust behind the door.

Of a sudden OBERON, TITANIA *and the fairy-host stream into the hall, with rounds of waxen tapers on their heads, which they swiftly kindle at the hearth as they pass it by, until the great chamber is full of light*

OBERON Through the house give glimmering light,
 By the dead and drowsy fire;
Every elf and fairy sprite
 Hop as light as bird from briar;
And this ditty after me
Sing, and dance it trippingly.

TITANIA [*to Oberon*]
First rehearse your song by rote,
To each word a warbling note;
Hand in hand, with fairy grace,
Will we sing and bless this place.

OBERON *leads and all the fairies sing in chorus; as they sing, they take hands and dance about the hall*

Now, until the break of day,
Through this house each fairy stray.
To the best bride-bed will we,
Which by us shall blessèd be:
And the issue there create
Ever shall be fortunate:
So shall all the couples three
Ever true in loving be:
And the blots of Nature's hand
Shall not in their issue stand.
Never mole, hare-lip, nor scar,

Nor mark prodigious, such as are
Despiséd in nativity,
Shall upon their children be.
With this field-dew consecrate,
Every fairy take his gait,
And each several chamber bless,
Through this palace, with sweet peace;
And the owner of it blest
Ever shall in safety rest.
    Trip away:
    Make no stay
Meet me all by break of day.

They pass out: the hall is dark and silent once again

Epilogue
spoken by PUCK

If we shadows have offended,
Think but this, and all is mended,
That you have but slumb'red here
While these visions did appear.
And this weak and idle theme,
No more yielding but a dream,
Gentles, do not reprehend.
If you pardon, we will mend.
And, as I am an honest Puck,
If we have unearnéd luck
Now to 'scape the serpent's tongue,
We will make amends, ere long:
Else the Puck a liar call.
So, good night unto you all.
Give me your hands, if we be friends:
And Robin shall restore amends. [*he vanishes*

MUCH ADO ABOUT NOTHING

INTRODUCTION

Much Ado About Nothing, like both *Othello* and *The Winter's Tale*, is a drama about a woman wrongfully accused of sexual infidelity. In all three plays, the wronged woman dies, or is thought to have died, under the weight of the accusations thrown at her. In the tragedy of *Othello* the heroine's death is irreversible. In both *Much Ado* and *The Winter's Tale*, however, a way out of the pain may be found: the slandered heroine may be resurrected and a comic ending by some means secured.

Much Ado flirts with the forms of tragedy – Hero, the slandered woman, undergoes a mock death that she may be lamented and pitied. The audience, however, knows at every stage that the death is counterfeited. 'One Hero died defil'd, but I do live . . . ' (5.2.63) she says once her reputation has been cleared. It is in no sense a play which makes light of the existence of pain in the world but, being a comedy, it optimistically chooses to believe that pain may nevertheless be dissipated, problems overcome and characters rescued even from the edge of catastrophe.

In this, Shakespeare differs from his principal sources in which the material is not treated as a comedy. The story of a lover believing a false report of the sexual infidelity of his beloved is derived from several variants of a fifth century bc Greek romance by Chariton. The two most significant sixteenth century versions of this are to be found in the fifth canto of Ariosto's *Orlando Furioso* (1516), and the twenty second story of Bandello's *La Prima Parte de le Novelle* (1554). From Ariosto Shakespeare borrows several key plot details – including the villain's exploitation of the maid's innocent impersonation of her mistress to convince the lover of his beloved's unfaithfulness. From Bandello Shakespeare takes the Messina setting, the names of Leonato and Don Pedro, and several more plot details – including the heroine's swoon, mock death, and subsequent restoration to her lover in disguise. The other main plot strand – following the fates of two disdainful antagonists to romance – equally springs from several sources, the most significant of which in relation to *Much Ado* is Castiglione's *Il Cortegiano* (1528).

It seems probable that the play was written in late 1598. In this period, the comic actor in Shakespeare's company, The Lord Chamberlain's Men, was Will Kemp. In the 1600 Quarto edition of the play (probably prepared for publication from Shakespeare's own manuscript), Kemp's name (variously spelt) appears in place of Dogberry's in some speech-headings. Shakespeare evidently wrote the part of Dogberry with Kemp fully in mind – so much so that he used Dogberry's and Kemp's names interchangeably in his writing. Kemp, however, was no longer in the employ of The Lord Chamberlain's Men by early 1599, so no Shakespearean part could have been written for him after that date. Since *Much Ado* does not appear in the entry in the Stationer's Register for 7 September 1598, it is therefore possible to place its composition with some confidence to late 1598.

Plot summary

A triumphant company of men, led by Don Pedro, returns to Messina from the wars. They are welcomed into the home of Leonato, the governor of Messina, where they determine to stay 'at least a month' (1.1.129–30). Hero, Leonato's only daughter, finds favour with Count Claudio, one of Don Pedro's company, and after a slight misunderstanding, it is arranged that they shall marry. Hero's cousin Beatrice resumes her 'merry war' (1.1.52) with Claudio's friend Signior Benedick, each vehemently protesting a complete antipathy to marriage. Don Pedro, Claudio and Hero resolve to trick these two cynics into falling in love with each other. By holding staged conversations within earshot of first Benedick and then Beatrice, they succeed in convincing each that s/he is dearly loved by the other. Beatrice and Benedick determine to reciprocate the love they each now believe the other secretly holds.

Meanwhile Don John, Don Pedro's misanthropic and villainous brother, schemes to disrupt the harmony of the community. With the aid of his mercenary friend Borachio, he manages to spoil Claudio's happiness by convincing him that Hero is unchaste. Borachio is then overheard by the night watch bragging to his companion Conrade about his part in the plot to discredit Hero. Despite the watch's astonishing ineptitude, they manage to arrest both Borachio and Conrade and take them away for questioning.

Claudio appears at the wedding in order to shame Hero publicly. He accuses her of being 'an approved wanton' (4.1.41) and Don Pedro accuses her of being 'a common stale' (4.1.62). Even her father, Leonato, becomes convinced that his daughter has behaved immodestly. Horrified at these accusations, Hero swoons. The Friar contrives a plan: it should be put about that Hero has in fact died, in the hope that 'slander' may change to 'remorse' (4.1.208). Beatrice is so incensed at the unfair treatment her cousin has received that she persuades Benedick to challenge Claudio to a duel.

Borachio and Conrade are cross-examined by Dogberry, the master constable. During the course of this chaotic interrogation, it emerges that Borachio has received a thousand ducats from Don John for his part in the conspiracy, that Don John has now fled, and that the slandered Hero is entirely innocent. Informed of all this, Leonato presents the news both of Hero's 'death' and of her established innocence to Claudio, who asks what he may do to make amends. He is told to mourn for Hero and then to be ready the next day to marry her (unnamed) cousin who happens to resemble her closely.

The next day Hero is presented to Claudio in disguise and he agrees to marry her in accordance with Leonato's will. Hero reveals her true identity and is greeted as one returned from the dead. The double marriage of Hero and Claudio and Beatrice and Benedick is delayed only by an all-inclusive dance and by the news that Don John has been taken in flight and so will be punished.

Soldiers and Lovers

Much Ado focuses on a military community in an off-duty moment. In the leisured calm after the wars, soldiers become lovers. Claudio says that before he went to war, he 'had a rougher task in hand':

> But now I am return'd, and that war-thoughts
> Have left their places vacant. In their rooms
> Come thronging soft and delicate desires . . . (1.1.264–66)

As 'soft and delicate desires' displace 'war-thoughts', the soldiers' established allegiances to each other are tested by their newly emerging allegiances to women. In the terms of the play, the life of a soldier is characterised by a shared pride in jocular camaraderie, masculine courage and a sense of honour. The life of a lover, by contrast, is the stuff of jokes – peace-loving, domestic, tame, emasculating. On one level there is a desire to trade in the military drum and fife for the recreational and romantic tabor and pipe (2.3.13–14). On another, however, there is a fear of the vulnerability acquired in the exchange. The prevalence of witticisms throughout the male community about cuckoldry and horns betrays a deep-seated anxiety. Once in thrall to women, men fear they may never again feel peace of mind. Thus, although they good-humouredly tease each other about becoming sexual 'double-dealers', their good-humour in this respect does *not* extend to any prospective 'double-dealing' on the part of women. In fact, their words and actions reveal an acute anxiety about female sexuality. When the suggestion arises that one of the women, the innocent Hero, may herself have been less than chaste, there is an immediate reaffirmation of the bonds of male friendship in collective contempt for, and unbridled aggression towards, the woman.

The degree of male aggression that Hero's supposed crime unleashes is shocking. Claudio and Don Pedro are ready, with troubling haste, to devise a plan for shaming Hero, before they have even been offered any proof of her infidelity:

> If I see anything tonight why I should not marry her, tomorrow, in the congregation, where I should wed, there will I shame her.

says Claudio, and Don Pedro replies:

> And as I wooed for thee to obtain her, I will join thee to disgrace her. (3.2.106–110)

Even Leonato, Hero's father, is ready to believe his daughter a wanton merely on the report of others. In common with many possessive Shakespearean fathers, he seems more obsessed with his own grief, loss and shame than he is with the pain suffered by Hero. When she swoons, he wishes her dead:

> Do not live, Hero, do not ope thine eyes;
> For did I think thou wouldst not quickly die,
> Thought I thy spirits were stronger than thy shames
> Myself would on the rearward of reproaches
> Strike at thy life. (4.1.120–24)

There is a male assumption that female sexuality is a commodity that belongs to them. Even after the slanderous nature of the accusations is known, Leonato's brother says to him: 'Make those that so offend you suffer too' (5.1.40), as if the offence committed had been primarily against him, not Hero. Men, it seems, can only conceive of crimes against men.

Beatrice, on the other hand, feels keenly the injustice that has been done to her cousin. In the early stages of the play she had poured scorn on Benedick's military prowess:

> I pray you, how many hath he killed and eaten in these wars? But how many hath he killed? For indeed I promised to eat all of his killing. (1.1.36–38)

Now, however, aware of her powerlessness in the face of an accumulation of male aggression, she decides to use Benedick's masculinity to strike back at the male perpetrators of the injustice done to Hero. In her instruction to Benedick that he should 'Kill Claudio' she re-directs male violence to act on behalf of women rather than against them. In doing so she breaks in on the male bonds of the regiment and challenges Benedick to assess where his primary allegiance now lies.

Balthasar's song in Act 2 blithely recommends that the best thing for women to do in life is, simply, to 'convert . . . all your sounds of woe' into a far merrier 'Hey nonny, nonny' (2.3.66–67). The violence and extremity of the male responses to Hero's 'guilt' ensures that there will indeed need to be some drastic 'converting' before the women can feel comfortable voicing anything as frolicsome as 'Hey nonny, nonny'. That the play does finally find such a carefree tone, making possible an untroubled comic ending, does not make light of the genuine 'sounds of woe' that have preceded it. Rather, it testifies to the transforming power of comic form, which insists that characters need not be fixed for ever in folly, but may instead be redeemed even from the depth of their own foolishness.

Unredeemable Villainy

Thus Claudio, Don Pedro and Leonato are all offered dignified routes out of their mistake in believing ill of Hero too quickly, and in acting on that belief too viciously. Don John, however, is not susceptible to such gentle realignment. Unlike *As You Like It*, in which both villains undergo dramatic conversions to lives of generosity and holiness in order to secure the comic ending, *Much Ado* boasts a villain whose wickedness proves to be beyond redemption.

> [I]t must not be denied but that I am a plain-speaking villain. (1.3.25–26)

says Don John, and the only definitive explanation for his acknowledged villainy seems to be a misanthropic distaste for the world.

> Will it serve for any model to build mischief on? (1.3.38–39)

he asks when told of Claudio's forthcoming marriage. He is committed to poisoning others' delight and constantly seeks 'food to [his] displeasure' (1.3.53–54). As a distant forerunner to Iago (the pernicious influence in *Othello*), Don John seems to derive his villainous momentum, in Coleridge's famous phrase, from a 'motiveless malignity'. Lacking a clear motive that might be divertible to some better purpose or accessible to redemption, Don John cannot, then, be converted and absorbed into the warmth and good humour of the Messina community for the final dance. Leonato had made a point of welcoming him specifically by name when the company first arrived in Messina, but, having abused that welcome, Don John must be excluded from the community. His attempt to exclude himself by fleeing is inadequate in the moral scheme of the play. He must be apprehended and brought back, that those who were so easily duped by him may themselves have the luxury of proclaiming his exclusion.

Don John is a moral convenience in the world of Messina: the blame for the near-catastrophe of the broken nuptials may be neatly placed on him. Castigating him implicitly exonerates all the other characters. Yet Don John's poisonous presence in Messina acts as a catalyst, exposing much that is ugly or morally suspect in other characters too. In their willingness to believe the worst of Hero, their violence of language and action towards her, and their apparent callous indifference to the news of her death, neither Don Pedro nor Claudio emerges unstained. Equally, Leonato publicly abhors his daughter's 'foul-tainted flesh' (4.1.140) before he has heard a single word from her. Don John's spite therefore uncovers a latent vein of misogyny in the world of Messina. Had he not provided so obvious an excuse for it, this tendency may well have found minimal opportunity for expression. Although he releases it, he certainly cannot be held responsible for generating it: the effectiveness of his villainous scheme is dependent upon an inherently prejudiced attitude in a patriarchal and military society. The last word we hear before the pipers are instructed to 'strike up' for the final dance is that 'brave punishments' (5.4.124–25) will be devised for Don John. Messina's morality requires that innocence is finally vindicated and self-proclaimed villainy punished. The presence of such an obvious scapegoat for all the evils in Messina, however, ensures that its pervasive misogynist values remain unchallenged.

Much Ado About Nothing

Much Ado has been very popular throughout its stage history. A large measure of the delight to be found in the play derives from the energetic, biting and flirtatious banter that crackles between Beatrice and Benedick. Each claims to be immune to the ravishes of love. Benedick laughs at the 'shallow follies' of lovers (2.3.10). Beatrice says she will not take a husband 'till God make men of some other metal than earth' (2.1.51–52). The comedy lies in watching them swallow their pride and grudgingly admit to loving each other. In their antagonism to romantic cliché and sentiment, and in their taste for unsparing exchanges of wit, they are well suited to each other. Their function in the play is to provide some relief from the seriousness of the Claudio-Hero plot. Dogberry's inability to select the appropriate word and his blundering effectiveness in apprehending and cross-examining villains constitutes the other centre of humour in the play. Unlike Beatrice, who claims she was 'born to speak all mirth and no matter' (2.1.292), *Much Ado About Nothing* offers a sophisticated mingling of mirth and matter. The genuineness of its mirth is not compromised by the seriousness of its matter; its 'sighs of woe' are not invalidated by the resounding 'Hey nonny, nonny' of its close. In its real engagement with pain and its refusal to let that pain ultimately obscure a life optimism, it points the way to the later tragicomedies.

The scene: Messina

CHARACTERS IN THE PLAY

DON PEDRO, *Prince of Arragon*

DON JOHN, *his bastard brother*

CLAUDIO, *a young lord of Florence*

BENEDICK, *a young lord of Padua*

LEONATO, *governor of Messina*

ANTONIO, *an old man, his brother*

BALTHAZAR, *a singer in the service of Don Pedro*

BORACHIO } *followers of Don John*
CONRADE }

A Messenger

FRIAR FRANCIS

DOGBERRY, *a constable*

VERGES, *a headborough*

First Watchman

Second Watchman

A Sexton

A Boy

A Lord

HERO, *daughter to Leonato*

BEATRICE, *niece to Leonato*

MARGARET } *waiting-gentlewomen to Hero*
URSULA }

Antonio's son, musicians, watchmen, attendants, etc.

MUCH ADO ABOUT NOTHING

ACT I SCENE I

An orchard, adjoining the house of Leonato; at one side a covered alley of thick-pleached fruit-trees; at the back an arbour overgrown with honeysuckle

'LEONATO, *governor of Messina,* HERO *his daughter, and* BEATRICE *his niece, with a messenger'*

LEONATO I learn in this letter that Don Pedro of Arragon comes this night to Messina.

MESSENG'R He is very near by this. He was not three leagues off when I left him.

LEONATO How many gentlemen have you lost in this action?

MESSENG'R But few of any sort, and none of name.

LEONATO A victory is twice itself when the achiever brings home full numbers. I find here that Don Pedro hath bestowed much honour on a young Florentine called Claudio.

MESSENG'R Much deserved on his part, and equally remembered by Don Pedro. He hath borne himself beyond the promise of his age, doing in the figure of a lamb the feats of a lion. He hath indeed better bettered expectation than you must expect of me to tell you how.

LEONATO He hath an uncle here in Messina will be very much glad of it.

MESSENG'R I have already delivered him letters, and there appears much joy in him – even so much, that joy could not show itself modest enough without a badge of bitterness.

LEONATO Did he break out into tears?

MESSENG'R In great measure.

LEONATO A kind overflow of kindness. There are no faces truer than those that are so washed. How much better is it to weep at joy than to joy at weeping!

BEATRICE I pray you, is Signior Mountanto returned from the wars or no?

MESSENG'R I know none of that name, lady. There was none such in the army of any sort.

LEONATO What is he that you ask for, niece?

HERO My cousin means Signior Benedick of Padua.

MESSENG'R O, he's returned, and as pleasant as ever he was.

BEATRICE He set up his bills here in Messina and challenged Cupid at the flight, and my uncle's fool reading the challenge subscribed for Cupid, and challenged him at the birdbolt. I pray you, how many hath he killed and eaten in these wars? But how many hath he killed? For indeed I promised to eat all of his killing.

LEONATO Faith, niece, you tax Signior Benedick too much – but he'll be meet with you, I doubt it not.

MESSENG'R He hath done good service, lady, in these wars.

BEATRICE You had musty victual, and he hath holp to eat it. He is a very valiant trencher-man, he hath an excellent stomach.

MESSENG'R And a good soldier too, lady.

BEATRICE And a good soldier to a lady, but what is he to a lord?

MESSENG'R A lord to a lord, a man to a man – stuffed with all honourable virtues.

BEATRICE It is so, indeed. He is no less than a stuffed man, but for the stuffing – well, we are all mortal.

LEONATO You must not, sir, mistake my niece. There is a kind of merry war betwixt Signior Benedick and her. They never meet but there's a skirmish of wit between them.

BEATRICE Alas, he gets nothing by that. In our last conflict, four of his five wits went halting off, and now is the whole man governed with one – so that if he have wit enough to keep himself warm, let him bear it for a difference between himself and his horse, for it is all the wealth that he hath left to be known a reasonable creature. Who is his companion now? He hath every month a new sworn brother.

MESSENG'R Is't possible?

BEATRICE Very easily possible. He wears his faith but as the fashion of his hat, it ever changes with the next block.

MESSENG'R I see, lady, the gentleman is not in your books.

BEATRICE No, an he were, I would burn my study. But I pray you who is his companion? Is there no young squarer now that will make a voyage with him to the devil?

MESSENG'R He is most in the company of the right noble Claudio.

BEATRICE O Lord, he will hang upon him like a disease – he is sooner caught than the pestilence, and the taker runs presently mad. God help the noble Claudio. If he have caught the Benedict, it will cost him a thousand pound ere a' be cured.

MESSENG'R I will hold friends with you, lady.

BEATRICE Do, good friend.

LEONATO You will never run mad, niece.

BEATRICE No, not till a hot January.

MESSENG'R Don Pedro is approached.

'DON PEDRO, CLAUDIO, BENEDICK, BALTHAZAR and JOHN the Bastard' enter the orchard

D. PEDRO Good Signior Leonato, are you come to meet your trouble? The fashion of the world is to avoid cost, and you encounter it.

LEONATO Never came trouble to my house in the likeness of your grace. For trouble being gone, comfort should remain: but when you depart from me, sorrow abides and happiness takes his leave.

D. PEDRO You embrace your charge too willingly. I think this is your daughter.

LEONATO Her mother hath many times told me so.

BENEDICK Were you in doubt, sir, that you asked her?

LEONATO Signior Benedick, no – for then were you a child.

D. PEDRO You have it full, Benedick – we may guess by this what you are, being a man. Truly the lady fathers herself. Be happy, lady, for you are like an honourable father.

[*he talks apart with Hero and Leonato*

BENEDICK If Signior Leonato be her father, she would not have his head on her shoulders for all Messina, as like him as she is.

BEATRICE I wonder that you will still be talking, Signior Benedick – nobody marks you.

BENEDICK What, my dear Lady Disdain! Are you yet living?

BEATRICE Is it possible Disdain should die, while she hath such meet food to feed it as Signior Benedick? Courtesy itself must convert to disdain, if you come in her presence.

BENEDICK Then is courtesy a turn-coat. But it is certain I am loved of all ladies, only you excepted: and I would I could find in my heart that I had not a hard heart, for truly I love none.

BEATRICE A dear happiness to women – they would else have been troubled with a pernicious suitor. I thank God and my cold blood, I am of your humour for that. I had rather hear my dog bark at a crow than a man swear he loves me.

BENEDICK God keep your ladyship still in that mind, so some gentleman or other shall 'scape a predestinate scratched face.

BEATRICE Scratching could not make it worse, an 'twere such a face as yours were.

BENEDICK Well, you are a rare parrot-teacher.

BEATRICE A bird of my tongue is better than a beast of yours.

BENEDICK I would my horse had the speed of your tongue, and so good a continuer. But keep your way a God's name – I have done.

BEATRICE You always end with a jade's trick. I know you of old.

D. PEDRO That is the sum of all, Leonato. [*he turns*] Signior Claudio and Signior Benedick, my dear friend Leonato hath invited you all. I tell him we shall stay here at the least a month, and he heartily prays some occasion may detain us longer. I dare swear he is no hypocrite, but prays from his heart.

LEONATO If you swear, my lord, you shall not be forsworn. [*to* DON JOHN] Let me bid you welcome, my lord – being reconciled to the prince your brother. [*bows*] I owe you all duty.

DON JOHN I thank you. I am not of many words, but I thank you.

LEONATO Please it your grace lead on?

D PEDRO Your hand, Leonato – we will go together.

[*all depart save Benedick and Claudio*

CLAUDIO Benedick, didst thou note the daughter of Signior Leonato?

BENEDICK I noted her not, but I looked on her.

CLAUDIO Is she not a modest young lady?

BENEDICK Do you question me as an honest man should do, for

my simple true judgement? Or would you have me speak after my custom, as being a professed tyrant to their sex?

CLAUDIO No, I pray thee speak in sober judgement.

BENEDICK Why, i'faith, methinks she's too low for a high praise, too brown for a fair praise, and too little for a great praise – only this commendation I can afford her, that were she other than she is, she were unhandsome, and being no other but as she is, I do not like her.

CLAUDIO Thou thinkest I am in sport. I pray thee tell me truly how thou lik'st her.

BENEDICK Would you buy her, that you inquire after her?

CLAUDIO Can the world buy such a jewel?

BENEDICK Yea, and a case to put it into. But speak you this with a sad brow? Or do you play the flouting Jack, to tell us Cupid is a good hare-finder, and Vulcan a rare carpenter? Come, in what key shall a man take you to go in the song?

CLAUDIO In mine eye, she is the sweetest lady that ever I looked on.

BENEDICK I can see yet without spectacles, and I see no such matter: there's her cousin, an she were not possessed with a fury, exceeds her as much in beauty as the first of May doth the last of December. But I hope you have no intent to turn husband, have you?

CLAUDIO I would scarce trust myself, though I had sworn the contrary, if Hero would be my wife.

BENEDICK Is't come to this? In faith hath not the world one man but he will wear his cap with suspicion? Shall I never see a bachelor of threescore again? Go to i'faith, an thou wilt needs thrust thy neck into a yoke, wear the print of it, and sigh away Sundays.

DON PEDRO *re-enters the orchard*

Look, Don Pedro is returned to seek you.

D. PEDRO What secret hath held you here, that you followed not to Leonato's?

BENEDICK I would your grace would constrain me to tell.

D. PEDRO I charge thee on thy allegiance.

BENEDICK You hear, Count Claudio. I can be secret as a dumb

man, I would have you think so – but on my allegiance, mark you this, on my allegiance! He is in love – with who? Now that is your grace's part. Mark, how short his answer is – with Hero, Leonato's short daughter.

CLAUDIO If this were so, so were it uttered.

BENEDICK Like the old tale, my lord – 'it is not so, nor 'twas not so: but indeed, God forbid it should be so.'

CLAUDIO If my passion change not shortly, God forbid it should be otherwise.

D. PEDRO Amen, if you love her – for the lady is very well worthy.

CLAUDIO You speak this to fetch me in, my lord.

D. PEDRO By my troth, I speak my thought.

CLAUDIO And in faith, my lord, I spoke mine.

BENEDICK And by my two faiths and troths, my lord, I spoke mine.

CLAUDIO That I love her, I feel.

D. PEDRO That she is worthy, I know.

BENEDICK That I neither feel how she should be loved, nor know how she should be worthy, is the opinion that fire cannot melt out of me – I will die in it at the stake.

D. PEDRO Thou wast ever an obstinate heretic in the despite of beauty.

CLAUDIO And never could maintain his part but in the force of his will.

BENEDICK That a woman conceived me, I thank her: that she brought me up, I likewise give her most humble thanks: but that I will have a recheat winded in my forehead, or hang my bugle in an invisible baldric, all women shall pardon me. Because I will not do them the wrong to mistrust any, I will do myself the right to trust none: and the fine is – for the which I may go the finer – I will live a bachelor.

D. PEDRO I shall see thee, ere I die, look pale with love.

BENEDICK With anger, with sickness, or with hunger, my lord – not with love: prove that ever I lose more blood with love than I will get again with drinking, pick out mine eyes with a ballad-maker's pen, and hang me up at the door of a brothel-house for the sign of blind Cupid.

D. PEDRO Well, if ever thou dost fall from this faith, thou wilt prove a notable argument.

BENEDICK If I do, hang me in a bottle like a cat and shoot at me, and he that hits me, let him be clapped on the shoulder and called Adam.

D. PEDRO Well, as time shall try:
'In time the savage bull doth bear the yoke.'

BENEDICK The savage bull may – but if ever the sensible Benedick bear it, pluck off the bull's horns and set them in my forehead. And let me be vilely painted – and in such great letters as they write, 'Here is good horse to hire,' let them signify under my sign, 'Here you may see Benedick the married man.'

CLAUDIO If this should ever happen, thou wouldst be horn-mad.

D. PEDRO Nay, if Cupid have not spent all his quiver in Venice, thou wilt quake for this shortly.

BENEDICK I look for an earthquake too then.

D. PEDRO Well, you will temporize with the hours. In the meantime, good Signior Benedick, repair to Leonato's, commend me to him, and tell him I will not fail him at supper – for indeed he hath made great preparation.

BENEDICK I have almost matter enough in me for such an embassage, and so I commit you –

CLAUDIO To the tuition of God: from my house if I had it –

D. PEDRO The sixth of July: your loving friend, Benedick.

BENEDICK Nay, mock not, mock not. The body of your discourse is sometime guarded with fragments, and the guards are but slightly basted on neither. Ere you flout old ends any further, examine your conscience – and so I leave you. [*he goes*

CLAUDIO My liege, your highness now may do me good.

D. PEDRO My love is thine to teach. Teach it but how,
And thou shalt see how apt it is to learn
Any hard lesson that may do thee good.

CLAUDIO Hath Leonato any son, my lord?

D. PEDRO No child but Hero, she's his only heir:
Dost thou affect her, Claudio

CLAUDIO O my lord,
When you went onward on this ended action,

I looked upon her with a soldier's eye,
That liked, but had a rougher task in hand
Than to drive liking to the name of love:
But now I am returned, and that war-thoughts
Have left their places vacant. In their rooms
Come thronging soft and delicate desires,
All prompting me how fair young Hero is,
Saying I liked her ere I went to wars.

D. PEDRO Thou wilt be like a lover presently,
And tire the hearer with a book of words.
If thou dost love fair Hero, cherish it,
And I will break with her, and with her father,
And thou shalt have her. Was't not to this end
That thou began'st to twist so fine a story?

CLAUDIO How sweetly you do minister to love,
That know love's grief by his complexion!
But lest my liking might too sudden seem,
I would have salved it with a longer treatise.

D. PEDRO What need the bridge much broader than the flood?
The fairest grant is the necessity:
Look, what will serve is fit: 'tis once, thou lovest,
And I will fit thee with the remedy.
I know we shall have revelling tonight –
I will assume thy part in some disguise,
And tell fair Hero I am Claudio,
And in her bosom I'll unclasp my heart,
And take her hearing prisoner with the force
And strong encounter of my amorous tale:
Then after to her father will I break –
And the conclusion is, she shall be thine.
In practice let us put it presently.

[*they leave the orchard*

SCENE 2

The hall of Leonato's house; three doors, one in the centre leading to the great chamber; above it a gallery with doors at the back. Servants preparing the room for a dance; ANTONIO *directing them*

LEONATO *enters in haste*

LEONATO How now brother, where is my cousin your son? Hath he provided this music?

ANTONIO He is very busy about it. But brother, I can tell you strange news that you yet dreamt not of.

LEONATO Are they good?

ANTONIO As the event stamps them, but they have a good cover. They show well outward. The prince and Count Claudio, walking in a thick-pleached alley in mine orchard, were thus much overheard by a man of mine: the prince discovered to Claudio that he loved my niece your daughter, and meant to acknowledge it this night in a dance – and if he found her accordant, he meant to take the present time by the top and instantly break with you of it.

LEONATO Hath the fellow any wit that told you this?

ANTONIO A good sharp fellow. I will send for him, and question him yourself.

LEONATO No, no, we will hold it as a dream till it appear itself: but I will acquaint my daughter withal, that she may be the better prepared for an answer, if peradventure this be true. Go you and tell her of it. [ANTONIO *goes out at one door; his son enters at another, followed by a musician*] Cousin, you know what you have to do – [*seeing the musician*] O, I cry you mercy friend, go you with me and I will use your skill. Good cousin, have a care this busy time.

[*he goes out with the musician; after a brief space Antonio's son and the servants depart likewise*

SCENE 3

A door opens in the gallery: DON JOHN *and* CONRADE *come forth*

CONRADE What the good-year, my lord! why are you thus out of measure sad?

DON JOHN There is no measure in the occasion that breeds, therefore the sadness is without limit.

CONRADE You should hear reason.

DON JOHN And when I have heard it, what blessing brings it?

CONRADE If not a present remedy, at least a patient sufferance.

DON JOHN I wonder that thou – being as thou say'st thou art born under Saturn – goest about to apply a moral medicine to a mortifying mischief. I cannot hide what I am: I must be sad when I have cause, and smile at no man's jests; eat when I have stomach, and wait for no man's leisure; sleep when I am drowsy, and tend on no man's business; laugh when I am merry, and claw no man in his humour.

CONRADE Yea, but you must not make the full show of this till you may do it without controlment. You have of late stood out against your brother, and he hath ta'en you newly into his grace, where it is impossible you should take true root but by the fair weather that you make yourself. It is needful that you frame the season for your own harvest.

DON JOHN I had rather be a canker in a hedge than a rose in his grace, and it better fits my blood to be disdained of all than to fashion a carriage to rob love from any: in this, though I cannot be said to be a flattering honest man, it must not be denied but I am a plain-dealing villain. I am trusted with a muzzle and enfranchised with a clog – therefore I have decreed not to sing in my cage. If I had my mouth, I would bite: if I had my liberty, I would do my liking: in the meantime, let me be that I am, and seek not to alter me.

CONRADE Can you make no use of your discontent?

DON JOHN I make all use of it, for I use it only. Who comes here?

BORACHIO *enters the gallery*

What news, Borachio?

BORACHIO I came yonder from a great supper. The prince your brother is royally entertained by Leonato, and I can give you intelligence of an intended marriage.

DON JOHN Will it serve for any model to build mischief on? What is he for a fool that betroths himself to unquietness?

BORACHIO Marry, it is your brother's right hand.

DON JOHN Who, the most exquisite Claudio?

BORACHIO Even he.

DON JOHN A proper squire! And who, and who, which way looks he?

BORACHIO Marry, on Hero the daughter and heir of Leonato.

DON JOHN A very forward March-chick! How came you to this?

BORACHIO Being entertained for a perfumer, as I was smoking a musty room, comes me the prince and Claudio, hand in hand in sad conference: I whipt me behind the arras, and there heard it agreed upon that the prince should woo Hero for himself, and having obtained her, give her to Count Claudio.

DON JOHN Come, come, let us thither – this may prove food to my displeasure. That young start-up hath all the glory of my overthrow: if I can cross him any way, I bless myself every way. You are both sure, and will assist me?

CONRADE To the death, my lord.

DON JOHN Let us to the great supper – their cheer is the greater that I am subdued. Would the cook were o' my mind. Shall we go prove what's to be done?

BORACHIO We'll wait upon your lordship.

[*they leave the gallery*

ACT 2 SCENE 1

The door of the great chamber opens; LEONATO, ANTONIO, HERO, BEATRICE, MARGARET, URSULA, *and others of Leonato's household come forth*

LEONATO Was not Count John here at supper?

ANTONIO I saw him not.

BEATRICE How tartly that gentleman looks. I never can see him but I am heart-burned an hour after.

HERO He is of a very melancholy disposition.

BEATRICE He were an excellent man that were made just in the mid-way between him and Benedick. The one is too like an image and says nothing, and the other too like my lady's eldest son, evermore tattling.

LEONATO Then half Signior Benedick's tongue in Count John's mouth, and half Count John's melancholy in Signior Benedick's face –

BEATRICE With a good leg and a good foot, uncle, and money enough in his purse, such a man would win any woman in the world if a' could get her good will.

LEONATO By my troth, niece, thou wilt never get thee a husband, if thou be so shrewd of thy tongue.

ANTONIO In faith, she's too curst.

BEATRICE Too curst is more than curst. I shall lessen God's sending that way, for it is said, 'God sends a curst cow short horns' – but to a cow too curst he sends none.

LEONATO So by being too curst, God will send you no horns?

BEATRICE Just, if he send me no husband – for the which blessing I am at him upon my knees every morning and evening. Lord! I could not endure a husband with a beard on his face – I had rather lie in the woollen!

LEONATO You may light on a husband that hath no beard.

BEATRICE What should I do with him? Dress him in my apparel and make him my waiting-gentlewoman? He that hath a beard is more than a youth; and he that hath no beard is less than a man: and he that is more than a youth is not for me, and he that is less than a man I am not for him. Therefore I will even take sixpence in earnest of the bear'ard and lead his apes into hell.

LEONATO Well then, go you into hell?

BEATRICE No – but to the gate, and there will the devil meet me like an old cuckold with horns on his head, and say, 'Get you to heaven, Beatrice, get you to heaven – here's no place for you maids.' So deliver I up my apes, and away to Saint Peter: for the heavens, he shows me where the bachelors sit, and there live we as merry as the day is long.

ANTONIO [*to* HERO] Well niece, I trust you will be ruled by your father.

BEATRICE Yes faith, it is my cousin's duty to make curtsy, and say, 'Father, as it please you'. But yet for all that, cousin, let him be a handsome fellow, or else make another curtsy, and say, 'Father, as it please me.'

LEONATO Well, niece, I hope to see you one day fitted with a husband.

BEATRICE Not till God make men of some other mettle than earth. Would it not grieve a woman to be over-mastered with a piece of valiant dust? To make an account of her life to a clod of wayward marl? No, uncle, I'll none: Adam's sons are my brethren, and truly I hold it a sin to match in my kindred.

LEONATO Daughter, remember what I told you. If the prince do solicit you in that kind, you know your answer.

BEATRICE The fault will be in the music, cousin, if you be not wooed in good time: if the prince be too important, tell him there is measure in every thing, and so dance out the answer. For hear me, Hero – wooing, wedding, and repenting, is as a Scotch jig, a measure, and a cinque-pace: the first suit is hot and hasty like a Scotch jig, and full as fantastical; the wedding mannerly-modest, as a measure, full of state and ancientry; and then comes Repentance, and with his bad legs falls into the cinque-pace faster and faster, till he sink into his grave.

LEONATO Cousin, you apprehend passing shrewdly.

BEATRICE I have a good eye, uncle – I can see a church by daylight.

LEONATO The revellers are ent'ring, brother. Make good room.

[ANTONIO *gives orders to the servants and goes out*

DON PEDRO, CLAUDIO, BENEDICK, DON JOHN, BORACHIO *and others of Don Pedro's party enter masked, with a drummer before them;* ANTONIO *returns later, also masked. Musicians enter the gallery and prepare to play; the couples take their places for a round dance*

D. PEDRO [*leading* HERO *forth*] Lady, will you walk a bout with your friend?

HERO So you walk softly and look sweetly and say nothing, I am yours for the walk – and especially when I walk away.

D. PEDRO With me in your company?

HERO I may say so when I please.

D. PEDRO And when please you to say so?

HERO When I like your favour, for God defend the lute should be like the case!

D. PEDRO My visor is Philemon's roof – within the house is Jove.

HERO Why, then your visor should be thatched.

D. PEDRO Speak low if you speak love.

[*they pass on round the room*

BORACHIO Well, I would you did like me.

MARGARET So would not I for your own sake, for I have many ill qualities.

BORACHIO Which is one?

MARGARET I say my prayers aloud.

BORACHIO I love you the better, the hearers may cry Amen.

MARGARET God match me with a good dancer.

BORACHIO Amen.

MARGARET And God keep him out of my sight when the dance is done: answer, clerk.

BORACHIO No more words – the clerk is answered.

[*they pass on round the room*

URSULA I know you well enough – you are Signior Antonio.

ANTONIO At a word, I am not.

URSULA I know you by the waggling of your head.

ANTONIO To tell you true, I counterfeit him.

URSULA You could never do him so ill-well, unless you were the very man: here's his dry hand up and down – you are he, you are he.

ANTONIO At a word, I am not.

URSULA Come, come, do you think I do not know you by your

excellent wit? Can virtue hide itself? Go to, mum, you are he. Graces will appear, and there's an end.

[*they pass on round the room*

BEATRICE Will you not tell me who told you so?

BENEDICK No, you shall pardon me.

BEATRICE Nor will you not tell me who you are?

BENEDICK Not now.

BEATRICE That I was disdainful, and that I had my good wit out of the 'Hundred Merry Tales'. Well, this was Signior Benedick that said so.

BENEDICK What's he?

BEATRICE I am sure you know him well enough.

BENEDICK Not I, believe me.

BEATRICE Did he never make you laugh?

BENEDICK I pray you, what is he?

BEATRICE Why, he is the prince's jester, a very dull fool – only his gift is in devising impossible slanders. None but libertines delight in him, and the commendation is not in his wit but in his villainy, for he both pleases men and angers them, and then they laugh at him and beat him. [*surveying the company*] I am sure he is in the fleet – I would he had boarded me.

BENEDICK When I know the gentleman, I'll tell him what you say.

BEATRICE Do, do. He'll but break a comparison or two on me, which peradventure, not marked or not laughed at, strikes him into melancholy – and then there's a partridge wing saved, for the fool will eat no supper that night. We must follow the leaders.

BENEDICK In every good thing.

BEATRICE Nay, if they lead to any ill, I will leave them at the next turning.

The musicians strike up, and the couples break into a lively dance; at the end thereof DON PEDRO *beckons to* LEONATO *and they go forth together. The door of the great chamber is thrown open;* HERO *leads the couples to the banquet,* DON JOHN, BORACHIO *and* CLAUDIO *remaining behind*

DON JOHN [*aloud*] Sure my brother is amorous on Hero, and hath withdrawn her father to break with him about it. The ladies follow her, and but one visor remains.

BORACHIO And that is Claudio. I know him by his bearing.

DON JOHN Are not you Signior Benedick?

CLAUDIO You know me well – I am he.

DON JOHN Signior, you are very near my brother in his love. He is enamoured on Hero. I pray you, dissuade him from her, she is no equal for his birth. You may do the part of an honest man in it.

CLAUDIO How know you he loves her?

DON JOHN I heard him swear his affection.

BORACHIO So did I too, and he swore he would marry her tonight.

DON JOHN Come, let us to the banquet.

[he goes within, followed by Borachio

CLAUDIO Thus answer I in name of Benedick,
But hear these ill news with the ears of Claudio.
'Tis certain so – the prince wooes for himself.
Friendship is constant in all other things
Save in the office and affairs of love:
Therefore all hearts in love use their own tongues.
Let every eye negotiate for itself,
And trust no agent: for beauty is a witch
Against whose charms faith melteth into blood:
This is an accident of hourly proof,
Which I mistrusted not. Farewell, therefore, Hero.

BENEDICK, *unmasked, comes from the great chamber to seek for* CLAUDIO

BENEDICK Count Claudio?

CLAUDIO Yea, the same.

BENEDICK Come, will you go with me?

CLAUDIO Whither?

BENEDICK Even to the next willow, about your own business, county. What fashion will you wear the garland of? About your neck, like an usurer's chain? Or under your arm, like a lieutenant's scarf? You must wear it one way, for the prince hath got your Hero.

CLAUDIO I wish him joy of her.

BENEDICK Why, that's spoken like an honest drover – so they sell bullocks: but did you think the prince would have served you thus?

CLAUDIO I pray you, leave me.

BENEDICK Ho, now you strike like the blind man. 'Twas the boy that stole your meat, and you'll beat the post.

CLAUDIO If it will not be, I'll leave you. [*he goes out*

BENEDICK Alas, poor hurt fowl – now will he creep into sedges. But, that my Lady Beatrice should know me, and not know me. The prince's fool! Ha, it may be I go under that title because I am merry: yea, but so I am apt to do myself wrong: I am not so reputed – it is the base, the bitter disposition of Beatrice that puts the world into her person, and so gives me out. Well, I'll be revenged as I may.

DON PEDRO *returns with* LEONATO *and* HERO; LEONATO *and* HERO *talk apart*

D. PEDRO Now, signior, where's the count? Did you see him?

BENEDICK Troth, my lord, I have played the part of Lady Fame. I found him here as melancholy as a lodge in a warren. I told him, and I think I told him true, that your grace had got the good will of this young lady – and I off'red him my company to a willow tree, either to make him a garland, as being forsaken, or to bind him up a rod, as being worthy to be whipped.

D. PEDRO To be whipped! What's his fault?

BENEDICK The flat transgression of a school-boy, who, being overjoyed with finding a bird's-nest, shows it his companion, and he steals it.

D. PEDRO Wilt thou make a trust a transgression? The transgression is in the stealer.

BENEDICK Yet it had not been amiss the rod had been made, and the garland too – for the garland he might have worn himself, and the rod he might have bestowed on you, who, as I take it, have stolen his bird's-nest.

D. PEDRO I will but teach them to sing, and restore them to the owner.

BENEDICK If their singing answer your saying, by my faith you say honestly.

D. PEDRO The Lady Beatrice hath a quarrel to you. The gentleman that danced with her told her she is much wronged by you.

BENEDICK O, she misused me past the endurance of a block: an oak but with one green leaf on it would have answered her: my very visor began to assume life and scold with her. She told me, not thinking I had been myself, that I was the prince's jester, that I was duller than a great thaw – huddling jest upon jest with such impossible conveyance upon me, that I stood like a man at a mark, with a whole army shooting at me. She speaks poniards, and every word stabs: if her breath were as terrible as her terminations, there were no living near her, she would infect to the north star. I would not marry her, though she were endowed with all that Adam had left him before he transgressed. She would have made Hercules have turned spit, yea, and have cleft his club to make the fire too. Come, talk not of her. You shall find her the infernal Ate in good apparel – I would to God some scholar would conjure her, for certainly, while she is here, a man may live as quiet in hell as in a sanctuary – and people sin upon purpose because they would go thither, so indeed all disquiet, horror, and perturbation follow her.

CLAUDIO *and* BEATRICE *enter, talking together*

D. PEDRO Look, here she comes.

BENEDICK Will your grace command me any service to the world's end? I will go on the slightest errand now to the Antipodes that you can devise to send me on: I will fetch you a tooth-picker now from the furthest inch of Asia: bring you the length of Prester John's foot: fetch you a hair off the great Cham's beard: do you any embassage to the Pigmies – rather than hold three words' conference with this harpy. You have no employment for me?

D. PEDRO None, but to desire your good company.

BENEDICK O God, sir, here's a dish I love not – I cannot endure my Lady Tongue. [*he goes within*

D. PEDRO Come, lady, come, you have lost the heart of Signior Benedick.

BEATRICE [*comes forward*] Indeed my lord, he lent it me awhile, and I gave him use for it – a double heart for his single one. Marry, once before he won it of me with false dice, therefore your grace may well say I have lost it.

D. PEDRO You have put him down, lady, you have put him down.

BEATRICE So I would not he should do me, my lord, lest I should prove the mother of fools. I have brought Count Claudio, whom you sent me to seek.

D. PEDRO Why, how now count, wherefore are you sad?

CLAUDIO Not sad, my lord.

D. PEDRO How then? Sick?

CLAUDIO Neither, my lord.

BEATRICE The count is neither sad, nor sick, nor merry, nor well: but civil count – civil as an orange, and something of that jealous complexion.

D. PEDRO I'faith lady, I think your blazon to be true, though I'll be sworn, if he be so, his conceit is false. Here, Claudio, I have wooed in thy name and fair Hero is won, I have broke with her father and his good will obtained. Name the day of marriage, and God give thee joy.

LEONATO [*leads* HERO *forward*] Count, take of me my daughter, and with her my fortunes: his grace hath made the match, and all grace say Amen to it.

BEATRICE Speak, count, 'tis your cue.

CLAUDIO Silence is the perfectest herald of joy – I were but little happy, if I could say how much! Lady, as you are mine, I am yours. I give away myself for you and dote upon the exchange.

BEATRICE Speak cousin, or, if you cannot, stop his mouth with a kiss, and let not him speak neither.

D. PEDRO In faith, lady, you have a merry heart.

BEATRICE Yea, my lord, I thank it – poor fool, it keeps on the windy side of care. My cousin tells him in his ear that he is in her heart.

CLAUDIO And so she doth, cousin.

BEATRICE Good Lord, for alliance! Thus goes every one to the world but I, and I am sun-burnt. I may sit in a corner and cry 'heigh-ho for a husband'.

D. PEDRO Lady Beatrice, I will get you one.

BEATRICE I would rather have one of your father's getting: hath your grace ne'er a brother like you? Your father got excellent husbands if a maid could come by them.

D. PEDRO Will you have me, lady?

BEATRICE No my lord, unless I might have another for working-days – your grace is too costly to wear every day. But I beseech your grace pardon me, I was born to speak all mirth and no matter.

D. PEDRO Your silence most offends me, and to be merry best becomes you, for out o' question you were born in a merry hour.

BEATRICE No, sure, my lord, my mother cried – but then there was a star danced, and under that was I born. Cousins, God give you joy!

LEONATO Niece, will you look to those things I told you of?

BEATRICE I cry you mercy, uncle. By your grace's pardon.

[*she bows and goes out*

D. PEDRO By my troth, a pleasant-spirited lady.

LEONATO There's little of the melancholy element in her, my lord. She is never sad but when she sleeps, and not ever sad then: for I have heard my daughter say, she hath often dreamt of unhappiness and waked herself with laughing.

D. PEDRO She cannot endure to hear tell of a husband.

LEONATO O by no means – she mocks all her wooers out of suit.

D. PEDRO She were an excellent wife for Benedick.

LEONATO O Lord, my lord, if they were but a week married, they would talk themselves mad.

D. PEDRO Count Claudio, when mean you to go to church?

CLAUDIO Tomorrow, my lord. Time goes on crutches till love have all his rites.

LEONATO Not till Monday, my dear son, which is hence a just seven-night – and a time too brief too, to have all things answer my mind.

D. PEDRO Come, you shake the head at so long a breathing – but I warrant thee, Claudio, the time shal not go dully by us. I will in the interim undertake one of Hercules' labours, which is, to bring Signior Benedick and the Lady Beatrice into a mountain of affection th'one with th'other. I would fain have it a match – and I doubt not but to fashion it, if you three will but minister such assistance as I shall give you direction.

LEONATO My lord, I am for you, though it cost me ten nights' watchings.

CLAUDIO And I, my lord.

D. PEDRO And you too, gentle Hero?

HERO I will do any modest office, my lord, to help my cousin to a good husband.

D. PEDRO And Benedick is not the unhopefullest husband that I know: thus far can I praise him – he is of a noble strain, of approved valour, and confirmed honesty. [*to Hero*] I will teach you how to humour your cousin, that she shall fall in love with Benedick. [*to Leonato and Claudio*] And I, with your two helps, will so practise on Benedick that, in despite of his quick wit and his queasy stomach, he shall fall in love with Beatrice. If we can do this, Cupid is no longer an archer, his glory shall be ours – for we are the only love-gods. Go in with me, and I will tell you my drift.

[*they go within, Hero on the arm of Claudio*

SCENE 2

DON JOHN *and* BORACHIO, *coming from the banquet, meet them in the door*

DON JOHN It is so – the Count Claudio shall marry the daughter of Leonato.

BORACHIO Yea my lord, but I can cross it.

DON JOHN Any bar, any cross, any impediment will be medicinable to me. I am sick in displeasure to him, and whatsoever comes athwart his affection ranges evenly with mine. How canst thou cross this marriage?

BORACHIO Not honestly, my lord – but so covertly that no dishonesty shall appear in me.

DON JOHN Show me briefly how.

BORACHIO I think I told your lordship, a year since, how much I am in the favour of Margaret, the waiting gentlewoman to Hero.

DON JOHN I remember.

BORACHIO I can, at any unseasonable instant of the night, appoint her to look out at her lady's chamber-window.

DON JOHN What life is in that to be the death of this marriage?

BORACHIO The poison of that lies in you to temper. Go you to the prince your brother, spare not to tell him that he hath wronged his honour in marrying the renowned Claudio – whose estimation do you mightily hold up – to a contaminated stale, such a one as Hero.

DON JOHN What proof shall I make of that?

BORACHIO Proof enough to misuse the prince, to vex Claudio, to undo Hero, and kill Leonato. Look you for any other issue?

DON JOHN Only to despite them, I will endeavour any thing.

BORACHIO Go then, find me a meet hour to draw Don Pedro and the Count Claudio alone, tell them that you know that Hero loves me, intend a kind of zeal both to the prince and Claudio, as in love of your brother's honour, who hath made this match, and his friend's reputation, who is thus like to be cozened with the semblance of a maid. That you have discovered this they will scarcely believe without trial: offer them instances, which shall bear no less likelihood than to see me at her chamber-window, hear me call Margaret Hero, hear Margaret term me Claudio – and bring them to see this the very night before the intended wedding. For in the meantime I will so fashion the matter that Hero shall be absent, and there shall appear such seeming truth of Hero's disloyalty, that jealousy shall be called assurance, and all the preparation overthrown.

DON JOHN Grow this to what adverse issue it can, I will put it in practice. Be cunning in the working this, and thy fee is a thousand ducats.

BORACHIO Be you constant in the accusation, and my cunning shall not shame me.

DON JOHN I will presently go learn their day of marriage. [*they go*

SCENE 3

The orchard adjoining the house of Leonato

BENEDICK *enters the orchard, musing; he yawns*

BENEDICK [*calls*] Boy! [*a boy runs up*

BOY Signior.

BENEDICK In my chamber-window lies a book, bring it hither to me in the orchard.

BOY I am here already, sir.

BENEDICK I know that – but I would have thee hence, and here again. [*the boy departs;* BENEDICK *sits*] I do much wonder, that one man seeing how much another man is a fool when he dedicates his behaviours to love, will after he hath laughed at such shallow follies in others, become the argument of his own scorn by falling in love. And such a man is Claudio. I have known when there was no music with him but the drum and the fife, and now had he rather hear the tabor and the pipe: I have known when he would have walked ten mile afoot, to see a good armour, and now will he lie ten nights awake carving the fashion of a new doublet: he was wont to speak plain, and to the purpose (like an honest man and a soldier) and now is he turned orthography – his words are a very fantastical banquet, just somany strange dishes. May I be so converted, and see with these eyes? I cannot tell – I think not: I will not be sworn but love may transform me to an oyster, but I'll take my oath on it, till he have made an oyster of me, he shall never make me such a fool. One woman is fair, yet I am well: another is wise, yet I am well: another virtuous, yet I am well: but till all graces be in one woman, one woman shall not come in my grace. Rich she shall be, that's certain: wise, or I'll none: virtuous, or I'll never cheapen her: fair, or I'll never look on her: mild, or come not near me: noble, or not I for an angel: of good discourse, an excellent musician, and her hair shall be of what colour it please God. [*voices heard*] Ha! The prince and Monsieur Love! I will hide me in the arbour. [*he does so*

DON PEDRO, LEONATO, *and* CLAUDIO *approach, followed by* BALTHAZAR *with a lute;* CLAUDIO *stands beside the arbour and peeps through the honeysuckle*

D. PEDRO Come, shall we hear this music?

CLAUDIO Yea, my good lord. How still the evening is,
As hushed on purpose to grace harmony!

D. PEDRO See you where Benedick hath hid himself?

CLAUDIO O very well, my lord: the music ended,
We'll fit the hid-fox with a pennyworth.

D. PEDRO Come Balthazar, we'll hear that song again.

BALTH'R O good my lord, tax not so bad a voice
To slander music any more than once.

D. PEDRO It is the witness still of excellency,
To put a strange face on his own perfection.
I pray thee sing, and let me woo no more.

BALTH'R Because you talk of wooing, I will sing –
Since many a wooer doth commence his suit
To her he thinks not worthy, yet he wooes,
Yet will he swear he loves.

D. PEDRO Nay, pray thee come,
Or if thou wilt hold longer argument,
Do it in notes.

BALTH'R Note this before my notes –
There's not a note of mine that's worth the noting.

D. PEDRO Why these are very crotchets that he speaks –
Note notes, forsooth, and nothing!

[*Balthazar begins to play*

BENEDICK Now, divine air! now is his soul ravished. Is it not strange that sheeps' guts should hale souls out of men's bodies Well, a horn for my money, when all's done.

Balthazar sings

Sigh no more, ladies, sigh no more,
Men were deceivers ever,
One foot in sea, and one on shore,
To one thing constant never.
Then sigh not so, but let them go,
And be you blithe and bonny,
Converting all your sounds of woe
Into Hey nonny, nonny.

Sing no more ditties, sing no moe
Of dumps so dull and heavy,
The fraud of men was ever so,
Since summer first was leavy.
Then sigh not so, but let them go,
And be you blithe and bonny,
Converting all your sounds of woe
Into Hey nonny, nonny.

D. PEDRO By my troth, a good song.

BALTH'R And an ill singer, my lord.

D. PEDRO Ha, no, no, faith – thou sing'st well enough for a shift. [*he talks apart with Claudio and Leonato*

BENEDICK An he had been a dog that should have howled thus, they would have hanged him. And I pray God his bad voice bode no mischief – I had as lief have heard the night-raven, come what plague could have come after it.

D. PEDRO Yea, marry. [*turns*] Dost thou hear, Balthazar? I pray thee get us some excellent music: for tomorrow night we would have it at the Lady Hero's chamber-window.

BALTH'R The best I can, my lord.

D. PEDRO Do so, farewell. [*Balthazar goes*
Come hither, Leonato. What was it you told me of today? That your niece Beatrice was in love with Signior Benedick?

BENEDICK *crouches close to the side of the arbour that he may hear the better*

CLAUDIO [*peeping*] O ay, stalk on, stalk on – the fowl sits. [*aloud*] I did never think that lady would have loved any man.

LEONATO No, nor I neither – but most wonderful that she should so dote on Signior Benedick, whom she hath in all outward behaviours seemed ever to abhor.

BENEDICK Is't possible? Sits the wind in that corner?

LEONATO By my troth, my lord, I cannot tell what to think of it, but that she loves him with an enraged affection. It is past the infinite of thought.

D. PEDRO May be she doth but counterfeit.

CLAUDIO Faith, like enough.

LEONATO O God! Counterfeit? There was never counterfeit of passion came so near the life of passion as she discovers it.

D. PEDRO Why, what effects of passion shows she?

CLAUDIO [*peeps again*] Bait the hook well – this fish will bite.

LEONATO What effects, my lord! She will sit you – [*to Claudio*] You heard my daughter tell you how.

CLAUDIO She did, indeed.

D. PEDRO How, how, I pray you! You amaze me. I would have thought her spirit had been invincible against all assaults of affection.

LEONATO I would have sworn it had, my lord – especially against Benedick.

BENEDICK I should think this a gull, but that the white-bearded fellow speaks it: knavery cannot, sure, hide himself in such reverence.

CLAUDIO He hath ta'en th'infection – hold it up.

D. PEDRO Hath she made her affection known to Benedick?

LEONATO No, and swears she never will. That's her torment.

CLAUDIO 'Tis true indeed, so your daughter says: 'Shall I,' says she, 'that have so oft encountered him with scorn, write to him that I love him?'

LEONATO This says she now when she is beginning to write to him, for she'll be up twenty times a night, and there will she sit in her smock till she have writ a sheet of paper: my daughter tells us all.

CLAUDIO Now you talk of a sheet of paper, I remember a pretty jest your daughter told us of.

LEONATO O, when she had writ it, and was reading it over, she found 'Benedick' and 'Beatrice' between the sheet?

CLAUDIO That.

LEONATO O, she tore the letter into a thousand half-pence, railed at herself that she should be so immodest to write to one that she knew would flout her. 'I measure him,' says she, 'by my own spirit, for I should flout him if he writ to me – yea, though I love him, I should.'

CLAUDIO Then down upon her knees she falls, weeps, sobs, beats her heart, tears her hair, prays, curses – 'O sweet Benedick! God give me patience!'

LEONATO She doth indeed – my daughter says so. And the ecstasy hath so much overborne her, that my daughter is sometime afeard she will do a desperate outrage to herself. It is very true.

D. PEDRO It were good that Benedick knew of it by some other, if she will not discover it.

CLAUDIO To what end? He would make but a sport of it, and torment the poor lady worse.

D. PEDRO An he should, it were an alms to hang him. She's an excellent sweet lady, and – out of all suspicion – she is virtuous.

CLAUDIO And she is exceeding wise.

D. PEDRO In every thing but in loving Benedick.

LEONATO O my lord, wisdom and blood combating in so tender a body, we have ten proofs to one that blood hath the victory. I am sorry for her, as I have just cause, being her uncle and her guardian.

D. PEDRO I would she had bestowed this dotage on me. I would have daffed all other respects, and made her half myself. I pray you tell Benedick of it, and hear what 'a will say.

LEONATO Were it good, think you?

CLAUDIO Hero thinks surely she will die – for she says she will die if he love her not, and she will die ere she make her love known, and she will die if he woo her rather than she will bate one breath of her accustomed crossness.

D. PEDRO She doth well. If she should make tender of her love, 'tis very possible he'll scorn it – for the man, as you know all, hath a contemptible spirit.

CLAUDIO He is a very proper man.

D. PEDRO He hath indeed a good outward happiness.

CLAUDIO Before God, and in my mind, very wise.

D. PEDRO He doth indeed show some sparks that are like wit.

CLAUDIO And I take him to be valiant.

D. PEDRO As Hector, I assure you. And in the managing of quarrels you may say he is wise, for either he avoids them with great discretion, or undertakes them with a most Christian-like fear.

LEONATO If he do fear God, 'a must necessarily keep peace. If he break the peace, he ought to enter into a quarrel with fear and trembling.

D. PEDRO And so will he do – for the man doth fear God, howsoever it seems not in him by some large jests he will make . . . Well, I am sorry for your niece. Shall we go seek Benedick, and tell him of her love?

CLAUDIO Never tell him, my lord. Let her wear it out with good counsel.

LEONATO Nay, that's impossible – she may wear her heart out first.

D. PEDRO Well, we will hear further of it by your daughter. Let it cool the while. I love Benedick well, and I could wish he would modestly examine himself, to see how much he is unworthy so good a lady.

LEONATO My lord, will you walk? Dinner is ready.

[*they draw away from the arbour*

CLAUDIO If he do not dote on her upon this, I will never trust my expectation.

D. PEDRO Let there be the same net spread for her – and that must your daughter and her gentlewomen carry. The sport will be, when they hold one an opinion of another's dotage, and no such matter. That's the scene that I would see, which will be merely a dumb-show. Let us send her to call him in to dinner.

They depart; BENEDICK *comes from the arbour*

BENEDICK This can be no trick. The conference was sadly borne. They have the truth of this from Hero. They seem to pity the lady. It seems her affections have their full bent. Love me! Why, it must be requited. I hear how I am censured – they say I will bear myself proudly, if I perceive the love come from her: they say too that she will rather die than give any sign of affection. I did never think to marry. I must not seem proud. Happy are they that hear their detractions, and can put them to mending. They say the lady is fair – 'tis a truth, I can bear them witness: and virtuous – 'tis so, I cannot reprove it: and wise, but for loving me – by my troth, it is no addition to her wit, nor no great argument of her folly, for I will be horribly in love with her. I may chance have some odd quirks and remnants of wit broken on me, because I have railed so long against marriage: but doth not the appetite alter? A man loves the meat in his youth that he cannot endure in his age. Shall quips and sentences and these paper bullets of the brain awe a man from the career of his humour? No – the world must be peopled. When I said I would die a bachelor, I did not think I should live till I were married.

BEATRICE *approaches*

Here comes Beatrice. By this day, she's a fair lady. I do spy some marks of love in her.

BEATRICE Against my will I am sent to bid you come in to dinner.

BENEDICK Fair Beatrice, I thank you for your pains.

BEATRICE I took no more pains for those thanks than you take pains to thank me. If it had been painful, I would not have come.

BENEDICK You take pleasure then in the message.

BEATRICE Yea, just so much as you may take upon a knife's point, and choke a daw withal. You have no stomach, signior – fare you well. *[she goes*

BENEDICK Ha! 'Against my will I am sent to bid you come in to dinner': there's a double meaning in that. 'I took no more pains for those thanks than you took pains to thank me' – that's as much as to say, Any pains that I take for you is as easy as thanks. If I do not take pity of her, I am a villain. If I do not love her, I am a Jew. I will go get her picture. *[he departs in haste*

A day passes

ACT 3 SCENE 1

The orchard; HERO, MARGARET, *and* URSULA *enter the alley of fruit-trees*

HERO Good Margaret, run thee to the parlour,
There shalt thou find my cousin Beatrice
Proposing with the prince and Claudio.
Whisper her ear, and tell her I and Ursley
Walk in the orchard, and our whole discourse
Is all of her. Say that thou overheard'st us,
And bid her steal into the pleachéd bower,
Where honeysuckles, ripened by the sun,
Forbid the sun to enter, like favourites,
Made proud by princes, that advance their pride
Against that power that bred it. There will she hide her,
To listen our propose. This is thy office –
Bear thee well in it and leave us alone.

MARGARET I'll make her come, I warrant you, presently.
[*she leaves them*

HERO Now, Ursula, when Beatrice doth come,
As we do trace this alley up and down,
Our talk must only be of Benedick.
When I do name him, let it be thy part
To praise him more than ever man did merit.
My talk to thee must be how Benedick
Is sick in love with Beatrice: of this matter
Is little Cupid's crafty arrow made,
That only wounds by hearsay.

BEATRICE *approaches, and stealing behind the walls of the alley, enters the arbour*

Now begin,
For look where Beatrice like a lapwing runs
Close by the ground, to hear our conference.

URSULA The pleasant'st angling is to see the fish
Cut with her golden oars the silver stream,
And greedily devour the treacherous bait:
So angle we for Beatrice, who even now

Is couchéd in the woodbine coverture.
Fear you not my part of the dialogue.

HERO Then go we near her, that her ear lose nothing
Of the false sweet bait that we lay for it.

[they draw nigh the arbour

No, truly, Ursula, she is too disdainful –
I know her spirits are as coy and wild
As haggards of the rock.

URSULA But are you sure
That Benedick loves Beatrice so entirely?

HERO So says the prince, and my new-trothéd lord.

URSULA And did they bid you tell her of it, madam?

HERO They did entreat me to acquaint her of it.
But I persuaded them, if they loved Benedick,
To wish him wrestle with affection,
And never to let Beatrice know of it.

URSULA Why did you so? Doth not the gentleman
Deserve at full as fortunate a bed
As ever Beatrice shall couch upon?

HERO O god of love! I know he doth deserve
As much as may be yielded to a man:
But nature never framed a woman's heart
Of prouder stuff than that of Beatrice
Disdain and scorn ride sparkling in her eyes,
Misprizing what they look on, and her wit
Values itself so highly, that to her
All matter else seems weak: she cannot love,
Nor take no shape nor project of affection,
She is so self-endeared.

URSULA Sure, I think so.
And therefore certainly it were not good
She knew his love, lest she'll make sport at it.

HERO Why, you speak truth. I never yet saw man,
How wise, how noble, young, how rarely featured,
But she would spell him backward: if fair-faced,
She would swear the gentleman should be her sister;
If black, why nature, drawing of an antic,
Made a foul blot: if tall, a lance ill-headed;
If low, an agate very vilely cut:

If speaking, why a vane blown with all winds;
If silent, why a block movéd with none.
So turns she every man the wrong side out,
And never gives to truth and virtue that
Which simpleness and merit purchaseth.

URSULA Sure, sure, such carping is not commendable.

HERO No, nor to be so odd and from all fashions,
As Beatrice is, cannot be commendable.
But who dare tell her so? If I should speak,
She would mock me into air – O, she would laugh me
Out of myself, press me to death with wit.
Therefore let Benedick, like covered fire,
Consume away in sighs, waste inwardly:
It were a better death than die with mocks,
Which is as bad as die with tickling.

URSULA Yet tell her of it, hear what she will say.

HERO No rather I will go to Benedick,
And counsel him to fight against his passion.
And, truly, I'll devise some honest slanders
To stain my cousin with. One doth not know,
How much an ill word may empoison liking.

URSULA O do not do your cousin such a wrong.
She cannot be so much without true judgment –
Having so swift and excellent a wit,
As she is prized to have – as to refuse
So rare a gentleman as Signior Benedick.

HERO He is the only man of Italy,
Always excepted my dear Claudio.

URSULA I pray you be not angry with me, madam,
Speaking my fancy: Signior Benedick,
For shape, for bearing, argument, and valour,
Goes foremost in report through Italy.

HERO Indeed, he hath an excellent good name.

URSULA His excellence did earn it, ere he had it.
When are you married, madam?

HERO Why, every day tomorrow! Come, go in.
I'll show thee some attires, and have thy counsel
Which is the best to furnish me tomorrow.

URSULA She's limed, I warrant you – we have caught her, madam.

HERO If it prove so, then loving goes by haps,
Some Cupid kills with arrows, some with traps.
[*they go*

BEATRICE *comes from the arbour*

BEATRICE What fire is in mine ears? Can this be true?
Stand I condemned for pride and scorn so much?
Contempt, farewell! And maiden pride, adieu!
No glory lives behind the back of such.
And, Benedick, love on, I will requite thee,
Taming my wild heart to thy loving hand:
If thou dost love, my kindness shall incite thee
To bind our loves up in a holy band:
For others say thou dost deserve, and I
Believe it better than reportingly. [*she goes*

SCENE 2

The parlour in Leonato's house

DON PEDRO, CLAUDIO, BENEDICK (*very spruce*), *and* LEONATO

D. PEDRO I do but stay till your marriage be consummate, and then go I toward Arragon.

CLAUDIO I'll bring you thither, my lord, if you'll vouchsafe me.

D. PEDRO Nay, that would be as great a soil in the new gloss of your marriage, as to show a child his new coat and forbid him to wear it. I will only be bold with Benedick for his company – for, from the crown of his head to the sole of his foot, he is all mirth. He hath twice or thrice cut Cupid's bowstring, and the little hangman dare not shoot at him. He hath a heart as sound as a bell, and his tongue is the clapper – for what his heart thinks his tongue speaks.

BENEDICK Gallants, I am not as I have been.

LEONATO So say I. Methinks you are sadder.

CLAUDIO I hope he be in love.

D. PEDRO Hang him, truant! There's no true drop of blood in him to be truly touched with love. If he be sad, he wants money.

BENEDICK I have the toothache.

D. PEDRO Draw it.

BENEDICK Hang it!

CLAUDIO You must hang it first, and draw it afterwards.

D. PEDRO What! Sigh for the toothache?

LEONATO Where is but a humour or a worm?

BENEDICK Well, every one can master a grief but he that has it.

CLAUDIO Yet say I, he is in love.

D. PEDRO There is no appearance of fancy in him, unless it be a fancy that he hath to strange disguises – as, to be a Dutchman today, a Frenchman tomorrow, or in the shape of two countries at once, as a German from the waist downward, all slops, and a Spaniard from the hip upward, no doublet. Unless he have a fancy to this foolery, as it appears he hath, he is no fool for fancy, as you would have it appear he is.

CLAUDIO If he be not in love with some woman, there is no believing old signs. A' brushes his hat a mornings – what should that bode?

D. PEDRO Hath any man seen him at the barber's?

CLAUDIO No, but the barber's man hath been seen with him, and the old ornament of his cheek hath already stuffed tennis-balls.

LEONATO Indeed, he looks younger than he did, by the loss of a beard.

D. PEDRO Nay, a' rubs himself with civet – can you smell him out by that?

CLAUDIO That's as much as to say the sweet youth's in love.

D. PEDRO The greatest note of it is his melancholy.

CLAUDIO And when was he wont to wash his face?

D. PEDRO Yea, or to paint himself? For the which, I hear what they say of him.

CLAUDIO Nay, but his jesting spirit, which is new-crept into a lute-string and now governed by stops.

D. PEDRO Indeed, that tells a heavy tale for him. Conclude, conclude, he is in love.

CLAUDIO Nay, but I know who loves him.

D. PEDRO That would I know too. I warrant, one that knows him not.

CLAUDIO Yes, and his ill conditions – and in despite of all, dies for him.

D. PEDRO She shall be buried with her face upwards.

BENEDICK Yet is this no charm for the toothache. Old signior, walk aside with me. I have studied eight or nine wise words to speak to you, which these hobby-horses must not hear. [*Benedick and Leonato go out*

D. PEDRO For my life, to break with him about Beatrice.

CLAUDIO 'Tis even so. Hero and Margaret have by this played their parts with Beatrice, and then the two bears will not bite one another when they meet.

DON JOHN *enters*

DON JOHN My lord and brother, God save you.

D. PEDRO Good-den, brother.

DON JOHN If your leisure served, I would speak with you.

D. PEDRO In private?

DON JOHN If it please you – yet Count Claudio may hear, for what I would speak of concerns him.

CLAUDIO What's the matter?

DON JOHN Means your lordship to be married tomorrow?

D. PEDRO You know he does.

DON JOHN I know not that, when he knows what I know.

CLAUDIO If there be any impediment, I pray you discover it.

DON JOHN You may think I love you not – let that appear hereafter, and aim better at me by that I now will manifest. For my brother, I think he holds you well, and in dearness of heart hath holp to effect your ensuing marriage: surely, suit ill spent, and labour ill bestowed.

D. PEDRO Why, what's the matter?

DON JOHN I came hither to tell you, and, circumstances shortened – for she has been too long a talking of – the lady is disloyal.

CLAUDIO Who, Hero?

DON JOHN Even she – Leonato's Hero, your Hero, every man's Hero.

CLAUDIO Disloyal?

DON JOHN The word is too good to paint out her wickedness. I could say she were worse. Think you of a worse title, and I will fit her to it. Wonder not till further warrant: go but with me tonight, you shall see her chamber-window entered, even the night before her wedding-day. If you love her then, tomorrow wed her. But it would better fit your honour to change your mind.

CLAUDIO May this be so?

D. PEDRO I will not think it.

DON JOHN If you dare not trust that you see, confess not that you know: if you will follow me, I will show you enough, and when you have seen more and heard more, proceed accordingly.

CLAUDIO If I see any thing tonight why I should not marry her, tomorrow, in the congregation, where I should wed, there will I shame her.

D. PEDRO And as I wooed for thee to obtain her, I will join with thee to disgrace her.

DON JOHN I will disparage her no farther till you are my witnesses. Bear it coldly but till midnight, and let the issue show itself.

D. PEDRO O day untowardly turned!

CLAUDIO O mischief strangely thwarting!

DON JOHN O plague right well prevented! So will you say, when you have seen the sequel. [*they go*

SCENE 3

A street in Messina: on one side the door of Leonato's house, in the centre the porch of a church, having a bench within it: midnight; rain and wind

The Watch, armed with bills, stand a-row before the porch; Master Constable DOGBERRY, *bearing a lantern, and* VERGES, *the Headborough, survey them*

DOGBERRY Are you good men and true?

VERGES Yea, or else it were pity but they should suffer salvation, body and soul.

DOGBERRY Nay, that were a punishment too good for them, if

they should have any allegiance in them, being chosen for the prince's watch.

VERGES Well, give them their charge, neighbour Dogberry.

DOGBERRY First, who think you the most desertless man to be constable?

1 WATCH. Hugh Oatcake, sir, or George Seacoal, for they can write and read.

DOGBERRY Come hither, neighbour Seacoal. God hath blessed you with a good name: to be a well-favoured man is the gift of fortune, but to write and read comes by nature.

2 WATCH. Both which, Master Constable –

DOGBERRY You have: I knew it would be your answer. Well, for your favour, sir, why give God thanks, and make no boast of it – and for your writing and reading, let that appear when there is no need of such vanity. You are thought here to be the most senseless and fit man for the constable of the watch: therefore bear you the lantern [*he gives it to him*]. This is your charge – you shall comprehend all vagrom men, you are to bid any man stand, in the prince's name.

2 WATCH. How if 'a will not stand?

DOGBERRY Why then take no note of him, but let him go, and presently call the rest of the watch together, and thank God you are rid of a knave.

VERGES If he will not stand when he is bidden, he is none of the prince's subjects.

DOGBERRY True, and they are to meddle with none but the prince's subjects. You shall also make no noise in the streets: for, for the watch to babble and to talk, is most tolerable and not to be endured.

2 WATCH. We will rather sleep than talk – we know what belongs to a watch.

DOGBERRY Why, you speak like an ancient and most quiet watchman, for I cannot see how sleeping should offend: only have a care that your bills be not stolen. Well, you are to call at all the ale-houses, and bid those that are drunk get them to bed.

2 WATCH. How if they will not?

DOGBERRY Why then, let them alone till they are sober. If they make you not then the better answer, you may say they are not the men you took them for.

2 WATCH. Well, sir.

DOGBERRY If you meet a thief, you may suspect him, by virtue of your office, to be no true man: and, for such kind of men, the less you meddle or make with them, why the more is for your honesty.

2 WATCH. If we know him to be a thief, shall we not lay hands on him?

DOGBERRY Truly by your office you may, but I think they that touch pitch will be defiled: the most peaceable way for you, if you do take a thief, is to let him show himself what he is, and steal out of your company.

VERGES You have been always called a merciful man, partner.

DOGBERRY Truly, I would not hang a dog by my will, much more a man who hath any honesty in him.

VERGES If you hear a child cry in the night, you must call to the nurse and bid her still it.

2 WATCH. How if the nurse be asleep and will not hear us?

DOGBERRY Why then, depart in peace, and let the child wake her with crying – for the ewe that will not hear her lamb when it baes, will never answer a calf when he bleats.

VERGES 'Tis very true.

DOGBERRY This is the end of the charge. You, constable, are to present the prince's own person – if you meet the prince in the night, you may stay him.

VERGES Nay, by'r lady, that I think 'a cannot.

DOGBERRY Five shillings to one on't with any man that knows the statutes, he may stay him – marry, not without the prince be willing, for indeed the watch ought to offend no man, and it is an offence to stay a man against his will.

VERGES By'r lady, I think it be so.

DOGBERRY Ha, ah, ha! Well, masters, good night. An there be any matter of weight chances, call up me. Keep your fellows' counsels and your own, and good night. Come, neighbour. [*they walk away*

2 WATCH. Well, masters, we hear our charge. Let us go sit here upon the church-bench till two, and then all to bed.

[they all enter the porch and prepare to sleep

DOGBERRY [*turns*] One word more, honest neighbours. I pray you, watch about Signior Leonato's door, for the wedding being there tomorrow, there is a great coil tonight. Adieu, be vigitant, I beseech you.

[Dogberry and Verges go

The door of Leonato's house opens and BORACHIO *staggers forth, followed after a short space by* CONRADE

BORACHIO [*stops*] What, Conrade!

2 WATCH. Peace, stir not.

BORACHIO Conrade, I say!

CONRADE Here, man, I am at thy elbow.

BORACHIO Mass, and my elbow itched – I thought there would a scab follow.

CONRADE I will owe thee an answer for that, and now forward with thy tale.

BORACHIO Stand thee close then under this pent-house, for it drizzles rain, and I will, like a true drunkard, utter all to thee. *[they stand beneath the eaves of the porch*

2 WATCH. Some treason, masters – yet stand close.

BORACHIO Therefore know, I have earned of Don John a thousand ducats.

CONRADE Is it possible that any villainy should be so dear?

BORACHIO Thou shouldst rather ask if it were possible any villainy should be so rich, for when rich villains have need of poor ones, poor ones may make what price they will.

CONRADE I wonder at it.

BORACHIO That shows thou art unconfirmed. Thou knowest that the fashion of a doublet, or a hat, or a cloak, is nothing to a man.

CONRADE Yes it is apparel.

BORACHIO I mean the fashion.

CONRADE Yes, the fashion is the fashion.

BORACHIO Tush, I may as well say the fool's the fool. But seest thou not what a deformed thief this fashion is?

2 WATCH. I know that Deformed, 'a has been a vile thief this

seven year, 'a goes up and down like a gentleman: I remember his name.

BORACHIO Didst thou not hear somebody?

CONRADE No, 'twas the vane on the house.

BORACHIO Seest thou not, I say, what a deformed thief this fashion is? How giddily 'a turns about all the hot-bloods between fourteen and five-and-thirty? Sometimes fashioning them like Pharaoh's soldiers in the reechy painting, sometime like god Bel's priests in the old church window, sometime like the shaven Hercules in the smirched worm-eaten tapestry, where his cod-piece seems as massy as his club?

CONRADE All this I see, and I see that the fashion wears out more apparel than the man. But art not thou thyself giddy with the fashion too, that thou hast shifted out of thy tale into telling me of the fashion?

BORACHIO Not so neither. But know that I have tonight wooed Margaret, the Lady Hero's gentlewoman, by the name of Hero. She leans me out at her mistress' chamber-window, bids me a thousand times good night. I tell this tale vilely – I should first tell thee how the prince, Claudio, and my master, planted and placed and possessed by my master Don John, saw afar off in the orchard this amiable encounter.

CONRADE And thought they Margaret was Hero?

BORACHIO Two of them did, the prince and Claudio. But the devil, my master, knew she was Margaret – and partly by his oaths, which first possessed them, partly by the dark night, which did deceive them, but chiefly by my villainy, which did confirm any slander that Don John had made, away went Claudio enraged, swore he would meet her as he was appointed next morning at the temple, and there, before the whole congregation, shame her with what he saw o'er-night, and send her home again without a husband. [*the watchmen sally forth*

2 WATCH. We charge you in the prince's name, stand.

1 WATCH. Call up the right Master Constable. We have here recovered the most dangerous piece of lechery that ever was known in the commonwealth.

2 WATCH. And one Deformed is one of them – I know him, 'a wears a lock.

CONRADE Masters, masters.

2 WATCH. You'll be made bring Deformed forth, I warrant you.

CONRADE Masters –

1 WATCH. Never speak, we charge you. Let us obey you to go with us.

BORACHIO We are like to prove a goodly commodity, being taken up of these men's bills.

CONRADE A commodity in question, I warrant you. Come, we'll obey you. [*the watchmen hale them away*

SCENE 4

A room opening into Hero's bed-chamber

HERO, *before a mirror,* MARGARET, *and* URSULA

HERO Good Ursula, wake my cousin Beatrice, and desire her to rise.

URSULA I will, lady.

HERO And bid her come hither.

URSULA Well. [*she goes out*

MARGARET Troth, I think your other rebato were better.

HERO No, pray thee good Meg, I'll wear this.

MARGARET By my troth's not so good, and I warrant your cousin will say so.

HERO My cousin's a fool, and thou art another. I'll wear none but this.

MARGARET I like the new tire within excellently, if the hair were a thought browner: and your gown's a most rare fashion i'faith. I saw the Duchess of Milan's gown that they praise so –

HERO O, that exceeds, they say.

MARGARET By my troth's but a night-gown in respect of yours – cloth o' gold and cuts, and laced with silver, set with pearls down sleeves, side-sleeves, and skirts, round underborne with a bluish tinsel – but for a fine quaint graceful and excellent fashion, yours is worth ten on't.

HERO God give me joy to wear it, for my heart is exceeding heavy.

MARGARET 'Twill be heavier soon by the weight of a man.

HERO Fie upon thee, art not ashamed?

MARGARET Of what, lady? Of speaking honourably? Is not marriage honourable in a beggar? Is not your lord honourable without marriage? I think you would have me say, 'saving your reverence, a husband': an bad thinking do not wrest true speaking – I'll offend nobody – is there any harm in 'the heavier for a husband'? None I think, an it be the right husband, and the right wife, otherwise 'tis light and not heavy – ask my Lady Beatrice else, here she comes.

BEATRICE *enters*

HERO Good morrow, coz.

BEATRICE Good morrow, sweet Hero.

HERO Why how now? Do you speak in the sick tune?

BEATRICE I am out of all other tune, methinks.

MARGARET Clap's into 'Light o' love' – that goes without a burden – do you sing it, and I'll dance it.

BEATRICE Yea, light o' love with your heels – then if your husband have stables enough you'll see he shall lack no barns.

MARGARET O illegitimate construction! I scorn that with my heels.

BEATRICE 'Tis almost five o'clock cousin, 'tis time you were ready. By my troth I am exceeding ill. Heigh-ho!

MARGARET For a hawk, a horse, or a husband?

BEATRICE For the letter that begins them all, H.

MARGARET Well, an you be not turned Turk, there's no more sailing by the star.

BEATRICE What means the fool, trow?

MARGARET Nothing I – but God send every one their heart's desire.

HERO These gloves the count sent me, they are an excellent perfume.

BEATRICE I am stuffed, cousin, I cannot smell.

MARGARET A maid and stuffed! There's goodly catching of cold.

BEATRICE O God help me, God help me, how long have you professed apprehension?

MARGARET Ever since you left it. Doth not my wit become me rarely?

BEATRICE It is not seen enough, you should wear it in your cap. By my troth I am sick.

MARGARET Get you some of this distilled Carduus Benedictus, and lay it to your heart – it is the only thing for a qualm.

HERO There thou prick'st her with a thistle.

BEATRICE Benedictus, why Benedictus? You have some moral in this Benedictus.

MARGARET Moral? No, by my troth, I have no moral meaning – I meant plain holy-thistle. You may think perchance that I think you are in love – nay by'r lady I am not such a fool to think what I list, nor I list not to think what I can, nor indeed I cannot think, if I would think my heart out of thinking, that you are in love, or that you will be in love, or that you can be in love: yet Benedick was such another and now is he become a man. He swore he would never marry, and yet now in despite of his heart he eats his meat without grudging – and how you may be converted I know not, but methinks you look with your eyes as other women do.

BEATRICE What pace is this that thy tongue keeps?

MARGARET Not a false gallop.

URSULA *returns in haste*

URSULA Madam, withdraw. The prince, the count, Signior Benedick, Don John, and all the gallants of the town are come to fetch you to church.

HERO Help to dress me, good coz, good Meg, good Ursula.

[*they hasten to the bed-chamber*

SCENE 5

The hall in Leonato's house

LEONATO, DOGBERRY *and* VERGES

LEONATO What would you with me, honest neighbour?

DOGBERRY Marry, sir, I would have some confidence with you, that decerns you nearly.

LEONATO Brief I pray you, for you see it is a busy time with me.

DOGBERRY Marry, this it is, sir.

VERGES Yes, in truth it is, sir.

LEONATO What is it, my good friends?

DOGBERRY Goodman Verges, sir, speaks a little off the matter – an old man, sir, and his wits are not so blunt, as God help I would desire they were, but in faith honest, as the skin between his brows.

VERGES Yes, I thank God, I am as honest as any man living, that is an old man, and no honester than I.

DOGBERRY Comparisons are odorous – palabras, neighbour Verges.

LEONATO Neighbours, you are tedious.

DOGBERRY It pleases your worship to say so, but we are the poor duke's officers. But truly for mine own part if I were as tedious as a king I could find in my heart to bestow it all of your worship.

LEONATO All thy tediousness on me, ah?

DOGBERRY Yea, an 'twere a thousand pound more than 'tis, for I hear as good exclamation on your worship as of any man in the city, and though I be but a poor man, I am glad to hear it.

VERGES And so am I.

LEONATO I would fain know what you have to say.

VERGES Marry sir, our watch tonight, excepting your worship's presence, ha' ta'en a couple of as arrant knaves as any in Messina.

DOGBERRY A good old man, sir, he will be talking – as they say, 'when the age is in, the wit is out.' God help us, it is a world to see. Well said, i'faith, neighbour Verges. Well, God's a good man – an two men ride of a horse, one must ride behind. An honest soul i'faith, sir, by my troth he is, as ever broke bread, but – God is to be worshipped – all men are not alike, alas, good neighbour.

LEONATO Indeed, neighbour, he comes too short of you.

DOGBERRY Gifts that God gives.

LEONATO I must leave you.

DOGBERRY One word, sir – our watch, sir, have indeed comprehended two aspicious persons, and we would have them this morning examined before your worship.

LEONATO Take their examination yourself, and bring it me, I am now in great haste, as it may appear unto you.

DOGBERRY It shall be suffigance.

LEONATO Drink some wine ere you go: fare you well.

[he meets a messenger at the door

MESSENG'R My lord, they stay for you to give your daughter to her husband.

LEONATO I'll wait upon them – I am ready.

[Leonato and the messenger go out

DOGBERRY Go good partner, go get you to Francis Seacoal, bid him bring his pen and inkhorn to the gaol: we are now to examination these men.

VERGES And we must do it wisely.

DOGBERRY We will spare for no wit, I warrant you: here's that [*touches his forehead*] shall drive some of them to a 'non-come'. Only get the learned writer to set down our excommunication, and meet me at the gaol.

[they depart

ACT 4 SCENE 1

Before the altar of a church

DON PEDRO, DON JOHN, LEONATO, FRIAR FRANCIS, CLAUDIO, BENEDICK, HERO, BEATRICE, *etc.*

LEONATO Come Friar Francis, be brief – only to the plain form of marriage, and you shall recount their particular duties afterwards.

FRIAR You come hither, my lord, to marry this lady?

CLAUDIO No.

LEONATO To be married to her: friar, you come to marry her.

FRIAR Lady, you come hither to be married to this count?

HERO I do.

FRIAR If either of you know any inward impediment why you should not be conjoined, I charge you on your souls to utter it.

CLAUDIO Know you any, Hero?

HERO None my lord.

FRIAR Know you any, count?

LEONATO I dare make his answer, 'none'.

CLAUDIO O, what men dare do! What men may do! What men daily do, not knowing what they do!

BENEDICK How now! Interjections? Why then, some be of laughing, as 'ah! ha! he!'

CLAUDIO Stand thee by, friar. Father, by your leave –
Will you with free and unconstrainéd soul
Give me this maid your daughter?

LEONATO As freely, son, as God did give her me.

CLAUDIO And what have I to give you back whose worth
May counterpoise this rich and precious gift?

D. PEDRO Nothing, unless you render her again.

CLAUDIO Sweet prince, you learn me noble thankfulness.
There Leonato, take her back again,
Give not this rotten orange to your friend,
She's but the sign and semblance of her honour.
Behold how like a maid she blushes here!
O, what authority and show of truth
Can cunning sin cover itself withal!

Comes not that blood, as modest evidence,
To witness simple virtue? Would you not swear,
All you that see her, that she were a maid,
By these exterior shows? But she is none:
She knows the heat of a luxurious bed
Her blush is guiltiness, not modesty.

LEONATO What do you mean my lord?

CLAUDIO Not to be married,
Not to knit my soul to an approvéd wanton.

LEONATO Dear my lord, if you in your own proof
Have vanquished the resistance of her youth,
And made defeat of her virginity –

CLAUDIO I know what you would say: if I have known her,
You will say she did embrace me as a husband,
And so extenuate the 'forehand sin:
No Leonato,
I never tempted her with word too large,
But as a brother to his sister showed
Bashful sincerity, and comely love.

HERO And seemed I ever otherwise to you?

CLAUDIO Out on the seeming, I will write against it.
You seem to me as Dian in her orb,
As chaste as is the bud ere it be blown:
But you are more intemperate in your blood
Than Venus, or those pamp'red animals
That rage in savage sensuality.

HERO Is my lord well that he doth speak so wide?

LEONATO Sweet prince, why speak not you?

D. PEDRO What should I speak?
I stand dishonoured that have gone about
To link my dear friend to a common stale.

LEONATO Are these things spoken, or do I but dream?

DON JOHN Sir, they are spoken, and these things are true.

BENEDICK This looks not like a nuptial.

HERO 'True,' O God!

CLAUDIO Leonato, stand I here?
Is this the prince? Is this the prince's brother?
Is this face Hero's? Are our eyes our own?

LEONATO All this is so, but what of this my lord?

CLAUDIO Let me but move one question to your daughter,
And by that fatherly and kindly power
That you have in her, bid her answer truly.
LEONATO I charge thee do so, as thou art my child.
HERO O God defend me how am I beset!
What kind of catechizing call you this?
CLAUDIO To make you answer truly to your name.
HERO Is it not Hero? Who can blot that name
With any just reproach?
CLAUDIO Marry, that can Hero –
Hero itself can blot out Hero's virtue.
What man was he talked with you yesternight,
Out at your window betwixt twelve and one?
Now if you are a maid, answer to this.
HERO I talked with no man at that hour my lord.
D. PEDRO Why then are you no maiden. Leonato,
I am sorry you must hear: upon mine honour,
Myself, my brother, and this grievéd count,
Did see her, hear her, at that hour last night,
Talk with a ruffian at her chamber-window –
Who hath indeed, most like a liberal villain,
Confessed the vile encounters they have had
A thousand times in secret.
DON JOHN Fie, fie! They are not to be named, my lord,
Not to be spoke of.
There is not chastity enough in language,
Without offence, to utter them. Thus, pretty lady,
I am sorry for thy much misgovernment.
CLAUDIO O Hero! What a Hero hadst thou been,
If half thy outward graces had been placed
About the thoughts and counsels of thy heart!
But, fare thee well, most foul, most fair – farewell,
Thou pure impiety, and impious purity.
For thee I'll lock up all the gates of love,
And on my eyelids shall conjecture hang,
To turn all beauty into thoughts of harm,
And never shall it more be gracious.
LEONATO Hath no man's dagger here a point for me?
[*Hero swoons*

BEATRICE Why, how now cousin, wherefore sink you down?
DON JOHN Come let us go: these things, come thus to light,
Smother her spirits up. *[Don Pedro, Don John, and Claudio leave the church*
BENEDICK How doth the lady?
BEATRICE Dead I think – help, uncle –
Hero – why Hero – uncle – Signior Benedick – Friar!
LEONATO O Fate! Take not away thy heavy hand.
Death is the fairest cover for her shame
That may be wished for.
BEATRICE How now cousin Hero?
FRIAR Have comfort lady.
LEONATO Dost thou look up?
FRIAR Yea, wherefore should she not?
LEONATO Wherefore? Why, doth not every earthly thing
Cry shame upon her? Could she here deny
The story that is printed in her blood?
Do not live Hero, do not ope thine eyes:
For did I think thou wouldst not quickly die,
Thought I thy spirits were stronger than thy shames,
Myself would on the rearward of reproaches
Strike at thy life. Grieved I, I had but one?
Chid I for that at frugal nature's frame?
O, one too much by thee. Why had I one?
Why ever wast thou lovely in my eyes?
Why had I not with charitable hand
Took up a beggar's issue at my gates,
Who smirchéd thus, and mired with infamy,
I might have said, 'No part of it is mine,
This shame derives itself from unknown loins'?
But mine, and mine I loved, and mine I praised,
And mine that I was proud on, mine so much
That I myself was to myself not mine,
Valuing of her – why she, O she is fall'n
Into a pit of ink, that the wide sea
Hath drops too few to wash her clean again,
And salt too little which may season give
To her foul tainted flesh.

BENEDICK Sir, sir, be patient. For my part, I am so
Attired in wonder, I know not what to say.

BEATRICE O, on my soul, my cousin is belied!

BENEDICK Lady, were you her bedfellow last night?

BEATRICE No, truly, not – although, until last night,
I have this twelvemonth been her bedfellow.

LEONATO Confirmed, confirmed – O, that is stronger made,
Which was before barred up with ribs of iron.
Would the two princes lie? And Claudio lie,
Who loved her so, that, speaking of her foulness,
Washed it with tears! Hence from her, let her die.

FRIAR Hear me a little –
[For I have only been silent so long,
And given way unto this course of fortune,]
By noting of the lady, I have marked
A thousand blushing apparitions
To start into her face, a thousand innocent shames
In angel whiteness beat away those blushes,
And in her eye there hath appeared a fire,
To burn the errors that these princes hold
Against her maiden truth. Call me a fool,
Trust not my reading, nor my observations,
Which with experimental seal doth warrant
The tenour of my book: trust not my age,
My reverence, calling, nor divinity,
If this sweet lady lie not guiltless here
Under some biting error.

LEONATO Friar, it cannot be.
Thou seest that all the grace that she hath left
Is that she will not add to her damnation
A sin of perjury – she not denies it:
Why seek'st thou then to cover with excuse
That which appears in proper nakedness?

FRIAR Lady, what man is he you are accused of?

HERO They know that do accuse me, I know none.
If I know more of any man alive
Than that which maiden modesty doth warrant,
Let all my sins lack mercy. O my father,
Prove you that any man with me conversed

At hours unmeet, or that I yesternight
Maintained the change of words with any creature –
Refuse me, hate me, torture me to death.

FRIAR There is some strange misprision in the princes.

BENEDICK Two of them have the very bent of honour.
And if their wisdoms be misled in this,
The practice of it lives in John the bastard,
Whose spirits toil in frame of villainies.

LEONATO I know not. If they speak but truth of her,
These hands shall tear her – if they wrong her honour,
The proudest of them shall well hear of it.
Time hath not yet so dried this blood of mine,
Nor age so eat up my invention,
Nor fortune made such havoc of my means,
Nor my bad life reft me so much of friends,
But they shall find, awaked in such a kind,
Both strength of limb, and policy of mind,
Ability in means, and choice of friends,
To quit me of them throughly.

FRIAR Pause awhile,
And let my counsel sway you in this case.
Your daughter here the princes left for dead.
Let her awhile be secretly kept in,
And publish it that she is dead indeed.
Maintain a mourning ostentation,
And on your family's old monument
Hang mournful epitaphs, and do all rites
That appertain unto a burial.

LEONATO What shall become of this? What will this do?

FRIAR Marry, this well carried, shall on her behalf
Change slander to remorse – that is some good.
But not for that dream I on this strange course,
But on this travail look for greater birth:
She dying, as it must be so maintained,
Upon the instant that she was accused,
Shall be lamented, pitied, and excused
Of every hearer: for it so falls out
That what we have we prize not to the worth,

Whiles we enjoy it, but being lacked and lost,
Why then we rack the value, then we find
The virtue that possession would not show us
Whiles it was ours – so will it fare with Claudio:
When he shall hear she died upon his words,
Th'idea of her life shall sweetly creep
Into his study of imagination,
And every lovely organ of her life
Shall come apparelled in more precious habit,
More moving-delicate and full of life,
Into the eye and prospect of his soul,
Than when she lived indeed: then shall he mourn –
If ever love had interest in his liver –
And wish he had not so accuséd her:
No, though he thought his accusation true.
Let this be so, and doubt not but success
Will fashion the event in better shape
Than I can lay it down in likelihood.
But if all aim but this be levelled false,
The supposition of the lady's death
Will quench the wonder of her infamy.
And if it sort not well, you may conceal her –
As best befits her wounded reputation –
In some reclusive and religious life,
Out of all eyes, tongues, minds, and injuries.

BENEDICK Signior Leonato, let the friar advise you,
And though you know my inwardness and love
Is very much unto the prince and Claudio,
Yet, by mine honour, I will deal in this
As secretly and justly as your soul
Should with your body.

LEONATO Being that I flow in grief,
The smallest twine may lead me.

FRIAR 'Tis well consented – presently away –
For to strange sores strangely they strain the cure.
Come lady, die to live – this wedding day
Perhaps is but prolonged – have patience and endure.
[*the Friar, Hero, and Leonato depart*

BENEDICK Lady Beatrice, have you wept all this while?

BEATRICE Yea, and I will weep a while longer.

BENEDICK I will not desire that.

BEATRICE You have no reason, I do it freely.

BENEDICK Surely I do believe your fair cousin is wronged.

BEATRICE Ah, how much might the man deserve of me that would right her!

BENEDICK Is there any way to show such friendship?

BEATRICE A very even way, but no such friend.

BENEDICK May a man do it?

BEATRICE It is a man's office, but not yours.

BENEDICK I do love nothing in the world so well as you – is not that strange?

BEATRICE As strange as the thing I know not. It were as possible for me to say I loved nothing so well as you – but believe me not – and yet I lie not – I confess nothing, nor I deny nothing – I am sorry for my cousin.

BENEDICK By my sword Beatrice, thou lovest me.

BEATRICE Do not swear and eat it.

BENEDICK I will swear by it that you love me, and I will make him eat it that says I love not you.

BEATRICE Will you not eat your word?

BENEDICK With no sauce that can be devised to it – I protest I love thee.

BEATRICE Why then God forgive me –

BENEDICK What offence sweet Beatrice?

BEATRICE You have stayed me in a happy hour, I was about to protest I loved you.

BENEDICK And do it with all thy heart.

BEATRICE I love you with so much of my heart, that none is left to protest.

BENEDICK Come bid me do any thing for thee.

BEATRICE Kill Claudio.

BENEDICK Ha! not for the wide world.

BEATRICE You kill me to deny it – farewell.

BENEDICK Tarry sweet Beatrice. [*he stays her*

BEATRICE I am gone, though I am here – there is no love in you – nay I pray you let me go.

BENEDICK Beatrice –

BEATRICE In faith I will go.

BENEDICK We'll be friends first.

BEATRICE You dare easier be friends with me than fight with mine enemy.

BENEDICK Is Claudio thine enemy?

BEATRICE Is 'a not approved in the height a villain, that hath slandered, scorned, dishonoured my kinswoman? O that I were a man! What, bear her in hand until they come to take hands, and then with public accusation, uncovered slander, unmitigated rancour – O God that I were a man! I would eat his heart in the market-place.

BENEDICK Hear me Beatrice –

BEATRICE Talk with a man out at a window – a proper saying!

BENEDICK Nay but Beatrice –

BEATRICE Sweet Hero, she is wronged, she is slandred, she is undone.

BENEDICK Beat –

BEATRICE Princes and counties! Surely a princely testimony, a goodly count, Count Comfect – a sweet gallant surely. O that I were a man for his sake! Or that I had any friend would be a man for my sake! But manhood is melted into curtsies, valour into complement, and men are only turned into tongue, and trim ones too: he is now as valiant as Hercules, that only tells a lie and swears it. I cannot be a man with wishing, therefore I will die a woman with grieving.

BENEDICK Tarry good Beatrice – by this hand I love thee.

BEATRICE Use it for my love some other way than swearing by it.

BENEDICK Think you in your soul the Count Claudio hath wronged Hero?

BEATRICE Yea, as sure as I have a thought or a soul.

BENEDICK Enough, I am engaged, I will challenge him. I will kiss your hand, and so I leave you. [*he takes her hand*] By this hand, Claudio shall render me a dear account. [*he kisses it*] As you hear of me, so think of me. Go comfort your cousin. I must say she is dead – and so farewell.

[*he departs; Beatrice follows slowly after*

SCENE 2

A room in a gaol

DOGBERRY *and* VERGES *in their robes of office, the Sexton in his clerk's gown, and the Watch guarding* CONRADE *and* BORACHIO

DOGBERRY Is our whole dissembly appeared?

VERGES O, a stool and a cushion for the sexton!

[*they are brought*

SEXTON [*sits*] Which be the malefactors?

DOGBERRY Marry, that am I, and my partner.

VERGES Nay, that's certain. We have the exhibition to examine.

SEXTON But which are the offenders that are to be examined? let them come before Master Constable.

DOGBERRY Yea marry, let them come before me.

[*Borachio and Conrade are led forward*

What is your name, friend?

BORACHIO Borachio.

DOGBERRY Pray write down 'Borachio'. Yours, sirrah?

[*the Sexton writes as Dogberry directs*

CONRADE I am a gentleman, sir, and my name is Conrade.

DOGBERRY Write down 'Master Gentleman Conrade'. Masters, do you serve God?

CONRADE, BORACHIO Yea, sir, we hope.

DOGBERRY Write down that they hope they serve God: and write 'God' first, for God defend but God should go before such villains. Masters, it is proved already that you are little better than false knaves, and it will go near to be thought so shortly. How answer you for yourselves?

CONRADE Marry, sir, we say we are none.

DOGBERRY A marvellous witty fellow, I assure you – but I will go about with him. Come you hither sirrah – a word in your ear. Sir, I say to you, it is thought you are false knaves.

BORACHIO Sir, I say to you, we are none.

DOGBERRY Well, stand aside. 'Fore God, they are both in a tale. Have you writ down, that they are none?

SEXTON Master Constable, you go not the way to examine. You must call forth the watch that are their accusers.

DOGBERRY Yea marry, that's the eftest way, let the watch come forth. Masters, I charge you in the prince's name, accuse these men.

1 WATCH. This man said, sir, that Don John the prince's brother was a villain.

DOGBERRY Write down 'Prince John a villain'. Why this is flat perjury, to call a prince's brother villain.

BORACHIO Master Constable –

DOGBERRY Pray thee fellow peace. I do not like thy look, I promise thee.

SEXTON What heard you him say else?

2 WATCH. Marry, that he had received a thousand ducats of Don John, for accusing the Lady Hero wrongfully.

DOGBERRY Flat burglary as ever was committed.

VERGES Yea by mass that it is.

SEXTON What else fellow?

1 WATCH. And that Count Claudio did mean, upon his words, to disgrace Hero before the whole assembly, and not marry her.

DOGBERRY O villain! Thou wilt be condemned into everlasting redemption for this.

SEXTON What else?

WATCHMEN This is all.

SEXTON And this is more, masters, than you can deny. Prince John is this morning secretly stolen away: Hero was in this manner accused, in this very manner refused, and upon the grief of this suddenly died. Master Constable, let these men be bound, and brought to Leonato's. I will go before and show him their examination.

[*he goes out*

DOGBERRY Come, let them be opinioned.

VERGES Let them be – in the hands. [*he offers to bind Conrade*

CONRADE Off, coxcomb!

DOGBERRY God's my life, where's the sexton? Let him write down the prince's officer 'coxcomb'. Come, bind them. Thou naughty varlet!

CONRADE Away! You are an ass, you are an ass.

[*the Watch bind them*

DOGBERRY Dost thou not suspect my place? Dost thou not suspect my years? O that he were here to write me down an ass! But, masters, remember that I am an ass – though it be not written down, yet forget not that I am an ass. No, thou villain, thou art full of piety, as shall be proved upon thee by good witness. I am a wise fellow, and which is more – an officer, and which is more – a householder, and which is more – as pretty a piece of flesh as any is in Messina, and one that knows the law, go to, and a rich fellow enough, go to, and a fellow that hath had losses, and one that hath two gowns and everything handsome about him. Bring him away. O that I had been writ down an ass!

[*he struts forth; the rest follow*

ACT 5 SCENE 1

The street before the house of Leonato

LEONATO *and* ANTONIO *appear, walking towards the house*

ANTONIO If you go on thus, you will kill yourself,
And 'tis not wisdom thus to second grief
Against yourself.

LEONATO I pray thee cease thy counsel,
Which falls into mine ears as profitless
As water in a sieve: give not me counsel,
Nor let no comforter delight mine ear,
But such a one whose wrongs do suit with mine.
Bring me a father that so loved his child,
Whose joy of her is overwhelmed like mine,
And bid him speak of patience,
Measure his woe the length and breadth of mine,
And let it answer every strain for strain,
As thus for thus, and such a grief for such,
In every lineament, branch, shape, and form:
If such a one will smile and stroke his beard,
And – sorry wag – cry 'hem' when he should groan,
Patch grief with proverbs, make misfortune drunk
With candle-wasters . . . bring him yet to me,
And I of him will gather patience.
But there is no such man – for, brother, men
Can counsel and speak comfort to that grief
Which they themselves not feel, but tasting it,
Their counsel turns to passion, which before
Would give preceptial medicine to rage,
Fetter strong madness in a silken thread,
Charm ache with air, and agony with words.
No, no – 'tis all men's office to speak patience
To those that wring under the load of sorrow,
But no man's virtue nor sufficiency
To be so moral when he shall endure
The like himself. Therefore give me no counsel.
My griefs cry louder than advertisement.

ANTONIO Therein do men from children nothing differ.

LEONATO I pray thee peace. I will be flesh and blood –
For there was never yet philosopher
That could endure the toothache patiently,
However they have writ the style of gods,
And made a 'push' at chance and sufferance.

ANTONIO Yet bend not all the harm upon yourself,
Make those that do offend you suffer too.

LEONATO There thou speak'st reason, nay I will do so.
My soul doth tell me Hero is belied –
And that shall Claudio know, so shall the prince,
And all of them that thus dishonour her.

DON PEDRO *and* CLAUDIO *approach*

ANTONIO Here comes the prince and Claudio hastily.

D. PEDRO Good-den, good-den.

CLAUDIO Good day to both of you.

[*they pass by*

LEONATO Hear you, my lords –

D. PEDRO We have some haste, Leonato.

LEONATO Some haste, my lord! Well, fare you well my lord.
Are you so hasty now? Well, all is one.

D. PEDRO [*turns*] Nay, do not quarrel with us, good old man.

ANTONIO If he could right himself with quarrelling,
Some of us would lie low.

CLAUDIO Who wrongs him?

LEONATO Marry, thou dost wrong me, thou dissembler, thou.
Nay, never lay thy hand upon thy sword,
I fear thee not.

CLAUDIO Marry, beshrew my hand,
If it should give your age such cause of fear.
In faith my hand meant nothing to my sword.

LEONATO Tush, tush, man, never fleer and jest at me.
I speak not like a dotard nor a fool,
As under privilege of age to brag
What I have done being young, or what would do
Were I not old. Know, Claudio, to thy head,
Thou hast so wronged mine innocent child and me,
That I am forced to lay my reverence by,
And with grey hairs and bruise of many days,

Do challenge thee to trial of a man.
I say thou hast belied mine innocent child,
Thy slander hath gone through and through her heart,
And she lies buried with her ancestors:
O in a tomb where never scandal slept,
Save this of hers, framed by thy villainy.

CLAUDIO My villainy!

LEONATO Thine Claudio, thine I say.

D. PEDRO You say not right, old man.

LEONATO My lord, my lord,
I'll prove it on his body if he dare –
Despite his nice fence and his active practice,
His May of youth and bloom of lustihood.

CLAUDIO Away, I will not have to do with you.

LEONATO Canst thou so daff me? Thou hast killed my child –
If thou kill'st me, boy, thou shalt kill a man.

ANTONIO He shall kill two of us, and men indeed –
But that's no matter, let him kill one first.
[he comes between them, and draws his sword
Win me and wear me! Let him answer me.
Come follow me boy, come sir boy, come follow me.
Sir boy, I'll whip you from your foining fence –
Nay, as I am a gentleman, I will.

LEONATO Brother –

ANTONIO Content yourself, God knows I loved my niece,
And she is dead, slandered to death by villains
That dare as well answer a man indeed
As I dare take a serpent by the tongue.
Boys, apes, braggarts, Jacks, milksops!

LEONATO Brother Antony –

ANTONIO Hold you content. What, man! I know them, yea,
And what they weigh, even to the utmost scruple –
Scambling, out-facing, fashion-monging boys,
That lie, and cog, and flout, deprave, and slander,
Go anticly, and show outward hideousness,
And speak off half a dozen dang'rous words,
How they might hurt their enemies, if they durst,
And this is all.

LEONATO But brother Antony –

ANTONIO Come, 'tis no matter –
Do not you meddle, let me deal in this.

D. PEDRO Gentlemen both, we will not wake your patience.
My heart is sorry for your daughter's death:
But on my honour she was charged with nothing
But what was true, and very full of proof.

LEONATO My lord, my lord –

D. PEDRO I will not hear you.

LEONATO No?
Come brother, away. [I will be heard.

ANTONIO And shall, or some of us will smart for it.]

[*Leonato and Antonio enter the house*

BENEDICK *comes up*

D. PEDRO See, see, here comes the man we went to seek.

CLAUDIO Now signior, what news?

BENEDICK Good day, my lord.

D. PEDRO Welcome, signior, you are almost come to part almost a fray.

CLAUDIO We had liked to have had our two noses snapped off with two old men without teeth.

D. PEDRO Leonato and his brother. What think'st thou? Had we fought I doubt we should have been too young for them.

BENEDICK In a false quarrel there is no true valour. I came to seek you both.

CLAUDIO We have been up and down to seek thee, for we are high-proof melancholy, and would fain have it beaten away. Wilt thou use thy wit?

BENEDICK It is in my scabbard – shall I draw it?

D. PEDRO Dost thou wear thy wit by thy side?

CLAUDIO Never any did so, though very many have been beside their wit. I will bid thee draw, as we do the minstrels – draw to pleasure us.

D. PEDRO As I am an honest man he looks pale. Art thou sick, or angry?

CLAUDIO What, courage, man: what though care killed a cat, thou hast mettle enough in thee to kill care.

BENEDICK Sir, I shall meet your wit in the career, an you charge it against me. I pray you choose another subject.

CLAUDIO Nay then, give him another staff – this last was broke cross.

D. PEDRO By this light, he changes more and more. I think he be angry indeed.

CLAUDIO If he be, he knows how to turn his girdle.

BENEDICK Shall I speak a word in your ear?

CLAUDIO God bless me from a challenge!

BENEDICK You are a villain – I jest not – I will make it good how you dare, with what you dare, and when you dare: do me right, or I will protest your cowardice: you have killed a sweet lady, and her death shall fall heavy on you. [*aloud*] Let me hear from you.

CLAUDIO Well, I will meet you, so I may have good cheer.

D. PEDRO What, a feast, a feast?

CLAUDIO I'faith, I thank him, he hath bid me to a calf's-head and a capon, the which if I do not carve most curiously, say my knife's naught. Shall I not find a woodcock too?

BENEDICK Sir, your wit ambles well – it goes easily.

D. PEDRO I'll tell thee how Beatrice praised thy wit the other day. I said, thou hadst a fine wit. 'True,' said she, 'a fine little one': 'No,' said I, 'a great wit': 'Right,' says she, 'a great gross one': 'Nay,' said I, 'a good wit': 'Just,' said she, 'it hurts nobody': 'Nay,' said I, 'the gentleman is wise': 'Certain,' said she, 'a wise gentleman': 'Nay,' said I, 'he hath the tongues': 'That I believe,' said she, 'for he swore a thing to me on Monday night, which he forswore on Tuesday morning – there's a double tongue, there's two tongues.' Thus did she an hour together trans-shape thy particular virtues – yet at last she concluded with a sigh, thou wast the proper'st man in Italy.

CLAUDIO For the which she wept heartily and said she cared not.

D. PEDRO Yea, that she did – but yet, for all that, an if she did not hate him deadly, she would love him dearly. The old man's daughter told us all.

CLAUDIO All, all – and moreover, God saw him when he was hid in the garden.

D. PEDRO But when shall we set the savage bull's horns on the sensible Benedick's head?

CLAUDIO Yea, and text underneath, 'Here dwells Benedick the married man'?

BENEDICK Fare you well, boy – you know my mind. I will leave you now to your gossip-like humour. You break jests as braggarts do their blades, which God be thanked hurt not. My lord, for your many courtesies I thank you. I must discontinue your company – your brother the bastard is fled from Messina: you have among you killed a sweet and innocent lady: for my Lord Lack-beard, there, he and I shall meet, and till then peace be with him. [*he passes on*

D. PEDRO He is in earnest.

CLAUDIO In most profound earnest, and I'll warrant you, for the love of Beatrice.

D. PEDRO And hath challenged thee?

CLAUDIO Most sincerely.

D. PEDRO What a pretty thing man is, when he goes in his doublet and hose and leaves off his wit!

CLAUDIO He is then a giant to an ape, but then is an ape a doctor to such a man.

D. PEDRO But soft you, let me be – pluck up, my heart, and be sad – did he not say my brother was fled?

DOGBERRY, VERGES *and the Watch approach, with* CONRADE *and* BORACHIO *in custody*

DOGBERRY Come you sir, if justice cannot tame you, she shall ne'er weigh more reasons in her balance. Nay, an you be a cursing hypocrite once, you must be looked to.

D. PEDRO How now, two of my brother's men bound? Borachio, one?

CLAUDIO Hearken after their offence, my lord.

D. PEDRO Officers, what offence have these men done?

DOGBERRY Marry sir, they have committed false report – moreover, they have spoken untruths – secondarily, they are slanders – sixth and lastly, they have belied a lady – thirdly, they have verified unjust things – and to conclude, they are lying knaves.

D. PEDRO First, I ask thee what they have done – thirdly, I ask thee what's their offence – sixth and lastly, why they are committed – and to conclude, what you lay to their charge.

CLAUDIO Rightly reasoned, and in his own division – and by my troth there's one meaning well suited.

D. PEDRO Who have you offended, masters, that you are thus bound to your answer? This learned constable is too cunning to be understood. What's your offence?

BORACHIO Sweet prince, let me go no farther to mine answer: do you hear me, and let this count kill me. I have deceived even your very eyes: what your wisdoms could not discover, these shallow fools have brought to light – who in the night overheard me confessing to this man how Don John your brother incensed me to slander the Lady Hero, how you were brought into the orchard and saw me court Margaret in Hero's garments, how you disgraced her when you should marry her. My villainy they have upon record, which I had rather seal with my death than repeat over to my shame. The lady is dead upon mine and my master's false accusation: and briefly, I desire nothing but the reward of a villain.

D. PEDRO Runs not this speech like iron through your blood?

CLAUDIO I have drunk poison whiles he uttered it.

D. PEDRO But did my brother set thee on to this?

BORACHIO Yea, and paid me richly for the practice of it.

D. PEDRO He is composed and framed of treachery,
And fled he is upon this villainy.

CLAUDIO Sweet Hero, now thy image doth appear
In the rare semblance that I loved it first.

DOGBERRY Come, bring away the plaintiffs. By this time our sexton hath reformed Signior Leonato of the matter. And masters, do not forget to specify, when time and place shall serve, that I am an ass.

VERGES Here, here comes Master Signior Leonato, and the sexton too.

LEONATO *and* ANTONIO *come from the house, with the Sexton*

LEONATO Which is the villain? Let me see his eyes,
That when I note another man like him,
I may avoid him: which of these is he?

BORACHIO If you would know your wronger, look on me.

LEONATO	Art thou the slave that with thy breath hast killed
	Mine innocent child?
BORACHIO	Yea, even I alone.
LEONATO	No, not so villain, thou beliest thyself,
	Here stand a pair of honourable men,
	A third is fled that had a hand in it.
	I thank you, princes, for my daughter's death,
	Record it with your high and worthy deeds,
	'Twas bravely done, if you bethink you of it.
CLAUDIO	I know not how to pray your patience,
	Yet I must speak. Choose your revenge yourself,
	Impose me to what penance your invention
	Can lay upon my sin – yet sinned I not,
	But in mistaking.
D. PEDRO	By my soul nor I,
	And yet to satisfy this good old man,
	I would bend under any heavy weight
	That he'll enjoin me to.
LEONATO	I cannot bid you bid my daughter live –
	That were impossible – but I pray you both,
	Possess the people in Messina here
	How innocent she died, and if your love
	Can labour aught in sad invention,
	Hang her an epitaph upon her tomb,
	And sing it to her bones – sing it tonight:
	Tomorrow morning come you to my house,
	And since you could not be my son-in-law,
	Be yet my nephew: my brother hath a daughter,
	Almost the copy of my child that's dead,
	And she alone is heir to both of us –
	Give her the right you should have giv'n her cousin,
	And so dies my revenge.
CLAUDIO	O noble sir!
	Your over-kindness doth wring tears from me.
	I do embrace your offer, and dispose
	For henceforth of poor Claudio.
LEONATO	Tomorrow then I will expect your coming,
	Tonight I take my leave. This naughty man
	Shall face to face be brought to Margaret,

Line numbers: 250, 260, 270, 280

Who I believe was packed in all this wrong,
Hired to it by your brother.

BORACHIO No, by my soul she was not,
Nor knew not what she did when she spoke to me,
But always hath been just and virtuous
In anything that I do know by her.

DOGBERRY Moreover, sir – which indeed is not under white and black – this plaintiff here, the offender, did call me ass. I beseech you let it be remembred in his punishment. And also the watch heard them talk of one Deformed – they say he wears a key in his ear and a lock hanging by it, and borrows money in God's name, the which he hath used so long and never paid, that now men grow hard-hearted and will lend nothing for God's sake. Pray you examine him upon that point.

LEONATO I thank thee for thy care and honest pains.

DOGBERRY Your worship speaks like a most thankful and reverend youth, and I praise God for you.

LEONATO There's for thy pains.

DOGBERRY God save the foundation!

LEONATO Go, I discharge thee of thy prisoner, and I thank thee.

DOGBERRY I leave an arrant knave with your worship, which I beseech your worship to correct yourself, for the example of others. God keep your worship, I wish your worship well, God restore you to health, I humbly give you leave to depart – and if a merry meeting may be wished, God prohibit it. Come neighbour.

[*Dogberry and Verges depart*

LEONATO Until tomorrow morning, lords, farewell.

ANTONIO Farewell my lords, we look for you tomorrow.

D. PEDRO We will not fail.

CLAUDIO Tonight I'll mourn with Hero.

[*Don Pedro and Claudio walk sadly away*

LEONATO Bring you these fellows on. We'll talk with Margaret,
How her acquaintance grew with this lewd fellow.

Leonato and Antonio go within, followed by the Sexton, the Watch and the prisoners

SCENE 2

BENEDICK *and* MARGARET *come up the street*

BENEDICK Pray thee sweet Mistress Margaret, deserve well at my hands, by helping me to the speech of Beatrice.

MARGARET Will you then write me a sonnet in praise of my beauty?

BENEDICK In so high a style, Margaret, that no man living shall come over it, for in most comely truth thou deservest it.

MARGARET To have no man come over me? Why, shall I always keep below stairs?

BENEDICK Thy wit is as quick as the greyhound's mouth, it catches.

MARGARET And yours – as blunt as the fencer's foils, which hit, but hurt not.

BENEDICK A most manly wit Margaret, it will not hurt a woman. And so I pray thee call Beatrice – I give thee the bucklers.

MARGARET Give us the swords, we have bucklers of our own.

BENEDICK If you use them, Margaret, you must put in the pikes with a vice – and they are dangerous weapons for maids.

MARGARET Well, I will call Beatrice to you, who I think hath legs.

[*Margaret enters the house*

BENEDICK And therefore will come.

[*sings*] The god of love,
That sits above,
And knows me, and knows me,
How pitiful I deserve.

I mean in singing. But in loving – Leander the good swimmer, Troilus the first employer of pandars, and a whole book full of these quondam carpet-mongers, whose names yet run smoothly in the even road of a blank verse, why, they were never so truly turned over and over as my poor self, in love. Marry, I cannot show it in rhyme – I have tried. I can find out no rhyme to 'lady' but 'baby,' an innocent rhyme: for 'scorn,' 'horn,' a hard rhyme: for 'school,' 'fool,' a babbling rhyme. Very ominous endings. No, I was not born under a rhyming planet, nor I cannot woo in festival terms.

BEATRICE *comes forth*

Sweet Beatrice, wouldst thou come when I called thee?

BEATRICE Yea signior, and depart when you bid me.

BENEDICK O stay but till then.

BEATRICE 'Then' is spoken: fare you well now – and yet, ere I go, let me go with that I came for, which is, with knowing what hath passed between you and Claudio.

BENEDICK Only foul words – and thereupon I will kiss thee.

BEATRICE Foul words is but foul wind, and foul wind is but foul breath, and foul breath is noisome – therefore I will depart unkissed.

BENEDICK Thou hast frighted the word out of his right sense, so forcible is thy wit. But I must tell thee plainly, Claudio undergoes my challenge, and either I must shortly hear from him, or I will subscribe him a coward. And I pray thee now tell me, for which of my bad parts didst thou first fall in love with me?

BEATRICE For them all together, which maintain so politic a state of evil that they will not admit any good part to intermingle with them. But for which of my good parts did you first suffer love for me?

BENEDICK 'Suffer love'! A good epithet. I do suffer love indeed, for I love thee against my will.

BEATRICE In spite of your heart, I think. Alas, poor heart, if you spite it for my sake, I will spite it for yours, for I will never love that which my friend hates.

BENEDICK Thou and I are too wise to woo peaceably.

BEATRICE It appears not in this confession – there's not one wise man among twenty that will praise himself.

BENEDICK An old, an old instance, Beatrice, that lived in the time of good neighbours. If a man do not erect in this age his own tomb ere he dies, he shall live no longer in monument than the bell rings and the widow weeps.

BEATRICE And how long is that, think you?

BENEDICK Question! Why, an hour in clamour and a quarter in rheum. Therefore is it most expedient for the wise – if Don Worm, his conscience, find no impediment to the contrary – to be the trumpet of his own virtues, as

I am to myself. So much for praising myself, who, I myself will bear witness, is praiseworthy. And now tell me, how doth your cousin?

BEATRICE Very ill.

BENEDICK And how do you?

BEATRICE Very ill too.

BENEDICK Serve God, love me, and mend. There will I leave you too, for here comes one in haste.

URSULA *runs forth*

URSULA Madam, you must come to your uncle – yonder's old coil at home. It is proved my Lady Hero hath been falsely accused, the prince and Claudio mightily abused, and Don John is the author of all, who is fled and gone. Will you come presently?

BEATRICE Will you go hear this news, signior?

BENEDICK I will live in thy heart, die in thy lap, and be buried in thy eyes: and moreover, I will go with thee to thy uncle's. [*they go within*

SCENE 3

A church-yard; before a sepulchre. Night

DON PEDRO, CLAUDIO *and other lords approach with tapers, followed by* BALTHAZAR *and musicians*

CLAUDIO Is this the monument of Leonato?

A LORD It is, my lord.

CLAUDIO [*reads from a scroll*]

Done to death by slanderous tongues
Was the Hero that here lies:
Death, in guerdon of her wrongs,
Gives her fame which never dies:
So the life that died with shame,
Lives in death with glorious fame.

Hang thou there upon the tomb, [*affixing it*
Praising her when I am dumb.

Now, music, sound, and sing your solemn hymn.

BALTHAZAR *sings*

Pardon, goddess of the night,
Those that slew thy virgin knight,
For the which, with songs of woe,
Round about her tomb they go:
  Midnight, assist our moan,
  Help us to sigh and groan,
    Heavily, heavily.
  Graves, yawn and yield your dead,
  Till death be utteréd,
    Heavily, heavily.

CLAUDIO Now, unto thy bones good night.
Yearly will I do this rite.

D. PEDRO Good morrow masters, put your torches out.
The wolves have preyed, and look, the gentle day,
Before the wheels of Phoebus, round about
Dapples the drowsy east with spots of grey:
Thanks to you all, and leave us. Fare you well.

CLAUDIO Good morrow masters – each his several way.
[*the musicians leave the church-yard*

D. PEDRO Come let us hence, and put on other weeds,
And then to Leonato's we will go.

CLAUDIO And Hymen now with luckier issue speeds,
Than this for whom we rendred up this woe! [*they go*

SCENE 4

The hall in Leonato's house; musicians seated in the gallery

LEONATO, ANTONIO, BENEDICK *and* FRIAR FRANCIS *enter, followed by* HERO, BEATRICE, MARGARET *and* URSULA, *who talk apart*

FRIAR Did I not tell you she was innocent?

LEONATO So are the prince and Claudio, who accused her
Upon the error that you heard debated:
But Margaret was in some fault for this,
Although against her will, as it appears
In the true course of all the question.

ANTONIO Well, I am glad that all things sort so well.
BENEDICK And so am I, being else by faith enforced
To call young Claudio to a reckoning for it.
LEONATO [*turns*] Well daughter, and you gentlewomen all,
Withdraw into a chamber by yourselves,
And when I send for you come hither masked.
[*the ladies go out*
The prince and Claudio promised by this hour
To visit me. You know your office, brother –
You must be father to your brother's daughter,
And give her to young Claudio.
ANTONIO Which I will do with confirmed countenance.
BENEDICK Friar, I must entreat your pains, I think.
FRIAR To do what, signior?
BENEDICK To bind me, or undo me – one of them
Signior Leonato, truth it is, good signior,
Your niece regards me with an eye of favour.
LEONATO That eye my daughter lent her. 'Tis most true.
BENEDICK And I do with an eye of love requite her.
LEONATO The sight whereof I think you had from me,
From Claudio, and the prince. But what's your will?
BENEDICK Your answer, sir, is enigmatical:
But for my will, my will is your good will
May stand with ours, this day to be conjoined
In the state of honourable marriage –
In which, good friar, I shall desire your help.
LEONATO My heart is with your liking.
FRIAR And my help.
Here comes the prince and Claudio.

DON PEDRO *and* CLAUDIO *enter with two or three other lords*

D. PEDRO Good morrow to this fair assembly.
LEONATO Good morrow prince, good morrow Claudio:
We here attend you. Are you yet determined
Today to marry with my brother's daughter?
CLAUDIO I'll hold my mind, were she an Ethiope.
LEONATO Call her forth, brother. Here's the friar ready.
[*Antonio goes*
D. PEDRO Good morrow Benedick. Why, what's the matter,
That you have such a February face,

So full of frost, of storm, and cloudiness?

CLAUDIO I think he thinks upon the savage bull:
Tush, fear not, man, we'll tip thy horns with gold,
And all Europa shall rejoice at thee,
As once Europa did at lusty Jove,
When he would play the noble beast in love.

BENEDICK Bull Jove, sir, had an amiable low –
And some such strange bull leaped your father's cow,
And got a calf in that same noble feat,
Much like to you, for you have just his bleat.

ANTONIO *returns, with the ladies masked*

CLAUDIO For this I owe you: here comes other reck'nings.
Which is the lady I must seize upon?

ANTONIO This same is she, and I do give you her.

CLAUDIO Why, then she's mine. Sweet, let me see your face.

LEONATO No, that you shall not, till you take her hand
Before this friar, and swear to marry her.

CLAUDIO Give me your hand before this holy friar –
I am your husband if you like of me.

HERO And when I lived I was your other wife – [*she unmasks*
And when you loved, you were my other husband.

CLAUDIO Another Hero!

HERO Nothing certainer.
One Hero died defiled, but I do live,
And surely as I live, I am a maid.

D. PEDRO The former Hero! Hero that is dead!

LEONATO She died, my lord, but whiles her slander lived.

FRIAR All this amazement can I qualify.
When after that the holy rites are ended,
I'll tell you largely of fair Hero's death,
Meantime let wonder seem familiar,
And to the chapel let us presently.

BENEDICK Soft and fair, friar. Which is Beatrice?

BEATRICE I answer to that name. [*unmasks*] What is your will?

BENEDICK Do not you love me?

BEATRICE Why no, no more than reason.

BENEDICK Why then your uncle, and the prince, and Claudio,
Have been deceivéd, for they swore you did.

BEATRICE Do not you love me?

BENEDICK Troth no, no more than reason.

BEATRICE Why then my cousin, Margaret, and Ursula,
Are much deceived, for they did swear you did.

BENEDICK They swore that you were almost sick for me.

BEATRICE They swore that you were well-nigh dead for me.

BENEDICK 'Tis no such matter. Then, you do not love me?

BEATRICE No, truly, but in friendly recompense.

LEONATO Come cousin, I am sure you love the gentleman.

CLAUDIO And I'll be sworn upon't, that he loves her,
For here's a paper written in his hand,
A halting sonnet of his own pure brain,
Fashioned to Beatrice.

HERO And here's another,
Writ in my cousin's hand, stol'n from her pocket,
Containing her affection unto Benedick.

BENEDICK A miracle! Here's our own hands against our hearts. Come, I will have thee – but by this light I take thee for pity.

BEATRICE I would not deny you – but by this good day I yield upon great persuasion, and partly to save your life, for I was told you were in a consumption.

BENEDICK Peace, I will stop your mouth. [*he kisses her*

D. PEDRO How dost thou, Benedick the married man?

BENEDICK I'll tell thee what, prince: a college of wit-crackers cannot flout me out of my humour. Dost thou think I care for a satire or an epigram? No, if a man will be beaten with brains, 'a shall wear nothing handsome about him. In brief, since I do purpose to marry, I will think nothing to any purpose that the world can say against it – and therefore never flout at me for what I have said against it: for man is a giddy thing, and this is my conclusion. For thy part, Claudio, I did think to have beaten thee, but in that thou art like to be my kinsman, live unbruised, and love my cousin.

CLAUDIO I had well hoped thou wouldst have denied Beatrice, that I might have cudgelled thee out of thy single life, to make thee a double-dealer – which out of question thou wilt be, if my cousin do not look exceeding narrowly to thee.

BENEDICK Come, come, we are friends. Let's have a dance ere we are married, that we may lighten our own hearts, and our wives' heels.

LEONATO We'll have dancing afterward.

BENEDICK First, of my word – therefore play music. Prince, thou art sad – get thee a wife, get thee a wife. There is no staff more reverend than one tipped with horn.

A messenger enters

MESSENG'R My lord, your brother John is ta'en in flight, and brought with armed men back to Messina.

BENEDICK Think not on him till tomorrow. I'll devise thee brave punishments for him. Strike up, pipers!

Music and dance

AS YOU LIKE IT

INTRODUCTION

As You Like It is both an extravagant play and a play about extravagance. It relishes its own romantic excesses of language and action, and enjoys mocking those excesses. Like *A Midsummer Night's Dream*, it dramatises an escape from the corruption of court life into a greenworld. Unlike the wood near Athens, however, *As You Like It*'s place of refuge – the forest of Arden – is thoroughly wholesome, reviving those who flee there weary from the pressures of the court. The play adheres to many of the conventions of the pastoral tradition – a range of courtly and rustic characters, a leisured existence in an idealised natural setting, quasi-philosophical debate, bucolic love stories, moments of song, an interest in gentle wit, and a broadly sentimental depiction of the shepherd's life. The refugees from the city repeatedly proclaim the simple beauties of their rural life in Arden. At the end of the play, however, they abandon it to return to the city, apparently without a moment of wistfulness. No attitude characterised in the play, not even an enthusiasm for the simple life, escapes criticism, since everything is juxtaposed with its contrary. However, the play is never savage in its exposure of folly, taking sympathetic delight in the foolish extravagances it depicts.

The main source for the play is Thomas Lodge's prose romance *Rosalynde* (1590). First performed in 1599 by Shakespeare's company, The Lord Chamberlain's Men, *As You Like It* may well have been one of the earliest plays presented in The Globe playhouse, newly opened that year. One character in the play, Duke Senior, describes life metaphorically as a series of plays, and the world as a stage. In doing so, he likens both his own and others' lives to different theatrical productions ('woeful pageants') being played in the same theatre:

> This wide and universal theatre
> Presents more woeful pageants than the scene
> Wherein we play in. (2.7.136–38)

Heard in the performance space of The Globe, the Duke's words may have sounded like a self-conscious reference to the expansive repertoire of the new playhouse. Jacques, famously, pursues the Duke's theatrical metaphor:

> All the world's a stage,
> And all the men and women merely players (2.7.138–39)

This too would, presumably, have resonated with particular piquancy in The Globe, itself a three-dimensional incarnation of the stage-as-world metaphor. *As You Like It* and one of its earliest performance contexts therefore trade upon a shared central metaphor: the interrelatedness of the theatre and the world. Another Shakespeare play, *Henry V*, also first performed in 1599, advertises its own theatricality yet more obviously, drawing its audience's attention explicitly and repeatedly to the possibilities and limitations of its staging. In 1599, the new theatrical facilities on offer in the The Globe were clearly considered worth vaunting.

Plot summary

At the opening of the play, two brothers are quarrelling. In direct contravention of their father's will, Orlando de Boys has been deprived of a gentleman's education and kept from his inheritance by his wicked elder brother, Oliver de Boys. Adam, the old family servant, attempts to intervene. He asks them to honour the memory of their dead father, Sir Rowland de Boys, by living at peace with each other, but he is verbally abused by Oliver for his trouble. Oliver discovers that Orlando is planning to engage in a sporting bout of wrestling with Charles, the Duke's wrestler. He slanders Orlando to Charles, persuading him to inflict the severest possible injury upon the upstart challenger.

Meanwhile the 'old news' from court is reiterated; Duke Senior has been banished by his younger brother Duke Frederick and is living in exile in the forest of Arden with a small group of faithful lords. Duke Senior's daughter Rosalind has been detained at court by Duke Frederick as a companion for his daughter Celia. The two girls are said to love each other dearly, 'being ever from their cradles bred together' (1.1.100).

At the scheduled wrestling match, Rosalind and Celia try to persuade the unknown challenger, Orlando, in the interests of his own safety, not to enter the ring. Both girls are agreeably taken with the strange young man's courtesy and demeanour. Since he will not be deterred, they wish him well instead. Against the odds, Orlando throws Charles and is declared the winner. The cousins congratulate him, and Rosalind gives him a necklace. He finds himself tongue-tied in response. Duke Frederick discovers that the victor is the son of Sir Rowland, Frederick's enemy of old. Orlando is advised to leave in order to avoid incurring the Duke's wrath, and is subsequently also informed that his brother Oliver means to burn him in his bed. He flees to the forest, accompanied by the good old servant Adam.

Duke Frederick, jealous of the love the people bear to Rosalind, accuses his niece of treachery and instructs her to leave the court on pain of death. Celia secretly resolves to flee with her cousin to the forest of Arden, where they will seek Rosalind's banished father. To ensure their own protection on their travels, they disguise themselves – Celia as Aliena, a peasant girl, Rosalind as Ganymede, her brother. They take with them Touchstone, the court clown, as a comfort and distraction in their banishment.

The action then shifts to the forest of Arden where the various refugees from the city run into each other and into the local inhabitants of the forest by turns. Rosalind's father, Duke Senior, holds court, commending the simple life away from the 'painted pomp' of the 'envious court' (2.1.3–4). Amiens, one of the lords in his rustic retinue, sings a song in celebration of their idyllic life spent 'under the greenwood tree', while Jaques, a cynical malcontent, lampoons this self-congratulatory approach to their primitive lifestyle.

While these courtly exiles are enjoying a rural banquet, they are rudely interrupted by Orlando, brandishing a sword and forbidding any to eat until he has taken food. He and Adam have arrived exhausted and weak in the forest, and Orlando has undertaken to find food for Adam. When his rough entrance is met with a courteous response, he realises the civility of the community upon which he has stumbled, apologises for his rudeness, and fetches Adam that they may both enjoy the gracious entertainment offered by Duke Senior.

Restored to full strength, Orlando hangs love poems on trees in the forest. These are addressed to Rosalind, who has by now herself arrived in the forest, with Celia and Touchstone. Rosalind is able, through a chance encounter, to exploit the impunity offered by her disguise to torment Orlando playfully about his lovelorn condition. In the guise of the boy Ganymede, she claims to be able to cure him of his love if he, Orlando, will pretend that s/he, Ganymede, is Rosalind. Orlando, unaware of the irony of the project, agrees to the game.

Rosalind/Ganymede stumbles across an amorous shepherd, Silvius, and his scornful love, Phebe, and cannot resist interfering in their love wrangles. S/he urges Phebe to make a realistic assessment of her own worth, and settle happily for this good man while she has the chance. Rather than heeding this advice, Phebe instead falls in love with Ganymede.

At court it is popularly believed that Orlando must have fled in company with Rosalind and Celia. Concerned for his own daughter's welfare, Duke Frederick commissions Oliver to find Orlando, that the girls may also be traced. Oliver enters the forest to seek Orlando, who generously saves him from wild animals. As a result of this rescue, Oliver undergoes an entertainingly instant conversion, is reconciled to Orlando, falls in love with Aliena, and gives up his estate and revenue to his brother.

Aliena is to marry Oliver, and Touchstone to marry a country woman, Audrey, the next day. Ganymede promises to arrange matters so that Orlando, Silvius and Phebe may each also marry to their satisfaction, even though their desires seem incompatible. They each promise to trust Ganymede until then.

The next day, in a mini-masque presentation, Hymen leads in Rosalind attired once again as herself. Duke Senior greets her as a daughter, Orlando as his bride, and Phebe, realising she has unwittingly fallen in love with a woman, gives up all claim on her and agrees instead to marry Silvius. Duke Frederick had been planning to take bloody vengeance on his exiled brother for luring so many lords to his rustic court. Instead of executing his plans, however, at the outskirts of the forest he is suddenly converted to a religious life, and hands back the dukedom to his banished brother. As the action dissolves into a nuptial dance, Jaques makes clear his intention to join the newly converted Duke Frederick, thus avoiding the festivities. Rosalind delivers the Epilogue, in which she makes a conventional apology for the play, and requests that it nevertheless meet with a kind reception.

The Forest of Arden

The play is diffuse in its attention and can, initially, be baffling in its range of characters, many of whose situations parody each other to some degree. Amidst such diversity, the most obvious point of unity is the play's strong geographical focus. Almost all characters in the play either live in the forest of Arden or are drawn there for one reason or another. As an Arcadian retreat from the corruption of court life, Arden assumes a set of identifiable values in the scheme of the play.

The journey into Arden is, almost universally, a tiring one. The rewards available once there, however, are considerable. Corin, a shepherd, articulates the pastoral ideal most clearly:

> I earn that I eat; get that I wear; owe no man hate, envy no man's happiness; glad of other men's good, content with my harm; and the greatest of my pride is to see my ewes graze and my lambs suck . . . (3.2.71–74)

Corin's pastoral philosophy is in large measure adopted by Duke Senior's rustic court. Amiens sings that in Arden those who are able to shun ambition may be easily content:

> Who doth ambition shun,
> And loves to live i'th'sun,
> Seeking the food he eats,
> And pleas'd with what he gets,
> Come hither, come hither, come hither.
> Here shall he see
> No enemy,
> But winter and rough weather. (2.5.34–41)

His idealistic vision does not seem misplaced in Arden. There is minimal strife of any sort in the forest, and, as Amiens claims, no enemies at all bar the elements. Life is governed principally by a taste for leisure (otium) and debate (negotium), and the action of the play alternates between these two conventions of the pastoral tradition. A pleasure in otium, in the suspension of action, absorbs most of the principal characters. Rosalind enjoys playfully exploring the discrepancy between her inner, feminine, self and the assumed 'doublet and hose' (3.2.189) of her outward appearance. Touchstone anticipates indulging his sensual appetites with Audrey. Duke Senior is content to be content with life. Orlando is satisfied writing dreadful love poetry and wooing by role-play. The only significant incongruity in Arden is the intensity of Jaques' melancholy. Few, however, stir themselves to take serious issue with his cynicism. They do not need to: the whole of Arden implicitly contradicts him.

Rosalind's, Celia's and Orlando's escape to the forest of Arden represents a temporary abandonment of the 'working-day world' (1.3.12) of restriction and injustice to which they had been subject. While still at court, Rosalind had been fretful about her life:

ROSALIND O how full of briars is this working-day world!

Celia encourages her to reconceive her trials as the passing inconveniences one might encounter during holiday festivities:

CELIA They are but burs, cousin, thrown upon thee in holiday foolery. (1.3.11–14)

Her advice is that they should think about whatever fortune throws at them not as significant obstacles (briers, thorns), but as part of the passing inconvenience and harmless foolery of a holiday moment (burs, sticky buds); in that way the world may be transformed into a more pleasant place. Rosalind, however, cannot make her problems evaporate simply by *thinking* herself into a holiday mood: 'these burs,' she says, 'are in my heart.' (1.3.16) It takes an actual displacement, a complete removal from the 'working-day world' of threats and injustice, for her to be able to adopt a more festive spirit. Her gleeful dressing up as the boy Ganymede (with 'a swashing and martial outside' (1.3.117)) offers her a new, and less troubled, perspective on the world, and so helps her to dislodge the burs that had settled in her heart. The freedom to act as a man in a man's world is in itself a holiday, and she even delays surrendering this newly expanded self since it affords her so much empowering entertainment. The restorative power of the greenworld and the liberation of assuming another identity work their combined healing magic on her: in Arden her heart is troubled by neither briers nor burs.

Having once escaped the courtly world of restriction, Rosalind is then happy to allow her thinking to be transformed. In the freedom of the new context she can take Celia's advice about adopting a holiday mentality, saying to Orlando:

> ROSALIND Come, woo me, woo me; for now I am in a
> holiday humour and like enough to consent.
> (4.1.61–62)

Being away from home puts her 'in a holiday humour', and this makes possible things that would not otherwise have been so. The clear distinction drawn in this play between the humdrum nature of the working day and the liberating nature of the holiday moment is characteristic of the festive comedies more generally. The time spent away from their set patterns of relating enables not just Rosalind, but all the characters in *As You Like It*, to experience a sense of psychological and social release.

Excepting a few stylised wrangles, life in Arden seems to recapture the idyllic patterns of an innocent past. In Act 1, Charles had reported that the exiled gentlemen in Arden 'fleet the time carelessly as they did in the golden world' (1.1.109–10). Duke Senior chooses to characterise the innocence of their communal life not in terms of a mythological golden age, but of an Edenic perfection: 'Here feel we not the penalty of Adam . . . ' (2.1.5) The penalty for disobedience that God imposed upon Adam and his descendants was that the ground should not bring forth food without an investment of sweat and labour; the natural world in general should thwart human purposes. It is as if in entering Arden, the refugees from the 'painted pomp' of the 'envious court' have slipped magically into a pre-fallen world in which these universal conditions of humanity somehow do not apply. Arden offers itself as a temporal anomaly, a space entirely apart from the corrupt world around it. In its playfulness and idealism, it alludes, through the conventions of the pastoral form, to the innocence of a pre-fallen world.

As You Like It – As You, Like It

As You Like It, in common with *Much Ado About Nothing* and *What You Will* (the alternative title for *Twelfth Night)*, has an impressively nonchalant play title. As J. Dover Wilson suggested in 1962, the offhand nature of these titles testifies to a playwright 'very sure of his public'. More specifically, *As You Like It* suggests, with casual confidence, that the play, and by extension, the world, can be whatever you want it to be – as you like it. At the end of Act 1, Celia asserts that the world may be transformed by being thought about in other terms:

> Now go we in content
> To liberty, and not to banishment. (1.3.134–35)

Through a change of attitude the girls are thus able to experience banishment as liberty – as if they had themselves chosen it. In Act 2 Amiens commends Duke Senior for having successfully managed a similar mental transformation:

> Happy is your Grace,
> That can translate the stubbornness of fortune
> Into so quiet and sweet a style. (2.1.18–20)

Since perception is evidently key in determining the nature and quality of an experience, the lesson of Arden seems to be to think positively about everything. Prickly briers may be converted into furry burs, banishment into liberty, and even the 'stubbornness of fortune' into 'so quiet and sweet a style', given the right frame of mind. Arden, as a realm which seems to take characters back to a state of innocence, fosters that positive frame of mind.

One of the features of life in Arden is that characters have a tendency to see themselves mirrored in the world around them. Hearing of Silvius' aching heart, Rosalind says:

> Alas, poor shepherd, searching of thy wound
> I have by hard adventure found mine own. (2.4.40–41)

To which Touchstone adds, 'And I mine.' Such a willingness to feel a kinship with the world is, typically for a play full of balanced opposites, both commended and ridiculed: commended as evidence of a sympathetic engagement with others, and ridiculed as indicative of a myopic self-absorption. Thus Rosalind is moved to help Silvius by the recognition that 'this shepherd's passion/ Is much upon my fashion' (2.4.55–6). Touchstone, however, equally eager to find his own reflection in the world, is gently rebuked for assuming that this shepherd's character is also much upon *his* fashion. So, when he addresses Silvius as 'clown' as an acknowledgement of kinship, Rosalind checks him with: 'Peace fool, he's not thy kinsman' (2.4.61). By greeting Silvius as a mirror of himself, Touchstone may be satirising Rosalind's rush of fellow feeling, or he may genuinely believe he has found a fellow clown. Either way the point is clear: the appreciation of others only to the extent to which they reflect oneself suggests a lack of genuine engagement with the world.

This tendency for characters to see their environment in self-reflexive terms, mirroring some truth about themselves, is cryptically alluded to in the title of the play. It hints that, seen in one particular sheen, things may easily be found to be like you – as you, like it. This glancing suggestion – that as you are, so will you find it to be – is made as much to the audience as it is to its own characters. Typically for the comedies, we too are invited to see our own reflection amidst the holiday foolery played out before us.

The ending

In the middle of Act 4, the play's two thorough-going villains – Oliver and Duke Frederick – still pose a threat to the happiness of the other characters. Oliver is seeking out his brother in order to rid himself of him, and Frederick raising an army with which he can defeat the exiles and kill Duke Senior. If the drama is to reach a point of satisfactory closure, a solution needs to be found to these problems, a way of deflecting or converting the impending threat. In a dramatic display of the hearty optimism of comic form, both these threats are made to dissolve into nothingness. Oliver, rescued from danger by Orlando, realises, with impressive suddenness, that kindness is nobler than revenge. Rosalind and Celia's astonishment at his transformation is only surpassed by Oliver's own sense of wonder at his volte-face:

CELIA Was't you that did so oft contrive to kill him?
OLIVER 'Twas I. But 'tis not I. I do not shame
To tell you what I was, since my conversion
So sweetly tastes, being the thing I am. (4.3.133–36)

Arden has, it seems, worked its natural magic on him. Duke Frederick's conversion, narrated in the closing moments of the play, is, if anything, even more dramatic:

JAQUES Duke Frederick hearing how that every day
Men of great worth resorted to this forest,
Address'd a mighty power, which were on foot
In his own conduct, purposely to take
His brother here, and put him to the sword.
And to the skirts of this wild wood he came,
Where, meeting with an old religious man,
After some question with him, was converted
Both from his enterprise and from the world,
His crown bequeathing to his banish'd brother,
And all their lands restor'd to them again
That were with him exil'd. (5.4.145–156)

This is the most extreme expression of the play's willingness simply to dispense with the problems it has generated. It makes no apology for the improbabilities of its solution: rather it delights in the cursory casting aside of potential irritants to its closing harmony. No psychological plausibility is sought in order to explain the dramatic shift in Duke Frederick's intentions. As Amiens's song attests, enmity cannot survive within the green-world of Arden: encountering its mere fringes ('the skirts of this wild wood') is, therefore, sufficient to divert Frederick from his vicious plan. Nevertheless, the redemptive character of Arden is rendered ludicrously fast-working here in order to complement the generic exigencies of comic form. It is a structural necessity that the threat evaporate to create space for a final, unclouded, celebratory dance: so evaporate it does, and with entertaining haste.

In the wood near Athens, the lovers had suffered from 'seething brains' (*A Midsummer Night's Dream* 5.1.4). In the forest of Arden, by contrast, the lovers' minds are pleasantly distracted by the pervasive 'holiday humour' of the place. *As You Like It* is, as its title suggests, a fantasy of wish-fulfilment. Its gentle tone takes characters towards their desires through the leisured distractions of play. Its villains, unlike those in *Much Ado About Nothing*, need not be brought to account. Instead, they are gloriously converted to lives of generosity and holiness. Even its cynical malcontent need not be vigorously contradicted since the wholesomeness of his environment implicitly contradicts his every fit of gloom. He chooses not to participate in the nuptial celebrations since he is 'for other than for dancing measures' (5.4.184), but no other character feels that his antagonism to the values of Arden should disqualify him from their community: Duke Senior even urges him to stay. Arden is secure enough to be able to accommodate contrary positions.

Despite its healing properties, Arden is, in the final analysis, a retreat from the world, and at some point that world needs to be re-engaged with. The forest offers the opportunity for recuperation and distraction from the anxieties of 'the working-day world'. Its value, however, is as a temporary haven, not as a permanent alternative way of life. At the end of *As You Like It*, there is a new-found willingness to return to the court and to reassume worldly responsibilities. It is not only the altered circumstances, but also the pleasant time spent 'under the greenwood tree', that has made this possible.

The scene: Oliver's house, Duke Frederick's court, and the Forest of Arden

CHARACTERS IN THE PLAY

A banished DUKE
FREDERICK, *his brother, and usurper of his dominions*
AMIENS, JAQUES — *lords attending on the banished Duke*
LE BEAU, *a courtier attending upon Frederick*
CHARLES, *wrestler to Frederick*
OLIVER, JAQUES, ORLANDO — *sons of Sir Rowland de Boys*
ADAM, DENNIS — *servants to Oliver*
TOUCHSTONE, *a clown*
SIR OLIVER MARTEXT, *a vicar*
CORIN, SILVIUS — *shepherds*
WILLIAM, *a country fellow, in love with Audrey*
A person representing Hymen
ROSALIND, *daughter to the banished Duke*
CELIA, *daughter to Frederick*
PHEBE, *a shepherdess*
AUDREY, *a country wench*

Lords, pages, foresters, and attendant

AS YOU LIKE IT

ACT I SCENE I

An orchard, near Oliver's house

ORLANDO *and* ADAM

ORLANDO As I remember, Adam, it was upon this fashion: 'a bequeathed me by will but poor thousand crowns and, as thou say'st, charged my brother on his blessing to breed me well: and there begins my sadness. My brother Jaques he keeps at school, and report speaks goldenly of his profit: for my part, he keeps me rustically at home, or, to speak more properly, stays me here at home unkept: for call you that 'keeping' for a gentleman of my birth, that differs not from the stalling of an ox? His horses are bred better – for, besides that they are fair with their feeding, they are taught their manage, and to that end riders dearly hired: but I, his brother, gain nothing under him but growth, for the which his animals on his dunghills are as much bound to him as I. Besides this nothing that he so plentifully gives me, the something that nature gave me his countenance seems to take from me: he lets me feed with his hinds, bars me the place of a brother, and, as much as in him lies, mines my gentility with my education. This is it, Adam, that grieves me – and the spirit of my father, which I think is within me, begins to mutiny against this servitude. I will no longer endure it, though yet I know no wise remedy how to avoid it.

OLIVER *enters the orchard*

ADAM Yonder comes my master, your brother.

ORLANDO Go apart, Adam, and thou shalt hear how he will shake me up. [*Adam withdraws a little*

OLIVER Now, sir! What make you here?

ORLANDO Nothing: I am not taught to make any thing.

OLIVER What mar you then, sir?

ORLANDO Marry, sir, I am helping you to mar that which God

made, a poor unworthy brother of yours, with idleness.

OLIVER Marry, sir, be better employed, and be naught awhile.

ORLANDO Shall I keep your hogs and eat husks with them? What prodigal portion have I spent, that I should come to such penury?

OLIVER Know you where you are, sir?

ORLANDO O sir, very well: here in your orchard.

OLIVER Know you before whom, sir?

ORLANDO Ay, better than him I am before knows me. I know you are my eldest brother, and in the gentle condition of blood you should so know me. The courtesy of nations allows you my better, in that you are the first-born, but the same tradition takes not away my blood, were there twenty brothers betwixt us: I have as much of my father in me as you, albeit I confess your coming before me is nearer to his reverence.

OLIVER What, boy! [*he strikes him*

ORLANDO Come, come, elder brother, you are too young in this. [*he takes him by the throat*

OLIVER Wilt thou lay hands on me, villain?

ORLANDO I am no villain: I am the youngest son of Sir Rowland de Boys, he was my father, and he is thrice a villain that says such a father begot villains. Wert thou not my brother, I would not take this hand from thy throat, till this other had pulled out thy tongue for saying so – thou hast railed on thyself.

[*Adam comes forward*

ADAM Sweet masters, be patient. For your father's remembrance, be at accord.

OLIVER [*struggles*] Let me go, I say.

ORLANDO I will not till I please: you shall hear me. My father charged you in his will to give me good education: you have trained me like a peasant, obscuring and hiding from me all gentleman-like qualities. The spirit of my father grows strong in me, and I will no longer endure it: therefore allow me such exercises as may become a gentleman, or give me the poor allottery my father left me by testament – with that I will go buy my fortunes. [*he releases him*

OLIVER And what wilt thou do? Beg when that is spent? Well, sir, get you in: I will not long be troubled with you: you shall have some part of your 'will'. I pray you, leave me.

ORLANDO I will no further offend you than becomes me for my good. [*he turns to go*

OLIVER Get you with him, you old dog.

ADAM Is 'old dog' my reward? Most true, I have lost my teeth in your service. God be with my old master! He would not have spoke such a word.

[*Orlando and Adam depart*

OLIVER Is it even so? Begin you to grow upon me? I will physic your rankness, and yet give no thousand crowns neither. Holla, Dennis!

DENNIS *comes from the house*

DENNIS Calls your worship?

OLIVER Was not Charles, the duke's wrestler, here to speak with me?

DENNIS So please you, he is here at the door, and importunes access to you.

OLIVER Call him in. [*Dennis goes*] 'Twill be a good way; and tomorrow the wrestling is.

DENNIS *returns, bringing* CHARLES

CHARLES Good morrow to your worship.

OLIVER Good Monsieur Charles. [*they salute*] What's the new news at the new court?

CHARLES There's no news at the court, sir, but the old news: that is, the old duke is banished by his younger brother the new duke, and three or four loving lords have put themselves into voluntary exile with him, whose lands and revenues enrich the new duke, therefore he gives them good leave to wander.

OLIVER Can you tell if Rosalind, the duke's daughter, be banished with her father?

CHARLES O, no; for the duke's daughter, her cousin, so loves her – being ever from their cradles bred together – that she would have followed her exile, or have died to stay behind her. She is at the court, and no less beloved of her uncle than his own daughter – and never two ladies loved as they do.

OLIVER Where will the old duke live?

CHARLES They say he is already in the forest of Arden, and a many merry men with him; and there they live like the old Robin Hood of England: they say many young gentlemen flock to him every day, and fleet the time carelessly as they did in the golden world.

OLIVER What, you wrestle tomorrow before the new duke?

CHARLES Marry, do I, sir: and I came to acquaint you with a matter. I am given, sir, secretly to understand that your younger brother, Orlando, hath a disposition to come in disguised against me to try a fall: tomorrow, sir, I wrestle for my credit, and he that escapes me without some broken limb shall acquit him well: your brother is but young and tender, and for your love I would be loath to foil him, as I must for my own honour if he come in: therefore, out of my love to you, I came hither to acquaint you withal, that either you might stay him from his intendment, or brook such disgrace well as he shall run into, in that it is a thing of his own search, and altogether against my will.

OLIVER Charles, I thank thee for thy love to me, which thou shalt find I will most kindly requite. I had myself notice of my brother's purpose herein, and have by underhand means laboured to dissuade him from it; but he is resolute. I'll tell thee, Charles – it is the stubbornest young fellow of France, full of ambition, an envious emulator of every man's good parts, a secret and villanous contriver against me his natural brother: therefore use thy discretion; I had as lief thou didst break his neck as his finger. And thou wert best look to't; for if thou dost him any slight disgrace, or if he do not mightily grace himself on thee, he will practise against thee by poison, entrap thee by some treacherous device, and never leave thee till he hath ta'en thy life by some indirect means or other: for, I assure thee (and almost with tears I speak it), there is not one so young and so villanous this day living. I speak but brotherly of him, but should I anatomize him to thee as he is, I must blush and weep, and thou must look pale and wonder.

CHARLES I am heartily glad I came hither to you. If he come tomorrow, I'll give him his payment: if ever he go alone again, I'll never wrestle for prize more: and so, God keep your worship!

OLIVER Farewell, good Charles. [*Charles takes his leave*] Now will I stir this gamester: I hope I shall see an end of him; for my soul (yet I know not why) hates nothing more than he. Yet he's gentle, never schooled and yet learned, full of noble device, of all sorts enchantingly beloved, and indeed so much in the heart of the world, and especially of my own people, who best know him, that I am altogether misprised: but it shall not be so long – this wrestler shall clear all. Nothing remains but that I kindle the boy thither, which now I'll go about.

[*he goes within*

SCENE 2

A lawn near the palace of Duke Frederick

ROSALIND *and* CELIA, *seated*

CELIA I pray thee, Rosalind, sweet my coz, be merry.

ROSALIND Dear Celia, I show more mirth than I am mistress of, and would you yet I were merrier? Unless you could teach me to forget a banished father, you must not learn me how to remember any extraordinary pleasure.

CELIA Herein, I see, thou lov'st me not with the full weight that I love thee; if my uncle, thy banished father, had banished thy uncle, the duke my father, so thou hadst been still with me, I could have taught my love to take thy father for mine; so wouldst thou, if the truth of thy love to me were so righteously tempered as mine is to thee.

ROSALIND Well, I will forget the condition of my estate, to rejoice in yours.

CELIA You know my father hath no child but I, nor none is like to have; and truly when he dies, thou shalt be his heir: for what he hath taken away from thy father perforce, I will render thee again in affection. By mine honour I will, and when I break that oath, let me turn monster: therefore, my sweet Rose, my dear Rose, be merry.

ROSALIND From henceforth I will, coz, and devise sports. Let me see – what think you of falling in love?

CELIA Marry, I prithee, do, to make sport withal: but love no man in good earnest, nor no further in sport neither, than with safety of a pure blush thou mayst in honour come off again.

ROSALIND What shall be our sport then?

CELIA Let us sit and mock the good housewife Fortune from her wheel, that her gifts may henceforth be bestowed equally.

ROSALIND I would we could do so; for her benefits are mightily misplaced, and the bountiful blind woman doth most mistake in her gifts to women.

CELIA 'Tis true, for those that she makes fair she scarce makes honest, and those that she makes honest she makes very ill-favouredly.

ROSALIND Nay, now thou goest from Fortune's office to Nature's: Fortune reigns in gifts of the world, not in the lineaments of Nature.

TOUCHSTONE *approaches*

CELIA No? When Nature hath made a fair creature, may she not by Fortune fall into the fire? Though Nature hath given us wit to flout at Fortune, hath not Fortune sent in this fool to cut off the argument?

ROSALIND Indeed, there is Fortune too hard for Nature, when Fortune makes Nature's natural the cutter-off of Nature's wit.

CELIA Peradventure this is not Fortune's work neither, but Nature's, who perceiveth our natural wits too dull to reason of such goddesses and hath sent this natural for our whetstone: for always the dulness of the fool is the whetstone of the wits. How now, wit! Whither wander you?

TOUCH. Mistress, you must come away to your father.

CELIA Were you made the messenger?

TOUCH. No, by mine honour, but I was bid to come for you.

ROSALIND Where learned you that oath, fool?

TOUCH. Of a certain knight, that swore by his honour they were good pancakes, and swore by his honour the mustard was naught: now I'll stand to it, the pancakes were naught and the mustard was good, and yet was not the knight forsworn.

CELIA How prove you that, in the great heap of your knowledge?

ROSALIND Ay, marry, now unmuzzle your wisdom.

TOUCH. Stand you both forth now: stroke your chins, and swear by your beards that I am a knave.

CELIA By our beards (if we had them) thou art.

TOUCH. By my knavery (if I had it) then I were: but if you swear by that that is not, you are not forsworn: no more was this knight, swearing by his honour, for he never had any; or if he had, he had sworn it away, before ever he saw those pancakes or that mustard.

CELIA Prithee, who is't that thou mean'st?

TOUCH. [*to Rosalind*] One that old Frederick, your father, loves.

ROSALIND My father's love is enough to honour him. Enough! Speak no more of him – you'll be whipped for taxation one of these days.

TOUCH. The more pity, that fools may not speak wisely what wise men do foolishly.

CELIA By my troth, thou sayest true: for since the little wit that fools have was silenced, the little foolery that wise men have makes a great show. Here comes Monsieur Le Beau.

LE BEAU *is seen hurrying towards them*

ROSALIND With his mouth full of news.

CELIA Which he will put on us, as pigeons feed their young.

ROSALIND Then shall we be news-crammed.

CELIA All the better: we shall be the more marketable. Bon jour, Monsieur Le Beau! What's the news?

LE BEAU Fair princess, you have lost much good sport.

CELIA Sport? Of what colour?

LE BEAU What colour, madam? How shall I answer you?

ROSALIND As wit and fortune will.

TOUCH. [*mocking him*] Or as the Destinies decree.

CELIA Well said, that was laid on with a trowel.

TOUCH. Nay, if I keep not my rank –

ROSALIND Thou losest thy old smell.

LE BEAU You amaze me, ladies: I would have told you of good wrestling, which you have lost the sight of.

ROSALIND Yet tell us the manner of the wrestling.

LE BEAU I will tell you the beginning, and, if it please your ladyships, you may see the end – for the best is yet to do, and here, where you are, they are coming to perform it.

CELIA Well, the beginning, that is dead and buried?

LE BEAU There comes an old man and his three sons –

CELIA I could match this beginning with an old tale.

LE BEAU Three proper young men, of excellent growth and presence.

ROSALIND With bills on their necks: 'Be it known unto all men by these presents.'

LE BEAU The eldest of the three wrestled with Charles, the duke's wrestler, which Charles in a moment threw him and broke three of his ribs, that there is little hope of life in him: so he served the second, and so the third . . . Yonder they lie, the poor old man their father making such pitiful dole over them that all the beholders take his part with weeping.

ROSALIND Alas!

TOUCH. But what is the sport, monsieur, that the ladies have lost?

LE BEAU Why, this that I speak of.

TOUCH. Thus men may grow wiser every day. It is the first time that ever I heard breaking of ribs was sport for ladies.

CELIA Or I, I promise thee.

ROSALIND But is there any else longs to see this broken music in his sides? Is there yet another dotes upon rib-breaking? Shall we see this wrestling, cousin?

LE BEAU You must if you stay here, for here is the place appointed for the wrestling, and they are ready to perform it.

CELIA Yonder, sure, they are coming. Let us now stay and see it.

A flourish of trumpets. Duke FREDERICK *with his lords,* ORLANDO, CHARLES, *and attendants cross the lawn towards a plot prepared for the wrestling*

DUKE F. Come on. Since the youth will not be entreated, his own peril on his forwardness.

ROSALIND Is yonder the man?

LE BEAU Even he, madam.

CELIA Alas, he is too young: yet he looks successfully.

DUKE How now, daughter and cousin! Are you crept hither to see the wrestling?

ROSALIND Ay, my liege, so please you give us leave.

DUKE F. You will take little delight in it, I can tell you, there is such odds in the man. In pity of the challenger's youth I would fain dissuade him, but he will not be entreated. Speak to him, ladies – see if you can move him.

CELIA Call him hither, good Monsieur Le Beau.

DUKE F. Do so: I'll not be by. [*he takes his seat*

LE BEAU Monsieur the challenger, the princess calls for you.

ORLANDO [*comes forward*]. I attend them with all respect and duty.

ROSALIND Young man, have you challenged Charles the wrestler?

ORLANDO [*bows*] No, fair princess: he is the general challenger. I come but in, as others do, to try with him the strength of my youth.

CELIA Young gentleman, your spirits are too bold for your years. You have seen cruel proof of this man's strength. If you saw yourself with your eyes, or knew yourself with your judgment, the fear of your adventure would counsel you to a more equal enterprise. We pray you, for your own sake, to embrace your own safety, and give over this attempt.

ROSALIND Do, young sir, your reputation shall not therefore be misprised: we will make it our suit to the duke that the wrestling might not go forward.

ORLANDO I beseech you, punish me not with your hard thoughts, wherein I confess me much guilty to deny so fair and excellent ladies anything. But let your fair eyes and gentle wishes go with me to my trial: wherein if I be foiled, there is but one shamed that was never gracious; if killed, but one dead that is willing to be so: I shall do my friends no wrong, for I have none to lament me; the world no injury, for in it I have nothing: only in the world I fill up a place, which may be better supplied when I have made it empty.

ROSALIND The little strength that I have, I would it were with you.

CELIA And mine, to eke out hers.

ROSALIND Fare you well. Pray heaven, I be deceived in you!

CELIA Your heart's desires be with you!

CHARLES [*calls*] Come, where is this young gallant that is so desirous to lie with his mother earth?

ORLANDO Ready, sir, but his will hath in it a more modest working.

DUKE F. You shall try but one fall.

CHARLES No, I warrant your grace, you shall not entreat him to a second, that have so mightily persuaded him from a first.

ORLANDO An you mean to mock me after, you should not have mocked me before: but come your ways.

ROSALIND Now, Hercules be thy speed, young man!

CELIA I would I were invisible, to catch the strong fellow by the leg. [*the wrestling begins: they close, Orlando skilfully securing the better hold*

ROSALIND O excellent young man!

CELIA If I had a thunderbolt in mine eye, I can tell who should down. [*the wrestlers sway and strain to and fro, till of a sudden Charles is thrown heavily to the ground; a great shout*

DUKE F. [*rises*] No more, no more.

ORLANDO Yes, I beseech your grace – I am not yet well breathed.

DUKE F. How dost thou, Charles?

LE BEAU He cannot speak, my lord.

DUKE F. Bear him away. [*they take up Charles and carry him forth*
What is thy name, young man?

ORLANDO Orlando, my liege; the youngest son of Sir Rowland de Boys.

DUKE F. I would thou hadst been son to some man else.
The world esteemed thy father honourable,
But I did find him still mine enemy:
Thou shouldst have better pleased me with this deed,
Hadst thou descended from another house:

But fare thee well, thou art a gallant youth.
I would thou hadst told me of another father.
[*Duke Frederick, Le Beau and the other lords depart*

CELIA Were I my father, coz, would I do this?

ORLANDO I am more proud to be Sir Rowland's son,
His youngest son, and would not change that calling
To be adopted heir to Frederick.

ROSALIND My father loved Sir Rowland as his soul,
And all the world was of my father's mind.
Had I before known this young man his son,
I should have given him tears unto entreaties,
Ere he should thus have ventured.

CELIA Gentle cousin,
Let us go thank him, and encourage him:
My father's rough and envious disposition
Sticks me at heart. [*they rise and accost Orlando*]
Sir, you have well deserved.
If you do keep your promises in love
But justly as you have exceeded promise,
Your mistress shall be happy.

ROSALIND [*takes a chain from her neck*] Gentleman,
Wear this for me – one out of suits with fortune,
That could give more, but that her hand lacks means
Shall we go, coz? [*she turns and walks away*

CELIA [*follows*] Ay: fare you well, fair gentleman.

ORLANDO Can I not say, 'I thank you'? My better parts
Are all thrown down, and that which here stands up
Is but a quintain, a mere lifeless block.

ROSALIND He calls us back: my pride fell with my fortunes –
I'll ask him what he would. [*she turns again*]
Did you call, sir?
Sir, you have wrestled well and overthrown
More than your enemies. [*they gaze upon each other*

CELIA [*plucks her sleeve*] Will you go, coz?

ROSALIND Have with you. Fare you well.
[*she hastens away, Celia following*

ORLANDO What passion hangs these weights upon my tongue?
I cannot speak to her, yet she urged conference.

LE BEAU *returns*

O poor Orlando, thou art overthrown!
Or Charles, or something weaker, masters thee.

LE BEAU Good sir, I do in friendship counsel you
To leave this place. Albeit you have deserved
High commendation, true applause, and love,
Yet such is now the duke's condition,
That he misconstrues all that you have done.
The duke is humorous – what he is, indeed,
More suits you to conceive than I to speak of.

ORLANDO I thank you, sir: and, pray you, tell me this,
Which of the two was daughter of the duke,
That here was at the wrestling?

LE BEAU Neither his daughter, if we judge by manners,
But yet, indeed, the smaller is his daughter.
The other is daughter to the banished duke,
And here detained by her usurping uncle,
To keep his daughter company – whose loves
Are dearer than the natural bond of sisters.
But I can tell you that of late this duke
Hath ta'en displeasure 'gainst his gentle niece,
Grounded upon no other argument
But that the people praise her for her virtues,
And pity her for her good father's sake;
And, on my life, his malice 'gainst the lady
Will suddenly break forth. Sir, fare you well.
Hereafter, in a better world than this,
I shall desire more love and knowledge of you.

ORLANDO I rest much bounden to you: fare you well.
[*Le Beau goes*
Thus must I from the smoke into the smother,
From tyrant duke unto a tyrant brother.
But heavenly Rosalind!
[*he departs, musing*

SCENE 3

A room in the palace of Duke Frederick

ROSALIND *on a couch with her face to the wall,* CELIA *bending over her*

CELIA Why cousin, why Rosalind. Cupid have mercy! Not a word?

ROSALIND Not one to throw at a dog.

CELIA No, thy words are too precious to be cast away upon curs: throw some of them at me; come, lame me with reasons.

ROSALIND Then there were two cousins laid up, when the one should be lamed with reasons, and the other mad without any.

CELIA But is all this for your father?

ROSALIND No, some of it is for my child's father. [*rises*] O, how full of briars is this working-day world!

CELIA They are but burs, cousin, thrown upon thee in holiday foolery. If we walk not in the trodden paths, our very petticoats will catch them.

ROSALIND I could shake them off my coat – these burs are in my heart.

CELIA Hem them away.

ROSALIND I would try, if I could cry 'hem' and have him.

CELIA Come, come, wrestle with thy affections.

ROSALIND O, they take the part of a better wrestler than myself.

CELIA O, a good wish upon you! You will try in time, in despite of a fall. But turning these jests out of service, let us talk in good earnest: is it possible, on such a sudden, you should fall into so strong a liking with old Sir Rowland's youngest son?

ROSALIND The duke my father loved his father dearly.

CELIA Doth it therefore ensue that you should love his son dearly? By this kind of chase, I should hate him, for my father hated his father dearly; yet I hate not Orlando.

ROSALIND No, faith, hate him not, for my sake.

CELIA Why should I not? Doth he not deserve well?

ROSALIND Let me love him for that, and do you love him because
I do. [*the door is flung open and* DUKE FREDERICK *enters, preceded by attendants and the lords of his council*]
Look, here comes the duke.

CELIA With his eyes full of anger.

DUKE F. [*pausing in the doorway*]
Mistress, dispatch you with your safest haste
And get you from our court.

ROSALIND Me, uncle?

DUKE F. You, cousin.
Within these ten days if that thou be'st found
So near our public court as twenty miles,
Thou diest for it.

ROSALIND I do beseech your grace,
Let me the knowledge of my fault bear with me:
If with myself I hold intelligence
Or have acquaintance with mine own desires,
If that I do not dream or be not frantic –
As I do trust I am not – then, dear uncle,
Never so much as in a thought unborn
Did I offend your highness.

DUKE F. Thus do all traitors!
If their purgation did consist in words,
They are as innocent as grace itself:
Let it suffice thee that I trust thee not.

ROSALIND Yet your mistrust cannot make me a traitor:
Tell me whereon the likelihood depends.

DUKE F. Thou art thy father's daughter, there's enough.

ROSALIND So was I when your highness took his dukedom,
So was I when your highness banished him;
Treason is not inherited, my lord,
Or, if we did derive it from our friends,
What's that to me? My father was no traitor.
Then, good my liege, mistake me not so much
To think my poverty is treacherous.

CELIA Dear sovereign, hear me speak.

DUKE F. Ay, Celia, we stayed her for your sake,
Else had she with her father ranged along.

CELIA I did not then entreat to have her stay,

It was your pleasure and your own remorse.
I was too young that time to value her,
But now I know her: if she be a traitor,
Why so am I: we still have slept together,
Rose at an instant, learned, played, eat together,
And wheresoe'er we went, like Juno's swans,
Still we went coupled and inseparable.

DUKE F. She is too subtle for thee, and her smoothness,
Her very silence and her patience
Speak to the people, and they pity her.
Thou art a fool – she robs thee of thy name,
And thou wilt show more bright and seem more virtuous
When she is gone: then open not thy lips.
Firm and irrevocable is my doom
Which I have passed upon her – she is banished.

CELIA Pronounce that sentence then on me, my liege.
I cannot live out of her company.

DUKE F. You are a fool. You, niece, provide yourself.
If you outstay the time, upon mine honour,
And in the greatness of my word, you die.
[he turns and leaves the room, his lords following him

CELIA O my poor Rosalind, whither wilt thou go?
Wilt thou change fathers? I will give thee mine.
I charge thee, be not thou more grieved than I am.

ROSALIND I have more cause.

CELIA Thou hast not, cousin.
Prithee, be cheerful; know'st thou not, the duke
Hath banished me his daughter?

ROSALIND That he hath not.

CELIA No, hath not? Rosalind lacks then the love
Which teacheth thee that thou and I am one.
Shall we be sund'red? Shall we part, sweet girl?
No, let my father seek another heir.
Therefore devise with me how we may fly,
Whither to go and what to bear with us,
And do not seek to take your change upon you,
To bear your griefs yourself and leave me out;
For, by this heaven, now at our sorrows pale,

Say what thou canst, I'll go along with thee.

ROSALIND Why, whither shall we go?

CELIA To seek my uncle in the forest of Arden.

ROSALIND Alas, what danger will it be to us,
Maids as we are, to travel forth so far!
Beauty provoketh thieves sooner than gold.

CELIA I'll put myself in poor and mean attire,
And with a kind of umber smirch my face.
The like do you, so shall we pass along
And never stir assailants.

ROSALIND Were it not better,
Because that I am more than common tall,
That I did suit me all points like a man?
A gallant curtle-axe upon my thigh,
A boar-spear in my hand, and in my heart
Lie there what hidden woman's fear there will,
We'll have a swashing and a martial outside,
As many other mannish cowards have
That do outface it with their semblances.

CELIA What shall I call thee when thou art a man?

ROSALIND I'll have no worse a name than Jove's own page,
And therefore look you call me Ganymede.
But what will you be called?

CELIA Something that hath a reference to my state;
No longer Celia, but Aliena.

ROSALIND But, cousin, what if we assayed to steal
The clownish fool out of your father's court?
Would he not be a comfort to our travel?

CELIA He'll go along o'er the wide world with me,
Leave me alone to woo him. Let's away,
And get our jewels and our wealth together,
Devise the fittest time and safest way
To hide us from pursuit that will be made
After my flight. Now go we in content
To liberty, and not to banishment. [*they go*

ACT 2 SCENE 1

The forest of Arden

The entrance to a cave, with a spreading tree before it. The exiled Duke, 'AMIENS and two or three Lords like foresters' come from the cave

DUKE Now, my co-mates and brothers in exile,
Hath not old custom made this life more sweet
Than that of painted pomp? Are not these woods
More free from peril than the envious court?
Here feel we not the penalty of Adam,
The seasons' difference? As the icy fang
And churlish chiding of the winter's wind,
Which, when it bites and blows upon my body,
Even till I shrink with cold, I smile and say
'This is no flattery: these are counsellors
That feelingly persuade me what I am.'
Sweet are the uses of adversity,
Which like the toad, ugly and venomous,
Wears yet a precious jewel in his head:
And this our life, exempt from public haunt,
Finds tongues in trees, books in the running brooks,
Sermons in stones, and good in every thing.
I would not change it.

AMIENS Happy is your grace,
That can translate the stubbornness of fortune
Into so quiet and so sweet a style.

DUKE Come, shall we go and kill us venison?
And yet it irks me the poor dappled fools,
Being native burghers of this desert city,
Should in their own confines with forkéd heads
Have their round haunches gored.

1 LORD Indeed, my lord,
The melancholy Jaques grieves at that,
And, in that kind, swears you do more usurp
Than doth your brother that hath banished you:
Today my Lord of Amiens and myself
Did steal behind him as he lay along
Under an oak, whose antique root peeps out

Upon the brook that brawls along this wood,
To the which place a poor sequest'red stag,
That from the hunter's aim had ta'en a hurt,
Did come to languish; and, indeed, my lord,
The wretched animal heaved forth such groans,
That their discharge did stretch his leathern coat
Almost to bursting, and the big round tears
Coursed one another down his innocent nose
In piteous chase: and thus the hairy fool,
Much markéd of the melancholy Jaques,
Stood on th'extremest verge of the swift brook,
Augmenting it with tears.

DUKE But what said Jaques?
Did he not moralize this spectacle?

1 LORD O yes, into a thousand similes.
First, for his weeping in the needless stream;
'Poor deer,' quoth he, 'thou mak'st a testament
As worldlings do, giving thy sum of more
To that which had too much': then, being there alone,
Left and abandoned of his velvet friends;
' 'Tis right,' quoth he, 'thus misery doth part
The flux of company': anon a careless herd,
Full of the pasture, jumps along by him
And never stays to greet him; 'Ay,' quoth Jaques,
'Sweep on, you fat and greasy citizens!
'Tis just the fashion; wherefore do you look
Upon that poor and broken bankrupt there?'
Thus most invectively he pierceth through
The body of the country, city, court,
Yea, and of this our life, swearing that we
Are mere usurpers, tyrants, and what's worse,
To fright the animals and to kill them up
In their assigned and native dwelling-place.

DUKE And did you leave him in this contemplation?

2 LORD We did, my lord, weeping and commenting
Upon the sobbing deer.

DUKE Show me the place.
I love to cope him in these sullen fits,
For then he's full of matter.

1 LORD I'll bring you to him straight. [*they go*

SCENE 2

A room in the palace of Duke Frederick

Duke FREDERICK, *lords, and attendants*

DUKE F. Can it be possible that no man saw them?
It cannot be. Some villains of my court
Are of consent and sufferance in this.

I LORD I cannot hear of any that did see her.
The ladies, her attendants of her chamber,
Saw her abed, and in the morning early
They found the bed untreasured of their mistress.

2 LORD My lord, the roynish clown, at whom so oft
Your grace was wont to laugh, is also missing.
Hisperia, the princess' gentlewoman,
Confesses that she secretly o'erheard
Your daughter and her cousin much commend
The parts and graces of the wrestler
That did but lately foil the sinewy Charles,
And she believes wherever they are gone
That youth is surely in their company.

DUKE F. Send to his brother, fetch that gallant hither.
If he be absent, bring his brother to me –
I'll make him find him: do this suddenly;
And let not search and inquisition quail
To bring again these foolish runaways. [*they go*

SCENE 3

The orchard near Oliver's house

ORLANDO *and* ADAM, *meeting*

ORLANDO Who's there?

ADAM What! My young master? O my gentle master,
O my sweet master, O you memory
Of old Sir Rowland. Why, what make you here?
Why are you virtuous? Why do people love you?
And wherefore are you gentle, strong, and valiant?

Why would you be so fond to overcome
The bonny prizer of the humorous duke?
Your praise is come too swiftly home before you.
Know you not, master, to some kind of men
Their graces serve them but as enemies?
No more do yours; your virtues, gentle master,
Are sanctified and holy traitors to you.
O, what a world is this, when what is comely
Envenoms him that bears it!

ORLANDO Why, what's the matter?

ADAM O unhappy youth,
Come not within these doors; within this roof
The enemy of all your graces lives.
Your brother – no, no brother – yet the son
(Yet not the son, I will not call him son)
Of him I was about to call his father –
Hath heard your praises, and this night he means
To burn the lodging where you use to lie,
And you within it: if he fail of that,
He will have other means to cut you off:
I overheard him, and his practices.
This is no place, this house is but a butchery;
Abhor it, fear it, do not enter it.

ORLANDO Why, whither, Adam, wouldst thou have me go?

ADAM No matter whither, so you come not here.

ORLANDO What, wouldst thou have me go and beg my food?
Or with a base and boisterous sword enforce
A thievish living on the common road?
This I must do, or know not what to do:
Yet this I will not do, do how I can –
I rather will subject me to the malice
Of a diverted blood and bloody brother.

ADAM But do not so: I have five hundred crowns,
The thrifty hire I saved under your father,
Which I did store to be my foster-nurse
When service should in my old limbs lie lame,
And unregarded age in corners thrown.
Take that, and He that doth the ravens feed,
Yea providently caters for the sparrow,

Be comfort to my age. [*he gives him a bag*]
Here is the gold;
All this I give you. Let me be your servant.
Though I look old, yet I am strong and lusty;
For in my youth I never did apply
Hot and rebellious liquors in my blood,
Nor did not with unbashful forehead woo
The means of weakness and debility.
Therefore my age is as a lusty winter,
Frosty, but kindly: let me go with you.
I'll do the service of a younger man
In all your business and necessities.

ORLANDO O good old man, how well in thee appears
The constant service of the antique world,
When service sweat for duty, not for meed!
Thou art not for the fashion of these times,
Where none will sweat but for promotion,
And having that do choke their service up
Even with the having – it is not so with thee.
But, poor old man, thou prun'st a rotten tree,
That cannot so much as a blossom yield,
In lieu of all thy pains and husbandry.
But come thy ways, we'll go along together,
And ere we have thy youthful wages spent,
We'll light upon some settled low content.

ADAM Master, go on, and I will follow thee
To the last gasp with truth and loyalty.
From seventeen years till now almost fourscore
Here lived I, but now live here no more.
At seventeen years many their fortunes seek,
But at fourscore it is too late a week.
Yet fortune cannot recompense me better
Than to die well, and not my master's debtor.

[*they leave the orchard*

SCENE 4

A clearing in the outskirts of the forest

ROSALIND *(as* GANYMEDE*) clad as a boy in forester's dress, and* CELIA *(as* ALIENA*) clad as a shepherdess, together with* TOUCHSTONE, *approach slowly and fling themselves upon the ground under a tree*

ROSALIND O Jupiter! How weary are my spirits!

TOUCH. I care not for my spirits, if my legs were not weary.

ROSALIND I could find in my heart to disgrace my man's apparel, and to cry like a woman: but I must comfort the weaker vessel, as doublet-and-hose ought to show itself courageous to petticoat: therefore courage, good Aliena!

CELIA I pray you, bear with me, I cannot go no further.

TOUCH. For my part, I had rather bear with you than bear you: yet I should bear no cross if I did bear you, for I think you have no money in your purse.

ROSALIND Well, this is the forest of Arden!

TOUCH. Ay, now am I in Arden, the more fool I. When I was at home I was in a better place, but travellers must be content.

ROSALIND Ay.
Be so, good Touchstone.

CORIN *and* SILVIUS *draw near*

Look you, who comes here –
A young man and an old in solemn talk.

CORIN That is the way to make her scorn you still.

SILVIUS O Corin, that thou knew'st how I do love her!

CORIN I partly guess: for I have loved ere now.

SILVIUS No, Corin, being old, thou canst not guess,
Though in thy youth thou wast as true a lover
As ever sighed upon a midnight pillow:
But if thy love were ever like to mine –
As sure I think did never man love so –
How many actions most ridiculous
Hast thou been drawn to by thy fantasy?

CORIN Into a thousand that I have forgotten.

SILVIUS O thou didst then ne'er love so heartily.
If thou remembrest not the slightest folly
That ever love did make thee run into,
Thou hast not loved . . .
Or if thou hast not sat as I do now,
Wearing thy hearer in thy mistress' praise,
Thou hast not loved
Or if thou hast not broke from company
Abruptly, as my passion now makes me,
Thou hast not loved
O Phebe, Phebe, Phebe!

[he buries his face in his hands and runs into the forest

ROSALIND Alas, poor shepherd! Searching of thy wound,
I have by hard adventure found mine own.

TOUCH. And I mine: I remember, when I was in love I broke my sword upon a stone, and bid him take that for coming a-night to Jane Smile, and I remember the kissing of her batler and the cow's dugs that her pretty chopt hands had milked; and I remember the wooing of a peascod instead of her, from whom I took two cods, and giving her them again, said with weeping tears, 'Wear these for my sake'. We that are true lovers run into strange capers; but as all is mortal in nature, so is all nature in love mortal in folly.

ROSALIND Thou speak'st wiser than thou art ware of.

TOUCH. Nay, I shall ne'er be ware of mine own wit till I break my shins against it.

ROSALIND Jove, Jove! This shepherd's passion
Is much upon my fashion.

TOUCH. And mine – but it grows something stale with me.

CELIA I pray you, one of you question yond man
If he for gold will give us any food.
I faint almost to death.

TOUCH. Holla; you, clown!

ROSALIND Peace, fool, he's not thy kinsman.

CORIN Who calls?

TOUCH. Your betters, sir.

CORIN Else are they very wretched.

ROSALIND Peace, I say. Good even to you, friend.

CORIN And to you, gentle sir, and to you all.
ROSALIND I prithee, shepherd, if that love or gold
Can in this desert place buy entertainment,
Bring us where we may rest ourselves and feed:
Here's a young maid with travel much oppressed,
And faints for succour.
CORIN Fair sir, I pity her,
And wish for her sake more than for mine own,
My fortunes were more able to relieve her:
But I am shepherd to another man,
And do not shear the fleeces that I graze:
My master is of churlish disposition,
And little recks to find the way to heaven
By doing deeds of hospitality:
Besides, his cote, his flocks and bounds of feed
Are now on sale, and at our sheepcote now
By reason of his absence there is nothing
That you will feed on; but what is, come see,
And in my voice most welcome shall you be.
ROSALIND What is he that shall buy his flock and pasture?
CORIN That young swain that you saw here but erewhile,
That little cares for buying anything.
ROSALIND I pray thee, if it stand with honesty,
Buy thou the cottage, pasture, and the flock,
And thou shalt have to pay for it of us.
CELIA And we will mend thy wages: I like this place,
And willingly could waste my time in it.
CORIN Assuredly, the thing is to be sold.
Go with me. If you like upon report
The soil, the profit, and this kind of life,
I will your very faithful feeder be,
And buy it with your gold right suddenly.
[*he goes; they rise and follow him*

SCENE 5

Before the cave of the exiled Duke

'AMIENS, JAQUES *and others', seated beneath the tree*

AMIENS [*sings*] Under the greenwood tree,
Who loves to lie with me,
And turn his merry note
Unto the sweet bird's throat,
Come hither, come hither, come hither:
Here shall he see
No enemy,
But winter and rough weather.

JAQUES More, more, I prithee, more.

AMIENS It will make you melancholy, Monsieur Jaques.

JAQUES I thank it. More, I prithee, more. I can suck melancholy out of a song, as a weasel sucks eggs. More, I prithee, more.

AMIENS My voice is ragged, I know I cannot please you.

JAQUES I do not desire you to please me, I do desire you to sing. Come, more, another stanzo: call you 'em stanzos?

AMIENS What you will, Monsieur Jaques.

JAQUES Nay, I care not for their names, they owe me nothing. Will you sing?

AMIENS More at your request than to please myself.

JAQUES Well then, if ever I thank any man, I'll thank you: but that they call compliment is like th'encounter of two dog-apes; and when a man thanks me heartily, methinks I have given him a penny and he renders me the beggarly thanks. Come, sing; and you that will not, hold your tongues.

AMIENS Well, I'll end the song. Sirs, cover the while – the duke will drink under this tree. He hath been all this day to look you.

[*Some of the company prepare a meal beneath the tree*

JAQUES And I have been all this day to avoid him. He is too disputable for my company. I think of as many matters as he, but I give heaven thanks, and make no boast of them. Come, warble, come.

They sing 'altogether here'

Who doth ambition shun,
And loves to live i'th' sun,
Seeking the food he eats,
And pleased with what he gets,
Come hither, come hither, come hither:
Here shall he see
No enemy,
But winter and rough weather.

JAQUES I'll give you a verse to this note, that I made yesterday in despite of my invention.

AMIENS And I'll sing it.

JAQUES Thus it goes:

If it do come to pass,
That any man turn ass,
Leaving his wealth and ease,
A stubborn will to please,
Ducdame, ducdame, ducdame:
Here shall he see,
Gross fools as he,
An if he will come to me.

AMIENS What's that 'ducdame'?

JAQUES 'Tis a Greek invocation, to call fools into a circle. I'll go sleep, if I can: if I cannot, I'll rail against all the first-born of Egypt.

AMIENS And I'll go seek the duke; his banquet is prepared.

[*they depart in different directions*

SCENE 6

The clearing in the outskirts of the forest

ORLANDO *and* ADAM *approach*

ADAM Dear master, I can go no further: O, I die for food. [*he falls*] Here lie I down, and measure out my grave. Farewell, kind master.

ORLANDO Why, how now, Adam! No greater heart in thee? Live a little, comfort a little, cheer thyself a little. If this uncouth forest yield anything savage, I will either be food for it or bring it for food to thee. Thy conceit is nearer death than thy powers. [*he lifts him tenderly and props him against a tree*] For my sake be comfortable – hold death awhile at the arm's end: I will here be with thee presently, and if I bring thee not something to eat, I will give thee leave to die: but if thou diest before I come, thou art a mocker of my labour. [*Adam smiles a little*] Well said! Thou look'st cheerly, and I'll be with thee quickly. Yet thou liest in the bleak air. [*he takes him in his arms*] Come, I will bear thee to some shelter – and thou shalt not die for lack of a dinner, if there live any thing in this desert. Cheerly, good Adam! [*he carries him away*

SCENE 7

Before the cave of the exiled Duke

A meal of fruit and wine set out under the tree; the DUKE *and some of his lords reclining thereat*

DUKE I think he be transformed into a beast,
For I can nowhere find him like a man.

I LORD My lord, he is but even now gone hence.
Here was he merry, hearing of a song.

DUKE If he, compact of jars, grow musical,
We shall have shortly discord in the spheres:
Go, seek him, tell him I would speak with him.

JAQUES *is seen coming through the trees, a smile upon his face, and shortly behind him* AMIENS, *who silently takes his seat next to the Duke at the meal when he comes up*

I LORD He saves my labour by his own approach.

DUKE Why, how now, monsieur! What a life is this,
That your poor friends must woo your company?
What, you look merrily!

JAQUES [*breaks into laughter*].
A fool, a fool! I met a fool i'th' forest,

A motley fool – a miserable world!
As I do live by food, I met a fool,
Who laid him down and basked him in the sun,
And railed on Lady Fortune in good terms,
In good set terms, and yet a motley fool.
'Good morrow, fool,' quoth I: 'No, sir,' quoth he,
'Call me not fool till heaven hath sent me fortune.'
And then he drew a dial from his poke,
And looking on it with lack-lustre eye,
Says very wisely, 'It is ten o'clock:
Thus we may see,' quoth he, 'how the world wags:
'Tis but an hour ago since it was nine,
And after one hour more 'twill be eleven,
And so from hour to hour, we ripe, and ripe,
And then from hour to hour, we rot, and rot –
And thereby hangs a tale.' When I did hear
The motley fool thus moral on the time,
My lungs began to crow like chanticleer,
That fools should be so deep-contemplative;
And I did laugh, sans intermission,
An hour by his dial. O noble fool!
O worthy fool! Motley's the only wear.

DUKE What fool is this?

JAQUES A worthy fool. One that hath been a courtier,
And says, if ladies be but young and fair,
They have the gift to know it: and in his brain,
Which is as dry as the remainder biscuit
After a voyage, he hath strange places crammed
With observation, the which he vents
In mangled forms. O, that I were a fool!
I am ambitious for a motley coat.

DUKE Thou shalt have one.

JAQUES It is my only suit –
Provided that you weed your better judgments
Of all opinion that grows rank in them
That I am wise. I must have liberty
Withal, as large a charter as the wind,
To blow on whom I please, for so fools have:
And they that are most galléd with my folly,

They most must laugh: and why, sir, must they so?
The 'why' is plain as way to parish church:
He that a fool doth very wisely hit
Doth very foolishly, although he smart,
Not to seem senseless of the bob: if not,
The wise man's folly is anatomized
Even by the squand'ring glances of the fool.
Invest me in my motley; give me leave
To speak my mind, and I will through and through
Cleanse the foul body of th'infected world,
If they will patiently receive my medicine.

DUKE Fie on thee! I can tell what thou wouldst do.

JAQUES What, for a counter, would I do but good?

DUKE Most mischievous foul sin, in chiding sin:
For thou thyself hast been a libertine,
As sensual as the brutish sting itself,
And all th'embosséd sores and headed evils,
That thou with licence of free foot hast caught,
Wouldst thou disgorge into the general world.

JAQUES Why, who cries out on pride,
That can therein tax any private party?
Doth it not flow as hugely as the sea,
Till that the weary very means do ebb?
What woman in the city do I name,
When that I say the city-woman bears
The cost of princes on unworthy shoulders?
Who can come in and say that I mean her,
When such a one as she, such is her neighbour?
Or what is he of basest function,
That says his bravery is not on my cost,
Thinking that I mean him, but therein suits
His folly to the mettle of my speech?
There then! How then? What then? Let me see wherein
My tongue hath wronged him: if it do him right,
Then he hath wronged himself; if he be free,
Why then my taxing like a wild-goose flies,
Unclaimed of any man. But who comes here?

ORLANDO *appears before them, with his sword drawn*

ORLANDO Forbear, and eat no more.
JAQUES Why, I have eat none yet.
ORLANDO Nor shalt not, till necessity be served.
JAQUES Of what kind should this cock come of?
DUKE Art thou thus boldened, man, by thy distress?
Or else a rude despiser of good manners,
That in civility thou seem'st so empty?
ORLANDO You touched my vein at first. The thorny point
Of bare distress hath ta'en from me the show
Of smooth civility: yet am I inland bred,
And know some nurture. But forbear, I say,
He dies that touches any of this fruit
Till I and my affairs are answeréd.
JAQUES [*taking up a bunch of raisins*]
An you will not be answered with reason, I must die.
DUKE What would you have? Your gentleness shall force,
More than your force move us to gentleness.
ORLANDO I almost die for food, and let me have it.
DUKE Sit down and feed, and welcome to our table.
ORLANDO Speak you so gently? Pardon me, I pray you –
I thought that all things had been savage here,
And therefore put I on the countenance
Of stern commandment. But whate'er you are
That in this desert inaccessible,
Under the shade of melancholy boughs,
Lose and neglect the creeping hours of time;
If ever you have looked on better days,
If ever been where bells have knolled to church,
If ever sat at any good man's feast,
If ever from your eyelids wiped a tear,
And know what 'tis to pity and be pitied,
Let gentleness my strong enforcement be:
In the which hope I blush, and hide my sword.
DUKE True is it that we have seen better days,
And have with holy bell been knolled to church,
And sat at good men's feasts, and wiped our eyes
Of drops that sacred pity hath engendred:
And therefore sit you down in gentleness,

And take upon command what help we have
That to your wanting may be ministred.

ORLANDO Then but forbear your food a little while,
Whiles, like a doe, I go to find my fawn,
And give it food. There is an old poor man,
Who after me hath many a weary step
Limped in pure love: till he be first sufficed,
Oppressed with two weak evils, age and hunger,
I will not touch a bit.

DUKE Go find him out,
And we will nothing waste till you return.

ORLANDO I thank ye, and be blessed for your good comfort!
[he goes

DUKE Thou seest we are not all alone unhappy:
This wide and universal theatre
Presents more woeful pageants than the scene
Wherein we play in.

JAQUES All the world's a stage,
And all the men and women merely players;
They have their exits and their entrances,
And one man in his time plays many parts,
His acts being seven ages. At first the infant,
Mewling and puking in the nurse's arms:
Then the whining school-boy, with his satchel
And shining morning face, creeping like snail
Unwillingly to school: and then the lover,
Sighing like furnace, with a woeful ballad
Made to his mistress' eyebrow: then a soldier,
Full of strange oaths and bearded like the pard,
Jealous in honour, sudden and quick in quarrel,
Seeking the bubble reputation
Even in the cannon's mouth: and then the justice,
In fair round belly with good capon lined,
With eyes severe and beard of formal cut,
Full of wise saws and modern instances,
And so he plays his part. The sixth age shifts
Into the lean and slippered pantaloon,
With spectacles on nose and pouch on side,
His youthful hose, well saved, a world too wide

For his shrunk shank, and his big manly voice,
Turning again toward childish treble, pipes
And whistles in his sound. Last scene of all,
That ends this strange eventful history,
Is second childishness, and mere oblivion,
Sans teeth, sans eyes, sans taste, sans every thing.

ORLANDO *returns with* ADAM *in his arms*

DUKE Welcome. Set down your venerable burden,
And let him feed.

ORLANDO I thank you most for him.

ADAM So had you need,
I scarce can speak to thank you for myself.

DUKE Welcome, fall to: I will not trouble you
As yet to question you about your fortunes:
Give us some music, and good cousin, sing.

AMIENS [*sings*] Blow, blow, thou winter wind,
Thou art not so unkind
As man's ingratitude:
Thy tooth is not so keen,
Because thou art not seen,
Although thy breath be rude.
Hey-ho, sing hey-ho, unto the green holly,
Most friendship is feigning; most loving mere folly:
Then hey-ho, the holly,
This life is most jolly.

Freeze, freeze, thou bitter sky,
That dost not bite so nigh
As benefits forgot:
Though thou the waters warp,
Thy sting is not so sharp
As friend remembred not.
Hey-ho, sing hey-ho, unto the green holly,
Most friendship is feigning; most loving mere folly:
Then hey-ho, the holly,
This life is most jolly.

DUKE If that you were the good Sir Rowland's son,
As you have whispered faithfully you were,
And as mine eye doth his effigies witness

Most truly limned and living in your face,
Be truly welcome hither: I am the duke
That loved your father. The residue of your fortune,
Go to my cave and tell me. Good old man,
Thou art right welcome as thy master is:
Support him by the arm. Give me your hand,
And let me all your fortunes understand.

[*they enter the cave*

ACT 3 SCENE 1

A room in the palace of Duke Frederick

Enter Duke FREDERICK, *lords, and* OLIVER, *guarded by attendants*

DUKE F. Not see him since? Sir, sir, that cannot be:
But were I not the better part made mercy,
I should not seek an absent argument
Of my revenge, thou present: but look to it,
Find out thy brother wheresoe'er he is –
Seek him with candle; bring him dead or living
Within this twelvemonth, or turn thou no more
To seek a living in our territory.
Thy lands and all things that thou dost call thine
Worth seizure do we seize into our hands,
Till thou canst quit thee by thy brother's mouth
Of what we think against thee.

OLIVER O that your highness knew my heart in this!
I never loved my brother in my life.

DUKE F. More villain thou. Well, push him out of doors,
And let my officers of such a nature
Make an extent upon his house and lands:
Do this expediently and turn him going. [*they go*

SCENE 2

The clearing in the outskirts of the forest, near the sheepcote

ORLANDO *with a paper, which he fixes to the trunk of a tree*

ORLANDO Hang there, my verse, in witness of my love,
And thou, thrice-crownéd queen of night, survey
With thy chaste eye, from thy pale sphere above,
Thy huntress' name that my full life doth sway.
O Rosalind! These trees shall be my books,
And in their barks my thoughts I'll character,
That every eye which in this forest looks
Shall see thy virtue witnessed everywhere.

Run, run, Orlando, carve on every tree
The fair, the chaste and unexpressive she. [*he passes on*

CORIN *and* TOUCHSTONE *come up*

CORIN And how like you this shepherd's life, Master Touchstone?

TOUCH. Truly, shepherd, in respect of itself, it is a good life; but in respect that it is a shepherd's life, it is naught. In respect that it is solitary, I like it very well; but in respect that it is private, it is a very vile life. Now in respect it is in the fields, it pleaseth me well; but in respect it is not in the court, it is tedious. As it is a spare life, look you, it fits my humour well; but as there is no more plenty in it, it goes much against my stomach. Hast any philosophy in thee, shepherd?

CORIN No more, but that I know the more one sickens, the worse at ease he is; and that he that wants money, means and content is without three good friends; that the property of rain is to wet and fire to burn; that good pasture makes fat sheep; and that a great cause of the night, is lack of the sun; that he that hath learned no wit by nature nor art may complain of good breeding, or comes of a very dull kindred.

TOUCH. Such a one is a natural philosopher. Wast ever in court, shepherd?

CORIN No, truly.

TOUCH. Then thou art damned.

CORIN Nay, I hope –

TOUCH. Truly thou art damned, like an ill-roasted egg all on one side.

CORIN For not being at court? Your reason.

TOUCH. Why, if thou never wast at court, thou never saw'st good manners; if thou never saw'st good manners, then thy manners must be wicked, and wickedness is sin, and sin is damnation. Thou art in a parlous state, shepherd.

CORIN Not a whit, Touchstone. Those that are good manners at the court are as ridiculous in the country, as the behaviour of the country is most mockable at the court. You told me you salute not at the court, but you kiss your hands; that courtesy would be uncleanly, if courtiers were shepherds.

TOUCH. Instance, briefly; come, instance.

CORIN Why, we are still handling our ewes, and their fells you know are greasy.

TOUCH. Why, do not your courtier's hands sweat? And is not the grease of a mutton as wholesome as the sweat of a man? Shallow, shallow: a better instance, I say: come.

CORIN Besides, our hands are hard.

TOUCH. Your lips will feel them the sooner. Shallow, again: a more sounder instance, come.

CORIN And they are often tarred over with the surgery of our sheep; and would you have us kiss tar? The courtier's hands are perfumed with civet.

TOUCH. Most shallow man! Thou worms-meat, in respect of a good piece of flesh indeed! Learn of the wise, and perpend: civet is of a baser birth than tar, the very uncleanly flux of a cat. Mend the instance, shepherd.

CORIN You have too courtly a wit for me, I'll rest.

TOUCH. Wilt thou rest damned? God help thee, shallow man! God make incision in thee! Thou art raw.

CORIN Sir, I am a true labourer. I earn that I eat, get that I wear, owe no man hate, envy no man's happiness, glad of other men's good, content with my harm; and the greatest of my pride is to see my ewes graze and my lambs suck.

TOUCH. That is another simple sin in you, to bring the ewes and the rams together, and to offer to get your living by the copulation of cattle – to be bawd to a bell-wether, and to betray a she-lamb of a twelvemonth to a crooked-pated, old, cuckoldly ram, out of all reasonable match. If thou beest not damned for this, the devil himself will have no shepherds – I cannot see else how thou shouldst 'scape.

CORIN Here comes young Master Ganymede, my new mistress's brother.

ROSALIND, *unwitting of their presence, comes up, sees* ORLANDO*'s paper on the tree and, plucking it down, begins to read it*

ROSALIND 'From the east to western Ind,
No jewel is like Rosalind.
Her worth, being mounted on the wind,
Through all the world bears Rosalind.
All the pictures fairest lined
Are but black to Rosalind.
Let no face be kept in mind
But the fair of Rosalind.'

TOUCH. [*taps her on the arm with his bauble*] I'll rhyme you so eight years together, dinners, and suppers, and sleeping-hours excepted: it is the right butter women's rank to market.

ROSALIND Out, fool!

TOUCH. For a taste:
If a hart do lack a hind,
Let him seek out Rosalind:
If the cat will after kind,
So be sure will Rosalind:
Winter garments must be lined,
So must slender Rosalind.
They that reap must sheaf and bind,
Then to cart with Rosalind.
Sweetest nut hath sourest rind,
Such a nut is Rosalind.
He that sweetest rose will find,
Must find love's prick and Rosalind.
This is the very false gallop of verses. Why do you infect yourself with them?

ROSALIND Peace, you dull fool! I found them on a tree.

TOUCH. Truly, the tree yields bad fruit.

ROSALIND I'll graff it with you, and then I shall graff it with a medlar: then it will be the earliest fruit i'th' country: for you'll be rotten ere you be half ripe, and that's the right virtue of the medlar.

TOUCH. You have said: but whether wisely or no, let the forest judge.

CELIA *draws near, likewise reading a paper*

ROSALIND Peace!

Here comes my sister, reading. Stand aside.

[*they hide behind a tree*

CELIA 'Why should this a desert be?
For it is unpeopled? No;
Tongues I'll hang on every tree,
That shall civil sayings show.
Some, how brief the life of man
Runs his erring pilgrimage,
That the stretching of a span
Buckles in his sum of age;
Some, of violated vows
'Twixt the souls of friend and friend:
But upon the fairest boughs,
Or at every sentence end,
Will I Rosalinda write,
Teaching all that read to know
The quintessence of every sprite
Heaven would in little show.
Therefore Heaven Nature charged,
That one body should be filled
With all graces wide-enlarged:
Nature presently distilled
Helen's cheek, but not her heart,
Cleopatra's majesty,
Atalanta's better part,
Sad Lucretia's modesty
Thus Rosalind of many parts
By heavenly synod was devised,
Of many faces, eyes, and hearts.
To have the touches dearest prized . . .
Heaven would that she these gifts should have,
And I to live and die her slave.'

ROSALIND O most gentle pulpiter, what tedious homily of love have you wearied your parishioners withal, and never cried, 'Have patience, good people!'

CELIA [*starts and turns, dropping the paper*] How now, back-friends! Shepherd, go off a little. Go with him, sirrah.

TOUCH. Come, shepherd, let us make an honourable retreat – though not with bag and baggage, yet with scrip and scrippage.

[*Touchstone picks up the verses and departs with Corin*

CELIA Didst thou hear these verses?

ROSALIND O yes, I heard them all, and more too, for some of them had in them more feet than the verses would bear.

CELIA That's no matter: the feet might bear the verses.

ROSALIND Ay, but the feet were lame, and could not bear themselves without the verse, and therefore stood lamely in the verse.

CELIA But didst thou hear without wondering how thy name should be hanged and carved upon these trees?

ROSALIND I was seven of the nine days out of the wonder before you came; for look here what I found on a palm-tree. I was never so be-rhymed since Pythagoras' time, that I was an Irish rat, which I can hardly remember.

CELIA Trow you who hath done this?

ROSALIND Is it a man?

CELIA And a chain that you once wore about his neck! Change you colour?

ROSALIND I prithee, who?

CELIA O Lord, Lord! It is a hard matter for friends to meet; but mountains may be removed with earthquakes and so encounter.

ROSALIND Nay, but who is it?

CELIA Is it possible?

ROSALIND Nay, I prithee now with most petitionary vehemence, tell me who it is.

CELIA O wonderful, wonderful, and most wonderful wonderful! And yet again wonderful, and after that out of all whooping!

ROSALIND Good my complexion! Dost thou think, though I am caparisoned like a man, I have a doublet and-hose in my disposition? One inch of delay more is a South-sea of discovery. I prithee, tell me who is it quickly, and speak apace: I would thou couldst stammer, that thou mightst pour this concealed man out of thy mouth, as wine comes out of a narrow-mouthed bottle; either too much at once, or none at all. I prithee take the cork out of thy mouth, that I may drink thy tidings.

CELIA So you may put a man in your belly.

ROSALIND Is he of God's making? What manner of man? Is his head worth a hat? Or his chin worth a beard?

CELIA Nay, he hath but a little beard.

ROSALIND Why, God will send more, if the man will be thankful: let me stay the growth of his beard, if thou delay me not the knowledge of his chin.

CELIA It is young Orlando, that tripped up the wrestler's heels, and your heart, both in an instant.

ROSALIND Nay, but the devil take mocking; speak sad brow and true maid.

CELIA I'faith, coz, 'tis he.

ROSALIND Orlando?

CELIA Orlando.

ROSALIND Alas the day, what shall I do with my doublet and hose? What did he when thou saw'st him? What said he? How looked he? Wherein went he? What makes he here? Did he ask for me? Where remains he? How parted he with thee? And when shalt thou see him again? Answer me in one word.

CELIA You must borrow me Gargantua's mouth first: 'tis a word too great for any mouth of this age's size. To say ay and no to these particulars is more than to answer in a catechism.

ROSALIND But doth he know that I am in this forest and in man's apparel? Looks he as freshly as he did the day he wrestled?

CELIA It is as easy to count atomies as to resolve the propositions of a lover: but take a taste of my finding him, and relish it with good observance. I found him under a tree, like a dropped acorn.

ROSALIND It may well be called Jove's tree, when it drops such fruit.

CELIA Give me audience, good madam.

ROSALIND Proceed.

CELIA There lay he, stretched along, like a wounded knight.

ROSALIND Though it be pity to see such a sight, it well becomes the ground.

CELIA Cry 'holla' to thy tongue, I prithee; it curvets unseasonably. He was furnished like a hunter.

ROSALIND O ominous! He comes to kill my heart.

CELIA I would sing my song without a burden – thou bring'st me out of tune.

ROSALIND Do you not know I am a woman? When I think, I must speak. Sweet, say on.

ORLANDO *and* JAQUES *are seen coming through the trees*

CELIA You bring me out. Soft! comes he not here?

ROSALIND 'Tis he – slink by, and note him.

[*Celia and Rosalind steal behind a tree, within earshot*

JAQUES I thank you for your company – but, good faith,
I had as lief have been myself alone.

ORLANDO And so had I: but yet, for fashion sake,
I thank you too for your society.

JAQUES God buy you, let's meet as little as we can.

ORLANDO I do desire we may be better strangers.

JAQUES I pray you, mar no more trees with writing love-songs in their barks.

ORLANDO I pray you, mar no more of my verses with reading them ill-favouredly.

JAQUES Rosalind is your love's name?

ORLANDO Yes, just.

JAQUES I do not like her name.

ORLANDO There was no thought of pleasing you when she was christened.

JAQUES What stature is she of?

ORLANDO Just as high as my heart.

JAQUES You are full of pretty answers: have you not been acquainted with goldsmiths' wives, and conned them out of rings?

ORLANDO Not so; but I answer you right painted cloth, from whence you have studied your questions.

JAQUES You have a nimble wit; I think 'twas made of Atalanta's heels. Will you sit down with me? And we two will rail against our mistress the world, and all our misery.

ORLANDO I will chide no breather in the world but myself, against whom I know most faults.

JAQUES The worst fault you have is to be in love.

ORLANDO 'Tis a fault I will not change for your best virtue. I am weary of you.

JAQUES By my troth, I was seeking for a fool when I found you.

ORLANDO He is drowned in the brook – look but in, and you shall see him.

JAQUES There I shall see mine own figure.

ORLANDO Which I take to be either a fool or a cipher.

JAQUES I'll tarry no longer with you. Farewell, good Signior Love. [*he bows*

ORLANDO I am glad of your departure. [*he bows likewise*] Adieu, good Monsieur Melancholy. [*Jaques departs*

ROSALIND I will speak to him like a saucy lackey, and under that habit play the knave with him. [*calls*] Do you hear, forester?

ORLANDO [*turns*] Very well. What would you?

ROSALIND I pray you, what is't o'clock?

ORLANDO You should ask me what time o'day: there's no clock in the forest.

ROSALIND Then there is no true lover in the forest, else sighing every minute and groaning every hour would detect the lazy foot of Time as well as a clock.

ORLANDO And why not the swift foot of Time? Had not that been as proper?

ROSALIND By no means, sir: Time travels in divers paces with divers persons. I'll tell you who Time ambles withal, who Time trots withal, who Time gallops withal, and who he stands still withal.

ORLANDO I prithee, who doth he trot withal?

ROSALIND Marry, he trots hard with a young maid between the contract of her marriage and the day it is solemnized: if the interim be but a se'nnight, Time's pace is so hard that it seems the length of seven year.

ORLANDO Who ambles Time withal?

ROSALIND With a priest that lacks Latin, and a rich man that hath not the gout: for the one sleeps easily because he cannot study, and the other lives merrily because he feels no pain: the one lacking the burden of lean and wasteful learning; the other knowing no burden of heavy tedious penury. These Time ambles withal.

ORLANDO Who doth he gallop withal?

ROSALIND With a thief to the gallows: for though he go as softly as foot can fall, he thinks himself too soon there.

ORLANDO Who stays it still withal?

ROSALIND With lawyers in the vacation: for they sleep between term and term, and then they perceive not how Time moves.

ORLANDO Where dwell you, pretty youth?

ROSALIND With this shepherdess, my sister; here in the skirts of the forest, like fringe upon a petticoat.

ORLANDO Are you native of this place?

ROSALIND As the cony that you see dwell where she is kindled.

ORLANDO Your accent is something finer than you could purchase in so removed a dwelling.

ROSALIND I have been told so of many: but indeed an old religious uncle of mine taught me to speak, who was in his youth an inland man – one that knew courtship too well, for there he fell in love. I have heard him read many lectures against it, and I thank God I am not a woman, to be touched with so many giddy offences as he hath generally taxed their whole sex withal.

ORLANDO Can you remember any of the principal evils that he laid to the charge of women?

ROSALIND There were none principal; they were all like one another as halfpence are, every one fault seeming monstrous till his fellow-fault came to match it.

ORLANDO I prithee, recount some of them.

ROSALIND No: I will not cast away my physic but on those that are sick. There is a man haunts the forest, that abuses our young plants with carving 'Rosalind' on their barks; hangs odes upon hawthorns and elegies on brambles; all, forsooth, deifying the name of Rosalind: if I could meet that fancy-monger, I would give him some good counsel, for he seems to have the quotidian of love upon him.

ORLANDO I am he that is so love-shaked. I pray you, tell me your remedy.

ROSALIND There is none of my uncle's marks upon you: he taught me how to know a man in love; in which cage of rushes I am sure you are not prisoner.

ORLANDO What were his marks?

ROSALIND A lean cheek, which you have not: a blue eye and

sunken, which you have not: an unquestionable spirit, which you have not: a beard neglected, which you have not – but I pardon you for that, for simply your having in beard is a younger brother's revenue. Then your hose should be ungartered, your bonnet unbanded, your sleeve unbuttoned, your shoe untied, and every thing about you demonstrating a careless desolation: but you are no such man; you are rather point-device in your accoutrements, as loving yourself than seeming the lover of any other.

ORLANDO Fair youth, I would I could make thee believe I love.

ROSALIND Me believe it! You may as soon make her that you love believe it, which I warrant she is apter to do than to confess she does: that is one of the points in the which women still give the lie to their consciences. But, in good sooth, are you he that hangs the verses on the trees, wherein Rosalind is so admired?

ORLANDO I swear to thee, youth, by the white hand of Rosalind, I am that he, that unfortunate he.

ROSALIND But are you so much in love as your rhymes speak?

ORLANDO Neither rhyme nor reason can express how much.

ROSALIND Love is merely a madness, and I tell you deserves as well a dark house and a whip as madmen do: and the reason why they are not so punished and cured is, that the lunacy is so ordinary that the whippers are in love too. Yet I profess curing it by counsel.

ORLANDO Did you ever cure any so?

ROSALIND Yes, one, and in this manner. He was to imagine me his love, his mistress; and I set him every day to woo me: at which time would I, being but a moonish youth, grieve, be effeminate, changeable, longing and liking, proud, fantastical, apish, shallow, inconstant, full of tears, full of smiles; for every passion something, and for no passion truly anything, as boys and women are for the most part cattle of this colour: would now like him, now loathe him; then entertain him, then forswear him; now weep for him, then spit at him; that I drave my suitor from his mad humour of love to a living humour of madness – which was, to forswear the full stream of the world and to live in a nook merely monastic. And thus I cured him, and this way will I take upon me to wash your liver as clean as a sound sheep's heart, that there shall not be one spot of love in't.

ORLANDO I would not be cured, youth.

ROSALIND I would cure you, if you would but call me Rosalind, and come every day to my cote, and woo me.

ORLANDO Now, by the faith of my love, I will. Tell me where it is.

ROSALIND Go with me to it, and I'll show it you: and by the way you shall tell me where in the forest you live. Will you go?

ORLANDO With all my heart, good youth.

ROSALIND Nay, you must call me Rosalind. Come, sister will you go? *[they go*

Some days pass

SCENE 3

The clearing near the sheepcote (as before)

TOUCHSTONE *and* AUDREY *approach;* JAQUES *following at a little distance*

TOUCH. Come apace, good Audrey. I will fetch up your goats, Audrey. And how, Audrey? Am I the man yet? Doth my simple feature content you?

AUDREY Your features! Lord warrant us! What features?

TOUCH. I am here with thee and thy goats, as the most capricious poet, honest Ovid, was among the Goths.

JAQUES O knowledge ill-inhabited! Worse than Jove in a thatched house!

TOUCH. When a man's verses cannot be understood, nor a man's good wit seconded with the forward child, understanding, it strikes a man more dead than a great reckoning in a little room. Truly, I would the gods had made thee poetical.

AUDREY I do not know what 'poetical' is; is it honest in deed and word? Is it a true thing?

TOUCH. No, truly; for the truest poetry is the most feigning;

and lovers are given to poetry; and what they swear in poetry it may be said as lovers they do feign.

AUDREY Do you wish then that the gods had made me poetical?

TOUCH. I do, truly: for thou swear'st to me thou art honest; now, if thou wert a poet, I might have some hope thou didst feign.

AUDREY Would you not have me honest?

TOUCH. No truly, unless thou wert hard-favoured: for honesty coupled to beauty is to have honey a sauce to sugar.

JAQUES A material fool!

AUDREY Well, I am not fair, and therefore I pray the gods make me honest.

TOUCH. Truly, and to cast away honesty upon a foul slut were to put good meat into an unclean dish.

AUDREY I am not a slut, though I thank the gods I am foul.

TOUCH. Well, praised be the gods for thy foulness! Sluttishness may come hereafter. But be it as it may be, I will marry thee: and to that end, I have been with Sir Oliver Martext the vicar of the next village, who hath promised to meet me in this place of the forest and to couple us.

JAQUES I would fain see this meeting

AUDREY Well, the gods give us joy!

TOUCH. Amen. A man may, if he were of a fearful heart, stagger in this attempt; for here we have no temple but the wood, no assembly but horn-beasts. But what though? Courage! As horns are odious, they are necessary. It is said, 'many a man knows no end of his goods'. Right! Many a man has good horns, and knows no end of them. Well, that is the dowry of his wife; 'tis none of his own getting. Horns? Even so. Poor men alone? No, no, the noblest deer hath them as huge as the rascal. Is the single man therefore blessed? No, as a walled town is more worthier than a village, so is the forehead of a married man more honourable than the bare brow of a bachelor: and by how much defence is better than no skill, by so much is a horn more precious than to want.

SIR OLIVER MARTEXT *comes up*

Here comes Sir Oliver. Sir Oliver Martext, you are

well met. Will you dispatch us here under this tree, or shall we go with you to your chapel?

MARTEXT Is there none here to give the woman?

TOUCH. I will not take her on gift of any man.

MARTEXT Truly, she must be given, or the marriage is not lawful.

JAQUES [*comes forward, doffing his hat*] Proceed, proceed; I'll give her.

TOUCH. Good even, good Master What-ye-call't: how do you, sir? You are very well met: God'ild you for your last company – I am very glad to see you – even a toy in hand here, sir. Nay, pray be covered.

JAQUES Will you be married, motley?

TOUCH. As the ox hath his bow, sir, the horse his curb, and the falcon her bells, so man hath his desires; and as pigeons bill, so wedlock would be nibbling.

JAQUES And will you, being a man of your breeding, be married under a bush like a beggar? Get you to church, and have a good priest that can tell you what marriage is – this fellow will but join you together as they join wainscot; then one of you will prove a shrunk panel, and like green timber warp, warp.

TOUCH. I am not in the mind but I were better to be married of him than of another; for he is not like to marry me well, and not being well married, it will be a good excuse for me hereafter to leave my wife.

JAQUES Go thou with me, and let me counsel thee.

TOUCH. Come, sweet Audrey,
We must be married, or we must live in bawdry. Farewell, good Master Oliver: not – [*sings and dances*
O sweet Oliver,
O brave Oliver,
Leave me not behind thee:
but –
Wind away,
Begone, I say,
I will not to wedding with thee.

[*he dances off, Jaques and Audrey following*

MARTEXT 'Tis no matter; ne'er a fantastical knave of them all shall flout me out of my calling. [*he goes*

SCENE 4

ROSALIND *and* CELIA *comes along the path from the cottage; Rosalind drops upon a bank*

ROSALIND Never talk to me, I will weep.

CELIA Do, I prithee – but yet have the grace to consider that tears do not become a man.

ROSALIND But have I not cause to weep?

CELIA As good cause as one would desire; therefore, weep.

ROSALIND His very hair is of the dissembling colour.

CELIA Something browner than Judas's: marry, his kisses are Judas's own children.

ROSALIND I'faith, his hair is of a good colour.

CELIA An excellent colour: your chestnut was ever the only colour.

ROSALIND And his kissing is as full of sanctity as the touch of holy bread.

CELIA He hath bought a pair of cast lips of Diana: a nun of winter's sisterhood kisses not more religiously, the very ice of chastity is in them.

ROSALIND But why did he swear he would come this morning, and comes not?

CELIA Nay, certainly, there is no truth in him.

ROSALIND Do you think so?

CELIA Yes, I think he is not a pick-purse nor a horse-stealer, but for his verity in love I do think him as concave as a covered goblet or a worm-eaten nut.

ROSALIND Not true in love?

CELIA Yes, when he is in – but I think he is not in.

ROSALIND You have heard him swear downright he was.

CELIA 'Was' is not 'is': besides, the oath of a lover is no stronger than the word of a tapster; they are both the confirmer of false reckonings. He attends here in the forest on the duke your father.

ROSALIND I met the duke yesterday and had much question with him: he asked me of what parentage I was; I told him, of as good as he – so he laughed and let me go. But what talk we of fathers, when there is such a man as Orlando?

CELIA O that's a brave man! He writes brave verses, speaks brave words, swears brave oaths and breaks them bravely, quite traverse, athwart the heart of his lover – as a puny tilter, that spurs his horse but on one side, breaks his staff like a noble goose; but all's brave that youth mounts and folly guide. Who comes here?

CORIN *draws near and accosts them*

CORIN Mistress and master, you have oft inquired
After the shepherd that complained of love,
Who you saw sitting by me on the turf,
Praising the proud disdainful shepherdess
That was his mistress.

CELIA Well: and what of him?

CORIN If you will see a pageant truly played,
Between the pale complexion of true love
And the red glow of scorn and proud disdain,
Go hence a little and I shall conduct you,
If you will mark it.

ROSALIND O, come, let us remove.
The sight of lovers feedeth those in love:
Bring us to this sight, and you shall say
I'll prove a busy actor in their play.

[*they go*

SCENE 5

Another part of the forest

PHEBE, *followed by* SILVIUS *who entreats her*

SILVIUS [*kneels*] Sweet Phebe, do not scorn me, do not, Phebe:
Say that you love me not, but say not so
In bitterness. The common executioner,
Whose heart th'accustomed sight of death makes hard,
Falls not the axe upon the humbled neck
But first begs pardon: will you sterner be
Than he that dies and lives by bloody drops?

ROSALIND, CELIA, *and* CORIN *come up behind unseen*

PHEBE I would not be thy executioner.
I fly thee, for I would not injure thee.
Thou tell'st me there is murder in mine eye –
'Tis pretty, sure, and very probable,
That eyes, that are the frail'st and softest things,
Who shut their coward gates on atomies,
Should be called tyrants, butchers, murderers!
Now I do frown on thee with all my heart,
And if mine eyes can wound, now let them kill thee;
Now counterfeit to swoon, why now fall down,
Or if thou canst not, O for shame, for shame,
Lie not, to say mine eyes are murderers!
Now show the wound mine eye hath made in thee.
Scratch thee but with a pin, and there remains
Some scar of it: lean but upon a rush,
The cicatrice and capable impressure
Thy palm some moment keeps: but now mine eyes,
Which I have darted at thee, hurt thee not,
Nor, I am sure, there is no force in eyes
That can do hurt.

SILVIUS O dear Phebe,
If ever – as that ever may be near –
You meet in some fresh cheek the power of fancy,
Then shall you know the wounds invisible

That love's keen arrows make.

PHEBE But till that time
Come not thou near me: and when that time comes
Afflict me with thy mocks, pity me not,
As till that time I shall not pity thee.

ROSALIND [*advancing*].
And why, I pray you? Who might be your mother,
That you insult, exult, and all at once,
Over the wretched? What though you have no beauty –
As, by my faith, I see no more in you
Than without candle may go dark to bed –
Must you be therefore proud and pitiless?
Why, what means this? Why do you look on me?
I see no more in you than in the ordinary
Of nature's sale-work! 'Od's my little life,
I think she means to tangle my eyes too:
No, faith, proud mistress, hope not after it.
'Tis not your inky brows, your black silk hair,
Your bugle eyeballs, nor your cheek of cream,
That can entame my spirits to your worship.
You foolish shepherd, wherefore do you follow her,
Like foggy south, puffing with wind and rain?
You are a thousand times a properer man
Than she a woman: 'tis such fools as you
That makes the world full of ill-favoured children:
'Tis not her glass, but you, that flatters her,
And out of you she sees herself more proper
Than any of her lineaments can show her.
But, mistress, know yourself – down on your knees,
And thank heaven, fasting, for a good man's love;
[*Phebe kneels to Rosalind*
For I must tell you friendly in your ear,
Sell when you can – you are not for all markets:
Cry the man mercy, love him, take his offer.
Foul is most foul, being foul to be a scoffer.
So take her to thee, shepherd – fare you well.

PHEBE Sweet youth, I pray you chide a year together.
I had rather hear you chide than this man woo.

ROSALIND [*to Phebe*] He's fallen in love with your foulness, [*to Silvius*] and she'll fall in love with my anger. If it be so, as fast as she answers thee with frowning looks, I'll sauce her with bitter words. [*to Phebe*] Why look you so upon me?

PHEBE For no ill will I bear you.

ROSALIND I pray you, do not fall in love with me,
For I am falser than vows made in wine:
Besides, I like you not. If you will know my house,
'Tis at the tuft of olives here hard by.
Will you go, sister? Shepherd, ply her hard.
Come, sister. Shepherdess, look on him better,
And be not proud – though all the world could see,
None could be so abused in sight as he.
Come, to our flock.

[*she stalks away, followed by Celia and Corin*

PHEBE [*gazing after them*]
Dead Shepherd, now I find thy saw of might,
'Who ever loved that loved not at first sight?'

SILVIUS Sweet Phebe –

PHEBE Ha! What say'st thou, Silvius?

SILVIUS Sweet Phebe, pity me.

PHEBE Why, I am sorry for thee, gentle Silvius.

SILVIUS Wherever sorrow is, relief would be:
If you do sorrow at my grief in love,
By giving love your sorrow and my grief
Were both extermined.

PHEBE Thou hast my love – is not that neighbourly?

SILVIUS I would have you.

PHEBE Why, that were covetousness.
Silvius, the time was that I hated thee,
And yet it is not that I bear thee love;
But since that thou canst talk of love so well,
Thy company, which erst was irksome to me,
I will endure; and I'll employ thee too:
But do not look for further recompense
Than thine own gladness that thou art employed.

SILVIUS So holy and so perfect is my love,
And I in such a poverty of grace,
That I shall think it a most plenteous crop

To glean the broken ears after the man
That the main harvest reaps: loose now and then
A scattered smile, and that I'll live upon.

PHEBE Know'st thou the youth that spoke to me erewhile?

SILVIUS Not very well, but I have met him oft,
And he hath bought the cottage and the bounds
That the old carlot once was master of.

PHEBE Think not I love him, though I ask for him.
'Tis but a peevish boy Yet he talks well –
But what care I for words? Yet words do well,
When he that speaks them pleases those that hear:
It is a pretty youth – not very pretty –
But, sure, he's proud, and yet his pride becomes him:
He'll make a proper man: the best thing in him
Is his complexion; and faster than his tongue
Did make offence, his eye did heal it up:
He is not very tall – yet for his years he's tall:
His leg is but so so – and yet 'tis well:
There was a pretty redness in his lip,
A little riper and more lusty red
Than that mixed in his check; 'twas just the difference
Betwixt the constant red and mingled damask.
There be some women, Silvius, had they marked him
In parcels as I did, would have gone near
To fall in love with him: but, for my part,
I love him not, nor hate him not; and yet
I have more cause to hate him than to love him,
For what had he to do to chide at me?
He said mine eyes were black and my hair black,
And, now I am remembered, scorn'd at me:
I marvel why I answered not again:
But that's all one; omittance is no quittance:
I'll write to him a very taunting letter,
And thou shalt bear it – wilt thou, Silvius?

SILVIUS Phebe, with all my heart.

PHEBE I'll write it straight;
The matter's in my head and in my heart.
I will be bitter with him and passing short:
Go with me, Silvius. [*they go*

ACT 4 SCENE 1

The clearing near the sheepcote

Enter ROSALIND, CELIA, *and* JACQUES

JAQUES I prithee, pretty youth, let me be better acquainted with thee.

ROSALIND They say you are a melancholy fellow.

JAQUES I am so: I do love it better than laughing.

ROSALIND Those that are in extremity of either are abominable fellows, and betray themselves to every modern censure worse than drunkards.

JAQUES Why, 'tis good to be sad and say nothing.

ROSALIND Why then, 'tis good to be a post.

JAQUES I have neither the scholar's melancholy, which is emulation; nor the musician's, which is fantastical; nor the courtier's, which is proud; nor the soldier's, which is ambitious; nor the lawyer's, which is politic; nor the lady's, which is nice; nor the lover's, which is all these: but it is a melancholy of mine own, compounded of many simples, extracted from many objects, and indeed the sundry contemplation of my travels, in which my often rumination wraps me in a most humorous sadness.

ROSALIND A traveller! By my faith, you have great reason to be sad: I fear you have sold your own lands to see other men's; then, to have seen much, and to have nothing, is to have rich eyes and poor hands.

JAQUES Yes, I have gained my experience.

ORLANDO *draws near*

ROSALIND And your experience makes you sad: I had rather have a fool to make me merry than experience to make me sad – and to travel for it too!

ORLANDO Good day, and happiness, dear Rosalind!

[*she takes no heed of him*

JAQUES Nay then, God buy you, an you talk in blank verse.

[*he turns from them*

ROSALIND Farewell, Monsieur Traveller: look you lisp and wear strange suits; disable all the benefits of your own country; be out of love with your nativity, and almost chide God for making you that countenance you are; or I will scarce think you have swam in a gondola. [*Jaques passes out of earshot; she sits*] Why, how now, Orlando! Where have you been all this while? You a lover! An you serve me such another trick, never come in my sight more.

ORLANDO My fair Rosalind, I come within an hour of my promise.

ROSALIND Break an hour's promise in love? He that will divide a minute into a thousand parts, and break but a part of the thousandth part of a minute in the affairs of love, it may be said of him that Cupid hath clapped him o'th' shoulder, but I'll warrant him heart whole.

ORLANDO Pardon me, dear Rosalind.

ROSALIND Nay, an you be so tardy, come no more in my sight. I had as lief be wooed of a snail.

ORLANDO Of a snail?

ROSALIND Ay, of a snail; for though he comes slowly, he carries his house on his head; a better jointure, I think, than you make a woman: besides, he brings his destiny with him.

ORLANDO What's that? [*he sits beside her*

ROSALIND Why, horns; which such as you are fain to be beholding to your wives for: but he comes armed in his fortune, and prevents the slander of his wife.

ORLANDO Virtue is no horn-maker. [*musing*] And my Rosalind is virtuous.

ROSALIND And I am your Rosalind.

[*she puts her arm about his neck*

CELIA It pleases him to call you so; but he hath a Rosalind of a better leer than you.

ROSALIND Come, woo me, woo me; for now I am in a holiday humour, and like enough to consent. What would you say to me now, an I were your very very Rosalind?

ORLANDO I would kiss before I spoke.

ROSALIND Nay, you were better speak first, and when you were gravelled for lack of matter, you might take occasion to kiss: very good orators, when they are out, they will spit; and for lovers, lacking (God warr'nt us!) matter, the cleanliest shift is to kiss.

ORLANDO How if the kiss be denied?

ROSALIND Then she puts you to entreaty and there begins new matter.

ORLANDO Who could be out, being before his beloved mistress?

ROSALIND Marry, that should you if I were your mistress, or I should think my honesty ranker than my wit.

ORLANDO What, of my suit?

ROSALIND Not out of your apparel, and yet out of your suit. Am not I your Rosalind?

ORLANDO I take some joy to say you are, because I would be talking of her.

ROSALIND Well, in her person, I say I will not have you.

ORLANDO Then in mine own person, I die.

ROSALIND No, faith, die by attorney: the poor world is almost six thousand years old, and in all this time there was not any man died in his own person, videlicet, in a love-cause: Troilus had his brains dashed out with a Grecian club, yet he did what he could to die before, and he is one of the patterns of love: Leander, he would have lived many a fair year, though Hero had turned nun, if it had not been for a hot midsummer night; for, good youth, he went but forth to wash him in the Hellespont, and being taken with the cramp was drowned, and the foolish chroniclers of that age found it was 'Hero of Sestos'. But these are all lies. Men have died from time to time, and worms have eaten them, but not for love.

ORLANDO I would not have my right Rosalind of this mind, for I protest her frown might kill me.

ROSALIND By this hand, it will not kill a fly. [*draws closer to him*] But come, now I will be your Rosalind in a more coming-on disposition; and ask me what you will, I will grant it.

ORLANDO Then love me, Rosalind.

ROSALIND Yes, faith will I, Fridays and Saturdays and all.

ORLANDO And wilt thou have me?

ROSALIND Ay, and twenty such.

ORLANDO What sayest thou?

ROSALIND Are you not good?

ORLANDO I hope so.

ROSALIND Why then, can one desire too much of a good thing? [*she rises*] Come, sister, you shall be the priest and marry us. Give me your hand, Orlando. What do you say, sister?

ORLANDO Pray thee, marry us.

CELIA I cannot say the words.

ROSALIND You must begin, 'Will you, Orlando' –

CELIA Go to. Will you, Orlando, have to wife this Rosalind?

ORLANDO I will.

ROSALIND Ay, but when?

ORLANDO Why now, as fast as she can marry us.

ROSALIND Then you must say, 'I take thee, Rosalind, for wife.'

ORLANDO I take thee, Rosalind, for wife.

ROSALIND I might ask you for your commission, but I do take thee, Orlando, for my husband. There's a girl goes before the priest, and certainly a woman's thought runs before her actions.

ORLANDO So do all thoughts, they are winged.

ROSALIND Now tell me how long you would have her after you have possessed her.

ORLANDO For ever and a day.

ROSALIND Say 'a day' without the 'ever'. No, no, Orlando, men are April when they woo, December when they wed; maids are May when they are maids, but the sky changes when they are wives. I will be more jealous of thee than a Barbary cock-pigeon over his hen, more clamorous than a parrot against rain, more new-fangled than an ape, more giddy in my desires than a monkey: I will weep for nothing, like Diana in the fountain, and I will do that when you are disposed to be merry; I will laugh like a hyen, and that when thou art inclined to sleep.

ORLANDO But will my Rosalind do so?

ROSALIND By my life, she will do as I do.

ORLANDO O, but she is wise.

ROSALIND Or else she could not have the wit to do this: the wiser, the waywarder: make the doors upon a woman's wit, and it will out at the casement; shut that, and 'twill out at the key-hole; stop that, 'twill fly with the smoke out at the chimney.

ORLANDO A man that had a wife with such a wit, he might say 'Wit, whither wilt?'

ROSALIND Nay, you might keep that check for it, till you met your wife's wit going to your neighbour's bed.

ORLANDO And what wit could wit have to excuse that?

ROSALIND Marry, to say she came to seek you there. You shall never take her without her answer, unless you take her without her tongue: O, that woman that cannot make her fault her husband's occasion, let her never nurse her child herself, for she will breed it like a fool.

ORLANDO For these two hours, Rosalind, I will leave thee.

ROSALIND Alas, dear love, I cannot lack thee two hours!

ORLANDO I must attend the duke at dinner. By two o'clock I will be with thee again.

ROSALIND Ay, go your ways, go your ways; I knew what you would prove, my friends told me as much, and I thought no less: that flattering tongue of yours won me: 'tis but one cast away, and so, come death. Two o'clock is your hour?

ORLANDO Ay, sweet Rosalind.

ROSALIND By my troth, and in good earnest, and so God mend me, and by all pretty oaths that are not dangerous, if you break one jot of your promise, or come one minute behind your hour, I will think you the most pathetical break-promise, and the most hollow lover, and the most unworthy of her you call Rosalind, that may be chosen out of the gross band of the unfaithful: therefore beware my censure, and keep your promise.

ORLANDO With no less religion than if thou wert indeed my Rosalind: so adieu.

ROSALIND Well, Time is the old justice that examines all such offenders, and let Time try: adieu! [*he goes*

CELIA You have simply misused our sex in your love-prate: we must have your doublet and hose plucked over your head, and show the world what the bird hath done to her own nest.

ROSALIND O coz, coz, coz, my pretty little coz, that thou didst know how many fathom deep I am in love! But it cannot be sounded; my affection hath an unknown bottom, like the bay of Portugal.

CELIA Or rather, bottomless – that as fast as you pour affection in, it runs out.

ROSALIND No, that same wicked bastard of Venus, that was begot of thought, conceived of spleen, and born of madness – that blind rascally boy that abuses every one's eyes because his own are out – let him be judge how deep I am in love. I'll tell thee, Aliena, I cannot be out of the sight of Orlando: I'll go find a shadow and sigh till he come.

CELIA And I'll sleep. [*they go*

ACT 4 SCENE 2

Before the cave of the exiled Duke. A noise as of huntsmen approaching. Presently AMIENS *and other lords appear, dressed as foresters, with* JAQUES *in their midst to whom they are telling of their morning's sport*

JAQUES Which is he that killed the deer?

A LORD Sir, it was I.

JAQUES Let's present him to the duke, like a Roman conqueror. And it would do well to set the deer's horns upon his head, for a branch of victory. Have you no song, forester, for this purpose?

AMIENS Yes, sir.

JAQUES Sing it: 'tis no matter how it be in tune, so it make noise enough.

He that killed the deer is first clad in horns and skin, and then raised aloft by the company, who 'sing him home', Amiens leading and the rest joining in chorus

The Song

What shall he have that killed the deer?
His leather skin and horns to wear:
Then sing him home – the rest shall bear

This burden.
Take thou no scorn to wear the horn,
It was a crest ere thou wast born.
Thy father's father wore it,
And thy father bore it.
The horn, the horn, the lusty horn,
Is not a thing to laugh to scorn.

They march thrice around the tree, repeating the burthen again and again; then they turn into the Duke's cave

SCENE 3

The clearing near the sheepcote

ROSALIND *and* CELIA *return*

ROSALIND How say you now? Is it not past two o'clock? And here much Orlando!

CELIA I warrant you, with pure love and troubled brain, he hath ta'en his bow and arrows, and is gone forth to sleep. Look, who comes here.

SILVIUS *approaches*

SILVIUS My errand is to you, fair youth –
My gentle Phebe bid me give you this:
[he gives Rosalind a letter
I know not the contents, but as I guess
By the stern brow and waspish action
Which she did use as she was writing of it,
It bears an angry tenour: pardon me,
I am but as a guiltless messenger.

ROSALIND Patience herself would startle at this letter,
And play the swaggerer – bear this, bear all:
She says I am not fair, that I lack manners,
She calls me proud, and that she could not love me
Were man as rare as phoenix: 'od's my will!
Her love is not the hare that I do hunt.
Why writes she so to me? Well, shepherd, well,
This is a letter of your own device.

SILVIUS No, I protest, I know not the contents –

Phebe did write it.

ROSALIND Come, come, you are a fool,
And turned into the extremity of love.
I saw her hand – she has a leathern hand,
A freestone-coloured hand: I verily did think
That her old gloves were on, but 'twas her hands:
She has a huswife's hand – but that's no matter:
I say she never did invent this letter.
This is a man's invention, and his hand.

SILVIUS Sure, it is hers.

ROSALIND Why, 'tis a boisterous and a cruel style,
A style for challengers; why, she defies me,
Like Turk to Christian: women's gentle brain
Could not drop forth such giant-rude invention,
Such Ethiop words, blacker in their effect
Than in their countenance. Will you hear the letter?

SILVIUS So please you, for I never heard it yet;
Yet heard too much of Phebe's cruelty.

ROSALIND She Phebes me: mark how the tyrant writes.
[*reads*] 'Art thou god to shepherd turned,
That a maiden's heart hath burned?'
Can a woman rail thus?

SILVIUS Call you this railing?

ROSALIND 'Why, thy godhead laid apart,
Warr'st thou with a woman's heart?'
Did you ever hear such railing?
'Whiles the eye of man did woo me,
That could do no vengeance to me.'
Meaning me a beast.
'If the scorn of your bright eyne
Have power to raise such love in mine,
Alack, in me what strange effect
Would they work in mild aspect?
Whiles you chid me I did love,
How then might your prayers move?
He that brings this love to thee
Little knows this love in me:
And by him seal up thy mind,
Whether that thy youth and kind

Will the faithful offer take
Of me and all that I can make,
Or else by him my love deny,
And then I'll study how to die.'

SILVIUS Call you this chiding?

CELIA Alas, poor shepherd!

ROSALIND Do you pity him? No, he deserves no pity. Wilt thou love such a woman? What, to make thee an instrument and play false strains upon thee! Not to be endured! Well, go your way to her (for I see love hath made thee a tame snake) and say this to her: that if she love me, I charge her to love thee: if she will not, I will never have her, unless thou entreat for her. If you be a true lover, hence, and not a word; for here comes more company. [*he goes*

OLIVER *comes up hastily by another path*

OLIVER Good morrow, fair ones: pray you, if you know,
Where in the purlieus of this forest stands
A sheepcote fenced about with olive-trees?

CELIA West of this place, down in the neighbour bottom –
The rank of osiers by the murmuring stream
Left on your right hand brings you to the place.
But at this hour the house doth keep itself,
There's none within.

OLIVER If that an eye may profit by a tongue,
Then should I know you by description –
Such garments and such years: 'The boy is fair,
Of female favour, and bestows himself
Like a ripe forester: the woman low,
And browner than her brother.' Are not you
The owner of the house I did inquire for?

CELIA It is no boast, being asked, to say we are.

OLIVER Orlando doth commend him to you both,
And to that youth he calls his Rosalind
He sends this bloody napkin; are you he?

ROSALIND I am: what must we understand by this?

OLIVER Some of my shame, if you will know of me
What man I am, and how, and why, and where
This handkercher was stained.

CELIA I pray you, tell it.

OLIVER When last the young Orlando parted from you
He left a promise to return again
Within an hour, and pacing through the forest,
Chewing the food of sweet and bitter fancy,
Lo, what befel! He threw his eye aside,
And mark what object did present itself!
Under an oak, whose boughs were mossed with age
And high top bald with dry antiquity,
A wretched ragged man, o'ergrown with hair,
Lay sleeping on his back: about his neck
A green and gilded snake had wreathed itself,
Who with her head nimble in threats approached
The opening of his mouth; but suddenly
Seeing Orlando, it unlinked itself,
And with indented glides did slip away
Into a bush: under which bush's shade
A lioness, with udders all drawn dry,
Lay couching, head on ground, with catlike watch,
When that the sleeping man should stir; for 'tis
The royal disposition of that beast
To prey on nothing that doth seem as dead:
This seen, Orlando did approach the man,
And found it was his brother, his elder brother.

CELIA O I have heard him speak of that same brother,
And he did render him the most unnatural
That lived 'mongst men.

OLIVER And well he might so do,
For well I know he was unnatural.

ROSALIND But, to Orlando: did he leave him there,
Food to the sucked and hungry lioness?

OLIVER Twice did he turn his back and purposed so:
But kindness, nobler ever than revenge,
And nature, stronger than his just occasion,
Made him give battle to the lioness,
Who quickly fell before him: in which hurtling
From miserable slumber I awaked.

CELIA Are you his brother?

ROSALIND Was't you he rescued?

CELIA Was't you that did so oft contrive to kill him?
OLIVER 'Twas I; but 'tis not I: I do not shame
To tell you what I was, since my conversion
So sweetly tastes, being the thing I am.
ROSALIND But, for the bloody napkin?
OLIVER By and by.
When from the first to last betwixt us two
Tears our recountments had most kindly bathed,
As how I came into that desert place,
In brief, he led me to the gentle duke,
Who gave me fresh array and entertainment,
Committing me unto my brother's love,
Who led me instantly unto his cave,
There stripped himself, and here upon his arm
The lioness had torn some flesh away,
Which all this while had bled; and now he fainted,
And cried, in fainting, upon Rosalind
Brief, I recovered him, bound up his wound,
And after some small space being strong at heart,
He sent me hither, stranger as I am,
To tell this story, that you might excuse
His broken promise, and to give this napkin,
Dyed in his blood, unto the shepherd youth
That he in sport doth call his Rosalind. [*Rosalind faints*
CELIA Why, how now, Ganymede! Sweet Ganymede!
OLIVER Many will swoon when they do look on blood.
CELIA There is more in it. Cousin, Ganymede!
OLIVER Look, he recovers.
ROSALIND I would I were at home.
CELIA We'll lead you thither.
I pray you, will you take him by the arm?
OLIVER Be of good cheer, youth: you a man!
You lack a man's heart.
ROSALIND I do so, I confess it
Ah, sirrah, a body would think this was well counterfeited. I pray you, tell your brother how well I counterfeited. Heigh-ho!
OLIVER This was not counterfeit. There is too great testimony in your complexion that it was a passion of earnest.

ROSALIND Counterfeit, I assure you.

OLIVER Well then, take a good heart, and counterfeit to be a man.

ROSALIND So I do: but, i'faith, I should have been a woman by right.

CELIA Come, you look paler and paler; pray you, draw homewards. Good sir, go with us.

OLIVER That will I: for I must bear answer back how you excuse my brother, Rosalind.

ROSALIND I shall devise something: but I pray you, commend my counterfeiting to him. Will you go?

[*they descend towards the cottage*

ACT 5 SCENE 1

TOUCHSTONE *and* AUDREY *come through the trees*

TOUCH. We shall find a time, Audrey – patience, gentle Audrey.

AUDREY Faith, the priest was good enough, for all the old gentleman's saying.

TOUCH. A most wicked Sir Oliver, Audrey, a most vile Martext. But, Audrey, there is a youth here in the forest lays claim to you.

AUDREY Ay, I know who 'tis; he hath no interest in me in the world: here comes the man you mean.

WILLIAM *enters the clearing*

TOUCH. It is meat and drink to me to see a clown. By my troth, we that have good wits have much to answer for; we shall be flouting; we cannot hold.

WILLIAM Good ev'n, Audrey.

AUDREY God ye good ev'n, William.

WILLIAM And good ev'n to you, sir.

TOUCH. [*with mock dignity*] Good ev'n, gentle friend. Cover thy head, cover thy head; nay, prithee, be covered. How old are you, friend?

WILLIAM Five-and-twenty, sir.

TOUCH. A ripe age. Is thy name William?

WILLIAM William, sir.

TOUCH. A fair name. Wast born i'th' forest here?

WILLIAM Ay sir, I thank God.

TOUCH. 'Thank God'; a good answer. Art rich?

WILLIAM Faith sir, so so.

TOUCH. 'So so' is good, very good, very excellent good: and yet it is not, it is but so so. Art thou wise?

WILLIAM Ay sir, I have a pretty wit.

TOUCH. Why, thou say'st well. I do now remember a saying: 'The fool doth think he is wise, but the wise man knows himself to be a fool.' [*By this William's mouth is wide open with amazement*] The heathen philosopher, when he had a desire to eat a grape, would open his lips when he put it into his mouth, meaning thereby that grapes were made to eat and lips to open. You do love this maid?

WILLIAM I do, sir.

TOUCH. Give me your hand. Art thou learned?

WILLIAM No, sir.

TOUCH. Then learn this of me – to have, is to have; for it is a figure in rhetoric that drink, being poured out of a cup into a glass, by filling the one doth empty the other; for all your writers do consent that ipse is he: now, you are not ipse, for I am he.

WILLIAM Which he, sir?

TOUCH. He, sir, that must marry this woman. Therefore, you clown, abandon (which is in the vulgar 'leave') the society (which in the boorish is 'company') of this female (which in the common is 'woman'); which together is, 'abandon the society of this female,' or, clown, thou perishest; or, to thy better understanding, diest; or, to wit, I kill thee, make thee away, translate thy life into death, thy liberty into bondage: I will deal in poison with thee, or in bastinado, or in steel; I will bandy with thee in faction; I will o'er-run thee with policy; I will kill thee a hundred and fifty ways – therefore tremble and depart.

AUDREY Do, good William.

WILLIAM God rest you merry, sir. [*he goes*

CORIN *appears and calls*

CORIN Our master and mistress seek you: come, away, away.

TOUCH. Trip, Audrey, trip, Audrey – I attend, I attend.

[*they run off towards the cottage*

A night passes

SCENE 2

OLIVER *and* ORLANDO *(his arm in a scarf) seated on a bank*

ORLANDO Is't possible that on so little acquaintance you should like her? That but seeing you should love her? And loving woo? And, wooing, she should grant? And will you persever to enjoy her?

OLIVER Neither call the giddiness of it in question, the poverty of her, the small acquaintance, my sudden wooing, nor her sudden consenting; but say with me, I love Aliena; say with her that she loves me; consent with both that we may enjoy each other: it shall be to your good; for my father's house and all the revenue that was old Sir Rowland's will I estate upon you, and here live and die a shepherd.

ROSALIND *is seen coming in the distance*

ORLANDO You have my consent. Let your wedding be tomorrow: thither will I invite the duke and all's contented followers. Go you and prepare Aliena; for look you, here comes my Rosalind.

ROSALIND God save you, brother.

OLIVER And you, fair sister. [*he goes*

ROSALIND O my dear Orlando, how it grieves me to see thee wear thy heart in a scarf.

ORLANDO It is my arm.

ROSALIND I thought thy heart had been wounded with the claws of a lion.

ORLANDO Wounded it is, but with the eyes of a lady.

ROSALIND Did your brother tell you how I counterfeited to swoon, when he showed me your handkercher?

ORLANDO Ay and greater wonders than that.

ROSALIND O, I know where you are: nay, 'tis true: there was never any thing so sudden but the fight of two rams, and Caesar's thrasonical brag of 'I came, saw, and overcame': for your brother and my sister no sooner met but they looked; no sooner looked but they loved; no sooner loved but they sighed; no sooner sighed but they asked one another the reason; no sooner knew the reason but they sought the remedy: and in these degrees have they made a pair of stairs to marriage, which they will climb incontinent, or else be incontinent before marriage: they are in the very wrath of love, and they will together; clubs cannot part them.

ORLANDO They shall be married tomorrow; and I will bid the duke to the nuptial. But, O, how bitter a thing it is to look into happiness through another man's eyes! By so much the more shall I tomorrow be at the height of heart-heaviness, by how much I shall think my brother happy in having what he wishes for.

ROSALIND Why then, tomorrow I cannot serve your turn for Rosalind?

ORLANDO I can live no longer by thinking.

ROSALIND I will weary you then no longer with idle talking. Know of me then, for now I speak to some purpose, that I know you are a gentleman of good conceit: I speak not this that you should bear a good opinion of my knowledge, insomuch I say I know you are; neither do I labour for a greater esteem than may in some little measure draw a belief from you, to do yourself good, and not to grace me. Believe then, if you please, that I can do strange things: I have, since I was three year old, conversed with a magician, most profound in his art, and yet not damnable. If you do love Rosalind so near the heart as your gesture cries it out, when your brother marries Aliena, shall you marry her. I know into what straits of fortune she is driven, and it is not impossible to me, if it appear not inconvenient to you, to set her before your eyes tomorrow, human as she is, and without any danger.

ORLANDO Speak'st thou in sober meanings?

ROSALIND By my life I do, which I tender dearly, though I say I am a magician. Therefore, put you in your best array, bid your friends; for if you will be married tomorrow, you shall; and to Rosalind, if you will.

SILVIUS *and* PHEBE *draw near*

Look, here comes a lover of mine and a lover of hers.

PHEBE Youth, you have done me much ungentleness,
To show the letter that I writ to you.

ROSALIND I care not if I have: it is my study
To seem despiteful and ungentle to you:
You are there followed by a faithful shepherd –
Look upon him, love him; he worships you.

PHEBE Good shepherd, tell this youth what 'tis to love.

SILVIUS It is to be all made of sighs and tears,
And so am I for Phebe.

PHEBE And I for Ganymede.

ORLANDO And I for Rosalind.

ROSALIND And I for no woman.

SILVIUS It is to be all made of faith and service,
And so am I for Phebe.

PHEBE And I for Ganymede.

ORLANDO And I for Rosalind.

ROSALIND And I for no woman.

SILVIUS It is to be all made of fantasy,
All made of passion, and all made of wishes,
All adoration, duty and observance,
All humbleness, all patience, and impatience,
All purity, all trial, all obedience;
And so am I for Phebe.

PHEBE And so am I for Ganymede.

ORLANDO And so am I for Rosalind.

ROSALIND And so am I for no woman.

PHEBE [*to Rosalind*].
If this be so, why blame you me to love you?

SILVIUS [*to Phebe*].
If this be so, why blame you me to love you?

ORLANDO If this be so, why blame you me to love you?

ROSALIND Who do you speak to, 'Why blame you me to love you?'

ORLANDO To her that is not here, nor doth not hear.

ROSALIND Pray you no more of this, 'tis like the howling of Irish wolves against the Moon. [*to Silvius*] I will help you, if I can. [*to Phebe*] I would love you, if I could. To-morrow meet me all together. [*to Phebe*] I will marry you, if ever I marry woman, and I'll be married tomorrow. [*to Orlando*] I will satisfy you, if ever I satisfied man, and you shall be married tomorrow. [*to Silvius*] I will content you, if what pleases you contents you, and you shall be married to morrow. [*to Orlando*] As you love Rosalind, meet. [*to Silvius*] As you love Phebe, meet. And as I love no woman, I'll meet. So, fare you well; I have left you commands.

SILVIUS I'll not fail, if I live.

PHEBE Nor I.

ORLANDO Nor I. [*they disperse*

SCENE 3

TOUCHSTONE *and* AUDREY *enter the clearing*

TOUCH. Tomorrow is the joyful day, Audrey.
Tomorrow will we be married.

AUDREY I do desire it with all my heart: and I hope it is no dishonest desire to desire to be a woman of the world. Here come two of the banished duke's pages.

Two pages run up

1 PAGE Well met, honest gentleman.

TOUCH. By my troth, well met. Come, sit, sit, and a song.

2 PAGE We are for you: sit i'th' middle.

1 PAGE Shall we clap into't roundly, without hawking or spitting or saying we are hoarse, which are the only prologues to a bad voice?

2 PAGE I'faith i'faith; and both in a tune, like two gipsies on a horse.

Song

It was a lover and his lass,
With a hey, and a ho, and a hey nonino:
That o'er the green corn-field did pass,
In spring time, the only pretty ring time,
When birds do sing, hey ding a ding, ding,
Sweet lovers love the spring.

Between the acres of the rye,
With a hey, and a ho, and a hey nonino:

These pretty country folks would lie,
In spring time, the only pretty ring time,
When birds do sing, hey ding a ding, ding,
Sweet lovers love the spring.

This carol they began that hour,
With a hey, and a ho, and a hey nonino:
How that life was but a flower,
In spring time, the only pretty ring time,
When birds do sing, hey ding a ding, ding,
Sweet lovers love the spring.

And therefore take the present time,
With a hey, and a ho, and a hey nonino:
For love is crownéd with the prime,
In spring time, the only pretty ring time.
When birds do sing, hey ding a ding, ding,
Sweet lovers love the spring.

TOUCH. Truly, young gentlemen, though there was no great matter in the ditty, yet the note was very untuneable.

I PAGE You are deceived, sir – we kept time, we lost not our time.

TOUCH. By my troth, yes; I count it but time lost to hear such a foolish song. God buy you, and God mend your voices! Come, Audrey. [*they go*

A night passes

SCENE 4

The clearing near the sheepcote (as before)

The exiled DUKE, AMIENS, JAQUES, ORLANDO, OLIVER, *and* CELIA

DUKE Dost thou believe, Orlando, that the boy
Can do all this that he hath promised?

ORLANDO I sometimes do believe, and sometimes do not,
As those that fear they hope, and know they fear.

ROSALIND, SILVIUS, *and* PHEBE *join the company*

ROSALIND Patience once more, whiles our compact is urged:

You say, if I bring in your Rosalind,
You will bestow her on Orlando here?

DUKE That would I, had I kingdoms to give with her.

ROSALIND And you say you will have her, when I bring her?

ORLANDO That would I, were I of all kingdoms king.

ROSALIND You say you'll marry me, if I be willing?

PHEBE That will I, should I die the hour after.

ROSALIND But if you do refuse to marry me,
You'll give yourself to this most faithful shepherd?

PHEBE So is the bargain.

ROSALIND You say that you'll have Phebe, if she will?

SILVIUS Though to have her and death were both one thing.

ROSALIND I have promised to make all this matter even.
Keep you your word, O duke, to give your daughter –
You yours, Orlando, to receive his daughter:
Keep your word, Phebe, that you'll marry me,
Or else refusing me, to wed this shepherd:
Keep your word, Silvius, that you'll marry her,
If she refuse me – and from hence I go,
To make these doubts all even.

[she beckons to Celia and they depart together

DUKE I do remember in this shepherd-boy
Some lively touches of my daughter's favour.

ORLANDO My lord, the first time that I ever saw him,
Methought he was a brother to your daughter:
But, my good lord, this boy is forest-born,
And hath been tutored in the rudiments
Of many desperate studies by his uncle,
Whom he reports to be a great magician,
Obscured in the circle of this forest.

TOUCHSTONE *and* AUDREY *enter the clearing*

JAQUES There is, sure, another flood toward, and these couples are coming to the ark. Here comes a pair of very strange beasts, which in all tongues are called fools.

TOUCH. Salutation and greeting to you all!

JAQUES Good my lord, bid him welcome: this is the motley-minded gentleman that I have so often met in the forest: he hath been a courtier, he swears.

TOUCH. If any man doubt that, let him put me to my purgation.

I have trod a measure; I have flattered a lady; I have been politic with my friend, smooth with mine enemy; I have undone three tailors; I have had four quarrels, and like to have fought one.

JAQUES And how was that ta'en up?

TOUCH. Faith, we met, and found the quarrel was upon the seventh cause.

JAQUES How seventh cause? Good my lord, like this fellow.

DUKE I like him very well.

TOUCH. God'ild you, sir, I desire you of the like. I press in here, sir, amongst the rest of the country copulatives, to swear and to forswear, according as marriage binds and blood breaks. [*he waves towards Audrey*] A poor virgin, sir, an ill-favoured thing, sir but mine own – a poor humour of mine, sir, to take that that no man else will: rich honesty dwells like a miser, sir, in a poor house, as your pearl in your foul oyster.

DUKE By my faith, he is very swift and sententious.

TOUCH. According to the fool's bolt, sir, and such dulcet diseases.

JAQUES But, for the seventh cause. How did you find the quarrel on the seventh cause?

TOUCH. Upon a lie seven times removed – bear your body more seeming, Audrey – as thus, sir: I did dislike the cut of a certain courtier's beard: he sent me word, if I said his beard was not cut well, he was in the mind it was: this is called the Retort Courteous. If I sent him word again 'it was not well cut', he would send me word, he cut it to please himself: this is called the Quip Modest. If again 'it was not well cut', he disabled my judgment: this is called the Reply Churlish. If again 'it was not well cut', he would answer, I spake not true: this is called the Reproof Valiant. If again 'it was not well cut', he would say, I lie: this is called the Countercheck Quarrelsome: and so to the Lie Circumstantial and the Lie Direct.

JAQUES And how oft did you say his beard was not well cut?

TOUCH. I durst go no further than the Lie Circumstantial: nor he durst not give me the Lie Direct: and so we measured swords and parted.

JAQUES Can you nominate in order now the degrees of the lie?

TOUCH. O sir, we quarrel in print – by the book, as you have books for good manners. I will name you the degrees. The first, the Retort Courteous; the second, the Quip Modest; the third, the Reply Churlish; the fourth, the Reproof Valiant; the fifth, the Countercheck Quarrelsome; the sixth, the Lie with Circumstance; the seventh, the Lie Direct. All these you may avoid, but the Lie Direct; and you may avoid that too, with an If. I knew when seven justices could not take up a quarrel, but when the parties were met themselves, one of them thought but of an If; as, 'If you said so, then I said so': and they shook hands and swore brothers. Your If is the only peace-maker; much virtue in If.

JAQUES Is not this a rare fellow, my lord? He's as good at any thing, and yet a fool!

DUKE He uses his folly like a stalking-horse, and under the presentation of that he shoots his wit.

Enter, as in a masque, persons representing HYMEN *and his train, together with* ROSALIND *and* CELIA *in their proper habits. Still music'*

HYMEN [*sings*] Then is there mirth in heaven,
When earthly things made even
Atone together.
Good duke, receive thy daughter,
Hymen from heaven brought her,
Yea, brought her hither,
That thou mightst join her hand with his
Whose heart within her bosom is.

ROSALIND [*to the Duke*] To you I give myself, for I am yours.
[*to Orlando*] To you I give myself, for I am yours.

DUKE If there be truth in sight, you are my daughter.

ORLANDO If there be truth in sight, you are my Rosalind.

PHEBE If sight and shape be true,
Why then, my love adieu!

ROSALIND I'll have no father, if you be not he:
I'll have no husband, if you be not he:
Nor ne'er wed woman, if you be not she.

HYMEN Peace, ho! I bar confusion.
'Tis I must make conclusion

Of these most strange events:
Here's eight that must take hands,
To join in Hymen's bands,
If truth holds true contents.
You and you no cross shall part:
You and you are heart in heart:
You to his love must accord,
Or have a woman to your lord.
You and you are sure together,
As the winter to foul weather.
Whiles a wedlock-hymn we sing,
Feed yourselves with questioning;
That reason wonder may diminish,
How thus we met, and these things finish.

Choric song

Wedding is great Juno's crown,
O blessèd bond of board and bed:
'Tis Hymen peoples every town,
High wedlock then be honourèd:
Honour, high honour and renown,
To Hymen, god of every town!

DUKE O my dear niece, welcome thou art to me.
Even daughter, welcome, in no less degree.

PHEBE [*to Silvius*]
I will not eat my word, now thou art mine,
Thy faith my fancy to thee doth combine.

Enter JAQUES DE BOYS

JAQ. DE B. Let me have audience for a word or two:
I am the second son of old Sir Rowland,
That bring these tidings to this fair assembly.
Duke Frederick, hearing how that every day
Men of great worth resorted to this forest,
Addressed a mighty power, which were on foot,
In his own conduct, purposely to take
His brother here and put him to the sword:
And to the skirts of this wild wood he came;
Where, meeting with an old religious man,
After some question with him, was converted

Both from his enterprise and from the world:
His crown bequeathing to his banished brother,
And all their lands restored to them again
That were with him exiled. This to be true,
I do engage my life.

DUKE Welcome, young man;
Thou offer'st fairly to thy brothers' wedding:
To one his lands withheld, and to the other
A land itself at large, a potent dukedom.
First, in this forest, let us do those ends
That here were well begun and well begot:
And after, every of this happy number,
That have endured shrewd days and nights with us,
Shall share the good of our returnéd fortune,
According to the measure of their states.
Meantime, forget this new-fall'n dignity,
And fall into our rustic revelry.
Play, music! And you brides and bridegrooms all,
With measure heaped in joy, to th' measures fall.

JAQUES Sir, by your patience – [*he stays the music*
[*to Jaques de Boys*] If I heard you rightly,
The duke hath put on a religious life,
And thrown into neglect the pompous court?

JAQUES B. He hath.

JAQUES To him will I: out of these convertites
There is much matter to be heard and learned . . .
[*to the Duke*] You to your former honour I bequeath,
Your patience and your virtue well deserves it:
[*to Orlando*]
You to a love, that your true faith doth merit:
[*to Oliver*] You to your land, and love, and great allies:
[*to Silvius*] You to a long and well-deservéd bed:
[*to Touchstone*]
And you to wrangling, for thy loving voyage
Is but for two months victualled. So to your
pleasures;
I am for other than for dancing measures.

DUKE Stay, Jaques, stay.

JAQUES To see no pastime, I: what you would have

I'll stay to know at your abandoned cave.

[*he turns from them*

DUKE Proceed, proceed: we will begin these rites,
As we do trust they'll end, in true delights.

Music and dance

EPILOGUE

spoken by ROSALIND

It is not the fashion to see the lady the epilogue: but it is no more unhandsome than to see the lord the prologue. If it be true that good wine needs no bush, 'tis true that a good play needs no epilogue: yet to good wine they do use good bushes; and good plays prove the better by the help of good epilogues . . . What a case am I in then, that am neither a good epilogue nor cannot insinuate with you in the behalf of a good play! I am not furnished like a beggar, therefore to beg will not become me: my way is to conjure you, and I'll begin with the women. I charge you, O women, for the love you bear to men, to like as much of this play as please you; and I charge you, O men, for the love you bear to women – as I perceive by your simpering, none of you hates them – that between you and the women the play may please. If I were a woman, I would kiss as many of you as had beards that pleased me, complexions that liked me, and breaths that I defied not: and, I am sure, as many as have good beards, or good faces, or sweet breaths, will, for my kind offer, when I make curtsy, bid me farewell.

TWELFTH NIGHT

INTRODUCTION

The title of *Twelfth Night* calls to mind the festivities traditionally held on 6 January, the twelfth night after Christmas. Twelfth night marks the end of the Christmas season and in Elizabethan England was a holiday characterised by revelry, excess, and a temporary but joyous overturning of the social structures and codes of behaviour that usually regulated life. It constituted a moment of licensed anarchy before the harsher regime of winter and self-denial once again closed in. Hence the title of *Twelfth Night* draws upon the associations that accompany it to enrich an understanding of the play. A tussle between the ordered regulation of society on the one hand, and a hearty disregard for such stifling influences on the other, forms its thematic backdrop.

Romantics like to believe that the play was first performed on twelfth night (6 January), 1601 at the royal palace of Whitehall. A play, not referred to specifically by title but described as both comic and musical, certainly was performed in front of Queen Elizabeth that night, and this play *may* have been *Twelfth Night.* The evidence, however, is far from conclusive. What is beyond doubt is that a year later, in early February 1602, a law student, John Manningham, made a diary entry in which he referred specifically to a performance of *Twelfth Night* given at the Middle Temple. Although there is nothing to suggest that this was its first performance, there is sufficient internal evidence to suggest that it was still relatively new when Manningham saw it. An Italian nobleman named Don Virginio Orsino had been Queen Elizabeth's guest for the night of the unnamed comic and musical performance at the end of the Christmas season the previous year. It is reasonable to assume that the name Orsino in Shakespeare's play is intended as a reference to Elizabeth's guest. The intelligibility of this reference for a contemporary audience would have depended upon the real Orsino's visit already having become a matter of comment. It therefore seems probable that the play's first performance fell, less romantically than some would have it, at some point between twelfth night 1601 and early February 1602.

No text of *Twelfth Night* has survived from its early years of production. The text of the play we now have is taken from the First Folio edition of Shakespeare's plays, published seven years after his death in 1623.

Plot Summary

Twelfth Night is driven by two interrelated plots. The main plot concerns the tangled relationships of four noble lovers. We discover, at the opening of the play, that there has been a shipwreck off the shores of Illyria. From this wreck Viola and her twin brother Sebastian are separately washed ashore. Each is unharmed, although distressed at the thought that the other may have been drowned. Viola decides to disguise herself as a eunuch, taking the name Cesario, in order to enable her to find employment in a foreign land. She is duly taken on in the service of the Duke Orsino. Believing that she is indeed a boy, he commissions her to deliver declarations of love on his behalf to the Lady Olivia, a neighbouring countess in mourning for her dead brother. This commission becomes increasingly vexing to Viola as she realises both that she herself is in love with Orsino and that Olivia, unaware that the messenger before her is in fact a woman, is in turn falling in love with her. This unhappy triangle is rescued from impasse by the arrival of Viola's twin brother Sebastian. Sebastian pleases Olivia just as much as Viola had done, and, unlike Viola, is happy to reciprocate Olivia's feelings. Viola's subsequent revelation that she is a woman in disguise prompts Orsino to declare his love for her. Thus these four characters are able to end the play happily as two newly-formed couples.

The sub-plot concerns the fates of a more mixed assembly of characters, all of whom form part of Olivia's household for one reason or another, and the various developments of their preposterous ventures. Olivia's impoverished uncle, Sir Toby Belch, is a bon viveur who manages to live off the generosity of his niece and the stupidity of his rich friend Sir Andrew Aguecheek. Sir Andrew is persuaded to stay at Olivia's, bankrolling Sir Toby's drinking, under the delusion that Olivia will one day reciprocate his love for her. These two form an alliance with Maria, Olivia's gentlewoman, and Feste, the peripatetic clown, in common antipathy towards Malvolio, Olivia's pompous steward. So irritated are they by his superciliousness that they engineer a plan to teach him a lesson. They convince him, via a forged letter, that Olivia loves him. The letter instructs him to show himself amenable to her love by wearing cross-gartered yellow stockings. When he appears in this ludicrous garb, Olivia is baffled by the excesses of his behaviour and orders that he be kept, in his own interests, under a careful surveillance. The conspirators take this as justification for locking Malvolio in a dark room and tormenting him almost out of his wits. When he is finally released from imprisonment, and discovers that not only does Olivia not love him but in fact is by then already married to Sebastian, he feels understandably embittered at the humiliating treatment he has received. Meanwhile Sir Andrew's futile courtship of Olivia necessarily comes to an end, and Sir Toby marries Maria by way of recompense for his mischief-making.

In common with the unnamed play performed on twelfth night 1601, *Twelfth Night is* both comic and musical. It depends for much of its humour upon the Shakespearean comic convention of impenetrable disguises and consequent mistaken identities. The comedy, however, is far less consistently skittish than it is in the bulk of Shakespeare's earlier comedies. Much of the play is marked by a wistfulness, and even a poignant sadness, that signals a shift in the dramatic tone of his comedies. In an untroubled comedy, all tangles may be untangled, all wrongs righted, all separated characters reunited, and all love found to be gloriously requited in the final resolution of the traumas generated by the preceding action. *Twelfth Night*, by contrast, does not end so neatly. The four fortunate lovers *are*, after all their misunderstandings, finally enveloped in a warm romantic haze. Several key characters are, however, bleakly excluded from the cosiness. Indeed, it is symptomatic of the uneasiness at the end of the play that there is no equivalent to the inclusive dance found, for example, at the end of *Much Ado About Nothing*. *Twelfth Night* closes instead with a rueful little song about the persistent presence of the wind and rain, sung by the solitary figure of Feste, the play's embittered and (in ironic contrast to his name) very *un*festive clown. Thus, at the end of the play, the characters are starkly divided into those whom the comic ending can accommodate, and those whom it refuses, who are left loveless and aggrieved for one reason or another. These excluded misfits disrupt the harmony of the close of this play and, more generally, introduce signs of fracture into the idea of a fully harmonious ending to Shakespeare's comedies. *Twelfth Night* marks a watershed in Shakespeare's comic writing: the comic ending would never again be unclouded by anxiety.

The Four Lovers

At the beginning of *Romeo and Juliet*, Romeo believes himself in love with the remote Rosaline. Similarly, for most of *Twelfth Night* the Duke Orsino believes himself in love with the inaccessible Lady Olivia. Like Romeo, Orsino proves to be more self-indulgently fascinated by the nature of his own languishing soul than in the supposed object of his affections. Indeed, so adept has Orsino become at navel-gazing that Olivia is frequently little more than the excuse for further maudlin contemplation of his own lovelorn condition:

> That instant was I turn'd into a hart,
> And my desires, like fell and cruel hounds,
> Ever since pursue me. (1.1.20–22)

Conventionally, in a hunting metaphor uttered by a lover, the lady would be represented as the hunted object of her lover's desires. Here, however, Orsino instinctively claims for himself the metaphorical roles both of the hunter ('fell and cruel hounds') *and* of the hunted ('a hart'). He thereby unconsciously, but tellingly, excludes Olivia from the ground of the chase entirely. His love for Olivia is much more about himself than it is about her. As is evident from Act 1 scene 4 and Act 2 scene 4, he is more attentive, and in much more sensuous detail, to the particularity of his page Cesario (whom the audience knows to be Viola in disguise) than he is to the reality of Olivia. Olivia remains a remote ideal. Cesario, on the other hand, becomes for Orsino not only a trusted confidant but a disconcertingly attractive person. Orsino cannot allow himself to admit that he is in love with a boy. Whatever label he chooses to attach to his feelings, however, the warmth of his affection is undeniable. Orsino is fortunate in being spared the uncomfortable implications of this unacknowledged love since it is, conveniently, legitimated for him at the end when Cesario is discovered to be a woman – and, because a comic ending requires that things resolve themselves optimally for those on the inside, not just any woman but a woman of noble parentage.

Orsino believes Olivia to be both as physically enclosed and as psychologically turned in upon herself as we have seen him to be:

> . . . like a cloistress she will veiled walk,
> And water once a day her chamber round
> With eye-offending brine. (1.1.27–29)

In fact, Olivia is not as emotionally constrained as her pose of mourning suggests. Her household is much more chaotic and lively than Orsino's, and she herself is considerably more inclined to mirth than is her elegiac, lack-lustre suitor. Whereas he seeks ways of nurturing and intensifying his feelings ('If music be the food of love, play on . . .' 1.1.1), she welcomes distraction from hers. So much so that when Viola arrives to woo her in Orsino's name, Olivia feels obliged to reach for her veil in the vain hope of sustaining the pretence of grief (1.5). This reliance on props, however, fails to convince Viola that she is indeed grief-stricken, and the props are quickly discarded. Olivia asks of Viola repeatedly:

> What are you? What would you?

and these questions, interrogating another's identity and purpose, carry a larger significance that resonates throughout the whole play. Both who Viola *is,* and what she *would* in Olivia's house, are complicated by layers of dissemblance and of disjuncture between what seems and what is. But when, later, Viola starts trying to alert her audience to this disjuncture – 'I am not what I am' (3.1.138) – Olivia quickly veers away from an interest in the world as it is and pursues instead a desperate attempt to make it conform to what she would like it to be:

> I would you were as I would have you be. (3.1.144)

Twelfth Night is unique among Shakespeare's plays in having an alternative title, *What You Will*. This self-consciously casual title is peculiarly apt in relation to a play in which so many things, including notions of the self, seem to be changeable according to whim. In transforming herself into the boy Cesario, for example, Viola demonstrates that 'what you will' may redefine what you are. In her exchange with Viola, Olivia tries to extend the formula so that what *she* wills may transform what someone *else* is. Her 'What are you? What would you?' questions are therefore left hanging. Choosing to ignore the half-answers that Viola supplies saves her from confronting the inadequacy of her trust in appearances. That which she seeks is, simply, a husband whom she may adore. Viola, for reasons she cannot guess at, repeatedly scorns her advances. Sebastian, by contrast, having been mistaken by Olivia for his twin, welcomes her bafflingly enthusiastic attentions. Olivia does not stop to query what must seem to her like an inexplicable volte-face in the object of her affections, but rather marches her now miraculously compliant lover straight off to a priest to be married. What she wills is, after all, essentially straightforward and she is fortunate, albeit through the most improbable of circumstances, in finding someone else whose will happens to coincide with her own – or at least to be readily bendable to it:

> OLIVIA ... would thou'dst be rul'd by me!
> SEBASTIAN Madam, I will. (4.1.60–61)

Prior to Sebastian's arrival, the problems in Illyria had become intensified to a point of maximum confusion and potential distress. Only the division of Viola into a male and female self, to satisfy Olivia and Orsino respectively, could possibly have ensured any harmony at the play's close. Sebastian's arrival makes it seem that just such a cleaving has been miraculously achieved, causing Antonio to exclaim:

> How have you made division of yourself? (5.1.214)

Sebastian is, in effect, the *deus ex machina* of the play – the late and dramatic arrival, as if from heaven, to solve otherwise insoluble difficulties. It is his presence that rescues Olivia from unknowingly (and unrequitedly) loving a woman, that enables Orsino to acknowledge his attraction to a person he had thought denied him, and that liberates Viola to be a woman once more by replacing her feigned manhood with its real counterpart.

Viola initially adopted her male disguise in the interests of self-protection while friendless in a foreign land. Like Rosalind in *As You Like It*, she enjoys a conspiratorial alliance with the audience in discussing her role-playing:

> A little thing would make me tell them how much I lack of a man. (3.4.283–84)

The audience is consequently 'in' on all the misunderstandings, jokes and ironies generated by the situation. As much expression as suppression of herself is detectable in her act as she draws upon latent potential within herself that would, presumably, have remained largely unexpressed in her female self. Thus she is resourceful, energetic, witty, impudent, stubborn. In the interests of womankind at large, and of herself in particular, she uses her role in a gentle crusade to jostle Orsino out of some of his more rigid and unthinking prejudices. Moreover, her male social identity enables her to do this without being suspected of herself having a vested interest:

> ORSINO There is no woman's sides
> Can bide the beating of so strong a passion
> As love doth give my heart . . .
>
> VIOLA . . . In faith, they are as true of heart as we.
> (2.4.92–94,105)

In other crucial ways, however, the role trammels her, preventing her from expressing her love for Orsino (in whose courtship of Olivia she finds herself the reluctant agent). Ultimately, therefore, she believes that the concealment of her love 'like a worm i'th' bud' (2.4.110) is destroying her from within.

At the end of *Twelfth Night* Viola admits to the deceit that she has practised on the inhabitants of Illyria by means of her disguise. She does not, however, (unlike Rosalind at the close of *As You Like It*) exchange her 'masculine usurp'd attire' for 'maiden weeds' (5.1.242,247) before the end of the play. The disclosure in itself is sufficient to render acceptable Orsino's attraction to her. Even in the subsequent overtures of love that he makes towards her, however, he persists in referring to her as 'boy' and in addressing her as 'Cesario':

> For so you shall be, while you are a man; (5.1.374)

He will, of course, delight in adjusting his naming and treatment of 'Cesario' when a womanly appearance makes it clear that such an adjustment is necessary. Until such time as his eyes confirm for him that this is indeed a woman before him, however, he cannot even say, 'For so you shall be awhile you *seem* a man', since in Orsino's mind there is minimal discrepancy between seeming and being.

For Orsino, then, the appearance of things *is* their reality, or at least creates the only expression of reality that can be sensibly engaged with. And indeed, on one level he is right. Through regular social interaction, Viola has created for herself a new, male self with a new name. That self and the name that represents it have been consolidated through recognition and usage by others. From the point of view of the inhabitants of Illyria, therefore, her revelation of herself as Viola is the creation of a new self, not the reversion to an old one, for they have no prior knowledge of the existence of a Viola. Orsino's inability to adjust his naming of Viola at the end of the play questions what self there can be independent of societal recognition. Although in Illyria Viola is as much a woman as she ever was back in Messaline (a womanhood complicated on the Elizabethan stage by the fact that her part would have been played by a boy actor), her socially recognised identity in this new land is male. The play therefore poses a question about the extent to which gender, and the expectations that accompany it, are socially constructed entities. By stepping across the gender divide, and proving to be virtually interchangeable with Sebastian, Viola highlights two, apparently contradictory, truths. The first is that some of the more rigid distinctions between the sexes derive only from social restriction and lack of opportunity, rather than from innate difference. The second is that the attempt to deny one's gender for a time can make one, by reaction, more fully cognisant of its significance to who one is. Viola is therefore glad at the prospect of once again seeming to be the thing she actually is, since, in her male role, she found that some of the things that most define her were necessarily suppressed.

These four lovers – Orsino, Olivia, Sebastian, Viola – create the warmth for the play's ending. Their union, however, is won at a cost, and the play suggests that the cost is borne by others.

The Misfits

Antonio, the sea-captain washed ashore from the shipwreck with Sebastian, generally receives very little critical attention. However, he is noteworthy for delivering some of the most strongly felt and affecting declarations of love in the play. His self-effacing adoration of Sebastian makes him long to be with him, if only to do him service:

> If you will not murder me for my love, let me be your servant. (2.1.31–32)

This self-sacrificial love carries a far more acute charge than mere friendship:

> I could not stay behind you: my desire
> More sharp than filéd steel, did spur me forth. (3.3.4–5)

He offers up his own purse, and indeed his own safety, in the service and protection of his beloved young master, yet these dramatic gestures meet with minimal acknowledgement. At one painful moment, arising from one of the Viola-Sebastian confusions (2.4), he even thinks he is being publicly disowned by the man he has faithfully served. At the end of the play, Antonio is supernumerary. Neither he, nor the intensity of his love for another man, can be absorbed into an harmonious ending. Instead he is obliged to observe from the margins as his beloved gives himself without reservation to a woman whom he has only just met. In Act 1 Olivia herself had drawn attention to the random nature of love that cannot be guaranteed to follow merit, or even suitability:

> Your lord does know my mind. I cannot love him.
> Yet I suppose him virtuous, know him noble,
> Of great estate, of fresh and stainless youth;
> In voices well divulg'd, free, learn'd, and valiant,
> And in dimension, and the shape of nature,
> A gracious person. But yet I cannot love him (1.5.244–49)

It is the cruel irony of love that it is rarely born of deserving, following instead its own more haphazard whims. Antonio suffers directly from exactly this injustice when he is cast aside by Sebastian, and with cavalier negligence, in favour of Olivia. If the rain which, as Feste says, 'raineth every day' (5.1.380) is to be taken as indicating anything about this world beyond simply its weather, Antonio is certainly among those most vulnerable to its emotional ravages.

Feste is very aware of the unpleasantness and wilful delusions at the heart of much of society. He is a clown of the most unfrolicsome kind. Rather he makes piquant comment, with the impunity offered to 'an allowed fool' (1.5.88), on the unacknowledged folly of those around him. He interrogates and lampoons the trust that others have in appearances, and does not himself seem to believe in the stable identity of anything. In a world in which little is what it seems, Feste's refusal to treat anything as reliable cannot be considered an unreasonable response. His maverick exchange with Viola at the beginning of Act 3 demonstrates that Feste's scepticism in this respect extends to his attitude to words, which are, of course, the very stuff of his trade as professional wit and wordsmith. Just as people may not be trusted as reliable communicators of a reality that transcends superficial appearance, neither, argues Feste, can words:

> Words are very rascals since bonds disgraced them. (3.1.19)

The bonds which might be expected to connect a word to a specific meaning, that might ground it in a knowable semantic place have, claims Feste, abandoned their responsibilities in this respect. Cut free of these bonds, words in Illyria operate amidst the plethora of deceptive appearances as further untrustworthy agents of meaning. A sentence may as easily be turned inside out as 'a chev'ril glove' (3.1.12). By a little deft manipulation, it can be made to mean something other than – even the opposite of – what at first seems. In Illyria, a eunuch may be found to be a girl, a self-proclaimed lover to have an unattached heart, a woman apparently in mourning to be a thoroughly mirthful spirit, the most rigid upholder of societal structures to be himself yearning to break free of them, and the words that might otherwise have given some stability to a world thus in flux to be slippery and chameleon.

Feste himself is as free of any 'bonds' as are the words whose 'wantonness' he proclaims to Viola (3.1.14). He does not belong precisely either in Olivia's or in Orsino's household, but floats between them motivated apparently by a whimsical pursuit of distraction and financial reward. He does not even necessarily belong in Illyria, and at his first appearance is upbraided for his long and unexplained absence. Feste is, then, from the first an outsider, an observer not a participator, acknowledging no bond to person or place. It is appropriate that at the play's close it should fall to him, a natural commentator on the behaviour of others, to deliver the final wistfully detached comment.

Malvolio, the self-important steward in Olivia's household, has a gift for making enemies. He humiliates Feste in front of Olivia and irritates Sir Toby, Sir Andrew and Maria by pompously pouring scorn on their late night revelling. The confrontation between these noisy revellers and Malvolio (2.2) represents one of the central conflicts of the play – that between licence and rule, revelry and regulation, decadence and puritanism. Malvolio, with puritanical fervour, would like everything to be regulated. Sir Toby, with an extravagant joie de vivre, would like everything to be licensed. Malvolio believes in rigidly upholding the structures of society and so objects to 'this uncivil rule' (2.3.117). Sir Toby believes in living according to the festival spirit and so champions the cause of 'cakes and ale' (2.3.110). As recompense for his high-handedness, Maria and the others decide to make Malvolio their dupe. They appeal directly to his vanity by persuading him that Olivia loves him, and he proves to be entirely susceptible to such flattery. He is induced to wear cross-gartered yellow stockings in order to signal to Olivia his compliance with her supposed will. The arch-upholder of established social structures is thus convinced that he himself should disrupt them by aspiring to rise above his allotted position. He aims, therefore, to become what he (secretly) wills – a nobleman by marriage. The festive yellow garb he is instructed to wear is entirely out of keeping with his usual severe demeanour. What the revellers seem to be attempting is to construct a revelling spirit out of the most unpromising and unfestive of raw materials. Olivia is understandably baffled by the self-contradictory version of Malvolio that is produced by this mischievous project. And Malvolio himself, far from being liberated by abandoning his new style of dress and demeanour, feels himself literally constricted by it:

> This does make some obstruction in the blood, this cross-gartering; but what of that? (3.4.20–21)

Malvolio demonstrates that someone cannot be *made* festive by external interference. His instinct is always to curb festivity, and those whose festivities he has curbed make a mockery of him by converting him into an unwitting item of entertainment himself. Sir Toby makes explicit at the beginning of Act 2 scene 5 that their plan is to bait Malvolio like a bear. Bear-baiting was a popular form of Elizabethan entertainment staged in an open-air galleried theatre, very similar to the public playhouses. So similar, in fact, that The Hope, close to the more famous Globe, doubled as both baiting house and playhouse. A bear would be chained to a stake in the pit and a pack of dogs would be set upon it. Bets would be laid about whether the dogs would kill the bear, and how long it would take them to do so. The spectacle for the crowd lay in the gradual destruction of a noble and once powerful beast.

The taunting of Malvolio is, similarly, laid on for the entertainment of the galleries. He is bound and locked in a dark room where he is visited by tormentors. And thus the joke goes too far. The gulling which had seemed funny when Malvolio merely appeared in yellow stockings makes an audience increasingly uncomfortable as the torments increase. In Act 1, Malvolio had himself, in discussing Feste, drawn attention to the crucial role of an appreciative audience in the life of a joke:

> . . . unless you laugh and minister occasion to him, he is gagged. (1.5.80–81)

Part of the discomfort involved in watching Twelft*h Night* is that it is an audience's initial laughter at the gulling of Malvolio, and consequent complicity in it, that can seem to have encouraged the tormenting revellers to persist with their mischief. It is we, the audience, who are 'laugh[ing] and minister[ing] occasion' to this particular joke.

At the very end of the play, having been rescued from his imprisonment, Malvolio's bitter parting line is:

I'll be reveng'd on the whole pack of you! (5.1.366)

His use of the word 'pack', suggestive of dogs, testifies to his awareness of exactly the sort of sport that has been had at his expense. Within a few years of the first performance of *Twelfth Night*, Shakespeare was to write *King Lear* (1605) and *Macbeth* (1606). In each of these plays a grander character – Gloucester and Macbeth – represents himself by the same image, as a bear tied to the stake who must stand the course (*King Lear* 3.7.53 and *Macbeth* 5.7.1–2). Malvolio, in his one moment of painful clear-sightedness about his own tormented position, temporarily transcends his previous pomposity and assumes a stature that attaches him credibly to a line of later, more weighty characters. This legacy of feeling and insight is traceable in the first instance through the inherited bear-baiting imagery. Malvolio's threat of revenge is a troubling moment for an audience, since his complaint against 'the whole pack of you' can reverberate with his offstage, as well as his onstage, tormentors. We were happy to see the early stages of the gulling. Shakespeare pulls us into a complicity with the mischief-makers in order then to make us feel guilty at the way our sympathy has tended. As ever in Shakespeare comedies, the audience is made very self-conscious about its own role in having colluded to make the dramatic event happen. The event is even, in some sense, 'what we will', pursuing our fantasies about love, and in Malvolio's case, revenge. Where the absurdly contrived coming together of the four lovers illustrates how plastic and ridiculous our romantic fantasies can be, Malvolio's fall gives us a glimpse of the ugly consequences of our revenge impulse. The romantic union of the rich and beautiful on the one hand, and the humbling of the petty and arrogant on the other, are, suggests the end of *Twelfth Night* to its audience, merely the exaggerated expression of 'what you will'. The uneasiness at the end of the play therefore derives from a recognition that achieving what we will, seeing where our fantasies tend, may not always be entirely pleasant.

In the overall scheme of *Twelfth Night*, notions of confinement and restriction are pitted against an aspiration towards liberty and excess. Olivia's apparent desire for a cloistered existence illustrates a broader belief, in the world of the play, in the value of containment and denial. By repeatedly articulating the need for containment, the inhabitants of Illyria struggle to keep life 'within the modest limits of order' (1.3.7–8). Such a project is a struggle precisely because it is not the way things naturally tend there. Sir Toby is the most explicit mouthpiece for those influences which pull the other way, replying to the request that he moderate his behaviour by saying:

> I'll confine myself no finer than I am. (1.3.9)

Sir Toby's desire to resist confinement, and his symptomatic celebration of 'cakes and ale' as a gesture of defiance against restraint, is a fairly pervasive attitude in Illyria. Feste, for example, epitomises the will to be free of restriction, moving easily between houses, between paymasters and professional engagements, and owing allegiance to no-one. The most obvious proponents of order and restriction, on the other hand, are Olivia (who tries to closet herself away and admit no mirth into her environment) and Malvolio (who attempts to support the prescribed hierarchies with pedantic inflexibility). Even in these two characters, however, there is a discernible gap between the disciplined position they theoretically wish to adopt and their ability to sustain such a position. Olivia is soon revealed as a woman relieved to exchange her cloistered existence for a life of romance and passion, and Malvolio as a man who wishes to flout the appointed order of things by allowing himself to be plucked by fortune from mediocrity into the ranks of the nobility. The struggle to maintain a disciplined order is undertaken *against* the natural inclinations even of those who most vociferously promote it.

Orsino instructs Viola to 'leap all civil bounds' (1.4.21) in pursuing his suit to Olivia, and the play in some sense dramatises both the placing and the infringement of such 'civil bounds' by exploring the limits of courteous and civilised behaviour. The festival of twelfth night was itself an opportunity to test the limits of social conventions through a joyous overturning of the regulations that usually governed social engagements. However, the abandonment of decorum and civilised restraint was, by the very terms of the celebration, only temporary. The delight to be had in the subversiveness of the festivities was in large part dependent upon an understanding that the world would be restored to a more sober and restrained version of itself the following day. It needed, that is, to be understood as a transient holiday moment, not a revolution. Similarly, the experimental and risky ways of relating to people that have been explored in the play are at its close abandoned in a reaffirmation of more orthodox social patterns. The play may have flirted with more daring categories of social interaction, but at its close it provides a ringing endorsement of establishment values. The playful experiments of the holiday festivities are over. Women are to appear and behave as women once again, marriage to be seen as a desirable way of giving shape and stability to a society, stewards to remain stewards, and any figures of challenge to the solidity of these structures (a homosexual suitor, a servant who aspires to rise) to be necessarily, and vigorously, excluded from the heart of the community.

The scene: Illyria

CHARACTERS IN THE PLAY

ORSINO, *Duke of Illyria*
SEBASTIAN, *brother to Viola*
ANTONIO, *a sea-captain, friend to Sebastian*
Another sea-captain, friend to Viola
VALENTINE, CURIO } *gentlemen attending on the Duke*
SIR TOBY BELCH, kinsman to Olivia
SIR ANDREW AGUECHEEK
MALVOLIO, *steward to Olivia*
FABIAN, *a gentleman in the service of Olivia*
FESTE, *fool to Olivia*
OLIVIA, *a rich countess*
VIOLA, *in love with the Duke*
MARIA, *Olivia's gentlewoman (small of stature)*

Lords, priests, sailors, officers, musicians, and other attendants

TWELFTH NIGHT *or* WHAT YOU WILL

ACT I SCENE I

A room in the Duke's palace

The Duke ORSINO, CURIO *and Lords, hearing music; the music ceases*

DUKE If music be the food of love, play on,
Give me excess of it; that, surfeiting,
The appetite may sicken, and so die.
That strain again! It had a dying fall:
O, it came o'er my ear like the sweet sound
That breathes upon a bank of violets,
Stealing and giving odour. [*music again*]
Enough, no more!
'Tis not so sweet now as it was before.
O spirit of love, how quick and fresh art thou,
That, notwithstanding thy capacity
Receiveth as the sea, nought enters there,
Of what validity and pitch soe'er,
But falls into abatement and low price,
Even in a minute. So full of shapes is fancy,
That it alone is high fantastical.

CURIO Will you go hunt, my lord?

DUKE What, Curio?

CURIO The hart.

DUKE Why, so I do, the noblest that I have:
O, when mine eyes did see Olivia first,
Methought she purged the air of pestilence;
That instant was I turned into a hart,
And my desires, like fell and cruel hounds,
E'er since pursue me.

VALENTINE *enters*

How now? what news from her?

VALENT. So please my lord, I might not be admitted,
But from her handmaid do return this answer:
The element itself, till seven years hence,
Shall not behold her face at ample view;

But like a cloistress she will veiléd walk,
And water once a day her chamber round
With eye-offending brine: all this to season
A brother's dead love, which she would keep fresh
And lasting, in her sad remembrance.

DUKE O, she that hath a heart of that fine frame
To pay this debt of love but to a brother,
How will she love, when the rich golden shaft
Hath killed the flock of all affections else
That live in her; when liver, brain and heart,
These sovereign thrones, are all supplied and filled,
Her sweet perfections, with one self king!
Away before me to sweet beds of flowers –
Love-thoughts lie rich when canopied with bowers.

[*they go*

SCENE 2

Near the sea-coast

VIOLA, CAPTAIN, *and sailors*

VIOLA What country, friends, is this?

CAPTAIN This is Illyria, lady.

VIOLA And what should I do in Illyria?
My brother he is in Elysium.
Perchance he is not drowned: what think you, sailors?

CAPTAIN It is perchance that you yourself were saved.

VIOLA O my poor brother! And so perchance may he be.

CAPTAIN True, madam, and to comfort you with chance,
Assure yourself, after our ship did split,
When you and those poor number saved with you
Hung on our driving boat, I saw your brother,
Most provident in peril, bind himself –
Courage and hope both teaching him the practice –
To a strong mast that lived upon the sea;
Where, like Arion on the dolphin's back,
I saw him hold acquaintance with the waves
So long as I could see.

VIOLA For saying so, there's gold:

Mine own escape unfoldeth to my hope,
Whereto thy speech serves for authority,
The like of him. Know'st thou this country?

CAPTAIN Ay, madam, well, for I was bred and born
Not three hours' travel from this very place.

VIOLA Who governs here?

CAPTAIN A noble duke, in nature as in name.

VIOLA What is his name?

CAPTAIN: Orsino.

VIOLA Orsino: I have heard my father name him.
He was a bachelor then.

CAPTAIN And so is now, or was so very late:
For but a month ago I went from hence,
And then 'twas fresh in murmur – as, you know,
What great ones do the less will prattle of –
That he did seek the love of fair Olivia.

VIOLA What's she?

CAPTAIN A virtuous maid, the daughter of a count
That died some twelvemonth since – then leaving her
In the protection of his son, her brother,
Who shortly also died: for whose dear love,
They say, she hath abjured the company
And sight of men.

VIOLA O, that I served that lady,
And might not be delivered to the world,
Till I had made mine own occasion mellow,
What my estate is.

CAPTAIN That were hard to compass,
Because she will admit no kind of suit,
No, not the duke's.

VIOLA There is a fair behaviour in thee, captain,
And though that nature with a beauteous wall
Doth oft close in pollution, yet of thee
I will believe thou hast a mind that suits
With this thy fair and outward character.
I prithee, and I'll pay thee bounteously,
Conceal me what I am, and be my aid
For such disguise as haply shall become
The form of my intent. I'll serve this duke,

Thou shalt present me as an eunuch to him,
It may be worth thy pains: for I can sing,
And speak to him in many sorts of music,
That will allow me very worth his service.
What else may hap to time I will commit,
Only shape thou thy silence to my wit.

DUKE Be you his eunuch, and your mute I'll be,
When my tongue blabs, then let mine eyes not see!

VIOLA I thank thee: lead me on. [*they go*

SCENE 3

A room in Olivia's house

SIR TOBY BELCH *seated with drink before him, and* MARIA

SIR TOBY What a plague means my niece, to take the death of her brother thus? I am sure care's an enemy to life.

MARIA By my troth, Sir Toby, you must come in earlier o' nights: your cousin, my lady, takes great exceptions to your ill hours.

SIR TOBY Why, let her except before excepted.

MARIA Ay, but you must confine yourself within the modest limits of order.

SIR TOBY Confine? I'll confine myself no finer than I am: these clothes are good enough to drink in, and so be these boots too: an they be not, let them hang themselves in their own straps.

MARIA That quaffing and drinking will undo you: I heard my lady talk of it yesterday: and of a foolish knight, that you brought in one night here, to be her wooer.

SIR TOBY Who? Sir Andrew Aguecheek?

MARIA Ay, he.

SIR TOBY He's as tall a man as any's in Illyria.

MARIA What's that to th' purpose?

SIR TOBY Why, he has three thousand ducats a year.

MARIA Ay, but he'll have but a year in all these ducats; he's a very fool and a prodigal.

SIR TOBY Fie, that you'll say so! He plays o'th' viol-de-gamboys, and speaks three or four languages word for word without book, and hath all the good gifts of nature.

MARIA He hath, indeed almost natural: for, besides that he's a fool, he's a great quarreller: and but that he hath the gift of a coward to allay the gust he hath in quarrelling, 'tis thought among the prudent he would quickly have the gift of a grave.

SIR TOBY By this hand, they are scoundrels and substractors that say so of him. Who are they?

MARIA They that add, moreover, he's drunk nightly in your company.

SIR TOBY With drinking healths to my niece: I'll drink to her as long as there is a passage in my throat and drink in Illyria: he's a coward and a coystrill that will not drink to my niece, till his brains turn o'th' toe like a parish-top. [*he seizes her about the waist and they dance a turn*] What, wench! Castiliano vulgo; for here comes Sir Andrew Agueface.

SIR ANDREW AGUECHEEK *enters*

SIR AND. Sir Toby Belch! How now, Sir Toby Belch?

SIR TOBY Sweet Sir Andrew!

SIR AND. Bless you, fair shrew.

MARIA [*curtsies*] And you too, sir!

SIR TOBY Accost, Sir Andrew, accost.

SIR AND. What's that?

SIR TOBY My niece's chambermaid.

SIR AND. Good Mistress Accost, I desire better acquaintance.

MARIA My name is Mary, sir.

SIR AND. Good Mistress Mary Accost –

SIR TOBY You mistake, knight: 'accost' is front her, board her, woo her, assail her.

SIR AND. By my troth, I would not undertake her in this company. Is that the meaning of 'accost'?

MARIA Fare you well, gentlemen. [*she turns to go*

SIR TOBY An thou let part so, Sir Andrew, would thou mightst never draw sword again.

SIR AND. An you part so, mistress, I would I might never draw sword again. Fair lady, do you think you have fools in hand?

MARIA Sir, I have not you by th'hand

SIR AND. Marry, but you shall have – and here's my hand.

[*he holds it out*

MARIA [*takes it*] Now, sir, 'thought is free'. [*she looks at his palm*] I pray you, bring your hand to th' buttery-bar and let it drink.

SIR AND. Wherefore, sweet-heart? What's your metaphor?

MARIA It's dry, sir.

SIR AND. Why, I think so; I am not such an ass, but I can keep my hand dry. But what's your jest?

MARIA A dry jest, sir.

SIR AND. Are you full of them?

MARIA Ay, sir; I have them at my fingers' ends: marry, now I let go your hand, I am barren.

[*she drops his hand, curtsies and trips away*

SIR TOBY [*sits*] O knight, thou lack'st a cup of canary: when did I see thee so put down ?

SIR AND. Never in your life, I think, unless you see canary put me down. [*sits beside him*] Methinks sometimes I have no more wit than a Christian or an ordinary man has: but I am a great eater of beef and I believe that does harm to my wit.

SIR TOBY No question.

SIR AND. An I thought that, I'd forswear it. I'll go ride home tomorrow, Sir Toby.

SIR TOBY Pourquoi, my dear knight?

SIR AND. What is 'pourquoi'? Do or not do? I would I had bestowed that time in the tongues, that I have in fencing, dancing and bear-baiting: O, had I but followed the arts!

SIR TOBY [*fondles him*]
Then hadst thou had an excellent head of hair.

SIR AND. Why, would that have mended my hair?

SIR TOBY Past question, for thou seest it will not curl by nature.

SIR AND. But it becomes me well enough, does't not?

SIR TOBY Excellent! it hangs like flax on a distaff and I hope to see a housewife take thee between her legs and spin it off.

SIR AND. Faith, I'll home tomorrow, Sir Toby. Your niece will not be seen, or if she be it's four to one she'll none of me: the count himself here hard by woos her.

SIR TOBY She'll none o'th' count – she'll not match above her degree, neither in estate, years, nor wit; I have heard her swear't. Tut, there's life in't, man.

SIR AND. I'll stay a month longer. I am a fellow o'th' strangest mind i'th' world: I delight in masques and revels sometimes altogether.

SIR TOBY Art thou good at these kickshawses, knight?

SIR AND. As any man in Illyria, whatsoever he be, under the degree of my betters, and yet I will not compare with an old man.

SIR TOBY What is thy excellence in a galliard, knight?

SIR AND. Faith, I can cut a caper.

SIR TOBY And I can cut the mutton to't.

SIR AND. And I think I have the back-trick simply as strong as any man in Illyria.

SIR TOBY Wherefore are these things hid? Wherefore have these gifts a curtain before 'em? Are they like to take dust, like Mistress Mall's picture? Why dost thou not go to church in a galliard and come home in a coranto? My very walk should be a jig; I would not so much as make water but in a sink-a-pace. What dost thou mean? Is it a world to hide virtues in? I did think, by the excellent constitution of thy leg, it was formed under the star of a galliard.

SIR AND. Ay, 'tis strong, and it does indifferent well in a dun-coloured stock. Shall we set about some revels?

SIR TOBY What shall we do else? Were we not born under Taurus?

SIR AND. Taurus! That's sides and heart.

SIR TOBY No, sir, it is legs and thighs. Let me see thee caper. [*Sir Andrew leaps*] Ha! Higher: ha, ha! Excellent!

[*they go*

SCENE 4

A room in the Duke's palace

'Enter VALENTINE, *and* VIOLA *in man's attire'*

VALENT. If the duke continue these favours towards you, Cesario, you are like to be much advanced. He hath known you but three days, and already you are no stranger.

VIOLA You either fear his humour or my negligence, that you call in question the continuance of his love. Is he inconstant, sir, in his favours?

VALENT. No, believe me.

VIOLA I thank you. Here comes the count.

'Enter DUKE, CURIO *and attendants'*

DUKE Who saw Cesario, ho!
VIOLA On your attendance, my lord, here.
DUKE Stand you awhile aloof. [*Curio and attendants withdraw*
Cesario,
Thou know'st no less but all: I have unclasped
To thee the book even of my secret soul.
Therefore, good youth, address thy gait unto her,
Be not denied access, stand at her doors,
And tell them, there thy fixéd foot shall grow
Till thou have audience.
VIOLA Sure, my noble lord,
If she be so abandoned to her sorrow
As it is spoke, she never will admit me.
DUKE Be clamorous and leap all civil bounds
Rather than make unprofited return.
VIOLA Say I do speak with her, my lord, what then?
DUKE O, then unfold the passion of my love,
Surprise her with discourse of my dear faith;
It shall become thee well to act my woes;
She will attend it better in thy youth
Than in a nuncio's of more grave aspect.
VIOLA I think not so, my lord.

DUKE Dear lad, believe it;
For they shall yet belie thy happy years,
That say thou art a man: Diana's lip
Is not more smooth and rubious; thy small pipe
Is as the maiden's organ, shrill and sound –
And all is semblative a woman's part.
I know thy constellation is right apt
For this affair. [*he beckons attendants*]
Some four or five attend him,
All if you will; for I myself am best
When least in company. Prosper well in this,
And thou shalt live as freely as thy lord,
To call his fortunes thine.

VIOLA I'll do my best
To woo your lady. [*aside*] Yet, a barful strife!
Whoe'er I woo, myself would be his wife. [*they go*

SCENE 5

A room in Olivia's house; at the back a chair of state

MARIA *and* CLOWN

MARIA Nay, either tell me where thou hast been, or I will not open my lips so wide as a bristle may enter in way of thy excuse: my lady will hang thee for thy absence.

CLOWN Let her hang me: he that is well hanged in this world needs to fear no colours.

MARIA Make that good.

CLOWN He shall see none to fear.

MARIA A good lenten answer: I can tell thee where that saying was born, of 'I fear no colours'.

CLOWN Where, good Mistress Mary?

MARIA In the wars – and that may you be bold to say in your foolery.

CLOWN Well, God give them wisdom that have it; and those that are fools, let them use their talents.

MARIA Yet you will be hanged for being so long absent; or to be turned away, is not that as good as a hanging to you?

CLOWN Many a good hanging prevents a bad marriage; and,

for turning away, let summer bear it out.

MARIA You are resolute, then?

CLOWN Not so neither, but I am resolved on two points –

MARIA That if one break, the other will hold; or if both break, your gaskins fall.

CLOWN Apt in good faith, very apt. [*she turns to go*] Well, go thy way – if Sir Toby would leave drinking, thou wert as witty a piece of Eve's flesh as any in Illyria.

MARIA Peace, you rogue, no more o' that: here comes my lady: make your excuse wisely, you were best [*she goes*

The Lady OLIVIA *enters in black,* MALVOLIO *and attendants following; she sits in her chair of state*

CLOWN [*feigns not to see them*] Wit, an't be thy will, put me into good fooling! Those wits that think they have thee, do very oft prove fools; and I, that am sure I lack thee, may pass for a wise man. For what says Quinapalus? 'Better a witty fool than a foolish wit.' [*turns*] God bless thee, lady!

OLIVIA Take the fool away.

CLOWN Do you not hear, fellows? Take away the lady.

OLIVIA Go to, y'are a dry fool: I'll no more of you: besides, you grow dishonest.

CLOWN Two faults, madonna, that drink and good counsel will amend: for give the dry fool drink, then is the fool not dry: bid the dishonest man mend himself; if he mend, he is no longer dishonest; if he cannot, let the botcher mend him: any thing that's mended is but patched: virtue that transgresses, is but patched with sin, and sin that amends is but patched with virtue. If that this simple syllogism will serve, so: if it will not, what remedy? As there is no true cuckold but calamity, so beauty's a flower: the lady bade take away the fool, therefore I say again, take her away.

OLIVIA Sir, I bade them take away you.

CLOWN Misprision in the highest degree! Lady, 'Cucullus non facit monachum'; that's as much to say as I wear not motley in my brain. Good madonna, give me leave to prove you a fool.

OLIVIA Can you do it?

CLOWN Dexteriously, good madonna.

OLIVIA Make your proof.

CLOWN I must catechize you for it, madonna. Good my mouse of virtue, answer me.

OLIVIA Well, sir, for want of other idleness, I'll bide your proof.

CLOWN Good madonna, why mourn'st thou?

OLIVIA Good fool, for my brother's death.

CLOWN I think his soul is in hell, madonna.

OLIVIA I know his soul is in heaven, fool.

CLOWN The more fool, madonna, to mourn for your brother's soul being in heaven. Take away the fool, gentlemen.

OLIVIA What think you of this fool, Malvolio? Doth he not mend?

MALVOLIO Yes, and shall do, till the pangs of death shake him: infirmity, that decays the wise, doth ever make the better fool.

CLOWN God send you, sir, a speedy infirmity, for the better increasing your folly! Sir Toby will be sworn that I am no fox, but he will not pass his word for two pence that you are no fool.

OLIVIA How say you to that, Malvolio?

MALVOLIO I marvel your ladyship takes delight in such a barren rascal: I saw him put down the other day with an ordinary fool that has no more brain than a stone. Look you now, he's out of his guard already; unless you laugh and minister occasion to him, he is gagged. I protest, I take these wise men, that crow so at these set kind of fools, no better than the fools' zanies.

OLIVIA O, you are sick of self-love, Malvolio, and taste with a distempered appetite. To be generous, guiltless, and of free disposition, is to take those things for bird-bolts that you deem cannon-bullets: there is no slander in an allowed fool, though he do nothing but rail; nor no railing in a known discreet man, though he do nothing but reprove.

CLOWN Now Mercury endue thee with leasing, for thou speakest well of fools!

MARIA *returns*

MARIA Madam, there is at the gate a young gentleman much desires to speak with you.

OLIVIA From the Count Orsino, is it?

MARIA I know not, madam – 'tis a fair young man, and well attended.

OLIVIA Who of my people hold him in delay?

MARIA Sir Toby, madam, your kinsman.

OLIVIA Fetch him off, I pray you! He speaks nothing but madman: fie on him. [*Maria hurries away*] Go you, Malvolio: if it be a suit from the count, I am sick, or not at home. What you will, to dismiss it. [*Malvolio goes*] Now you see, sir, how your fooling grows old, and people dislike it.

CLOWN Thou hast spoke for us, madonna, as if thy eldest son should be a fool: whose skull Jove cram with brains! For – here he comes – one of thy kin, has a most weak pia mater.

SIR TOBY BELCH *staggers in*

OLIVIA By mine honour, half drunk. What is he at the gate, cousin?

SIR TOBY [*speaks thick*] A gentleman.

OLIVIA A gentleman? What gentleman?

SIR TOBY 'Tis a gentlemen here. [*hiccoughs*] A plague o'these pickle-herring. [*Clown laughs*] How now, sot!

CLOWN Good Sir Toby –

OLIVIA Cousin, cousin, how have you come so early by this lethargy?

SIR TOBY Lechery! I defy lechery. There's one at the gate.

OLIVIA Ay, marry, what is he?

SIR TOBY Let him be the devil, an he will, I care not: give me 'faith', say I. [*he totters to the door*] Well, it's all one. [*he goes*

OLIVIA What's a drunken man like, fool?

CLOWN Like a drowned man, a fool, and a mad man: one draught above heat makes him a fool, the second mads him, and a third drowns him.

OLIVIA Go thou and seek the crowner, and let him sit o' my

coz; for he's in the third degree of drink: he's drowned: go look after him.

CLOWN He is but mad yet, madonna, and the fool shall look to the madman. [*he follows Sir Toby*

MALVOLIO *returns*

MALVOLIO Madam, yon young fellow swears he will speak with you. I told him you were sick, he takes on him to understand so much, and therefore comes to speak with you. I told him you were asleep, he seems to have a foreknowledge of that too, and therefore comes to speak with you. What is to be said to him, lady? He's fortified against any denial.

OLIVIA Tell him he shall not speak with me.

MALVOLIO Has been told so; and he says he'll stand at your door like a sheriff's post, and be the supporter to a bench, but he'll speak with you.

OLIVIA What kind o' man is he?

MALVOLIO Why, of mankind.

OLIVIA What manner of man?

MALVOLIO Of very ill manner; he'll speak with you, will you or no.

OLIVIA Of what personage and years is he?

MALVOLIO Not yet old enough for a man, nor young enough for a boy; as a squash is before 'tis a peascod, or a codling when 'tis almost an apple: 'tis with him in standing water between boy and man. He is very well-favoured and he speaks very shrewishly; one would think his mother's milk were scarce out of him.

OLIVIA Let him approach. Call in my gentlewoman.

MALVOLIO [*goes to the door*] Gentlewoman, my lady calls. [*he departs*

MARIA *returns*

OLIVIA Give me my veil: come, throw it o'er my face – we'll once more hear Orsino's embassy. [*Maria veils her*

VIOLA *(as Cesario) enters*

VIOLA The honourable lady of the house, which is she?

OLIVIA Speak to me, I shall answer for her: your will?

VIOLA Most radiant, exquisite, and unmatchable beauty! I pray you, tell me if this be the lady of the house, for I never saw her. I would be loath to cast away my speech; for besides that it is excellently well penned, I have taken great pains to con it. Good beauties, let me sustain no scorn; I am very comptible, even to the least sinister usage.

OLIVIA Whence came you, sir?

VIOLA I can say little more than I have studied, and that question's out of my part. Good gentle one, give me modest assurance if you be the lady of the house, that I may proceed in my speech.

OLIVIA Are you a comedian?

VIOLA No, my profound heart: and yet, by the very fangs of malice I swear, I am not that I play. Are you the lady of the house?

OLIVIA If I do not usurp myself, I am.

VIOLA Most certain, if you are she, you do usurp yourself; for what is yours to bestow, is not yours to reserve. But this is from my commission: I will on with my speech in your praise, and then show you the heart of my message.

OLIVIA Come to what is important in't: I forgive you the praise.

VIOLA Alas, I took great pains to study it, and 'tis poetical.

OLIVIA It is the more like to be feigned, I pray you keep it in. I heard you were saucy at my gates, and allowed your approach rather to wonder at you than to hear you. If you be not mad, be gone; if you have reason, be brief: 'tis not that time of moon with me to make one in so skipping a dialogue.

MARIA [*points to the hat in Viola's hand*] Will you hoist sail, sir? Here lies your way. [*she opens the door to thrust her out*

VIOLA [*resists*] No, good swabber; I am to hull here a little longer. Some mollification for your giant, sweet lady!

OLIVIA Tell me your mind.

VIOLA I am a messenger.

OLIVIA Sure, you have some hideous matter to deliver, when the courtesy of it is so fearful. Speak your office.

VIOLA It alone concerns your ear. I bring no overture of war, no taxation of homage; I hold the olive in my hand: my words are as full of peace as matter.

OLIVIA Yet you began rudely. What are you? What would you?

VIOLA The rudeness that hath appeared in me have I learned from my entertainment. What I am, and what I would, are as secret as maidenhead: to your ears, divinity; to any other's, profanation.

OLIVIA Give us the place alone: we will hear this divinity. [*Maria and attendants withdraw*] Now, sir, what is your text?

VIOLA Most sweet lady –

OLIVIA A comfortable doctrine, and much may be said of it. Where lies your text?

VIOLA In Orsino's bosom.

OLIVIA In his bosom! In what chapter of his bosom?

VIOLA To answer by the method, in the first of his heart.

OLIVIA O, I have read it; it is heresy. Have you no more to say?

VIOLA Good madam, let me see your face.

OLIVIA Have you any commission from your lord to negotiate with my face? You are now out of your text: but we will draw the curtain, and show you the picture. [*she unveils*] Look you, sir, such a one I was – this present! Is't not well done?

VIOLA Excellently done, if God did all.

OLIVIA 'Tis in grain, sir, 'twill endure wind and weather.

VIOLA 'Tis beauty truly blent, whose red and white
Nature's own sweet and cunning hand laid on:
Lady, you are the cruell'st she alive,
If you will lead these graces to the grave,
And leave the world no copy.

OLIVIA O, sir, I will not be so hard-hearted; I will give out divers schedules of my beauty: it shall be inventoried, and every particle and utensil labelled to my will: as, *Item*, Two lips indifferent red; *Item*, Two grey eyes with lids to them; *Item*, One neck, one chin, and so forth. Were you sent hither to praise me?

VIOLA I see you what you are, you are too proud;
But, if you were the devil, you are fair.
My lord and master loves you; O, such love
Could be but recompensed, though you were crowned

The nonpareil of beauty!
OLIVIA How does he love me?
VIOLA With adorations, fertile tears,
With groans that thunder love, with sighs of fire.
OLIVIA Your lord does know my mind, I cannot love him:
Yet I suppose him virtuous, know him noble,
Of great estate, of fresh and stainless youth;
In voices well divulged, free, learned and valiant,
And in dimension and the shape of nature
A gracious person: but yet I cannot love him;
He might have took his answer long ago.
VIOLA If I did love you in my master's flame,
With such a suff'ring, such a deadly life,
In your denial I would find no sense,
I would not understand it.
OLIVIA Why, what would you?
VIOLA Make me a willow cabin at your gate,
And call upon my soul within the house,
Write loyal cantons of contemnéd love,
And sing them loud even in the dead of night;
Holla your name to the reverberate hills,
And make the babbling gossip of the air
Cry out 'Olivia!' O, you should not rest
Between the elements of air and earth,
But you should pity me.
OLIVIA You might do much
What is your parentage?
VIOLA Above my fortunes, yet my state is well:
I am a gentleman.
OLIVIA Get you to your lord;
I cannot love him: let him send no more,
Unless – perchance – you come to me again,
To tell me how he takes it. Fare you well:
I thank you for your pains: spend this for me.
[*offers money*
VIOLA I am no fee'd post, lady; keep your purse.
My master, not myself, lacks recompense.
Love make his heart of flint that you shall love,
And let your fervour like my master's be

Placed in contempt! Farewell, fair cruelty. [*she goes*

OLIVIA 'What is your parentage?'
'Above my fortunes, yet my state is well:
I am a gentleman'. I'll be sworn thou art!
Thy tongue, thy face, thy limbs, actions, and spirit,
Do give thee five-fold blazon. Not too fast: soft, soft!
Unless the master were the man. [*she muses*] How now!
Even so quickly may one catch the plague?
Methinks I feel this youth's perfections
With an invisible and subtle stealth
To creep in at mine eyes. Well, let it be.
What, ho, Malvolio!

MALVOLIO *returns*

MALVOLIO Here, madam, at your service.

OLIVIA Run after that same peevish messenger,
The county's man: he left this ring behind him,
Would I or not; tell him I'll none of it.
Desire him not to flatter with his lord,
Nor hold him up with hopes – I am not for him:
If that the youth will come this way tomorrow,
I'll give him reasons for't. Hie thee, Malvolio.

MALVOLIO Madam, I will. [*he hurries forth*

OLIVIA I do I know not what, and fear to find
Mine eye too great a flatterer for my mind.
Fate, show thy force – ourselves we do not owe –
What is decreed, must be; and be this so! [*she goes*

ACT 2 SCENE 1

At the door of Antonio's house

ANTONIO *and* SEBASTIAN

ANTONIO Will you stay no longer? Nor will you not that I go with you?

SEBASTIAN By your patience, no: my stars shine darkly over me; the malignancy of my fate might perhaps distemper yours; therefore I shall crave of you your leave that I may bear my evils alone: it were a bad recompense for your love, to lay any of them on you.

ANTONIO Let me yet know of you whither you are bound.

SEBASTIAN No, sooth, sir: my determinate voyage is mere extravagancy. But I perceive in you so excellent a touch of modesty, that you will not extort from me what I am willing to keep in; therefore it charges me in manners the rather to express myself. You must know of me then, Antonio, my name is Sebastian, which I called Roderigo. My father was that Sebastian of Messaline, whom I know you have heard of. He left behind him myself and a sister, both born in an hour: if the heavens had been pleased, would we had so ended! But you, sir, altered that, for some hour before you took me from the breach of the sea was my sister drowned.

ANTONIO Alas, the day!

SEBASTIAN A lady, sir, though it was said she much resembled me, was yet of many accounted beautiful: but, though I could not with such estimable wonder overfar believe that, yet thus far I will boldly publish her – she bore a mind that envy could not but call fair. She is drowned already, sir, with salt water, though I seem to drown her remembrance again with more.

ANTONIO Pardon me, sir, your bad entertainment.

SEBASTIAN O, good Antonio, forgive me your trouble.

ANTONIO If you will not murder me for my love, let me be your servant.

SEBASTIAN If you will not undo what you have done, that is, kill him whom you have recovered, desire it not. Fare ye well at once. My bosom is full of kindness, and I am yet so near the manners of my mother, that upon the least occasion more mine eyes will tell tales of me. [*they clasp hands*] I am bound to the Count Orsino's court – farewell! [*he goes*

ANTONIO The gentleness of all the gods go with thee!
I have many enemies in Orsino's court,
Else would I very shortly see thee there:
But, come what may, I do adore thee so,
That danger shall seem sport, and I will go. [*he goes in*

SCENE 2

A street near Olivia's house

VIOLA *approaches,* MALVOLIO *following after*

MALVOLIO [*comes up*] Were not you e'en now with the Countess Olivia?

VIOLA Even now, sir. On a moderate pace I have since arrived but hither.

MALVOLIO [*sharply*] She returns this ring to you, sir; you might have saved me my pains, to have taken it away yourself. She adds moreover, that you should put your lord into a desperate assurance she will none of him: and one thing more, that you be never so hardy to come again in his affairs, unless it be to report your lord's taking of this. [*he holds out the ring*] Receive it so.

VIOLA She took the ring of me. I'll none of it.

MALVOLIO Come, sir, you peevishly threw it to her; and her will is, it should be so returned: [*he throws it at her feet*] if it be worth stooping for, there it lies in your eye; if not, be it his that finds it. [*he walks off*

VIOLA I left no ring with her: what means this lady?
Fortune forbid my outside have not charmed her!
She made good view of me, indeed so much,
That as methought her eyes had lost her tongue,
For she did speak in starts distractedly.
She loves me, sure – the cunning of her passion

Invites me in this churlish messenger.
None of my lord's ring! Why, he sent her none.
I am the man – if it be so, as 'tis,
Poor lady, she were better love a dream.
Disguise, I see thou art a wickedness,
Wherein the pregnant enemy does much.
How easy is it for the proper-false
In women's waxen hearts to set their forms!
Alas, our frailty is the cause, not we,
For such as we are made of, such we be.
How will this fadge? My master loves her dearly,
And I (poor monster!) fond as much on him:
And she, mistaken, seems to dote on me:
What will become of this? As I am man,
My state is desperate for my master's love;
As I am woman – now alas the day! –
What thriftless sighs shall poor Olivia breathe?
O time, thou must untangle this, not I,
It is too hard a knot for me t'untie. [*she goes*

SCENE 3

A room in Olivia's house; a bench and a table with cold viands and drinking-vessels thereon

SIR TOBY BELCH *and* SIR ANDREW AGUECHEEK *enter, drunk*

SIR TOBY [*sits at table*] Approach, sir Andrew: [*Sir Andrew follows with difficulty*] not to be a-bed after midnight is to be up betimes; and 'diluculo surgere', thou know'st –

SIR AND. [*sits beside him*] Nay, by my troth, I know not: but I know, to be up late is to be up late. [*he eats*

SIR TOBY [*takes up a pot and finds it empty*] A false conclusion: I hate it as an unfilled can. To be up after midnight and to go to bed then, is early; so that to go to bed after midnight is to go to bed betimes. Does not our life consist of the four elements?

SIR AND. [*his mouth full*] Faith, so they say – but I think it rather consists of eating and drinking.

SIR TOBY Th'art a scholar; let us therefore eat and drink. [*bawls*]

Marian, I say! A stoup of wine!

The CLOWN *comes in*

SIR AND. Here comes the fool, i'faith.

CLOWN [*sits between them upon the bench*] How now, my hearts! Did you never see the picture of 'we three'?

SIR TOBY Welcome, ass. Now let's have a catch.

SIR AND. By my troth, the fool has an excellent breast. I had rather than forty shillings I had such a leg, and so sweet a breath to sing, as the fool has. In sooth, thou wast in very gracious fooling last night, when thou spok'st of Pigrogromitus, of the Vapians passing the equinoctial of Queubus; 'twas very good, i'faith. I sent thee sixpence for thy leman – hadst it?

CLOWN I did impetticoat thy gratillity: for Malvolio's nose is no whipstock: my lady has a white hand, and the Myrmidons are no bottle-ale houses.

SIR AND. Excellent! why, this is the best fooling, when all is done. Now, a song.

SIR TOBY Come on, there is sixpence for you. Let's have a song.

SIR AND. There's a testril of me too: if one knight give a –

CLOWN Would you have a love-song, or a song of good life?

SIR TOBY A love-song, a love-song.

SIR AND. Ay, I care not for good life.

CLOWN [*sings*] O mistress mine, where are you roaming?
O, stay and hear, your true love's coming,
That can sing both high and low.
Trip no further pretty sweeting:
Journeys end in lovers meeting,
Every wise man's son doth know.

SIR AND. Excellent good, i'faith!

SIR TOBY Good, good.

CLOWN [*sings*] What is love, 'tis not hereafter,
Present mirth hath present laughter
What's to come is still unsure.
In delay there lies no plenty,
Then come kiss me, sweet and twenty:
Youth's a stuff will not endure.

SIR AND. A mellifluous voice, as I am true knight.

SIR TOBY A contagious breath.

SIR AND. Very sweet and contagious, i'faith.

SIR TOBY To hear by the nose, it is dulcet in contagion. But shall we make the welkin dance indeed? Shall we rouse the night-owl in a catch, that will draw three souls out of one weaver? Shall we do that?

SIR AND. An you love me, let's do't: I am dog at a catch.

CLOWN By'r lady, sir, and some dogs will catch well.

SIR AND. Most certain. Let our catch be, 'Thou knave'.

CLOWN 'Hold thy peace, thou knave,' knight? I shall be constrained in't to call thee knave, knight.

SIR AND. 'Tis not the first time I have constrained one to call me knave. Begin, fool; it begins, 'Hold thy peace.'

CLOWN I shall never begin if I hold my peace.

SIR AND. Good, i'faith! Come, begin. [*they sing the catch*

MARIA *enters with wine*

MARIA What a caterwauling do you keep here! If my lady have not called up her steward Malvolio and bid him turn you out of doors, never trust me.

SIR TOBY My lady's a Cataian, we are politicians, Malvolio's a Peg-a-Ramsey, and
[*sings*] 'Three merry men be we.'
Am not I consanguineous? Am I not of her blood? Tillyvally! 'Lady'!
[*sings*] 'There dwelt a man in Babylon,
Lady, Lady!'

CLOWN Beshrew me, the knight's in admirable fooling.

SIR AND. Ay, he does well enough, if he be disposed, and so do I too; he does it with a better grace, but I do it more natural.

SIR TOBY [*sings*] 'O' the twelfth day of December' –

MARIA For the love o' God, peace.

MALVOLIO *enters*

MALVOLIO My masters, are you mad? Or what are you? Have you no wit, manners, nor honesty, but to gabble like tinkers at this time of night? Do ye make an ale-house of my lady's house, that ye squeak out your coziers' catches without any mitigation or remorse of voice? Is there no respect of place, persons, nor time in you?

SIR TOBY We did keep time, sir, in our catches. Sneck up!

MALVOLIO Sir Toby, I must be round with you. My lady bade me tell you, that though she harbours you as her kinsman, she's nothing allied to your disorders. If you can separate yourself and your misdemeanours, you are welcome to the house; if not, an it would please you to take leave of her, she is very willing to bid you farewell.

SIR TOBY [*sings to Maria*] 'Farewell, dear heart, since I must needs be gone.' [*he embraces her*

MARIA Nay, good Sir Toby.

CLOWN [*sings*] 'His eyes do show his days are almost done.'

MALVOLIO Is't even so?

SIR TOBY [*sings*] 'But I will never die.' [*he falls to the ground*

CLOWN [*sings*] 'Sir Toby, there you lie.'

MALVOLIO This is much credit to you.

SIR TOBY [*rising, sings*] 'Shall I bid him go?'

CLOWN [*sings*] 'What an if you do?'

SIR TOBY [*sings*] 'Shall I bid him go, and spare not?'

CLOWN [*sings*] 'O no, no, no, no, you dare not.'

SIR TOBY [*to Clown*] Out o' tune, sir! Ye lie. [*to Malvolio*] Art any more than a steward? Dost thou think because thou art virtuous, there shall be no more cakes and ale?

CLOWN Yes, by Saint Anne, and ginger shall be hot i'th' mouth too.

SIR TOBY Th'art i'th' right. Go, sir, rub your chain with crumbs. A stoup of wine, Maria! [*she fills their vessels*

MALVOLIO Mistress Mary, if you prized my lady's favour at any thing more than contempt, you would not give means for this uncivil rule; she shall know of it, by this hand. [*he departs*

MARIA Go shake your ears.

SIR AND. 'Twere as good a deed as to drink when a man's a-hungry, to challenge him the field, and then to break promise with him and make a fool of him.

SIR TOBY Do't, knight. I'll write thee a challenge; or I'll deliver thy indignation to him by word of mouth.

MARIA Sweet Sir Toby, be patient for tonight: since the youth of the count's was today with my lady, she is much out of quiet. For Monsieur Malvolio, let me alone with him: if I do not gull him into a nayword, and make him a common recreation, do not think I have wit enough to lie straight in my bed: I know I can do it.

SIR TOBY Possess us, possess us, tell us something of him.

MARIA Marry, sir, sometimes he is a kind of puritan.

SIR AND. O, if I thought that, I'd beat him like a dog.

SIR TOBY What, for being a puritan? Thy exquisite reason, dear knight?

SIR AND. I have no exquisite reason for't, but I have reason good enough.

MARIA The devil a puritan that he is, or any thing constantly but a time-pleaser, an affectioned ass, that cons state without book and utters it by great swarths: the best persuaded of himself, so crammed, as he thinks, with excellencies, that it is his ground of faith that all that look on him love him; and on that vice in him will my revenge find notable cause to work.

SIR TOBY What wilt thou do?

MARIA I will drop in his way some obscure epistles of love, wherein by the colour of his beard, the shape of his leg, the manner of his gait, the expressure of his eye, forehead, and complexion, he shall find himself most feelingly personated. I can write very like my lady your niece, on a forgotten matter we can hardly make distinction of our hands.

SIR TOBY Excellent! I smell a device.

SIR AND. I have't in my nose too.

SIR TOBY He shall think by the letters that thou wilt drop that they come from my niece, and that she's in love with him.

MARIA My purpose is, indeed, a horse of that colour.

SIR AND. And your horse now would make him an ass.

MARIA Ass, I doubt not.

SIR AND. O, 'twill be admirable.

MARIA Sport royal, I warrant you: I know my physic will work with him. I will plant you two, and let the fool make a third, where he shall find the letter: observe his construction of it. For this night, to bed, and dream on the event. Farewell. [*she goes out*

SIR TOBY Good night, Penthesilea.

SIR AND. Before me, she's a good wench.

SIR TOBY She's a beagle, true-bred, and one that adores me. What o' that? [*he sighs*

SIR AND. I was adored once too. [*he sighs also*

SIR TOBY Let's to bed, knight. Thou hadst need send for more money.

SIR AND. If I cannot recover your niece, I am a foul way out.

SIR TOBY Send for money, knight. If thou hast her not i'th'end, call me cut.

SIR AND. If I do not, never trust me, take it how you will.

SIR TOBY Come, come, I'll go burn some sack, 'tis too late to go to bed now: come knight; come knight. [*they go*

SCENE 4

A room in the Duke's palace

'Enter DUKE, VIOLA, CURIO *and others'*

DUKE [*to Viola*] Give me some music. Now –
[*musicians enter*] good morrow, friends.
Now, good Cesario, but that piece of song,
That old and antic song we heard last night:
Methought it did relieve my passion much,
More than light airs and recollected terms
Of these most brisk and giddy-pacéd times.
Come, but one verse.

CURIO He is not here, so please your lordship, that should sing it.

DUKE Who was it?

CURIO Feste, the jester, my lord, a fool that the Lady Olivia's father took much delight in. He is about the house.

DUKE Seek him out, and play the tune the while.
[*Curio goes; music plays*
Come hither, boy – if ever thou shalt love,
In the sweet pangs of it remember me:
For, such as I am all true lovers are,
Unstaid and skittish in all motions else,

Save in the constant image of the creature
That is beloved. How dost thou like this tune?

VIOLA It gives a very echo to the seat
Where Love is throned.

DUKE Thou dost speak masterly.
My life upon't, young though thou art, thine eye
Hath stayed upon some favour that it loves:
Hath it not, boy?

VIOLA A little, by your favour.

DUKE What kind of woman is't?

VIOLA Of your complexion.

DUKE She is not worth thee then. What years, i'faith?

VIOLA About your years, my lord.

DUKE Too old, by heaven: let still the woman take
An elder than herself; so wears she to him,
So sways she level in her husband's heart:
For, boy, however we do praise ourselves,
Our fancies are more giddy and unfirm,
More longing, wavering, sooner lost and won,
Than women's are.

VIOLA I think it well, my lord.

DUKE Then let thy love be younger than thyself,
Or thy affection cannot hold the bent:
For women are as roses, whose fair flower
Being once displayed doth fall that very hour.

VIOLA And so they are: alas, that they are so;
To die, even when they to perfection grow!

CURIO *re-enters with* CLOWN

DUKE O fellow, come, the song we had last night.
Mark it, Cesario, it is old and plain:
The spinsters and the knitters in the sun,
And the free maids that weave their thread with bones
Do use to chant it; it is silly sooth,
And dallies with the innocence of love,
Like the old age.

CLOWN Are you ready, sir?

DUKE Ay, prithee, sing. [*music*

CLOWN [*sings*] Come away, come away death,
And in sad cypress let me be laid:
Fly away, fly away breath,
I am slain by a fair cruel maid:
My shroud of white, stuck all with yew,
O, prepare it!
My part of death no one so true
Did share it.

Not a flower, not a flower sweet
On my black coffin let there be strown:
Not a friend, not a friend greet
My poor corpse, where my bones shall be thrown:
A thousand thousand sighs to save,
Lay me O where
Sad true lover never find my grave,
To weep there.

DUKE [*gives money*] There's for thy pains.

CLOWN No pains, sir, I take pleasure in singing, sir.

DUKE I'll pay thy pleasure then.

CLOWN Truly, sir, and pleasure will be paid, one time or another.

DUKE Give me now leave to leave thee.

CLOWN Now, the melancholy god protect thee, and the tailor make thy doublet of changeable taffeta, for thy mind is a very opal. I would have men of such constancy put to sea, that their business might be everything and their intent everywhere, for that's it that always makes a good voyage of nothing. Farewell. [*he goes*

DUKE Let all the rest give place. [*Curio and attendants depart*
Once more, Cesario,
Get thee to yon same sovereign cruelty
Tell her my love, more noble than the world,
Prizes not quantity of dirty lands;
The parts that fortune hath bestowed upon her,
Tell her I hold as giddily as fortune;
But 'tis that miracle and queen of gems
That nature pranks her in attracts my soul.

VIOLA But if she cannot love you, sir?
DUKE I cannot be so answered.
VIOLA Sooth, but you must.
Say that some lady, as perhaps there is,
Hath for your love as great a pang of heart
As you have for Olivia: you cannot love her;
You tell her so; must she not then be answered?
DUKE There is no woman's sides
Can bide the beating of so strong a passion
As love doth give my heart: no woman's heart
So big, to hold so much, they lack retention.
Alas, their love may be called appetite –
No motion of the liver, but the palate –
That suffers surfeit, cloyment and revolt;
But mine is all as hungry as the sea,
And can digest as much. Make no compare
Between that love a woman can bear me
And that I owe Olivia.
VIOLA Ay, but I know –
DUKE What dost thou know?
VIOLA Too well what love women to men may owe:
In faith they are as true of heart as we.
My father had a daughter loved a man,
As it might be, perhaps, were I a woman,
I should your lordship.
DUKE And what's her history?
VIOLA A blank, my lord: she never told her love,
But let concealment like a worm i'th' bud
Feed on her damask cheek: she pined in thought,
And with a green and yellow melancholy
She sat like Patience on a monument,
Smiling at grief. Was not this love, indeed?
We men may say more, swear more – but indeed
Our shows are more than will; for still we prove
Much in our vows, but little in our love.
DUKE But died thy sister of her love, my boy?
VIOLA I am all the daughters of my father's house,
And all the brothers too. and yet I know not. [*they muse*
Sir, shall I to this lady?

DUKE [*starts and rouses*] Ay, that's the theme.
To her in haste; give her this jewel; say,
My love can give no place, bide no denay. [*they go*

SCENE 5

A walled garden adjoining the house of Olivia; two doors, one leading out of the garden, the other opening: into the house whence there runs a broad walk with great box-trees on either side and a stone seat next the wall

The house-door opens and SIR TOBY BELCH *comes out with* SIR ANDREW AGUECHEEK

SIR TOBY [*turns and calls*] Come thy ways, Signior Fabian.

FABIAN [*follows through the door*] Nay, I'll come: if I lose a scruple of this sport, let me be boiled to death with melancholy.

SIR TOBY Wouldst thou not be glad to have the niggardly rascally sheep-biter come by some notable shame?

FABIAN I would exult, man: you know, he brought me out o' favour with my lady about a bear-baiting here.

SIR TOBY To anger him, we'll have the bear again, and we will fool him black and blue – shall we not, Sir Andrew?

SIR AND. An we do not, it is pity of our lives.

MARIA *appears, hurrying down the walk*

SIR TOBY Here comes the little villain. How now, my metal of India?

MARIA Get ye all three into the box-tree: Malvolio's coming down this walk. He has been yonder i'the sun practising behaviour to his own shadow this half hour: observe him, for the love of mockery; for I know this letter will make a contemplative idiot of him. Close, in the name of jesting! [*the men hide in a box-tree*] Lie thou there [*throws down a letter*] for here comes the trout that must be caught with tickling. [*she goes within*

MALVOLIO, *in plumed hat, comes slowly along the path, musing*

MALVOLIO 'Tis but fortune, all is fortune. Maria once told me she did affect me, and I have heard herself come thus near, that should she fancy it should be one of my complexion. Besides, she uses me with a more exalted respect than any one else that follows her. What should I think on't?

SIR TOBY Here's an overweening rogue!

FABIAN O, peace! Contemplation makes a rare turkey-cock of him. How he jets under his advanced plumes!

SIR AND. 'Slight, I could so beat the rogue!

FABIAN Peace, I say.

MALVOLIO To be Count Malvolio!

SIR TOBY Ah, rogue!

SIR AND. Pistol him, pistol him.

FABIAN Peace, peace!

MALVOLIO There is example for't; the lady of the Strachy married the yeoman of the wardrobe.

SIR TOBY Fie on him, Jezebel!

FABIAN O, peace! Now he's deeply in: look, how imagination blows him.

MALVOLIO Having been three months married to her, sitting in my state –

SIR TOBY O, for a stone-bow, to hit him in the eye!

MALVOLIO Calling my officers about me, in my branched velvet gown; having come from a day-bed, where I have left Olivia sleeping –

SIR TOBY Fire and brimstone!

FABIAN O, peace, peace!

MALVOLIO And then to have the humour of state: and after a demure travel of regard, telling them I know my place as I would they should do theirs, to ask for my kinsman Toby –

SIR TOBY Bolts and shackles!

FABIAN O, peace, peace, peace! Now, now.

MALVOLIO Seven of my people, with an obedient start, make out for him: I frown the while, and perchance wind up my watch, or play with my [*touches his steward's chain an instant*] – some rich jewel. Toby approaches; curtsies there to me –

SIR TOBY Shall this fellow live?

FABIAN Though our silence be drawn from us with cars, yet peace.

MALVOLIO I extend my hand to him thus; quenching my familiar smile with an austere regard of control –

SIR TOBY And does not 'Toby' take you a blow o'the lips then?

MALVOLIO Saying, 'Cousin Toby, my fortunes having cast me on your niece give me this prerogatlve of speech' –

SIR TOBY What, what?

MALVOLIO 'You must amend your drunkenness.'

SIR TOBY Out, scab! [*Malvolio turns as at a sound*

FABIAN Nay, patience, or we break the sinews of our plot.

MALVOLIO 'Besides, you waste the treasure of your time with a foolish knight' –

SIR AND. That's me, I warrant you.

MALVOLIO 'One Sir Andrew' – [*he sees the letter*

SIR AND. I knew 'twas I, for many do call me fool.

MALVOLIO [*takes up the letter*] What employment have we here?

FABIAN Now is the woodcock near the gin.

SIR TOBY O, peace! And the spirit of humours intimate reading aloud to him!

MALVOLIO By my life, this is my lady's hand: these be her very c's, her u's, and her t's, and thus makes go she her great P's. It is, in contempt of question, her hand.

SIR AND. Her c's, her u's, and her t's: why that?

MALVOLIO [*reads the superscription*] 'To the unknown beloved, this, and my good wishes'. Her very phrases! By your leave, wax. Soft! And the impressure her Lucrece, with which she uses to seal: 'tis my lady. To whom should this be?

[*he opens the letter*

FABIAN This wins him, liver and all.

MALVOLIO [*reads*] 'Jove knows I love
But who?
Lips, do not move!
No man must know.'

'No man must know'. What follows? The numbers altered. [*he muses*] 'No man must know' – if this should be thee, Malvolio!

SIR TOBY Marry, hang thee, brock!

MALVOLIO [*reads*] 'I may command where I adore:
But silence, like a Lucrece knife,
With bloodless stroke my heart doth gore
M, O, A, I, doth sway my life.'

FABIAN A fustian riddle!

SIR TOBY Excellent wench, say I.

MALVOLIO 'M, O, A, I, doth sway my life.' – Nay, but first, let me see, let me see, let me see.

FABIAN What dish o' poison has she dressed him!

SIR TOBY And with what wing the stallion checks at it!

MALVOLIO 'I may command where I adore'. Why she may command me; I serve her, she is my lady. Why, this is evident to any formal capacity. There is no obstruction in this. And the end: what should that alphabetical position portend? If I could make that resemble something in me! Softly! 'M, O, A, I' –

SIR TOBY O, ay, make up that – he is now at a cold scent.

FABIAN Sowter will cry upon't for all this, though it be as rank as a fox.

MALVOLIO 'M' – Malvolio – 'M' – why, that begins my name.

FABIAN Did not I say he would work it out? The cur is excellent at faults.

MALVOLIO 'M' – but then there is no consonancy in the sequel that suffers under probation: 'A' should follow, but 'O' does.

FABIAN And O shall end, I hope.

SIR TOBY Ay, or I'll cudgel him, and make him cry 'O!'

MALVOLIO And then 'I' comes behind.

FABIAN Ay, an you had any eye behind you, you might see more detraction at your heels, than fortunes before you.

MALVOLIO 'M, O, A, I'. This simulation is not as the former: and yet, to crush this a little, it would bow to me, for every one of these letters are in my name. Soft! Here follows prose.

[*reads*] 'If this fall into thy hand, revolve. In my stars I am above thee, but be not afraid of greatness: some are born great, some achieve greatness, and some have greatness thrust upon 'em. Thy Fates open their hands,

let thy blood and spirit embrace them; and to inure thyself to what thou art like to be, cast thy humble slough, and appear fresh. Be opposite with a kinsman, surly with servants; let thy tongue tang arguments of state; put thyself into the trick of singularity. She thus advises thee that sighs for thee. Remember who commended thy yellow stockings, and wished to see thee ever cross-gartered: I say, remember. Go to, thou art made, if thou desir'st to be so; if not, let me see thee a steward still, the fellow of servants, and not worthy to touch Fortune's fingers. Farewell. She, that would alter services with thee,

THE FORTUNATE-UNHAPPY

Daylight and champian discovers not more: this is open. I will be proud, I will read politic authors, I will baffle Sir Toby, I will wash off gross acquaintance, I will be point-devise the very man. I do not now fool myself, to let imagination jade me; for every reason excites to this, that my lady loves me. She did commend my yellow-stockings of late, she did praise my leg being cross-gartered, and in this she manifests herself to my love, and with a kind of injunction drives me to these habits of her liking. I thank my stars, I am happy. I will be strange, stout, in yellow stockings, and cross-gartered, even with the swiftness of putting on. Jove, and my stars be praised! Here is yet a postscript.

[*reads*] 'Thou canst not choose but know who I am. If thou entertain'st my love, let it appear in thy smiling, thy smiles become thee well. Therefore in my presence still smile, dear, O my sweet, I prithee.'

Jove I thank thee! [*he lifts his hands towards heaven*] I will smile, I will do everything that thou wilt have me.

[*he goes within*

FABIAN I will not give my part of this sport for a pension of thousands to be paid from the Sophy.

SIR TOBY I could marry this wench for this device –

SIR AND. So could I too.

SIR TOBY And ask no other dowry with her but such another jest.

SIR AND. Nor I neither.

MARIA *comes from the house*

FABIAN Here comes my noble gull-catcher.

SIR TOBY Wilt thou set thy foot o' my neck?

SIR AND. Or o' mine either?

SIR TOBY Shall I play my freedom at trey-trip, and become thy bond-slave?

SIR AND. I'faith or I either?

SIR TOBY Why, thou hast put him in such a dream, that when the image of it leaves him he must run mad.

MARIA Nay, but say true, does it work upon him?

SIR TOBY Like aqua-vitae with a midwife.

MARIA If you will then see the fruits of the sport, mark his first approach before my lady: he will come to her in yellow stockings, and 'tis a colour she abhors, and cross-gartered, a fashion she detests; and he will smile upon her, which will now be so unsuitable to her disposition, being addicted to a melancholy as she is, that it cannot but turn him into a notable contempt: if you will see it, follow me.

SIR TOBY To the gates of Tartar, thou most excellent devil of wit!

SIR AND. I'll make one too. [*they enter the house*

ACT 3 SCENE 1

The CLOWN *enters the garden with his pipe and tabor; he plays. Viola comes in through the outer door as he finishes*

VIOLA Save thee, friend, and thy music: dost thou live by thy tabor?

CLOWN No, sir, I live by the church.

VIOLA Art thou a churchman?

CLOWN No such matter, sir. I do live by the church: for I do live at my house, and my house doth stand by the church.

VIOLA So thou mayst say the king lies by a beggar, if a beggar dwell near him: or the church stands by thy tabor, if thy tabor stand by the church.

CLOWN You have said, sir. To see this age! A sentence is but a cheveril glove to a good wit – how quickly the wrong side may be turned outward!

VIOLA Nay, that's certain; they that dally nicely with words may quickly make them wanton.

CLOWN I would therefore my sister had had no name, sir.

VIOLA Why, man?

CLOWN Why, sir, her name's a word, and to dally with that word might make my sister want one. But indeed words are very rascals since bonds disgraced them.

VIOLA Thy reason, man?

CLOWN Troth, sir, I can yield you none without words, and words are grown so false I am loath to prove reason with them.

VIOLA I warrant thou art a merry fellow and car'st for nothing.

CLOWN Not so, sir, I do care for something: but in my conscience, sir, I do not care for you: if that be to care for nothing, sir, I would it would make you invisible.

VIOLA Art not thou the Lady Olivia's fool?

CLOWN No indeed sir, the Lady Olivia has no folly. She will keep no fool, sir, till she be married, and fools are as like husbands as pilchards are to herrings – the husband's the bigger. I am, indeed, not her fool, but her corrupter of words.

VIOLA I saw thee late at the Count Orsino's.

CLOWN Foolery, sir, does walk about the orb like the sun, it shines everywhere. I would be sorry, sir, but the fool should be as oft with your master as with my mistress: I think I saw your wisdom there.

VIOLA Nay, an thou pass upon me, I'll no more with thee. Hold, there's expenses for thee. [*she gives him a coin*

CLOWN [*gazes at the coin in his palm*] Now Jove, in his next commodity of hair, send thee a beard!

VIOLA By my troth I'll tell thee, I am almost sick for one – [*aside*] though I would not have it grow on my chin. Is thy lady within?

CLOWN [*still gazes at the coin*] Would not a pair of these have bred, sir?

VIOLA Yes, being kept together and put to use.

CLOWN I would play Lord Pandarus of Phrygia, sir, to bring a Cressida to this Troilus.

VIOLA I understand you, sir, 'tis well begged.

[*she gives another coin*

CLOWN The matter, I hope, is not great, sir; begging but a beggar: Cressida was a beggar. My lady is within, sir. I will conster to them whence you come, who you are and what you would are out of my welkin – I might say 'element,' but the word is over-worn.

[*he goes within*

VIOLA This fellow is wise enough to play the fool,
And to do that well craves a kind of wit:
He must observe their mood on whom he jests,
The quality of persons, and the time;
And, like the haggard, check at every feather
That comes before his eye. This is a practice,
As full of labour as a wise man's art:
For folly that he wisely shows is fit;
But wise men, folly-fall'n, quite taint their wit.

SIR TOBY BELCH *and* SIR ANDREW AGUECHEEK *come forth*

SIR TOBY Save you, gentleman.

VIOLA And you, sir.

SIR AND. [*bows*] Dieu vous garde, monsieur.

VIOLA [*bows*] Et vous aussi; votre serviteur.

SIR AND. I hope, sir, you are – and I am yours.

SIR TOBY Will you encounter the house? My niece is desirous you should enter, if your trade be to her.

VIOLA I am bound to your niece, sir. I mean, she is the list of my voyage.

SIR TOBY Taste your legs, sir, put them to motion.

VIOLA My legs do better under-stand me, sir, than I understand what you mean by bidding me taste my legs.

SIR TOBY I mean, to go, sir, to enter.

VIOLA I will answer you with gate and entrance – but we are prevented.

OLIVIA *comes from the house with* MARIA

Most excellent accomplished lady, the heavens rain odours on you!

SIR AND. That youth's a rare courtier – 'Rain odours' – well!

VIOLA My matter hath no voice, lady, but to your own most pregnant and vouchsafed ear.

SIR AND. 'Odours,' 'pregnant', and 'vouchsafed': I'll get 'em all three all ready.

OLIVIA Let the garden door be shut, and leave me to my hearing. [*Sir Toby, Sir Andrew and Maria depart*
Give me your hand, sir.

VIOLA [*bows low*] My duty, madam, and most humble service.

OLIVIA What is your name?

VIOLA Cesario is your servant's name, fair princess.

OLIVIA My servant, sir! 'Twas never merry world,
Since lowly feigning was called compliment:
Y'are servant to the Count Orsino, youth.

VIOLA And he is yours, and his must needs be yours;
Your servant's servant is your servant, madam.

OLIVIA For him, I think not on him: for his thoughts,
Would they were blanks, rather than filled with me!

VIOLA Madam, I come to whet your gentle thoughts
On his behalf.

OLIVIA O, by your leave, I pray you;
I bade you never speak again of him:
But, would you undertake another suit,

I had rather hear you to solicit that
Than music from the spheres.

VIOLA Dear lady –

OLIVIA Give me leave, beseech you: I did send,
After the last enchantment you did here,
A ring in chase of you; so did I abuse
Myself, my servant and, I fear me, you:
Under your hard construction must I sit,
To force that on you in a shameful cunning
Which you knew none of yours: what might you think?
Have you not set mine honour at the stake,
And baited it with all th'unmuzzled thoughts
That tyrannous heart can think?
To one of your receiving enough is shown,
A cypress, not a bosom, hides my heart:
So let me hear you speak.

VIOLA I pity you.

OLIVIA That's a degree to love.

VIOLA No, not a grise;
For 'tis a vulgar proof,
That very oft we pity enemies.

OLIVIA Why then methinks 'tis time to smile again:
O world, how apt the poor are to be proud!
If one should be a prey, how much the better
To fall before the lion than the wolf? ['*clock strikes*'
The clock upbraids me with the waste of time.
Be not afraid, good youth, I will not have you:
And yet, when wit and youth is come to harvest,
Your wife is like to reap a proper man:
There lies your way, due west.

VIOLA Then westward-ho!
Grace and good disposition attend your ladyship!
You'll nothing, madam, to my lord by me?

OLIVIA Stay:
I prithee, tell me what thou think'st of me.

VIOLA That you do think you are not what you are.

OLIVIA If I think so, I think the same of you.

VIOLA Then think you right; I am not what I am.

OLIVIA I would you were as I would have you be!

VIOLA Would it be better, madam, than I am?
I wish it might, for now I am your fool.

OLIVIA O, what a deal of scorn looks beautiful
In the contempt and anger of his lip!
A murderous guilt shows not itself more soon
Than love that would seem hid: love's night is noon.
Cesario, by the roses of the spring,
By maidhood, honour, truth, and everything,
I love thee so, that, maugre all thy pride,
Nor wit nor reason can my passion hide.
Do not extort thy reasons from this clause,
For that I woo, thou therefore hast no cause:
But rather reason thus with reason fetter,
Love sought is good, but given unsought is better.

VIOLA By innocence I swear, and by my youth,
I have one heart, one bosom, and one truth,
And that no woman has, nor never none
Shall mistress be of it, save I alone.
And so adieu, good madam! Never more
Will I my master's tears to you deplore.

OLIVIA Yet come again: for thou perhaps mayst move
That heart, which now abhors, to like his love. [*they go*

SCENE 2

A room in Olivia's house

SIR TOBY BELCH, SIR ANDREW AGUECHEEK *and* FABIAN

SIR AND. No, faith, I'll not stay a jot longer.

SIR TOBY Thy reason, dear venom, give thy reason.

FABIAN You must needs yield your reason, Sir Andrew.

SIR AND. Marry, I saw your niece do more favours to the count's serving-man than ever she bestowed upon me; I saw't i'th'orchard.

SIR TOBY Did she see thee the while, old boy? Tell me that.

SIR AND. As plain as I see you now.

FABIAN This was a great argument of love in her toward you.

SIR AND. 'Slight! will you make an ass o' me?

FABIAN I will prove it legitimate, sir, upon the oaths of judgment and reason.

SIR TOBY And they have been grand-jurymen since before Noah was a sailor.

FABIAN She did show favour to the youth in your sight, only to exasperate you, to awake your dormouse valour, to put fire in your heart, and brimstone in your liver: you should then have accosted her, and with some excellent jests, fire-new from the mint, you should have banged the youth into dumbness: this was looked for at your hand, and this was balked: the double gilt of this opportunity you let time wash off, and you are now sailed into the north of my lady's opinion, where you will hang like an icicle on a Dutchman's beard, unless you do redeem it by some laudable attempt, either of valour or policy.

SIR AND. An't be any way, it must be with valour, for policy I hate: I had as lief be a Brownist, as a politician.

SIR TOBY Why then, build me thy fortunes upon the basis of valour. Challenge me the count's youth to fight with him, hurt him in eleven places – my niece shall take note of it, and assure thyself there is no love-broker in the world can more prevail in man's commendation with woman than report of valour.

FABIAN There is no way but this, Sir Andrew.

SIR AND. Will either of you bear me a challenge to him?

SIR TOBY Go, write it in a martial hand, be curst and brief; it is no matter how witty, so it be eloquent and full of invention: taunt him with the license of ink: if thou 'thou'st' him some thrice, it shall not be amiss; and as many lies as will lie in thy sheet of paper, although the sheet were big enough for the bed of Ware in England, set 'em down – go, about it. Let there be gall enough in thy ink, though thou write with a goose-pen, no matter: about it.

SIR AND. Where shall I find you?

SIR TOBY We'll call thee at thy cubicle: go. [*Sir Andrew goes*

FABIAN This is a dear manakin to you, Sir Toby.

SIR TOBY I have been dear to him, lad – some two thousand strong, or so.

FABIAN We shall have a rare letter from him. But you'll not deliver't?

SIR TOBY Never trust me then; and by all means stir on the youth to an answer. I think oxen and wainropes cannot hale them together. For Andrew, if he were opened and you find so much blood in his liver as will clog the foot of a flea, I'll eat the rest of th'anatomy.

FABIAN And his opposite, the youth, bears in his visage no great presage of cruelty.

MARIA *comes tripping in, holding her sides for laughter*

SIR TOBY Look, where the youngest wren of nine comes.

MARIA If you desire the spleen, and will laugh yourselves into stitches, follow me. Yon gull Malvolio is turned heathen, a very renegado; for there is no Christian, that means to be saved by believing rightly, can ever believe such impossible passages of grossness. [*overcome with laughter*] He's in yellow stockings!

SIR TOBY [*shouts*] And cross-gartered?

MARIA Most villainously; like a pedant that keeps a school i'th' church. I have dogged him like his murderer. He does obey every point of the letter that I dropped to betray him: he does smile his face into more lines than is in the new map, with the augmentation of the Indies: you have not seen such a thing as 'tis. I can hardly forbear hurling things at him. I know my lady will strike him: if she do, he'll smile and take't for a great favour.

SIR TOBY Come, bring us, bring us where he is.

[*they rush forth*

SCENE 3

A street

ANTONIO *and* SEBASTIAN *approach*

SEBASTIAN I would not by my will have troubled you,
But since you make your pleasure of your pains,
I will no further chide you.

ANTONIO I could not stay behind you: my desire,
More sharp than filéd steel, did spur me forth;
And not all love to see you, though so much
As might have drawn one to a longer voyage,
But jealousy what might befall your travel,
Being skilless in these parts; which to a stranger,
Unguided and unfriended, often prove
Rough and unhospitable: my willing love,
The rather by these arguments of fear,
Set forth in your pursuit.

SEBASTIAN My kind Antonio,
I can no other answer make but thanks,
And thanks, and ever thanks; and oft good turns
Are shuffled off with such uncurrent pay:
But, were my worth as is my conscience firm,
You should find better dealing. What's to do?
Shall we go see the relics of this town?

ANTONIO Tomorrow sir – best first go see your lodging.

SEBASTIAN I am not weary, and 'tis long to night:
I pray you, let us satisfy our eyes
With the memorials and the things of fame
That do renown this city.

ANTONIO Would you'ld pardon me;
I do not without danger walk these streets.
Once in a sea-fight 'gainst the count his galleys
I did some service, of such note indeed
That were I ta'en here it would scarce be answered.

SEBASTIAN Belike you slew great number of his people.

ANTONIO Th'offence is not of such a bloody nature,
Albeit the quality of the time and quarrel

Might well have given us bloody argument:
It might have since been answered in repaying
What we took from them, which for traffic's sake
Most of our city did: only myself stood out,
For which, if I be lapséd in this place,
I shall pay dear.

SEBASTIAN Do not then walk too open.

ANTONIO It doth not fit me. Hold, sir, here's my purse.
[*he gives it*
In the south suburbs, at the Elephant,
Is best to lodge: I will bespeak our diet,
Whiles you beguile the time and feed your knowledge
With viewing of the town; there shall you have me.

SEBASTIAN Why I your purse?

ANTONIO Haply your eye shall light upon some toy
You have desire to purchase; and your store,
I think, is not for idle markets, sir.

SEBASTIAN I'll be your purse-bearer, and leave you for an hour.

ANTONIO To th'Elephant.

SEBASTIAN I do remember. [*they go off in different directions*

SCENE 4

Olivia's garden

OLIVIA *enters musing, followed by* MARIA; *Olivia sits*

OLIVIA I have sent after him, he says he'll come;
How shall I feast him? What bestow of him?
For youth is bought more oft than begged or borrowed.
I speak too loud.
[*to Maria*] Where's Malvolio? He is sad and civil,
And suits well for a servant with my fortunes –
Where is Malvolio?

MARIA He's coming, madam; but in very strange manner. He is, sure, possessed, madam.

OLIVIA Why, what's the matter? Does he rave?

MARIA No, madam, he does nothing but smile: your ladyship were best to have some guard about you, if he come, for sure the man is tainted in's wits.

OLIVIA Go, call him hither.

MALVOLIO, *in yellow stockings and with awkward gait, is seen coming down the walk*

I am as mad as he,
If sad and merry madness equal be.
How now, Malvolio?

MALVOLIO Sweet lady, ho, ho.

OLIVIA Smil'st thou?
I sent for thee upon a sad occasion.

MALVOLIO Sad, lady? I could be sad: this does make some obstruction in the blood, this cross-gartering – but what of that? If it please the eye of one, it is with me as the very true sonnet is: 'Please one and please all.'

OLIVIA Why, how dost thou, man? What is the matter with thee?

MALVOLIO Not black in my mind, though yellow in my legs. It did come to his hands, and commands shall be executed. I think we do know the sweet Roman hand.

OLIVIA Wilt thou go to bed, Malvolio?

MALVOLIO To bed! Ay, sweet-heart, and I'll come to thee.

OLIVIA God comfort thee! Why dost thou smile so, and kiss thy hand so oft?

MARIA How do you, Malvolio?

MALVOLIO [*disdainful*] At your request! Yes, nightingales answer daws.

MARIA Why appear you with this ridiculous boldness before my lady?

MALVOLIO [*to Olivia*] 'Be not afraid of greatness': 'twas well writ.

OLIVIA What mean'st thou by that, Malvolio?

MALVOLIO 'Some are born great' –

OLIVIA Ha?

MALVOLIO 'Some achieve greatness' –

OLIVIA What say'st thou?

MALVOLIO 'And some have greatness thrust upon them.'

OLIVIA Heaven restore thee!

MALVOLIO 'Remember, who commended thy yellow stockings' –

OLIVIA Thy yellow stockings!

MALVOLIO 'And wished to see thee cross-gartered.'

OLIVIA Cross-gartered?

MALVOLIO 'Go to, thou art made, if thou desir'st to be so' –

OLIVIA Am I made?

MALVOLIO 'If not, let me see thee a servant still.'

OLIVIA Why, this is very midsummer madness.

A servant comes from the house

SERVANT Madam, the young gentleman of the Count Orsino's is returned – I could hardly entreat him back: he attends your ladyship's pleasure.

OLIVIA I'll come to him. [*the servant goes*] Good Maria, let this fellow be looked to. Where's my cousin Toby? Let some of my people have a special care of him. I would not have him miscarry for the half of my dowry.

[*she enters the house followed by Maria*

MALVOLIO O, ho! Do you come near me now? No worse man than Sir Toby to look to me! This concurs directly with the letter – she sends him on purpose, that I may appear stubborn to him; for she incites me to that in the letter. 'Cast thy humble slough,' says she; 'be opposite with a kinsman, surly with servants, let thy tongue tang with arguments of state, put thyself into the trick of singularity'; and consequently sets down the manner how; as, a sad face, a reverend carriage, a slow tongue, in the habit of some sir of note, and so forth. I have limed her, but it is Jove's doing, and Jove make me thankful! And when she went away now, 'Let this fellow be looked to': fellow! Not Malvolio, nor after my degree, but 'fellow'. Why, every thing adheres together, that no dram of a scruple, no scruple of a scruple, no obstacle, no incredulous or unsafe circumstance – what can be said? Nothing that can be, can come between me and the full prospect of my hopes. Well, Jove, not I, is the doer of this, and he is to be thanked.

MARIA *returns with* SIR TOBY BELCH *and* FABIAN

SIR TOBY Which way is he, in the name of sanctity? If all the devils of hell be drawn in little, and Legion himself possessed him, yet I'll speak to him.

FABIAN Here he is, here he is. How is't with you, sir?

SIR TOBY How is't with you, man?

MALVOLIO Go off, I discard you; let me enjoy my private: go off.

MARIA Lo, how hollow the fiend speaks within him! Did not I tell you? Sir Toby, my lady prays you to have a care of him.

MALVOLIO Ah, ha! Does she so!

SIR TOBY Go to, go to: peace, peace, we must deal gently with him: let me alone. How do you, Malvolio? How is't with you? What, man! Defy the devil: consider, he's an enemy to mankind.

MALVOLIO Do you know what you say?

MARIA La you! An you speak ill of the devil, how he takes it at heart! Pray God, he be not bewitched!

FABIAN Carry his water to th'wise woman.

MARIA Marry, and it shall be done tomorrow morning, if I live. My lady would not lose him for more than I'll say.

MALVOLIO How now, mistress!

MARIA [*chokes*] O Lord!

SIR TOBY Prithee, hold thy peace, this is not the way: do you not see you move him? Let me alone with him.

FABIAN No way but gentleness, gently, gently: the fiend is rough, and will not be roughly used.

SIR TOBY Why, how now, my bawcock! How dost thou, chuck?

MALVOLIO Sir!

SIR TOBY Ay, Biddy, come with me. What, man! 'Tis not for gravity to play at cherry-pit with Satan. Hang him, foul collier!

MARIA Get him to say his prayers, good Sir Toby, get him to pray.

MALVOLIO My prayers, minx!

MARIA No, I warrant you, he will not hear of godliness.

MALVOLIO Go, hang yourselves all! You are idle shallow things – I am not of your element – You shall know more hereafter. [*he goes; they gaze after him in amazement*

SIR TOBY Is't possible?

FABIAN If this were played upon a stage now, I could condemn it as an improbable fiction.

SIR TOBY His very genius hath taken the infection of the device, man.

MARIA Nay, pursue him now, lest the device take air and taint.

FABIAN Why, we shall make him mad indeed.

MARIA The house will be the quieter.

SIR TOBY Come, we'll have him in a dark room and bound. My niece is already in the belief that he's mad; we may carry it thus, for our pleasure and his penance, till our very pastime, tired out of breath, prompt us to have mercy on him: at which time we will bring the device to the bar and crown thee for a finder of madmen. But see, but see.

SIR ANDREW AGUECHEEK *comes forth, a letter in his hand*

FABIAN More matter for a May morning!

SIR AND Here's the challenge, read it: I warrant there's vinegar and pepper in't.

FABIAN Is't so saucy?

SIR AND Ay, is't! I warrant him: do but read.

SIR TOBY Give me. [*he reads*] 'Youth, whatsoever thou art, thou art but a scurvy fellow.'

FABIAN Good, and valiant.

SIR TOBY 'Wonder not, nor admire not in thy mind, why I do call thee so, for I will show thee no reason for't.'

FABIAN A good note, that keeps you from the blow of the law.

SIR TOBY 'Thou com'st to the Lady Olivia, and in my sight she uses thee kindly: but thou liest in thy throat, that is not the matter I challenge thee for.'

FABIAN Very brief, and to exceeding good sense – [*aside*] less.

SIR TOBY 'I will waylay thee going home, where if it be thy chance to kill me,' –

FABIAN Good.

SIR TOBY 'Thou kill'st me like a rogue and a villain.'

FABIAN Still you keep o'th' windy side of the law: good.

SIR TOBY 'Fare thee well, and God have mercy upon one of our souls! He may have mercy upon mine, but my hope is better, and so look to thyself. Thy friend, as thou usest him, and thy sworn enemy, ANDREW AGUECHEEK'

If this letter move him not, his legs cannot: I'll give't him.

MARIA You may have very fit occasion for't: he is now in some commerce with my lady, and will by and by depart.

SIR TOBY Go, sir Andrew; scout me for him at the corner of the orchard like a bum-baily: so soon as ever thou seest him, draw, and as thou draw'st, swear horrible; for it comes to pass oft that a terrible oath, with a swaggering accent sharply twanged off, gives manhood more approbation than ever proof itself would have earned him. Away!

SIR AND Nay, let me alone for swearing.

[he leaves the garden by the outer door

SIR TOBY Now will not I deliver his letter: for the behaviour of the young gentleman gives him out to be of good capacity and breeding; his employment between his lord and my niece confirms no less; therefore this letter, being so excellently ignorant, will breed no terror in the youth: he will find it comes from a clodpole. But, sir, I will deliver his challenge by word of mouth; set upon Aguecheek a notable report of valour; and drive the gentleman, as I know his youth will aptly receive it, into a most hideous opinion of his rage, skill, fury and impetuosity. This will so fright them both, that they will kill one another by the look, like cockatrices.

OLIVIA *and* VIOLA *come from the house*

FABIAN Here he comes with your niece – give them way till he take leave, and presently after him.

SIR TOBY I will meditate the while upon some horrid message for a challenge.

[Sir Toby, Fabian and Maria go off into the garden

OLIVIA I have said too much unto a heart of stone,
And laid mine honour too unchary out:
There's something in me that reproves my fault;
But such a headstrong potent fault it is,
That it but mocks reproof.

VIOLA With the same 'haviour that your passion bears
Goes on my master's grief.

OLIVIA Here, wear this jewel for me, 'tis my picture;
Refuse it not, it hath no tongue to vex you:
And I beseech you come again tomorrow.
What shall you ask of me, that I'll deny,
That honour saved may upon asking give?

VIOLA Nothing but this – your true love for my master.

OLIVIA How with mine honour may I give him that
Which I have given to you?

VIOLA I will acquit you.

OLIVIA Well, come again tomorrow: fare thee well.
A fiend, like thee, might bear my soul to hell.
[*she goes within; Viola walks toward the outer gate*

SIR TOBY BELCH *and* FABIAN *come up*

SIR TOBY Gentleman, God save thee.

VIOLA [*turns*] And you, sir.

SIR TOBY That defence thou hast, betake thee to't: of what nature the wrongs are thou hast done him, I know not; but thy intercepter, full of despite, bloody as the hunter, attends thee at the orchard-end: dismount thy tuck, be yare in thy preparation, for thy assailant is quick, skilful and deadly.

VIOLA You mistake, sir. I am sure no man hath any quarrel to me; my remembrance is very free and clear from any image of offence done to any man.

SIR TOBY You'll find it otherwise, I assure you: therefore, if you hold your life at any price, betake you to your guard; for your opposite hath in him what youth, strength, skill and wrath can furnish man withal.

VIOLA I pray you, sir, what is he?

SIR TOBY He is knight, dubbed with unhatched rapier and on carpet consideration, but he is a devil in private brawl: souls and bodies hath he divorced three, and his incensement at this moment is so implacable, that satisfaction can be none but by pangs of death and sepulchre. Hob, nob, is his word; give't or take't.

VIOLA I will return again into the house and desire some conduct of the lady. I am no fighter. I have heard of some kind of men that put quarrels purposely on others to taste their valour: belike this is a man of that quirk.

SIR TOBY Sir, no; his indignation derives itself out of a very competent injury, therefore get you on and give him his desire. Back you shall not to the house, unless you undertake that with me which with as much safety you might answer him: therefore on, or strip your sword stark naked; for meddle you must, that's certain, or forswear to wear iron about you.

VIOLA This is as uncivil as strange. I beseech you, do me this courteous office, as to know of the knight what my offence to him is; it is something of my negligence, nothing of my purpose.

SIR TOBY I will do so. Signior Fabian, [*he winks*] stay you by this gentleman till my return. [*he departs by the outer door*

VIOLA Pray you, sir, do you know of this matter?

FABIAN I know the knight is incensed against you, even to a mortal arbitrement, but nothing of the circumstance more.

VIOLA I beseech you, what manner of man is he?

FABIAN Nothing of that wonderful promise, to read him by his form, as you are like to find him in the proof of his valour. He is indeed, sir, the most skilful, bloody and fatal opposite that you could possibly have found in any part of Illyria. [*he takes her by the arm*] Will you walk towards him? I will make your peace with him if I can.

VIOLA I shall be much bound to you for't: I am one, that had rather go with sir priest than sir knight: I care not who knows so much of my mettle. [*they leave the garden*

A quiet street at the back of Olivia's walled garden, with a gate leading thereto; trees and shrubs

SIR TOBY *and* SIR ANDREW

SIR TOBY Why, man, he's a very devil, I have not seen such a firago. I had a pass with him, rapier, scabbard and all, and he gives me the stuck in with such a mortal motion that it is inevitable; and on the answer, he pays you as surely as your feet hit the ground they step on. They say he has been fencer to the Sophy.

SIR AND. Pox on't, I'll not meddle with him.

SIR TOBY Ay, but he will not now be pacified: Fabian can scarce hold him yonder.

SIR AND. Plague on't, an I thought he had been valiant and so cunning in fence, I'd have seen him damned ere I'd have challenged him. Let him let the matter slip, and I'll give him my horse, grey Capilet.

SIR TOBY I'll make the motion: stand here, make a good show on't – this shall end without the perdition of souls. [*aside*] Marry, I'll ride your horse as well as I ride you.

FABIAN *and* VIOLA *come from the garden; Sir Toby beckons Fabian aside*

I have his horse to take up the quarrel; I have persuaded him the youth's a devil.

FABIAN He is as horribly conceited of him, and pants and looks pale, as if a bear were at his heels.

SIR TOBY [*to Viola*] There's no remedy, sir, he will fight with you for's oath sake: marry, he hath better bethought him of his quarrel, and he finds that now scarce to be worth talking of: therefore draw for the supportance of his vow, he protests he will not hurt you.

VIOLA Pray God defend me! A little thing would make me tell them how much I lack of a man.

FABIAN Give ground, if you see him furious.

SIR TOBY Come, Sir Andrew, there's no remedy, the gentleman will for his honour's sake have one bout with you: he cannot by the duello avoid it: but he has promised me, as he is a gentleman and a soldier, he will not hurt you. Come on, to't!

SIR AND. Pray God, he keep his oath!

VIOLA I do assure you, 'tis against my will.

They make ready to fight; ANTONIO *comes up*

ANTONIO [*to Sir Andrew*]
Put up your sword: if this young gentleman
Have done offence, I take the fault on me;
If you offend him, I for him defy you.

SIR TOBY You, sir! Why, what are you?

ANTONIO One, sir, that for his love dares yet do more
Than you have heard him brag to you he will.

SIR TOBY Nay, if you be an undertaker, I am for you. *[they draw*

Two officers approach

FABIAN O good Sir Toby, hold; here come the officers.

SIR TOBY *[to Antonio]* I'll be with you anon. *[he hides from the officers behind a tree*

VIOLA *[to Sir Andrew]* Pray, sir, put your sword up, if you please.

SIR AND. Marry, will I, sir; and, for that I promised you, I'll be as good as my word. *[he sheathes his sword]* He will bear you easily, and reins well.

1 OFFICER This is the man, do thy office.

2 OFFICER Antonio, I arrest thee at the suit
Of Count Orsino.

ANTONIO You do mistake me, sir.

1 OFFICER No, sir, no jot; I know your favour well:
Though now you have no sea-cap on your head.
Take him away, he knows I know him well.

ANTONIO I must obey. *[to Viola]* This comes with seeking you;
But there's no remedy, I shall answer it.
What will you do, now my necessity
Makes me to ask you for my purse? It grieves me
Much more for what I cannot do for you
Than what befalls myself. You stand amazed,
But be of comfort.

2 OFFICER Come, sir, away.

ANTONIO I must entreat of you some of that money.

VIOLA What money, sir?
For the fair kindness you have showed me here,
And part being prompted by your present trouble,
Out of my lean and low ability
I'll lend you something. *[opens her purse]*
My having is not much,
I'll make division of my present with you:
Hold, there's half my coffer. *[she proffers coin*

ANTONIO *[refuses it]* Will you deny me now?
Is't possible that my deserts to you
Can lack persuasion? Do not tempt my misery,

Lest that it make me so unsound a man
As to upbraid you with those kindnesses
That I have done for you.

VIOLA I know of none,
Nor know I you by voice or any feature:
I hate ingratitude more in a man,
Than lying vainness, babbling drunkenness,
Or any taint of vice whose strong corruption
Inhabits our frail blood.

ANTONIO O heavens themselves!

2 OFFICER Come, sir, I pray you, go.

ANTONIO Let me speak a little.
This youth that you see here
I snatched one half out of the jaws of death,
Relieved him with such sanctity of love
And to his image, which methought did promise
Most venerable worth, did I devotion.

1 OFFICER What's that to us? The time goes by: away!

ANTONIO But, O, how vile an idol proves this god!
Thou hast, Sebastian, done good feature shame.
In nature there's no blemish but the mind;
None can be called deformed but the unkind:
Virtue is beauty, but the beauteous evil
Are empty trunks o'erflourished by the devil.

1 OFFICER The man grows mad, away with him!
Come, come, sir.

ANTONIO Lead me on. [*they carry him off*

VIOLA Methinks his words do from such passion fly,
That he believes himself – so do not I?
Prove true, imagination, O prove true,
That I, dear brother, be now ta'en for you!

SIR TOBY [*peeps from behind the tree*] Come hither, knight – come hither, Fabian; we'll whisper o'er a couplet or two of most sage saws.

VIOLA He named Sebastian; I my brother know
Yet living in my glass; even such and so
In favour was my brother, and he went
Still in this fashion, colour, ornament,
For him I imitate: O, if it prove,

Tempests are kind and salt waves fresh in love!

[*she goes*

SIR TOBY A very dishonest paltry boy, and more a coward than a hare. His dishonesty appears in leaving his friend here in necessity and denying him; and for his cowardship, ask Fabian.

FABIAN A coward, a most devout coward, religious in it.

SIR AND. 'Slid, I'll after him again and beat him.

SIR TOBY Do, cuff him soundly, but never draw thy sword.

SIR AND. An I do not – [*he draws his sword and hurries after Viola*

FABIAN Come, let's see the event.

SIR TOBY I dare lay any money, 'twill be nothing yet.

[*they follow Sir Andrew*

ACT 4 SCENE 1

A square before Olivia's house

SEBASTIAN *and* CLOWN

CLOWN Will you make me believe that I am not sent for you?

SEBASTIAN Go to, go to, thou art a foolish fellow;
Let me be clear of thee.

CLOWN Well held out, i'faith! No, I do not know you, nor I am not sent to you by my lady to bid you come speak with her, nor your name is not Master Cesario, nor this is not my nose neither: nothing that is so, is so.

SEBASTIAN I prithee, vent thy folly somewhere else,
Thou know'st not me.

CLOWN Vent my folly! He has heard that word of some great man and now applies it to a fool. Vent my folly! I am afraid this great lubber, the world, will prove a cockney. I prithee now, ungird thy strangeness and tell me what I shall vent to my lady: [*whispers, winking*] shall I vent to her that thou art coming?

SEBASTIAN I prithee, foolish Greek, depart from me.
There's money for thee [*he gives a coin*]
– if you tarry longer
I shall give worse payment.

CLOWN By my troth, thou hast an open hand. These wise men that give fools money get themselves a good report – after fourteen years' purchase.

SIR ANDREW *with drawn sword enters the square,*
SIR TOBY *and* FABIAN *following*

SIR AND. Now, sir, have I met you again? There's for you.
[*he strikes wide*

SEBASTIAN [*replies with his fists*]
Why, there's for thee, and there, and there!
[*he knocks him down*
Are all the people mad? [*his hand upon his dagger*

SIR TOBY [*seizes him from behind*]
Hold, sir, or I'll throw your dagger o'er the house.

CLOWN This will I tell my lady straight: I would not be in some of your coats for two pence. [*he goes within*

SIR TOBY Come on, sir! Hold! [*Sebastian struggles*

SIR AND. [*rubbing his bruises*] Nay, let him alone, I'll go another way to work with him: I'll have an action of battery against him, if there be any law in Illyria: though I struck him first, yet it's no matter for that.

SEBASTIAN Let go thy hand!

SIR TOBY Come, sir, I will not let you go. [*to Sir Andrew*] Come, my young soldier, put up your iron: you are well fleshed. [*to Sebastian*] Come on.

SEBASTIAN I will be free from thee. [*he throws him off*
What wouldst thou now?
[*he draws*
If thou dar'st tempt me further, draw thy sword.

SIR TOBY What, what? [*he also draws*] Nay, then I must have an ounce or two of this malapert blood from you.
[*they begin to fight*

OLIVIA *comes from the house*

OLIVIA Hold, Toby! On thy life, I charge thee, hold!

SIR TOBY Madam! [*they break off*

OLIVIA Will it be ever thus? Ungracious wretch,
Fit for the mountains and the barbarous caves,
Where manners newer were preached! Out of my sight!
Be not offended, dear Cesario.
Rudesby, be gone! [*Sir Toby, Sir Andrew and Fabian slink off*
I prithee, gentle friend,
Let thy fair wisdom, not thy passion, sway
In this uncivil and unjust extent
Against thy peace. Go with me to my house,
And hear thou there how many fruitless pranks
This ruffian hath botched up, that thou thereby
Mayst smile at this. [*he draws back*]
Thou shalt not choose but go;
Do not deny. Beshrew his soul for me,
He started one poor heart of mine in thee.

SEBASTIAN What relish is in this? How runs the stream?
Or I am mad, or else this is a dream:

Let fancy still my sense in Lethe steep –
If it be thus to dream, still let me sleep!

OLIVIA Nay, come, I prithee: would thou'dst be ruled by me!

SEBASTIAN Madam, I will.

OLIVIA O, say so, and so be! [*they go in*

SCENE 2

A room in Olivia's house; at the back a closet with a curtain before it

CLOWN *and* MARIA, *holding a black gown and a false beard in his hand*

MARIA Nay, I prithee, put on this gown and this beard, make him believe thou art Sir Topas the curate, do it quickly. I'll call Sir Toby the whilst. [*she goes out*

CLOWN Well, I'll put it on, and I will dissemble myself in't, and I would I were the first that ever dissembled in such a gown. [*he dons the gown and the beard*] I am not tall enough to become the function well, nor lean enough to be thought a good student: but to be said an honest man and a good housekeeper goes as fairly as to say a careful man and a great scholar. The competitors enter.

MARIA *returns with Sir* TOBY

SIR TOBY Jove bless thee, Master Parson!

CLOWN [*in frightened voice*] Bonos dies, Sir Toby: for as the old hermit of Prague, that never saw pen and ink, very wittily said to a niece of King Gorboduc, 'That that is, is': so I, being Master Parson, am Master Parson; for what is 'that' but that? and 'is' but is?

SIR TOBY To him, Sir Topas.

CLOWN [*draws near the curtain*] What, ho, I say! Peace in this prison!

SIR TOBY The knave counterfeits well; a good knave.

MALVOLIO [*from the closet*] Who calls there?

CLOWN Sir Topas the curate, who comes to visit Malvolio the lunatic.

MALVOLIO Sir Topas, Sir Topas, good Sir Topas, go to my lady.

CLOWN Out, hyperbolical fiend! How vexest thou this man?

Talkest thou nothing but of ladies?

SIR TOBY Well said, Master Parson.

MALVOLIO Sir Topas, never was man thus wronged – good Sir Topas, do not think I am mad; they have laid me here in hideous darkness.

CLOWN Fie, thou dishonest Satan! I call thee by the most modest terms, for I am one of those gentle ones that will use the devil himself with courtesy: say'st thou that house is dark?

MALVOLIO As hell, Sir Topas.

CLOWN Why, it hath bay windows transparent as barricadoes, and the clerestories toward the south-north are as lustrous as ebony; and yet complainest thou of obstruction?

MALVOLIO I am not mad, Sir Topas. I say to you, this house is dark.

CLOWN Madman, thou errest: I say, there is no darkness but ignorance, in which thou art more puzzled than the Egyptians in their fog.

MALVOLIO I say, this house is as dark as ignorance, though ignorance were as dark as hell; and I say, there was never man thus abused. I am no more mad than so you are – make the trial of it in any constant question.

CLOWN What is the opinion of Pythagoras concerning wild fowl?

MALVOLIO That the soul of our grandam might haply inhabit a bird.

CLOWN What think'st thou of his opinion?

MALVOLIO I think nobly of the soul, and no way approve his opinion.

CLOWN Fare thee well: remain thou still in darkness. Thou shalt hold th'opinion of Pythagoras ere I will allow of thy wits, and fear to kill a woodcock, lest thou dispossess the soul of thy grandam. Fare thee well.

[*he turns back from before the curtain*

MALVOLIO [*calls*] Sir Topas, Sir Topas!

SIR TOBY My most exquisite Sir Topas!

CLOWN Nay, I am for all waters. [*he puts off the disguise*

MARIA Thou mightst have done this without thy beard and gown, he sees thee not.

SIR TOBY To him in thine own voice, and bring me word how thou find'st him. [*to Maria*] I would we were well rid of this knavery. If he may be conveniently delivered, I would he were, for I am now so far in offence with my niece, that I cannot pursue with any safety this sport to the upshot. Come by and by to my chamber.

[*Sir Toby and Maria go out by different doors*

CLOWN [*sings*] 'Hey Robin, jolly Robin,
Tell me how thy lady does.'

MALVOLIO Fool, –

CLOWN [*sings*] 'My lady is unkind, perdy.'

MALVOLIO Fool –

CLOWN [*sings*] 'Alas, why is she so?'

MALVOLIO Fool, I say –

CLOWN [*sings*] 'She loves another' – Who calls, ha?

MALVOLIO Good fool, as ever thou wilt deserve well at my hand, help me to a candle, and pen, ink and paper; as I am a gentleman, I will live to be thankful to thee for't.

CLOWN Master Malvolio!

MALVOLIO Ay, good fool.

CLOWN Alas, sir, how fell you besides your five wits?

MALVOLIO Fool, there was never man so notoriously abused: I am as well in my wits, fool, as thou art.

CLOWN But as well? Then you are mad indeed, if you go be no better in your wits than a fool.

MALVOLIO They have here propertied me; keep me in darkness, send ministers to me, asses, and do all they can to face me out of my wits.

CLOWN Advise you what you say; the minister is here. [*he changes his voice*] Malvolio, Malvolio, thy wits the heavens restore! Endeavour thyself to sleep, and leave thy vain bibble babble.

MALVOLIO Sir Topas –

CLOWN Maintain no words with him, good fellow. – Who, I, sir? Not I, sir. God buy you, good sir Topas – Marry, amen – I will, sir, I will.

MALVOLIO Fool, fool, fool, I say –

CLOWN Alas, sir, be patient. What say you, sir? I am shent for speaking to you.

MALVOLIO Good fool, help me to some light and some paper. I tell thee, I am as well in my wits, as any man in Illyria.

CLOWN Well-a-day that you were, sir!

MALVOLIO By this hand, I am. Good fool, some ink, paper and light: and convey what I will set down to my lady; it shall advantage thee more than ever the bearing of letteer did.

CLOWN I will help you to't. But tell me true, are you not mad indeed? Or do you but counterfeit?

MALVOLIO Believe me, I am not – I tell thee true.

CLOWN Nay, I'll ne'er believe a madman till I see his brains. I will fetch you light and paper and ink.

MALVOLIO Fool, I'll requite it in the highest degree: I prithee, be gone.

CLOWN [*sings as he dances from the room*]

I am gone, sir, and anon, sir,
I'll be with you again:
  In a trice, like to the old Vice,
Your need to sustain.
Who with dagger of lath,
In his rage and his wrath,
  Cries ah ha, to the devil:
Like a mad lad,
Pare thy nails dad,
  Adieu goodman devil. [*he goes*

SCENE 3

Olivia's garden

SEBASTIAN *comes from the house*

SEBASTIAN This is the air, that is the glorious sun,
This pearl she gave me, I do feel't and see't,
And though 'tis wonder that enwraps me thus,
Yet 'tis not madness. Where's Antonio then?
I could not find him at the Elephant,
Yet there he was, and there I found this credit,
That he did range the town to seek me out.
His counsel now might do me golden service,

For though my soul disputes well with my sense,
That this may be some error, but no madness,
Yet doth this accident and flood of fortune
So far exceed all instance, all discourse,
That I am ready to distrust mine eyes
And wrangle with my reason, that persuades me
To any other trust but that I am mad,
Or else the lady's mad; yet, if 'twere so,
She could not sway her house, command her followers,
Take and give back affairs and their dispatch,
With such a smooth, discreet, and stable bearing
As I perceive she does: there's something in't
That is deceivable. But here the lady comes.

OLIVIA *comes forth with a priest*

OLIVIA Blame not this haste of mine. If you mean well,
Now go with me and with this holy man
Into the chantry by: there, before him,
And underneath that consecrated roof,
Plight me the full assurance of your faith,
That my most jealous and too doubtful soul
May live at peace. He shall conceal it,
Whiles you are willing it shall come to note,
What time we will our celebration keep
According to my birth. What do you say?

SEBASTIAN I'll follow this good man and go with you,
And having sworn truth, ever will be true.

OLIVIA Then lead the way, good father, and heavens so shine,
That they may fairly note this act of mine!

[*they go*

ACT 5 SCENE 1

The square before Olivia's house

CLOWN *and* FABIAN

FABIAN Now, as thou lov'st me, let me see his letter.

CLOWN Good Master Fabian, grant me another request.

FABIAN Anything.

CLOWN Do not desire to see this letter.

FABIAN This is, to give a dog, and in recompense desire my dog again.

The DUKE *and* VIOLA *(as Cesario) enter the square with attendants*

DUKE Belong you to the Lady Olivia, friends?

CLOWN Ay, sir, we are some of her trappings.

DUKE I know thee well: how dost thou, my good fellow.

CLOWN Truly, sir, the better for my foes and the worse for my friends.

DUKE Just the contrary; the better for thy friends.

CLOWN No, sir, the worse.

DUKE How can that be?

CLOWN Marry, sir, they praise me and make an ass of me; now my foes tell me plainly I am an ass: so that by my foes, sir, I profit in the knowledge of myself, and by my friends I am abused: so that, conclusions to be as kisses, if your four negatives make your two affirmatives, why then – the worse for my friends and the better for my foes.

DUKE Why, this is excellent.

CLOWN By my troth, sir, no; though it please you to be one of my friends.

DUKE Thou shalt not be the worse for me – there's gold.

[*he gives him money*

CLOWN But that it would be double-dealing, sir, I would you could make it another.

DUKE O, you give me ill counsel.

CLOWN Put your grace in your pocket, sir, for this once, and let your flesh and blood obey it.

DUKE Well, I will be so much a sinner, to be a double-dealer; there's another. [*he gives more money*

CLOWN Primo, secundo, tertio, is a good play, and the old saying is, the third pays for all: the triplex, sir, is a good tripping measure, or the bells of St Bennet, sir, may put you in mind – one, two, three!

DUKE You can fool no more money out of me at this throw: if you will let your lady know I am here to speak with her, and bring her along with you, it may awake my bounty further.

CLOWN Marry, sir, lullaby to your bounty till I come again. I go, sir, but I would not have you to think that my desire of having is the sin of covetousness: but, as you say, sir, let your bounty take a nap, I will awake it anon. [*he goes within*

Officers approach with ANTONIO *bound*

VIOLA Here comes the man, sir, that did rescue me.

DUKE That face of his I do remember well,
Yet when I saw it last it was besmeared
As black as Vulcan in the smoke of war:
A baubling vessel was he captain of,
For shallow draught and bulk unprizable,
With which such scathful grapple did he make
With the most noble bottom of our fleet,
That very envy and the tongue of loss
Cried fame and honour on him. What's the matter?

1 OFFICER Orsino, this is that Antonio
That took the Phoenix and her fraught from Candy,
And this is he that did the Tiger board,
When your young nephew Titus lost his leg:
Here in the streets, desperate of shame and state,
In private brabble did we apprehend him.

VIOLA He did me kindness, sir, drew on my side,
But in conclusion put strange speech upon me,
I know not what 'twas but distraction.

DUKE Notable pirate! Thou salt-water thief!
What foolish boldness brought thee to their mercies,
Whom thou, in terms so bloody and so dear,

Hast made thine enemies?

ANTONIO Orsino, noble sir,
Be pleased that I shake off these names you give me;
Antonio never yet was thief or pirate,
Though I confess, on base and ground enough,
Orsino's enemy. A witchcraft drew me hither:
That most ingrateful boy there by your side,
From the rude sea's enraged and foamy mouth
Did I redeem; a wrack past hope he was:
His life I gave him and did thereto add
My love, without retention or restraint,
All his in dedication. For his sake
Did I expose myself – pure for his love! –
Into the danger of this adverse town,
Drew to defend him when he was beset:
Where being apprehended, his false cunning,
Not meaning to partake with me in danger,
Taught him to face me out of his acquaintance,
And grew a twenty years removéd thing
While one would wink; denied me mine own purse,
Which I had recommended to his use
Not half an hour before.

VIOLA How can this be?

DUKE When came he to this town?

ANTONIO Today, my lord; and for three months before,
No interim, not a minute's vacancy,
Both day and night did we keep company.

OLIVIA *comes from the house, attended*

DUKE Here comes the countess! Now heaven walks on earth.
But for thee, fellow – fellow, thy words are madness,
Three months this youth hath tended upon me.
But more of that anon. Take him aside. [*the officers obey*

OLIVIA [*draws near*]
What would my lord, but that he may not have,
Wherein Olivia may seem serviceable?
Cesario, you do not keep promise with me.

VIOLA Madam?

DUKE Gracious Olivia –
OLIVIA What do you say, Cesario? Good my lord –
VIOLA My lord would speak, my duty hushes me.
OLIVIA If it be aught to the old tune, my lord,
It is as fat and fulsome to mine ear
As howling after music.
DUKE Still so cruel?
OLIVIA Still so constant, lord.
DUKE What, to perverseness? You uncivil lady,
To whose ingrate and unauspicious altars
My soul the faithfull'st off'rings hath breathed out,
That e'er devotion tendered! What shall I do?
OLIVIA Even what it please my lord, that shall become him.
DUKE Why should I not, had I the heart to do it,
Like to th'Egyptian thief, at point of death,
Kill what I love? A savage jealousy
That sometime savours nobly. But hear me this:
Since you to non-regardance cast my faith,
And that I partly know the instrument
That screws me from my true place in your favour,
Live you, the marble-breasted tyrant, still;
But this your minion, whom I know you love,
And whom, by heaven I swear, I tender dearly,
Him will I tear out of that cruel eye,
Where he sits crownéd in his master's spite.
Come boy with me. My thoughts are ripe in mischief:
I'll sacrifice the lamb that I do love,
To spite a raven's heart within a dove. [*he turns away*
VIOLA [*follows*] And I, most jocund, apt and willingly,
To do you rest, a thousand deaths would die.
OLIVIA Where goes Cesario?
VIOLA After him I love
More than I love these eyes, more than my life,
More, by all mores, than e'er I shall love wife.
If I do feign, you witnesses above
Punish my life for tainting of my love!
OLIVIA Ay me, detested! How am I beguiled!
VIOLA Who does beguile you? Who does do you wrong?
OLIVIA Hast thou forgot thyself? Is it so long?

Call forth the holy father. [*an attendant goes within*

DUKE [*to Viola*] Come, away!

OLIVIA Whither, my lord? Cesario, husband, stay.

DUKE Husband?

OLIVIA Ay, husband. Can he that deny?

DUKE Her husband, sirrah?

VIOLA No, my lord, not I.

OLIVIA Alas, it is the baseness of thy fear,
That makes thee strangle thy propriety:
Fear not, Cesario, take thy fortunes up,
Be that thou know'st thou art, and then thou art
As great as that thou fear'st.

The priest comes forth

O, welcome, father!
Father, I charge thee, by thy reverence,
Here to unfold – though lately we intended
To keep in darkness, what occasion now
Reveals before 'tis ripe – what thou dost know
Hath newly passed between this youth and me.

PRIEST A contract of eternal bond of love,
Confirmed by mutual joinder of your hands,
Attested by the holy close of lips,
Strength'ned by interchangement of your rings,
And all the ceremony of this compact
Sealed in my function, by my testimony
Since when, my watch hath told me, toward my grave,
I have travelled but two hours.

DUKE O, thou dissembling cub! What wilt thou be
When time hath sowed a grizzle on thy case?
Or will not else thy craft so quickly grow,
That thine own trip shall be thine overthrow?
Farewell, and take her, but direct thy feet
Where thou and I henceforth may never meet.

VIOLA My lord, I do protest –

OLIVIA O, do not swear!
Hold little faith, though thou hast too much fear.

SIR ANDREW AGUECHEEK *comes up with his head broke*

SIR AND. For the love of God, a surgeon! Send one presently to

Sir Toby.

OLIVIA What's the matter?

SIR AND. H'as broke my head across and has given Sir Toby a bloody coxcomb too: for the love of God, your help! I had rather than forty pound I were at home.

[*he sinks to the ground*

OLIVIA Who has done this, Sir Andrew?

SIR AND. The count's gentleman, one Cesario: we took him for a coward, but he's the very devil incardinate.

DUKE My gentleman, Cesario?

SIR AND. 'Od's lifelings, here he is! You broke my head for nothing, and that that I did, I was set on to do't by Sir Toby.

VIOLA Why do you speak to me? I never hurt you:
You drew your sword upon me without cause,
But I bespake you fair, and hurt you not.

SIR AND. If a bloody coxcomb be a hurt, you have hurt me; I think you set nothing by a bloody coxcomb.

SIR TOBY *approaches bleeding, led by the* CLOWN

Here comes Sir Toby halting, you shall hear more: but if he had not been in drink, he would have tickled you othergates than he did.

DUKE How now, gentleman! How is't with you?

SIR TOBY That's all one – has hurt me, and there's th'end on't. [*to Clown*] Sot, didst see Dick surgeon, sot?

CLOWN O he's drunk, Sir Toby, an hour agone; his eyes were set at eight i'th' morning.

SIR TOBY Then he's a rogue, and a passy-measures pavin: I hate a drunken rogue.

OLIVIA Away with him! Who hath made this havoc with them?

SIR AND. [*rises*] I'll help you, Sir Toby, because we'll be dressed together.

SIR TOBY Will you help? An ass-head, and a coxcomb, and a knave! A thin-faced knave, a gull!

OLIVIA Get him to bed, and let his hurt be looked to.

[*Clown, Sir Toby, and Sir Andrew go within*

SEBASTIAN *enters the square*

SEBASTIAN I am sorry, madam, I have hurt your kinsman;

But, had it been the brother of my blood,
I must have done no less with wit and safety.
[*all stand in amaze*
You throw a strange regard upon me, and by that
I do perceive it hath offended you;
Pardon me, sweet one, even for the vows
We made each other but so late ago.

DUKE One face, one voice, one habit, and two persons,
A natural perspective, that is and is not.

SEBASTIAN Antonio! O my dear Antonio!
How have the hours racked and tortured me,
Since I have lost thee!

ANTONIO Sebastian are you?

SEBASTIAN Fear'st thou that, Antonio?

ANTONIO How have you made division of yourself?
An apple, cleft in two, is not more twin
Than these two creatures. Which is Sebastian?

OLIVIA Most wonderful!

SEBASTIAN Do I stand there? I never had a brother:
Nor can there be that deity in my nature
Of here and every where. I had a sister,
Whom the blind waves and surges have devoured.
Of charity, what kin are you to me?
What countryman? What name? What parentage?

VIOLA Of Messaline: Sebastian was my father –
Such a Sebastian was my brother too:
So went he suited to his watery tomb-
If spirits can assume both form and suit,
You come to fright us.

SEBASTIAN A spirit I am indeed,
But am in that dimension grossly clad,
Which from the womb I did participate.
Were you a woman, as the rest goes even,
I should my tears let fall upon your cheek,
And say 'Thrice-welcome, drownéd Viola!'

VIOLA My father had a mole upon his brow.

SEBASTIAN And so had mine.

VIOLA And died that day when Viola from her birth
Had numb'red thirteen years.

SEBASTIAN O, that record is lively in my soul!
He finishéd indeed his mortal act,
That day that made my sister thirteen years.

VIOLA If nothing lets to make us happy both,
But this my masculine usurped attire,
Do not embrace me till each circumstance
Of place, time, fortune, do cohere and jump
That I am Viola – which to confirm,
I'll bring you to a captain in this town,
Where lie my maiden weeds; by whose gentle help
I was preserved to serve this noble count.
All the occurrence of my fortune since
Hath been between this lady and this lord.

SEBASTIAN [*to Olivia*] So comes it, lady, you have been mistook;
But nature to her bias drew in that.
You would have been contracted to a maid,
Nor are you therein, by my life, deceived,
You are betrothed both to a maid and man.

DUKE Be not amazed – right noble is his blood.
If this be so, as yet the glass seems true,
I shall have share in this most happy wrack.
[*to Viola*] Boy, thou hast said to me a thousand times
Thou never shouldst love woman like to me.

VIOLA And all those sayings will I over-swear,
And all those swearings keep as true in soul,
As doth that orbéd continent the fire
That severs day from night.

DUKE Give me thy hand,
And let me see thee in thy woman's weeds.

VIOLA The captain that did bring me first on shore,
Hath my maid's garments: he upon some action
Is now in durance, at Malvolio's suit,
A gentleman and follower of my lady's.

OLIVIA He shall enlarge him. Fetch Malvolio hither –
And yet, alas, now I remember me,
They say, poor gentleman, he's much distract.

The CLOWN *returns with a letter in his hand,* FABIAN *following*

A most extracting frenzy of mine own

From my remembrance clearly banished his.
How does he, sirrah?

CLOWN Truly, madam, he holds Belzebub at the stave's end as well as a man in his case may do: has here writ a letter to you, I should have given't you today morning: but as a madman's epistles are no gospels, so it skills not much when they are delivered.

OLIVIA Open't, and read it.

CLOWN Look then to be well edified, when the fool delivers the madman. [*he shrieks*] 'By the Lord, madam' –

OLIVIA How now! Art thou mad?

CLOWN No, madam, I do but read madness: an your ladyship will have it as it ought to be, you must allow Vox.

OLIVIA Prithee, read i'thy right wits.

CLOWN So I do, madonna; but to read his right wits, is to read thus: therefore perpend, my princess, and give ear.

OLIVIA [*snatches the letter and gives it to Fabian*] Read it you, sirrah.

FABIAN ['*reads*'] 'By the Lord, madam, you wrong me, and the world shall know it: though you have put me into darkness, and given your drunken cousin rule over me, yet have I the benefit of my senses as well as your ladyship. I have your own letter that induced me to the semblance I put on; with the which I doubt not but to do myself much right, or you much shame. Think of me as you please. I leave my duty a little unthought of, and speak out of my injury.

THE MADLY-USED MALVOLIO'

OLIVIA Did he write this?

CLOWN Ay, madam.

DUKE This savours not much of distraction.

OLIVIA See him delivered, Fabian, bring him hither.

[*Fabian goes within*

My lord, so please you, these things further thought on,
To think me as well a sister as a wife,
One day shall crown th'alliance on't, so please you,
Here at my house and at my proper cost.

DUKE Madam, I am most apt t'embrace your offer.

[*to Viola*]
Your master quits you; and for your service done him,
So much against the mettle of your sex,
So far beneath your soft and tender breeding,
And since you called me master for so long,
Here is my hand – you shall from this time be
Your master's mistress.

OLIVIA A sister! You are she.

FABIAN *returns with* MALVOLIO

DUKE Is this the madman?

OLIVIA Ay, my lord, this same:
How now, Malvolio?

MALVOLIO Madam, you have done me wrong,
Notorious wrong.

OLIVIA Have I, Malvolio? No!

MALVOLIO Lady, you have. Pray you, peruse that letter.
[*he takes a letter from his bosom*
You must not now deny it is your hand,
Write from it, if you can, in hand or phrase,
Or say 'tis not your seal, not your invention:
You can say none of this. Well, grant it then,
And tell me, in the modesty of honour,
Why you have given me such clear lights of favour,
Bade me come smiling and cross-gartered to you,
To put on yellow stockings and to frown
Upon Sir Toby and the lighter people:
And, acting this in an obedient hope,
Why have you suffered me to be imprisoned,
Kept in a dark house, visited by the priest,
And made the most notorious geck and gull
That e'er invention played on? Tell me why.

OLIVIA Alas, Malvolio, this is not my writing,
Though, I confess, much like the character:
But, out of question, 'tis Maria's hand.
And now I do bethink me, it was she
First told me thou wast mad; then cam'st in smiling,
And in such forms which here were presupposed
Upon thee in the letter. Prithee, be content –

This practice hath most shrewdly passed upon thee;
But, when we know the grounds and authors of it,
Thou shalt be both the plaintiff and the judge
Of thine own cause.

FABIAN Good madam, hear me speak;
And let no quarrel nor no brawl to come
Taint the condition of this present hour,
Which I have wond'red at. In hope it shall not,
Most freely I confess, myself and Toby
Set this device against Malvolio here,
Upon some stubborn and uncourteous parts
We had conceived in him: Maria writ
The letter at Sir Toby's great importance,
In recompense whereof he hath married her.
How with a sportful malice it was followed,
May rather pluck on laughter than revenge,
If that the injuries be justly weighed
That have on both sides passed.

OLIVIA Alas, poor fool! How have they baffled thee!

CLOWN Why, 'Some are born great, some achieve greatness, and some have greatness thrown upon them.' I was one, sir, in this interlude, one Sir Topas, sir – but that's all one. 'By the Lord, fool, I am not mad!' But do you remember? 'Madam, why laugh you at such a barren rascal? An you smile not, he's gagged'. And thus the whirligig of time brings in his revenges.

MALVOLIO I'll be revenged on the whole pack of you.
[*he turns upon his heel and goes*

OLIVIA He hath been most notoriously abused.

DUKE Pursue him, and entreat him to a peace:
He hath not told us of the captain yet.
When that is known, and golden time convents,
A solemn combination shall be made
Of our dear souls. Meantime, sweet sister,
We will not part from hence. Cesario, come!
For so you shall be, while you are a man;
But, when in other habits you are seen,
Orsino's mistress and his fancy's queen.
[*all save the Clown go within*

CLOWN [*sings*] When that I was and a little tiny boy,
With hey, ho, the wind and the rain:
A foolish thing was but a toy,
For the rain it raineth every day.

But when I came to man's estate,
With hey, ho, the wind and the rain:
'Gainst knaves and thieves men shut their gate,
For the rain it raineth every day.

But when I came alas to wive,
With hey, ho, the wind and the rain:
By swaggering could I never thrive,
For the rain it raineth every day.

But when I came unto my beds,
With hey, ho, the wind and the rain:
With toss-pots still had drunken heads,
For the rain it raineth every day.

A great while ago the world begun,
With hey, ho, the wind and the rain:
But that's all one, our play is done,
And we'll strive to please you every day.

[*he goes*

INTRODUCTION TO THE FIVE TRAGEDIES

When Shakespeare's works were gathered together for posthumous publication in the First Folio edition of 1623, the volume's title-page divided them into comedies, histories and tragedies. How John Heminges and Henry Condell, Shakespeare's fellow-actors who collected the plays, came at this tripartite division, we will never really know, but as an early attempt at categorisation it has been remarkably resilient. However, what was understood by the genres, especially by the label 'tragedy', can only be surmised. It is unlikely that Shakespeare wrote with any tragic blueprint in mind, still less that Aristotle's influential pronouncements on Greek tragedy's flawed hero, whose downfall arouses pity and fear among the spectators, were a consideration. Among the eleven plays which the First Folio calls tragedies there are as many differences as similarities, and by 1623 there has been some shifting so that a play such as *Richard II*, described as a tragedy when it was first published in 1597, is catalogued as a history, whereas the opposite has happened to *King Lear*, a history in 1608 but a tragedy by 1623. This fluidity may register the fluidity of generic boundaries in the period, and Polonius's ridiculous subdivision of drama – 'tragedy, comedy, history, pastoral, pastoral-comical, historical-pastoral, tragical-historical, tragical-comical-historical-pastoral' (*Hamlet* 2.2.388–91) is a cautionary reminder both that genres are frequently indistinct and that any attempt to list all their possible permutations is folly.

This is not to say that there is no such thing as tragedy, rather that its definition, both in the context of Renaissance England and more modern times, is itself open to debate. In fact, the heterogeneity of tragedy is probably the only firm conclusion to be drawn from the welter of differing, even contradictory, assertions about its particular qualities. The Elizabethan courtier-poet Sir Philip Sidney called 'the high and excellent tragedy' a form that 'showeth forth the ulcers that are covered with tissue', making 'kings fear to be tyrants' and showing 'upon how weak foundations gilden roofs are builded'. Some years later, Sidney's friend and biographer Fulke Greville described contemporary tragedy's demonstration of 'God's revenging aspect upon every particular sin, to the despair, or confusion, of mortality'. About the same date, the playwright Thomas Heywood put forward a definition based on formal, rather than thematic or moral, criteria, defining tragedy with reference to its apparent opposite, comedy. According to Heywood, the two forms 'differ thus: in comedies *turbulenta prima, tranquilla ultima*; in tragedies *tranquilla prima, turbulenta ultima*: comedies begin in trouble and end in peace; tragedies begin in calms and end in tempest'. Set against Shakespeare's tragedies, these contemporary definitions seem at best inadequate and at worst misleading. Greville's belief that tragedy displays God's omniscient vengeance on mortal sin sits uneasily with the conclusion of, say, *King Lear*; *Macbeth*'s supernatural opening or the brawl which begins *Romeo and Juliet* do not seem to fit Heywood's 'tragedies begin in calms' formula; and it seems unlikely that Shakespeare's nuanced and complex representations of internal and external conflict could ever be didactic in the uncomplicated way Sidney asserts.

If definitions are evasive, however, the plays themselves give some sense of a unified grouping. There is no doubt that we approach a tragedy with different expectations from those with which we approach a comedy, and that these expectations may include a fundamental seriousness, high tone, and corpse-strewn finale. The five plays in this volume, *Romeo and Juliet*, *Hamlet*, *Othello*, *King Lear* and *Macbeth*, encompass all these elements to differing degrees, but they also contain a surprising amount of black humour, and wordplay, as well as a taste for the sensational. The often-cited porter scene in *Macbeth* (2.3), Hamlet's wit, the shock of Gloucester's blinding in *King Lear*, all push at tragic expectations in different ways. Together the plays span about a dozen years of Shakespeare's writing career over the reigns of two monarchs, Elizabeth I and James I. Although the continuing popularity of the tragedies, and their exalted place in the literary canon, mean that those aspects which seem to transcend the historical moment of their composition tend to be the most valued, the plays are, in their different ways, indelibly marked with the concerns of their period. Such concerns are registered in many ways, from the specific topicality of *Macbeth*'s Scottishness to the more general resonances of the plays' concern with the operations of authority and governance. Specific details of language or plot may seem obscure, and the fact that, since the seventeenth century, the plays have been repeatedly rewritten for contemporary audiences is evidence that elements of their particular historical mindset do not always travel across time and cultures. A version of *King Lear*, for example, adapted in 1681 by Nahum Tate to spare Cordelia and end with her marriage to Edgar, held the stage for almost a century and a half, and more recently the play has been updated in Jane Smiley's novel *A Thousand Acres* (1992). On the other hand, the tragedies' capacity to speak to modern concerns ensures their lasting relevance, especially in performance. From a Soviet film of *Hamlet* by Grigori Kozintsev (1964), in which the tortured hero stood for a generation of dissident intellectuals oppressed by the Stalinist regime, to a production of *Othello* directed by Janet Suzman in Johannesburg under apartheid, a context in which the kiss of a white Desdemona and a black Othello was charged with social taboo and legal prohibition, Shakespeare's tragedies maintain the power to express and to challenge social, personal and political realities.

EMMA SMITH
New Hall, Cambridge

FURTHER READING

Dympna Callaghan, *Women and Gender in Renaissance Tragedy* (1989)

John Drakakis (ed.), *Shakespearean Tragedy* (1992)

Michael Mangan, *A Preface to Shakespeare's Tragedies* (1991)

Tom McAlindon, *Shakespeare's Tragic Cosmos* (1991)

Adrian Poole, *Tragedy: Shakespeare and the Greek Example* (1987)

ROMEO AND JULIET

INTRODUCTION

The Most Excellent and Lamentable Tragedy of Romeo and Juliet was first printed in 1597, and probably written in 1594 or 1595. Shakespeare based his tale of 'star-cross'd lovers' on a well-known story. Arthur Brooke's long poem 'The Tragicall Historye of Romeus and Juliet' was translated from the Italian and first printed in 1562, although the tale of fated young love is archetypal and has numerous mythic analogues. Brooke's version of the tale has a definite didactic impulse, as is conveyed in its prefatory epistle 'To the Reader': 'this tragical matter [is] written to describe unto thee a couple of unfortunate lovers, thralling themselves to unhonest desire, neglecting the authority and advice of parents and friends, conferring their principal counsels with drunken gossips, and superstitious friars (the naturally fit instruments of unchastity) attempting all adventures of peril, for the attaining of their wished lust, using auricular confession (the key of whoredom, and treason) for furtherance of their purpose, abusing the honourable name of lawful marriage, to cloak the shame of stolen contracts, finally, by all means of unhonest life, hasting to most unhappy death.' Shakespeare takes the main narrative elements of Brooke's poem and develops them into a much warmer, more sympathetic play whose central couple are the victims, rather than the perpetrators, of wickedness.

The play tells the story of Romeo, a Montague, and Juliet, a Capulet. They meet, fall in love, and secretly marry despite the implacable feuding of their two families. In a fight with Tybalt, Juliet's cousin, Romeo kills him and is banished from Verona. To avoid marrying Paris, her father's choice of husband, Juliet takes a drug given her by a friar, and the sleep which results so resembles death that she is placed in her family tomb. The friar's plan to bring back Romeo, wake Juliet and reunite the pair misfires. Romeo finds Juliet and believes her dead; he kills himself with poison and she wakes to find him dead, only to kill herself on his dagger. The couple are buried together as the Montagues and Capulets vow to bury their enmity with them.

The choric sonnet which prefaces the play establishes what follows as a tragedy of fate. Two causes, one immediate and human (the warring families), the other distant and horoscopic (the 'star-crossed lovers'), are intertwined to form the governing dynamic of the story. The audience is given a superior knowledge of events at the outset, and thus the tragic effectiveness of the play rests on the inevitability of its conclusion rather than on suspense. We know what will happen in the end, but what is compulsive, in one of tragedy's most unpleasant truths, is watching its horror unfold. The familiarity of its story together with this statement of predetermination gives a double sense of unavoidable destiny, although many viewers and readers of the play have found it difficult to accept the role of coincidence in bringing about its catastrophe. As Michael Attenborough, who directed the play for the Royal Shakespeare Company in Stratford-on-Avon in 1997–8, put it: 'Most directors would try and persuade Shakespeare to find something more profound to cause everything to go so appallingly wrong. The erratic nature of the ecclesiastical postal service seems a bit limp as a dramatic device.' One of the play's characteristic features, and one of its great challenges in the theatre, is this audacious incorporation of banality and accident into its tragic mode.

In fact the play can claim a kind of hybrid generic status. Setting aside the Prologue (which was omitted from the play when it was printed in the First Folio of 1623), it begins more in a spirit of comedy than tragedy. The story of parental opposition to young love is a common theme of Shakespeare's comedies. *A Midsummer Night's Dream*, for example, written at about the same time as *Romeo and Juliet*, fulfils its comic promise as the lovers are united in the end. Even its inset tragedy, the play-within-a-play of Pyramus and Thisbe which probably also informed Shakespeare's conception of his own love tragedy *Romeo and Juliet*, is an opportunity for merriment. *Romeo and Juliet* ends, too, with the union of the lovers but subverts the comic finale by staging this as an entombed nuptial with death. Perhaps it is the death of Mercutio, Shakespeare's most brilliant addition to his source material, at almost exactly halfway through the play, which shifts its hitherto comic mood into irreversible tragedy. His dying curse 'A plague o' both your houses' (3.1.89) hangs in the air as the play lurches towards catastrophe through Romeo's revenge killing of Tybalt and his subsequent banishment. The play manages to combine inevitability – things are bound to go wrong – with the tantalising but never-allowed possibility that tragedy can be avoided. There is always the feeling that perhaps this time Juliet will wake up just a fraction sooner, and the awful spectacle of the double sacrifice to the 'ancient grudge' between the Montagues and the Capulets may thus be avoided. It is a hope which, of course, the play must always cruelly dash.

The events which lead to the final tragedy seem to gain momentum and become unstoppable as the play proceeds. Time is a crucial player in Shakespeare's play, where the dilatory narrative of Brooke's poem is tightened into a compact drama, which, while not quite the 'two hours' promised by the prologue, is characterised by a fierce energy. Time is inescapable, and seems to speed up as the play progresses. Juliet wills time onwards in the famous headlong cadences of her impatient 'Gallop apace, you fiery-footed steeds' (3.2.1), but then cannot put off the dawn and Romeo's flight after their wedding night together; Capulet tells Paris that Juliet will not be of marriageable age for 'two more summers' and then, a couple of acts later, brings their wedding forward to Thursday; Friar Lawrence's *sententiae* advise caution ('Wisely and slow. They stumble that run fast' 2.3.94; 'Too swift arrives as tardy as too slow' 2.6.15), but go unheeded in the helter-skelter pace towards the play's denouement.

This momentum contributes to the play's careful structure and symmetry. The dual focus suggested by its title is emphasised in the Prologue's 'Two households, both alike in dignity'. Brawls between the warring families punctuate the brief narrative of Romeo and Juliet's meeting, secret marriage, consummation, separation and reunion in the Capulet tomb. Within this structure, Shakespeare incorporates a diversity of language, from the regular rhyming of the Prologue, appropriately delivered in the anodyne cadences of a newscaster at the start of Baz Luhrmann's 1996 film *William Shakespeare's Romeo & Juliet*, to the weird inventiveness of

Mercutio's Queen Mab reverie, 'begot of nothing but vain fantasy' (1.4.98). The inspired bawdy of the Nurse's rambling prose contrasts with the formal sonnet the young lovers complete as their first exchange (1.5.90–103); the menacing prose exchanges of encounters between the two families are emphasised by their juxtaposition with the lyric intensity of love poetry; Tybalt's vaunting tragic idiom is matched by Mercutio's punning. Language is also a theme in a play concerned with the fatal consequences of names. Juliet's 'what's in a name' marks her naivety: names are all-important in a play which turns, fatally, on their inescapability. The language of *Romeo and Juliet* includes both formal verse and colloquial prose, and thus marks a development of the rhetorical artifice of Shakespeare's early plays and points towards the muscular lyricism and emotional immediacy of the mature playwright. Images of light and of fire suggest the 'violent passions' which, quite literally, burn themselves out. The symphonic quality of the play's variety and linguistic leitmotifs may explain the popularity of musical renditions of the story, from Berlioz, Prokofiev and Tchaikovsky to Dire Straits and Leonard Bernstein's *West Side Story*.

Romeo and Juliet's familiarity may be misleading. Like the play's original audiences, we almost all know the story before we read or see it. The two lovers have become cultural icons, embodiments of love in countless stories and songs. Every year from around the world thousands of letters, mostly asking for advice on matters of the heart or telling of other forbidden courtships, are sent to Verona for the attention of 'Juliet', and the town employs a team to answer them. A 1990s advertisement for a British dating agency offered to find lonely hearts their Romeo or Juliet, apparently unaware of the practical unsuitability, and fatal consequences, of the famous match. Romeo and Juliet represent a kind of perfect love immune to the rhythms of real life, fixed in the exquisite masochism of their double death in the tomb. Reading the play itself, however, we find that the characters do not quite stand up to their towering reputations. For one thing, they are very young. It is not accidental that both use comparisons drawn from childhood to articulate their new feelings, as their only experiences are those of children. For Romeo, parting from Juliet is like a boy's unwilling steps 'toward school with heavy looks' (2.2.157), and Juliet likens her frustration waiting for news of her lover 'As is the night before some festival To an impatient child that hath new robes And may not wear them' (3.2.29–31). The pace of their love may suggest an infatuation of which, were it allowed to run its natural course, they would soon tire. The illicit nature of their relationship gives it an added frisson; they are married within days – minutes, in performance – of meeting, egged on by the dubious encouragement of the Nurse, whose role retains some vestigial ambiguity from her culpability in Brooke's poem. Romeo is an incurable romantic, who is lovesick for the quickly-forgotten 'fair Rosaline' at the beginning of the play. He may seem to be in love less with Juliet as an individual than with love itself, a rather narcissistic young man whose earnest protestations satirise the hyperbolic rhetoric of Elizabethan sonnets and love conventions. Juliet is the younger of the pair, captivated by her ardent lover, rapt with the bittersweet emotions of first love. Neither seems fully to appreciate what they are doing, nor to know the other save as an idealised object of teenage desire. Characterisation, particularly of the central couple, is subservient to the relentless plot; Romeo and Juliet represent lovers rather than rounded personalities. Perhaps only the Nurse and Mercutio really take full flight as dramatic characters against a background of duller plot functionaries: lovers, parents, servants. *Romeo and Juliet* is a young person's play, a play about the integrity and intensity of immaturity in an irrational and powerful adult world, and perhaps its immediacy and energy can only be fully appreciated by young people. This is not to say that the play looks down on its heroes: they represent, more than any of Shakespeare's other tragic characters, the innocent victims of a malign machinery they did nothing to activate and can do nothing to avert.

The scene: Verona and Mantua

CHARACTERS IN THE PLAY

ESCALUS, *prince of Verona*

PARIS, *a young nobleman, kinsman to the prince*

MONTAGUE } *heads of two houses at enmity with each other*
CAPULET }

An old man, kinsman to Capulet

ROMEO, *son to Montague*

MERCUTIO, *kinsman to the prince, and friend to Romeo*

BENVOLIO, *nephew to Montague, and friend to Romeo*

TYBALT, *nephew to Lady Capulet*

FRIAR LAWRENCE, *a Franciscan*

FRIAR JOHN, *of the same order*

BALTHASAR, *servant to Romeo*

SAMPSON } *servants to Capulet*
GREGORY }

PETER, *servant to Juliet's Nurse*

ABRAHAM, *servant to Montague*

An Apothecary

Three Musicians

Page to Paris, another Page, an Officer

LADY MONTAGUE, *wife to Montague*

LADY CAPULET, *wife to Capulet*

JULIET, *daughter to Capulet*

Nurse to Juliet

Citizens, Kinsfolk of both houses, Guards, Watchmen, Servants and Attendants

CHORUS

ROMEO AND JULIET

The Prologue

Enter Chorus

CHORUS Two households, both alike in dignity,
In fair Verona, where we lay our scene,
From ancient grudge break to new mutiny,
Where civil blood makes civil hands unclean.
From forth the fatal loins of these two foes
A pair of star-crossed lovers take their life;
Whose misadventured piteous overthrows
Doth with their death bury their parents' strife.
The fearful passage of their death-marked love,
And the continuance of their parents' rage,
Which, but their children's end, nought could remove,
Is now the two hours' traffic of our stage;
The which if you with patient ears attend,
What here shall miss, our toil shall strive to mend.

[*exit*

ACT I SCENE I

Verona. A public place

'Enter SAMPSON *and* GREGORY *of the house of* CAPULET, *with swords and bucklers'*

SAMPSON Gregory, on my word we'll not carry coals.

GREGORY No, for then we should be colliers.

SAMPSON I mean, an we be in choler we'll draw.

GREGORY Ay, while you live draw your neck out of collar.

SAMPSON I strike quickly, being moved.

GREGORY But thou art not quickly moved to strike.

SAMPSON A dog of the house of Montague moves me.

GREGORY To move is to stir, and to be valiant is to stand: therefore if thou art moved thou runn'st away.

SAMPSON A dog of that house shall move me to stand: I will take the wall of any man or maid of Montague's.

GREGORY That shows thee a weak slave, for the weakest goes to the wall.

SAMPSON 'Tis true, and therefore women, being the weaker vessels, are ever thrust to the wall: therefore I will push Montague's men from the wall, and thrust his maids to the wall.

GREGORY The quarrel is between our masters, and us their men.

SAMPSON 'Tis all one; I will show myself a tyrant: when I have fought with the men, I will be cruel with the maids; I will cut off their heads.

GREGORY The heads of the maids?

SAMPSON Ay, the heads of the maids, or their maidenheads; take it in what sense thou wilt.

GREGORY They must take it in sense that feel it.

SAMPSON Me they shall feel while I am able to stand, and 'tis known I am a pretty piece of flesh.

GREGORY 'Tis well thou art not fish; if thou hadst, thou hadst been poor John. Draw thy tool; here comes two of the house of Montagues.

Enter ABRAHAM *and another serving man*

SAMPSON My naked weapon is out: quarrel; I will back thee.

GREGORY How? Turn thy back and run?

SAMPSON Fear me not.

GREGORY No, marry; I fear thee!

SAMPSON Let us take the law of our sides; let them begin.

GREGORY I will frown as I pass by, and let them take it as they list.

SAMPSON Nay, as they dare. I will bite my thumb at them, which is disgrace to them if they bear it.

ABRAHAM Do you bite your thumb at us, sir?

SAMPSON I do bite my thumb, sir.

ABRAHAM Do you bite your thumb at us, sir?

SAMPSON Is the law of our side if I say ay?

GREGORY No.

SAMPSON No, sir, I do not bite my thumb at you, sir, but I bite my thumb, sir.

GREGORY Do you quarrel, sir?

ABRAHAM Quarrel, sir? No, sir.

SAMPSON But if you do, sir, I am for you: I serve as good a man as you.

ABRAHAM No better.

SAMPSON Well, sir.

'Enter BENVOLIO*' on one side,* TYBALT *on the other*

GREGORY [*seeing Tybalt*] Say 'better': here comes one of my master's kinsmen.

SAMPSON Yes, better, sir.

ABRAHAM You lie.

SAMPSON Draw, if you be men. Gregory, remember thy washing blow. [*'they fight'*

BENVOLIO: [*intervening from behind*] Part, fools!
Put up your swords; you know not what you do.

TYBALT *comes up*

TYBALT: What, art thou drawn among these heartless hinds?
Turn thee, Benvolio; look upon thy death.

BENVOLIO I do but keep the peace: put up thy sword,
Or manage it to part these men with me.

TYBALT What, drawn, and talk of peace? I hate the word,
As I hate hell, all Montagues, and thee:
Have at thee, coward.

They fight. Enter several of both houses, joining in the fray. Then 'enter three or four Citizens with clubs or partisans', and an Officer

OFFICER Clubs, bills, and partisans! Strike, beat them down.
Down with the Capulets, down with the Montagues!

'Enter old CAPULET *in his gown, and his wife'*

CAPULET What noise is this? Give me my long sword, ho!

LADY CAP. A crutch, a crutch! Why call you for a sword?

CAPULET My sword, I say! Old Montague is come,
And flourishes his blade in spite of me.

'Enter old MONTAGUE *and his wife'*

MONTAG. Thou villain Capulet! – Hold me not, let me go.

LADY MON. Thou shalt not stir one foot to seek a foe.

'Enter PRINCE ESCALUS*, with his train'*

PRINCE Rebellious subjects, enemies to peace,
Profaners of this neighbour-stainèd steel, –
Will they not hear? What ho! you men, you beasts,

That quench the fire of your pernicious rage
With purple fountains issuing from your veins,
On pain of torture, from those bloody hands
Throw your mistempered weapons to the ground,
And hear the sentence of your movèd prince.
Three civil brawls, bred of an airy word
By thee, old Capulet, and Montague,
Have thrice disturbed the quiet of our streets,
And made Verona's ancient citizens
Cast by their grave beseeming ornaments
To wield old partisans, in hands as old,
Cankered with peace, to part your cankered hate:
If ever you disturb our streets again,
Your lives shall pay the forfeit of the peace.
For this time, all the rest depart away:
You, Capulet, shall go along with me;
And, Montague, come you this afternoon,
To know our farther pleasure in this case,
To old Freetown, our common judgment-place.
Once more, on pain of death, all men depart.
[all but Montague, Lady Montague, and Benvolio depart

MONTAG. Who set this ancient quarrel new abroach?
Speak, nephew, were you by when it began?

BENVOLIO Here were the servants of your adversary
And yours, close fighting ere I did approach:
I drew to part them; in the instant came
The fiery Tybalt, with his sword prepared,
Which, as he breathed defiance to my ears,
He swung about his head, and cut the winds,
Who, nothing hurt withal, hissed him in scorn:
While we were interchanging thrusts and blows,
Came more and more, and fought on part and part,
Till the prince came, who parted either part.

LADY MON. O where is Romeo? Saw you him today?
Right glad I am he was not at this fray.

BENVOLIO Madam, an hour before the worshipped sun
Peered forth the golden window of the east,
A troubled mind drave me to walk abroad,
Where, underneath the grove of sycamore

That westward rooteth from this city's side,
So early walking did I see your son:
Towards him I made, but he was ware of me,
And stole into the covert of the wood:
I, measuring his affections by my own,
Which then most sought where most might not be found,
Being one too many by my weary self,
Pursued my humour, not pursuing his,
And gladly shunned who gladly fled from me.

MONTAG. Many a morning hath he there been seen,
With tears augmenting the fresh morning's dew,
Adding to clouds more clouds with his deep sighs;
But all so soon as the all-cheering sun
Should in the farthest east begin to draw
The shady curtains from Aurora's bed,
Away from light steals home my heavy son,
And private in his chamber pens himself,
Shuts up his windows, locks fair daylight out,
And makes himself an artificial night:
Black and portentous must this humour prove,
Unless good counsel may the cause remove.

BENVOLIO My noble uncle, do you know the cause?

MONTAG. I neither know it, nor can learn of him.

BENVOLIO Have you importuned him by any means?

MONTAG. Both by myself and many other friends:
But he, his own affections' counsellor,
Is to himself – I will not say how true –
But to himself so secret and so close,
So far from sounding and discovery,
As is the bud bit with an envious worm,
Ere he can spread his sweet leaves to the air,
Or dedicate his beauty to the sun.
Could we but learn from whence his sorrows grow,
We would as willingly give cure as know.

'Enter ROMEO*'*

BENVOLIO See where he comes: so please you, step aside;
I'll know his grievance or be much denied.

MONTAG. I would thou wert so happy by thy stay

To hear true shrift. Come, madam, let's away.
[*Montague and his wife depart*

BENVOLIO Good morrow, cousin.
ROMEO Is the day so young?
BENVOLIO But new struck nine.
ROMEO Ay me, sad hours seem long.
Was that my father that went hence so fast?
BENVOLIO It was. What sadness lengthens Romeo's hours?
ROMEO Not having that which, having, makes them short.
BENVOLIO In love?
ROMEO Out –
BENVOLIO Of love?
ROMEO Out of her favour where I am in love.
BENVOLIO Alas that Love, so gentle in his view,
Should be so tyrannous and rough in proof!
ROMEO Alas that Love, whose view is muffled still,
Should without eyes see pathways to his will!
Where shall we dine? – O me! What fray was here?
Yet tell me not, for I have heard it all:
Here's much to do with hate, but more with love:
Why, then, O brawling love, O loving hate,
O anything of nothing first create!
O heavy lightness, serious vanity,
Misshapen chaos of well-seeming forms,
Feather of lead, bright smoke, cold fire, sick health,
Still-waking sleep, that is not what it is!
This love feel I, that feel no love in this.
Dost thou not laugh?
BENVOLIO No, coz, I rather weep.
ROMEO Good heart, at what?
BENVOLIO At thy good heart's oppression.
ROMEO Why, such is love's transgression.
Griefs of mine own lie heavy in my breast,
Which thou wilt propagate, to have it pressed
With more of thine. This love that thou hast shown
Doth add more grief to too much of mine own.
Love is a smoke made with the fume of sighs:
Being purged, a fire sparkling in lovers' eyes;
Being vexed, a sea nourished with lovers' tears.

What is it else? A madness most discreet,
A choking gall and a preserving sweet.
Farewell, my coz.

BENVOLIO Soft, I will go along:
And if you leave me so, you do me wrong.

ROMEO Tut, I have lost myself, I am not here,
This is not Romeo, he's some other where.

BENVOLIO Tell me in sadness, who is that you love?

ROMEO What, shall I groan and tell thee?

BENVOLIO Groan? Why no:
But sadly tell me, who?

ROMEO Bid a sick man in sadness make his will –
A word ill urged to one that is so ill.
In sadness, cousin, I do love a woman.

BENVOLIO I aimed so near when I supposed you loved.

ROMEO A right good markman! And she's fair I love.

BENVOLIO A right fair mark, fair coz, is soonest hit.

ROMEO Well, in that hit you miss. She'll not be hit
With Cupid's arrow: she hath Dian's wit,
And, in strong proof of chastity well armed,
From Love's weak childish bow she lives unharmed.
She will not stay the siege of loving terms,
Nor bide th' encounter of assailing eyes,
Nor ope her lap to saint-seducing gold.
O, she is rich in beauty, only poor
That, when she dies, with beauty dies her store.

BENVOLIO Then she hath sworn that she will still live chaste?

ROMEO She hath, and in that sparing makes huge waste:
For beauty, starved with her severity,
Cuts beauty off from all posterity.
She is too fair, too wise, wisely too fair,
To merit bliss by making me despair:
She hath forsworn to love, and in that vow
Do I live dead, that live to tell it now.

BENVOLIO Be ruled by me; forget to think of her.

ROMEO O, teach me how I should forget to think.

BENVOLIO By giving liberty unto thine eyes;
Examine other beauties.

ROMEO 'Tis the way

To call hers (exquisite) in question more.
These happy masks that kiss fair ladies' brows,
Being black, puts us in mind they hide the fair.
He that is strucken blind cannot forget
The precious treasure of his eyesight lost.
Show me a mistress that is passing fair:
What doth her beauty serve but as a note
Where I may read who passed that passing fair?
Farewell, thou canst not teach me to forget.

BENVOLIO I'll pay that doctrine, or else die in debt. *[they go*

SCENE 2

The same; later in the day

'Enter CAPULET, *County* PARIS, *and the* CLOWN', *servant to Capulet*

CAPULET But Montague is bound as well as I,
In penalty alike; and 'tis not hard, I think,
For men so old as we to keep the peace.

PARIS Of honourable reckoning are you both,
And pity 'tis you lived at odds so long.
But now, my lord, what say you to my suit?

CAPULET But saying o'er what I have said before:
My child is yet a stranger in the world ;
She hath not seen the change of fourteen years:
Let two more summers wither in their pride
Ere we may think her ripe to be a bride.

PARIS Younger than she are happy mothers made.

CAPULET And too soon marred are those so early made.
Earth hath swallowed all my hopes but she;
She is the hopeful lady of my earth.
But woo her, gentle Paris, get her heart;
My will to her consent is but a part:
And, she agreed, within her scope of choice
Lies my consent and fair according voice.
This night I hold an old accustomed feast,
Whereto I have invited many a guest,
Such as I love; and you among the store,
One more most welcome, makes my number more.

At my poor house look to behold this night
Earth-treading stars that make dark heaven light.
Such comfort as do lusty young men feel
When well-apparelled April on the heel
Of limping winter treads, even such delight
Among fresh female buds shall you this night
Inherit at my house: hear all, all see,
And like her most whose merit most shall be:
Which on more view, of many mine being one
May stand in number, though in reckoning none.
Come, go with me. [*To the Clown*] Go, sirrah,
trudge about
Through fair Verona; find those persons out
Whose names are written there, [*giving him a paper*]
and to them say
My house and welcome on their pleasure stay.
[*Capulet and Paris go*

CLOWN [*turns the paper about*] Find them out whose names are written here! It is written that the shoemaker should meddle with his yard and the tailor with his last, the fisher with his pencil and the painter with his nets. But I am sent to find those persons whose names are here writ, and can never find what names the writing person hath here writ. I must to the learned. In good time!

'*Enter* BENVOLIO AND ROMEO'

BENVOLIO Tut, man, one fire burns out another's burning,
One pain is lessened by another's anguish;
Turn giddy, and be holp by backward turning;
One desperate grief cures with another's languish;
Take thou some new infection to thy eye,
And the rank poison of the old will die.
ROMEO Your plantain leaf is excellent for that.
BENVOLIO For what, I pray thee?
ROMEO For your broken shin.
BENVOLIO Why, Romeo, art thou mad?
ROMEO Not mad, but bound more than a madman is:
Shut up in prison, kept without my food,
Whipped and tormented, and – God-den, good fellow.
CLOWN God gi' god-den. I pray, sir, can you read?

ROMEO Ay, mine own fortune in my misery.

CLOWN Perhaps you have learned it without book: but, I pray, can you read anything you see?

ROMEO Ay, if I know the letters and the language.

CLOWN Ye say honestly: rest you merry.

[he turns to go

ROMEO Stay, fellow; I can read. *[he reads the list*
'Signior Martino and his wife and daughters,
County Anselmo and his beauteous sisters,
The lady widow of Vitruvio,
Signior Placentio and his lovely nieces,
Mercutio and his brother Valentine,
Mine uncle Capulet, his wife and daughters,
My fair niece Rosaline and Livia,
Signior Valentio and his cousin Tybalt,
Lucio and the lively Helena.'
A fair assembly: whither should they come?

CLOWN Up.

ROMEO Whither?

CLOWN To supper; to our house.

ROMEO Whose house?

CLOWN My master's.

ROMEO Indeed I should have asked thee that before.

CLOWN Now I'll tell you without asking. My master is the great rich Capulet; and, if you be not of the house of Montagues, I pray come and crush a cup of wine. Rest you merry. *[goes*

BENVOLIO At this same ancient feast of Capulet's
Sups the fair Rosaline whom thou so loves,
With all the admirèd beauties of Verona:
Go thither, and with unattainted eye
Compare her face with some that I shall show,
And I will make thee think thy swan a crow.

ROMEO When the devout religion of mine eye
Maintains such falsehood, then turn tears to fires:
And these who, often drowned, could never die,
Transparent heretics, be burnt for liars.
One fairer than my love! The all-seeing sun
Ne'er saw her match since first the world begun.

BENVOLIO Tut, you saw her fair, none else being by,
Herself poised with herself in either eye:
But in that crystal scales let there be weighed
Your lady's love against some other maid
That I will show you shining at this feast,
And she shall scant show well that now seems best.

ROMEO I'll go along, no such sight to be shown,
But to rejoice in splendour of mine own. [*they go*

SCENE 3

Within Capulet's house

'Enter Capulet's Wife, and NURSE*'*

LADY CAP. Nurse, where's my daughter? Call her forth to me.

NURSE Now, by my maidenhead at twelve year old,
I bade her come. What, lamb! What, lady-bird!
God forbid! Where's this girl? What, Juliet!

'Enter JULIET*'*

JULIET How now, who calls?

NURSE Your mother.

JULIET Madam, I am here. What is your will?

LADY CAP. This is the matter. Nurse, give leave awhile:
We must talk in secret. Nurse, come back again:
I have remembered me; thou's hear our counsel.
Thou knowest my daughter's of a pretty age.

NURSE Faith, I can tell her age unto an hour.

LADY CAP. She's not fourteen.

NURSE I'll lay fourteen of my teeth –
And yet, to my teen be it spoken, I have but four –
She's not fourteen. How long is it now
To Lammas-tide?

LADY CAP. A fortnight and odd days.

NURSE Even or odd, of all days in the year,
Come Lammas-Eve at night shall she be fourteen.
Susan and she – God rest all Christian souls –
Were of an age. Well, Susan is with God;
She was too good for me. But, as I said,

On Lammas-Eve at night shall she be fourteen:
That shall she, marry; I remember it well.
'Tis since the earthquake now eleven years,
And she was weaned – I never shall forget it –
Of all the days of the year, upon that day:
For I had then laid wormwood to my dug,
Sitting in the sun under the dove-house wall.
My lord and you were then at Mantua –
Nay, I do bear a brain! But, as I said,
When it did taste the wormwood on the nipple
Of my dug, and felt it bitter, pretty fool,
To see it tetchy and fall out with the dug!
'Shake,' quoth the dove-house: 'twas no need, I trow,
To bid me trudge.
And since that time it is eleven years:
For then she could stand high-lone; nay, by th' rood,
She could have run and waddled all about:
For even the day before, she broke her brow,
And then my husband – God be with his soul,
'A was a merry man – took up the child:
'Yea,' quoth he, 'dost thou fall upon thy face?
Thou wilt fall backward when thou hast more wit;
Wilt thou not, Jule?' And, by my holidame,
The pretty wretch left crying, and said 'Ay'.
To see now how a jest shall come about!
I warrant, an I should live a thousand years,
I never should forget it: 'Wilt thou not, Jule?' quoth he;
And, pretty fool, it stinted, and said 'Ay'.

LADY CAP. Enough of this; I pray thee hold thy peace.

NURSE Yes, madam, yet I cannot choose but laugh,
To think it should leave crying, and say 'Ay':
And yet, I warrant, it had upon it brow
A bump as big as a young cockerel's stone,
A perilous knock: and it cried bitterly.
'Yea', quoth my husband, 'fallst upon thy face?
Thou wilt fall backward when thou comest to age:
Wilt thou not, Jule?' It stinted, and said 'Ay'.

JULIET And stint thou too, I pray thee, Nurse, say I.

NURSE Peace, I have done. God mark thee to his grace!

Thou wast the prettiest babe that e'er I nursed:
An I might live to see thee married once,
I have my wish.

LADY CAP. Marry, that 'marry' is the very theme
I came to talk of. Tell me, daughter Juliet,
How stands your dispositions to be married?

JULIET It is an honour that I dream not of.

NURSE An honour! Were not I thine only nurse,
I would say thou hadst sucked wisdom from thy teat.

LADY CAP. Well, think of marriage now; younger than you
Here in Verona, ladies of esteem,
Are made already mothers. By my count,
I was your mother much upon these years
That you are now a maid. Thus then in brief:
The valiant Paris seeks you for his love.

NURSE A man, young lady! Lady, such a man
As all the world – Why, he's a man of wax.

LADY CAP. Verona's summer hath not such a flower.

NURSE Nay, he's a flower; in faith, a very flower.

LADY CAP. What say you? Can you love the gentleman?
This night you shall behold him at our feast:
Read o'er the volume of young Paris' face,
And find delight writ there with beauty's pen;
Examine every married lineament,
And see how one another lends content;
And what obscured in this fair volume lies
Find written in the margent of his eyes.
This precious book of love, this unbound lover,
To beautify him, only lacks a cover.
The fish lives in the sea; and 'tis much pride
For fair without the fair within to hide.
That book in many's eyes doth share the glory,
That in gold clasps locks in the golden story:
So shall you share all that he doth possess,
By having him making yourself no less.

NURSE No less! Nay, bigger women grow by men!

LADY CAP. Speak briefly, can you like of Paris' love?

JULIET I'll look to like, if looking liking move;
But no more deep will I endart mine eye

Than your consent gives strength to make it fly.

'Enter Servingman'

SERV'MAN Madam, the guests are come, supper served up, you called, my young lady asked for, the nurse cursed in the pantry, and everything in extremity. I must hence to wait; I beseech you follow straight.

LADY CAP. We follow thee. Juliet, the County stays.

NURSE Go, girl, seek happy nights to happy days. *[they go*

SCENE 4

Without Capulet's house

'Enter ROMEO, MERCUTIO, BENVOLIO, *with five or six other masquers; torch-bearers'*

ROMEO What, shall this speech be spoke for our excuse?
Or shall we on without apology?

BENVOLIO The date is out of such prolixity:
We'll have no Cupid hoodwinked with a scarf,
Bearing a Tartar's painted bow of lath,
Scaring the ladies like a crow-keeper:
Nor no without-book prologue, faintly spoke
After the prompter, for our entrance:
But, let them measure us by what they will,
We'll measure them a measure and be gone.

ROMEO Give me a torch: I am not for this ambling;
Being but heavy, I will bear the light.

MERCUTIO Nay, gentle Romeo, we must have you dance.

ROMEO Not I, believe me: you have dancing shoes
With nimble soles; I have a soul of lead
So stakes me to the ground I cannot move.

MERCUTIO You are a lover: borrow Cupid's wings,
And soar with them above a common bound.

ROMEO I am too sore enpiercèd with his shaft
To soar with his light feathers and so bound;
I cannot bound a pitch above dull woe:
Under love's heavy burden do I sink.

MERCUTIO And, to sink in it, should you burden love –

Too great oppression for a tender thing.

ROMEO Is love a tender thing? It is too rough,
Too rude, too boisterous, and it pricks like thorn.

MERCUTIO If love be rough with you, be rough with love;
Prick love for pricking, and you beat love down.
Give me a case to put my visage in:
A visor for a visor! What care I
What curious eye doth quote deformities?
Here are the beetle-brows shall blush for me.
[*putting on a mask*

BENVOLIO Come, knock and enter, and no sooner in
But every man betake him to his legs.

ROMEO A torch for me; let wantons light of heart
Tickle the senseless rushes with their heels.
For I am proverbed with a grandsire phrase,
I'll be a candle-holder, and look on.
The game was ne'er so fair, and I am done.

MERCUTIO Tut, dun's the mouse, the constable's own word
If thou art Dun, we'll draw thee from the mire,
Or save-your-reverence love, wherein thou stickest
Up to the ears. Come, we burn daylight, ho.

ROMEO Nay, that's not so.

MERCUTIO I mean, sir, in delay
We waste our lights in vain, like lights by day.
Take our good meaning, for our judgment sits
Five times in that ere once in our five wits.

ROMEO And we mean well in going to this masque,
But 'tis no wit to go.

MERCUTIO Why, may one ask?

ROMEO I dreamt a dream tonight.

MERCUTIO And so did I.

ROMEO Well, what was yours?

MERCUTIO That dreamers often lie.

ROMEO In bed asleep while they do dream things true.

MERCUTIO O then I see Queen Mab hath been with you.
She is the fairies' midwife, and she comes
In shape no bigger than an agate-stone
On the fore-finger of an alderman,
Drawn with a team of little atomi

Over men's noses as they lie asleep.
Her chariot is an empty hazel-nut,
Made by the joiner squirrel or old grub
Time out o' mind the fairies' coachmakers:
Her waggon-spokes made of long spinners' legs,
The cover of the wings of grasshoppers,
Her traces of the smallest spider-web,
Her collars of the moonshine's watery beams,
Her whip of cricket's bone, the lash of film;
Her waggoner a small grey-coated gnat,
Not half so big as a round little worm
Pricked from the lazy finger of a maid.
And in this state she gallops night by night
Through lovers' brains, and then they dream of love;
O'er courtiers' knees, that dream on curtsies straight;
O er lawyers' fingers who straight dream on fees;
O'er ladies' lips, who straight on kisses dream,
Which oft the angry Mab with blisters plagues
Because their breaths with sweetmeats tainted are.
Sometime she gallops o'er a courtier's nose,
And then dreams he of smelling out a suit:
And sometime comes she with a tithe-pig's tail
Tickling a parson's nose as 'a lies asleep,
Then dreams he of another benefice.
Sometime she driveth o'er a soldier's neck,
And then dreams he of cutting foreign threats,
Of breaches, ambuscadoes, Spanish blades,
Of healths five fathom deep; and then anon
Drums in his ear, at which he starts and wakes,
And being thus frighted swears a prayer or two,
And sleeps again. This is that very Mab
That plats the manes of horses in the night,
And bakes the elf-locks in foul sluttish hairs,
Which once untangled much misfortune bodes:
This is the hag, when maids lie on their backs,
That presses them and learns them first to bear,
Making them women of good carriage:
This is she –

ROMEO Peace, peace, Mercutio, peace!

Thou talkst of nothing.

MERCUTIO True, I talk of dreams,
Which are the children of an idle brain,
Begot of nothing but vain fantasy,
Which is as thin of substance as the air,
And more inconstant than the wind, who woos
Even now the frozen bosom of the north,
And, being angered, puffs away from thence,
Turning his side to the dew-dropping south.

BENVOLIO This wind you talk of blows us from ourselves:
Supper is done, and we shall come too late.

ROMEO I fear, too early: for my mind misgives
Some consequence, yet hanging in the stars,
Shall bitterly begin his fearful date
With this night's revels, and expire the term
Of a despisèd life closed in my breast,
By some vile forfeit of untimely death.
But He that hath the steerage of my course
Direct my sail! On, lusty gentlemen.

BENVOLIO Strike, drum.

[*they march into the house*

SCENE 5

The hall in Capulet's house; musicians waiting.
Enter the masquers, march round the hall, and stand aside.
'Servingmen come forth with napkins'

1 SER'MAN Where's Potpan, that he helps not to take away? He shift a trencher! He scrape a trencher!

2 SER'MAN When good manners shall lie all in one or two men's hands, and they unwashed too, 'tis a foul thing.

1 SER'MAN Away with the joined-stools, remove the court-cupboard, look to the plate – Good thou, save me a piece of marchpane; and, as thou loves me, let the porter let in Susan Grindstone and Nell – Antony and Potpan!

3 SER'MAN Ay, boy, ready.

1 SER'MAN You are looked for and called for, asked for and sought for, in the great chamber.

4 SER'MAN We cannot be here and there too. Cheerly, boys; be brisk a while, and the longer liver take all.

[*Servingmen withdraw*

'Enter' CAPULET, *and* JULIET, *with 'all the guests and gentlewomen to the masquers'*

CAPULET Welcome, gentlemen! Ladies that have their toes
Unplagued with corns will walk a bout with you.
Ah, my mistresses, which of you all
Will now deny to dance? She that makes dainty,
She I'll swear hath corns: am I come near ye now?
Welcome, gentlemen! I have seen the day
That I have worn a visor and could tell
A whispering tale in a fair lady's ear,
Such as would please: 'tis gone, 'tis gone, 'tis gone.
You are welcome, gentlemen! Come, musicians, play.
A hall, a hall! Give room. And foot it, girls.

[*'music plays and they dance'*

More light, you knaves, and turn the tables up,
And quench the fire – the room is grown too hot.
Ah, sirrah, this unlooked-for sport comes well. –
Nay sit, nay sit, good cousin Capulet,
For you and I are past our dancing days.
How long is't now since last yourself and I
Were in a masque?

2 CAPUL'T By'r Lady, thirty years.

CAPULET What, man! 'tis not so much, 'tis not so much:
'Tis since the nuptial of Lucentio,
Come Pentecost as quickly as it will,
Some five and twenty years, and then we masqued.

2 CAPUL'T 'Tis more, 'tis more; his son is elder, sir:
His son is thirty.

CAPULET Will you tell me that?
His son was but a ward two years ago.

ROMEO [*to a servingman*]
What lady's that which doth enrich the hand
Of yonder knight?

SERV'MAN I know not, sir.

ROMEO O she doth teach the torches to burn bright!
It seems she hangs upon the cheek of night

As a rich jewel in an Ethiop's ear –
Beauty too rich for use, for earth too dear!
So shows a snowy dove trooping with crows,
As yonder lady o'er her fellows shows.
The measure done, I'll watch her place of stand,
And, touching hers, make blessèd my rude hand.
Did my heart love till now? Forswear it, sight!
For I ne'er saw true beauty till this night.

TYBALT This, by his voice, should be a Montague.
Fetch me my rapier, boy. [*his page goes*]
What dares the slave
Come hither, covered with an antic face,
To fleer and scorn at our solemnity?
Now, by the stock and honour of my kin,
To strike him dead I hold it not a sin.

CAPULET Why, how now, kinsman! wherefore storm you so?

TYBALT Uncle, this is a Montague, our foe:
A villain that is hither come in spite,
To scorn at our solemnity this night.

CAPULET Young Romeo is it?

TYBALT 'Tis he, that villain Romeo.

CAPULET Content thee, gentle coz, let him alone,
'A bears him like a portly gentleman:
And, to say truth, Verona brags of him
To be a virtuous and well-governed youth.
I would not for the wealth of all this town
Here in my house do him disparagement
Therefore be patient, take no note of him.
It is my will, the which if thou respect,
Show a fair presence and put off these frowns,
An ill-beseeming semblance for a feast.

TYBALT It fits when such a villain is a guest:
I'll not endure him.

CAPULET He shall be endured.
What, goodman boy? I say he shall. Go to,
Am I the master here, or you? Go to,
You'll not endure him? God shall mend my soul!
You'll make a mutiny among my guests!
You will set cock-a-hoop! You'll be the man!

TYBALT Why, uncle, 'tis a shame.
CAPULET Go to, go to,
You are a saucy boy. Is't so indeed?
This trick may chance to scathe you, I know what.
You must contrary me! Marry, 'tis time –
Well said, my hearts! – You are a princox: go,
Be quiet, or – More light, more light, for shame! –
I'll make you quiet. What, cheerly, my hearts!
TYBALT Patience perforce with wilful choler meeting
Makes my flesh tremble in their different greeting.
I will withdraw, but this intrusion shall,
Now seeming sweet, convert to bitterest gall. [*goes*
ROMEO [*takes Juliet's hand*]
If I profane with my unworthiest hand
This holy shrine, the gentle pain is this:
My lips, two blushing pilgrims, ready stand
To smooth that rough touch with a tender kiss.
JULIET Good pilgrim, you do wrong your hand too much,
Which mannerly devotion shows in this:
For saints have hands that pilgrims' hands do touch,
And palm to palm is holy palmers' kiss.
ROMEO Have not saints lips, and holy palmers too?
JULIET Ay, pilgrim, lips that they must use in prayer.
ROMEO O then, dear saint, let lips do what hands do,
They pray: grant thou, lest faith turn to despair.
JULIET Saints do not move, though grant for prayers' sake.
ROMEO Then move not, while my prayer's effect I take.
Thus from my lips by thine my sin is purged.
[*kissing her*
JULIET Then have my lips the sin that they have took.
ROMEO Sin from my lips? O trespass sweetly urged!
Give me my sin again. [*kissing her*
JULIET You kiss by th' book.
NURSE Madam, your mother craves a word with you.
ROMEO What is her mother?
NURSE Marry, bachelor,
Her mother is the lady of the house,
And a good lady, and a wise and virtuous.
I nursed her daughter that you talked withal.

I tell you, he that can lay hold of her
Shall have the chinks.

ROMEO Is she a Capulet?
O dear account! My life is my foe's debt.

BENVOLIO Away be gone; the sport is at the best.

ROMEO Ay, so I fear; the more is my unrest.

CAPULET Nay, gentlemen, prepare not to be gone;
We have a trifling foolish banquet towards.

The masquers excuse themselves, whispering in his ear

Is it e'en so? Why, then, I thank you all:
I thank you, honest gentlemen; good night.
More torches here; come on! then let's to bed.

Servants bring torches to escort the masquers out

Ah, sirrah, by my fay, it waxes late:
I'll to my rest. [*all leave but Juliet and Nurse*

JULIET Come hither, nurse. What is yond gentleman?

NURSE The son and heir of old Tiberio.

JULIET What's he that now is going out of door?

NURSE Marry, that I think be young Petruchio.

JULIET What's he that follows there, that would not dance?

NURSE I know not.

JULIET Go ask his name. – If he be marrièd,
My grave is like to be my wedding bed.

NURSE His name is Romeo, and a Montague,
The only son of your great enemy.

JULIET My only love sprung from my only hate!
Too early seen unknown, and known too late!
Prodigious birth of love it is to me,
That I must love a loathèd enemy.

NURSE What's this, what's this?

JULIET A rhyme I learned even now
Of one I danced withal.

'One calls within, "Juliet" '

NURSE Anon, anon!
Come, let's away; the strangers all are gone.

[*they go*

ACT 2

Prologue

Enter Chorus

CHORUS Now old desire doth in his deathbed lie,
And young affection gapes to be his heir;
That fair for which love groaned for and would die,
With tender Juliet matched, is now not fair.
Now Romeo is beloved and loves again,
Alike bewitchèd by the charm of looks,
But to his foe supposed he must complain,
And she steal love's sweet bait from fearful hooks:
Being held a foe, he may not have access
To breathe such vows as lovers use to swear;
And she as much in love, her means much less
To meet her new belovèd anywhere:
But passion lends them power, time means, to meet,
Tempering extremities with extreme sweet. [*exit*

SCENE I

Capulet's orchard; to the one side the outer wall with a lane beyond, to the other Capulet's house showing an upper window

'Enter ROMEO *alone' in the lane*

ROMEO Can I go forward when my heart is here?
Turn back, dull earth, and find thy centre out.
[*he climbs the wall and leaps into the orchard*

'Enter BENVOLIO *with* MERCUTIO*' in the lane. Romeo listens behind the wall*

BENVOLIO Romeo, my cousin Romeo!
MERCUTIO He is wise,
And on my life hath stolen him home to bed.
BENVOLIO He ran this way and leapt this orchard wall.
Call, good Mercutio.
MERCUTIO: Nay, I'll conjure too.

Romeo, humours, madman, passion, lover!
Appear thou in the likeness of a sigh;
Speak but one rhyme and I am satisfied:
Cry but 'Ay me!', pronounce but 'love' and 'dove';
Speak to my gossip Venus one fair word,
One nickname for her purblind son and heir,
Young Abraham Cupid, he that shot so trim
When King Cophetua loved the beggar maid.
He heareth not, he stirreth not, he moveth not;
The ape is dead, and I must conjure him.
I conjure thee by Rosaline's bright eyes,
By her high forehead and her scarlet lip,
By her fine foot, straight leg, and quivering thigh,
And the demesnes that there adjacent lie,
That in thy likeness thou appear to us.

BENVOLIO An if he hear thee, thou wilt anger him.

MERCUTIO This cannot anger him. 'Twould anger him
To raise a spirit in his mistress' circle
Of some strange nature, letting it there stand
Till she had laid it and conjured it down;
That were some spite. My invocation
Is fair and honest; in his mistress' name
I conjure only but to raise up him.

BENVOLIO Come! He hath hid himself among these trees
To be consorted with the humorous night:
Blind is his love and best befits the dark.

MERCUTIO If love be blind, love cannot hit the mark.
Now will he sit under a medlar tree,
And wish his mistress were that kind of fruit
As maids call medlars when they laugh alone.
O Romeo, that she were, O that she were
An open-arse and thou a poperin pear!
Romeo, goodnight. I'll to my truckle-bed;
This field-bed is too cold for me to sleep.
Come, shall we go?

BENVOLIO Go then, for 'tis in vain
To seek him here that means not to be found.

[*they go*

SCENE 2

ROMEO He jests at scars that never felt a wound.

JULIET *appears aloft at the window*

But soft! What light through yonder window breaks?
It is the east, and Juliet is the sun.
Arise, fair sun, and kill the envious moon,
Who is already sick and pale with grief
That thou, her maid, art far more fair than she.
Be not her maid, since she is envious.
Her vestal livery is but sick and green,
And none but fools do wear it: cast it off.
It is my lady, O it is my love;
O that she knew she were.
She speaks, yet she says nothing. What of that?
Her eye discourses: I will answer it.
I am too bold: 'tis not to me she speaks.
Two of the fairest stars in all the heaven,
Having some business, do entreat her eyes
To twinkle in their spheres till they return.
What if her eyes were there, they in her head?
The brightness of her cheek would shame those stars
As daylight doth a lamp; her eyes in heaven
Would through the airy region stream so bright
That birds would sing and think it were not night.
See how she leans her cheek upon her hand!
O that I were a glove upon that hand,
That I might touch that cheek.

JULIET Ay me!

ROMEO She speaks.

O speak again, bright angel, for thou art
As glorious to this night, being o'er my head,
As is a wingèd messenger of heaven
Unto the white-upturnèd wondering eyes
Of mortals that fall back to gaze on him
When he bestrides the lazy-passing clouds

And sails upon the bosom of the air.

JULIET O Romeo, Romeo! Wherefore art thou Romeo?
Deny thy father and refuse thy name:
Or, if thou wilt not, be but sworn my love,
And I'll no longer be a Capulet.

ROMEO Shall I hear more, or shall I speak at this?

JULIET 'Tis but thy name that is my enemy.
Thou art thy self, though not a Montague.
O be some other name! What's Montague?
It is nor hand, nor foot, nor arm, nor face,
Nor any part belonging to a man.
What's in a name? That which we call a rose
By any other name would smell as sweet.
So Romeo would, were he not Romeo called,
Retain that dear perfection which he owes,
Without that title. Romeo, doff thy name;
And for thy name, which is no part of thee,
Take all myself.

ROMEO I take thee at thy word.
Call me but love, and I'll be new baptized;
Henceforth I never will be Romeo.

JULIET What man art thou that, thus bescreened in night,
So stumblest on my counsel?

ROMEO By a name
I know not how to tell thee who I am.
My name, dear saint, is hateful to myself
Because it is an enemy to thee.
Had I it written, I would tear the word.

JULIET My ears have yet not drunk a hundred words
Of thy tongue's uttering, yet I know the sound.
Art thou not Romeo, and a Montague?

ROMEO Neither, fair maid, if either thee dislike.

JULIET How camest thou hither, tell me, and wherefore?
The orchard walls are high and hard to climb,
And the place death, considering who thou art,
If any of my kinsmen find thee here.

ROMEO With love's light wings did I o'erperch these walls;
For stony limits cannot hold love out,
And what love can do, that dares love attempt:

Therefore thy kinsmen are no stop to me.

JULIET If they do see thee, they will murther thee.

ROMEO Alack, there lies more peril in thine eye
Than twenty of their swords. Look thou but sweet,
And I am proof against their enmity.

JULIET I would not for the world they saw thee here.

ROMEO I have night's cloak to hide me from their eyes;
And but thou love me, let them find me here:
My life were better ended by their hate
Than death proroguèd, wanting of thy love.

JULIET By whose direction foundst thou out this place?

ROMEO By love, that first did prompt me to enquire.
He lent me counsel, and I lent him eyes.
I am no pilot; yet, wert thou as far
As that vast shore washed with the farthest sea,
I should adventure for such merchandise.

JULIET Thou knowest the mask of night is on my face;
Else would a maiden blush bepaint my cheek,
For that which thou hast heard me speak tonight.
Fain would I dwell on form; fain, fain deny
What I have spoke: but farewell compliment!
Dost thou love me? I know thou wilt say 'Ay',
And I will take thy word. Yet, if thou swearst,
Thou mayst prove false. At lovers' perjuries
They say Jove laughs. O gentle Romeo,
If thou dost love, pronounce it faithfully.
Or, if thou think'st I am too quickly won,
I'll frown and be perverse and say thee nay,
So thou wilt woo; but else, not for the world.
In truth, fair Montague, I am too fond,
And therefore thou mayst think my haviour light;
But trust me, gentleman, I'll prove more true
Than those that have more cunning to be strange.
I should have been more strange, I must confess,
But that thou overheardst, ere I was ware,
My true-love passion. Therefore pardon me,
And not impute this yielding to light love,
Which the dark night hath so discoverèd.

ROMEO Lady, by yonder blessèd moon I vow,

That tips with silver all these fruit tree tops –
JULIET O swear not by the moon, th' inconstant moon,
That monthly changes in her circled orb,
Lest that thy love prove likewise variable.
ROMEO What shall I swear by?
JULIET Do not swear at all:
Or, if thou wilt, swear by thy gracious self,
Which is the god of my idolatry,
And I'll believe thee.
ROMEO If my heart's dear love –
JULIET Well, do not swear. Although I joy in thee,
I have no joy of this contract tonight:
It is too rash, too unadvised, too sudden,
Too like the lightning, which doth cease to be
Ere one can say 'It lightens'. Sweet, goodnight:
This bud of love, by summer's ripening breath,
May prove a beauteous flower when next we meet.
Goodnight, goodnight! As sweet repose and rest
Come to thy heart as that within my breast.
ROMEO O wilt thou leave me so unsatisfied?
JULIET What satisfaction canst thou have tonight?
ROMEO Th'exchange of thy love's faithful vow for mine.
JULIET I gave thee mine before thou didst request it:
And yet I would it were to give again.
ROMEO Would'st thou withdraw it? For what purpose, love?
JULIET But to be frank and give it thee again:
And yet I wish but for the thing I have.
My bounty is as boundless as the sea,
My love as deep: the more I give to thee,
The more I have: for both are infinite.
I hear some noise within. Dear love, adieu –
[*Nurse calls within*
Anon, good nurse! – sweet Montague, be true.
Stay but a little; I will come again. [*Juliet goes in*
ROMEO O blessed, blessed night! I am afeared,
Being in night, all this is but a dream,
Too flattering sweet to be substantial.

JULIET *reappears at the window*

JULIET Three words, dear Romeo, and good night indeed.

If that thy bent of love be honourable,
Thy purpose marriage, send me word tomorrow,
By one that I'll procure to come to thee,
Where and what time thou wilt perform the rite;
And all my fortunes at thy foot I'll lay,
And follow thee my lord throughout the world.

NURSE [*within*] Madam!

JULIET I come, anon. – But if thou meanest not well,
I do beseech thee –

NURSE [*within*] Madam!

JULIET By and by I come –
To cease thy suit, and leave me to my grief.
Tomorrow will I send.

ROMEO So thrive my soul –

JULIET A thousand times good night!
[*she goes in*

ROMEO A thousand times the worse, to want thy light!
Love goes toward love as schoolboys from their books,
But love from love, toward school with heavy looks.

JULIET *returns to the window*

JULIET Hist, Romeo, hist! O for a falconer's voice
To lure this tassel-gentle back again!
Bondage is hoarse and may not speak aloud,
Else would I tear the cave where Echo lies,
And make her airy tongue more hoarse than mine
With repetition of my "Romeo!"

ROMEO It is my soul that calls upon my name.
How silver-sweet sound lovers' tongues by night,
Like softest music to attending ears!

JULIET Romeo!

ROMEO My niëss!

JULIET What o'clock tomorrow
Shall I send to thee?

ROMEO By the hour of nine.

JULIET I will not fail. 'Tis twenty year till then.
I have forgot why I did call thee back.

ROMEO Let me stand here till thou remember it.

JULIET I shall forget, to have thee still stand there,

Rememb'ring how I love thy company.

ROMEO And I'll still stay, to have thee still forget,
Forgetting any other home but this.

JULIET 'Tis almost morning. I would have thee gone,
And yet no farther than a wanton's bird,
That lets it hop a little from her hand,
Like a poor prisoner in his twisted gyves,
And with a silk thread plucks it back again,
So loving-jealous of his liberty.

ROMEO I would I were thy bird.

JULIET Sweet, so would I;
Yet I should kill thee with much cherishing.
Goodnight, goodnight! Parting is such sweet sorrow,
That I shall say goodnight till it be morrow.

ROMEO Sleep dwell upon thine eyes, peace in thy breast!
Would I were sleep and peace, so sweet to rest!
[*she goes in*
Hence will I to my ghostly sire's close cell,
His help to crave, and my dear hap to tell. [*he goes*

SCENE 3

Friar Lawrence's cell

'Enter FRIAR *alone with a basket'*

FRIAR The grey-eyed morn smiles on the frowning night,
Check'ring the eastern clouds with streaks of light:
And darkness fleckèd like a drunkard reels
From forth day's pathway, made by Titan's wheels:
Now ere the sun advance his burning eye,
The day to cheer and night's dank dew to dry,
I must upfill this osier cage of ours,
With baleful weeds and precious-juicèd flowers.
The earth that's nature's mother is her tomb;
What is her burying grave, that is her womb;
And from her womb children of divers kind
We sucking on her natural bosom find:
Many for many virtues excellent,
None but for some, and yet all different.

O mickle is the powerful grace that lies
In plants, herbs, stones, and their true qualities:
For nought so vile that on the earth doth live
But to the earth some special good doth give:
Nor aught so good but, strained from that fair use,
Revolts from true birth, stumbling on abuse.
Virtue itself turns vice, being misapplied,
And vice sometime by action dignified.

ROMEO *approaches, unseen by the Friar*

Within the infant rind of this weak flower
Poison hath residence, and medicine power:
For this, being smelt, with that part cheers each part;
Being tasted, stays all senses with the heart.
Two such opposèd kings encamp them still
In man as well as herbs – grace and rude will:
And where the worser is predominant,
Full soon the canker death eats up that plant.

ROMEO Good morrow, father.

FRIAR Benedicite!
What early tongue so sweet saluteth me?
Young son, it argues a distempered head,
So soon to bid goodmorrow to thy bed.
Care keeps his watch in every old man's eye,
And where care lodges sleep will never lie:
But where unbruisèd youth with unstuffed brain
Doth couch his limbs, there golden sleep doth reign.
Therefore thy earliness doth me assure
Thou art uproused with some distemperature
Or if not so, then here I hit it right –
Our Romeo hath not been in bed tonight.

ROMEO That last is true – the sweeter rest was mine.

FRIAR God pardon sin! Wast thou with Rosaline?

ROMEO With Rosaline? My ghostly father, no;
I have forgot that name, and that name's woe.

FRIAR That's my good son! But where hast thou been then?

ROMEO I'll tell thee ere thou ask it me again.
I have been feasting with mine enemy,
Where on a sudden one hath wounded me
That's by me wounded. Both our remedies

Within thy help and holy physic lies.
I bear no hatred, blessed man, for lo,
My intercession likewise steads my foe.

FRIAR Be plain, good son, and homely in thy drift.
Riddling confession finds but riddling shrift.

ROMEO Then plainly know my heart's dear love is set
On the fair daughter of rich Capulet:
As mine on hers, so hers is set on mine,
And all combined save what thou must combine
By holy marriage: when and where and how
We met, we wooed, and made exchange of vow
I'll tell thee as we pass; but this I pray,
That thou consent to marry us today.

FRIAR Holy Saint Francis, what a change is here!
Is Rosaline, that thou didst love so dear,
So soon forsaken? Young men's love then lies
Not truly in their hearts but in their eyes.
Jesu Maria, what a deal of brine
Hath washed thy sallow cheeks for Rosaline!
How much salt water thrown away in waste
To season love, that of it doth not taste!
The sun not yet thy sighs from heaven clears,
Thy old groans ring yet in mine ancient ears;
Lo, here upon thy cheek the stain doth sit
Of an old tear that is not washed off yet.
If e'er thou wast thyself, and these woes thine,
Thou and these woes were all for Rosaline.
And art thou changed? Pronounce this sentence, then –
Women may fall, when there's no strength in men.

ROMEO Thou chid'st me oft for loving Rosaline.

FRIAR For doting, not for loving, pupil mine.

ROMEO And bad'st me bury love.

FRIAR Not in a grave
To lay one in, another out to have.

ROMEO I pray thee chide me not. Her I love now
Doth grace for grace and love for love allow:
The other did not so.

FRIAR O, she knew well
Thy love did read by rote, that could not spell.

But come, young waverer, come go with me;
In one respect I'll thy assistant be:
For this alliance may so happy prove
To turn your households' rancour to pure love.

ROMEO O let us hence! I stand on sudden haste.

FRIAR Wisely and slow. They stumble that run fast. [*they go*

SCENE 4

A public place

'Enter BENVOLIO *and* MERCUTIO*'*

MERCUTIO Where the devil should this Romeo be? Came he not home tonight?

BENVOLIO Not to his father's; I spoke with his man.

MERCUTIO Why, that same pale hard-hearted wench, that Rosaline,
Torments him so, that he will sure run mad.

BENVOLIO Tybalt, the kinsman to old Capulet,
Hath sent a letter to his father's house.

MERCUTIO A challenge, on my life.

BENVOLIO Romeo will answer it.

MERCUTIO Any man that can write may answer a letter.

BENVOLIO Nay, he will answer the letter's master, how he dares being dared.

MERCUTIO Alas, poor Romeo, he is already dead – stabbed with a white wench's black eye, run through the ear with a love-song, the very pin of his heart cleft with the blind bow-boy's butt-shaft; and is he a man to encounter Tybalt?

BENVOLIO Why, what is Tybalt?

MERCUTIO More than Prince of Cats. O, he's the courageous captain of compliments. He fights as you sing pricksong – keeps time, distance, and proportion; he rests his minim rests – one, two, and the third in your bosom. The very butcher of a silk button, a duellist, a duellist, a gentleman of the very first house, of the first and second cause! Ah, the immortal passado, the punto reverso, the hai!

BENVOLIO The what?

MERCUTIO The pox of such antic, lisping, affecting fantasticoes, these new tuners of accent! 'By Jesu, a very good blade! a very tall man! a very good whore!' Why, is not this a lamentable thing, grandsire, that we should be thus afflicted with these strange flies, these fashion-mongers, these pardon-me's, who stand so much on the new form that they cannot sit at ease on the old bench? O, their bones, their bones!

'Enter ROMEO*'*

BENVOLIO Here comes Romeo, here comes Romeo!

MERCUTIO Without his roe, like a dried herring. O flesh, flesh, how art thou fishified! Now is he for the numbers that Petrarch flowed in. Laura to his lady was a kitchen wench – marry, she had a better love to be-rhyme her! – Dido a dowdy, Cleopatra a gipsy, Helen and Hero hildings and harlots, Thisbe a gray eye or so, but not to the purpose. Signior Romeo, bon jour! There's a French salutation to your French slop. You gave us the counterfeit fairly last night.

ROMEO Good morrow to you both. What counterfeit did I give you?

MERCUTIO The slip, sir, the slip. Can you not conceive?

ROMEO Pardon, good Mercutio. My business was great, and in such a case as mine a man may strain courtesy.

MERCUTIO That's as much as to say, such a case as yours constrains a man to bow in the hams.

ROMEO Meaning to curtsy?

MERCUTIO Thou hast most kindly hit it.

ROMEO A most courteous exposition.

MERCUTIO Nay, I am the very pink of courtesy.

ROMEO Pink for flower?

MERCUTIO Right.

ROMEO Why, then is my pump well flowered.

MERCUTIO Sure wit! Follow me this jest now till thou hast worn out thy pump, that, when the single sole of it is worn, the jest may remain, after the wearing, solely singular.

ROMEO O single-soled jest, solely singular for the singleness!

MERCUTIO Come between us, good Benvolio; my wits faints.

ROMEO Switch and spurs, switch and spurs; or I'll cry a match.

MERCUTIO Nay, if our wits run the wild-goose chase, I am done: for thou hast more of the wild goose in one of thy wits than, I am sure, I have in my whole five. Was I with you there for the goose?

ROMEO Thou wast never with me for anything when thou wast not there for the goose.

MERCUTIO I will bite thee by the ear for that jest.

ROMEO Nay, good goose, bite not.

MERCUTIO Thy wit is a very bitter sweeting; it is a most sharp sauce.

ROMEO And is it not then well served in to a sweet goose?

MERCUTIO O, here's a wit of cheveril, that stretches from an inch narrow to an ell broad.

ROMEO I stretch it out for that word 'broad', which, added to the goose, proves thee far and wide a broad goose.

MERCUTIO Why, is not this better now than groaning for love? Now art thou sociable, now art thou Romeo: now art thou what thou art, by art as well as by nature. For this drivelling love is like a great natural that runs lolling up and down to hide his bauble in a hole.

BENVOLIO Stop there, stop there!

MERCUTIO Thou desirest me to stop in my tale, against the hair?

BENVOLIO Thou wouldst else have made thy tale large.

MERCUTIO O, thou art deceived! I would have made it short, for I was come to the whole depth of my tale, and meant indeed to occupy the argument no longer.

The NURSE *in her best array is seen approaching with her man* PETER

ROMEO Here's goodly gear! A sail, a sail!

MERCUTIO Two, two! a shirt and a smock.

NURSE Peter!

PETER Anon.

NURSE My fan, Peter.

MERCUTIO Good Peter, to hide her face; for her fan's the fairer face.

NURSE God ye good morrow, gentlemen.

MERCUTIO God ye good-den, fair gentlewoman.

NURSE Is it good-den?

MERCUTIO 'Tis no less, I tell ye; for the bawdy hand of the dial is now upon the prick of noon.

NURSE Out upon you! What a man are you?

ROMEO One, gentlewoman, that God hath made, himself to mar.

NURSE By my troth, it is well said. 'For himself to mar,' quoth 'a? Gentlemen, can any of you tell me where I may find the young Romeo?

ROMEO I can tell you; but young Romeo will be older when you have found him than he was when you sought him. I am the youngest of that name, for fault of a worse.

NURSE You say well.

MERCUTIO Yea, is the worst well? Very well took, i' faith! Wisely, wisely!

NURSE If you be he, sir, I desire some confidence with you.

BENVOLIO She will indite him to some supper.

MERCUTIO A bawd, a bawd, a bawd! So ho!

ROMEO What, hast thou found?

MERCUTIO No hare, sir; unless a hare, sir, in a lenten pie, that is something stale and hoar ere it be spent.

'He walks by them and sings'

An old hare hoar
And an old hare hoar
Is very good meat in Lent.
But a hare that is hoar
Is too much for a score
When it hoars ere it be spent.

Romeo, will you come to your father's? We'll to dinner thither.

ROMEO I will follow you.

MERCUTIO Farewell, ancient lady; farewell, [*singing*] 'lady, lady, lady'. [*Mercutio and Benvolio go off*

NURSE I pray you, sir, what saucy merchant was this that was so full of his ropery?

ROMEO A gentleman, Nurse, that loves to hear himself talk, and will speak more in a minute than he will stand to in a month.

NURSE And 'a speak anything against me, I'll take him down

and 'a were lustier than he is, and twenty such Jacks: and if I cannot, I'll find those that shall. Scurvy knave! I am none of his flirt-gills, I am none of his skains-mates. [*To Peter*] And thou must stand by too, and suffer every knave to use me at his pleasure!

PETER I saw no man use you at his pleasure. If I had, my weapon should quickly have been out. I warrant you I dare draw as soon as another man, if I see occasion in a good quarrel, and the law on my side.

NURSE Now afore God, I am so vexed that every part about me quivers. Scurvy knave! Pray you, sir, a word. And as I told you, my young lady bid me enquire you out. What she bid me say I will keep to myself: but first let me tell ye, if ye should lead her in a fool's paradise, as they say, it were a very gross kind of behaviour, as they say: for the gentlewoman is young; and therefore, if you should deal double with her, truly it were an ill thing to be offered to any gentlewoman, and very weak dealing.

ROMEO Nurse, commend me to thy lady and mistress. I protest unto thee –

NURSE Good heart! and i' faith I will tell her as much. Lord, Lord! she will be a joyful woman.

ROMEO What wilt thou tell her, Nurse? Thou dost not mark me!

NURSE I will tell her, sir, that you do protest, which, as I take it, is a gentlemanlike offer.

ROMEO Bid her devise
Some means to come to shrift this afternoon,
And there she shall at Friar Lawrence' cell
Be shrived and married. Here is for thy pains.

NURSE No, truly, sir; not a penny.

ROMEO Go to, I say you shall.

NURSE This afternoon, sir; well, she shall be there.

ROMEO And stay, good Nurse, behind the abbey wall.
Within this hour my man shall be with thee
And bring thee cords made like a tackled stair,
Which to the high topgallant of my joy
Must be my convoy in the secret night.
Farewell. Be trusty, and I'll quit thy pains.

Farewell. Commend me to thy mistress.

NURSE Now God in heaven bless thee! Hark you, sir.

ROMEO What sayst thou, my dear Nurse?

NURSE Is your man secret? Did you ne'er hear say,
'Two may keep counsel, putting one away'?

ROMEO I warrant thee my man's as true as steel.

NURSE Well, sir, my mistress is the sweetest lady. Lord, Lord! when 'twas a little prating thing – O, there is a nobleman in town, one Paris, that would fain lay knife aboard: but she, good soul, had as lief see a toad, a very toad, as see him. I anger her sometimes, and tell her that Paris is the properer man; but I'll warrant you, when I say so, she looks as pale as any clout in the versal world. Doth not rosemary and Romeo begin both with a letter?

ROMEO Ay, Nurse; what of that? Both with an R.

NURSE Ah, mocker, that's the dog-name; R is for the – No; I know it begins with some other letter; and she hath the prettiest sententious of it, of you and rosemary, that it would do you good to hear it.

ROMEO Commend me to thy lady.

NURSE Ay, a thousand times. [*Romeo goes*] Peter!

PETER Anon.

NURSE Before and apace. [*they go*

SCENE 5

Capulet's orchard

'Enter JULIET*'*

JULIET The clock struck nine when I did send the Nurse;
In half an hour she promised to return.
Perchance she cannot meet him. That's not so.
O, she is lame! Love's heralds should be thoughts,
Which ten times faster glides than the sun's beams
Driving back shadows over louring hills.
Therefore do nimble-pinioned doves draw Love,
And therefore hath the wind-swift Cupid wings.
Now is the sun upon the highmost hill

Of this day's journey, and from nine till twelve
Is three long hours; yet she is not come.
Had she affections and warm youthful blood,
She would be swift in motion as a ball;
My words would bandy her to my sweet love,
And his to me.
But old folks, many feign as they were dead –
Unwieldy, slow, heavy, and pale as lead.

'Enter NURSE*', with* PETER

O God, she comes! O honey Nurse, what news?
Hast thou met with him? Send thy man away.

NURSE Peter, stay at the gate. [*Peter withdraws*

JULIET Now good sweet Nurse – O Lord, why look'st thou sad?
Though news be sad, yet tell them merrily;
If good, thou shamest the music of sweet news
By playing it to me with so sour a face.

NURSE I am aweary, give me leave a while.
Fie, how my bones ache! What a jaunce have I!

JULIET I would thou hadst my bones, and I thy news:
Nay, come, I pray thee speak; good, good Nurse, speak.

NURSE Jesu, what haste! Can you not stay awhile?
Do you not see that I am out of breath?

JULIET How art thou out of breath when thou hast breath
To say to me that thou art out of breath?
The excuse that thou dost make in this delay
Is longer than the tale thou dost excuse.
Is thy news good or bad? Answer to that.
Say either, and I'll stay the circumstance.
Let me be satisfied; is't good or bad?

NURSE Well, you have made a simple choice; you know not how to choose a man. Romeo? No, not he. Though his face be better than any man's, yet his leg excels all men's; and for a hand and a foot and a body, though they be not to be talked on, yet they are past compare. He is not the flower of courtesy, but, I'll warrant him, as gentle as a lamb. Go thy ways, wench; serve God. What, have you dined at home?

JULIET No, no. But all this did I know before.
What says he of our marriage, what of that?

NURSE Lord, how my head aches! what a head have I!
It beats as it would fall in twenty pieces.
My back o' t'other side; ah, my back, my back!
Beshrew your heart for sending me about
To catch my death with jauncing up and down.

JULIET I' faith, I am sorry that thou art not well.
Sweet, sweet, sweet Nurse, tell me, what says my love?

NURSE Your love says, like an honest gentleman, and a courteous, and a kind, and a handsome, and, I warrant, a virtuous – Where is your mother?

JULIET Where is my mother? Why, she is within.
Where should she be? How oddly thou repliest:
'Your love says, like an honest gentleman,
"Where is your mother?" '

NURSE O God's Lady dear!
Are you so hot? Marry come up, I trow!
Is this the poultice for my aching bones?
Henceforward do your messages yourself.

JULIET Here's such a coil! Come, what says Romeo?

NURSE Have you got leave to go to shrift today?

JULIET I have.

NURSE Then hie you hence to Friar Lawrence' cell;
There stays a husband to make you a wife.
Now comes the wanton blood up in your cheeks;
They'll be in scarlet straight at any news.
Hie you to church; I must another way,
To fetch a ladder, by the which your love
Must climb a bird's nest soon when it is dark.
I am the drudge, and toil in your delight:
But you shall bear the burden soon at night.
Go; I'll to dinner; hie you to the cell.

JULIET Hie to high fortune! Honest Nurse, farewell. [*they go*

SCENE 6

Friar Lawrence's cell

'Enter FRIAR *and* ROMEO

FRIAR So smile the heavens upon this holy act
That after-hours with sorrow chide us not.
ROMEO Amen, amen. But come what sorrow can,
It cannot countervail the exchange of joy
That one short minute gives me in her sight.
Do thou but close our hands with holy words,
Then love-devouring death do what he dare;
It is enough I may but call her mine.
FRIAR These violent delights have violent ends,
And in their triumph die like fire and powder
Which, as they kiss, consume. The sweetest honey
Is loathsome in his own deliciousness,
And in the taste confounds the appetite.
Therefore love moderately; long love doth so:
Too swift arrives as tardy as too slow.
Here comes the lady.

'Enter JULIET*'*

O, so light a foot
Will ne'er wear out the everlasting flint!
A lover may bestride the gossamers
That idles in the wanton summer air,
And yet not fall; so light is vanity.
JULIET Good even to my ghostly confessor.
FRIAR Romeo shall thank thee, daughter, for us both.
JULIET As much to him, else is his thanks too much.
[*they embrace*
ROMEO Ah, Juliet, if the measure of thy joy
Be heaped like mine, and that thy skill be more
To blazon it, then sweeten with thy breath
This neighbour air, and let rich music's tongue
Unfold the imagined happiness that both
Receive in either by this dear encounter.

JULIET Conceit, more rich in matter than in words,
Brags of his substance, not of ornament.
They are but beggars that can count their worth;
But my true love is grown to such excess
I cannot sum up sum of half my wealth.

FRIAR Come, come with me, and we will make short work;
For, by your leaves, you shall not stay alone
Till Holy Church incorporate two in one. [*they go*

ACT 3 SCENE 1

A public place

'Enter MERCUTIO, BENVOLIO, *and men'*

BENVOLIO I pray thee, good Mercutio, let's retire;
The day is hot, the Capels are abroad:
And if we meet we shall not scape a brawl,
For now, these hot days, is the mad blood stirring.

MERCUTIO Thou art like one of these fellows that, when he enters the confines of a tavern, claps me his sword upon the table and says 'God send me no need of thee'; and, by the operation of the second cup, draws him on the drawer, when indeed there is no need.

BENVOLIO Am I like such a fellow?

MERCUTIO Come, come, thou art as hot a Jack in thy mood as any in Italy; and as soon moved to be moody, and as soon moody to be moved.

BENVOLIO And what to?

MERCUTIO Nay, an there were two such, we should have none shortly, for one would kill the other. Thou? Why, thou wilt quarrel with a man that hath a hair more or a hair less in his beard than thou hast. Thou wilt quarrel with a man for cracking nuts, having no other reason but because thou hast hazel eyes. What eye but such an eye would spy out such a quarrel? Thy head is as full of quarrels as an egg is full of meat, and yet thy head hath been beaten as addle as an egg for quarrelling. Thou hast quarrelled with a man for coughing in the street, because he hath wakened thy dog that hath lain asleep in the sun. Didst thou not fall out with a tailor for wearing his new doublet before Easter? With another for tying his new shoes with old riband? And yet thou wilt tutor me from quarrelling?

BENVOLIO An I were so apt to quarrel as thou art, any man should buy the fee-simple of my life for an hour and a quarter.

MERCUTIO The fee-simple? O simple!

'Enter TYBALT*', 'and others'*

BENVOLIO By my head, here comes the Capulets.

MERCUTIO By my heel, I care not.

TYBALT Follow me close, for I will speak to them.
Gentlemen, good-den: a word with one of you.

MERCUTIO And but one word with one of us? Couple it with something; make it a word and a blow.

TYBALT You shall find me apt enough to that, sir, an you will give me occasion.

MERCUTIO Could you not take some occasion without giving?

TYBALT Mercutio, thou consort'st with Romeo –

MERCUTIO Consort? What, dost thou make us minstrels? An thou make minstrels of us, look to hear nothing but discords. Here's my fiddlestick; here's that shall make you dance. Zounds, consort!

BENVOLIO We talk here in the public haunt of men.
Either withdraw unto some private place
And reason coldly of your grievances,
Or else depart: here all eyes gaze on us.

MERCUTIO Men's eyes were made to look, and let them gaze.
I will not budge for no man's pleasure, I.

'Enter ROMEO*'*

TYBALT Well, peace be with you, sir; here comes my man.

MERCUTIO But I'll be hanged, sir, if he wears your livery.
Marry, go before to field, he'll be your follower!
Your worship in that sense may call him man.

TYBALT Romeo, the love I bear thee can afford
No better term than this: thou art a villain.

ROMEO Tybalt, the reason that I have to love thee
Doth much excuse the appertaining rage
To such a greeting. Villain am I none –
Therefore farewell; I see thou knowest me not.

TYBALT Boy, this shall not excuse the injuries
That thou hast done me; therefore turn and draw.

ROMEO I do protest I never injured thee,
But love thee better than thou canst devise
Till thou shalt know the reason of my love:
And so, good Capulet, which name I tender

As dearly as mine own, be satisfied.

MERCUTIO O calm, dishonourable, vile submission!
'Alla stoccata' carries it away. [*draws*
Tybalt, you rat-catcher, will you walk?

TYBALT What wouldst thou have with me?

MERCUTIO Good King of Cats, nothing but one of your nine lives that I mean to make bold withal and, as you shall use me hereafter, dry-beat the rest of the eight. Will you pluck your sword out of his pilcher by the ears? Make haste, lest mine be about your ears ere it be out.

TYBALT I am for you. [*draws*

ROMEO Gentle Mercutio, put thy rapier up.

MERCUTIO Come, sir, your passado. [*they fight*

ROMEO Draw, Benvolio; beat down their weapons.
Gentlemen, for shame forbear this outrage.
Tybalt, Mercutio, the prince expressly hath
Forbid this bandying in Verona streets.
Hold, Tybalt! good Mercutio!

'Tybalt under Romeo's arm thrusts Mercutio in and flies'

MERCUTIO I am hurt.
A plague o' both your houses! I am sped.
Is he gone and hath nothing?

BENVOLIO What, art thou hurt?

MERCUTIO Ay, ay, a scratch, a scratch; marry, 'tis enough.
Where is my page? Go, villain, fetch a surgeon.
[*Page goes*

ROMEO Courage, man; the hurt cannot be much.

MERCUTIO No, 'tis not so deep as a well, nor so wide as a church door, but 'tis enough, 'twill serve. Ask for me tomorrow and you shall find me a grave man. I am peppered, I warrant, for this world. A plague o' both your houses! Zounds! A dog, a rat, a mouse, a cat, to scratch a man to death! A braggart, a rogue, a villain, that fights by the book of arithmetic! Why the devil came you between us? I was hurt under your arm.

ROMEO I thought all for the best.

MERCUTIO Help me into some house, Benvolio,
Or I shall faint. A plague o' both your houses!

They have made worms' meat of me. I have it,
And soundly too. Your houses!

[*Benvolio helps him away*

ROMEO This gentleman, the prince's near ally,
My very friend, hath got this mortal hurt
In my behalf, my reputation stained
With Tybalt's slander – Tybalt that an hour
Hath been my cousin. O sweet Juliet,
Thy beauty hath made me effeminate,
And in my temper softened valour's steel!

BENVOLIO *returns*

BENVOLIO O Romeo, Romeo, brave Mercutio's dead.
That gallant spirit hath aspired the clouds,
Which too untimely here did scorn the earth.

ROMEO This day's black fate on moe days doth depend;
This but begins the woe others must end.

TYBALT *returns*

BENVOLIO Here comes the furious Tybalt back again.

ROMEO Again! in triumph, and Mercutio slain!
Away to heaven, respective lenity,
And fire-eyed fury be my conduct now!
Now, Tybalt, take the 'villain' back again
That late thou gavest me, for Mercutio's soul
Is but a little way above our heads,
Staying for thine to keep him company.
Either thou or I, or both, must go with him.

TYBALT Thou wretched boy that didst consort him here
Shalt with him hence.

ROMEO This shall determine that.

[*'they fight, Tybalt falls'*

BENVOLIO Romeo, away, be gone!
The citizens are up, and Tybalt slain.
Stand not amazed. The prince will doom thee death
If thou art taken. Hence, be gone, away!

ROMEO O, I am Fortune's fool.

BENVOLIO Why dost thou stay?

[*Romeo goes*

'Enter Citizens'

A CITIZEN Which way ran he that killed Mercutio?
Tybalt, that murderer, which way ran he?

BENVOLIO There lies that Tybalt.

A CITIZEN Up, sir, go with me:
I charge thee in the prince's name obey.

'Enter PRINCE, *old* MONTAGUE, CAPULET, *their wives and all'*

PRINCE Where are the vile beginners of this fray?

BENVOLIO O noble Prince, I can discover all
The unlucky manage of this fatal brawl.
There lies the man, slain by young Romeo,
That slew thy kinsman, brave Mercutio.

LADY CAP. Tybalt, my cousin, O my brother's child!
O prince! O husband! O, the blood is spilled
Of my dear kinsman. Prince, as thou art true,
For blood of ours shed blood of Montague.
O cousin, cousin!

PRINCE Benvolio, who began this bloody fray?

BENVOLIO Tybalt, here slain, whom Romeo's hand did slay.
Romeo, that spoke him fair, bid him bethink
How nice the quarrel was, and urged withal
Your high displeasure. All this – utterèd
With gentle breath, calm look, knees humbly bowed –
Could not take truce with the unruly spleen
Of Tybalt deaf to peace, but that he tilts
With piercing steel at bold Mercutio's breast,
Who, all as hot, turns deadly point to point,
And, with a martial scorn, with one hand beats
Cold death aside and with the other sends
It back to Tybalt, whose dexterity
Retorts it. Romeo he cries aloud,
'Hold, friends! friends, part!' and, swifter than his tongue,
His agile arm beats down their fatal points,
And 'twixt them rushes; underneath whose arm
An envious thrust from Tybalt hit the life
Of stout Mercutio, and then Tybalt fled,
But by and by comes back to Romeo

Who had but newly entertained revenge,
And to 't they go like lightning; for, ere I
Could draw to part them, was stout Tybalt slain,
And, as he fell, did Romeo turn and fly:
This is the truth, or let Benvolio die.

LADY CAP. He is a kinsman to the Montague;
Affection makes him false, he speaks not true.
Some twenty of them fought in this black strife,
And all those twenty could but kill one life.
I beg for justice, which thou, Prince, must give:
Romeo slew Tybalt; Romeo must not live.

PRINCE Romeo slew him; he slew Mercutio.
Who now the price of his dear blood doth owe?

MONTAG. Not Romeo, Prince; he was Mercutio's friend;
His fault concludes but what the law should end –
The life of Tybalt.

PRINCE And for that offence
Immediately we do exile him hence.
I have an interest in your hearts' proceeding:
My blood for your rude brawls doth lie a-bleeding.
But I'll amerce you with so strong a fine
That you shall all repent the loss of mine.
I will be deaf to pleading and excuses;
Nor tears nor prayers shall purchase out abuses.
Therefore use none. Let Romeo hence in haste,
Else, when he is found, that hour is his last.
Bear hence this body, and attend our will.
Mercy but murders, pardoning those that kill.

[*they go*

SCENE 2

Capulet's house

'Enter JULIET *alone'*

JULIET Gallop apace, you fiery-footed steeds,
Towards Phoebus' lodging! Such a waggoner
As Phaëton would whip you to the west
And bring in cloudy night immediately.

Spread thy close curtain, love-performing night,
That runaways' eyes may wink, and Romeo
Leap to these arms untalked of and unseen.
Lovers can see to do their amorous rites
By their own beauties; or, if love be blind,
It best agrees with night. Come, civil Night,
Thou sober-suited matron all in black,
And learn me how to lose a winning match,
Played for a pair of stainless maidenhoods.
Hood my unmanned blood, bating in my cheeks,
With thy black mantle till strange love, grown bold,
Think true love acted simple modesty.
Come, Night! Come, Romeo! Come, thou day in night;
For thou wilt lie upon the wings of night
Whiter than snow upon a raven's back.
Come, gentle Night; come, loving, black-browed
Night:
Give me my Romeo; and, when he shall die,
Take him and cut him out in little stars,
And he will make the face of heaven so fine
That all the world will be in love with night
And pay no worship to the garish sun.
O, I have bought the mansion of a love,
But not possessed it; and though I am sold,
Not yet enjoyed. So tedious is this day
As is the night before some festival
To an impatient child that hath new robes
And may not wear them. O, here comes my nurse,

'Enter NURSE *with cords'*

And she brings news; and every tongue that speaks
But Romeo's name speaks heavenly eloquence.
Now, Nurse, what news? What hast thou there?
The cords
That Romeo bid thee fetch?

NURSE Ay, ay, the cords.
[*throws them down*

JULIET Ay me, what news? Why dost thou wring thy hands?

NURSE Ah, weraday! He's dead, he's dead, he's dead!
We are undone, lady, we are undone.

Alack the day, he's gone, he's killed, he's dead!

JULIET Can heaven be so envious?

NURSE Romeo can,
Though heaven cannot. O Romeo, Romeo!
Who ever would have thought it? Romeo!

JULIET What devil art thou that dost torment me thus?
This torture should be roared in dismal hell.
Hath Romeo slain himself? Say thou but 'ay',
And that bare vowel 'I' shall poison more
Than the death-darting eye of cockatrice.
I am not I if there be such an 'I',
Or those eyes shut that makes thee answer 'ay'.
If he be slain, say 'ay', or, if not, 'no'.
Brief sounds determine of my weal or woe.

NURSE I saw the wound, I saw it with mine eyes,
(God save the mark!) here on his manly breast.
A piteous corse, a bloody piteous corse,
Pale, pale as ashes, all bedaubed in blood,
All in gore blood; I swounded at the sight.

JULIET O break, my heart! Poor bankrout, break at once!
To prison, eyes; ne'er look on liberty.
Vile earth, to earth resign, end motion here,
And thou and Romeo press one heavy bier!

NURSE O Tybalt, Tybalt, the best friend I had!
O courteous Tybalt, honest gentleman,
That ever I should live to see thee dead!

JULIET What storm is this that blows so contrary?
Is Romeo slaught'red? And is Tybalt dead?
My dearest cousin, and my dearer lord?
Then, dreadful trumpet, sound the general doom;
For who is living if those two are gone?

NURSE Tybalt is gone and Romeo banishèd;
Romeo that killed him, he is banishèd.

JULIET O God! did Romeo's hand shed Tybalt's blood?

NURSE It did, it did! alas the day, it did!

JULIET O serpent heart, hid with a flowering face!
Did ever dragon keep so fair a cave?
Beautiful tyrant, fiend angelical,
Dove-feathered raven, wolvish-ravening lamb!

Despisèd substance of divinest show,
Just opposite to what thou justly seemst –
A damnèd saint, an honourable villain!
O nature, what hadst thou to do in hell
When thou didst bower the spirit of a fiend
In mortal paradise of such sweet flesh?
Was ever book containing such vile matter
So fairly bound? O that deceit should dwell
In such a gorgeous palace!

NURSE
There's no trust,
No faith, no honesty in men; all perjured,
All forsworn, all naught, all dissemblers.
Ah, where's my man? Give me some aqua vitae.
These griefs, these woes, these sorrows make me old.
Shame come to Romeo!

JULIET
Blistered be thy tongue
For such a wish! He was not born to shame.
Upon his brow shame is ashamed to sit:
For 'tis a throne where honour may be crowned
Sole monarch of the universal earth.
O what a beast was I to chide at him!

NURSE
Will you speak well of him that killed your cousin?

JULIET
Shall I speak ill of him that is my husband?
Ah, poor my lord, what tongue shall smooth thy name
When I, thy three-hours wife, have mangled it?
But wherefore, villain, didst thou kill my cousin?
That villain cousin would have killed my husband.
Back, foolish tears, back to your native spring!
Your tributary drops belong to woe
Which you, mistaking, offer up to joy.
My husband lives, that Tybalt would have slain,
And Tybalt's dead that would have slain my husband:
All this is comfort; wherefore weep I then?
Some word there was, worser than Tybalt's death,
That murd'red me. I would forget it fain,
But oh, it presses to my memory
Like damnèd guilty deeds to sinners' minds –
'Tybalt is dead and Romeo banishèd'.
That 'banishèd', that one word 'banishèd',

Hath slain ten thousand Tybalts. Tybalt's death
Was woe enough if it had ended there:
Or, if sour woe delights in fellowship
And needly will be ranked with other griefs,
Why followed not, when she said 'Tybalt's dead',
'Thy father', or 'thy mother', nay, or both,
Which modern lamentation might have moved?
But, with a rearward following Tybalt's death,
'Romeo is banishèd'! To speak that word
Is father, mother, Tybalt, Romeo, Juliet,
All slain, all dead: 'Romeo is banishèd'!
There is no end, no limit, measure, bound,
In that word's death; no words can that woe sound.
Where is my father and my mother, Nurse?

NURSE Weeping and wailing over Tybalt's corse.
Will you go to them? I will bring you thither.

JULIET Wash they his wounds with tears? Mine shall be spent,
When theirs are dry, for Romeo's banishment.
Take up those cords. Poor ropes, you are beguiled,
Both you and I, for Romeo is exiled.
He made you for a highway to my bed,
But I, a maid, die maiden-widowèd.
Come, cords; come, Nurse: I'll to my wedding bed,
And death, not Romeo, take my maidenhead!

NURSE Hie to your chamber. I'll find Romeo
To comfort you: I wot well where he is.
Hark ye, your Romeo will be here at night:
I'll to him; he is hid at Lawrence' cell.

JULIET O find him! Give this ring to my true knight
And bid him come to take his last farewell.

[*they go*

SCENE 3

Friar Lawrence's cell with his study at the back

Enter FRIAR

FRIAR Romeo, come forth; come forth, thou fearful man.
Affliction is enamoured of thy parts,
And thou art wedded to calamity.

Enter ROMEO *from the study*

ROMEO Father, what news? What is the prince's doom?
What sorrow craves acquaintance at my hand
That I yet know not?
FRIAR Too familiar
Is my dear son with such sour company!
I bring thee tidings of the prince's doom.
ROMEO What less than doomsday is the prince's doom?
FRIAR A gentler judgment vanished from his lips;
Not body's death, but body's banishment.
ROMEO Ha, banishment? Be merciful, say 'death':
For exile hath more terror in his look,
Much more than death: do not say 'banishment'.
FRIAR Hence from Verona art thou banishèd.
Be patient, for the world is broad and wide.
ROMEO There is no world without Verona walls,
But purgatory, torture, hell itself:
Hence banishèd is banished from the world,
And world's exile is death. Then 'banishèd'
Is death mis-termed. Calling death 'banishèd',
Thou cut'st my head off with a golden axe,
And smilest upon the stroke that murders me.
FRIAR O deadly sin! O rude unthankfulness!
Thy fault our law calls death, but the kind Prince,
Taking thy part, hath rushed aside the law,
And turned that black word 'death' to 'banishment'.
This is dear mercy, and thou seest it not.
ROMEO 'Tis torture and not mercy. Heaven is here
Where Juliet lives, and every cat and dog

And little mouse, every unworthy thing,
Live here in heaven and may look on her,
But Romeo may not. More validity,
More honourable state, more courtship, lives
In carrion flies than Romeo: they may seize
On the white wonder of dear Juliet's hand,
And steal immortal blessing from her lips,
Who even in pure and vestal modesty
Still blush, as thinking their own kisses sin;
This may flies do, when I from this must fly;
And say'st thou yet that exile is not death?
[But Romeo may not – he is banishèd.
Flies may do this, but I from this must fly:
They are free men, but I am banishèd.]
Hadst thou no poison mixed, no sharp-ground knife,
No sudden mean of death, though ne'er so mean,
But 'banishèd' to kill me? 'Banishèd'!
O friar, the damnèd use that word in hell:
Howling attends it. How hast thou the heart,
Being a divine, a ghostly confessor,
A sin-absolver, and my friend professed,
To mangle me with that word 'banishèd'?

FRIAR Thou fond mad man, hear me a little speak.

ROMEO O thou wilt speak again of banishment.

FRIAR I'll give thee armour to keep off that word –
Adversity's sweet milk, philosophy,
To comfort thee though thou art banishèd.

ROMEO Yet 'banishèd'? Hang up philosophy!
Unless philosophy can make a Juliet,
Displant a town, reverse a prince's doom,
It helps not, it prevails not; talk no more.

FRIAR O then I see that madmen have no ears.

ROMEO How should they, when that wise men have no eyes?

FRIAR Let me dispute with thee of thy estate.

ROMEO Thou canst not speak of that thou dost not feel.
Wert thou as young as I, Juliet thy love,
An hour but married, Tybalt murderèd,
Doting like me, and like me banishèd,

Then mightst thou speak, then mightst thou tear
thy hair,
And fall upon the ground as I do now,
Taking the measure of an unmade grave.
[*knocking without*

FRIAR Arise; one knocks. Good Romeo, hide thyself.

ROMEO Not I, unless the breath of heartsick groans
Mist-like infold me from the search of eyes.
[*knocking again*

FRIAR Hark, how they knock! – Who's there? – Romeo, arise;
Thou wilt be taken. – Stay awhile! – Stand up;
[*louder knocking*
Run to my study. – By and by! – God's will,
What simpleness is this? – I come, I come.
[*knocking yet again*
Who knocks so hard? Whence come you? What's
your will?

NURSE [*from without*]
Let me come in and you shall know my errand
I come from Lady Juliet.

FRIAR Welcome then.

'Enter NURSE*'*

NURSE O holy friar, O tell me, holy friar,
Where is my lady's lord? Where's Romeo?

FRIAR There on the ground, with his own tears made drunk.

NURSE O he is even in my mistress' case,
Just in her case.

FRIAR O woeful sympathy:
Piteous predicament!

NURSE Even so lies she,
Blubbering and weeping, weeping and blubbering.
Stand up, stand up! Stand an you be a man;
For Juliet's sake, for her sake rise and stand
Why should you fall into so deep an O?

ROMEO [*rising*] Nurse!

NURSE Ah sir, ah sir, death's the end of all.

ROMEO Spakest thou of Juliet? How is it with her?
Doth not she think me an old murderer,
Now I have stained the childhood of our joy

With blood removed but little from her own?
Where is she? And how doth she? And what says
My concealed lady to our cancelled love?

NURSE O she says nothing, sir, but weeps and weeps,
And now falls on her bed, and then starts up,
And Tybalt calls, and then on Romeo cries,
And then down falls again.

ROMEO As if that name,
Shot from the deadly level of a gun,
Did murder her, as that name's cursèd hand
Murdered her kinsman. O tell me, friar, tell me,
In what vile part of this anatomy
Doth my name lodge? Tell me, that I may sack
The hateful mansion. [*'he offers to stab himself, and Nurse snatches the dagger away'*

FRIAR Hold thy desperate hand!
Art thou a man? Thy form cries out thou art:
Thy tears are womanish, thy wild acts denote
The unreasonable fury of a beast.
Unseemly woman in a seeming man,
And ill-beseeming beast in seeming both!
Thou hast amazed me. By my holy order,
I thought thy disposition better tempered.
Hast thou slain Tybalt? Wilt thou slay thyself?
And slay thy lady, that in thy life lives,
By doing damnèd hate upon thyself?
Why rail'st thou on thy birth, the heaven, and earth,
Since birth, and heaven, and earth, all three do meet
In thee at once, which thou at once wouldst lose?
Fie, fie! thou sham'st thy shape, thy love, thy wit,
Which like a usurer abound'st in all,
And usest none in that true use indeed
Which should bedeck thy shape, thy love, thy wit.
Thy noble shape is but a form of wax,
Digressing from the valour of a man;
Thy dear love sworn but hollow perjury,
Killing that love which thou hast vowed to cherish;
Thy wit, that ornament to shape and love,
Misshapen in the conduct of them both,

Like powder in a skilless soldier's flask
Is set afire by thine own ignorance,
And thou dismembered with thine own defence.
What, rouse thee, man! Thy Juliet is alive,
For whose dear sake thou wast but lately dead.
There art thou happy. Tybalt would kill thee,
But thou slewest Tybalt. There art thou happy.
The law that threatened death becomes thy friend,
And turns it to exile. There art thou happy too.
A pack of blessings light upon thy back;
Happiness courts thee in her best array;
But, like a misbehaved and sullen wench,
Thou pouts upon thy fortune and thy love.
Take heed, take heed, for such die miserable.
Go get thee to thy love, as was decreed;
Ascend her chamber; hence and comfort her.
But look thou stay not till the watch be set,
For then thou canst not pass to Mantua,
Where thou shalt live till we can find a time
To blaze your marriage, reconcile your friends,
Beg pardon of the prince, and call thee back
With twenty hundred thousand times more joy
Than thou wentst forth in lamentation.
Go before, Nurse. Commend me to thy lady,
And bid her hasten all the house to bed,
Which heavy sorrow makes them apt unto.
Romeo is coming.

NURSE O Lord, I could have stayed here all the night
To hear good counsel; O what learning is!
My lord, I'll tell my lady you will come.

ROMEO Do so, and bid my sweet prepare to chide.

'Nurse offers to go in and turns again'

NURSE Here, sir, a ring she bid me give you, sir.
Hie you, make haste, for it grows very late. [*she goes*

ROMEO How well my comfort is revived by this.

FRIAR Go hence; goodnight; and here stands all your state:
Either be gone before the watch be set,
Or by the break of day disguised from hence.
Sojourn in Mantua. I'll find out your man,

And he shall signify from time to time
Every good hap to you that chances here.
Give me thy hand. 'Tis late; farewell, goodnight.

ROMEO But that a joy past joy calls out on me,
It were a grief so brief to part with thee.
Farewell. *[they go*

SCENE 4

Capulet's house

'Enter old CAPULET, *his wife, and* PARIS*'*

CAPULET Things have fall'n out, sir, so unluckily
That we have had no time to move our daughter.
Look you, she loved her kinsman Tybalt dearly,
And so did I. Well, we were born to die.
'Tis very late; she'll not come down tonight.
I promise you, but for your company,
I would have been abed an hour ago.

PARIS These times of woe afford no times to woo.
Madam, goodnight; commend me to your daughter.

LADY CAP. I will, and know her mind early tomorrow;
Tonight she's mewed up to her heaviness.

Paris offers to go; Capulet calls him again

CAPULET Sir Paris, I will make a desperate tender
Of my child's love: I think she will be ruled
In all respects by me: nay more, I doubt it not.
Wife, go you to her ere you go to bed;
Acquaint her ear of my son Paris' love,
And bid her, mark you me, on Wednesday next –
But soft, what day is this?

PARIS Monday, my lord.

CAPULET: Monday, ha, ha; well, Wednesday is too soon;
O' Thursday let it be – O' Thursday, tell her,
She shall be married to this noble earl –
Will you be ready? Do you like this haste?
We'll keep no great ado; a friend or two:
For hark you, Tybalt being slain so late,

It may be thought we held him carelessly,
Being our kinsman, if we revel much:
Therefore we'll have some half a dozen friends,
And there an end. But what say you to Thursday?

PARIS My lord, I would that Thursday were tomorrow.

CAPULET Well, get you gone. O' Thursday be it then.
Go you to Juliet ere you go to bed;
Prepare her, wife, against this wedding day.
Farewell, my lord. Light to my chamber, ho!
Afore me, 'tis so very late, that we
May call it early by and by. Goodnight. *[they go*

SCENE 5

Juliet's bedroom: to one side the window above the orchard; to the other a door

ROMEO *and* JULIET *stand by the window*

JULIET Wilt thou be gone? It is not yet near day.
It was the nightingale, and not the lark,
That pierced the fearful hollow of thine ear.
Nightly she sings on yond pomegranate tree.
Believe me, love, it was the nightingale.

ROMEO It was the lark, the herald of the morn;
No nightingale. Look, love, what envious streaks
Do lace the severing clouds in yonder east.
Night's candles are burnt out, and jocund day
Stands tiptoe on the misty mountain tops.
I must be gone and live, or stay and die.

JULIET Yond light is not daylight; I know it, I:
It is some meteor that the sun exhaled
To be to thee this night a torchbearer
And light thee on thy way to Mantua.
Therefore stay yet; thou needst not to be gone.

ROMEO Let me be ta'en, let me be put to death;
I am content, so thou wilt have it so.
I'll say yon gray is not the morning's eye,
'Tis but the pale reflex of Cynthia's brow;
Nor that is not the lark whose notes do beat

The vaulty heaven so high above our heads.
I have more care to stay than will to go:
Come, death, and welcome! Juliet wills it so.
How is't, my soul? Let's talk; it is not day.

JULIET It is, it is! Hie hence, be gone, away!
It is the lark that sings so out of tune,
Straining harsh discords and unpleasing sharps.
Some say the lark makes sweet division:
This doth not so, for she divideth us.
Some say the lark and loathèd toad changed eyes;
O now I would they had changed voices too,
Since arm from arm that voice doth us affray,
Hunting thee hence with hunt's-up to the day.
O now be gone! More light and light it grows.

ROMEO More light and light, more dark and dark our woes.

'Enter NURSE *hastily'*

NURSE Madam!

JULIET Nurse?

NURSE Your lady mother is coming to your chamber.
The day is broke; be wary, look about.
[*she goes; Juliet bolts the door*

JULIET Then, window, let day in and let life out.

ROMEO Farewell, farewell; one kiss, and I'll descend.
[*he lowers the ladder and descends*

JULIET Art thou gone so, love, lord, ay husband, friend?
I must hear from thee every day in the hour,
For in a minute there are many days.
O, by this count I shall be much in years
Ere I again behold my Romeo.

ROMEO [*from the orchard*] Farewell!
I will omit no opportunity
That may convey my greetings, love, to thee.

JULIET O, think'st thou we shall ever meet again?

ROMEO I doubt it not; and all these woes shall serve
For sweet discourses in our times to come.

JULIET O God, I have an ill-divining soul!
Methinks I see thee, now thou art so low,
As one dead in the bottom of a tomb.
Either my eyesight fails or thou look'st pale.

ROMEO And trust me, love, in my eye so do you.
Dry sorrow drinks our blood. Adieu, adieu!
[*he goes*

JULIET O Fortune, Fortune, all men call thee fickle;
If thou art fickle, what dost thou with him
That is renowned for faith? Be fickle, Fortune:
For then I hope thou wilt not keep him long,
But send him back.

LADY CAP. [*without the door*] Ho, daughter, are you up?

JULIET [*pulls up and conceals the ladder*]
Who is't that calls? It is my lady mother.
Is she not down so late, or up so early?
What unaccustomed cause procures her hither?
[*she unlocks the door*

Enter LADY CAPULET

LADY CAP. Why, how now, Juliet?

JULIET Madam, I am not well.

LADY CAP. Evermore weeping for your cousin's death?
What, wilt thou wash him from his grave with tears?
An if thou couldst, thou couldst not make him live:
Therefore have done – some grief shows much of love,
But much of grief shows still some want of wit.

JULIET Yet let me weep for such a feeling loss.

LADY CAP. So shall you feel the loss, but not the friend
Which you weep for.

JULIET Feeling so the loss,
I cannot choose but ever weep the friend.

LADY CAP. Well, girl, thou weep'st not so much for his death,
As that the villain lives which slaughtered him.

JULIET What villain, madam?

LADY CAP. That same villain Romeo,

JULIET Villain and he be many miles asunder.
[*aloud*] God pardon him; I do, with all my heart:
And yet no man like he doth grieve my heart.

LADY CAP. That is because the traitor murderer lives.

JULIET Ay, madam, from the reach of these my hands.
Would none but I might venge my cousin's death!

LADY CAP. We will have vengeance for it, fear thou not.
Then weep no more. I'll send to one in Mantua,

Where that same banished runagate doth live,
Shall give him such an unaccustomed dram
That he shall soon keep Tybalt company;
And then I hope thou wilt be satisfied.

JULIET Indeed I never shall be satisfied
With Romeo till I behold him – dead –
Is my poor heart so for a kinsman vexed.
Madam, if you could find out but a man
To bear a poison, I would temper it
That Romeo should upon receipt thereof
Soon sleep in quiet. O how my heart abhors
To hear him named and cannot come to him
To wreak the love I bore my cousin
Upon his body that hath slaughtered him.

LADY CAP. Find thou the means and I'll find such a man.
But now I'll tell thee joyful tidings, girl.

JULIET And joy comes well in such a needy time.
What are they, I beseech your ladyship?

LADY CAP. Well, well, thou hast a careful father, child;
One who, to put thee from thy heaviness,
Hath sorted out a sudden day of joy
That thou expects not, nor I looked not for.

JULIET Madam, in happy time! What day is that?

LADY CAP. Marry, my child, early next Thursday morn
The gallant, young, and noble gentleman,
The County Paris, at Saint Peter's Church
Shall happily make thee there a joyful bride.

JULIET Now by Saint Peter's Church, and Peter too,
He shall not make me there a joyful bride.
I wonder at this haste, that I must wed
Ere he that should be husband comes to woo.
I pray you tell my lord and father, madam,
I will not marry yet; and when I do, I swear
It shall be Romeo, whom you know I hate,
Rather than Paris. These are news indeed!

LADY CAP. Here comes your father; tell him so yourself,
And see how he will take it at your hands.

'Enter CAPULET *and* NURSE*'*

CAPULET When the sun sets, the air doth drizzle dew;

But for the sunset of my brother's son
It rains downright.
How now, a conduit, girl? What, still in tears?
Evermore showering? In one little body
Thou counterfeits a bark, a sea, a wind:
For still thy eyes, which I may call the sea,
Do ebb and flow with tears; the bark thy body is,
Sailing in this salt flood; the winds thy sighs,
Who raging with thy tears, and they with them,
Without a sudden calm will overset
Thy tempest-tossèd body. How now, wife?
Have you delivered to her our decree?

LADY CAP. Ay, sir; but she will none, she gives you thanks.
I would the fool were married to her grave!

CAPULET Soft, take me with you, take me with you, wife.
How? Will she none? Doth she not give us thanks?
Is she not proud? Doth she not count her blest,
Unworthy as she is, that we have wrought
So worthy a gentleman to be her bride?

JULIET Not proud you have, but thankful that you have.
Proud can I never be of what I hate,
But thankful even for hate that is meant love.

CAPULET How how! how how, chop-logic! What is this?
'Proud', and 'I thank you', and 'I thank you not',
And yet 'not proud', mistress minion you?
Thank me no thankings nor proud me no prouds,
But fettle your fine joints 'gainst Thursday next
To go with Paris to Saint Peter's Church,
Or I will drag thee on a hurdle thither.
Out, you green-sickness carrion! Out, you baggage!
You tallow-face!

LADY CAP. Fie, fie! what, are you mad?

JULIET [*kneeling*] Good father, I beseech you on my knees,
Hear me with patience but to speak a word.

CAPULET Hang thee, young baggage! disobedient wretch!
I tell thee what; get thee to church o' Thursday,
Or never after look me in the face.
Speak not, reply not, do not answer me!
My fingers itch. Wife, we scarce thought us blest

That God had lent us but this only child;
But now I see this one is one too much,
And that we have a curse in having her.
Out on her, hilding!

NURSE God in heaven bless her!
You are to blame, my lord, to rate her so.

CAPULET And why, my Lady Wisdom? Hold your tongue,
Good Prudence. Smatter with your gossips, go!

NURSE I speak no treason.

CAPULET O Godigoden!

NURSE May not one speak?

CAPULET Peace, you mumbling fool!
Utter your gravity o'er a gossip's bowl,
For here we need it not.

LADY CAP. You are too hot.

CAPULET God's bread! It makes me mad. Day, night, work, play,
Alone, in company, still my care hath been
To have her matched; and having now provided
A gentleman of noble parentage,
Of fair demesnes, youthful and nobly trained,
Stuffed, as they say, with honourable parts,
Proportioned as one's thought would wish a man –
And then to have a wretched puling fool,
A whining mammet, in her fortune's tender,
To answer 'I'll not wed, I cannot love;
I am too young, I pray you pardon me.'
But, an you will not wed, I'll pardon you –
Graze where you will; you shall not house with me.
Look to't, think on't; I do not use to jest.
Thursday is near. Lay hand on heart; advise.
An you be mine, I'll give you to my friend;
An you be not, hang, beg, starve, die in the streets,
For by my soul I'll ne'er acknowledge thee,
Nor what is mine shall never do thee good:
Trust to't; bethink you; I'll not be forsworn.

[*he goes*

JULIET Is there no pity sitting in the clouds
That sees into the bottom of my grief?
O sweet my mother, cast me not away!

Delay this marriage for a month, a week;
Or, if you do not, make the bridal bed
In that dim monument where Tybalt lies.

LADY CAP. Talk not to me, for I'll not speak a word;
Do as thou wilt, for I have done with thee. [*she goes*

JULIET O God! – O nurse, how shall this be prevented?
My husband is on earth, my faith in heaven;
How shall that faith return again to earth,
Unless that husband send it me from heaven
By leaving earth? Comfort me, counsel me.
Alack, alack, that heaven should practise stratagems
Upon so soft a subject as myself!
What sayst thou? Hast thou not a word of joy?
Some comfort, nurse.

NURSE Faith, here it is. Romeo
Is banishèd; and all the world to nothing
That he dares ne'er come back to challenge you;
Or, if he do, it needs must be by stealth.
Then, since the case so stands as now it doth,
I think it best you married with the County.
O, he's a lovely gentleman!
Romeo's a dishclout to him. An eagle, madam,
Hath not so green, so quick, so fair an eye
As Paris hath. Beshrew my very heart,
I think you are happy in this second match,
For it excels your first; or, if it did not,
Your first is dead – or 'twere as good he were
As living here and you no use of him.

JULIET Speakst thou from thy heart?

NURSE And from my soul too; else beshrew them both.

JULIET Amen!

NURSE What?

JULIET Well, thou hast comforted me marvellous much.
Go in and tell my lady I am gone,
Having displeased my father, to Lawrence' cell
To make confession and to be absolved.

NURSE Marry, I will; and this is wisely done. [*she goes*

JULIET Ancient damnation! O most wicked fiend!
Is it more sin to wish me thus forsworn,

Or to dispraise my lord with that same tongue
Which she hath praised him with above compare
So many thousand times? Go, counsellor!
Thou and my bosom henceforth shall be twain.
I'll to the friar to know his remedy.
If all else fail, myself have power to die. [*she goes*

ACT 4 SCENE 1

Friar Lawrence's cell

'Enter FRIAR *and County* PARIS*'*

FRIAR On Thursday, sir? The time is very short.
PARIS My father Capulet will have it so,
And I am nothing slow to slack his haste.
FRIAR You say you do not know the lady's mind?
Uneven is the course; I like it not.
PARIS Immoderately she weeps for Tybalt's death,
And therefore have I little talked of love,
For Venus smiles not in a house of tears.
Now, sir, her father counts it dangerous
That she do give her sorrow so much sway,
And in his wisdom hastes our marriage
To stop the inundation of her tears,
Which, too much minded by herself alone,
May be put from her by society.
Now do you know the reason of this haste.
FRIAR I would I knew not why it should be slowed –
Look, sir, here comes the lady toward my cell.

'Enter JULIET*'*

PARIS Happily met, my lady and my wife!
JULIET That may be, sir, when I may be a wife.
PARIS That 'may be' must be, love, on Thursday next.
JULIET What must be shall be.
FRIAR That's a certain text.
PARIS Come you to make confession to this father?
JULIET To answer that, I should confess to you.
PARIS Do not deny to him that you love me.
JULIET I will confess to you that I love him.
PARIS So will ye, I am sure, that you love me.
JULIET If I do so, it will be of more price,
Being spoke behind your back, than to your face.
PARIS Poor soul, thy face is much abused with tears.
JULIET The tears have got small victory by that,

For it was bad enough before their spite.

PARIS Thou wrong'st it more than tears with that report.

JULIET That is no slander, sir, which is a truth;
And what I spake, I spake it to my face.

PARIS Thy face is mine, and thou hast sland'red it.

JULIET It may be so, for it is not mine own. –
Are you at leisure, holy father, now,
Or shall I come to you at evening mass?

FRIAR My leisure serves me, pensive daughter, now.
My lord, we must entreat the time alone.

PARIS God shield I should disturb devotion!
Juliet, on Thursday early will I rouse ye;
Till then adieu, and keep this holy kiss.
[*kisses her, and departs*

JULIET O shut the door, and, when thou hast done so,
Come weep with me – past hope, past cure, past help.

FRIAR O Juliet, I already know thy grief;
It strains me past the compass of my wits.
I hear thou must, and nothing may prorogue it,
On Thursday next be married to this County.

JULIET Tell me not, friar, that thou hearest of this,
Unless thou tell me how I may prevent it.
If in thy wisdom thou canst give no help,
Do thou but call my resolution wise
And with this knife I'll help it presently.
God joined my heart and Romeo's, thou our hands;
And ere this hand, by thee to Romeo's sealed,
Shall be the label to another deed,
Or my true heart with treacherous revolt
Turn to another, this shall slay them both:
Therefore, out of thy long-experienced time,
Give me some present counsel; or, behold,
'Twixt my extremes and me this bloody knife
Shall play the umpire, arbitrating that
Which the commission of thy years and art
Could to no issue of true honour bring.
Be not so long to speak: I long to die
If what thou speak'st speak not of remedy.

FRIAR Hold, daughter. I do spy a kind of hope,

Which craves as desperate an execution
As that is desperate which we would prevent.
If, rather than to marry County Paris,
Thou hast the strength of will to slay thyself,
Then is it likely thou wilt undertake
A thing like death to chide away this shame,
That copest with death himself to scape from it;
And, if thou darest, I'll give thee remedy.

JULIET O bid me leap, rather than marry Paris,
From off the battlements of any tower,
Or walk in thievish ways, or bid me lurk
Where serpents are; chain me with roaring bears,
Or hide me nightly in a charnel house,
O'ercovered quite with dead men's rattling bones,
With reeky shanks and yellow chapless skulls;
Or bid me go into a new-made grave
And lay me with a dead man in his shroud –
Things that, to hear them told, have made me tremble –
And I will do it without fear or doubt,
To live an unstained wife to my sweet love.

FRIAR Hold, then. Go home, be merry, give consent
To marry Paris. Wednesday is tomorrow.
Tomorrow night look that thou lie alone;
Let not the nurse lie with thee in thy chamber.
Take thou this vial, being then in bed,
And this distillèd liquor drink thou off,
When presently through all thy veins shall run
A cold and drowsy humour, for no pulse
Shall keep his native progress, but surcease;
No warmth, no breath, shall testify thou livest;
The roses in thy lips and cheeks shall fade
To wanny ashes, thy eyes' windows fall
Like death when he shuts up the day of life.
Each part, deprived of supple government,
Shall stiff and stark and cold appear like death;
And in this borrowed likeness of shrunk death
Thou shalt continue two and forty hours,
And then awake as from a pleasant sleep.

Now, when the bridegroom in the morning comes
To rouse thee from thy bed, there art thou dead.
Then, as the manner of our country is,
In thy best robes, uncovered on the bier,
Thou shalt be borne to that same ancient vault
Where all the kindred of the Capulets lie.
In the meantime, against thou shalt awake,
Shall Romeo by my letters know our drift,
And hither shall he come; and he and I
Will watch thy waking, and that very night
Shall Romeo bear thee hence to Mantua.
And this shall free thee from this present shame,
If no inconstant toy nor womanish fear
Abate thy valour in the acting it.

JULIET Give me, give me! O tell not me of fear!

FRIAR Hold, get you gone! Be strong and prosperous
In this resolve. I'll send a friar with speed
To Mantua with my letters to thy lord.

JULIET Love give me strength! And strength shall help afford.
Farewell, dear father. [*they go*

SCENE 2

Capulet's house

Enter CAPULET, LADY CAPULET, NURSE
and two or three Servingmen

CAPULET [*giving a paper*]
So many guests invite as here are writ.
[*Servingman goes out with it*
[*to another*] Sirrah, go hire me twenty cunning cooks.

SERV'MAN You shall have none ill, sir; for I'll try if they can lick their fingers.

CAPULET How canst thou try them so?

SERV'MAN Marry, sir, 'tis an ill cook that cannot lick his own fingers: therefore he that cannot lick his fingers goes not with me.

CAPULET Go, be gone. [*he goes*
We shall be much unfurnished for this time.

What, is my daughter gone to Friar Lawrence?

NURSE Ay, forsooth.

CAPULET Well, he may chance to do some good on her.
A peevish self-willed harlotry it is.

'Enter JULIET*'*

NURSE See where she comes from shrift with merry look.

CAPULET How now, my headstrong? Where have you been gadding?

JULIET Where I have learned me to repent the sin
Of disobedient opposition
To you and your behests, and am enjoined
By holy Lawrence to fall prostrate here
To beg your pardon. [*abasing herself*] Pardon, I beseech you!
Henceforward I am ever ruled by you.

CAPULET Send for the County: go tell him of this.
I'll have this knot knit up tomorrow morning.

JULIET I met the youthful lord at Lawrence' cell
And gave him what becomèd love I might,
Not stepping o'er the bounds of modesty.

CAPULET Why, I am glad on't; this is well. Stand up.
This is as 't should be. Let me see, the County:
Ay, marry, go, I say, and fetch him hither.
Now, afore God, this reverend holy friar,
All our whole city is much bound to him.

JULIET Nurse, will you go with me into my closet
To help me sort such needful ornaments
As you think fit to furnish me tomorrow?

LADY CAP. No, not till Thursday; there is time enough.

CAPULET Go, nurse, go with her; we'll to church tomorrow.

[*Nurse departs with Juliet*

LADY CAP. We shall be short in our provision;
'Tis now near night.

CAPULET Tush, I will stir about,
And all things shall be well, I warrant thee, wife.
Go thou to Juliet; help to deck up her.
I'll not to bed tonight. Let me alone;
I'll play the housewife for this once. What, ho!
They are all forth; well, I will walk myself

To County Paris, to prepare up him
Against tomorrow. My heart is wondrous light
Since this same wayward girl is so reclaimed. [*they go*

SCENE 3

Juliet's chamber; at the back a bed with curtains

'*Enter* JULIET *and* NURSE'

JULIET Ay, those attires are best. But, gentle nurse,
I pray thee leave me to myself tonight:
For I have need of many orisons
To move the heavens to smile upon my state,
Which well thou knowest is cross and full of sin.

Enter LADY CAPULET

LADY CAP. What, are you busy, ho? Need you my help?
JULIET No, madam, we have culled such necessaries
As are behoveful for our state tomorrow.
So please you, let me now be left alone,
And let the nurse this night sit up with you,
For I am sure you have your hands full all
In this so sudden business.
LADY CAP. Good night.
Get thee to bed and rest, for thou hast need.
[*she departs with the Nurse*
JULIET Farewell! God knows when we shall meet again.
I have a faint cold fear thrills through my veins
That almost freezes up the heat of life.
I'll call them back again to comfort me.
Nurse! – What should she do here?
My dismal scene I needs must act alone.
Come, vial!
What if this mixture do not work at all?
Shall I be married then tomorrow morning?
No, no! This shall forbid it. Lie thou there.
[*laying down her knife*
What if it be a poison which the friar
Subtly hath minist'red to have me dead,

Lest in this marriage he should be dishonoured
Because he married me before to Romeo?
I fear it is; and yet methinks it should not,
For he hath still been tried a holy man.
How if, when I am laid into the tomb,
I wake before the time that Romeo
Come to redeem me? There's a fearful point!
Shall I not then be stifled in the vault,
To whose foul mouth no healthsome air breathes in,
And there die strangled ere my Romeo comes?
Or, if I live, is it not very like
The horrible conceit of death and night,
Together with the terror of the place –
As in a vault, an ancient receptacle
Where for this many hundred years the bones
Of all my buried ancestors are packed;
Where bloody Tybalt, yet but green in earth,
Lies festering in his shroud; where, as they say,
At some hours in the night spirits resort –
Alack, alack, is it not like that I,
So early waking – what with loathsome smells,
And shrieks like mandrakes' torn out of the earth,
That living mortals, hearing them, run mad –
O, if I wake, shall I not be distraught,
Environèd with all these hideous fears,
And madly play with my forefathers' joints,
And pluck the mangled Tybalt from his shroud,
And, in this rage, with some great kinsman's bone,
As with a club, dash out my desp'rate brains?
O, look! Methinks I see my cousin's ghost
Seeking out Romeo, that did spit his body
Upon a rapier's point. Stay, Tybalt, stay!
Romeo, I come! This do I drink to thee.

[*'she falls upon her bed within the curtains'*

SCENE 4

Hall in Capulet's house

Enter LADY CAPULET *and* 'NURSE, *with herbs'*

LADY CAP. Hold, take these keys and fetch more spices, nurse.
NURSE They call for dates and quinces in the pastry.

'Enter old CAPULET*'*

CAPULET Come, stir, stir, stir! The second cock hath crowed:
The curfew bell hath rung, 'tis three o'clock.
Look to the baked meats, good Angelica;
Spare not for cost.
NURSE Go, you cot-quean, go,
Get you to bed. Faith, you'll be sick tomorrow
For this night's watching.
CAPULET No, not a whit. What, I have watched ere now
All night for lesser cause, and ne'er been sick.
LADY CAP. Ay, you have been a mouse-hunt in your time,
But I will watch you from such watching now.
[*she hurries out with Nurse*
CAPULET A jealous hood, a jealous hood!

'Enter three or four with spits and logs and baskets'

Now, fellow, what is there?
1 SER'MAN Things for the cook, sir; but I know not what.
CAPULET Make haste, make haste. [*1 Servingman goes*]
Sirrah, fetch drier logs.
Call Peter; he will show thee where they are.
2 SER'MAN I have a head, sir, that will find out logs
And never trouble Peter for the matter.
CAPULET Mass, and well said; a merry whoreson, ha!
Thou shalt be loggerhead. [*2 Servingman goes*]
Good faith, 'tis day!
The County will be here with music straight,
For so he said he would. [*music*] I hear him near.
Nurse! Wife! What, ho! What, nurse, I say!

'Enter NURSE*'*

Go waken Juliet; go and trim her up.
I'll go and chat with Paris. Hie, make haste,
Make haste! The bridegroom he is come already:
Make haste, I say. *[they go*

SCENE 5

Juliet's chamber; the curtains closed about the bed

Enter NURSE

NURSE Mistress! What, mistress! Juliet! Fast, I warrant her, she.
Why, lamb! why, lady! Fie, you slug-a-bed!
Why, love, I say! madam! sweetheart! why, bride!
What, not a word? You take your pennyworths now!
Sleep for a week; for the next night, I warrant,
The County Paris hath set up his rest
That you shall rest but little. God forgive me!
Marry, and amen! How sound is she asleep!
I needs must wake her. Madam, madam, madam!
Ay, let the County take you in your bed,
He'll fright you up, i'faith! Will it not be?
[draws back the curtains
What, dressed, and in your clothes, and down again?
I must needs wake you. Lady, lady, lady! *[shakes her*
Alas, alas! Help, help! My lady's dead!
O weraday that ever I was born!
Some aqua vitae, ho! My lord! My lady!

Enter LADY CAPULET

LADY CAP. What noise is here?
NURSE O lamentable day!
LADY CAP. What is the matter?
NURSE Look, look! O heavy day!
LADY CAP. O me, O me! My child, my only life!
Revive, look up, or I will die with thee!
Help, help! Call help.

Enter CAPULET

CAPULET For shame, bring Juliet forth; her lord is come.
NURSE She's dead, deceased: she's dead, alack the day!
LADY CAP. Alack the day, she's dead, she's dead, she's dead!
CAPULET Ha, let me see her. Out, alas! She's cold,
Her blood is settled, and her joints are stiff:
Life and these lips have long been separated;
Death lies on her like an untimely frost
Upon the sweetest flower of all the field.
NURSE O lamentable day!
LADY CAP. O woeful time!
CAPULET Death, that hath ta'en her hence to make me wail,
Ties up my tongue and will not let me speak.

'Enter FRIAR *and the* COUNTY*' with Musicians*

FRIAR Come, is the bride ready to go to church?
CAPULET Ready to go, but never to return.
O son, the night before thy wedding day
Hath Death lain with thy wife. There she lies,
Flower as she was, deflowerèd by him.
Death is my son-in-law, Death is my heir;
My daughter he hath wedded! I will die
And leave him all; life, living, all is Death's.
PARIS Have I thought long to see this morning's face,
And doth it give me such a sight as this?
LADY CAP. Accursed, unhappy, wretched, hateful day!
Most miserable hour that e'er time saw
In lasting labour of his pilgrimage!
But one, poor one, one poor and loving child,
But one thing to rejoice and solace in,
And cruel Death hath catched it from my sight!
NURSE O woe! O woeful, woeful, woeful day!
Most lamentable day, most woeful day
That ever, ever I did yet behold!
O day, O day, O day, O hateful day!
Never was seen so black a day as this.
O woeful day, O woeful day!
PARIS Beguiled, divorcèd, wrongèd, spited, slain!
Most detestable Death, by thee beguiled,

By cruel, cruel thee quite overthrown!
O love! O life! Not life, but love in death!

CAPULET Despised, distressèd, hated, martyred, killed!
Uncomfortable time, why cam'st thou now
To murder, murder our solemnity?
O child, O child! My soul, and not my child!
Dead art thou. Alack, my child is dead,
And with my child my joys are burièd!

FRIAR Peace, ho, for shame! Confusion's cure lives not
In these confusions. Heaven and yourself
Had part in this fair maid; now heaven hath all,
And all the better is it for the maid.
Your part in her you could not keep from death,
But heaven keeps his part in eternal life.
The most you sought was her promotion,
For 'twas your heaven she should be advanced;
And weep ye now, seeing she is advanced
Above the clouds as high as heaven itself?
O, in this love you love your child so ill
That you run mad, seeing that she is well.
She's not well married that lives married long,
But she's best married that dies married young.
Dry up your tears and stick your rosemary
On this fair corse, and as the custom is,
All in her best array, bear her to church:
For though fond nature bids us all lament,
Yet nature's tears are reason's merriment.

CAPULET All things that we ordainèd festival
Turn from their office to black funeral,
Our instruments to melancholy bells,
Our wedding cheer to a sad burial feast;
Our solemn hymns to sullen dirges change,
Our bridal flowers serve for a buried corse,
And all things change them to the contrary.

FRIAR Sir, go you in; and, madam, go with him;
And go, Sir Paris. Everyone prepare
To follow this fair corse unto her grave.
The heavens do lour upon you for some ill;
Move them no more by crossing their high will.

[*'all but the Nurse' and the Musicians 'go forth, casting rosemary upon her and shutting the curtains'*

1 MUSIC'N Faith, we may put up our pipes and be gone.

NURSE Honest good fellows, ah, put up, put up!
For well you know this is a pitiful case.

1 MUSIC'N Ay, by my troth, the case may be amended.

[*Nurse goes*

Enter PETER

PETER Musicians, O musicians, 'Heart's ease', 'Heart's ease'! O, an you will have me live, play 'Heart's ease'.

1 MUSIC'N Why 'Heart's ease'?

PETER O musicians, because my heart itself plays 'My heart is full of woe'. O play me some merry dump to comfort me.

1 MUSIC'N Not a dump we! 'Tis no time to play now.

PETER You will not then?

1 MUSIC'N No.

PETER I will then give it you soundly.

1 MUSIC'N What will you give us?

PETER No money, on my faith, but the gleek. I will give you the minstrel.

1 MUSIC'N Then will I give you the serving-creature.

PETER Then will I lay the serving-creature's dagger on your pate. I will carry no crotchets. I'll re you, I'll fa you. Do you note me?

1 MUSIC'N An you re us and fa us, you note us.

2 MUSIC'N Pray you put up your dagger, and put out your wit.

PETER Then have at you with my wit! I will dry-beat you with an iron wit, and put up my iron dagger. Answer me like men:

'When griping grief the heart doth wound,
And doleful dumps the mind oppress,
Then music with her silver sound – '

Why 'silver sound'? Why 'music with her silver sound'? What say you, Simon Catling?

1 MUSIC'N Marry, sir, because silver hath a sweet sound.

PETER Pretty! What say you, Hugh Rebeck?

2 MUSIC'N I say 'silver sound', because musicians sound for silver.

PETER Pretty too! What say you, James Soundpost?

3 MUSIC'N Faith, I know not what to say.

PETER O, I cry you mercy! You are the singer. I will say for you. It is 'music with her silver sound', because musicians have no gold for sounding.

'Then music with her silver sound
With speedy help doth lend redress.'

[*he goes*

1 MUSIC'N What a pestilent knave is this same!

2 MUSIC'N Hang him, Jack! Come, we'll in here, tarry for the mourners, and stay dinner.

[*they go also*

ACT 5 SCENE I

Mantua. A street with shops

'Enter ROMEO*'*

ROMEO If I may trust the flattering truth of sleep,
My dreams presage some joyful news at hand.
My bosom's lord sits lightly in his throne,
And all this day an unaccustomed spirit
Lifts me above the ground with cheerful thoughts.
I dreamt my lady came and found me dead –
Strange dream that gives a dead man leave to think! –
And breathed such life with kisses in my lips
That I revived and was an emperor.
Ah me! How sweet is love itself possessed,
When but love's shadows are so rich in joy!

Enter BALTHASAR, *Romeo's man, booted*

News from Verona! How now, Balthasar?
Dost thou not bring me letters from the friar?
How doth my lady? Is my father well?
How fares my Juliet? That I ask again,
For nothing can be ill if she be well.

BALTH'SAR Then she is well, and nothing can be ill.
Her body sleeps in Capel's monument,
And her immortal part with angels lives.
I saw her laid low in her kindred's vault,
And presently took post to tell it you.
O pardon me for bringing these ill news,
Since you did leave it for my office, sir.

ROMEO Is it e'en so? Then I defy you, stars!
Thou know'st my lodging. Get me ink and paper,
And hire post-horses; I will hence tonight.

BALTH'SAR I do beseech you, sir, have patience.
Your looks are pale and wild and do import
Some misadventure.

ROMEO Tush, thou art deceived.
Leave me, and do the thing I bid thee do.

Hast thou no letters to me from the friar?

BALTH'SAR No, my good lord.

ROMEO No matter. Get thee gone,
And hire those horses; I'll be with thee straight.
[Balthasar goes
Well, Juliet, I will lie with thee tonight.
Let's see for means. O mischief, thou art swift
To enter in the thoughts of desperate men!
I do remember an apothecary,
And hereabouts 'a dwells, which late I noted
In tatt'red weeds, with overwhelming brows,
Culling of simples. Meagre were his looks;
Sharp misery had worn him to the bones:
And in his needy shop a tortoise hung,
An alligator stuffed, and other skins
Of ill-shaped fishes; and about his shelves
A beggarly account of empty boxes,
Green earthen pots, bladders, and musty seeds,
Remnants of packthread, and old cakes of roses
Were thinly scattered, to make up a show.
Noting this penury, to myself I said,
'An if a man did need a poison now,
Whose sale is present death in Mantua,
Here lives a caitiff wretch would sell it him.'
O, this same thought did but forerun my need,
And this same needy man must sell it me.
As I remember, this should be the house.
Being holiday, the beggar's shop is shut.
What ho, apothecary!

Enter APOTHECARY

APOTH'ARY Who calls so loud?

ROMEO Come hither, man. I see that thou art poor.
Hold, there is forty ducats; let me have
A dram of poison, such soon-speeding gear
As will disperse itself through all the veins
That the life-weary taker may fall dead,
And that the trunk may be discharged of breath
As violently as hasty powder fired
Doth hurry from the fatal cannon's womb.

APOTH'ARY Such mortal drugs I have, but Mantua's law
Is death to any he that utters them.

ROMEO Art thou so bare and full of wretchedness
And fear'st to die? Famine is in thy cheeks,
Need and oppression starveth in thy eyes,
Contempt and beggary hangs upon thy back:
The world is not thy friend, nor the world's law;
The world affords no law to make thee rich:
Then be not poor, but break it and take this.

APOTH'ARY My poverty but not my will consents.

ROMEO I pay thy poverty and not thy will.

APOTH'ARY [*giving a phial*] Put this in any liquid thing you will
And drink it off, and if you had the strength
Of twenty men it would dispatch you straight.

ROMEO There is thy gold – worse poison to men's souls,
Doing more murder in this loathsome world,
Than these poor compounds that thou mayst not sell.
I sell thee poison; thou hast sold me none.
Farewell; buy food and get thyself in flesh.
[*Apothecary goes in*
Come, cordial and not poison, go with me
To Juliet's grave, for there must I use thee.
[*he passes on*

SCENE 2

Verona. Friar Lawrence's cell

Enter FRIAR JOHN

FRIAR J. Holy Franciscan friar, brother, ho!

Enter FRIAR LAWRENCE

FRIAR L. This same should be the voice of Friar John.
Welcome from Mantua. What says Romeo?
Or, if his mind be writ, give me his letter.

FRIAR J. Going to find a barefoot brother out,
One of our order, to associate me,
Here in this city visiting the sick,
And finding him, the searchers of the town,

Suspecting that we both were in a house
Where the infectious pestilence did reign,
Sealed up the doors, and would not let us forth,
So that my speed to Mantua there was stayed.

FRIAR L. Who bare my letter then to Romeo?

FRIAR J. I could not send it – here it is again –
Nor get a messenger to bring it thee,
So fearful were they of infection.

FRIAR L. Unhappy fortune! By my brotherhood,
The letter was not nice, but full of charge,
Of dear import; and the neglecting it
May do much danger. Friar John, go hence,
Get me an iron crow and bring it straight
Unto my cell.

FRIAR J. Brother, I'll go and bring it thee. [*goes*

FRIAR L. Now must I to the monument alone.
Within this three hours will fair Juliet wake.
She will beshrew me much that Romeo
Hath had no notice of these accidents;
But I will write again to Mantua,
And keep her at my cell till Romeo come.
Poor living corse, closed in a dead man's tomb!
[*he goes*

SCENE 3

Verona. A churchyard; in it the monument of the Capulets

'Enter PARIS *and his* PAGE*', bearing flowers and a torch*

PARIS Give me thy torch, boy. Hence, and stand aloof.
Yet put it out, for I would not be seen.
Under yond yew-trees lay thee all along,
Holding thine ear close to the hollow ground;
So shall no foot upon the churchyard tread,
Being loose, unfirm with digging up of graves,
But thou shalt hear it. Whistle then to me
As signal that thou hear'st some thing approach.
Give me those flowers. Do as I bid thee; go.

PAGE I am almost afraid to stand alone

Here in the churchyard, yet I will adventure. [*retires*

PARIS Sweet flower, with flowers thy bridal bed I strew –
O woe, thy canopy is dust and stones! –
Which with sweet water nightly I will dew,
Or, wanting that, with tears distilled by moans.
The obsequies that I for thee will keep
Nightly shall be to strew thy grave and weep.
[*Page whistles*
The boy gives warning something doth approach.
What cursèd foot wanders this way tonight
To cross my obsequies and true love's rite?
What, with a torch? Muffle me, night, awhile. [*retires*

'Enter ROMEO *and* BALTHASAR, *with a torch, a mattock, and a crow of iron'*

ROMEO Give me that mattock and the wrenching iron.
Hold, take this letter. Early in the morning
See thou deliver it to my lord and father.
Give me the light. Upon thy life I charge thee,
Whate'er thou hear'st or seest, stand all aloof
And do not interrupt me in my course.
Why I descend into this bed of death
Is partly to behold my lady's face,
But chiefly to take thence from her dead finger
A precious ring, a ring that I must use
In dear employment. Therefore hence, be gone.
But if thou, jealous, dost return to pry
In what I farther shall intend to do,
By heaven, I will tear thee joint by joint
And strew this hungry churchyard with thy limbs.
The time and my intents are savage-wild,
More fierce and more inexorable far
Than empty tigers or the roaring sea.

BALTH'SAR I will be gone, sir, and not trouble ye.

ROMEO So shalt thou show me friendship. Take thou that;
[*gives money*
Live and be prosperous; and farewell, good fellow.

BALTH'SAR For all this same, I'll hide me hereabout.
His looks I fear, and his intents I doubt. [*retires*

ROMEO Thou detestable maw, thou womb of death,
Gorged with the dearest morsel of the earth,
Thus I enforce thy rotten jaws to open,
[*begins to open the tomb*
And in despite I'll cram thee with more food.

PARIS This is that banished haughty Montague
That murd'red my love's cousin – with which grief
It is supposèd the fair creature died –
And here is come to do some villainous shame
To the dead bodies: I will apprehend him. –
[*comes forward*
Stop thy unhallowed toil, vile Montague!
Can vengeance be pursued further than death?
Condemnèd villain, I do apprehend thee.
Obey, and go with me, for thou must die.

ROMEO I must indeed, and therefore came I hither.
Good gentle youth, tempt not a desp'rate man.
Fly hence and leave me. Think upon these gone;
Let them affright thee. I beseech thee, youth,
Put not another sin upon my head
By urging me to fury. O be gone!
By heaven, I love thee better than myself,
For I come hither armed against myself.
Stay not, be gone. Live, and hereafter say
A madman's mercy bid thee run away.

PARIS I do defy thy conjuration,
And apprehend thee for a felon here.

ROMEO Wilt thou provoke me? Then have at thee, boy!
[*they fight*

PAGE O Lord, they fight! I will go call the watch. [*runs off*

PARIS O, I am slain! [*falls*] If thou be merciful,
Open the tomb, lay me with Juliet. [*dies*

ROMEO In faith, I will. Let me peruse this face.
Mercutio's kinsman, noble County Paris!
What said my man when my betossèd soul
Did not attend him as we rode? I think
He told me Paris should have married Juliet.
Said he not so? Or did I dream it so?
Or am I mad, hearing him talk of Juliet,

To think it was so? O give me thy hand,
One writ with me in sour misfortune's book!
I'll bury thee in a triumphant grave.
A grave? O no! – a lanthorn, slaught'red youth:
For here lies Juliet, and her beauty makes
This vault a feasting presence full of light.
Dead, lie thou there, by a dead man interred.
[lays Paris within the tomb
How oft when men are at the point of death
Have they been merry, which their keepers call
A light'ning before death! O how may I
Call this a light'ning? O my love, my wife!
Death, that hath sucked the honey of thy breath,
Hath had no power yet upon thy beauty.
Thou art not conquered; beauty's ensign yet
Is crimson in thy lips and in thy cheeks,
And death's pale flag is not advancèd there.
Tybalt, liest thou there in thy bloody sheet?
O, what more favour can I do to thee
Than with that hand that cut thy youth in twain
To sunder his that was thine enemy?
Forgive me, cousin! Ah, dear Juliet,
Why art thou yet so fair? Shall I believe
That unsubstantial Death is amorous,
And that the lean abhorrèd monster keeps
Thee here in dark to be his paramour?
For fear of that I still will stay with thee,
And never from this palace of dim night
Depart again. Here, here will I remain
With worms that are thy chambermaids. O, here
Will I set up my everlasting rest,
And shake the yoke of inauspicious stars
From this world-wearied flesh. Eyes, look your last!
Arms, take your last embrace! And lips, O you,
The doors of breath, seal with a righteous kiss
A dateless bargain to engrossing Death!
Come, bitter conduct; come, unsavoury guide!
Thou desperate pilot, now at once run on
The dashing rocks thy seasick weary bark!

Here's to my love! [*drinks*] O true apothecary!
Thy drugs are quick. Thus with a kiss I die. [*dies*

'Enter Friar' LAWRENCE *'with lanthorn, crow, and spade'*

FRIAR Saint Francis be my speed! how oft tonight
Have my old feet stumbled at graves! Who's there?

BALTH'SAR Here's one, a friend, and one that knows you well.

FRIAR Bliss be upon you! Tell me, good my friend,
What torch is yond that vainly lends his light
To grubs and eyeless skulls? As I discern,
It burneth in the Capels' monument.

BALTH'SAR It doth so, holy sir; and there's my master,
One that you love.

FRIAR Who is it?

BALTH'SAR Romeo.

FRIAR How long hath he been there?

BALTH'SAR Full half an hour.

FRIAR Go with me to the vault.

BALTH'SAR I dare not, sir.
My master knows not but I am gone hence,
And fearfully did menace me with death
If I did stay to look on his intents.

FRIAR Stay then; I'll go alone. Fear comes upon me.
O, much I fear some ill unthrifty thing.

BALTH'SAR As I did sleep under this yew-tree here,
I dreamt my master and another fought,
And that my master slew him.

FRIAR Romeo! [*advances*
Alack, alack, what blood is this which stains
The stony entrance of this sepulchre?
What mean these masterless and gory swords
To lie discoloured by this place of peace?
[*enters the tomb*
Romeo! O, pale! Who else? What, Paris too?
And steeped in blood? Ah, what an unkind hour
Is guilty of this lamentable chance!
The lady stirs. [*Juliet wakes*

JULIET O comfortable friar, where is my lord?
I do remember well where I should be,
And there I am. Where is my Romeo? [*voices afar off*

FRIAR I hear some noise, lady. Come from that nest
Of death, contagion, and unnatural sleep.
A greater power than we can contradict
Hath thwarted our intents. Come, come away.
Thy husband in thy bosom there lies dead:
And Paris too. Come, I'll dispose of thee
Among a sisterhood of holy nuns.
Stay not to question, for the watch is coming.
Come, go, good Juliet; I dare no longer stay.

JULIET Go, get thee hence, for I will not away. [*he goes*
What's here? A cup, closed in my true love's hand?
Poison, I see, hath been his timeless end,
O churl! Drunk all, and left no friendly drop
To help me after? I will kiss thy lips.
Haply some poison yet doth hang on them
To make me die with a restorative. [*kisses him*
Thy lips are warm!

The Page of Paris enters the graveyard with Watchmen

1 WATCH Lead, boy. Which way?

JULIET Yea, noise? Then I'll be brief. O happy dagger,
[*snatching Romeo's dagger*
This is thy sheath [*stabs herself*]; there rest, and let me die.
[*falls on Romeo's body and dies*

PAGE This is the place, there where the torch doth burn.

1 WATCH The ground is bloody. Search about the churchyard.
Go, some of you; whoe'er you find attach.
[*some Watchmen depart*
Pitiful sight! Here lies the County slain:
And Juliet bleeding, warm and newly dead,
Who here hath lain this two days burièd.
Go tell the Prince; run to the Capulets;
Raise up the Montagues; some others search.
[*other Watchmen depart*
We see the ground whereon these woes do lie,
But the true ground of all these piteous woes
We cannot without circumstance descry.

Re-enter some of the Watch, with BALTHASAR

2 WATCH Here's Romeo's man; we found him in the churchyard.

I WATCH: Hold him in safety till the Prince come hither.

Re-enter another Watchman, with FRIAR LAWRENCE

3 WATCH Here is a friar that trembles, sighs, and weeps.
We took this mattock and this spade from him
As he was coming from this churchyard's side.

I WATCH A great suspicion! Stay the friar too.

'Enter the Prince' and attendants

PRINCE What misadventure is so early up,
That calls our person from our morning rest?

Enter CAPULET *and his wife*

CAPULET What should it be that is so shrieked abroad?

LADY CAP. O, the people in the street cry 'Romeo',
Some 'Juliet', and some 'Paris', and all run
With open outcry toward our monument.

PRINCE What fear is this which startles in our ears?

I WATCH Sovereign, here lies the County Paris slain;
And Romeo dead; and Juliet, dead before,
Warm and new killed.

PRINCE Search, seek, and know how this foul murder comes.

I WATCH Here is a friar, and slaughtered Romeo's man,
With instruments upon them fit to open
These dead men's tombs.

CAPULET O heaven! O wife, look how our daughter bleeds!
This dagger hath mista'en, for, lo, his house
Is empty on the back of Montague,
And it mis-sheathèd in my daughter's bosom.

LADY CAP. O me! this sight of death is as a bell
That warns my old age to a sepulchre.

'Enter MONTAGUE*'*

PRINCE Come Montague; for thou art early up
To see thy son and heir more early down.

MONTAG. Alas, my liege, my wife is dead tonight;
Grief of my son's exile hath stopped her breath.
What further woe conspires against mine age?

PRINCE Look and thou shalt see.

MONTAG. O thou untaught! what manners is in this,
To press before thy father to a grave?

PRINCE Seal up the mouth of outrage for a while,
Till we can clear these ambiguities,
And know their spring, their head, their true descent;
And then will I be general of your woes,
And lead you even to death. Meantime forbear,
And let mischance be slave to patience.
Bring forth the parties of suspicion.

[*Watchmen bring forward Friar Lawrence and Balthasar*

FRIAR I am the greatest; able to do least,
Yet most suspected, as the time and place
Doth make against me, of this direful murder:
And here I stand both to impeach and purge
Myself condemnèd and myself excused.

PRINCE Then say at once what thou dost know in this.

FRIAR I will be brief, for my short date of breath
Is not so long as is a tedious tale.
Romeo there dead was husband to that Juliet;
And she, there dead, that Romeo's faithful wife.
I married them; and their stol'n marriage day
Was Tybalt's doomsday, whose untimely death
Banished the new-made bridegroom from this city;
For whom, and not for Tybalt, Juliet pined.
You, to remove that siege of grief from her,
Betrothed and would have married her perforce
To County Paris. Then comes she to me,
And with wild looks bid me devise some mean
To rid her from this second marriage,
Or in my cell there would she kill herself.
Then gave I her (so tutored by my art)
A sleeping potion; which so took effect
As I intended, for it wrought on her
The form of death. Meantime I writ to Romeo
That he should hither come as this dire night
To help to take her from her borrowed grave,
Being the time the potion's force should cease.
But he which bore my letter, Friar John,
Was stayed by accident, and yesternight
Returned my letter back. Then all alone

At the prefixèd hour of her waking
Came I to take her from her kindred's vault,
Meaning to keep her closely at my cell
Till I conveniently could send to Romeo.
But when I came, some minute ere the time
Of her awakening, here untimely lay
The noble Paris and true Romeo dead.
She wakes; and I entreated her come forth,
And bear this work of heaven with patience;
But then a noise did scare me from the tomb,
And she, too desperate, would not go with me,
But, as it seems, did violence on herself.
All this I know; and to the marriage
Her nurse is privy: and if aught in this
Miscarried by my fault, let my old life
Be sacrificed, some hour before his time,
Unto the rigour of severest law.

PRINCE We still have known thee for a holy man.
Where's Romeo's man? What can he say to this?

BALTH'SAR I brought my master news of Juliet's death,
And then in post he came from Mantua
To this same place, to this same monument.
This letter he early bid me give his father,
And threat'ned me with death, going in the vault,
If I departed not and left him there.

PRINCE Give me the letter; I will look on it.
Where is the County's page, that raised the watch?
[*Page comes forward*
Sirrah, what made your master in this place?

PAGE He came with flowers to strew his lady's grave,
And bid me stand aloof, and so I did.
Anon comes one with light to ope the tomb,
And by and by my master drew on him,
And then I ran away to call the watch.

PRINCE This letter doth make good the friar's words,
Their course of love, the tidings of her death;
And here he writes that he did buy a poison
Of a poor pothecary, and therewithal
Came to this vault to die, and lie with Juliet.

Where be these enemies? Capulet, Montague?
See what a scourge is laid upon your hate,
That heaven finds means to kill your joys with love!
And I, for winking at your discords too,
Have lost a brace of kinsmen. All are punished.

CAPULET O brother Montague, give me thy hand.
This is my daughter's jointure, for no more
Can I demand.

MONTAG. But I can give thee more;
For I will raise her statue in pure gold,
That, whiles Verona by that name is known,
There shall no figure at such rate be set
As that of true and faithful Juliet.

CAPULET As rich shall Romeo's by his lady's lie –
Poor sacrifices of our enmity!

PRINCE A glooming peace this morning with it brings;
The sun for sorrow will not show his head.
Go hence, to have more talk of these sad things.
Some shall be pardoned, and some punishèd;
For never was a story of more woe
Than this of Juliet and her Romeo.

[*they go*

HAMLET

INTRODUCTION

Putting a date to *Hamlet* is complicated by the existence of conflicting evidence and three distinct printed versions of the play. There may have been a Hamlet play before Shakespeare's, which belongs to the period of around 1600, although this, like much else in the play, has been the subject of endless scholarly debate. *Hamlet* is at once familiar – the moody prince addressing a skull, or 'To be or not to be' (3.1.56) – and yet opaque and intractable, requiring explanation and amplification. The fragments are well-known, but the whole is elusive. A standard critical work on the play has the title 'What happens in *Hamlet*' (J. Dover Wilson, first published in 1935 and still in print in the U.K.), attesting to both the necessity and the difficulty of paraphrase. Laurence Olivier's 1948 film of the play took as a prologue Hamlet's speech beginning 'So, oft it chances in particular men, That for some vicious mole in nature in them' (1.4.23–24) and constructed the play rather reductively as 'the tragedy of a man who could not make up his mind'. Horatio's attempt to tell the story in the final scene is marked by a similar inadequacy, as he reduces the play we have just read or watched to an inventory of 'carnal, bloody and unnatural acts, Of accidental judgments, casual slaughters, Of deaths put on by cunning and forced cause' (5.2.368–70). The play may have been these things but it is also ineffably more than their melodramatic sum. The challenge of 'pluck[ing] out the heart of [its] mystery' (3.2.354) has contributed to its central and profoundly influential position in western culture.

The play tells the story of Hamlet, Prince of Denmark, who is mourning the death of his father and his mother's remarriage to his uncle, Claudius. The ghost of Hamlet's father appears to his son and tells him that he was murdered by Claudius and must be avenged. When some travelling actors visit the Danish court, Hamlet gets them to perform a play about the murder of a king by his brother, in order to test Claudius's reaction. Later, Hamlet has the chance to murder Claudius, but refrains because his uncle is praying. Visiting his mother Gertrude in her chamber, Hamlet kills the old courtier Polonius, whose daughter Ophelia, with whom Hamlet may have been in love, runs mad and also dies. Polonius' son Laertes returns to Denmark to avenge these deaths. Claudius attempts to get rid of Hamlet by sending him to England with secret orders that he be murdered, but Hamlet escapes. He fights a duel with Laertes, whose foil has been tipped with poison by Claudius. Both die, as do Claudius and Gertrude. Into the scene of carnage marches the army of the Norwegian prince Fortinbras who has been advancing on Denmark, and in his dying speech, Hamlet prophesies Fortinbras's appointment as next Danish king.

An early reference to the play in 1602 gives it an interestingly extended title. Modern editors of the tragedies have tended to standardise their titles as single (or occasionally double) names, and thus to lose certain nuances of the plays' early reception. *The Revenge of Hamlet Prince [of] Denmark* identifies Shakespeare's play within the popular dramatic genre of revenge tragedy, inaugurated by Thomas Kyd's *The Spanish Tragedy* (1592). Revenge plays focused on an injured individual – in Kyd's play the main revenger is Hieronimo, whose son Horatio has been murdered – who must gain redress, often urged on by a ghost, outside a legal system which is frequently implicated in the original crime. The revenge process is rarely neatly accomplished, however, and there are usually supernumerary casualties swept up in its bloody path. The ethics of revenge were then, as now, complex, and it is hard to reconstruct the attitudes of contemporary audiences to the bloodletting represented in plays of the genre. What is clear from the plays is that revenge tragedies themselves began to debate the right and wrongs of private revenge, in relation both to judicial and divine punishment. All revenge plays had a kind of sympathy for their hero but could not countenance his survival after taking his revenge, invariably including him in the final tableau of bloody bodies. Hamlet's conscience, therefore, may be dissected in extreme detail by Shakespeare, but he is by no means the first play hero caught between impulses towards revenge and away from violence. Nor is he the first revenger to delay. Revenge tragedy was dependent on delay for its dramatic form and tension, for if a wrong were immediately avenged, the play would, of necessity, be a very short one. Like other revenge plays including Kyd's, revenge in *Hamlet* is not confined to one individual. Hamlet is charged to 'revenge his [father's] foul and most unnatural murder' (1.5.25), and Laertes is spurred on by the deaths of his father and sister. Their final fatal duel is the clash of two revengers who must die. Hamlet is both revenger and villain – the injured and the injuring party. Even Fortinbras could be seen to be on a kind of revenge quest, another son putting right the wrongs done to a father by pressing for 'the surrender of those lands Lost by his father' (1.2.23–24). Revenge, like bloodshed, multiplies in the play until it consumes the whole Danish court.

The play's double-figure death count may sit awkwardly with the impression of *Hamlet* as a philosophical play of words rather than action. In fact, the play is both. Hamlet himself shifts from the bloody and excessive rhetoric of the stage-revenger in his 'now could I drink hot blood, And do such bitter business as the day Would quake to look on' (3.2.378–80) to the contemplative metaphysics of 'What a piece of work is a man, how noble in reason, how infinite in faculties [. . .] how like a god: the beauty of the world [. . .] and yet to me, what is this quintessence of dust?' (2.2.298–303). In asking Laertes' forgiveness at the last, Hamlet solidifies a view of himself as a divided personality, and is thus able to deny culpability for his actions, blaming them on 'his madness'. He distances himself through the repeated use of the third person: 'Was't Hamlet wronged Laertes? Never Hamlet. If Hamlet from himself be ta'en away, And when he's not himself does wrong Laertes, Then Hamlet does it not.' (5.2.219–22) Despite this denial, Hamlet is both bloodthirsty and contemplative, impulsive and havering. His is a play about action, and about the psychological and cultural impediments to action; Hamlet seems paralysed by the gap between the senses of acting as doing something and acting as pretending to do something, and the implications of these contradictory meanings become most evident in conversation with the troupe of players.

The players and their play 'The Murder of Gonzago' force

Hamlet, and *Hamlet*, into highly self-conscious musings on the differences between appearance and reality, art and life. All these reflections are infinitely complicated by the material fact of the artistry, the artificiality, of the play *Hamlet*. Hamlet berates himself for not showing his true grief to the extent of the Player King's 'dream of passion': 'what would he do, Had he the motive and the cue for passion That I have?' (2.2.543–45). But the characteristic self-consciousness of the early modern stage must impinge on Hamlet's theatrical assertion of his own 'reality' within a play, a 'fiction'. Throughout Hamlet, appearance and reality, superficiality and depth, are contrasted, but often their distinctness is blurred. Take Hamlet's first appearance, for example, in the second scene of the play, dressed ostentatiously in black. 'Why seems it so particular with thee?' his mother asks, referring to the death of the old king, and Hamlet immediately questions her use of the word 'seems'. He then reviles outer appearances – 'customary suits of solemn black', 'fruitful river in the eye', 'dejected haviour of the visage' – as, in suitably theatrical terminology, 'actions that a man might play'. He himself, however, announces that he is not playing at grief. He has 'that within which passes show', in the first assertion of his own secret inner self which he reiterates later in the play. Hamlet seems to need to believe that there is more to him than his exterior appearances, yet he is a skilful operator of those appearances, such that we do not and cannot know whether, for example, he 'feigns' madness or 'is' mad, nor, indeed, whether these two states are ever distinct. Despite his concern for a private subjectivity, Hamlet is not averse to the visible gestures which manifest these hidden depths. Here, Hamlet's 'that within which passes show' is implicitly identical with the show itself. Inside he is feeling what the outside denotes: the grief which expresses itself in black clothes, tears, and gloomy looks. Appearance and reality turn out to be the same, rather slippery, thing. At his first entry in the play, Hamlet has made a conscious decision to look like he feels, or to imply his feelings through his looks. Clearly, however, his adoption of dark clothes in the festive post-wedding celebrations of Claudius and Gertrude is not the involuntary result of the continuum of inner and outer, but an intentional and premeditated public reproach. (Such a reading of the scene is beautifully rendered in Kenneth Branagh's 1996 film of the play, in which

Hamlet is depicted as an immature spoilsport determined to wreck the celebrations.) Hamlet has used his appearance theatrically, to great visual and verbal effect, while simultaneously admitting that others in less pain might also do this – but not he. His manipulation of the dramatic situation and our perceptions is consummate: he must have been a very sharp student at Wittenburg university, known to play audiences since Christopher Marlowe's *Dr Faustus* (1592) as the *alma mater* of those rather too clever for their own good.

While the character of Hamlet holds the stage throughout, as Shakespeare's longest and most demanding role, the play is not simply an individual tragedy. In twentieth-century performances, however, there has been a tendency to focus on the central character to the exclusion of all else, and this narrowness has frequently been achieved through cutting the more political aspects of the play, especially the role of Fortinbras, whose 'promised march' (4.4.3) over Denmark is in the background for much of the play and takes centre stage in its final moments. When Marcellus states that 'something is rotten in the state of Denmark' (1.4.90), this extends the tragedy into the public sphere. Ultimately the price of Claudius' actions is the loss of Denmark itself, as the advance of the Norwegian army is counterpoised with the events at court. The early modern idea that the body of the monarch symbolised the body of the country meant that an ailing or wicked king affected, even infected, the kingdom. This analogy is highlighted by the use of 'Denmark' as a title for old Hamlet (1.1.48) and then for Claudius (1.2.69). Alongside Hamlet's personal tragedy is the tragedy of state, as Denmark itself is destroyed in the violence bred in its royal house. There are also other individual tragedies which the extraordinary power of Hamlet's ego can obscure. Gertrude, for example, is often harshly treated by critics of the play, who unfairly load much of the blame for events on her shoulders. Given, however, that there is no evidence that she suspects her new husband, her remarriage may be a pragmatic survival technique, both for herself and her son. Claudius seems to have the whole court in his pocket; it is hard to see what resistance Gertrude might have made, nor what her life would have been worth had she not married the ambitious new king. Ophelia, too, is a tragic character, and her relationship with Hamlet is an early casualty of the prince's obsession with his mother's remarriage. Denmark – arguably like Shakespeare's tragedies in general – seems a place inhospitable to women, and Gertrude and Ophelia are isolated figures – pawns of male politicking and victims of male opprobrium. It would be interesting to look at tragic events of the play from their perspective, in order to recentre them in a play determined to push them to its margins. Ultimately, however, the play is crowded by the force of Hamlet's personality, until the other characters seem merely the ciphers to his story. 'The rest is silence' (5.2.345), says the dying Prince; but as the fascination with the story of *Hamlet* shows no sign of abating, such quiet seems indefinitely postponed.

The Scene: Denmark

CHARACTERS IN THE PLAY

CLAUDIUS, *King of Denmark*
HAMLET, *Prince of Denmark, son to the late, and nephew to the present king*
POLONIUS, *Principal Secretary of State*
HORATIO, *friend to Hamlet*
LAERTES, *son to Polonius*
VALTEMAND, CORNELIUS } *ambassadors to Norway*
ROSENCRANTZ, GUILDENSTERN } *formerly fellow-students with Hamlet*
OSRIC, *a fantastic fop*
A Gentleman
A Doctor of Divinity
MARCELLUS, BARNARDO, FRANCISCO } *Gentlemen of the Guard*
REYNALDO, *servant to Polonius*
Four or five Players
Two Grave-diggers
FORTINBRAS, *Prince of Norway*
A Norwegian Captain
English Ambassadors

GERTRUDE, *Queen of Denmark, mother to Hamlet*
OPHELIA, *daughter to Polonius*

Lords, Ladies, Soldiers, Sailors, Messenger, and Attendants

The GHOST *of Hamlet's father*

THE TRAGEDY OF HAMLET PRINCE OF DENMARK

ACT I SCENE I

The castle at Elsinore. A narrow platform upon the battlements; turret-doors to right and left. Starlight, very cold

FRANCISCO, *a sentinel armed with a partisan, paces to and fro. A bell tolls twelve. Presently* BARNARDO, *another sentinel likewise armed, comes from the castle; he starts, hearing Francisco's tread in the darkness*

BARNARDO Who's there?
FRANCISCO Nay, answer me. Stand and unfold yourself.
BARNARDO Long live the King!
FRANCISCO Barnardo?
BARNARDO He.
FRANCISCO You come most carefully upon your hour.
BARNARDO 'Tis now struck twelve, get thee to bed, Francisco.
FRANCISCO For this relief much thanks, 'tis bitter cold,
And I am sick at heart.
BARNARDO Have you had quiet guard?
FRANCISCO Not a mouse stirring.
BARNARDO Well, good night:
If you do meet Horatio and Marcellus,
The rivals of my watch, bid them make haste.

HORATIO *and* MARCELLUS *come forth*

FRANCISCO [*listens*] I think I hear them. Stand ho, who is there?
HORATIO Friends to this ground.
MARCEL. And liegemen to the Dane.
FRANCISCO Give you good night.
MARCEL. O, farewell honest soldier,
Who hath relieved you?
FRANCISCO Barnardo hath my place;
Give you good night. [*Francisco goes*
MARCEL. Holla, Barnardo!
BARNARDO Say,
What, is Horatio there?
HORATIO A piece of him.

BARNARDO Welcome Horatio, welcome good Marcellus.
HORATIO What, has this thing appeared again tonight?
BARNARDO I have seen nothing.
MARCEL. Horatio says 'tis but our fantasy,
And will not let belief take hold of him
Touching this dreaded sight twice seen of us,
Therefore I have entreated him along
With us to watch the minutes of this night,
That if again this apparition come,
He may approve our eyes and speak to it.
HORATIO Tush, tush, 'twill not appear.
BARNARDO Sit down awhile,
And let us once again assail your ears,
That are so fortified against our story,
What we have two nights seen.
HORATIO Well, sit we down,
And let us hear Barnardo speak of this.
BARNARDO Last night of all,
When yon same star that's westward from the pole
Had made his course t' illume that part of heaven
Where now it burns, Marcellus and myself,
The bell then beating one –

A GHOST *appears; it is clad in armour from head to foot, and bears a marshal's truncheon*

MARCEL. Peace, break thee off, look where it comes again!
BARNARDO In the same figure like the King that's dead.
MARCEL. Thou art a scholar, speak to it, Horatio.
BARNARDO Looks 'a not like the King? Mark it, Horatio.
HORATIO Most like, it harrows me with fear and wonder.
BARNARDO It would be spoke to.
MARCEL. Question it, Horatio.
HORATIO What art thou that usurp'st this time of night,
Together with that fair and warlike form
In which the majesty of buried Denmark
Did sometimes march? by heaven I charge thee speak.
MARCEL. It is offended.
BARNARDO See, it stalks away.
HORATIO Stay, speak, speak, I charge thee speak.
[the Ghost vanishes

MARCEL. 'Tis gone and will not answer.
BARNARDO How now Horatio, you tremble and look pale,
Is not this something more than fantasy?
What think you on't?
HORATIO Before my God, I might not this believe
Without the sensible and true avouch
Of mine own eyes.
MARCEL. Is it not like the King?
HORATIO As thou art to thyself.
Such was the very armour be had on,
When he the ambitious Norway combated,
So frowned he once, when in an angry parle
He smote the sledded Polacks on the ice.
'Tis strange.
MARCEL. Thus twice before, and jump at the dead hour,
With martial stalk hath he gone by our watch.
HORATIO In what particular thought to work I know not,
But in the gross and scope of mine opinion,
This bodes some strange eruption to our state.
MARCEL. Good now sit down, and tell me he that knows,
Why this same strict and most observant watch
So nightly toils the subject of the land,
And why such daily cast of brazen cannon
And foreign mart for implements of war,
Why such impress of shipwrights, whose sore task
Does not divide the Sunday from the week,
What might be toward that this sweaty haste
Doth make the night joint-labourer with the day,
Who is't that can inform me?
HORATIO That can I,
At least the whisper goes so; our last king,
Whose image even but now appeared to us,
Was as you know by Fortinbras of Norway,
Thereto pricked on by a most emulate pride,
Dared to the combat; in which our valiant Hamlet
(For so this side of our known world esteemed him)
Did say this Fortinbras, who by a sealed compact,
Well ratified by law and heraldry,
Did forfeit (with his life) all those his lands

Which he stood seized of, to the conqueror,
Against the which a moiety competent
Was gagèd by our king, which had returned
To the inheritance of Fortinbras,
Had he been vanquisher; as by the same co-mart,
And carriage of the article designed,
His fell to Hamlet; now sir, young Fortinbras,
Of unimprovèd mettle hot and full,
Hath in the skirts of Norway here and there
Sharked up a list of lawless resolutes
For food and diet to some enterprise
That hath a stomach in't, which is no other,
As it doth well appear unto our state,
But to recover of us by strong hand
And terms compulsatory, those foresaid lands
So by his father lost; and this, I take it,
Is the main motive of our preparations,
The source of this our watch, and the chief head
Of this post-haste and romage in the land.

BARNARDO I think it be no other but e'en so;
Well may it sort that this portentous figure
Comes armèd through our watch so like the king
That was and is the question of these wars.

HORATIO A mote it is to trouble the mind's eye:
In the most high and palmy state of Rome,
A little ere the mightiest Julius fell,
The graves stood tenantless, and the sheeted dead
Did squeak and gibber in the Roman streets,
And even the like precurse of fierce events,
As harbingers preceding still the fates
And prologue to the omen coming on,
Have heaven and earth together demonstrated
Unto our climatures and countrymen,
As stars with trains of fire and dews of blood,
Disasters in the sun; and the moist star,
Upon whose influence Neptune's empire stands,
Was sick almost to doomsday with eclipse.

The GHOST *reappears*

But soft, behold, lo where it comes again!

I'll cross it though it blast me. [*he 'spreads his arms'*
Stay, illusion!
If thou hast any sound or use of voice,
Speak to me.
If there be any good thing to be done
That may to thee do ease, and grace to me,
Speak to me.
If thou art privy to thy country's fate
Which happily foreknowing may avoid,
O, speak!
Or if thou hast uphoarded in thy life
Extorted treasure in the womb of earth,
For which they say you spirits oft walk in death,
[*a cock crows*
Speak of it – stay and speak – stop it, Marcellus!

MARCEL. Shall I strike at it with my partisan?

HORATIO Do if it will not stand.

BARNARDO 'Tis here!

HORATIO 'Tis here!

MARCEL. 'Tis gone! [*the Ghost vanishes*
We do it wrong being so majestical
To offer it the show of violence,
For it is as the air, invulnerable,
And our vain blows malicious mockery.

BARNARDO It was about to speak when the cock crew.

HORATIO And then it started like a guilty thing,
Upon a fearful summons; I have heard
The cock that is the trumpet to the morn
Doth with his lofty and shrill-sounding throat
Awake the god of day, and at his warning
Whether in sea or fire, in earth or air,
Th'extravagant and erring spirit hies
To his confine, and of the truth herein
This present object made probation.

MARCEL. It faded on the crowing of the cock.
Some say that ever 'gainst that season comes
Wherein our Saviour's birth is celebrated
This bird of dawning singeth all night long,
And then they say no spirit dare stir abroad,

The nights are wholesome, then no planets strike,
No fairy takes, nor witch hath power to charm,
So hallowed, and so gracious is that time.

HORATIO So have I heard and do in part believe it.
But look, the morn in russet mantle clad
Walks o'er the dew of yon high eastward hill.
Break we our watch up and by my advice
Let us impart what we have seen tonight
Unto young Hamlet, for upon my life
This spirit, dumb to us, will speak to him:
Do you consent we shall acquaint him with it,
As needful in our loves, fitting our duty?

MARCEL. Let's do't, I pray, and I this morning know
Where we shall find him most convenient. [*they go*

SCENE 2

The Council Chamber in the castle

A 'flourish' of trumpets. 'Enter CLAUDIUS *King of Denmark,* GERTRUDE *the Queen, Councillors,* POLONIUS *and his son* LAERTES*',* VALTEMAND *and* CORNELIUS*, all clad in gay apparel, as from the coronation; and last of all Prince* HAMLET *in black, with downcast eyes. The King and Queen ascend steps to the thrones*

KING Though yet of Hamlet our dear brother's death
The memory be green, and that it us befitted
To bear our hearts in grief, and our whole kingdom
To be contracted in one brow of woe,
Yet so far hath discretion fought with nature,
That we with wisest sorrow think on him
Together with remembrance of ourselves:
Therefore our sometime sister, now our queen,
Th'imperial jointress to this warlike state,
Have we as 'twere with a defeated joy,
With an auspicious, and a dropping eye,
With mirth in funeral, and with dirge in marriage,
In equal scale weighing delight and dole,
Taken to wife: nor have we herein barred

Your better wisdoms, which have freely gone
With this affair along – for all, our thanks.
Now follows that you know, young Fortinbras,
Holding a weak supposal of our worth,
Or thinking by our late dear brother's death
Our state to be disjoint and out of frame,
Colleaguèd with this dream of his advantage,
He hath not failed to pester us with message
Importing the surrender of those lands
Lost by his father, with all bands of law,
To our most valiant brother – so much for him:
Now for ourself, and for this time of meeting,
Thus much the business is. We have here writ
To Norway, uncle of young Fortinbras –
Who impotent and bed-rid scarcely hears
Of this his nephew's purpose – to suppress
His further gait herein, in that the levies,
The lists, and full proportions, are all made
Out of his subject. And we here dispatch
You good Cornelius, and you Valtemand,
For bearers of this greeting to old Norway,
Giving to you no further personal power
To business with the king, more than the scope
Of these delated articles allow:
Farewell, and let your haste commend your duty.

CORNEL., VALTEM'D In that, and all things, will we show our duty.

KING We doubt it nothing, heartily farewell.

[*Valtemand and Cornelius bow, and depart*

And now, Laertes, what's the news with you?
You told us of some suit, what is't, Laertes?
You cannot speak of reason to the Dane,
And lose your voice; what wouldst thou beg, Laertes,
That shall not be my offer, not thy asking?
The head is not more native to the heart,
The hand more instrumental to the mouth,
Than is the throne of Denmark to thy father.
What wouldst thou have, Laertes?

LAERTES My dread lord,

Your leave and favour to return to France,
From whence though willingly I came to Denmark,
To show my duty in your coronation;
Yet now I must confess, that duty done,
My thoughts and wishes bend again toward France,
And bow them to your gracious leave and pardon.

KING Have you your father's leave? What says Polonius?

POLONIUS He hath my lord, wrung from me my slow leave
By laboursome petition, and at last
Upon his will I sealed my hard consent.
I do beseech you give him leave to go.

KING Take thy fair hour, Laertes, time be thine,
And thy best graces spend it at thy will.
But now my cousin Hamlet, and my son –

HAMLET A little more than kin, and less than kind.

KING How is it that the clouds still hang on you?

HAMLET Not so, my lord, I am too much in the sun.

QUEEN Good Hamlet, cast thy nighted colour off,
And let thine eye look like a friend on Denmark;
Do not for ever with thy vailèd lids
Seek for thy noble father in the dust;
Thou know'st 'tis common, all that lives must die,
Passing through nature to eternity.

HAMLET Ay, madam, it is common.

QUEEN If it be,
Why seems it so particular with thee?

HAMLET Seems, madam! Nay it is, I know not 'seems'.
'Tis not alone my inky cloak, good mother,
Nor customary suits of solemn black,
Nor windy suspiration of forced breath,
No, nor the fruitful river in the eye,
Nor the dejected haviour of the visage,
Together with all forms, motes, shapes of grief,
That can denote me truly. These indeed seem,
For they are actions that a man might play,
But I have that within which passes show,
These but the trappings and the suits of woe.

KING 'Tis sweet and commendable in your nature, Hamlet,
To give these mourning duties to your father,

But you must know your father lost a father,
That father lost, lost his, and the survivor bound
In filial obligation for some term
To do obsequious sorrow. But to persever
In obstinate condolement is a course
Of impious stubbornness, 'tis unmanly grief,
It shows a will most incorrect to heaven,
A heart unfortified, a mind impatient,
An understanding simple and unschooled.
For what we know must be and is as common
As any the most vulgar thing to sense,
Why should we in our peevish opposition
Take it to heart? Fie, 'tis a fault to heaven,
A fault against the dead, a fault to nature,
To reason most absurd, whose common theme
Is death of fathers, and who still hath cried,
From the first corse till he that died today,
'This must be so'. We pray you throw to earth
This unprevailing woe, and think of us
As of a father, for let the world take note
You are the most immediate to our throne,
And with no less nobility of love
Than that which dearest father bears his son,
Do I impart toward you. For your intent
In going back to school in Wittenberg,
It is most retrograde to our desire,
And we beseech you, bend you to remain
Here in the cheer and comfort of our eye,
Our chiefest courtier, cousin, and our son.

QUEEN Let not thy mother lose her prayers, Hamlet;
I pray thee stay with us, go not to Wittenberg.

HAMLET I shall in all my best obey you, madam.

KING Why, 'tis a loving and a fair reply,
Be as ourself in Denmark. Madam, come.
This gentle and unforced accord of Hamlet,
Sits smiling to my heart, in grace whereof,
No jocund health that Denmark drinks today,
But the great cannon to the clouds shall tell,
And the king's rouse the heaven shall bruit again,

Re-speaking earthly thunder; come away.
[*'Flourish. Exeunt all but Hamlet'*

HAMLET O, that this too too solid flesh would melt,
Thaw and resolve itself into a dew,
Or that the Everlasting had not fixed
His canon 'gainst self-slaughter. O God, God,
How weary, stale, flat, and unprofitable
Seem to me all the uses of this world!
Fie on't, ah fie, 'tis an unweeded garden
That grows to seed, things rank and gross in nature
Possess it merely. That it should come to this,
But two months dead, nay not so much, not two,
So excellent a king, that was to this
Hyperion to a satyr, so loving to my mother,
That he might not beteem the winds of heaven
Visit her face too roughly – heaven and earth,
Must I remember? Why, she would hang on him
As if increase of appetite had grown
By what it fed on, and yet within a month,
Let me not think on't. Frailty, thy name is woman!
A little month or ere those shoes were old
With which she followed my poor father's body,
Like Niobe all tears, why she, even she –
O God, a beast that wants discourse of reason
Would have mourned longer – married with my uncle,
My father's brother, but no more like my father
Than I to Hercules, within a month,
Ere yet the salt of most unrighteous tears
Had left the flushing in her gallèd eyes
She married. O most wicked speed, to post
With such dexterity to incestuous sheets!
It is not, nor it cannot come to good,
But break my heart, for I must hold my tongue.

HORATIO, MARCELLUS *and* BARNARDO *enter*

HORATIO Hail to your lordship!

HAMLET I am glad to see you well;
Horatio – or I do forget myself!

HORATIO The same, my lord, and your poor servant ever.

HAMLET Sir, my good friend, I'll change that name with you.
[they clasp hands
And what make you from Wittenberg, Horatio?
Marcellus. *[he gives his hand*
MARCEL. My good lord!
HAMLET I am very glad to see you – good even, sir.
[he bows to Barnardo
But what in faith make you from Wittenberg?
[he draws Horatio apart
HORATIO A truant disposition, good my lord.
HAMLET I would not hear your enemy say so,
Nor shall you do mine ear that violence
To make it truster of your own report
Against yourself. I know you are no truant,
But what is your affair in Elsinore?
We'll teach you to drink deep ere you depart.
HORATIO My lord, I came to see your father's funeral.
HAMLET I prithee do not mock me, fellow-student,
I think it was to see my mother's wedding.
HORATIO Indeed, my lord, it followed hard upon.
HAMLET Thrift, thrift, Horatio, the funeral baked meats
Did coldly furnish forth the marriage tables.
Would I had met my dearest foe in heaven
Or ever I had seen that day, Horatio –
My father, methinks I see my father.
HORATIO Where, my lord?
HAMLET In my mind's eye, Horatio.
HORATIO I saw him once, 'a was a goodly king –
HAMLET 'A was a man, take him for all in all,
I shall not look upon his like again.
HORATIO My lord, I think I saw him yesternight.
HAMLET Saw, who?
HORATIO My lord, the king your father.
HAMLET The king my father!
HORATIO Season your admiration for a while
With an attent ear till I may deliver
Upon the witness of these gentlemen
This marvel to you.
[he turns to Marcellus and Barnardo

HAMLET For God's love let me hear!
HORATIO Two nights together had these gentlemen,
Marcellus and Barnardo, on their watch
In the dead waste and middle of the night,
Been thus encountered. A figure like your father,
Armèd at point exactly, cap-a-pe,
Appears before them, and with solemn march,
Goes slow and stately by them; thrice he walked
By their oppressed and fear-surprisèd eyes
Within his truncheon's length, whilst they distilled
Almost to jelly with the act of fear,
Stand dumb and speak not to him; this to me
In dreadful secrecy impart they did,
And I with them the third night kept the watch,
Where, as they had delivered, both in time,
Form of the thing, each word made true and good,
The apparition comes: I knew your father,
These hands are not more like.
HAMLET But where was this?
MARCEL. My lord, upon the platform where we watch.
HAMLET Did you not speak to it?
HORATIO My lord, I did,
But answer made it none, yet once methought
It lifted up it head, and did address
Itself to motion like as it would speak:
But even then the morning cock crew loud,
And at the sound it shrunk in haste away
And vanished from our sight.
HAMLET 'Tis very strange.
HORATIO As I do live, my honoured lord, 'tis true,
And we did think it writ down in our duty
To let you know of it.
HAMLET Indeed, indeed, sirs, but this troubles me.
Hold you the watch tonight?
ALL We do, my lord.
HAMLET Armed, say you?
ALL Armed, my lord.
HAMLET From top to toe?
ALL My lord, from head to foot.

HAMLET Then saw you not his face.

HORATIO O yes, my lord, he wore his beaver up.

HAMLET What, looked he frowningly?

HORATIO A countenance more in sorrow than in anger.

HAMLET Pale, or red?

HORATIO Nay, very pale.

HAMLET And fixed his eyes upon you?

HORATIO Most constantly.

HAMLET I would I had been there.

HORATIO It would have much amazed you.

HAMLET Very like, very like. Stayed it long?

HORATIO While one with moderate haste might tell a hundred.

MARCEL., BARN. Longer, longer.

HORATIO Not when I saw't.

HAMLET His beard was grizzled, no?

HORATIO It was as I have seen it in his life,
A sable silvered.

HAMLET I will watch tonight,
Perchance 'twill walk again.

HORATIO I war'nt it win.

HAMLET If it assume my noble father's person,
I'll speak to it though hell itself should gape
And bid me hold my peace; I pray you all
If you have hitherto concealed this sight,
Let it be tenable in your silence still,
And whatsomever else shall hap tonight,
Give it an understanding but no tongue.
I will requite your loves, so fare you well:
Upon the platform 'twixt eleven and twelve
I'll visit you.

ALL Our duty to your honour.

HAMLET Your loves, as mine to you. Farewell.

[*they bow and depart*

My father's spirit (in arms!); all is not well,
I doubt some foul play. Would the night were come;
Till then sit still my soul, foul deeds will rise,
Though all the earth o'erwhelm them, to men's eyes.

[*he goes*

SCENE 3

A room in the house of Polonius

'Enter LAERTES *and* OPHELIA *his sister'*

LAERTES My necessaries are embarked, farewell,
And sister, as the winds give benefit
And convoy is assistant, do not sleep,
But let me hear from you.
OPHELIA Do you doubt that?
LAERTES For Hamlet, and the trifling of his favour,
Hold it a fashion, and a toy in blood,
A violet in the youth of primy nature,
Forward, not permanent, sweet, not lasting,
The perfume and suppliance of a minute,
No more.
OPHELIA No more but so?
LAERTES Think it no more.
For nature crescent does not grow alone
In thews and bulk, but as this temple waxes
The inward service of the mind and soul
Grows wide withal. Perhaps he loves you now,
And now no soil nor cautel doth besmirch
The virtue of his will. But you must fear,
His greatness weighed, his will is not his own,
For he himself is subject to his birth.
He may not, as unvalued persons do,
Carve for himself, for on his choice depends
The sanity and health of this whole state,
And therefore must his choice be circumscribed
Unto the voice and yielding of that body
Whereof he is the head. Then if he says he loves you,
It fits your wisdom so far to believe it
As he in his particular act and place
May give his saying deed, which is no further
Than the main voice of Denmark goes withal.
Then weigh what loss your honour may sustain
If with too credent ear you list his songs,

Or lose your heart, or your chaste treasure open
To his unmast'red importunity.
Fear it Ophelia, fear it my dear sister,
And keep you in the rear of your affection,
Out of the shot and danger of desire.
'The chariest maid is prodigal enough
If she unmask her beauty to the moon.'
'Virtue itself 'scapes not calumnious strokes.'
'The canker galls the infants of the spring
Too oft before their buttons be disclosed,
And in the morn and liquid dew of youth
Contagious blastments are most imminent.'
Be wary then – best safety lies in fear,
Youth to itself rebels, though none else near.

OPHELIA I shall the effect of this good lesson keep
As watchman to my heart. But good my brother,
Do not, as some ungracious pastors do,
Show me the steep and thorny way to heaven,
Whiles like a puffed and reckless libertine
Himself the primrose path of dalliance treads,
And recks not his own rede.

POLONIUS *enters*

LAERTES O fear me not;
I stay too long – but here my father comes.
A double blessing is a double grace, [*he kneels*
Occasion smiles upon a second leave.

POLONIUS Yet here, Laertes? Aboard, aboard for shame!
The wind sits in the shoulder of your sail,
And you are stayed for. There – my blessing with thee,
[*he lays his hand on Laertes' head*
And these few precepts in thy memory
Look thou character. Give thy thoughts no tongue,
Nor any unproportioned thought his act.
Be thou familiar, but by no means vulgar;
Those friends thou hast, and their adoption tried,
Grapple them unto thy soul with hoops of steel,
But do not dull thy palm with entertainment
Of each new-hatched unfledged courage. Beware
Of entrance to a quarrel, but being in,

Bear't that th'opposèd may beware of thee.
Give every man thy ear, but few thy voice;
Take each man's censure, but reserve thy judgment.
Costly thy habit as thy purse can buy,
But not expressed in fancy; rich not gaudy.
For the apparel oft proclaims the man,
And they in France of the best rank and station,
Or of a most select and generous, chief in that.
Neither a borrower nor a lender be,
For loan oft loses both itself and friend,
And borrowing dulls the edge of husbandry;
This above all, to thine own self be true
And it must follow as the night the day
Thou canst not then be false to any man.
Farewell – my blessing season this in thee.

LAERTES Most humbly do I take my leave, my lord.

POLONIUS The time invites you, go, your servants tend.

LAERTES [*rises*] Farewell, Ophelia, and remember well
What I have said to you.

OPHELIA 'Tis in my memory locked,
And you yourself shall keep the key of it. [*they embrace*

LAERTES Farewell. [*he goes*

POLONIUS What is't, Ophelia, he hath said to you?

OPHELIA So please you, something touching the Lord Hamlet.

POLONIUS Marry, well bethought.
'Tis told me he hath very oft of late
Given private time to you, and you yourself
Have of your audience been most free and bounteous.
If it be so – as so 'tis put on me,
And that in way of caution – I must tell you,
You do not understand yourself so clearly
As it behoves my daughter and your honour.
What is between you? Give me up the truth.

OPHELIA He hath, my lord, of late made many tenders
Of his affection to me.

POLONIUS Affection, pooh! You speak like a green girl
Unsifted in such perilous circumstance.
Do you believe his tenders, as you call them?

OPHELIA I do not know, my lord, what I should think.

POLONIUS Marry, I will teach you – think yourself a baby
That you have ta'en these tenders for true pay
Which are not sterling. Tender yourself more dearly,
Or (not to crack the wind of the poor phrase,
Running it thus) you'll tender me a fool.

OPHELIA My lord, he hath importuned me with love
In honourable fashion.

POLONIUS Ay, fashion you may call it, go to, go to.

OPHELIA And hath given countenance to his speech, my lord,
With almost all the holy vows of heaven.

POLONIUS Ay, springes to catch woodcocks. I do know
When the blood burns, how prodigal the soul
Lends the tongue vows. These blazes, daughter,
Giving more light than heat, extinct in both,
Even in their promise, as it is a-making,
You must not take for fire. From this time
Be something scanter of your maiden presence,
Set your entreatments at a higher rate
Than a command to parle; for Lord Hamlet,
Believe so much in him that he is young,
And with a larger tether may he walk
Than may be given you: in few, Ophelia,
Do not believe his vows, for they are brokers
Not of that dye which their investments show,
But mere implorators of unholy suits,
Breathing like sanctified and pious bonds
The better to beguile. This is for all,
I would not in plain terms from this time forth
Have you so slander any moment leisure
As to give words or talk with the Lord Hamlet.
Look to't, I charge you, come your ways.

OPHELIA I shall obey, my lord. [*they go*

SCENE 4

The platform on the battlements

HAMLET, HORATIO *and* MARCELLUS *come from one of the turrets*

HAMLET The air bites shrewdly, it is very cold.
HORATIO It is a nipping and an eager air.
HAMLET What hour now?
HORATIO I think it lacks of twelve.
MARCEL. No, it is struck.
HORATIO Indeed? I heard it not – it then draws near the season,
Wherein the spirit held his wont to walk.
[*'a flourish of trumpets', and ordnance shot off*
What does this mean, my lord?
HAMLET The King doth wake tonight and takes his rouse,
Keeps wassail and the swagg'ring upspring reels:
And as he drains his draughts of Rhenish down,
The kettle-drum and trumpet thus bray out
The triumph of his pledge.
HORATIO Is it a custom?
HAMLET Ay marry is't,
But to my mind, though I am native here
And to the manner born, it is a custom
More honoured in the breach than the observance.
This heavy-headed revel east and west
Makes us traduced and taxed of other nations.
They clepe us drunkards, and with swinish phrase
Soil our addition, and indeed it takes
From our achievements, though performed at height,
The pith and marrow of our attribute.
So, oft it chances in particular men,
That for some vicious mole of nature in them,
As in their birth, wherein they are not guilty
(Since nature cannot choose his origin),
By the o'ergrowth of some complexion,
Oft breaking down the pales and forts of reason,
Or by some habit, that too much o'er-leavens

The form of plausive manners – that these men,
Carrying I say the stamp of one defect,
Being nature's livery, or fortune's star,
His virtues else be they as pure as grace,
As infinite as man may undergo,
Shall in the general censure take corruption
From that particular fault: the dram of evil
Doth all the noble substance of a doubt,
To his own scandal.

The GHOST *appears*

HORATIO Look, my lord, it comes!

HAMLET Angels and ministers of grace defend us!
Be thou a spirit of health, or goblin damned,
Bring with thee airs from heaven, or blasts from hell,
Be thy intents wicked, or charitable,
Thou com'st in such a questionable shape,
That I will speak to thee. I'll call thee Hamlet,
King, father, royal Dane. O, answer me!
Let me not burst in ignorance, but tell
Why thy canonized bones hearsèd in death
Have burst their cerements? Why the sepulchre,
Wherein we saw thee quietly inurned,
Hath oped his ponderous and marble jaws
To cast thee up again? What may this mean
That thou, dead corse, again in complete steel
Revisits thus the glimpses of the moon,
Making night hideous, and we fools of nature
So horridly to shake our disposition
With thoughts beyond the reaches of our souls?
Say why is this? Wherefore? What should we do?
[*the Ghost 'beckons'*

HORATIO It beckons you to go away with it,
As if it some impartment did desire
To you alone.

MARCEL. Look with what courteous action
It wares you to a more removèd ground,
But do not go with it.

HORATIO No, by no means.

HAMLET It will not speak, then I will follow it.
HORATIO Do not my lord.
HAMLET Why, what should be the fear?
I do not set my life at a pin's fee,
And for my soul, what can it do to that
Being a thing immortal as itself;
It waves me forth again, I'll follow it.
HORATIO What if it tempt you toward the flood, my lord,
Or to the dreadful summit of the cliff
That beetles o'er his base into the sea,
And there assume some other horrible form,
Which might deprive your sovereignty of reason,
And draw you into madness? Think of it –
The very place puts toys of desperation,
Without more motive, into every brain
That looks so many fathoms to the sea
And hears it roar beneath.
HAMLET It waves me still.
Go on, I'll follow thee.
MARCEL. You shall not go, my lord.
HAMLET Hold off your hands.
HORATIO Be ruled, you shall not go.
HAMLET My fate cries out,
And makes each petty artere in this body
As hardy as the Nemean lion's nerve;
Still am I called, unhand me gentlemen,
[he breaks from them, drawing his sword
By heaven, I'll make a ghost of him that lets me!
I say, away! Go on, I'll follow thee.
[the Ghost passes into one of the turrets, Hamlet following
HORATIO He waxes desperate with imagination.
MARCEL. Lets follow, 'tis not fit thus to obey him.
HORATIO Have after – to what issue will this come?
MARCEL. Something is rotten in the state of Denmark.
HORATIO Heaven will direct it.
MARCEL. Nay, let's follow him.
[they follow

SCENE 5

An open space at the foot of the castle wall

A door in the wall opens; the GHOST *comes forth and* HAMLET *after, the hilt of his drawn sword held crosswise before him*

HAMLET Whither wilt thou lead me? speak, I'll go no further.
GHOST [*turns*] Mark me.
HAMLET I will.
GHOST My hour is almost come,
When I to sulph'rous and tormenting flames
Must render up myself.
HAMLET Alas, poor ghost!
GHOST Pity me not, but lend thy serious hearing
To what I shall unfold.
HAMLET Speak, I am bound to hear.
GHOST So art thou to revenge, when thou shalt hear.
HAMLET What?
GHOST I am thy father's spirit,
Doomed for a certain term to walk the night,
And for the day confined to fast in fires,
Till the foul crimes done in my days of nature
Are burnt and purged away: but that I am forbid
To tell the secrets of my prison-house,
I could a tale unfold whose lightest word
Would harrow up thy soul, freeze thy young blood,
Make thy two eyes like stars start from their spheres,
Thy knotted and combinèd locks to part,
And each particular hair to stand an end,
Like quills upon the fretful porpentine.
But this eternal blazon must not be
To ears of flesh and blood. List, list, O list!
If thou didst ever thy dear father love –
HAMLET O God!
GHOST Revenge his foul and most unnatural murder.
HAMLET Murder!
GHOST Murder most foul, as in the best it is,
But this most foul, strange and unnatural.

HAMLET Haste me to know't, that I with wings as swift
As meditation or the thoughts of love,
May sweep to my revenge.

GHOST I find thee apt,
And duller shouldst thou be than the fat weed
That rots itself in ease on Lethe wharf,
Wouldst thou not stir in this; now Hamlet hear,
'Tis given out, that sleeping in my orchard,
A serpent stung me, so the whole ear of Denmark
Is by a forgèd process of my death
Rankly abused: but know, thou noble youth,
The serpent that did sting thy father's life
Now wears his crown.

HAMLET O, my prophetic soul!
My uncle?

GHOST Ay, that incestuous, that adulterate beast,
With witchcraft of his wit, with traitorous gifts,
O wicked wit and gifts, that have the power
So to seduce; won to his shameful lust
The will of my most seeming-virtuous queen;
O Hamlet, what a falling-off was there!
From me whose love was of that dignity,
That it went hand in hand even with the vow
I made to her in marriage, and to decline
Upon a wretch whose natural gifts were poor
To those of mine;
But virtue, as it never will be moved,
Though lewdness court it in a shape of heaven,
So lust, though to a radiant angel linked,
Will sate itself in a celestial bed
And prey on garbage.
But soft, methinks I scent the morning air,
Brief let me be; sleeping within my orchard,
My custom always of the afternoon,
Upon my secure hour thy uncle stole
With juice of cursed hebona in a vial,
And in the porches of my ears did pour
The leperous distilment, whose effect
Holds such an enmity with blood of man,

That swift as quicksilver it courses through
The natural gates and alleys of the body,
And with a sudden vigour it doth posset
And curd, like eager droppings into milk,
The thin and wholesome blood; so did it mine,
And a most instant tetter barked about
Most lazar-like with vile and loathsome crust
All my smooth body.
Thus was I sleeping by a brother's hand,
Of life, of crown, of queen at once dispatched,
Cut off even in the blossoms of my sin,
Unhouseled, disappointed, unaneled,
No reck'ning made, but sent to my account
With all my imperfections on my head.
O, horrible! O, horrible! Most horrible !
If thou hast nature in thee bear it not,
Let not the royal bed of Denmark be
A couch for luxury and damnèd incest.
But howsomever thou pursues this act,
Taint not thy mind, nor let thy soul contrive
Against thy mother aught – leave her to heaven,
And to those thorns that in her bosom lodge
To prick and sting her. Fare thee well at once,
The glow-worm shows the matin to be near,
And 'gins to pale his uneffectual fire.
Adieu, adieu, adieu, remember me.
[*the Ghost vanishes into the ground; Hamlet falls distraught upon his knees*

HAMLET O all you host of heaven! O earth! What else?
And shall I couple hell? O fie! Hold, hold, my heart,
And you, my sinews, grow not instant old,
But bear me stiffly up. [*he rises*] Remember thee?
Ay thou poor ghost, whiles memory holds a seat
In this distracted globe. Remember thee?
Yea, from the table of my memory
I'll wipe away all trivial fond records,
All saws of books, all forms, all pressures past
That youth and observation copied there,
And thy commandment all alone shall live

Within the book and volume of my brain,
Unmixed with baser matter – yes by heaven!
O most pernicious woman!
O villain, villain, smiling damnèd villain!
My tables, meet it is I set it down [*he writes*
That one may smile, and smile, and be a villain,
At least I am sure it may be so in Denmark.
So, uncle, there you are. Now, to my word,
It is 'Adieu, adieu, remember me.'
[*he kneels and lays his hand upon the hilt of his sword*
I have sworn't. [*he prays*

HORATIO *and* MARCELLUS *come from the castle, calling in the darkness*

HORATIO My lord, my lord!
HAMLET Lord Hamlet!
HORATIO Heaven secure him!
HAMLET So be it! [*he rises*
MARCEL. Illo, ho, ho, my lord!
HAMLET Hillo, ho, ho, boy! Come, bird, come.
[*they see Hamlet*
MARCEL. How is't, my noble lord?
HORATIO What news, my lord?
HAMLET O, wonderful!
HORATIO Good my lord, tell it.
HAMLET No, you will reveal it.
HORATIO Not I, my lord, by heaven.
MARCEL. Nor I, my lord.
HAMLET How say you then, would heart of man once think it?
But you'll be secret?
HORATIO, MARCEL. Ay, by heaven, my lord.
HAMLET There's ne'er a villain dwelling in all Denmark
But he's an arrant knave.
HORATIO There needs no ghost, my lord, come from the grave,
To tell us this.
HAMLET Why right, you are in the right,
And so without more circumstance at all
I hold it fit that we shake hands and part,
You, as your business and desire shall point you,

For every man hath business and desire
Such as it is, and for my own poor part,
Look you, I will go pray.

HORATIO These are but wild and whirling words, my lord.

HAMLET I am sorry they offend you, heartily,
Yes, faith, heartily.

HORATIO There's no offence, my lord.

HAMLET [*to Horatio*] Yes, by Saint Patrick, but there is, Horatio,
And much offence too – touching this vision here,
It is an honest ghost, that let me tell you –
For your desire to know what is between us,
O'ermaster't as you may.
[*to both*] And now, good friends,
As you are friends, scholars, and soldiers,
Give me one poor request.

HORATIO What is't, my lord? We will.

HAMLET Never make known what you have seen tonight.

BOTH My lord, we will not.

HAMLET Nay, but swear't.

HORATIO In faith,
My lord, not I.

MARCEL. Nor I, my lord, in faith.

HAMLET [*draws*] Upon my sword.

MARCEL. We have sworn, my lord, already.

HAMLET Indeed, upon my sword, indeed.

GHOST [*beneath*] Swear.

HAMLET Ha, ha, boy! Say'st thou so? Art thou there, truepenny?
Come on, you hear this fellow in the cellarage,
Consent to swear.

HORATIO Propose the oath, my lord.

HAMLET Never to speak of this that you have seen,
Swear by my sword.
[*they lay their hands upon the hilt*

GHOST [*beneath*] Swear.

HAMLET Hic et ubique? Then we'll shift our ground:
Come hither gentlemen,
And lay your hands again upon my sword.
Swear by my sword,
Never to speak of this that you have heard.

GHOST [*beneath*] Swear by his sword.

HAMLET Well said, old mole! Canst work i'th'earth so fast?
[*they swear again in silence*
A worthy pioneer! Once more remove, good friends.

HORATIO O day and night, but this is wondrous strange!

HAMLET And therefore as a stranger give it welcome.
There are more things in heaven and earth, Horatio,
Than are dreamt of in your philosophy.
But come –
Here as before, never, so help you mercy
(How strange or odd some'er I bear myself;
As I perchance hereafter shall think meet
To put an antic disposition on)
That you at such times seeing me, never shall
With arms encumbered thus, or this head-shake,
Or by pronouncing of some doubtful phrase,
As 'Well, well, we know', or 'We could an if we would',
Or 'If we list to speak', or 'There be an if they might',
Or such ambiguous giving out, to note
That you know aught of me – this do swear,
So grace and mercy at your most need help you!

GHOST [*beneath*] Swear.

HAMLET Rest, rest, perturbèd spirit! [*they swear a third time*]
So, gentlemen,
With all my love I do commend me to you,
And what so poor a man as Hamlet is
May do t'express his love and friending to you
God willing shall not lack. Let us go in together,
And still your fingers on your lips I pray.
The time is out of joint, O cursèd spite,
That ever I was born to set it right!
Nay come, let's go together. [*they enter the castle*

[*Some weeks pass*]

ACT 2 SCENE 1

A room in the house of Polonius

POLONIUS *and* REYNALDO

POLONIUS Give him this money, and these notes, Reynaldo,
REYNALDO I will, my lord.
POLONIUS You shall do marvellous wisely, good Reynaldo,
Before you visit him, to make inquire
Of his behaviour.
REYNALDO: My lord, I did intend it.
POLONIUS Marry, well said, very well said; look you sir,
Inquire me first what Danskers are in Paris,
And how, and who, what means, and where they keep,
What company, at what expense, and finding
By this encompassment and drift of question
That they do know my son, come you more nearer
Than your particular demands will touch it,
Take you as 'twere some distant knowledge of him,
As thus, 'I know his father, and his friends,
And in part him' – do you mark this, Reynaldo?
REYNALDO Ay, very well, my lord.
POLONIUS 'And in part him, but,' you may say, 'not well,
But if't be he I mean, he's very wild,
Addicted so and so.' And there put on him
What forgeries you please, marry none so rank
As may dishonour him, take heed of that,
But sir such wanton, wild, and usual slips
As are companions noted and most known
To youth and liberty.
REYNALDO As gaming, my lord.
POLONIUS Ay, or drinking, fencing, swearing, quarrelling,
Drabbing – you may go so far.
REYNALDO My lord, that would dishonour him.
POLONIUS Faith no, as you may season it in the charge.
You must not put another scandal on him,
That he is open to incontinency,

That's not my meaning, but breathe his faults so quaintly
That they may seem the taints of liberty,
The flash and outbreak of a fiery mind,
A savageness in unreclaimed blood,
Of general assault.

REYNALDO But, my good lord –

POLONIUS Wherefore should you do this?

REYNALDO Ay my lord,
I would know that.

POLONIUS Marry sir, here's my drift,
And I believe it is a fetch of warrant,
You laying these slight sullies on my son,
As 'twere a thing a little soiled i'th' working,
Mark you, your party in converse, him you would sound,
Having ever seen in the prenominate crimes
The youth you breathe of guilty, be assured
He closes with you in this consequence,
'Good sir', or so, or 'friend', or 'gentleman',
According to the phrase, or the addition
Of man and country.

REYNALDO Very good, my lord.

POLONIUS And then sir, does 'a this, 'a does, what was I about to say?
By the mass I was about to say something.
Where did I leave?

REYNALDO At 'closes in the consequence',
At 'friend, or so, and gentleman'.

POLONIUS At 'closes in the consequence'. Ay marry –
He closes thus, 'I know the gentleman,
I saw him yesterday, or th'other day,
Or then, or then, with such or such, and as you say,
There was 'a gaming, there o'ertook in's rouse,
There falling out at tennis', or perchance,
'I saw him enter such a house of sale',
Videlicet, a brothel, or so forth. See you now,
Your bait of falsehood takes this carp of truth,
And thus do we of wisdom, and of reach,
With windlasses, and with assays of bias,

By indirections find directions out,
So by my former lecture and advice
Shall you my son; you have me, have you not?

REYNALDO My lord, I have.

POLONIUS God bye ye, fare ye well.

REYNALDO Good, my lord.

POLONIUS Observe his inclination in yourself.

REYNALDO I shall, my lord.

POLONIUS And let him ply his music.

REYNALDO Well, my lord. [*he goes*

POLONIUS Farewell.

OPHELIA *enters in perturbation*

How now Ophelia, what's the matter?

OPHELIA O my lord, my lord, I have been so affrighted!

POLONIUS With what, i'th'name of God?

OPHELIA My lord, as I was sewing in my closet,
Lord Hamlet with his doublet all unbraced,
No hat upon his head, his stockings fouled,
Ungart'red, and down-gyvèd to his ankle,
Pale as his shirt, his knees knocking each other,
And with a look so piteous in purport
As if he had been loosèd out of hell
To speak of horrors – he comes before me.

POLONIUS Mad for thy love?

OPHELIA My lord, I do not know,
But truly I do fear it.

POLONIUS What said he?

OPHELIA He took me by the wrist, and held me hard,
Then goes he to the length of all his arm,
And with his other hand thus o'er his brow,
He falls to such perusal of my face
As 'a would draw it. Long stayed he so,
At last, a little shaking of mine arm,
And thrice his head thus waving up and down,
He raised a sigh so piteous and profound
As it did seem to shatter all his bulk,
And end his being; that done, he lets me go,
And with his head over his shoulder turned
He seemed to find his way without his eyes,

For out adoors he went without their helps,
And to the last bended their light on me.

POLONIUS Come, go with me. I will go seek the king.
This is the very ecstasy of love,
Whose violent property fordoes itself,
And leads the will to desperate undertakings,
As oft as any passion under heaven
That does afflict our natures: I am sorry –
What, have you given him any hard words of late?

OPHELIA No, my good lord, but as you did command
I did repel his letters, and denied
His access to me.

POLONIUS That hath made him mad.
I am sorry that with better heed and judgment
I had not quoted him. I feared he did but trifle
And meant to wreck thee, but beshrew my jealousy
By heaven, it is as proper to our age
To cast beyond ourselves in our opinions,
As it is common for the younger sort
To lack discretion; come, go we to the king.
This must be known, which, being kept close, might move
More grief to hide, than hate to utter love.
Come. [*they go*

SCENE 2

An audience chamber in the castle; at the back a lobby, with curtains to left and right of the entry and a door to the rear within

A flourish of trumpets. The KING *and* QUEEN *enter followed by* ROSENCRANTZ, GUILDENSTERN, *and attendants*

KING Welcome, dear Rosencrantz and Guildenstern!
Moreover that we much did long to see you,
The need we have to use you did provoke
Our hasty sending. Something have you heard
Of Hamlet's transformation – so call it,
Sith nor th'exterior nor the inward man
Resembles that it was. What it should be,

More than his father's death, that thus hath put him
So much from th'understanding of himself,
I cannot dream of: I entreat you both,
That being of so young days brought up with him,
And sith so neighboured to his youth and haviour,
That you vouchsafe your rest here in our court
Some little time, so by your companies
To draw him on to pleasures, and to gather
So much as from occasion you may glean
Whether aught to us unknown afflicts him thus,
That opened lies within our remedy.

QUEEN Good gentlemen, he hath much talked of you,
And sure I am two men there are not living
To whom he more adheres. If it will please you
To show us so much gentry and good will
As to expend your time with us awhile,
For the supply and profit of our hope,
Your visitation shall receive such thanks
As fits a king's remembrance.

ROSENC'Z Both your majesties
Might by the sovereign power you have of us,
Put your dread pleasures more into command
Than to entreaty.

GUILD'RN But we both obey,
And here give up ourselves in the full bent,
To lay our service freely at your feet
To be commanded.

KING Thanks Rosencrantz, and gentle Guildenstern.

QUEEN Thanks Guildenstern, and gentle Rosencrantz,
And I beseech you instantly to visit
My too much changèd son. Go some of you
And bring these gentlemen where Hamlet is.

GUILD'RN Heavens make our presence and our practices
Pleasant and helpful to him!

QUEEN Ay, amen!
[*Rosencrantz and Guildenstern bow and depart*

POLONIUS *enters, and speaks with the King apart*

POLONIUS The ambassadors from Norway, my good lord,
Are joyfully returned.

KING Thou still hast been the father of good news.
POLONIUS Have I, my lord? Assure you, my good liege,
I hold my duty as I hold my soul,
Both to my God and to my gracious king;
And I do think, or else this brain of mine
Hunts not the trail of policy so sure
As it hath used to do, that I have found
The very cause of Hamlet's lunacy.
KING O speak of that, that do I long to hear.
POLONIUS Give first admittance to th'ambassadors.
My news shall be the fruit to that great feast.
KING Thyself do grace to them, and bring them in.
[*Polonius goes out*
He tells me, my dear Gertrude, he hath found
The head and source of all your son's distemper.
QUEEN I doubt it is no other but the main,
His father's death and our o'erhasty marriage.
KING Well, we shall sift him.

POLONIUS *returns with* VALTEMAND *and* CORNELIUS

Welcome, my good friends!
Say Valtemand, what from our brother Norway?
VALTEM'D Most fair return of greetings and desires; [*they bow*
Upon our first, he sent out to suppress
His nephew's levies, which to him appeared
To be a preparation 'gainst the Polack,
But better looked into, he truly found
It was against your highness, whereat grieved
That so his sickness, age and impotence
Was falsely borne in hand, sends out arrests
On Fortinbras, which he in brief obeys,
Receives rebuke from Norway, and in fine,
Makes vow before his uncle never more
To give th'assay of arms against your majesty:
Whereon old Norway, overcome with joy,
Gives him threescore thousand crowns in annual fee,
And his commission to employ those soldiers,
So levied, as before, against the Polack,
With an entreaty, herein further shown,
That it might please you to give quiet pass

Through your dominions for this enterprise,
On such regards of safety and allowance
As therein are set down. *[he proffers a paper*

KING *[takes it]* It likes us well,
And at our more considered time, we'll read,
Answer, and think upon this business:
Meantime, we thank you for your well-took labour.
Go to your rest, at night we'll feast together.
Most welcome home!
[Valtemand and Cornelius bow and depart

POLONIUS This business is well ended.
My liege and madam, to expostulate
What majesty should be, what duty is,
Why day is day, night night, and time is time,
Were nothing but to waste night, day and time.
Therefore since brevity is the soul of wit,
And tediousness the limbs and outward flourishes,
I will be brief – your noble son is mad:
Mad call I it, for to define true madness,
What is't but to be nothing else but mad?
But let that go.

QUEEN More matter, with less art.

POLONIUS Madam, I swear I use no art at all.
That he is mad 'tis true, 'tis true, 'tis pity,
And pity 'tis 'tis true – a foolish figure,
But farewell it, for I will use no art.
Mad let us grant him then, and now remains
That we find out the cause of this effect,
Or rather say, the cause of this defect,
For this effect defective comes by cause:
Thus it remains, and the remainder thus.
Perpend. *[he takes papers from his doublet*
I have a daughter, have while she is mine,
Who in her duty and obedience, mark,
Hath given me this, now gather and surmise. *[he reads]*
'To the celestial, and my soul's idol, the most beautified Ophelia,' –
That's an ill phrase, a vile phrase, 'beautified' is a vile phrase, but you shall hear. Thus: *[he reads]*

'In her excellent white bosom, these, etc.' –

QUEEN Came this from Hamlet to her?

POLONIUS Good madam, stay awhile, I will be faithful – [*he reads*]

'Doubt thou the stars are fire,
Doubt that the sun doth move,
Doubt truth to be a liar,
But never doubt I love.

O dear Ophelia, I am ill at these numbers, I have not art to reckon my groans, but that I love thee best, O most best, believe it. Adieu.

Thine evermore, most dear lady, whilst this machine is to him, Hamlet.'

This in obedience hath my daughter shown me,
And more above hath his solicitings,
As they fell out by time, by means, and place,
All given to mine ear.

KING But how hath she
Received his love?

POLONIUS What do you think of me ?

KING As of a man faithful and honourable.

POLONIUS I would fain prove so. But what might you think
When I had seen this hot love on the wing,
As I perceived it (I must tell you that)
Before my daughter told me, what might you,
Or my dear majesty your queen here think,
If I had played the desk or table-book,
Or given my heart a working mute and dumb,
Or looked upon this love with idle sight,
What might you think? No, I went round to work,
And my young mistress thus I did bespeak –
'Lord Hamlet is a prince out of thy star,
This must not be': and then I prescripts gave her
That she should lock herself from his resort,
Admit no messengers, receive no tokens.
Which done, she took the fruits of my advice:
And he repellèd, a short tale to make,
Fell into a sadness, then into a fast,
Thence to a watch, thence into a weakness,
Thence to a lightness, and by this declension,

Into the madness wherein now he raves,
And all we mourn for.

KING Do you think 'tis this?

QUEEN It may be, very like.

POLONIUS Hath there been such a time, I would fain know that,
That I have positively said ' 'Tis so',
When it proved otherwise?

KING Not that I know.

POLONIUS Take this from this, if this be otherwise;

[he points to his head and shoulder

If circumstances lead me, I will find
Where truth is hid, though it were hid indeed
Within the centre.

HAMLET, *disorderly attired and reading a book, enters the lobby by the door at the back; he hears voices from the chamber and pauses a moment beside one of the curtains, unobserved*

KING How may we try it further?

POLONIUS You know sometimes he walks four hours together
Here in the lobby.

QUEEN So he does, indeed.

POLONIUS At such a time I'll loose my daughter to him.
Be you and I behind an arras then;
Mark the encounter, if he love her not,
And be not from his reason fall'n thereon,
Let me be no assistant for a state,
But keep a farm and carters.

KING We will try it.

HAMLET *comes forward, his eyes on the book*

QUEEN But look where sadly the poor wretch comes reading.

POLONIUS Away, I do beseech you both away,
I'll board him presently, O give me leave.

[the King and Queen hurry forth

How does my good Lord Hamlet?

HAMLET Well, God-a-mercy.

POLONIUS Do you know me, my lord?

HAMLET Excellent well, you are a fishmonger.

POLONIUS Not I, my lord.

HAMLET Then I would you were so honest a man.

POLONIUS Honest, my lord?

HAMLET Ay sir, to be honest as this world goes, is to be one man picked out of ten thousand.

POLONIUS That's very true, my lord.

HAMLET For if the sun breed maggots in a dead dog, being a good kissing carrion. Have you a daughter?

POLONIUS I have, my lord.

HAMLET Let her not walk i'th'sun. Conception is a blessing, but as your daughter may conceive, friend look to't.

[he reads again

POLONIUS How say you by that? Still harping on my daughter, yet he knew me not at first, 'a said I was a fishmonger. 'A is far gone, far gone, and truly in my youth I suffered much extremity for love, very near this. I'll speak to him again – What do you read, my lord?

HAMLET Words, words, words.

POLONIUS What is the matter, my lord?

HAMLET Between who?

POLONIUS I mean the matter that you read, my lord.

HAMLET *[bears down upon him, Polonius retreating backwards]* Slanders, sir; for the satirical rogue says here that old men have grey beards, that their faces are wrinkled, their eyes purging thick amber and plum-tree gum, and that they have a plentiful lack of wit, together with most weak hams – all which, sir, though I most powerfully and potently believe, yet I hold it not honesty to have it thus set down, for yourself, sir, shall grow old as I am, if like a crab you could go backward.

[he reads again

POLONIUS Though this be madness, yet there is method in't. Will you walk out of the air, my lord?

HAMLET Into my grave.

POLONIUS Indeed, that's out of the air; how pregnant sometimes his replies are! A happiness that often madness hits on, which reason and sanity could not so prosperously be delivered of. I will leave him, and suddenly contrive the means of meeting between him and my daughter. – My honourable lord, I will most humbly take my leave of you.

HAMLET You cannot, sir, take from me anything that I will more willingly part withal: except my life, except my life, except my life.

POLONIUS Fare you well, my lord. [*he bows low*

HAMLET These tedious old fools! [*he returns to his book*

ROSENCRANTZ *and* GUILDENSTERN *enter*

POLONIUS You go to seek the Lord Hamlet, there he is.

ROSENC'Z [*to Polonius*] God save you, sir! [*Polonius goes out*

GUILD'RN My honoured lord!

ROSENC'Z My most dear lord!

HAMLET [*looks up*] My excellent good friends! How dost thou, Guildenstern? [*putting up the book*
Ah, Rosencrantz! Good lads, how do you both?

ROSENC'Z As the indifferent children of the earth.

GUILD'RN Happy, in that we are not over-happy,
On Fortune's cap we are not the very button.

HAMLET Nor the soles of her shoe?

ROSENC'Z Neither, my lord.

HAMLET Then you live about her waist or in the middle of her favours?

GUILD'RN Faith, her privates we.

HAMLET In the secret parts of fortune? O most true, she is a strumpet. What's the news?

ROSENC'Z None, my lord, but that the world's grown honest.

HAMLET Then is doomsday near. But your news is not true. Let me question more in particular: what have you, my good friends, deserved at the hands of Fortune, that she sends you to prison hither?

GUILD'RN Prison, my lord!

HAMLET Denmark's a prison.

ROSENC'Z Then is the world one.

HAMLET A goodly one, in which there are many confines, wards and dungeons; Denmark being one o'th'worst.

ROSENC'Z We think not so, my lord.

HAMLET Why, then 'tis none to you; for there is nothing either good or bad, but thinking makes it so: to me it is a prison.

ROSENC'Z Why, then your ambition makes it one: 'tis too narrow for your mind.

HAMLET O God! I could be bounded in a nut-shell, and count

myself a king of infinite space; were it not that I have bad dreams.

GUILD'RN Which dreams, indeed, are ambition: for the very substance of the ambitious is merely the shadow of a dream.

HAMLET A dream itself is but a shadow.

ROSENC'Z Truly, and I hold ambition of so airy and light a quality, that it is but a shadow's shadow.

HAMLET Then are our beggars bodies, and our monarchs and outstretched heroes the beggars' shadows. Shall we to th' court? For, by my fay, I cannot reason.

ROSENC'Z, GUILD'RN We'll wait upon you.

HAMLET No such matter: I will not sort you with the rest of my servants; for to speak to you like an honest man, I am most dreadfully attended. But, in the beaten way of friendship, what make you at Elsinore?

ROSENC'Z To visit you, my lord, no other occasion.

HAMLET Beggar that I am, I am even poor in thanks, but I thank you – and sure, dear friends, my thanks are too dear a halfpenny: were you not sent for? Is it your own inclining? Is it a free visitation? Come, come, deal justly with me, come, come, nay speak.

GUILD'RN What should we say, my lord?

HAMLET Why, anything but to th'purpose. You were sent for, and there is a kind of confession in your looks, which your modesties have not craft enough to colour – I know the good king and queen have sent for you.

ROSENC'Z To what end, my lord?

HAMLET That you must teach me: but let me conjure you, by the rights of our fellowship, by the consonancy of our youth, by the obligation of our ever-preserved love, and by what more dear a better proposer can charge you withal, be even and direct with me whether you were sent for or no?

ROSENC'Z What say you? [*to Guildenstern*

HAMLET Nay then, I have an eye of you!
[*aloud*] If you love me, hold not off.

GUILD'RN My lord, we were sent for.

HAMLET I will tell you why, so shall my anticipation prevent your discovery, and your secrecy to the king and queen moult no feather. I have of late, but wherefore I know not, lost all my mirth, forgone all custom of exercises: and indeed it goes so heavily with my disposition, that this goodly frame the earth, seems to me a sterile promontory, this most excellent canopy the air, look you, this brave o'erhanging firmament, this majestical roof fretted with golden fire, why it appeareth nothing to me but a foul and pestilent congregation of vapours. What a piece of work is a man, how noble in reason, how infinite in faculties, in form and moving, how express and admirable in action, how like an angel in apprehension, how like a god: the beauty of the world; the paragon of animals; and yet to me, what is this quintessence of dust? man delights not me, no, nor woman neither, though by your smiling you seem to say so.

ROSENC'Z My lord, there was no such stuff in my thoughts.

HAMLET Why did ye laugh then, when I said 'man delights not me'?

ROSENC'Z To think, my lord, if you delight not in man, what lenten entertainment the players shall receive from you. We coted them on the way, and hither are they coming to offer you service.

HAMLET He that plays the King shall be welcome, his majesty shall have tribute on me, the adventurous Knight shall use his foil and target, the Lover shall not sigh gratis, the Humorous Man shall end his part in peace, the Clown shall make those laugh whose lungs are tickle o'th'sere, and the Lady shall say her mind freely – or the blank verse shall halt for't. What players are they?

ROSENC'Z Even those you were wont to take such delight in, the tragedians of the city.

HAMLET How chances it they travel? Their residence both in reputation and profit was better both ways.

ROSENC'Z I think their inhibition comes by the means of the late innovation.

HAMLET Do they hold the same estimation they did when I was in the city? Are they so followed?

ROSENC'Z No, indeed, are they not.

HAMLET How comes it? do they grow rusty?

ROSENC'Z Nay, their endeavour keeps in the wonted pace; but there is, sir, an eyrie of children, little eyases, that cry out on the top of question, and are most tyrannically clapped for't: these are now the fashion, and so berattle the common stages (so they call them) that many wearing rapiers are afraid of goose-quills, and dare scarce come thither.

HAMLET What, are they children? Who maintains 'em? How are they escoted? Will they pursue the quality no longer than they can sing? will they not say afterwards if they should grow themselves to common players (as it is like most will if their means are not better) their writers do them wrong, to make them exclaim against their own succession?

ROSENC'Z Faith, there has been much to-do on both sides: and the nation holds it no sin to tarre them to controversy. There was, for a while, no money bid for argument, unless the Poet and the Player went to cuffs in the question.

HAMLET Is't possible?

GUILD'RN O, there has been much throwing about of brains.

HAMLET Do the boys carry it away?

ROSENC'Z Ay, that they do my lord, Hercules and his load too.

HAMLET It is not very strange, for my uncle is king of Denmark, and those that would make mows at him while my father lived, give twenty, forty, fifty, a hundred ducats apiece for his picture in little. 'Sblood, there is something in this more than natural, if philosophy could find it out. [*'A flourish' of trumpets heard*

GUILD'RN There are the players.

HAMLET Gentlemen, you are welcome to Elsinore. [*he bows*] Your hands? Come then, th'appurtenance of welcome is fashion and ceremony; let me comply with you in this garb [*he takes their hands*], lest my extent to the players, which I tell you must show fairly outwards, should more appear like entertainment than yours. You are welcome: but my uncle-father, and aunt-mother, are deceived.

GUILD'RN In what, my dear lord?

HAMLET I am but mad north-north-west; when the wind is southerly, I know a hawk from a handsaw.

POLONIUS *enters*

POLONIUS Well be with you, gentlemen!

HAMLET Hark you Guildenstern, and you too, at each ear a hearer – that great baby you see there is not yet out of his swaddling-clouts.

ROSENC'Z Happily he is the second time come to them, for they say an old man is twice a child.

HAMLET I will prophesy, he comes to tell me of the players, mark it. [*raises his voice*] You say right sir, a Monday morning, 'twas then indeed.

POLONIUS My lord, I have news to tell you.

HAMLET My lord, I have news to tell you. When Roscius was an actor in Rome –

POLONIUS The actors are come hither, my lord.

HAMLET Buz, buz!

POLONIUS Upon my honour –

HAMLET 'Then came each actor on his ass' –

POLONIUS The best actors in the world, either for tragedy, comedy, history, pastoral, pastoral-comical, historical-pastoral, tragical-historical, tragical-comical-historical-pastoral, scene individable, or poem unlimited. Seneca cannot be too heavy nor Plautus too light. For the law of writ and the liberty, these are the only men.

HAMLET O Jephthah, judge of Israel, what a treasure hadst thou!

POLONIUS What a treasure had he, my lord?

HAMLET Why,

'One fair daughter, and no more,
The which he lovèd passing well.'

POLONIUS Still on my daughter.

HAMLET Am I not i'th' right, old Jephthah?

POLONIUS If you call me Jephthah, my lord, I have a daughter that I love passing well.

HAMLET Nay, that follows not.

POLONIUS What follows then, my lord?

HAMLET Why,

'As by lot, God wot',
and then you know
'It came to pass, as most like it was.'
The first row of the pious chanson will show you more, for look where my abridgement comes.

'Enter four or five Players'

You are welcome masters, welcome all – I am glad to see thee well – Welcome, good friends – O, my old friend! Why, thy face is valanced since I saw thee last, com'st thou to beard me in Denmark? – What, my young lady and mistress! By'r lady, your ladyship is nearer to heaven than when I saw you last by the altitude of a chopine. Pray God your voice, like a piece of uncurrent gold, be not cracked within the ring. Masters, you are all welcome. We'll e'en to't like French falconers, fly at anything we see, we'll have a speech straight. [*to the First Player*] Come give us a taste of your quality, come, a passionate speech.

I PLAYER What speech, my good lord?

HAMLET I heard thee speak me a speech once, but it was never acted, or if it was, not above once, for the play I remember pleased not the million, 'twas caviary to the general, but it was – as I received it, and others, whose judgments in such matters cried in the top of mine – an excellent play, well digested in the scenes, set down with as much modesty as cunning. I remember one said there were no sallets in the lines, to make the matter savoury, nor no matter in the phrase that might indict the author of affection, but called it an honest method, as wholesome as sweet, and by very much more handsome than fine: one speech in't I chiefly loved, 'twas Aeneas' tale to Dido, and thereabout of it especially where he speaks of Priam's slaughter. If it live in your memory begin at this line, let me see, let me see –
'The rugged Pyrrhus, like th'Hyrcanian beast' –
'tis not so, it begins with Pyrrhus –
'The rugged Pyrrhus, he whose sable arms,
Black as his purpose, did the night resemble
When he lay couchèd in th'ominous horse,

Hath now this dread and black complexion smeared
With heraldry more dismal: head to foot
Now is he total gules, horridly tricked
With blood of fathers, mothers, daughters, sons,
Baked and impasted with the parching streets,
That lend a tyrannous and a damnèd light
To their lord's murder. Roasted in wrath and fire,
And thus o'er-sizèd with coagulate gore,
With eyes like carbuncles, the hellish Pyrrhus
Old grandsire Priam seeks.'
So proceed you.

POLONIUS 'Fore God, my lord, well spoken, with good accent and good discretion.

I PLAYER 'Anon he finds him
Striking too short at Greeks; his antique sword,
Rebellious to his arm, lies where it falls,
Repugnant to command; unequal matched,
Pyrrhus at Priam drives, in rage strikes wide,
But with the whiff and wind of his fell sword
Th'unnervèd father falls: then senseless Ilium,
Seeming to feel this blow, with flaming top
Stoops to his base; and with a hideous crash
Takes prisoner Pyrrhus' ear. For lo! his sword,
Which was declining on the milky head
Of reverend Priam, seemed i'th'air to stick,
So as a painted tyrant Pyrrhus stood,
And like a neutral to his will and matter,
Did nothing:
But as we often see, against some storm,
A silence in the heavens, the rack stand still,
The bold winds speechless, and the orb below
As hush as death, anon the dreadful thunder
Doth rend the region, so after Pyrrhus' pause,
A rousèd vengeance sets him new awork,
And never did the Cyclops' hammers fall
On Mars's armour, forged for proof eterne,
With less remorse than Pyrrhus' bleeding sword
Now falls on Priam.
Out, out, thou strumpet Fortune! All you gods,

In general synod take away her power,
Break all the spokes and fellies from her wheel,
And bowl the round nave down the hill of heaven
As low as to the fiends.'

POLONIUS This is too long.

HAMLET It shall to the barber's with your beard; prithee say on – he's for a jig, or a tale of bawdry, or he sleeps – say on, come to Hecuba.

I PLAYER 'But who, ah woe! had seen the mobled queen – '

HAMLET 'The mobled queen'?

POLONIUS That's good, 'mobled queen' is good.

I PLAYER 'Run barefoot up and down, threat'ning the flames
With bisson rheum, a clout upon that head
Where late the diadem stood, and for a robe,
About her lank and all o'er-teemèd loins,
A blanket in the alarm of fear caught up –
Who this had seen, with tongue in venom steeped,
'Gainst Fortune's state would treason have pronounced;
But if the gods themselves did see her then,
When she saw Pyrrhus make malicious sport
In mincing with his sword her husband's limbs,
The instant burst of clamour that she made,
Unless things mortal move them not at all,
Would have made milch the burning eyes of heaven,
And passion in the gods.'

POLONIUS Look whe'r he has not turned his colour, and has tears in's eyes – prithee no more.

HAMLET 'Tis well, I'll have thee speak out the rest of this soon. Good my lord, will you see the players well bestowed; do you hear, let them be well used, for they are the abstracts and brief chronicles of the time; after your death you were better have a bad epitaph than their ill report while you live.

POLONIUS My lord, I will use them according to their desert.

HAMLET God's bodkin, man, much better! Use every man after his desert, and who shall 'scape whipping? Use them after your own honour and dignity – the less they deserve the more merit is in your bounty. Take them in.

POLONIUS Come, sirs. [*he goes to the door*

HAMLET Follow him, friends, we'll hear a play tomorrow. [*he stops the First Player*] Dost thou hear me, old friend, can you play The Murder of Gonzago?

I PLAYER Ay, my lord.

HAMLET We'll ha't tomorrow night. You could for a need study a speech of some dozen or sixteen lines, which I would set down and insert in't, could you not?

I PLAYER Ay, my lord. [*Polonius and the Players go out*

HAMLET Very well. Follow that lord, and look you mock him not. [*to Rosencrantz and Guildenstern*] My good friends, I'll leave you till night. You are welcome to Elsinore.

ROSENC'Z Good my lord. [*they take their leave*

HAMLET Ay, so, God bye to you! Now I am alone.
O, what a rogue and peasant slave am I!
Is it not monstrous that this player here,
But in a fiction, in a dream of passion,
Could force his soul so to his own conceit
That from her working all his visage wanned,
Tears in his eyes, distraction in his aspect,
A broken voice, and his whole function suiting
With forms to his conceit; and all for nothing!
For Hecuba!
What's Hecuba to him, or he to Hecuba,
That he should weep for her? What would he do,
Had he the motive and the cue for passion
That I have? He would drown the stage with tears,
And cleave the general ear with horrid speech,
Make mad the guilty and appal the free,
Confound the ignorant, and amaze indeed
The very faculties of eyes and ears; yet I,
A dull and muddy-mettled rascal, peak
Like John-a-dreams, unpregnant of my cause,
And can say nothing; no, not for a king,
Upon whose property and most dear life
A damned defeat was made: am I a coward?
Who calls me villain, breaks my pate across,
Plucks off my beard and blows it in my face
Tweaks me by the nose, gives me the lie i'th'throat
As deep as to the lungs – who does me this,

Ha, 'swounds, I should take it: for it cannot be
But I am pigeon-livered, and lack gall
To make oppression bitter, or ere this
I should ha' fatted all the region kites
With this slave's offal. Bloody, bawdy villain!
Remorseless, treacherous, lecherous, kindless villain!
O, vengeance!
Why, what an ass am I. This is most brave,
That I, the son of a dear father murdered,
Prompted to my revenge by heaven and hell,
Must like a whore unpack my heart with words,
And fall a-cursing like a very drab;
A stallion! Fie upon't! Foh!
About, my brains; hum, I have heard
That guilty creatures sitting at a play
Have by the very cunning of the scene
Been struck so to the soul, that presently
They have proclaimed their malefactions:
For murder, though it have no tongue, will speak
With most miraculous organ: I'll have these players
Play something like the murder of my father
Before mine uncle, I'll observe his looks,
I'll tent him to the quick; if 'a do blench
I know my course. The spirit that I have seen
May be a devil, and the devil hath power
T'assume a pleasing shape, yea, and perhaps
Out of my weakness and my melancholy,
As he is very potent with such spirits,
Abuses me to damn me; I'll have grounds
More relative than this – the play's the thing
Wherein I'll catch the conscience of the king. [*he goes*

[*a day passes*]

ACT 3 SCENE 1

The lobby of the audience chamber, the walls hung with arras; a table in the midst; to one side a faldstool with a crucifix

The KING *and the* QUEEN *enter with* POLONIUS, ROSENCRANTZ, *and* GUILDENSTERN; OPHELIA *follows a little behind*

KING And can you by no drift of conference
Get from him why he puts on this confusion,
Grating so harshly all his days of quiet
With turbulent and dangerous lunacy?

ROSENC'Z He does confess he feels himself distracted,
But from what cause 'a will by no means speak.

GUILD'RN Nor do we find him forward to be sounded,
But with a crafty madness keeps aloof
When we would bring him on to some confession
Of his true state.

QUEEN Did he receive you well?

ROSENC'Z Most like a gentleman.

GUILD'RN But with much forcing of his disposition.

ROSENC'Z Niggard of question, but of our demands
Most free in his reply.

QUEEN Did you assay him
To any pastime?

ROSENC'Z Madam, it so fell out that certain players
We o'er-raught on the way. Of these we told him,
And there did seem in him a kind of joy
To hear of it: they are here about the court,
And as I think, they have already order
This night to play before him.

POLONIUS 'Tis most true,
And he beseeched me to entreat your majesties
To hear and see the matter.

KING With all my heart, and it doth much content me
To hear him so inclined.
Good gentlemen, give him a further edge,

And drive his purpose into these delights.
ROSENC'Z We shall, my lord.
[*Rosencrantz and Guildenstern go out*
KING Sweet Gertrude, leave us too,
For we have closely sent for Hamlet hither,
That he, as 'twere by accident, may here
Affront Ophelia;
Her father and myself, lawful espials,
Will so bestow ourselves, that seeing unseen,
We may of their encounter frankly judge,
And gather by him as he is behaved,
If't be th'affliction of his love or no
That thus he suffers for.
QUEEN I shall obey you –
And for your part, Ophelia, I do wish
That your good beauties be the happy cause
Of Hamlet's wildness, so shall I hope your virtues
Will bring him to his wonted way again,
To both your honours.
OPHELIA Madam, I wish it may.
[*the Queen goes*
POLONIUS Ophelia, walk you here. Gracious, so please you,
We will bestow ourselves. Read on this book,
[*he takes a book from the faldstool*
That show of such an exercise may colour
Your loneliness; we are oft to blame in this,
'Tis too much proved, that with devotion's visage
And pious action we do sugar o'er
The devil himself.
KING O, 'tis too true,
How smart a lash that speech doth give my conscience.
The harlot's cheek, beautied with plast'ring art,
Is not more ugly to the thing that helps it,
Than is my deed to my most painted word:
O heavy burden!
POLONIUS I hear him coming, let's withdraw, my lord.
[*they bestow themselves behind the arras;*
Ophelia kneels at the faldstool

HAMLET *enters*

HAMLET To be, or not to be, that is the question,
Whether 'tis nobler in the mind to suffer
The slings and arrows of outrageous fortune,
Or to take arms against a sea of troubles,
And by opposing, end them. To die, to sleep –
No more, and by a sleep to say we end
The heart-ache, and the thousand natural shocks
That flesh is heir to; 'tis a consummation
Devoutly to be wished to die to sleep!
To sleep, perchance to dream, ay there's the rub,
For in that sleep of death what dreams may come
When we have shuffled off this mortal coil
Must give us pause – there's the respect
That makes calamity of so long life:
For who would bear the whips and scorns of time,
Th'oppressor's wrong, the proud man's contumely,
The pangs of disprized love, the law's delay,
The insolence of office, and the spurns
That patient merit of th'unworthy takes,
When he himself might his quietus make
With a bare bodkin; who would fardels bear,
To grunt and sweat under a weary life,
But that the dread of something after death,
The undiscovered country, from whose bourn
No traveller returns, puzzles the will,
And makes us rather bear those ills we have,
Than fly to others that we know not of?
Thus conscience does make cowards of us all,
And thus the native hue of resolution
Is sicklied o'er with the pale cast of thought,
And enterprises of great pitch and moment
With this regard their currents turn awry,
And lose the name of action. Soft you now,
The fair Ophelia – Nymph, in thy orisons
Be all my sins remembered.

OPHELIA [*rises*] Good my lord,
How does your honour for this many a day?

HAMLET I humbly thank you, well, well, well.

OPHELIA My lord, I have remembrances of yours,
That I have longèd long to re-deliver.
I pray you now receive them.

HAMLET No, not I,
I never gave you aught.

OPHELIA My honoured lord, you know right well you did,
And with them words of so sweet breath composed
As made the things more rich. Their perfume lost,
Take these again, for to the noble mind
Rich gifts wax poor when givers prove unkind.
There, my lord. [*she takes jewels from her bosom and places them on the table before him*

HAMLET [*remembers the plot*] Ha, ha! Are you honest?

OPHELIA My lord?

HAMLET Are you fair?

OPHELIA What means your lordship?

HAMLET That if you be honest and fair, your honesty should admit no discourse to your beauty.

OPHELIA Could beauty, my lord, have better commerce than with honesty?

HAMLET Ay truly, for the power of beauty will sooner transform honesty from what it is to a bawd, than the force of honesty can translate beauty into his likeness. This was sometime a paradox, but now the time gives it proof. I did love you once.

OPHELIA Indeed, my lord, you made me believe so.

HAMLET You should not have believed me, for virtue cannot so inoculate our old stock, but we shall relish of it – I loved you not.

OPHELIA I was the more deceived.

HAMLET [*points to the faldstool*] Get thee to a nunnery, why wouldst thou be a breeder of sinners? I am myself indifferent honest, but yet I could accuse me of such things, that it were better my mother had not borne me: I am very proud, revengeful, ambitious, with more offences at my beck, than I have thoughts to put them in, imagination to give them shape, or time to act them in: what should such fellows as I do crawling between earth and heaven? We are arrant knaves all, believe none of us – go thy ways to a nunnery. [*suddenly*] Where's your father?

OPHELIA At home, my lord.

HAMLET Let the doors be shut upon him, that he may play the fool nowhere but in's own house. Farewell.

[*he goes out*

OPHELIA [*kneels before the crucifix*] O help him, you sweet heavens!

HAMLET [*returns, distraught*] If thou dost marry, I'll give thee this plague for thy dowry – be thou as chaste as ice, as pure as snow, thou shalt not escape calumny; get thee to a nunnery, go, farewell. [*he paces to and fro*] Or if thou wilt needs marry, marry a fool, for wise men know well enough what monsters you make of them: to a nunnery, go, and quickly too, farewell. [*he rushes out*

OPHELIA O heavenly powers, restore him!

HAMLET [*once more returning*] I have heard of your paintings too, well enough. God hath given you one face and you make yourselves another, you jig, you amble, and you lisp, you nickname God's creatures, and make your wantonness your ignorance; go to, I'll no more on't, it hath made me mad. I say we will have no mo marriage – those that are married already, all but one, shall live, the rest shall keep as they are: to a nunnery, go. [*he departs again*

OPHELIA O, what a noble mind is here o'erthrown!
The courtier's, soldier's, scholar's, eye, tongue, sword,
Th'expectancy and rose of the fair state,
The glass of fashion, and the mould of form,
Th'observed of all observers, quite quite down,
And I of ladies most deject and wretched,
That sucked the honey of his music vows,
Now see that noble and most sovereign reason
Like sweet bells jangled, out of tune and harsh,
That unmatched form and feature of blown youth,
Blasted with ecstasy! O, woe is me!
T'have seen what I have seen, see what I see!

[*she prays*

The KING *and* POLONIUS *steal forth from behind the arras*

KING Love! his affections do not that way tend,
Nor what he spake, though it lacked form a little,
Was not like madness – there's something in his soul
O'er which his melancholy sits on brood,
And I do doubt the hatch and the disclose
Will be some danger; which for to prevent,
I have in quick determination
Thus set it down: he shall with speed to England,
For the demand of our neglected tribute.
Haply the seas, and countries different,
With variable objects, shall expel
This something-settled matter in his heart,
Whereon his brains still beating puts him thus
From fashion of himself. What think you on't?
[*Ophelia comes forward*

POLONIUS It shall do well. But yet do I believe
The origin and commencement of his grief
Sprung from neglected love. How now, Ophelia?
You need not tell us what Lord Hamlet said,
We heard it all. My lord, do as you please,
But if you hold it fit, after the play,
Let his queen-mother all alone entreat him
To show his grief, let her be round with him,
And I'll be placed (so please you) in the ear
Of all their conference. If she find him not,
To England send him; or confine him where
Your wisdom best shall think.

KING It shall be so,
Madness in great ones must not unwatched go.
[*they depart*

SCENE 2

The hall of the castle, with seats set to both sides as for a spectacle; at the back a dais with curtains concealing an inner stage

'HAMLET, *and three of the Players' come from behind the curtains*

HAMLET [*to the First Player*] Speak the speech I pray you as I pronounced it to you, trippingly on the tongue, but if you mouth it as many of your players do, I had as lief the town-crier spoke my lines. Nor do not saw the air too much with your hand thus, but use all gently, for in the very torrent, tempest, and as I may say whirlwind of your passion, you must acquire and beget a temperance that may give it smoothness. O, it offends me to the soul, to hear a robustious periwig-pated fellow tear a passion to tatters, to very rags, to split the ears of the groundlings, who for the most part are capable of nothing but inexplicable dumb-shows and noise: I would have such a fellow whipped for o'erdoing Termagant, it out-herods Herod, pray you avoid it.

I PLAYER I warrant your honour.

HAMLET Be not too tame neither, but let your own discretion be your tutor, suit the action to the word, the word to the action, with this special observance, that you o'erstep not the modesty of nature: for anything so o'erdone is from the purpose of playing, whose end both at the first, and now, was and is, to hold as 'twere the mirror up to nature, to show virtue her own feature, scorn her own image, and the very age and body of the time his form and pressure. Now this overdone, or come tardy off, though it make the unskilful laugh, cannot but make the judicious grieve, the censure of the which one must in your allowance o'erweigh a whole theatre of others. O there be players that I have seen play – and heard others praise, and that highly – not to speak it profanely, that neither having th'accent of Christians, nor the gait of Christian, pagan, nor man, have so strutted and bellowed, that I have thought some of nature's journeymen had made men, and not made them well, they imitated humanity so abominably.

I PLAYER I hope we have reformed that indifferently with us, sir.

HAMLET O reform it altogether, and let those that play your clowns speak no more than is set down for them, for there be of them that will themselves laugh, to set on some quantity of barren spectators to laugh too, though in the mean time some necessary question of the play be then to be considered. That's villainous, and shows a most pitiful ambition in the fool that uses it. Go, make you ready.

[the Players retire behind the curtains

POLONIUS *enters with* ROSENCRANTZ *and* GUILDENSTERN

How now, my lord? Will the king hear this piece of work?

POLONIUS And the queen too, and that presently.

HAMLET Bid the players make haste.

[Polonius bows and departs

Will you two help to hasten them?

ROSENC'Z Ay, my lord.

[Rosencrantz and Guildenstern follow Polonius

HAMLET What, ho! Horatio!

HORATIO *comes in*

HORATIO Here, sweet lord, at your service.

HAMLET Horatio, thou art e'en as just a man
As e'er my conversation coped withal.

HORATIO O, my dear lord, –

HAMLET Nay, do not think I flatter,
For what advancement may I hope from thee,
That no revenue hast but thy good spirits
To feed and clothe thee? Why should the poor be flattered?
No, let the candied tongue lick absurd pomp,
And crook the pregnant hinges of the knee
Where thrift may follow fawning. Dost thou hear?
Since my dear soul was mistress of her choice,
And could of men distinguish her election,

Sh' hath sealed thee for herself, for thou hast been
As one in suff'ring all that suffers nothing,
A man that Fortune's buffets and rewards
Hast ta'en with equal thanks; and blest are those
Whose blood and judgment are so well co-meddled,
That they are not a pipe for Fortune's finger
To sound what stop she please: give me that man
That is not passion's slave, and I will wear him
In my heart's core, ay in my heart of heart,
As I do thee. Something too much of this –
There is a play tonight before the king,
One scene of it comes near the circumstance
Which I have told thee of my father's death.
I prithee when thou seest that act afoot,
Even with the very comment of thy soul
Observe my uncle – if his occulted guilt
Do not itself unkennel in one speech,
It is a damnèd ghost that we have seen,
And my imaginations are as foul
As Vulcan's stithy; give him heedful note,
For I mine eyes will rivet to his face,
And after we will both our judgments join
In censure of his seeming.

HORATIO Well, my lord,
If 'a steal aught the whilst this play is playing,
And 'scape detecting, I will pay the theft.

[*trumpets and kettle-drums heard*

HAMLET They are coming to the play. I must be idle. Get you a place.

The KING *and* QUEEN *enter, followed by* POLONIUS, OPHELIA, ROSENCRANTZ, GUILDENSTERN, *and other courtiers; they sit, the King, the Queen and Polonius on this side, Ophelia and Horatio and others on that*

KING How fares our cousin Hamlet?

HAMLET Excellent i'faith, of the chameleon's dish, I eat the air, promise-crammed – you cannot feed capons so.

KING I have nothing with this answer, Hamlet. These words are not mine.

HAMLET No, nor mine now. [*to Polonius*] My lord, you played once i'th'university, you say?

POLONIUS That did I, my lord, and was accounted a good actor.

HAMLET What did you enact?

POLONIUS I did enact Julius Caesar. I was killed i'th'Capitol, Brutus killed me.

HAMLET It was a brute part of him to kill so capital a calf there. Be the players ready?

ROSENC'Z Ay, my lord, they stay upon your patience.

QUEEN Come hither, my dear Hamlet, sit by me.

HAMLET No, good mother, here's metal more attractive.

[*he turns towards Ophelia*

POLONIUS [*to the King*] O ho! Do you mark that?

[*they whisper together, watching Hamlet*

HAMLET Lady, shall I lie in your lap?

OPHELIA No, my lord.

HAMLET I mean, my head upon your lap?

OPHELIA Ay, my lord. [*he lies at her feet*

HAMLET Do you think I meant country matters?

OPHELIA I think nothing, my lord.

HAMLET That's a fair thought to lie between maids' legs.

OPHELIA What is, my lord?

HAMLET Nothing.

OPHELIA You are merry, my lord.

HAMLET Who, I?

OPHELIA Ay, my lord.

HAMLET O God, your only jig-maker. What should a man do but be merry, for look you how cheerfully my mother looks, and my father died within's two hours.

[*the Queen turns away and whispers with the King and Polonius*

OPHELIA Nay, 'tis twice two months, my lord.

HAMLET So long? Nay, then let the devil wear black, for I'll have a suit of sables; O heavens, die two months ago, and not forgotten yet? Then there's hope a great man's memory may outlive his life half a year, but by'r lady 'a must build churches then, or else shall 'a suffer not thinking on, with the hobby-horse, whose epitaph is 'For O! for O! the hobby-horse is forgot.'

'The trumpets sound', the curtains are drawn aside, discovering the inner stage, and a Dumb-Show is performed thereon

The Dumb-Show

'Enter a King and a Queen, very lovingly, the Queen embracing him and he her, she kneels and makes show of protestation unto him, he takes her up and declines his head open her neck, he lies him down upon a bank of flowers, she seeing him asleep leaves him: anon comes in another man, takes off his crown, kisses it, and pours poison in the sleeper's ears and leaves him: the Queen returns, finds the King dead, and makes passionate action: the poisoner with some three or four mutes comes in again, seeming to condole with her: the dead body is carried away: the poisoner woos the Queen with gifts, she seems harsh awhile, but in the end accepts his love' [*the curtains are closed*

Hamlet seems troubled and casts glances at the King and Queen as the show goes forward; they continue in talk with Polonius throughout

OPHELIA What means this, my lord?

HAMLET Marry, this is miching mallecho, it means mischief.

OPHELIA Belike this show imports the argument of the play.

Enter a player before the curtains, the King and Queen turn to listen

HAMLET We shall know by this fellow. The players cannot keep counsel, they'll tell all.

OPHELIA Will 'a tell us what this show meant?

HAMLET [*savagely*] Ay, or any show that you will show him – be not you ashamed to show, he'll not shame to tell you what it means.

OPHELIA You are naught, you are naught, I'll mark the play.

PLAYER For us and for our tragedy,
Here stooping to your clemency,
We beg your hearing patiently. [*exit*

HAMLET Is this a prologue, or the posy of a ring?

OPHELIA 'Tis brief, my lord.

HAMLET As woman's love.

Enter on the dais two Players, a King and a Queen

PL. KING Full thirty times hath Phoebus' cart gone round
Neptune's salt wash, and Tellus' orbèd ground,
And thirty dozen moons with borrowed sheen
About the world have times twelve thirties been,

Since love our hearts and Hymen did our hands
Unite commutual in most sacred bands.

PL. QUEEN So many journeys may the sun and moon
Make us again count o'er ere love be done!
But woe is me, you are so sick of late,
So far from cheer, and from your former state,
That I distrust you. Yet though I distrust,
Discomfort you, my lord, it nothing must,
For women fear too much, even as they love,
And women's fear and love hold quantity,
In neither aught, or in extremity.
Now what my love is proof hath made you know,
And as my love is sized, my fear is so.
Where love is great, the littlest doubts are fear,
Where little fears grow great, great love grows there.

PL. KING Faith, I must leave thee, love, and shortly too.
My operant powers their functions leave to do,
And thou shalt live in this fair world behind,
Honoured, beloved, and haply one as kind
For husband shalt thou –

PL. QUEEN O, confound the rest!
Such love must needs be treason in my breast,
In second husband let me be accurst,
None wed the second, but who killed the first.

HAMLET That's wormwood, wormwood.

PL. QUEEN The instances that second marriage move
Are base respects of thrift, but none of love.
A second time I kill my husband dead,
When second husband kisses me in bed.

PL. KING I do believe you think what now you speak,
But what we do determine, oft we break.
Purpose is but the slave to memory,
Of violent birth but poor validity,
Which now like fruit unripe sticks on the tree,
But fall unshaken when they mellow be.
Most necessary 'tis that we forget
To pay ourselves what to ourselves is debt.
What to ourselves in passion we propose,
The passion ending, doth the purpose lose.

The violence of either grief or joy
Their own enactures with themselves destroy,
Where joy most revels, grief doth most lament,
Grief joys, joy grieves, on slender accident.
This world is not for aye, nor 'tis not strange
That even our loves should with our fortunes change:
For 'tis a question left us, yet to prove,
Whether love lead fortune, or else fortune love.
The great man down, you mark his favourite flies,
The poor advanced makes friends of enemies,
And hitherto doth love on fortune tend,
For who not needs shall never lack a friend,
And who in want a hollow friend doth try,
Directly seasons him his enemy.
But orderly to end where I begun,
Our wills and fates do so contrary run,
That our devices still are overthrown,
Our thoughts are ours, their ends none of our own –
So think thou wilt no second husband wed,
But die thy thoughts when thy first lord is dead.

PL. QUEEN Nor earth to me give food nor heaven light,
Sport and repose lock from me day and night,
To desperation turn my trust and hope,
An anchor's cheere in prison be my scope,
Each opposite that blanks the face of joy
Meet what I would have well and it destroy,
Both here and hence pursue me lasting strife,
If once a widow, ever I be wife!

HAMLET If she should break it now!

PL. KING 'Tis deeply sworn. Sweet, leave me here awhile,
My spirits grow dull, and fain I would beguile
The tedious day with sleep. [*he 'sleeps'*

PL. QUEEN Sleep rock thy brain,
And never come mischance between us twain! [*exit*

HAMLET Madam, how like you this play?

QUEEN The lady doth protest too much, methinks.

HAMLET O, but she'll keep her word.

KING Have you heard the argument? Is there no offence in't?

HAMLET No, no, they do but jest, poison in jest, no offence i'th'world.

KING What do you call the play?

HAMLET The Mouse-trap. Marry, how? – tropically. This play is the image of a murder done in Vienna. Gonzago is the duke's name, his wife Baptista, you shall see anon, 'tis a knavish piece of work, but what of that? Your majesty, and we that have free souls, it touches us not – let the galled jade wince, our withers are unwrung.

Enter First Player for LUCIANUS, *clad in a black doublet and with a vial in his hand; he struts towards the sleeping King making mouths and threatening gestures*

This is one Lucianus, nephew to the king.

OPHELIA You are as good as a chorus, my lord.

HAMLET I could interpret between you and your love, if I could see the puppets dallying.

OPHELIA You are keen, my lord, you are keen.

HAMLET It would cost you a groaning to take off mine edge.

OPHELIA Still better and worse.

HAMLET So you mis-take your husbands. [*he looks up*] Begin, murderer. Pox! Leave thy damnable faces and begin! Come – 'the croaking raven doth bellow for revenge.'

LUCIANUS Thoughts black, hands apt, drugs fit, and time agreeing,
Confederate season, else no creature seeing,
Thou mixture rank, of midnight weeds collected,
With Hecate's ban thrice blasted, thrice infected,
Thy natural magic and dire property
On wholesome life usurps immediately.

[*'pours the poison in his ears'*

HAMLET 'A poisons him i'th'garden for's estate, his name's Gonzago, the story is extant, and written in very choice Italian, you shall see anon how the murderer gets the love of Gonzago's wife.

[*the King, very pale, totters to his feet*

OPHELIA The king rises.

HAMLET What, frighted with false fire!

QUEEN How fares my lord?

POLONIUS Give o'er the play.

KING Give me some light – away! [*he rushes from the hall*

POLONIUS Lights, lights, lights!

[*all but Hamlet and Horatio depart*

HAMLET Why, let the stricken deer go weep,
The hart ungallèd play,
For some must watch while some must sleep,
Thus runs the world away.

Would not this, sir, and a forest of feathers, if the rest of my fortunes turn Turk with me, with two Provincial roses on my razed shoes, get me a fellowship in a cry of players, sir?

HORATIO Half a share.

HAMLET A whole one, I.
For thou dost know, O Damon dear,
This realm dismantled was
Of Jove himself, and now reigns here
A very, very – peacock.

HORATIO You might have rhymed.

HAMLET O good Horatio, I'll take the ghost's word for a thousand pound. Didst perceive?

HORATIO Very well, my lord.

HAMLET Upon the talk of the poisoning?

HORATIO I did very well note him.

ROSENCRANTZ *and* GUILDENSTERN *return*

HAMLET Ah, ha! [*turns his back upon them*] Come, some music! Come, the recorders!
For if the king like not the comedy,
Why then, belike, – he likes it not, perdy.
Come, some music!

GUILD'RN Good my lord, vouchsafe me a word with you.

HAMLET Sir, a whole history.

GUILD'RN The king, sir, –

HAMLET Ay, sir, what of him?

GUILD'RN Is in his retirement marvellous distempered.

HAMLET With drink, sir?

GUILD'RN No my lord, rather with choler.

HAMLET Your wisdom should show itself more richer to signify this to the doctor. For, for me to put him to his purgation, would perhaps plunge him into more choler.

GUILD'RN Good my lord, put your discourse into some frame, and start not so wildly from my affair.

HAMLET I am tame, sir – pronounce.

GUILD'RN The queen your mother, in most great affliction of spirit, hath sent me to you.

HAMLET You are welcome.

GUILD'RN Nay, good my lord, this courtesy is not of the right breed. If it shall please you to make me a wholesome answer, I will do your mother's commandment. If not, your pardon and my return shall be the end of my business. *[he bows and turns away*

HAMLET Sir, I cannot.

ROSENC'Z What, my lord?

HAMLET Make you a wholesome answer – my wit's diseased. But, sir, such answer as I can make, you shall command, or rather as you say, my mother. Therefore no more, but to the matter – my mother, you say –

ROSENC'Z Then thus she says, your behaviour hath struck her into amazement and admiration.

HAMLET O wonderful son that can so stonish a mother! But is there no sequel at the heels of this mother's admiration? Impart.

ROSENC'Z She desires to speak with you in her closet ere you go to bed.

HAMLET We shall obey, were she ten times our mother. Have you any further trade with us?

ROSENC'Z My lord, you once did love me.

HAMLET And do still, by these pickers and stealers.

ROSENC'Z Good my lord, what is your cause of distemper? You do surely bar the door upon your own liberty, if you deny your griefs to your friend.

HAMLET Sir, I lack advancement.

ROSENC'Z How can that be, when you have the voice of the king himself for your succession in Denmark?

HAMLET Ay, sir, but 'While the grass grows' – the proverb is something musty.

Players bring in recorders

O, the recorders, let me see one. [*he takes a recorder and leads Guildenstern aside*] To withdraw with you, why do you go about to recover the wind of me, as if you would drive me into a toil?

GUILD'RN O, my lord, if my duty be too bold, my love is too unmannerly.

HAMLET I do not well understand that – will you play upon this pipe?

GUILD'RN My lord, I cannot.

HAMLET I pray you.

GUILD'RN Believe me, I cannot.

HAMLET I do beseech you.

GUILD'RN I know no touch of it, my lord.

HAMLET It is as easy as lying; govern these ventages with your fingers and thumb, give it breath with your mouth, and it will discourse most eloquent music – look you, these are the stops.

GUILD'RN But these cannot I command to any utt'rance of harmony, I have not the skill.

HAMLET Why, look you now, how unworthy a thing you make of me! You would play upon me, you would seem to know my stops, you would pluck out the heart of my mystery, you would sound me from my lowest note to the top of my compass – and there is much music, excellent voice, in this little organ, yet cannot you make it speak. 'Sblood, do you think I am easier to be played on than a pipe? Call me what instrument you will, though you can fret me, you cannot play upon me.

POLONIUS *enters*

God bless you, sir!

POLONIUS My lord, the queen would speak with you, and presently.

HAMLET Do you see yonder cloud that's almost in shape of a camel?

POLONIUS By th'mass and 'tis, like a camel indeed.

HAMLET Methinks it is like a weasel.

POLONIUS It is backed like a weasel.

HAMLET Or, like a whale?

POLONIUS Very like a whale.

HAMLET Then I will come to my mother by and by. [*aside*] They fool me to the top of my bent – I will come by and by.

POLONIUS I will say so.

[*Polonius, Rosencrantz and Guildenstern depart*

HAMLET 'By and by' is easily said.
Leave me, friends. [*the rest go*
'Tis now the very witching time of night,
When churchyards yawn, and hell itself breathes out
Contagion to this world: now could I drink hot blood,
And do such bitter business as the day
Would quake to look on: soft, now to my mother –
O heart, lose not thy nature, let not ever
The soul of Nero enter this firm bosom,
Let me be cruel not unnatural.
I will speak daggers to her, but use none.
My tongue and soul in this be hypocrites,
How in my words somever she be shent,
To give them seals never, my soul, consent! [*he goes*

SCENE 3

The lobby, with the faldstool as before; the audience chamber without

The KING, ROSENCRANTZ *and* GUILDENSTERN

KING I like him not, nor stands it safe with us
To let his madness range. Therefore prepare you,
I your commission will forthwith dispatch,
And he to England shall along with you.
The terms of our estate may not endure
Hazard so near's as doth hourly grow
Out of his brows.

GUILD'RN We will ourselves provide.
Most holy and religious fear it is
To keep those many many bodies safe
That live and feed upon your majesty.

ROSENC'Z The single and peculiar life is bound
With all the strength and armour of the mind
To keep itself from noyance, but much more

That spirit upon whose weal depends and rests
The lives of many. The cess of majesty
Dies not alone; but like a gulf doth draw
What's near it with it. O, 'tis a massy wheel
Fixed on the summit of the highest mount,
To whose huge spokes ten thousand lesser things
Are mortised and adjoined, which when it falls,
Each small annexment, petty consequence,
Attends the boist'rous ruin. Never alone
Did the king sigh, but with a general groan.

GUILD'RN Arm you, I pray you, to this speedy voyage,
For we will fetters put about this fear,
Which now goes too free-footed.

ROSENC'Z We will haste us. [*they go*

POLONIUS *enters*

POLONIUS My lord, he's going to his mother's closet –
Behind the arras I'll convey myself
To hear the process – I'll warrant she'll tax him home,
And as you said, and wisely was it said,
'Tis meet that some more audience than a mother,
Since nature makes them partial, should o'erhear
The speech of vantage; fare you well, my liege,
I'll call upon you ere you go to bed,
And tell you what I know.

KING Thanks, dear my lord.
[*Polonius goes; the King paces to and fro*
O, my offence is rank, it smells to heaven,
It hath the primal eldest curse upon't,
A brother's murder! Pray can I not,
Though inclination be as sharp as will.
My stronger guilt defeats my strong intent,
And like a man to double business bound,
I stand in pause where I shall first begin,
And both neglect. What if this cursèd hand
Were thicker than itself with brother's blood,
Is there not rain enough in the sweet heavens
To wash it white as snow? Whereto serves mercy
But to confront the visage of offence?
And what's in prayer but this twofold force,

To be forestallèd ere we come to fall,
Or pardoned being down? Then I'll look up.
My fault is past, but O, what form of prayer
Can serve my turn? 'Forgive me my foul murder'?
That cannot be since I am still possessed
Of those effects for which I did the murder;
My crown, mine own ambition, and my queen;
May one be pardoned and retain th'offence?
In the corrupted currents of this world
Offence's gilded hand may shove by justice,
And oft 'tis seen the wicked prize itself
Buys out the law. But 'tis not so above,
There is no shuffling, there the action lies
In his true nature, and we ourselves compelled
Even to the teeth and forehead of our faults
To give in evidence. What then? What rests?
Try what repentance can – what can it not?
Yet what can it, when one can not repent?
O wretched state! O bosom black as death!
O limèd soul, that struggling to be free,
Art more engaged; help, angels! Make assay,
Bow stubborn knees, and heart, with strings of steel,
Be soft as sinews of the new-born babe –
All may be well. [*he kneels*

HAMLET *enters the audience chamber and pauses, seeing the King*

HAMLET [*approaches the entry to the lobby*]
Now might I do it pat, now 'a is a-praying –
And now I'll do't, [*he draws his sword*] and so a' goes to heaven,
And so am I revenged. That would be scanned:
A villain kills my father, and for that
I his sole son do this same villain send
To heaven.
Why, this is bait and salary, not revenge.
'A took my father grossly, full of bread,
With all his crimes broad blown, as flush as May,
And how his audit stands who knows save heaven?
But in our circumstance and course of thought,
'Tis heavy with him: and am I then revenged

To take him in the purging of his soul,
When he is fit and seasoned for his passage?
No. *[he sheathes his sword*
Up, sword, and know thou a more horrid hent,
When he is drunk asleep, or in his rage,
Or in th'incestuous pleasure of his bed,
At game, a-swearing, or about some act
That has no relish of salvation in't,
Then trip him that his heels may kick at heaven,
And that his soul may be as damned and black
As hell whereto it goes; my mother stays,
This physic but prolongs thy sickly days. *[he passes on*

KING [*rises*] My words fly up, my thoughts remain below.
Words without thoughts never to heaven go. *[he goes*

SCENE 4

The Queen's closet hung with arras, and with portraits of King Hamlet and Claudius upon one wall; seats and a couch

The QUEEN *and* POLONIUS

POLONIUS 'A will come straight. Look you lay home to him,
Tell him his pranks have been too broad to bear with,
And that your grace hath screened and stood between
Much heat and him. I'll silence me even here –
Pray you be round with him.

HAMLET [*without*] Mother, mother, mother!

QUEEN I'll war'nt you,
Fear me not. Withdraw, I hear him coming.
[Polonius hides behind the arras

HAMLET *enters*

HAMLET Now, mother, what's the matter?

QUEEN Hamlet, thou hast thy father much offended.

HAMLET Mother, you have my father much offended.

QUEEN Come, come, you answer with an idle tongue.

HAMLET Go, go, you question with a wicked tongue.

QUEEN Why, how now, Hamlet?

HAMLET What's the matter now?

QUEEN Have you forgot me?
HAMLET No, by the rood not so,
You are the queen, your husband's brother's wife,
And would it were not so, you are my mother.
QUEEN Nay then, I'll set those to you that can speak. [*going*
HAMLET [*seizes her arm*]
Come, come, and sit you down, you shall not budge,
You go not till I set you up a glass
Where you may see the inmost part of you.
QUEEN What wilt thou do? thou wilt not murder me?
Help, help, ho!
POLONIUS [*behind the arras*] What, ho! help, help, help!
HAMLET [*draws*] How now! A rat? Dead, for a ducat, dead.
[*he makes a pass through the arras*
POLONIUS [*falls*] O, I am slain!
QUEEN O me, what hast thou done?
HAMLET Nay, I know not,
Is it the king?
[*he lifts up the arras and discovers Polonius, dead*
QUEEN O what a rash and bloody deed is this!
HAMLET A bloody deed – almost as bad, good mother,
As kill a king, and marry with his brother.
QUEEN As kill a king!
HAMLET Ay, lady, it was my word.
[*to Polonius*] Thou wretched, rash, intruding fool, farewell!
I took thee for thy better, take thy fortune,
Thou find'st to be too busy is some danger.
[*he turns back, dropping the arras*
Leave wringing of your hands, peace, sit you down,
And let me wring your heart, for so I shall
If it be made of penetrable stuff,
If damnèd custom have not brassed it so,
That it be proof and bulwark against sense.
QUEEN What have I done, that thou dar'st wag thy tongue
In noise so rude against me?
HAMLET Such an act
That blurs the grace and blush of modesty,
Calls virtue hypocrite, takes off the rose

From the fair forehead of an innocent love
And sets a blister there, makes marriage vows
As false as dicers' oaths, O such a deed
As from the body of contraction plucks
The very soul, and sweet religion makes
A rhapsody of words; heaven's face does glow,
And this solidity and compound mass
With heated visage, as against the doom,
Is thought-sick at the act.

QUEEN Ay me, what act,
That roars so loud, and thunders in the index?

HAMLET [*leads her to the portraits on the wall*]
Look here, upon this picture, and on this,
The counterfeit presentment of two brothers.
See what a grace was seated on this brow –
Hyperion's curls, the front of Jove himself,
An eye like Mars to threaten and command,
A station like the herald Mercury,
New-lighted on a heaven-kissing hill,
A combination and a form indeed,
Where every god did seem to set his seal
To give the world assurance of a man.
This was your husband – Look you now what follows.
Here is your husband, like a mildewed ear,
Blasting his wholesome brother. Have you eyes?
Could you on this fair mountain leave to feed,
And batten on this moor? Ha! Have you eyes?
You cannot call it love, for at your age
The heyday in the blood is tame, it's humble,
And waits upon the judgment, and what judgment
Would step from this to this? Sense sure you have
Else could you not have motion, but sure that sense
Is apoplexed, for madness would not err,
Nor sense to ecstasy was ne'er so thralled,
But it reserved some quantity of choice
To serve in such a difference. What devil was't
That thus hath cozened you at hoodman-blind?
Eyes without feeling, feeling without sight,
Ears without hands or eyes, smelling sans all,

Or but a sickly part of one true sense
Could not so mope: O shame, where is thy blush?
Rebellious hell,
If thou canst mutine in a matron's bones,
To flaming youth let virtue be as wax
And melt in her own fire. Proclaim no shame
When the compulsive ardour gives the charge,
Since frost itself as actively doth burn,
And reason pandars will.

QUEEN O Hamlet, speak no more.
Thou turn'st my eyes into my very soul,
And there I see such black and grainèd spots
As will not leave their tinct.

HAMLET Nay, but to live
In the rank sweat of an enseamèd bed
Stewed in corruption, honeying and making love
Over the nasty sty –

QUEEN O speak to me no more,
These words like daggers enter in mine ears,
No more, sweet Hamlet.

HAMLET A murderer and a villain,
A slave that is not twentieth part the tithe
Of your precedent lord, a vice of kings,
A cutpurse of the empire and the rule,
That from a shelf the precious diadem stole
And put it in his pocket –

QUEEN No more.

HAMLET A king of shreds and patches –

'Enter the GHOST *in his night-gown'*

Save me and hover o'er me with your wings,
You heavenly guards! – What would your gracious figure?

QUEEN Alas, he's mad.

HAMLET Do you not come your tardy son to chide,
That lapsed in time and passion lets go by
Th'important acting of your dread command?
O, say!

GHOST Do not forget! this visitation
Is but to whet thy almost blunted purpose –

But look, amazement on thy mother sits,
O step between her and her fighting soul;
Conceit in weakest bodies strongest works,
Speak to her, Hamlet.

HAMLET How is it with you, lady?

QUEEN Alas, how is't with you,
That you do bend your eye on vacancy,
And with th'incorporal air do hold discourse?
Forth at your eyes your spirits wildly peep,
And as the sleeping soldiers in th'alarm,
Your bedded hairs like life in excrements
Start up and stand an end. O gentle son,
Upon the heat and flame of thy distemper
Sprinkle cool patience. Whereon do you look?

HAMLET On him! on him! Look you, how pale he glares!
His form and cause conjoined, preaching to stones,
Would make them capable. Do not look upon me,
Lest with this piteous action you convert
My stern effects, then what I have to do
Will want true colour, tears perchance for blood.

QUEEN To whom do you speak this?

HAMLET Do you see nothing there?

QUEEN Nothing at all, yet all that is I see.

HAMLET Nor did you nothing hear?

QUEEN No, nothing but ourselves.

HAMLET Why, look you there! Look how it steals away!
My father in his habit as he lived,
Look where he goes, even now, out at the portal.
[*the Ghost vanishes*

QUEEN This is the very coinage of your brain!
This bodiless creation ecstasy
Is very cunning in.

HAMLET Ecstasy!
My pulse as yours doth temperately keep time,
And makes as healthful music – it is not madness
That I have uttered; bring me to the test
And I the matter will re-word, which madness
Would gambol from. Mother, for love of grace,
Lay not that flattering unction to your soul,

That not your trespass but my madness speaks,
It will but skin and film the ulcerous place,
Whiles rank corruption mining all within
Infects unseen. Confess yourself to heaven,
Repent what's past, avoid what is to come,
And do not spread the compost on the weeds
To make them ranker. Forgive me this my virtue,
For in the fatness of these pursy times
Virtue itself of vice must pardon beg,
Yea curb and woo for leave to do him good.

QUEEN O Hamlet, thou hast cleft my heart in twain.

HAMLET O throw away the worser part of it,
And live the purer with the other half.
Good night, but go not to my uncle's bed,
Assume a virtue if you have it not.
That monster custom, who all sense doth eat
Of habits evil, is angel yet in this,
That to the use of actions fair and good
He likewise gives a frock or livery
That aptly is put on. Refrain tonight,
And that shall lend a kind of easiness
To the next abstinence, the next more easy:
For use almost can change the stamp of nature,
And either . . . the devil, or throw him out,
With wondrous potency: once more, good night,
And when you are desirous to be blessed,
I'll blessing beg of you. For this same lord,
[*pointing to Polonius*
I do repent; but heaven hath pleased it so,
To punish me with this, and this with me,
That I must be their scourge and minister.
I will bestow him and will answer well
The death I gave him; so, again, good night.
I must be cruel only to be kind.
This bad begins, and worse remains behind.
[*he makes to go, but returns*
One word more, good lady.

QUEEN What shall I do?

HAMLET Not this by no means that I bid you do –

Let the bloat king tempt you again to bed,
Pinch wanton on your cheek, call you his mouse,
And let him for a pair of reechy kisses,
Or paddling in your neck with his damned fingers,
Make you to ravel all this matter out
That I essentially am not in madness,
But mad in craft. 'Twere good you let him know,
For who that's but a queen, fair, sober, wise,
Would from a paddock, from a bat, a gib,
Such dear concernings hide? Who would do so?
No, in despite of sense and secrecy,
Unpeg the basket on the house's top,
Let the birds fly, and like the famous ape,
To try conclusions in the basket creep,
And break your own neck down.

QUEEN Be thou assured, if words be made of breath,
And breath of life, I have no life to breathe
What thou hast said to me.

HAMLET I must to England, you know that?

QUEEN Alack,
I had forgot, 'tis so concluded on.

HAMLET There's letters sealed, and my two school-fellows,
Whom I will trust as I will adders fanged,
They bear the mandate – they must sweep my way
And marshal me to knavery: let it work,
For 'tis the sport to have the engineer
Hoist with his own petar, and't shall go hard
But I will delve one yard below their mines,
And blow them at the moon: O, 'tis most sweet
When in one line two crafts directly meet.
This man shall set me packing,
I'll lug the guts into the neighbour room;
Mother, good night in deed. This counsellor
Is now most still, most secret, and most grave,
Who was in life a foolish prating knave.
Come, sir, to draw toward an end with you.
Good night, mother.

[he drags the body from the room; the Queen casts herself sobbing upon the couch

ACT 4 SCENE 1

After a short while the KING *enters with* ROSENCRANTZ *and* GUILDENSTERN

KING [*raises her*] There's matter in these sighs, these profound heaves,
You must translate, 'tis fit we understand them.
Where is your son?

QUEEN Bestow this place on us a little while.
[*Rosencrantz and Guildenstern depart*
Ah, mine own lord, what have I seen tonight!

KING What, Gertrude? How does Hamlet?

QUEEN Mad as the sea and wind when both contend
Which is the mightier – in his lawless fit,
Behind the arras hearing something stir,
Whips out his rapier, cries 'A rat, a rat!'
And in this brainish apprehension kills
The unseen good old man.

KING O heavy deed!
It had been so with us had we been there.
His liberty is full of threats to all,
To you yourself, to us, to everyone.
Alas, how shall this bloody deed be answered?
It will be laid to us, whose providence
Should have kept short, restrained, and out of haunt
This mad young man; but so much was our love,
We would not understand what was most fit,
But like the owner of a foul disease,
To keep it from divulging, let it feed
Even on the pith of life: where is he gone?

QUEEN To draw apart the body he hath killed,
O'er whom his very madness, like some ore
Among a mineral of metals base,
Shows itself pure – 'a weeps for what is done.

KING O, Gertrude, come away!
The sun no sooner shall the mountains touch,
But we will ship him hence, and this vile deed

We must with all our majesty and skill
Both countenance and excuse. Ho! Guildenstern!

ROSENCRANTZ *and* GUILDENSTERN *return*

Friends both, go join you with some further aid –
Hamlet in madness hath Polonius slain,
And from his mother's closet hath he dragged him –
Go, seek him out, speak fair, and bring the body
Into the chapel; I pray you, haste in this. [*they go*
Come, Gertrude, we'll call up our wisest friends,
And let them know both what we mean to do
And what's untimely done: [so haply slander,]
Whose whisper o'er the world's diameter,
As level as the cannon to his blank
Transports his poisoned shot, may miss our name,
And hit the woundless air. O, come away!
My soul is full of discord and dismay. [*they go*

SCENE 2

Another room of the castle

HAMLET *enters*

HAMLET Safely stowed.

CALLING WITHOUT Hamlet! Lord Hamlet!

HAMLET But soft, what noise, who calls on Hamlet?
O, here they come!

ROSENCRANTZ *and* GUILDENSTERN *enter in haste, with a guard*

ROSENC'Z What have you done, my lord, with the dead body?

HAMLET Compounded it with dust whereto 'tis kin.

ROSENC'Z Tell us where 'tis that we may take it thence,
And bear it to the chapel.

HAMLET Do not believe it.

ROSENC'Z Believe what?

HAMLET That I can keep your counsel and not mine own. Besides, to be demanded of a sponge, what replication should be made by the son of a king?

ROSENC'Z Take you me for a sponge, my lord?

HAMLET Ay, sir, that soaks up the king's countenance, his rewards, his authorities. But such officers do the king best service in the end, he keeps them like an apple, in the corner of his jaw, first mouthed to be last swallowed – when he needs what you have gleaned, it is but squeezing you, and, sponge, you shall be dry again.

ROSENC'Z I understand you not, my lord.

HAMLET I am glad of it – a knavish speech sleeps in a foolish ear.

ROSENC'Z My lord, you must tell us where the body is, and go with us to the king.

HAMLET The body is with the king, but the king is not with the body. The king is a thing –

GUILD'RN A thing, my lord!

HAMLET Of nothing, bring me to him. Hide fox, and all after.

[he runs out; they pursue with the guard

SCENE 3

The hall of the castle, as before

The KING *seated at a table on the dais with 'two or three' councillors of state*

KING I have sent to seek him, and to find the body.
How dangerous is it that this man goes loose!
Yet must not we put the strong law on him,
He's loved of the distracted multitude,
Who like not in their judgment but their eyes,
And where 'tis so, th'offender's scourge is weighed
But never the offence: to bear all smooth and even,
This sudden sending him away must seem
Deliberate pause. Diseases desperate grown
By desperate appliance are relieved,
Or not at all.

ROSENCRANTZ, GUILDENSTERN *and others enter*

How now! what hath befallen?

ROSENC'Z Where the dead body is bestowed, my lord,
We cannot get from him.

KING But where is he?

ROSENC'Z Without, my lord, guarded, to know your pleasure.

KING Bring him before us.

ROSENC'Z Ho! bring in the lord.

HAMLET *enters guarded by soldiers*

KING Now, Hamlet, where's Polonius?

HAMLET At supper.

KING At supper? Where?

HAMLET Not where he eats, but where 'a is eaten – a certain convocation of politic worms are e'en at him: your worm is your only emperor for diet, we fat all creatures else to fat us, and we fat ourselves for maggots. Your fat king and your lean beggar is but variable service, two dishes, but to one table – that's the end.

KING Alas, alas!

HAMLET A man may fish with the worm that hath eat of a king, and eat of the fish that hath fed of that worm.

KING What dost thou mean by this?

HAMLET Nothing but to show you how a king may go a progress through the guts of a beggar.

KING Where is Polonius?

HAMLET In heaven – send thither to see, if your messenger find him not there, seek him i'th'other place yourself. But if indeed you find him not within this month, you shall nose him as you go up the stairs into the lobby.

KING [*to attendants*] Go seek him there.

HAMLET 'A will stay till you come. [*they depart*

KING Hamlet, this deed, for thine especial safety,
Which we do tender, as we dearly grieve
For that which thou hast done, must send thee hence
With fiery quickness. Therefore prepare thyself,
The bark is ready, and the wind at help,
Th'associates tend, and everything is bent
For England.

HAMLET For England.

KING Ay, Hamlet.

HAMLET Good.

KING So is it if thou knew'st our purposes.

HAMLET I see a cherub that sees them. But, come, for England!
[*he bows*] Farewell, dear mother.

KING Thy loving father, Hamlet.

HAMLET My mother – father and mother is man and wife, man and wife is one flesh, and so my mother: [*he turns to his guards*] come, for England! [*they go*

KING [*to Rosencrantz and Guildenstern*]
Follow him at foot, tempt him with speed aboard,
Delay it not, I'll have him hence tonight.
Away! for everything is sealed and done
That else leans on th'affair – pray you, make haste.
[*all depart save the King*
And, England, if my love thou hold'st at aught –
As my great power thereof may give thee sense,
Since yet thy cicatrice looks raw and red
After the Danish sword, and thy free awe
Pays homage to us – thou mayst not coldly set
Our sovereign process, which imports at full
By letters congruing to that effect,
The present death of Hamlet. Do it, England,
For like the hectic in my blood he rages,
And thou must cure me; till I know 'tis done,
Howe'er my haps, my joys were ne'er begun. [*he goes*

SCENE 4

A plain near to a port in Denmark

Prince FORTINBRAS, *with his army on the march*

FORT'BRAS Go, captain, from me greet the Danish king,
Tell him that by his licence Fortinbras
Craves the conveyance of a promised march
Over his kingdom. You know the rendezvous.
If that his majesty would aught with us,
We shall express our duty in his eye,
And let him know so.

CAPTAIN I will do't, my lord.
[*he turns one way*

FORT'BRAS [*to the troops*] Go softly on.
[*Fortinbras and the army go forward another way*

The Captain meets HAMLET, ROSENCRANTZ, GUILDENSTERN *and the guard on their road to port*

HAMLET Good sir, whose powers are these?
CAPTAIN They are of Norway, sir.
HAMLET How purposed, sir, I pray you?
CAPTAIN Against some part of Poland.
HAMLET Who commands them, sir?
CAPTAIN The nephew to old Norway, Fortinbras.
HAMLET Goes it against the main of Poland, sir,
Or for some frontier?
CAPTAIN Truly to speak, and with no addition,
We go to gain a little patch of ground
That hath in it no profit but the name.
To pay five ducats, five, I would not farm it;
Nor will it yield to Norway or the Pole
A ranker rate should it be sold in fee.
HAMLET Why, then the Polack never will defend it.
CAPTAIN Yes, 'tis already garrisoned.
HAMLET Two thousand souls and twenty thousand ducats
Will not debate the question of this straw!
This is th'imposthume of much wealth and peace,
That inward breaks, and shows no cause without
Why the man dies. I humbly thank you, sir.
CAPTAIN God bye you, sir. [*he goes*
ROSENC'Z Will't please you go, my lord?
HAMLET I'll be with you straight, go a little before.
[*Rosencrantz, Guildenstern and the rest pass on*
How all occasions do inform against me,
And spur my dull revenge! What is a man,
If his chief good and market of his time
Be but to sleep and feed? A beast, no more:
Sure he that made us with such large discourse,
Looking before and after, gave us not
That capability and god-like reason
To fust in us unused. Now, whether it be
Bestial oblivion, or some craven scruple
Of thinking too precisely on th'event –
A thought which quartered hath but one part wisdom,

And ever three parts coward – I do not know
Why yet I live to say 'This thing's to do',
Sith I have cause, and will, and strength, and means,
To do't. Examples gross as earth exhort me.
Witness this army of such mass and charge,
Led by a delicate and tender prince,
Whose spirit with divine ambition puffed
Makes mouths at the invisible event,
Exposing what is mortal and unsure
To all that fortune, death and danger dare,
Even for an egg-shell. Rightly to be great
Is not to stir without great argument,
But greatly to find quarrel in a straw
When honour's at the stake. How stand I then,
That have a father killed, a mother stained,
Excitements of my reason and my blood,
And let all sleep? While to my shame I see
The imminent death of twenty thousand men,
That for a fantasy and trick of fame
Go to their graves like beds, fight for a plot
Whereon the numbers cannot try the cause,
Which is not tomb enough and continent
To hide the slain? O, from this time forth,
My thoughts be bloody, or be nothing worth!
[*he follows on*

[*Some weeks pass*]

SCENE 5

A room in the castle of Elsinore

The QUEEN *with her ladies,* HORATIO *and a gentleman*

QUEEN I will not speak with her.
GENT'MAN She is importunate, indeed distract,
Her mood will needs be pitied.
QUEEN What would she have?
GENT'MAN She speaks much of her father, says she hears
There's tricks i'th'world, and hems, and beats her heart,

Spurns enviously at straws, speaks things in doubt
That carry but half sense. Her speech is nothing,
Yet the unshapèd use of it doth move
The hearers to collection – they aim at it,
And botch the words up fit to their own thoughts,
Which as her winks and nods and gestures yield them,
Indeed would make one think there might be thought,
Though nothing sure, yet much unhappily.

HORATIO 'Twere good she were spoken with, for she may strew
Dangerous conjectures in ill-breeding minds.

QUEEN Let her come in. [*the gentleman goes out*
[*aside*] To my sick soul, as sin's true nature is,
Each toy seems prologue to some great amiss,
So full of artless jealousy is guilt,
It spills itself, in fearing to be spilt.

The gentleman returns with OPHELIA, *distracted, a lute in her hands and her hair about her shoulders*

OPHELIA Where is the beauteous majesty of Denmark?

QUEEN How now, Ophelia?

OPHELIA [*sings*] How should I your true love know
From another one?
By his cockle hat and staff,
And his sandal shoon.

QUEEN Alas, sweet lady, what imports this song?

OPHELIA Say you? Nay, pray you mark.
[*sings*] He is dead and gone, lady,
He is dead and gone,
At his head a grass-green turf,
At his heels a stone.
O, ho!

QUEEN Nay, but Ophelia –

OPHELIA Pray you mark.
[*sings*] White his shroud as the mountain snow –

The KING *enters*

QUEEN Alas, look here, my lord.

OPHELIA [*sings*] Larded all with sweet flowers,
Which bewept to the grave did not go,
With true-love showers.

KING How do you, pretty lady?

OPHELIA Well, God dild you! They say the owl was a baker's daughter. Lord, we know what we are, but know not what we may be. God be at your table!

KING Conceit upon her father.

OPHELIA Pray you let's have no words of this, but when they ask you what it means, say you this.

[*sings*] Tomorrow is Saint Valentine's day,
All in the morning betime,
And I a maid at your window
To be your Valentine.
Then up he rose, and donned his clo'es,
And dupped the chamber door,
Let in the maid, that out a maid
Never departed more.

KING Pretty Ophelia!

OPHELIA Indeed, la, without an oath, I'll make an end on't –

[*sings*] By Gis and by Saint Charity,
Alack and fie for shame!
Young men will do't, if they come to't,
By Cock, they are to blame.
Quoth she, Before you tumbled me,
You promised me to wed.

he answers

So would I ha' done, by yonder sun,
An thou hadst not come to my bed.

KING How long hath she been thus?

OPHELIA I hope all will be well. We must be patient, but I cannot choose but weep to think they would lay him i'th'cold ground. My brother shall know of it, and so I thank you for your good counsel. Come, my coach! Good night, ladies, good night. Sweet ladies, good night, good night. [*she goes*

KING Follow her close, give her good watch, I pray you.

[*Horatio and the gentleman follow her*

O, this is the poison of deep grief, it springs
All from her father's death – and now behold!
O Gertrude, Gertrude,
When sorrows come, they come not single spies,

But in battalions: first her father slain,
Next your son gone, and he most violent author
Of his own just remove, the people muddied,
Thick and unwholesome in their thoughts and whispers
For good Polonius' death – and we have done but greenly,
In hugger-mugger to inter him – poor Ophelia
Divided from herself and her fair judgment,
Without the which we are pictures or mere beasts,
Last, and as much containing as all these,
Her brother is in secret come from France,
Feeds on his wonder, keeps himself in clouds,
And wants not buzzers to infect his ear
With pestilent speeches of his father's death,
Wherein necessity, of matter beggared,
Will nothing stick our person to arraign
In ear and ear: O my dear Gertrude, this
Like to a murdering-piece in many places
Gives me superfluous death! [*a tumult without*

QUEEN Alack! what noise is this?

KING [*calls*] Attend! [*an attendant enters*
Where are my Switzers? let them guard the door.
What is the matter?

ATTENDANT Save yourself, my lord!
The ocean, overpeering of his list,
Eats not the flats with more impiteous haste
Than young Laertes in a riotous head
O'erbears your officers: the rabble call him lord,
And as the world were now but to begin,
Antiquity forgot, custom not known,
The ratifiers and props of every word,
They cry 'Choose we, Laertes shall be king!'
Caps, hands, and tongues applaud it to the clouds,
'Laertes shall be king, Laertes king!'
[*the shouts grow louder*

QUEEN How cheerfully on the false trail they cry!
O, this is counter, you false Danish dogs!

KING The doors are broke.

LAERTES, *armed, bursts into the room with Danes following*

LAERTES Where is this king? Sirs, stand you all without.

DANES No, let's come in.

LAERTES I pray you, give me leave.

DANES We will, we will.

[they retire without the door

LAERTES I thank you, keep the door. O thou vile king,
Give me my father.

QUEEN Calmly, good Laertes.

LAERTES That drop of blood that's calm proclaims me bastard,
Cries cuckold to my father, brands the harlot,
Even here, between the chaste unsmirchèd brows
Of my true mother. *[he advances upon them; the Queen throws herself in his path*

KING What is the cause, Laertes,
That thy rebellion looks so giant-like?
Let him go, Gertrude, do not fear our person,
There's such divinity doth hedge a king,
That treason can but peep to what it would,
Acts little of his will. Tell me, Laertes,
Why thou art thus incensed – let him go, Gertrude –
Speak, man.

LAERTES Where is my father?

KING Dead.

QUEEN But not by him.

KING Let him demand his fill.

LAERTES How came he dead? I'll not be juggled with.
To hell allegiance, vows to the blackest devil,
Conscience and grace to the profoundest pit!
I dare damnation. To this point I stand,
That both the worlds I give to negligence,
Let come what comes, only I'll be revenged
Most throughly for my father.

KING Who shall stay you.

LAERTES My will, not all the world's:
And for my means, I'll husband them so well,
They shall go far with little.

KING Good Laertes,
If you desire to know the certainty

Of your dear father, is't writ in your revenge,
That, sweepstake, you will draw both friend and foe,
Winner and loser?

LAERTES None but his enemies.

KING Will you know them then?

LAERTES To his good friends thus wide I'll ope my arms,
And like the kind life-rend'ring pelican,
Repast them with my blood.

KING Why, now you speak
Like a good child and a true gentleman.
That I am guiltless of your father's death,
And am most sensibly in grief for it,
It shall as level to your judgment 'pear,
As day does to your eye.

SHOUTING WITHOUT Let her come in.

LAERTES How now! What noise is that?

OPHELIA *re-enters with flowers in her hand*

O heat, dry up my brains, tears seven times salt,
Burn out the sense and virtue of mine eye!
By heaven, thy madness shall be paid with weight,
Till our scale turn the beam. O rose of May,
Dear maid, kind sister, sweet Ophelia!
O heavens, is't possible a young maid's wits
Should be as mortal as an old man's life?
Nature is fine in love, and where 'tis fine,
It sends some precious instance of itself
After the thing it loves.

OPHELIA [*sings*] They bore him barefaced on the bier,
Hey non nonny, nonny, hey nonny,
And in his grave rained many a tear –
Fare you well, my dove!

LAERTES Hadst thou thy wits, and didst persuade revenge,
It could not move thus.

OPHELIA You must sing 'Adown adown', an you call him adown-a. O, how the wheel becomes it! It is the false steward that stole his master's daughter.

LAERTES This nothing's more than matter.

OPHELIA [*to Laertes*] There's rosemary, that's for remembrance –

pray you, love, remember – and there is pansies, that's for thoughts.

LAERTES A document in madness, thoughts and remembrance fitted.

OPHELIA [*to the King*] There's fennel for you, and columbines. [*to the Queen*] There's rue for you, and here's some for me, we may call it herb of grace o'Sundays – O, you must wear your rue with a difference. There's a daisy. I would give you some violets, but they withered all, when my father died – they say 'a made a good end –
[*sings*] For bonny sweet Robin is all my joy –

LAERTES Thought and affliction, passion, hell itself,
She turns to favour and to prettiness.

OPHELIA [*sings*] And will 'a not come again?
And will 'a not come again?
No, no, he is dead,
Go to thy death-bed,
He never will come again.

His beard was as white as snow,
All flaxen was his poll,
He is gone, he is gone,
And we cast away moan,
God ha' mercy on his soul! –

And of all Christian souls I pray God. God bye you.
[*she goes*

LAERTES Do you see this, O God?

KING Laertes, I must commune with your grief,
Or you deny me right. Go but apart,
Make choice of whom your wisest friends you will
And they shall hear and judge 'twixt you and me.
If by direct or by collateral hand
They find us touched, we will our kingdom give,
Our crown, our life, and all that we call ours,
To you in satisfaction; but if not,
Be you content to lend your patience to us,
And we shall jointly labour with your soul
To give it due content.

LAERTES Let this be so.

His means of death, his obscure funeral,
No trophy, sword, nor hatchment o'er his bones,
No noble rite, nor formal ostentation,
Cry to be heard as 'twere from heaven to earth,
That I must call't in question.

KING So you shall,
And where th'offence is let the great axe fall.
I pray you, go with me. [*they go*

SCENE 6

'HORATIO *and others' enter*

HORATIO What are they that would speak with me?

GENT'MAN Seafaring men, sir. They say they have letters for you.

HORATIO Let them come in. [*an attendant goes out*
[*aside*] I do not know from what part of the world
I should be greeted, if not from Lord Hamlet.

The attendant brings in sailors

I SAILOR God bless you, sir.

HORATIO Let him bless thee too.

I SAILOR 'A shall, sir, an't please him. There's a letter for you, sir, it came from th'ambassador that was bound for England, if your name be Horatio, as I am let to know it is.

HORATIO [*turns aside and reads*] 'Horatio, when thou shalt have overlooked this, give these fellows some means to the king, they have letters for him. Ere we were two days old at sea, a pirate of very warlike appointment gave us chase. Finding ourselves too slow of sail, we put on a compelled valour, and in the grapple I boarded them. On the instant they got clear of our ship, so I alone became their prisoner. They have dealt with me like thieves of mercy, but they knew what they did; I am to do a good turn for them. Let the king have the letters I have sent, and repair thou to me with as much speed as thou wouldest fly death. I have words to speak in thine ear will make thee dumb, yet are they much too light for the bore of the matter. These good fellows will bring thee where I am. Rosencrantz and Guildenstern hold their course for England – of them I have much to tell thee. Farewell.

He that thou knowest thine, HAMLET.'

Come, I will give you way for these your letters,
And do't the speedier that you may direct me
To him from whom you brought them. [*they go*

SCENE 7

The KING *and* LAERTES *return*

KING
Now must your conscience my acquittance seal,
And you must put me in your heart for friend,
Sith you have heard and with a knowing ear
That he which hath your noble father slain
Pursued my life.

LAERTES
It well appears: but tell me,
Why you proceeded not against these feats,
So crimeful and so capital in nature,
As by your safety, greatness, wisdom, all things else,
You mainly were stirred up.

KING
O, for two special reasons,
Which may to you perhaps seem much unsinewed,
But yet to me they're strong. The queen his mother
Lives almost by his looks, and for myself,
My virtue or my plague, be it either which,
She is so conjunctive to my life and soul,
That as the star moves not but in his sphere
I could not but by her. The other motive,
Why to a public count I might not go,
Is the great love the general gender bear him,
Who dipping all his faults in their affection,
Would like the spring that turneth wood to stone,
Convert his gyves to graces, o that my arrows,
Too slightly timbered for so loud a wind,
Would have reverted to my bow again,
And not where I had aimed them.

LAERTES
And so have I a noble father lost,

A sister driven into desperate terms,
Whose worth, if praises may go back again,
Stood challenger on mount of all the age
For her perfections. But my revenge will come.

KING Break not your sleeps for that, you must not think
That we are made of stuff so flat and dull,
That we can let our beard be shook with danger
And think it pastime. You shortly shall hear more.
I loved your father, and we love ourself,
And that I hope will teach you to imagine –

'Enter a MESSENGER *with letters'*

How now! what news?

MESSENGER Letters, my lord, from Hamlet.
These to your majesty, these to the queen.

KING From Hamlet! who brought them?

MESSENGER Sailors, my lord, they say, I saw them not.
They were given me by Claudio, he received them
Of him that brought them.

KING Laertes, you shall hear them.
Leave us. [*the Messenger goes*
[*reads*] 'High and mighty, you shall know I am set naked on your kingdom. Tomorrow shall I beg leave to see your kingly eyes, when I shall, first asking your pardon thereunto, recount the occasion of my sudden and more strange return. HAMLET.'
What should this mean? Are all the rest come back?
Or is it some abuse, and no such thing?

LAERTES Know you the hand?

KING 'Tis Hamlet's character. 'Naked' –
And in a postscript here he says 'alone'.
Can you devise me?

LAERTES I am lost in it, my lord, but let him come!
It warms the very sickness in my heart
That I shall live and tell him to his teeth
'Thus diest thou.'

KING If it be so, Laertes, –
As how should it be so? How otherwise? –
Will you be ruled by me?

LAERTES Ay, my lord,

So you will not o'errule me to a peace.
KING To thine own peace. If he be now returned,
As checking at his voyage, and that he means
No more to undertake it, I will work him
To an exploit, now ripe in my device,
Under the which he shall not choose but fall:
And for his death no wind of blame shall breathe,
But even his mother shall uncharge the practice,
And call it accident.
LAERTES My lord, I will be ruled,
The rather if you could devise it so
That I might be the organ.
KING It falls right.
You have been talked of since your travel much,
And that in Hamlet's hearing, for a quality
Wherein they say you shine. Your sum of parts
Did not together pluck such envy from him,
As did that one, and that in my regard
Of the unworthiest siege.
LAERTES What part is that, my lord?
KING A very riband in the cap of youth,
Yet needful too, for youth no less becomes
The light and careless livery that it wears,
Than settled age his sables and his weeds
Importing health and graveness; two months since,
Here was a gentleman of Normandy –
I have seen myself, and served against, the French,
And they can well on horseback – but this gallant
Had witchcraft in't, he grew unto his seat,
And to such wondrous doing brought his horse,
As had he been incorpsed and demi-natured
With the brave beast. So far he topped my thought,
That I in forgery of shapes and tricks
Come short of what he did.
LAERTES A Norman, was't?
KING A Norman.
LAERTES Upon my life, Lamord.
KING The very same.
LAERTES I know him well, he is the brooch indeed

And gem of all the nation.

KING He made confession of you,
And gave you such a masterly report
For art and exercise in your defence,
And for your rapier most especial,
That he cried out 'twould be a sight indeed
If one could match you; the scrimers of their nation
He swore had neither motion, guard, nor eye,
If you opposed them; sir, this report of his
Did Hamlet so envenom with his envy,
That he could nothing do but wish and beg
Your sudden coming o'er to play with him.
Now, out of this –

LAERTES What out of this, my lord?

KING Laertes, was your father dear to you?
Or are you like the painting of a sorrow,
A face without a heart?

LAERTES Why ask you this?

KING Not that I think you did not love your father,
But that I know love is begun by time,
And that I see in passages of proof
Time qualifies the spark and fire of it.
There lives within the very flame of love
A kind of wick or snuff that will abate it,
And nothing is at a like goodness still,
For goodness, growing to a pleurisy,
Dies in his own too much. That we would do
We should do when we would: for this 'would' changes,
And hath abatements and delays as many
As there are tongues, are hands, are accidents,
And then this 'should' is like a spendthrift sigh,
That hurts by easing; but to the quick o'th'ulcer –
Hamlet comes back, what would you undertake
To show yourself your father's son in deed
More than in words?

LAERTES To cut his throat i'th'church.

KING No place indeed should murder sanctuarize,
Revenge should have no bounds: but, good Laertes,

Will you do this, keep close within your chamber.
Hamlet returned shall know you are come home.
We'll put on those shall praise your excellence,
And set a double varnish on the fame
The Frenchman gave you, bring you in fine together,
And wager on your heads; he being remiss,
Most generous, and free from all contriving,
Will not peruse the foils, so that with ease,
Or with a little shuffling, you may choose
A sword unbated, and in a pass of practice
Requite him for your father.

LAERTES I will do't,
And, for the purpose, I'll anoint my sword.
I bought an unction of a mountebank,
So mortal, that but dip a knife in it,
Where it draws blood, no cataplasm so rare,
Collected from all simples that have virtue
Under the moon, can save the thing from death
That is but scratched withal. I'll touch my point
With this contagion, that if I gall him slightly,
It may be death.

KING Let's further think of this,
Weigh what convenience both of time and means
May fit us to our shape. If this should fail,
And that our drift look through our bad performance,
'Twere better not assayed. Therefore this project
Should have a back or second that might hold,
If this did blast in proof; soft, let me see,
We'll make a solemn wager on your cunnings –
I ha't!
When in your motion you are hot and dry,
As make your bouts more violent to that end,
And that he calls for drink, I'll have preferred him
A chalice for the nonce, whereon but sipping,
If he by chance escape your venomed stuck,
Our purpose may hold there. But stay, what noise?

The QUEEN *enters weeping*

QUEEN One woe doth tread upon another's heel,

So fast they follow; your sister's drowned, Laertes.

LAERTES Drowned! O, where?

QUEEN There is a willow grows askant the brook,
That shows his hoar leaves in the glassy stream,
Therewith fantastic garlands did she make
Of crow-flowers, nettles, daisies, and long purples
That liberal shepherds give a grosser name,
But our cold maids do dead men's fingers call them.
There on the pendent boughs her crownet weeds
Clamb'ring to hang, an envious sliver broke,
When down her weedy trophies and herself
Fell in the weeping brook. Her clothes spread wide,
And mermaid-like awhile they bore her up,
Which time she chanted snatches of old lauds,
As one incapable of her own distress,
Or like a creature native and indued
Unto that element. But long it could not be
Till that her garments, heavy with their drink,
Pulled the poor wretch from her melodious lay
To muddy death.

LAERTES Alas then, she is drowned?

QUEEN Drowned, drowned.

LAERTES Too much of water hast thou, poor Ophelia,
And therefore I forbid my tears; but yet
It is our trick, nature her custom holds,
Let shame say what it will – when these are gone,
The woman will be out. Adieu, my lord!
I have a speech o' fire that fain would blaze,
But that this folly douts it. [*he goes*

KING Let's follow, Gertrude.
How much I had to do to calm his rage!
Now fear I this will give it start again,
Therefore let's follow. [*they follow*

ACT 5 SCENE 1

A graveyard, with a newly opened grave; yew-trees, and a gate

Two clowns (a sexton and his mate) enter with spades and mattocks; they make them ready to dig

1 CLOWN Is she to be buried in Christian burial when she wilfully seeks her own salvation?

2 CLOWN I tell thee she is, therefore make her grave straight. The crowner hath sat on her, and finds it Christian burial.

1 CLOWN How can that be, unless she drowned herself in her own defence?

2 CLOWN Why, 'tis found so.

1 CLOWN It must be 'se offendendo', it cannot be else. For here lies the point, if I drown myself wittingly, it argues an act, and an act hath three branches, it is to act, to do, and to perform – argal, she drowned herself wittingly.

2 CLOWN Nay, but hear you, goodman delver.

1 CLOWN Give me leave. Here lies the water – good. Here stands the man – good. If the man go to this water and drown himself, it is, will he nill he, he goes, mark you that. But if the water come to him, and drown him, he drowns not himself – argal, he that is not guilty of his own death, shortens not his own life.

2 CLOWN But is this law?

1 CLOWN Ay, marry is't, crowner's quest law.

2 CLOWN Will you ha' the truth an't? If this had not been a gentlewoman, she should have been buried out a Christian burial.

1 CLOWN Why, there thou say'st, and the more pity that great folk should have countenance in this world to drown or hang themselves more than their even-Christen. Come, my spade! there is no ancient gentlemen but gardeners, ditchers and grave-makers – they hold up Adam's profession.

[*he goes down into the open grave*

2 CLOWN Was he a gentleman?

1 CLOWN 'A was the first that ever bore arms.

2 CLOWN Why, he had none.

1 CLOWN What, art a heathen? How dost thou understand the Scripture? the Scripture says Adam digged; could he dig without arms? I'll put another question to thee. If thou answerest me not to the purpose, confess thyself –

2 CLOWN Go to.

1 CLOWN What is he that builds stronger than either the mason, the shipwright, or the carpenter?

2 CLOWN The gallows-maker, for that frame outlives a thousand tenants.

1 CLOWN I like thy wit well in good faith, the gallows does well – but how does it well? It does well to those that do ill. Now thou dost ill to say the gallows is built stronger than the church – argal, the gallows may do well to thee. To't again, come.

2 CLOWN 'Who builds stronger than a mason, a shipwright, or a carpenter?'

1 CLOWN Ay, tell me that, and unyoke.

2 CLOWN Marry, now I can tell.

1 CLOWN To't.

2 CLOWN Mass, I cannot tell.

1 CLOWN Cudgel thy brains no more about it, for your dull ass will not mend his pace with beating. And when you are asked this question next, say 'a grave-maker'. The houses he makes lasts till doomsday. Go, get thee to Yaughan, and fetch me a stoup of liquor.

[Second Clown goes

HAMLET *(clad in sailor's garb) and* HORATIO *are seen entering the graveyard*

First Clown digs and sings

In youth when I did love, did love,
Methought it was very sweet,
To contract o' the time for a my behove,
O, methought there a was nothing a meet.

HAMLET Has this fellow no feeling of his business that 'a sings in grave-making?

HORATIO Custom hath made it in him a property of easiness.

HAMLET 'Tis e'en so, the hand of little employment hath the daintier sense.

I CLOWN [*sings*] But age with his stealing steps
Hath clawed me in his clutch,
And hath shipped me intil the land,
As if I had never been such.

[*he throws up a skull*

HAMLET That skull had a tongue in it, and could sing once! How the knave jowls it to the ground, as if 'twere Cain's jaw-bone, that did the first murder! This might be the pate of a politician, which this ass now o'er-reaches; one that would circumvent God, might it not?

HORATIO It might, my lord.

HAMLET Or of a courtier, which could say 'Good morrow, sweet lord! How dost thou, good lord?' This might be my lord such-a-one, that praised my lord such a-one's horse, when 'a meant to beg it, might it not?

HORATIO Ay, my lord.

HAMLET Why, e'en so, and now my Lady Worm's, chopless and knocked about the mazzard with a sexton's spade; here's fine revolution an we had the trick to see't! Did these bones cost no more the breeding, but to play at loggats with them? Mine ache to think on't.

I CLOWN [*sings*] A pick-axe, and a spade, a spade,
For and a shrouding sheet,
O, a pit of clay for to be made
For such a guest is meet.

[*he throws up a second skull*

HAMLET There's another. Why may not that be the skull of a lawyer? Where be his quiddities now, his quillities, his cases, his tenures, and his tricks? Why does he suffer this rude knave now to knock him about the sconce with a dirty shovel, and will not tell him of his action of battery? [*he takes up the skull*] Hum! This fellow might be in's time a great buyer of land, with his statutes, his recognizances, his fines, his double vouchers, his recoveries: is this the fine of his fines, and the recovery of his recoveries, to have his fine pate full of fine dirt? Will his vouchers vouch him no more of his purchases, and double ones too, than the length and breadth of a pair of indentures? The very conveyances of his lands will scarcely lie in this box [*he taps the skull*], and must th'inheritor himself have no more, ha?

HORATIO Not a jot more, my lord.

HAMLET Is not parchment made of sheep-skins?

HORATIO Ay, my lord, and of calves'-skins too.

HAMLET They are sheep and calves which seek out assurance in that. I will speak to this fellow. [*they go forward*] Whose grave's this, sirrah?

1 CLOWN Mine, sir – [*sings*]

O, a pit of clay for to be made
For such a guest is meet.

HAMLET I think it be thine, indeed, for thou liest in't.

1 CLOWN You lie out on't sir, and therefore 'tis not yours; for my part I do not lie in't, and yet it is mine.

HAMLET Thou dost lie in't, to be in't and say it is thine. 'Tis for the dead, not for the quick – therefore thou liest.

1 CLOWN 'Tis a quick lie, sir, 'twill away again from me to you.

HAMLET What man dost thou dig it for?

1 CLOWN For no man, sir.

HAMLET What woman then?

1 CLOWN For none neither.

HAMLET Who is to be buried in't?

1 CLOWN One that was a woman, sir, but rest her soul she's dead.

HAMLET How absolute the knave is! We must speak by the card or equivocation will undo us. By the Lord, Horatio, this three years I have took note of it, the age is grown so picked, that the toe of the peasant comes so near the heel of the courtier he galls his kibe. How long hast thou been grave-maker?

1 CLOWN Of all the days i'th'year I came to't that day that our last king Hamlet overcame Fortinbras.

HAMLET How long is that since?

1 CLOWN Cannot you tell that? Every fool can tell that. It was that very day that young Hamlet was born: he that is mad and sent into England.

HAMLET Ay, marry, why was he sent into England?

1 CLOWN Why, because 'a was mad: 'a shall recover his wits there, or if 'a do not, 'tis no great matter there.

HAMLET Why?

1 CLOWN 'Twill not be seen in him there, there the men are as mad as he.

HAMLET How came he mad?

1 CLOWN Very strangely, they say.

HAMLET How strangely?

1 CLOWN Faith, e'en with losing his wits.

HAMLET Upon what ground?

1 CLOWN Why, here in Denmark: I have been sexton here man and boy thirty years.

HAMLET How long will a man lie i'th'earth ere he rot?

1 CLOWN Faith, if 'a be not rotten before 'a die, as we have many pocky corses nowadays that will scarce hold the laying in, 'a will last you some eight year, or nine year. A tanner will last you nine year.

HAMLET Why he more than another?

1 CLOWN Why sir, his hide is so tanned with his trade, that 'a will keep out water a great while; and your water is a sore decayer of your whoreson dead body Here's a skull now: this skull hath lien you i'th'earth three-and-twenty years.

HAMLET Whose was it?

1 CLOWN A whoreson mad fellow's it was, whose do you think it was?

HAMLET Nay, I know not.

1 CLOWN A pestilence on him for a mad rogue! 'A poured a flagon of Rhenish on my head once; this same skull, sir, was, sir, Yorick's skull, the king's jester.

HAMLET This?

1 CLOWN E'en that.

HAMLET Let me see. [*he takes the skull*] Alas, poor Yorick! I knew him, Horatio – a fellow of infinite jest, of most excellent fancy. He hath borne me on his back a thousand times, and now how abhorred in my imagination it is! My gorge rises at it. Here hung those lips that I have kissed I know not how oft. Where be your gibes now? Your gambols, your songs, your flashes of merriment, that were wont to set the table on a roar? Not one now to mock your own grinning? Quite chop fallen? Now get you to my lady's chamber, and tell her, let her paint an inch thick, to this favour she must come. Make her laugh at that. Prithee, Horatio, tell me one thing.

HORATIO What's that, my lord.

HAMLET Dost thou think Alexander looked o' this fashion i'th' earth?

HORATIO E'en so.

HAMLET And smelt so? Pah! *[he sets down the skull*

HORATIO E'en so, my lord.

HAMLET To what base uses we may return, Horatio! Why may not imagination trace the noble dust of Alexander, till 'a find it stopping a bung-hole?

HORATIO 'Twere to consider too curiously, to consider so.

HAMLET No, faith, not a jot, but to follow him thither with modesty enough, and likelihood to lead it; as thus – Alexander died, Alexander was buried, Alexander returneth to dust, the dust is earth, of earth we make loam, and why of that loam whereto he was converted might they not stop a beer-barrel?

Imperious Caesar, dead and turned to clay,
Might stop a hole to keep the wind away.
O, that that earth, which kept the world in awe,
Should patch a wall t'expel the winter's flaw!

But soft, but soft, awhile – here comes the king,
The queen, the courtiers.

A procession enters the graveyard: the corpse of OPHELIA *in an open coffin, with* LAERTES, *the* KING, *the* QUEEN, *courtiers and a Doctor of Divinity in cassock and gown following*

Who is this they follow?
And with such maimèd rites? This doth betoken
The corse they follow did with desperate hand
Fordo it own life. 'Twas of some estate.
Couch we awhile, and mark. *[they sit under a yew*

LAERTES What ceremony else?

HAMLET That is Laertes,
A very noble youth – mark.
LAERTES What ceremony else?
DOCTOR Her obsequies have been as far enlarged
As we have warranty. Her death was doubtful,
And but that great command o'ersways the order,
She should in ground unsanctified have lodged
Till the last trumpet: for charitable prayers,
Shards, flints and pebbles should be thrown on her:
Yet here she is allowed her virgin crants,
Her maiden strewments, and the bringing home
Of bell and burial.
LAERTES Must there no more be done?
DOCTOR No more be done!
We should profane the service of the dead
To sing sage requiem and such rest to her
As to peace-parted souls.
LAERTES Lay her i'th'earth,
And from her fair and unpolluted flesh
May violets spring! [*the coffin is laid within the grave*]
I tell thee, churlish priest,
A minist'ring angel shall my sister be,
When thou liest howling.
HAMLET What, the fair Ophelia!
QUEEN [*scattering flowers*] Sweets to the sweet. Farewell!
I hoped thou shouldst have been my Hamlet's wife:
I thought thy bride-bed to have decked, sweet maid,
And not have strewed thy grave.
LAERTES O, treble woe
Fall ten times treble on that cursèd head
Whose wicked deed thy most ingenious sense
Deprived thee of! Hold off the earth awhile,
Till I have caught her once more in mine arms;
[*'leaps in the grave'*
Now pile your dust upon the quick and dead,
Till of this flat a mountain you have made
T'o'ertop old Pelion, or the skyish head
Of blue Olympus.
HAMLET [*comes forward*] What is he whose grief

Bears such an emphasis? whose phrase of sorrow
Conjures the wand'ring stars, and makes them stand
Like wonder-wounded hearers? This is I,
Hamlet the Dane. [*'leaps in after Laertes'*

LAERTES [*grappling with him*] The devil take thy soul!

HAMLET Thou pray'st not well.
I prithee take thy fingers from my throat,
For though I am not splenitive and rash,
Yet have I in me something dangerous,
Which let thy wiseness fear; hold off thy hand.

KING Pluck them asunder.

QUEEN Hamlet, Hamlet!

ALL Gentlemen!

HORATIO Good my lord, be quiet.

[*Attendants part them, and they come up out of the grave*

HAMLET Why, I will fight with him upon this theme
Until my eyelids will no longer wag.

QUEEN O my son, what theme?

HAMLET I loved Ophelia, forty thousand brothers
Could not with all their quantity of love
Make up my sum. What wilt thou do for her?

KING O he is mad, Laertes.

QUEEN For love of God, forbear him.

HAMLET 'Swounds, show me what thou't do:
Woo't weep? Woo't fight? Woo't fast? Woo't tear thyself?
Woo't drink up eisel? Eat a crocodile?
I'll do't. Dost thou come here to whine?
To outface me with leaping in her grave?
Be buried quick with her, and so will I.
And if thou prate of mountains, let them throw
Millions of acres on us, till our ground,
Singeing his pate against the burning zone,
Make Ossa like a wart! Nay, an thou'lt mouth,
I'll rant as well as thou.

QUEEN This is mere madness,
And thus awhile the fit will work on him.
Anon as patient as the female dove

When that her golden couplets are disclosed
His silence will sit drooping.

HAMLET Hear you, sir,
What is the reason that you use me thus?
I loved you ever, but it is no matter,
Let Hercules himself do what he may,
The cat will mew, and dog will have his day. [*he goes*

KING I pray thee, good Horatio, wait upon him.
[*Horatio follows*
[*aside to Laertes*]
Strengthen your patience in our last night's speech,
We'll put the matter to the present push.
Good Gertrude, set some watch over your son.
This grave shall have a living monument;
An hour of quiet shortly shall we see,
Till then, in patience our proceeding be. [*they go*

SCENE 2

The hall of the castle; chairs of state, benches, tables, etc.

HAMLET *and* HORATIO *enter talking*

HAMLET So much for this, sir, now shall you see the other –
You do remember all the circumstance?

HORATIO Remember it, my lord!

HAMLET Sir, in my heart there was a kind of fighting
That would not let me sleep – methought I lay
Worse than the mutines in the bilboes. Rashly,
And praised be rashness for it. Let us know
Our indiscretion sometime serves us well,
When our deep plots do pall, and that should learn us
There's a divinity that shapes our ends,
Rough-hew them how we will –

HORATIO That is most certain.

HAMLET Up from my cabin,
My sea-gown scarfed about me, in the dark
Groped I to find out them, had my desire,
Fingered their packet, and in fine withdrew

To mine own room again, making so bold,
My fears forgetting manners, to unseal
Their grand commission; where I found, Horatio –
Ah, royal knavery! – an exact command,
Larded with many several sorts of reasons,
Importing Denmark's health and England's too,
With, ho! such bugs and goblins in my life,
That on the supervise, no leisure bated,
No, not to stay the grinding of the axe,
My head should be struck off.

HORATIO Is't possible?

HAMLET Here's the commission, read it at more leisure.
But wilt thou hear now how I did proceed?

HORATIO I beseech you.

HAMLET Being thus be-netted round with villainies –
Or I could make a prologue to my brains
They had begun the play. I sat me down,
Devised a new commission, wrote it fair –
I once did hold it, as our statists do,
A baseness to write fair, and laboured much
How to forget that learning, but, sir, now
It did me yeoman's service. Wilt thou know
Th'effect of what I wrote?

HORATIO Ay, good my lord.

HAMLET An earnest conjuration from the king,
As England was his faithful tributary,
As love between them like the palm might flourish,
As peace should still her wheaten garland wear
And stand a comma 'tween their amities,
And many such like 'as'es' of great charge,
That on the view and knowing of these contents
Without debatement further, more or less,
He should those bearers put to sudden death,
Not shriving-time allowed.

HORATIO How was this sealed?

HAMLET Why, even in that was heaven ordinant,
I had my father's signet in my purse,
Which was the model of that Danish seal,
Folded the writ up in the form of th'other,

Subscribed it, gave't th'impression, placed it safely,
The changeling never known: now, the next day
Was our sea-fight, and what to this was sequent
Thou knowest already.

HORATIO So Guildenstern and Rosencrantz go to't.

HAMLET Why, man, they did make love to this employment,
They are not near my conscience, their defeat
Does by their own insinuation grow.
'Tis dangerous when the baser nature comes
Between the pass and fell incensèd points
Of mighty opposites.

HORATIO Why, what a king is this!

HAMLET Does it not, think thee, stand me now upon –
He that hath killed my king, and whored my mother,
Popped in between th'election and my hopes,
Thrown out his angle for my proper life,
And with such cozenage – is't not perfect conscience
To quit him with this arm? And is't not to be damned,
To let this canker of our nature come
In further evil?

HORATIO It must be shortly known to him from England
What is the issue of the business there.

HAMLET It will be short, the interim is mine,
And a man's life's no more than to say 'one'.
But I am very sorry, good Horatio,
That to Laertes I forgot myself;
For by the image of my cause I see
The portraiture of his; I'll court his favours:
But sure the bravery of his grief did put me
Into a towering passion.

HORATIO Peace, who comes here?

OSRIC, *a diminutive and fantastical courtier, enters the hall, wearing a winged doublet and a hat of latest fashion*

OSRIC [*doffs his hat and bows low*] Your lordship is right welcome back to Denmark.

HAMLET I humbly thank you, sir. [*aside*] Dost know this water-fly?

HORATIO No, my good lord.

HAMLET Thy state is the more gracious, for 'tis a vice to know him. He hath much land, and fertile: let a beast be lord of beasts, and his crib shall stand at the king's mess. 'Tis a chough, but, as I say, spacious in the possession of dirt.

OSRIC [*bows again*] Sweet lord, if your lordship were at leisure, I should impart a thing to you from his majesty.

HAMLET I will receive it, sir, with all diligence of spirit. [*Osric continues bowing and waving his hat to and fro*] Put your bonnet to his right use, 'tis for the head.

OSRIC I thank your lordship, it is very hot.

HAMLET No, believe me, 'tis very cold, the wind is northerly.

OSRIC It is indifferent cold, my lord, indeed.

HAMLET But yet, methinks, it is very sultry and hot for my complexion.

OSRIC Exceedingly, my lord, it is very sultry – as 'twere – I cannot tell how. But, my lord, his majesty bade me signify to you that 'a has laid a great wager on your head. Sir, this is the matter, –

HAMLET [*again moves him to put on his hat*]
I beseech you remember –

OSRIC Nay, good my lord, for mine ease, in good faith. Sir, here is newly come to court Laertes – believe me, an absolute gentleman, full of most excellent differences, of very soft society, and great showing: indeed, to speak sellingly of him, he is the card or calendar of gentry; for you shall find in him the continent of what parts a gentleman would see.

HAMLET Sir, his definement suffers no perdition in you, though I know to divide him inventorially would dizzy th'arithmetic of memory, and yet but yaw neither in respect of his quick sail, but in the verity of extolment I take him to be a soul of great article, and his infusion of such dearth and rareness, as to make true diction of him, his semblable is his mirror, and who else would trace him? – his umbrage, nothing more.

OSRIC Your lordship speaks most infallibly of him.

HAMLET The concernancy, sir? Why do we wrap the gentleman in our more rawer breath?

OSRIC Sir?

HORATIO Is't not possible to understand in another tongue? You will to't, sir, really.

HAMLET What imports the nomination of this gentleman?

OSRIC Of Laertes?

HORATIO His purse is empty already, all's golden words are spent.

HAMLET Of him, sir.

OSRIC I know you are not ignorant –

hamlet I would you did, sir, yet in faith if you did, it would not much approve me. Well, sir?

OSRIC You are not ignorant of what excellence Laertes is –

HAMLET I dare not confess that, lest I should compare with him in excellence, but to know a man well were to know himself.

OSRIC I mean, sir, for his weapon, but in the imputation laid on him by them in his meed, he's unfellowed.

HAMLET What's his weapon?

OSRIC Rapier and dagger.

HAMLET That's two of his weapons – but, well.

OSRIC The king, sir, hath wagered with him six Barbary horses, against the which he has impawned, as I take it, six French rapiers and poniards, with their assigns, as girdle, hangers, and so. Three of the carriages in faith are very dear to fancy, very responsive to the hilts, most delicate carriages, and of very liberal conceit.

HAMLET What call you the carriages?

HORATIO I knew you must be edified by the margent ere you had done.

OSRIC The carriages, sir, are the hangers.

HAMLET The phrase would be more germane to the matter, if we could carry a cannon by our sides – I would it might be hangers till then. But on! Six Barbary horses against six French swords, their assigns, and three liberal-conceited carriages – that's the French bet against the Danish. Why is this all 'impawned' as you call it?

OSRIC The king, sir, hath laid, sir, that in a dozen passes between yourself and him he shall not exceed you three hits. He hath laid on twelve for nine. And it would come to immediate trial, if your lordship would vouchsafe the answer.

HAMLET How if I answer 'no'?

OSRIC I mean, my lord, the opposition of your person in trial.

HAMLET Sir, I will walk here in the hall, if it please his majesty. It is the breathing time of day with me. Let the foils be brought, the gentleman willing, and the king hold his purpose, I will win for him an I can, if not I will gain nothing but my shame and the odd hits.

OSRIC Shall I re-deliver you e'en so?

HAMLET To this effect, sir, after what flourish your nature will.

OSRIC [*bows*] I commend my duty to your lordship.

HAMLET Yours, yours. [*after another deep bow, Osric dons his hat and trips forth*

He does well to commend it himself, there are no tongues else for's turn.

HORATIO This lapwing runs away with the shell on his head.

HAMLET 'A did comply, sir, with his dug before 'a sucked it. Thus has he and many more of the same bevy that I know the drossy age dotes on – only got the tune of the time and, out of an habit of encounter, a kind of yeasty collection, which carries them through and through the most profound and winnowed opinions, and do but blow them to their trial, the bubbles are out.

A lord enters

LORD My lord, his majesty commended him to you by young Osric, who brings back to him that you attend him in the hall. He sends to know if your pleasure hold to play with Laertes, or that you will take longer time.

HAMLET I am constant to my purposes, they follow the king's pleasure. If his fitness speaks, mine is ready; now or whensoever, provided I be so able as now.

LORD The king, and queen, and all are coming down.

HAMLET In happy time.

LORD The queen desires you to use some gentle entertainment to Laertes before you fall to play.

HAMLET She well instructs me. [*the lord departs*

HORATIO You will lose this wager, my lord.

HAMLET I do not think so. Since he went into France, I have been in continual practice. I shall win at the odds; but thou wouldst not think how ill all's here about my heart – but it is no matter.

HORATIO Nay, good my lord –

HAMLET It is but foolery, but it is such a kind of gain-giving as would perhaps trouble a woman.

HORATIO If your mind dislike anything, obey it. I will forestall their repair hither, and say you are not fit.

HAMLET Not a whit, we defy augury. There is special providence in the fall of a sparrow. If it be now, 'tis not to come – if it be not to come, it will be now – if it be not now, yet it will come – the readiness is all. Since no man, of aught he leaves, knows what is't to leave betimes, let be.

Attendants enter to set benches and carry in cushions for the spectators; next follow trumpeters and drummers with kettle-drums, the KING, *the* QUEEN *and all the court,* OSRIC *and another lord, as judges, bearing foils and daggers which are placed upon a table near the walls, and last of all* LAERTES *dressed for the fence*

KING Come, Hamlet, come and take this hand from me.
[*he puts the hand of Laertes into the hand of Hamlet; and after leads the Queen to the chairs of state*

HAMLET Give me your pardon, sir. I have done you wrong,
But pardon't, as you are a gentleman.
This presence knows, and you must needs have heard,
How I am punished with a sore distraction.
What I have done
That might your nature, honour and exception
Roughly awake, I here proclaim was madness.
Was't Hamlet wronged Laertes? Never Hamlet.
If Hamlet from himself be ta'en away,
And when he's not himself does wrong Laertes,
Then Hamlet does it not, Hamlet denies it.
Who does it then? His madness. If't be so,
Hamlet is of the faction that is wronged,
His madness is poor Hamlet's enemy.
Sir, in this audience,
Let my disclaiming from a purposed evil
Free me so far in your most generous thoughts,
That I have shot my arrow o'er the house,
And hurt my brother.

LAERTES I am satisfied in nature,
Whose motive in this case should stir me most
To my revenge, but in my terms of honour
I stand aloof, and will no reconcilement,
Till by some elder masters of known honour
I have a voice and precedent of peace,
To keep my name ungored: but till that time,
I do receive your offered love like love,
And will not wrong it.

HAMLET I embrace it freely,
And will this brother's wager frankly play.
Give us the foils, come on.

LAERTES Come, one for me.

HAMLET I'll be your foil, Laertes. In mine ignorance
Your skill shall like a star i'th'darkest night
Stick fiery off indeed.

LAERTES You mock me, sir.

HAMLET No, by, this hand.

KING Give them the foils, young Osric.

[*Osric brings forward some four or five foils;*
Laertes takes one and makes a pass or two

Cousin Hamlet,
You know the wager?

HAMLET Very well, my lord.
Your grace has hid the odds o'th'weaker side.

KING I do not fear it, I have seen you both –
But since he is bettered, we have therefore odds.

LAERTES This is too heavy: let me see another.

[*he goes to the table and brings from it*
the poisoned and unbated rapier

HAMLET [*takes a foil from Osric*]
This likes me well. These foils have all a length?

OSRIC Ay, my good lord.

The judges and attendants prepare the floor for the fence; Hamlet makes ready; other servants bear in flagons of wine with cups

KING Set me the stoups of wine upon that table.
If Hamlet give the first or second hit,
Or quit in answer of the third exchange,

Let all the battlements their ordnance fire.
The king shall drink to Hamlet's better breath,
And in the cup an union shall he throw,
Richer than that which four successive kings
In Denmark's crown have worn: give me the cups,
And let the kettle to the trumpet speak,
The trumpet to the cannoneer without,
The cannons to the heavens, the heaven to earth,
'Now the king drinks to Hamlet.' Come, begin,
And you, the judges, bear a wary eye.

The cups are set at his side; trumpets sound; Hamlet and Laertes take their stations

HAMLET Come on, sir.

LAERTES Come, my lord,

They play

HAMLET One!

LAERTES No.

HAMLET Judgment?

OSRIC A hit, a very palpable hit.

[*they break off; the kettle-drum sounds, the trumpets blow, and a cannon-shot is heard without*

LAERTES Well, again.

KING Stay, give me drink. Hamlet, this pearl is thine.
Here's to thy health! [*he drinks and then seems to cast the pearl into the cup*
Give him the cup.

HAMLET I'll play this bout first, set it by a while.

[*the servant sets it on a table behind him*

Come. [*they play again*
Another hit! What say you?

LAERTES A touch, a touch, I do confess't. [*they break off*

KING Our son shall win.

QUEEN He's fat, and scant of breath.
Here, Hamlet, take my napkin, rub thy brows.

[*she gives it him, and going to the table takes up his cup of wine*

The queen carouses to thy fortune, Hamlet.

HAMLET Good madam!

KING Gertrude, do not drink.

QUEEN I will, my lord, I pray you pardon me.

[*she drinks and offers the cup to Hamlet*

KING It is the poisoned cup, it is too late!

HAMLET I dare not drink yet, madam – by and by.

QUEEN Come, let me wipe thy face. [*she does so*

LAERTES [*to the King*] My lord, I'll hit him now.

KING I do not think't.

LAERTES And yet 'tis almost 'gainst my conscience.

HAMLET Come, for the third, Laertes. You do but dally,
I pray you pass with your best violence.
I am afeard you make a wanton of me.

LAERTES Say you so? Come on.

They play the third bout

OSRIC Nothing neither way. [*they break off*

LAERTES [*suddenly*] Have at you now!

[*he takes Hamlet off his guard and wounds him slightly; Hamlet enraged closes with him, and 'in scuffling they change rapiers'*

KING Part them, they are incensed.

HAMLET [*attacks*] Nay, come again. [*the Queen falls*

OSRIC Look to the queen there, ho!

[*Hamlet wounds Laertes deeply*

HORATIO They bleed on both sides! – how is it, my lord?

[*Laertes falls*

OSRIC [*tending him*] How is't, Laertes?

LAERTES Why, as a woodcock to my own springe, Osric!
I am justly killed with mine own treachery.

HAMLET How does the queen?

KING She swoons to see them bleed.

QUEEN No, no, the drink, the drink – O my dear Hamlet –
The drink, the drink! I am poisoned! [*she dies*

HAMLET O villainy! Ho! Let the door be locked –
Treachery! Seek it out.

LAERTES It is here, Hamlet. Hamlet, thou art slain,
No medicine in the world can do thee good,
In thee there is not half an hour of life,

The treacherous instrument is in thy hand,
Unbated and envenomed. The foul practice
Hath turned itself on me, lo, here I lie,
Never to rise again – thy mother's poisoned –
I can no more – the king, the king's to blame.

HAMLET The point envenomed too! –
Then, venom, to thy work. [*he stabs the King*

ALL Treason! treason!

KING O, yet defend me, friends, I am but hurt.

HAMLET Here, thou incestuous, murderous, damnèd Dane,
[*he forces him to drink*
Drink off this potion. Is thy union here?
Follow my mother. [*the King dies*

LAERTES He is justly served,
It is a poison tempered by himself.
Exchange forgiveness with me, noble Hamlet,
Mine and my father's death come not upon thee,
Nor thine on me! [*he dies*

HAMLET Heaven make thee free of it! I follow thee. [*he falls*
I am dead, Horatio. Wretched queen, adieu!
You that look pale and tremble at this chance,
That are but mutes or audience to this act,
Had I but time, as this fell sergeant, Death,
Is strict in his arrest, O, I could tell you –
But let it be; Horatio, I am dead,
Thou livest, report me and my cause aright
To the unsatisfied.

HORATIO Never believe it;
I am more an antique Roman than a Dane –
Here's yet some liquor left. [*he seizes the cup*

HAMLET [*rises*] As thou'rt a man,
Give me the cup, let go, by heaven I'll ha't!
[*he dashes the cup to the ground and falls back*
O God, Horatio, what a wounded name,
Things standing thus unknown, shall live behind me!
If thou didst ever hold me in thy heart,
Absent thee from felicity awhile,
And in this harsh world draw thy breath in pain,
To tell my story.

[*the tread of soldiers marching heard afar off, and later a shot; Osric goes out*

What warlike noise is this?

OSRIC [*returning*] Young Fortinbras, with conquest come from Poland,
To th'ambassadors of England gives
This warlike volley.

HAMLET O, I die, Horatio,
The potent poison quite o'er-crows my spirit,
I cannot live to hear the news from England,
But I do prophesy th'election lights
On Fortinbras, he has my dying voice.
So tell him, with th'occurrents more and less
Which have solicited – the rest is silence. [*he dies*

HORATIO Now cracks a noble heart. Good night, sweet prince,
And flights of angels sing thee to thy rest!
Why does the drum come hither?

Prince FORTINBRAS, *the English ambassadors, and others enter*

FORT'BRAS Where is this sight?

HORATIO What is it you would see?
If aught of woe or wonder cease your search

FORT'BRAS This quarry cries on havoc. O proud death,
What feast is toward in thine eternal cell,
That thou so many princes at a shot
So bloodily hast struck?

1 AMBASS. The sight is dismal,
And our affairs from England come too late.
The ears are senseless that should give us hearing,
To tell him his commandment is fulfilled,
That Rosencrantz and Guildenstern are dead.
Where should we have our thanks?

HORATIO Not from his mouth
Had it th'ability of life to thank you;
He never gave commandment for their death;
But since, so jump upon this bloody question,
You from the Polack wars, and you from England,
Are here arrived, give order that these bodies
High on a stage be placèd to the view,

And let me speak to th'yet unknowing world
How these things came about; so shall you hear
Of carnal, bloody and unnatural acts,
Of accidental judgments, casual slaughters,
Of deaths put on by cunning and forced cause,
And, in this upshot, purposes mistook
Fall'n on th'inventors' heads: all this can I
Truly deliver.

FORT'BRAS Let us haste to hear it,
And call the noblest to the audience.
For me, with sorrow I embrace my fortune.
I have some rights of memory in this kingdom,
Which now to claim my vantage doth invite me.

HORATIO Of that I shall have also cause to speak,
And from his mouth whose voice will draw on more.
But let this same be presently performed,
Even while men's minds are wild, lest more mischance
On plots and errors happen.

FORT'BRAS Let four captains
Bear Hamlet like a soldier to the stage,
For he was likely, had he been put on,
To have proved most royal; and for his passage,
The soldiers' music and the rite of war
Speak loudly for him:
Take up the bodies – such a sight as this
Becomes the field, but here shows much amiss.
Go, bid the soldiers shoot.

The soldiers bear away the bodies, the while a dead march is heard; 'after the which a peal of ordnance is shot off'

OTHELLO

INTRODUCTION

The outline story of *Othello* is taken from the works of an Italian prose writer, Giambattista Cinthio Geraldi, published in 1564. Shakespeare also used Cinthio as his source for *Measure for Measure*, written at about the same time as *Othello*, around 1604. In Cinthio's story, an unnamed 'Moor', 'ensign' and 'corporal' stand for Othello, Iago and Cassio, although Desdemona is named. From this rather two-dimensional narrative, Shakespeare develops a complicated psychological portrait of jealousy and its effects, first performed at court before James I.

The play is the story of Othello, a black general in Venice who is renowned for his bravery and service to the state. Against her father's will, he marries Desdemona, and she immediately accompanies him to Cyprus, where it is feared the Turks are about to attack. Iago, Othello's companion, is passed over when the general makes Cassio his lieutenant. He engineers the downfall of Othello and Cassio by planting the seeds of suspicion about Desdemona's fidelity in Othello's fertile mind. Othello believes Desdemona has been unfaithful to him with Cassio, and the evidence, arranged by Iago with the inadvertent help of his wife Emilia, Desdemona's maid, seems to confirm his error. Othello smothers Desdemona, and then kills himself when he realises his mistake. Cassio becomes governor of Cyprus, and is left to decide the unrepentant Iago's punishment.

The most significant element of *Othello*, in literary-historical and plot terms, and in terms of its ongoing reception, is the blackness of its central character. On the stage, this fact cannot be overlooked, although it is possible to lose sight of it in reading the play. The cultural representation of blackness on which Shakespeare could draw dealt entirely in negative moral polarities: blackness was the property of the devil, the savage, the uncivilised. It was associated with sin, death, and villainy – and Shakespeare had not been averse to calling up these stereotypical associations in his characterisation of Aaron in *Titus Andronicus* (*c.*1593). Othello, however, offers a more complicated representation. Making a black man a hero was an intrepid development of the tragic form. The significance of Othello's colour cannot be overestimated, but its precise meanings are notoriously difficult to pin down. Certainly the play articulates, and seems to subvert, a conventional moral vocabulary which associated blackness with evil. As the Duke tells Brabantio, Desdemona's father, whose opposition to the match is entirely on racial grounds, 'your son-in-law is far more fair than black' (1.3.290), although for Brabantio, Othello is a 'sooty bosom' who has used 'foul charms' to ensnare his 'tender, fair, and happy' daughter and keep her from suitors 'of our nation' (1.2.66–71). Iago, Roderigo and Brabantio all voice their prejudices against Othello in racial terms, but the object of these remarks, Othello himself, is the representative of Venice in Cyprus, its loyal and decorated defender. Even Iago recognises Othello's 'free and open nature' (1.3.394) and uses this to plot his downfall. By contrast, it is Iago who is associated, particularly when his plotting is discovered, with the kind of qualities conventionally allied with and attributed to blackness: he is 'heathenish' (5.2.315) and 'hellish' (370). Clearly his terrible and destructive scheming is driven by a malevolence out of scale with his perceived slight by Othello over Cassio's promotion, even if his casual remark that ''twixt my sheets He's done my office' (1.3.382–83) is added to the supposed charges. In the representation of Othello and Iago, Shakespeare might be seen to have reversed stereotypical expectations that white equals good, black bad.

In another way, though, it seems that the stereotype is fulfilled. While Iago is single-minded in provoking Othello's jealousy, perhaps Othello must bear some of the responsibility also. Ultimately, he does kill his wife, at which Emilia calls him 'the blacker devil' (5.2.134). The justice of his own final self-exculpation is questionable: 'one that loved not wisely but too well' (5.2.346). Is Othello a stereotypical barbarian whose savagery is only thinly covered by Venetian manners, and whose excessive and uncontrollable jealousy prompts him to murder his innocent wife? Or is he an outsider, the black man grudgingly accepted for his military usefulness but under such personal pressure from a prejudiced society that he is particularly and tragically susceptible to Iago's provocation? Either way, the play seems to endorse the concept of blackness – as stereotypical moral inferiority, or as oppressed and brutalised minority – as crucial to any interpretation. For many modern readers, Othello emerges as the victim of prejudice, a representative sacrifice to the self-contained Venetian society whose agent is Iago. Shakespeare's Venice in *Othello*, as in *The Merchant of Venice*, is a seemingly cosmopolitan society policed by complex rules of incorporation and exclusion. Like Shylock, Othello is, ultimately, an outsider. It is likely that Venice functioned, on one level, as a kind of surrogate London in the dramatic geography of the late Elizabethan period, and, after reading *Othello*, it is no surprise to discover that, a couple of years before its first performances, Elizabeth I had formally banished from England all 'negars and blackamoors'. The play's representation of race has proved strikingly modern, and has tended to address contemporary racial concerns and attitudes. When the black actor Paul Robeson played the title role in a London production of the play in the 1930s, for example, he was not admitted to the hotel where the rest of the cast were celebrating. In the publicity for a 1995 film of the play (directed by Oliver Parker), parallels were drawn with the contemporaneous and public trial of the black American sportsman O. J. Simpson for the murder of his white girlfriend. One of the most interesting aspects of the play has to be its continued relevance to ongoing prejudices and racial politics.

Black and white are not the only polarities in the play, however, and not necessarily those which would have been most significant to its first audiences. The opposition between Christian Venice and Muslim ('infidel') Turkey is a crucial dynamic, and this geopolitical context extends the action beyond the claustrophobic, essentially domestic world of much of *Othello*. As long as Venice has Turkey as an external enemy against which it can unite, everything goes well enough. But the Turkish threat evaporates, thanks to a convenient storm, and the troops on Cyprus engage in drinking and mischief. 'Are we turned Turks?' thunders Othello, disturbed from the marital bed by his drunken soldiers. 'For Christian shame, put by this barbarous brawl' (2.3.157–59). It is cruelly apt that the *Oxford English Dictionary* includes among its definitions of the phrase 'to turn Turk' both anyone 'behaving as a barbarian or savage' and 'one who treats his wife hardly'. Suddenly barbarity is a threat from within, not without. Instead of being an externalised menace, it is insidiously ever-present. Iago personifies the enemy working within, but it is Othello himself who switches sides most startlingly. His final speech exemplifies the complex web of allegiances and social and cultural identities in which he is trapped. He likens himself to 'the base Indian' and then in a complex gesture of self-inscription and substitution, imagines his suicide as the act of the state's defender killing its enemy: 'in Aleppo once, Where a malignant and a turbaned Turk Beat a Venetian and traduced the state, I took by th'throat the circumcised dog And smote him – thus' (5.2.354–58). In this final act, Othello is the enemy and the victim within.

The play's insistence on reversals and revelations, on turning tables as well as Turks, rests on Iago, who speaks with uncanny skill to weaknesses and insecurities in those around him. Much psychologising about the play has focused on Iago's character, following Coleridge's influential statement of his 'motiveless malignity'. Iago's belief in his ruthless control over himself and others marks him as a distinctly modern dramatic subject. He asserts his own autonomy outside the structures of belief and hierarchy in which he refuses to be situated. Like gardeners, he argues, we each have responsibility for what grows in the soil of our character, for it is 'in ourselves that we are thus or thus' as 'the power and corrigible authority of this lies in our wills' (1.3.319–25). Iago is charismatic, and Cassio, Roderigo, and Othello himself, are all willing to respond to his force of personality. Othello's is a rather distant character, formal, unreachable, whereas Iago's tone is confiding, implicating, speaking in asides and soliloquies to the audience. In his asides, Iago operates both as a dramatic villain, like Richard III, or Edmund in *King Lear*, while his habit of soliloquising also links him with dramatic heroes like Hamlet or Macbeth. Othello, on the other hand, seems to be acted upon, rather than active. He takes the bait from Iago's hook, and all his actions, from his first appearance when he is summoned before the Duke's nocturnal council of war, seem to be dictated by others. Not until his suicide does he act autonomously, and even then, as has been seen, his sense of self is chronically fractured. Othello reacts; Iago acts. Othello's language is removed and oratorical; Iago soliloquises. Othello is a creature of the middle-stage, apparently unaware of his audience; Iago comes forward to fix us with an unsettlingly conspiratorial stare. For all Othello's tragic centrality in the plot, audience interest is largely located in Iago. Because we are given access to Iago's machiavellian plotting, we may lose sympathy with Othello's blind faith in his ensign, his unquestioning belief in 'honest Iago' and his willingness to accept the calumny against his new bride. He won Desdemona with his storytelling, and he commissions his own story, like so many tragic protagonists, in his dying speech. Othello is insistently self-dramatising but curiously uncertain of his own image. He recounts how he wooed Desdemona through his stories of himself, but he is then haunted by the fear that she loves an exotic idea of him rather than himself. His uncertainties make a gap into which Iago is able to insinuate his plots. Iago never voices any such self-doubt, and even when his role is discovered, he is unrepentant and unbroken.

Othello looks back and forward among Shakespeare's tragedies. Like *Romeo and Juliet*, it begins as a love story against a backdrop of a divided and sectarian society, and like that play, there is some hope that all may be well. (Shakespeare's apparent interest in this shift from comedy to tragedy is tellingly reversed in his revisiting of elements of the *Othello* story in *The Winter's Tale* (1611)). Like *Hamlet*, *Othello* has an element of the revenge tragedy, as Iago claims he is redressing wrongs done him by the Moor. The play looks forward, however, to the concerns of *King Lear* and *Macbeth* in its representation of the breakdown of its central personality. Othello undergoes a kind of mental collapse as all his worst fears seem to be realised, and he becomes his own destroyer. The extent to which he is a tragic victim, and the extent to which he is at least a partial architect of his downfall, are held in tension by the play and by critical reactions to it. *Othello* thus develops an idea of the tragic trajectory compelled by a destructive coalition of external and internal forces and agents: the external motor of *Romeo and Juliet* and the internal dynamic of *Hamlet* have been yoked together, as they will be again in *King Lear* and *Macbeth*.

The Scene: Venice; Cyprus

CHARACTERS IN THE PLAY

DUKE OF VENICE
BRABANTIO, *a senator, father to Desdemona*
Other Senators
GRATIANO, *brother to Brabantio*
LODOVICO, *kinsman to Brabantio*
OTHELLO, *a noble Moor in the service of the Venetian state*
CASSIO, *his lieutenant*
IAGO, *his ancient*
RODERIGO, *a Venetian gentleman*
MONTANO, *Othello's predecessor as governor of Cyprus*
Clown, servant to Othello

DESDEMONA, *daughter to Brabantio and wife to Othello*
EMILIA, *wife to Iago*
BIANCA, *mistress to Cassio*

Sailor, Messenger, Herald, Officers, Gentlemen, Musicians, and Attendants

OTHELLO

ACT I SCENE I

Venice. A street

Enter RODERIGO *and* IAGO

RODERIGO Tush, never tell me; I take it much unkindly
That thou, Iago, who hast had my purse
As if the strings were thine, shouldst know of this.

IAGO 'Sblood, but you'll not hear me.
If ever I did dream of such a matter,
Abhor me.

RODERIGO Thou told'st me thou didst hold him in thy hate.

IAGO Despise me if I do not. Three great ones of the city,
In personal suit to make me his lieutenant,
Off-capped to him; and, by the faith of man,
I know my price: I am worth no worse a place.
But he, as loving his own pride and purposes,
Evades them with a bombast circumstance
Horribly stuffed with epithets of war;
And, in conclusion,
Nonsuits my mediators: for, 'Certes,' says he,
'I have already chose my officer.'
And what was he?
Forsooth, a great arithmetician,
One Michael Cassio, a Florentine,
A fellow almost damned in a fair wife,
That never set a squadron in the field,
Nor the division of a battle knows
More than a spinster – unless the bookish theoric,
Wherein the togèd consuls can propose
As masterly as he; mere prattle without practice
Is all his soldiership. But he, sir, had th'election;
And I, of whom his eyes had seen the proof
At Rhodes, at Cyprus, and on other grounds
Christian and heathen, must be be-lee'd and calmed
By debitor-and-creditor: this counter-caster,
He, in good time, must his lieutenant be,

And I – God bless the mark! – His Moorship's ancient.

RODERIGO By heaven, I rather would have been his hangman.

IAGO Why, there's no remedy: 'tis the curse of service;
Preferment goes by letter and affection,
And not by old gradation, where each second
Stood heir to th'first. Now, sir, be judge yourself
Whether I in any just term am affined
To love the Moor.

RODERIGO I would not follow him then.

IAGO O, sir, content you.
I follow him to serve my turn upon him.
We cannot all be masters, nor all masters
Cannot be truly followed. You shall mark
Many a duteous and knee-crooking knave
That, doting on his own obsequious bondage,
Wears out his time, much like his master's ass,
For nought but provender, and, when he's old, cashiered.
Whip me such honest knaves. Others there are
Who, trimmed in forms and visages of duty,
Keep yet their hearts attending on themselves;
And, throwing but shows of service on their lords,
Do well thrive by them; and, when they've lined their coats,
Do themselves homage. These fellows have some soul,
And such a one do I profess myself:
For sir,
It is as sure as you are Roderigo,
Were I the Moor, I would not be Iago;
In following him, I follow but myself;
Heaven is my judge, not I for love and duty,
But seeming so, for my peculiar end;
For when my outward action doth demonstrate
The native act and figure of my heart
In compliment extern, 'tis not long after
But I will wear my heart upon my sleeve
For daws to peck at – I am not what I am.

RODERIGO What a full fortune does the thick-lips owe,
If he can carry't thus!

IAGO Call up her father,

Rouse him, make after him, poison his delight,
Proclaim him in the streets, incense her kinsmen,
And, though he in a fertile climate dwell,
Plague him with flies; though that his joy be joy,
Yet throw such changes of vexation on't
As it may lose some colour.

RODERIGO Here is her father's house; I'll call aloud.

IAGO Do; with like timorous accent and dire yell
As when, by night and negligence, the fire
Is spied in populous cities.

RODERIGO What, ho, Brabantio! Signior Brabantio, ho!

IAGO Awake! What, ho, Brabantio! Thieves! Thieves! Thieves!
Look to your house, your daughter, and your bags!
Thieves! Thieves!

BRABANTIO *appears above, at a window*

BRABANTIO What is the reason of this terrible summons?
What is the matter there?

RODERIGO Signior, is all your family within?

IAGO Are your doors locked?

BRABANTIO Why, wherefore ask you this?

IAGO 'Zounds, sir, you're robbed; for shame, put on your gown;
Your heart is burst; you have lost half your soul;
Even now, now, very now, an old black ram
Is tupping your white ewe. Arise, arise;
Awake the snorting citizens with the bell,
Or else the devil will make a grandsire of you.
Arise, I say.

BRABANTIO What, have you lost your wits?

RODERIGO Most reverend signior, do you know my voice?

BRABANTIO Not I; what are you?

RODERIGO My name is Roderigo.

BRABANTIO The worser welcome:
I have charged thee not to haunt about my doors;
In honest plainness thou hast heard me say
My daughter is not for thee; and now, in madness,
Being full of supper and distempering draughts,
Upon malicious knavery dost thou come
To start my quiet.

RODERIGO Sir, sir, sir –
BRABANTIO But thou must needs be sure
My spirit and my place have in them power
To make this bitter to thee.
RODERIGO Patience, good sir.
BRABANTIO What tell'st thou me of robbing? This is Venice:
My house is not a grange.
RODERIGO Most grave Brabantio,
In simple and pure soul I come to you.

IAGO 'Zounds, sir, you are one of those that will not serve God, if the devil bid you. Because we come to do you service and you think we are ruffians, you'll have your daughter covered with a Barbary horse; you'll have your nephews neigh to you; you'll have coursers for cousins, and jennets for germans.

BRABANTIO What profane wretch art thou?

IAGO I am one, sir, that comes to tell you your daughter and the Moor are now making the beast with two backs.

BRABANTIO Thou art a villain.
IAGO You are a senator.
BRABANTIO This thou shalt answer; I know thee, Roderigo.
RODERIGO Sir, I will answer anything. But I beseech you,
If't be your pleasure and most wise consent,
As partly I find it is, that your fair daughter,
At this odd-even and dull watch o' th'night,
Transported with no worse nor better guard
But with a knave of common hire, a gondolier,
To the gross clasps of a lascivious Moor –
If this be known to you, and your allowance,
We then have done you bold and saucy wrong;
But if you know not this, my manners tell me
We have your wrong rebuke. Do not believe
That, from the sense of all civility,
I thus would play and trifle with your reverence.
Your daughter, if you have not given her leave,
I say again, hath made a gross revolt,
Tying her duty, beauty, wit, and fortunes
In an extravagant and wheeling stranger
Of here and everywhere. Straight satisfy yourself.

If she be in her chamber or your house,
Let loose on me the justice of the state
For thus deluding you.

BRABANTIO Strike on the tinder, ho!
Give me a taper! Call up all my people!
This accident is not unlike my dream;
Belief of it oppresses me already.
Light, I say! Light! *[he goes in*

IAGO Farewell, for I must leave you:
It seems not meet nor wholesome to my place
To be produced – as, if I stay, I shall –
Against the Moor; for I do know the state,
However this may gall him with some check,
Cannot with safety cast him; for he's embarked
With such loud reason to the Cyprus wars,
Which even now stand in act, that, for their souls,
Another of his fathom they have none
To lead their business: in which regard,
Though I do hate him as I do hell-pains,
Yet, for necessity of present life,
I must show out a flag and sign of love,
Which is indeed but sign. That you shall surely find him,
Lead to the Sagittary the raisèd search,
And there will I be with him. So farewell. *[he goes*

Enter, below, BRABANTIO, *and Servants with torches*

BRABANTIO It is too true an evil: gone she is;
And what's to come of my despisèd time
Is nought but bitterness. Now, Roderigo,
Where didst thou see her? O unhappy girl!
With the Moor, say'st thou? Who would be a father!
How didst thou know 'twas she? O, she deceives me
Past thought! What said she to you? Get more tapers.
Raise all my kindred. Are they married, think you?

RODERIGO Truly, I think they are.

BRABANTIO O heaven! How got she out? O treason of the blood!
Fathers, from hence trust not your daughters' minds
By what you see them act! Is there not charms
By which the property of youth and maidhood
May be abused? Have you not read, Roderigo,

Of some such thing?

RODERIGO Yes, sir, I have indeed.

BRABANTIO Call up my brother. O, that you had had her!
Some one way, some another. Do you know
Where we may apprehend her and the Moor?

RODERIGO I think I can discover him, if you please
To get good guard and go along with me.

BRABANTIO Pray you, lead on. At every house I'll call;
I may command at most. Get weapons, ho!
And raise some special officers of night.
On, good Roderigo; I'll deserve your pains. *[they go*

SCENE 2

Another street

Enter OTHELLO, IAGO, *and Attendants with torches*

IAGO Though in the trade of war I have slain men,
Yet do I hold it very stuff o'th'conscience
To do no contrived murder. I lack iniquity
Sometimes to do me service. Nine or ten times
I had thought t'have jerked him here under the ribs.

OTHELLO 'Tis better as it is.

IAGO Nay, but he prated,
And spoke such scurvy and provoking terms
Against your honour
That, with the little godliness I have,
I did full hard forbear him. But I pray, sir,
Are you fast married? For be sure of this,
That the magnifico is much beloved,
And hath in his effect a voice potential
As double as the duke's. He will divorce you,
Or put upon you what restraint and grievance
The law, with all his might to enforce it on,
Will give him cable.

OTHELLO Let him do his spite;
My services which I have done the signiory
Shall out-tongue his complaints. 'Tis yet to know –
Which, when I know that boasting is an honour,

I shall promulgate – I fetch my life and being
From men of royal siege; and my demerits
May speak unbonneted to as proud a fortune
As this that I have reached. For know, Iago,
But that I love the gentle Desdemona,
I would not my unhousèd free condition
Put into circumscription and confine
For the sea's worth. But look what lights come yond!

IAGO Those are the raisèd father and his friends.
You were best go in.

OTHELLO Not I; I must be found.
My parts, my title, and my perfect soul,
Shall manifest me rightly. Is it they?

IAGO By Janus, I think no.

Enter CASSIO, *and certain Officers with torches*

OTHELLO The servants of the duke, and my lieutenant!
The goodness of the night upon you, friends!
What is the news?

CASSIO The duke does greet you, general,
And he requires your haste-post-haste appearance
Even on the instant.

OTHELLO What is the matter, think you?

CASSIO Something from Cyprus, as I may divine.
It is a business of some heat: the galleys
Have sent a dozen sequent messengers
This very night at one another's heels;
And many of the consuls, raised and met,
Are at the duke's already. You have been hotly called for;
When, being not at your lodging to be found,
The senate hath sent about three several quests
To search you out.

OTHELLO 'Tis well I am found by you.
I will but spend a word here in the house,
And go with you. [*he goes in*

CASSIO Ancient, what makes he here?

IAGO Faith, he tonight hath boarded a land carack;
If it prove lawful prize, he's made for ever.

CASSIO I do not understand.

IAGO He's married.

CASSIO To who?

Re-enter OTHELLO

IAGO Marry, to – Come, captain, will you go?

OTHELLO Have with you.

CASSIO Here comes another troop to seek for you.

IAGO It is Brabantio. General, be advised;
He comes to bad intent.

Enter BRABANTIO, RODERIGO, *and Officers with torches and weapons*

OTHELLO Holla! Stand there!

RODERIGO Signior, it is the Moor.

BRABANTIO Down with him, thief!

[*they draw on both sides*

IAGO You, Roderigo! Come sir, I am for you.

OTHELLO Keep up your bright swords, for the dew will rust them.
Good signior, you shall more command with years
Than with your weapons.

BRABANTIO O thou foul thief, where hast thou stowed my daughter?
Damned as thou art, thou hast enchanted her.
For I'll refer me to all things of sense,
If she in chains of magic were not bound,
Whether a maid so tender, fair, and happy,
So opposite to marriage that she shunned
The wealthy curlèd darlings of our nation,
Would ever have, t'incur a general mock,
Run from her guardage to the sooty bosom
Of such a thing as thou – to fear, not to delight.
Judge me the world, if 'tis not gross in sense
That thou hast practised on her with foul charms,
Abused her delicate youth with drugs or minerals
That weaken motion: I'll have't disputed on;
'Tis probable and palpable to thinking.
I therefore apprehend and do attach thee
For an abuser of the world, a practiser
Of arts inhibited and out of warrant.
Lay hold upon him. If he do resist,

Subdue him at his peril.

OTHELLO Hold your hands,
Both you of my inclining and the rest:
Were it my cue to fight, I should have known it
Without a prompter. Where will you that I go
To answer this your charge?

BRABANTIO To prison, till fit time
Of law and course of direct session
Call thee to answer.

OTHELLO What if I do obey?
How may the duke be therewith satisfied,
Whose messengers are here about my side,
Upon some present business of the state
To bring me to him?

I OFFICER 'Tis true, most worthy signior;
The duke's in council, and your noble self,
I am sure, is sent for.

BRABANTIO How! The duke in council!
In this time of the night! Bring him away.
Mine's not an idle cause: the duke himself,
Or any of my brothers of the state,
Cannot but feel this wrong as 'twere their own;
For if such actions may have passage free,
Bond-slaves and pagans shall our statesmen be.
[*they go*

SCENE 3

A council-chamber

The DUKE *and Senators sitting at a table; Officers attending*

DUKE There is no composition in these news
That gives them credit.

I SENATOR Indeed they are disproportioned:
My letters say a hundred and seven galleys.

DUKE And mine, a hundred and forty.

2 SENATOR And mine, two hundred;
But though they jump not on a just account –
As in these cases where the aim reports

'Tis oft with difference – yet do they all confirm
A Turkish fleet, and bearing up to Cyprus.

DUKE Nay, it is possible enough to judgment;
I do not so secure me in the error,
But the main article I do approve
In fearful sense.

SAILOR [*without*] What, ho! What, ho! What, ho!

I OFFICER A messenger from the galleys.

Enter Sailor

DUKE Now, what's the business?

SAILOR The Turkish preparation makes for Rhodes;
So was I bid report here to the state
By Signior Angelo.

DUKE How say you by this change?

I SENATOR This cannot be,
By no assay of reason; 'tis a pageant
To keep us in false gaze. When we consider
Th'importancy of Cyprus to the Turk,
And let ourselves again but understand
That, as it more concerns the Turk than Rhodes,
So may he with more facile question bear it,
For that it stands not in such warlike brace,
But altogether lacks th'abilities
That Rhodes is dressed in – if we make thought of this,
We must not think the Turk is so unskilful
To leave that latest which concerns him first,
Neglecting an attempt of ease and gain
To wake and wage a danger profitless.

DUKE Nay, in all confidence, he's not for Rhodes.

I OFFICER Here is more news.

Enter a Messenger

MESSENGER The Ottomites, reverend and gracious,
Steering with due course toward the isle of Rhodes,
Have there injointed with an after fleet.

I SENATOR Ay, so I thought. How many, as you guess?

MESSENGER Of thirty sail; and now they do re-stem
Their backward course, bearing with frank appearance
Their purposes toward Cyprus. Signior Montano,

Your trusty and most valiant servitor,
With his free duty recommends you thus,
And prays you to relieve him.

DUKE 'Tis certain then for Cyprus.
Marcus Luccicos, is not he in town?

I SENATOR He's now in Florence.

DUKE Write from us to him; post-post-haste dispatch.

I SENATOR Here comes Brabantio and the valiant Moor.

Enter BRABANTIO, OTHELLO, IAGO, RODERIGO, *and Officers*

DUKE Valiant Othello, we must straight employ you
Against the general enemy Ottoman.
[*to Brabantio*]
I did not see you; welcome, gentle signior;
We lacked your counsel and your help tonight.

BRABANTIO So did I yours. Good your grace, pardon me:
Neither my place nor aught I heard of business
Hath raised me from my bed, nor doth the general care
Take hold on me; for my particular grief
Is of so flood-gate and o'erbearing nature
That it engluts and swallows other sorrows,
And yet is still itself.

DUKE Why, what's the matter?

BRABANTIO My daughter! O, my daughter!

ALL Dead?

BRABANTIO Ay, to me:
She is abused, stolen from me and corrupted
By spells and medicines bought of mountebanks;
For nature so preposterously to err,
Being not deficient, blind, or lame of sense,
Sans witchcraft could not.

DUKE Whoe'er he be that in this foul proceeding
Hath thus beguiled your daughter of herself,
And you of her, the bloody book of law
You shall yourself read in the bitter letter
After your own sense, yea, though our proper son
Stood in your action.

BRABANTIO Humbly I thank your grace.
Here is the man: this Moor, whom now, it seems,
Your special mandate for the state affairs

Hath hither brought.

ALL We are very sorry for't.

DUKE [*to Othello*]
What in your own part can you say to this?

BRABANTIO Nothing, but this is so.

OTHELLO Most potent, grave, and reverend signiors,
My very noble and approved good masters,
That I have ta'en away this old man's daughter,
It is most true; true, I have married her:
The very head and front of my offending
Hath this extent, no more. Rude am I in my speech,
And little blest with the soft phrase of peace:
For since these arms of mine had seven years' pith
Till now some nine moons wasted, they have used
Their dearest action in the tented field;
And little of this great world can I speak
More than pertains to feats of broil and battle;
And therefore little shall I grace my cause
In speaking for myself. Yet, by your patience,
I will a round unvarnished tale deliver
Of my whole course of love: what drugs, what charms,
What conjuration, and what mighty magic –
For such proceedings I am charged withal –
I won his daughter.

BRABANTIO A maiden never bold;
Of spirit so still and quiet that her motion
Blushed at herself; and she – in spite of nature,
Of years, of country, credit, everything –
To fall in love with what she feared to look on!
It is a judgment maimed and most imperfect
That will confess perfection so could err
Against all rules of nature, and must be driven
To find out practices of cunning hell
Why this should be. I therefore vouch again
That with some mixtures powerful o'er the blood,
Or with some dram conjured to this effect,
He wrought upon her.

DUKE To vouch this is no proof,
Without more wider and more overt test

Than these thin habits and poor likelihoods
Of modern seeming do prefer against him.

I SENATOR But, Othello, speak:
Did you by indirect and forcèd courses
Subdue and poison this young maid's affections?
Or came it by request and such fair question
As soul to soul affordeth?

OTHELLO I beseech you,
Send for the lady to the Sagittary,
And let her speak of me before her father;
If you do find me foul in her report,
The trust, the office I do hold of you,
Not only take away, but let your sentence
Even fall upon my life.

DUKE Fetch Desdemona hither.

OTHELLO Ancient, conduct them; you best know the place.
[Iago departs with attendants
And till she come, as truly as to heaven
I do confess the vices of my blood,
So justly to your grave ears I'll present
How I did thrive in this fair lady's love,
And she in mine.

DUKE Say it, Othello.

OTHELLO Her father loved me, oft invited me,
Still questioned me the story of my life
From year to year – the battles, sieges, fortunes,
That I have passed.
I ran it through, even from my boyish days
To th' very moment that he bade me tell it:
Wherein I spake of most disastrous chances,
Of moving accidents by flood and field,
Of hair-breadth scapes i'th'imminent deadly breach,
Of being taken by the insolent foe,
And sold to slavery; of my redemption thence,
And portance in my travels' history:
Wherein of antres vast and deserts idle,
Rough quarries, rocks, and hills whose heads touch heaven,
It was my hint to speak – such was the process;

And of the Cannibals that each other eat,
The Anthropophagi, and men whose heads
Do grow beneath their shoulders. This to hear
Would Desdemona seriously incline;
But still the house affairs would draw her thence,
Which ever as she could with haste dispatch
She'ld come again, and with a greedy ear
Devour up my discourse; which I observing,
Took once a pliant hour, and found good means
To draw from her a prayer of earnest heart
That I would all my pilgrimage dilate,
Whereof by parcels she had something heard,
But not intentively. I did consent,
And often did beguile her of her tears
When I did speak of some distressful stroke
That my youth suffered. My story being done,
She gave me for my pains a world of sighs:
She swore, in faith 'twas strange, 'twas passing strange;
'Twas pitiful, 'twas wondrous pitiful;
She wished she had not heard it, yet she wished
That heaven had made her such a man; she thanked me,
And bade me, if I had a friend that loved her,
I should but teach him how to tell my story,
And that would woo her. Upon this hint I spake;
She loved me for the dangers I had passed,
And I loved her that she did pity them.
This only is the witchcraft I have used.
Here comes the lady; let her witness it.

Enter DESDEMONA, IAGO, *and Attendants*

DUKE I think this tale would win my daughter too.
Good Brabantio,
Take up this mangled matter at the best:
Men do their broken weapons rather use
Than their bare hands.

BRABANTIO I pray you, hear her speak.
If she confess that she was half the wooer,
Destruction on my head, if my bad blame
Light on the man! Come hither, gentle mistress:
Do you perceive in all this company

Where most you owe obedience?

DESDEM. My noble father,
I do perceive here a divided duty.
To you I am bound for life and education;
My life and education both do learn me
How to respect you. You are the lord of duty;
I am hitherto your daughter. But here's my husband;
And so much duty as my mother showed
To you, preferring you before her father,
So much I challenge that I may profess
Due to the Moor my lord.

BRABANTIO God bu'y! I've done.
Please it your grace, on to the state affairs.
I had rather to adopt a child than get it.
Come hither, Moor:
I here do give thee that with all my heart,
Which, but thou hast already, with all my heart
I would keep from thee. For your sake, jewel,
I am glad at soul I have no other child;
For thy escape would teach me tyranny,
To hang clogs on them. I have done, my Lord.

DUKE Let me speak like yourself, and say a sentence
Which, as a grise or step, may help these lovers
Into your favour.
When remedies are past, the griefs are ended
By seeing the worst, which late on hopes depended.
To mourn a mischief that is past and gone
Is the next way to draw new mischief on.
What cannot be preserved when Fortune takes,
Patience her injury a mockery makes.
The robbed that smiles steals something from the thief;
He robs himself that spends a bootless grief.

BRABANTIO So let the Turk of Cyprus us beguile,
We lose it not so long as we can smile.
He bears the sentence well that nothing bears
But the free comfort which from thence he hears;
But he bears both the sentence and the sorrow
That to pay grief must of poor patience borrow.
These sentences, to sugar or to gall,

Being strong on both sides, are equivocal.
But words are words: I never yet did hear
That the bruised heart was piercèd through the ear.
I humbly beseech you, proceed to th'affairs of state.

DUKE The Turk with a most mighty preparation makes for Cyprus. Othello, the fortitude of the place is best known to you; and though we have there a substitute of most allowed sufficiency, yet opinion, a sovereign mistress of effects, throws a more safer voice on you: you must therefore be content to slubber the gloss of your new fortunes with this more stubborn and boisterous expedition.

OTHELLO The tyrant Custom, most grave senators,
Hath made the flinty and steel couch of war
My thrice-driven bed of down. I do agnize
A natural and prompt alacrity
I find in hardness; and do undertake
These present wars against the Ottomites.
Most humbly therefore bending to your state,
I crave fit disposition for my wife,
Due reference of place and exhibition,
With such accommodation and besort
As levels with her breeding.

DUKE Why, if you please,
Be't at her father's.

BRABANTIO I'll not have it so.

OTHELLO Nor I.

DESDEM. Nor I; I would not there reside,
To put my father in impatient thoughts
By being in his eye. Most gracious duke,
To my unfolding lend your prosperous ear,
And let me find a charter in your voice
T'assist my simpleness.

DUKE What would you, Desdemona?

DESDEM. That I did love the Moor to live with him,
My downright violence and scorn of fortunes
May trumpet to the world. My heart's subdued
Even to the very quality of my lord.
I saw Othello's visage in his mind,

And to his honours and his valiant parts
Did I my soul and fortunes consecrate.
So that, dear lords, if I be left behind,
A moth of peace, and he go to the war,
The rights for why I love him are bereft me,
And I a heavy interim shall support
By his dear absence. Let me go with him.

OTHELLO Let her have your voice.
Vouch with me, heaven, I therefore beg it not
To please the palate of my appetite;
Nor to comply with heat and young affects
In my distinct and proper satisfaction;
But to be free and bounteous to her mind.
And heaven defend your good souls that you think
I will your serious and great business scant
For she is with me. No, when light-winged toys
Of feathered Cupid seel with wanton dullness
My speculative and officed instruments,
That my disports corrupt and taint my business,
Let housewives make a skillet of my helm,
And all indign and base adversities
Make head against my estimation!

DUKE Be it as you shall privately determine,
Either for her stay or going; th'affair cries haste,
And speed must answer it.

I SENATOR You must away tonight.

OTHELLO With all my heart.

DUKE At nine i'th'morning here we'll meet again.
Othello, leave some officer behind,
And he shall our commission bring to you;
With such things else of quality and respect
As doth import you.

OTHELLO So please your grace, my ancient:
A man he is of honesty and trust;
To his conveyance I assign my wife,
With what else needful your good grace shall think
To be sent after me.

DUKE Let it be so.
Good night to everyone. And, noble signior,

If virtue no delighted beauty lack,
Your son-in-law is far more fair than black.

I SENATOR Adieu, brave Moor; use Desdemona well.

BRABANTIO Look to her, Moor, if thou hast eyes to see:
She has deceived her father, and may thee.

OTHELLO My life upon her faith! [*Duke, Senators, Officers, etc. go*
Honest Iago,
My Desdemona must I leave to thee;
I prithee, let thy wife attend on her,
And bring them after in the best advantage.
Come, Desdemona, I have but an hour
Of love, of worldly matter and direction,
To spend with thee: we must obey the time.
[*Othello and Desdemona go out*

RODERIGO Iago!

IAGO What say'st thou, noble heart?

RODERIGO What will I do, think'st thou?

IAGO Why, go to bed and sleep.

RODERIGO I will incontinently drown myself.

IAGO If thou dost, I shall never love thee after. Why, thou silly gentleman!

RODERIGO It is silliness to live when to live is torment; and then have we a prescription to die when death is our physician.

IAGO O villainous! I have looked upon the world for four times seven years; and since I could distinguish betwixt a benefit and an injury, I never found a man that knew how to love himself. Ere I would say I would drown myself for the love of a guinea-hen, I would change my humanity with a baboon.

RODERIGO What should I do? I confess it is my shame to be so fond, but it is not in my virtue to amend it.

IAGO Virtue! A fig! 'tis in ourselves that we are thus or thus. Our bodies are gardens, to the which our wills are gardeners; so that if we will plant nettles or sow lettuce, set hyssop and weed up tine, supply it with one gender of herbs or distract it with many, either to have it sterile with idleness or manured with industry – why, the power and corrigible authority of this lies in our wills. If the beam of our lives had not one scale of reason to poise another of sensuality, the blood and baseness of our natures would conduct us to most preposterous conclusions. But we have reason to cool our raging motions, our carnal stings, our unbitted lusts; whereof I take this, that you call love, to be a set or scion.

RODERIGO It cannot be.

IAGO It is merely a lust of the blood and a permission of the will. Come, be a man. Drown thyself! Drown cats and blind puppies. I have professed me thy friend, and I confess me knit to thy deserving with cables of perdurable toughness. I could never better stead thee than now. Put money in thy purse; follow thou these wars; defeat thy favour with an usurped beard. I say, put money in thy purse. It cannot be that Desdemona should long continue her love to the Moor – put money in thy purse – nor he his to her: it was a violent commencement, and thou shalt see an answerable sequestration – put but money in thy purse. These Moors are changeable in their wills – fill thy purse with money. The food that to him now is as luscious as locusts, shall be to him shortly as bitter as coloquintida. She must change for youth: when she is sated with his body, she will find the error of her choice. Therefore put money in thy purse. If thou wilt needs damn thyself, do it a more delicate way than drowning. Make all the money thou canst. If sanctimony and a frail vow betwixt an erring barbarian and a supersubtle Venetian be not too hard for my wits and all the tribe of hell, thou shalt enjoy her; therefore make money. A pox of drowning thyself! 'Tis clean out of the way. Seek thou rather to be hanged in compassing thy joy than to be drowned and go without her.

RODERIGO Wilt thou be fast to my hopes, if I depend on the issue?

IAGO Thou art sure of me. Go, make money. I have told thee often, and I retell thee again and again, I hate the Moor. My cause is hearted; thine hath no less reason. Let us be conjunctive in our revenge against him. If thou canst cuckold him, thou dost thyself a pleasure, me a sport. There are many events in the womb of time, which will be delivered. Traverse! Go; provide thy money. We will have more of this tomorrow. Adieu.

RODERIGO Where shall we meet i'th'morning?

IAGO At my lodging.

RODERIGO I'll be with thee betimes.

IAGO Go to; farewell. Do you hear, Roderigo?

RODERIGO What say you?

IAGO No more of drowning, do you hear?

RODERIGO I am changed.

IAGO Go to; farewell. Put money enough in your purse.

RODERIGO I'll sell all my land. [*goes*

IAGO Thus do I ever make my fool my purse;
For I mine own gained knowledge should profane
If I would time expend with such a snipe
But for my sport and profit. I hate the Moor;
And it is thought abroad that 'twixt my sheets
He's done my office. I know not if't be true;
Yet I, for mere suspicion in that kind,
Will do as if for surety. He holds me well;
The better shall my purpose work on him.
Cassio's a proper man: let me see now;
To get his place, and to plume up my will
In double knavery. How? How? Let's see:
After some time to abuse Othello's ear
That he is too familiar with his wife;
He hath a person and a smooth dispose
To be suspected – framed to make women false.
The Moor is of a free and open nature
That thinks men honest that but seem to be so,
And will as tenderly be led by th'nose
As asses are.
I have't. It is engendered. Hell and night
Must bring this monstrous birth to the world's light.
[*goes*

ACT 2 SCENE 1

A sea-port in Cyprus. An open place near the quay

Enter MONTANO *and two Gentlemen*

MONTANO What from the cape can you discern at sea?
1 GENT'MAN Nothing at all: it is a high-wrought flood;
I cannot 'twixt the heaven and the main
Descry a sail.
MONTANO Methinks the wind hath spoke aloud at land;
A fuller blast ne'er shook our battlements.
If it hath ruffianed so upon the sea,
What ribs of oak, when mountains melt on them,
Can hold the mortise? What shall we hear of this?
2 GENT'MAN A segregation of the Turkish fleet:
For do but stand upon the foaming shore,
The chidden billow seems to pelt the clouds;
The wind-shaked surge, with high and monstrous mane,
Seems to cast water on the burning Bear,
And quench the guards of th'ever-fixèd pole.
I never did like molestation view
On the enchafèd flood.
MONTANO If that the Turkish fleet
Be not ensheltered and embayed, they are drowned;
It is impossible they bear it out.

Enter a third Gentleman

3 GENT'MAN News, lads! Our wars are done:
The desperate tempest hath so banged the Turks
That their designment halts. A noble ship of Venice
Hath seen a grievous wreck and sufferance
On most part of their fleet.
MONTANO How! Is this true?
3 GENT'MAN The ship is here put in,
A Veronesa; Michael Cassio,
Lieutenant to the warlike Moor Othello,
Is come on shore; the Moor himself at sea,
And is in full commission here for Cyprus.

MONTANO I am glad on't; 'tis a worthy governor.
3 GENT'MAN But this same Cassio, though he speak of comfort
Touching the Turkish loss, yet he looks sadly,
And prays the Moor be safe; for they were parted
With foul and violent tempest.
MONTANO Pray heaven he be;
For I have served him, and the man commands
Like a full soldier. Let's to the sea-side, ho!
As well to see the vessel that's come in
As to throw out our eyes for brave Othello,
Even till we make the main and th'aerial blue
An indistinct regard.
3 GENT'MAN Come, let's do so;
For every minute is expectancy
Of more arrivance.

Enter CASSIO

CASSIO Thanks you, the valiant of this warlike isle,
That so approve the Moor! O, let the heavens
Give him defence against the elements,
For I have lost him on a dangerous sea.
MONTANO Is he well shipped?
CASSIO His bark is stoutly timbered, and his pilot
Of very expert and approved allowance;
Therefore my hopes, not forfeited to death,
Stand in bold cure.
[*a cry heard:* 'A sail, a sail, a sail!'

Enter a fourth Gentleman

CASSIO What noise?
4 GENT'MAN The town is empty; on the brow o'th'sea
Stand ranks of people, and they cry 'A sail!'
CASSIO My hopes do shape him for the Governor. [*guns heard*
2 GENT'MAN They do discharge their shot of courtesy:
Our friends at least.
CASSIO I pray you, sir, go forth,
And give us truth who 'tis that is arrived.
2 GENT'MAN I shall. [*goes*
MONTANO But, good lieutenant, is your general wived?
CASSIO Most fortunately: he hath achieved a maid

That paragons description and wild fame;
One that excels the quirks of blazoning pens,
And in th'essential vesture of creation
Does tire the ingener.

Re-enter second Gentleman

How now! Who has put in?

2 GENT'MAN 'Tis one Iago, ancient to the general.

CASSIO He's had most favourable and happy speed:
Tempests themselves, high seas, and howling winds,
The guttered rocks, and congregated sands,
Traitors insteeped to clog the guiltless keel,
As having sense of beauty, do omit
Their mortal natures, letting go safely by
The divine Desdemona.

MONTANO What is she?

CASSIO She that I spake of, our great captain's captain,
Left in the conduct of the bold Iago;
Whose footing here anticipates our thoughts
A se'nnight's speed. Great Jove, Othello guard,
And swell his sail with thine own powerful breath
That he may bless this bay with his tall ship,
Make love's quick pants in Desdemona's arms,
Give renewed fire to our extincted spirits,
And bring all Cyprus comfort.

Enter DESDEMONA, EMILIA, IAGO, RODERIGO, *and Attendants*

O, behold,
The riches of the ship is come on shore!
You men of Cyprus, let her have your knees.
Hail to thee, lady! And the grace of heaven,
Before, behind thee, and on every hand,
Enwheel thee round!

DESDEM. I thank you, valiant Cassio.
What tidings can you tell me of my lord?

CASSIO He is not yet arrived; nor know I aught
But that he's well and will be shortly here.

DESDEM. O, but I fear – How lost you company?

CASSIO The great contention of the sea and skies
Parted our fellowship. But, hark! A sail!

[*a cry heard,* 'A sail, a sail!', *and then guns*

2 GENT. They give their greeting to the citadel:
This likewise is a friend.

CASSIO See for the news.

[*Gentleman goes*

Good ancient, you are welcome.
[*to Emilia*] Welcome, mistress.
Let it not gall your patience, good Iago,
That I extend my manners; 'tis my breeding
That gives me this bold show of courtesy. [*kisses her*

IAGO Sir, would she give you so much of her lips
As of her tongue she oft bestows on me,
You'ld have enough.

DESDEM. Alas, she has no speech.

IAGO In faith, too much;
I find it still when I have list to sleep.
Marry, before your ladyship, I grant,
She puts her tongue a little in her heart
And chides with thinking.

EMILIA You have little cause to say so.

IAGO Come on, come on; you are pictures out of doors, bells in your parlours, wild-cats in your kitchens; saints in your injuries, devils being offended; players in your housewifery, and hussies in your beds.

DESDEM. O, fie upon thee, slanderer!

IAGO Nay, it is true, or else I am a Turk:
You rise to play, and go to bed to work.

EMILIA You shall not write my praise.

IAGO No, let me not.

DESDEM. What wouldst thou write of me, if thou shouldst praise me?

IAGO O gentle lady, do not put me to't;
For I am nothing if not critical.

DESDEM. Come on, assay – There's one gone to the harbour?

IAGO Ay, madam.

DESDEM. I am not merry; but I do beguile
The thing I am by seeming otherwise.
Come, how wouldst thou praise me?

IAGO I am about it; but indeed my invention comes from my

pate as birdlime does from frieze – it plucks out brains and all. But my muse labours, and thus she is delivered.
If she be fair and wise, fairness and wit,
The one's for use, the other useth it.

DESDEM. Well praised! How if she be black and witty?

IAGO If she be black, and thereto have a wit,
She'll find a white that shall her blackness hit.

DESDEM. Worse and worse.

EMILIA How if fair and foolish?

IAGO She never yet was foolish that was fair;
For even her folly helped her to an heir.

DESDEM. These are old fond paradoxes to make fools laugh i'th'alehouse. What miserable praise hast thou for her that's foul and foolish?

IAGO There's none so foul, and foolish thereunto,
But does foul pranks which fair and wise ones do.

DESDEM. O heavy ignorance! Thou praisest the worst best. But what praise couldst thou bestow on a deserving woman indeed – one that in the authority of her merit did justly put on the vouch of very malice?

IAGO She that was ever fair, and never proud,
Had tongue at will, and yet was never loud,
Never lacked gold, and yet went never gay,
Fled from her wish, and yet said 'Now I may';
She that, being angered, her revenge being nigh,
Bade her wrong stay, and her displeasure fly;
She that in wisdom never was so frail
To change the cod's head for the salmon's tail;
She that could think, and ne'er disclose her mind,
See suitors following, and not look behind;
She was a wight, if ever such wight were –

DESDEM. To do what?

IAGO To suckle fools and chronicle small beer.

DESDEM. O most lame and impotent conclusion! Do not learn of him, Emilia, though he be thy husband. How say you, Cassio? Is he not a most profane and liberal counsellor?

CASSIO He speaks home, madam. You may relish him more in the soldier than in the scholar.

IAGO [*aside*] He takes her by the palm. Ay, well said, whisper.

With as little a web as this will I ensnare as great a fly as Cassio. Ay, smile upon her, do; I will gyve thee in thine own courtship. You say true: 'tis so, indeed. If such tricks as these strip you out of your lieutenantry, it had been better you had not kissed your three fingers so oft, which now again you are most apt to play the sir in. Very good; well kissed! An excellent courtesy! 'Tis so, indeed. Yet again your fingers to your lips? Would they were clyster-pipes for your sake!

[*trumpets within*

[*aloud*] The Moor! I know his trumpet.

CASSIO 'Tis truly so.

DESDEM. Let's meet him and receive him.

CASSIO Lo where he comes!

Enter OTHELLO *and Attendants*

OTHELLO O my fair warrior!

DESDEM. My dear Othello!

OTHELLO It gives me wonder great as my content
To see you here before me. O my soul's joy!
If after every tempest come such calms,
May the winds blow till they have wakened death!
And let the labouring bark climb hills of seas
Olympus-high and duck again as low
As hell's from heaven! If it were now to die,
'Twere now to be most happy; for I fear,
My soul hath her content so absolute
That not another comfort like to this
Succeeds in unknown fate.

DESDEM. The heavens forbid
But that our loves and comforts should increase
Even as our days do grow!

OTHELLO Amen to that, sweet powers!
I cannot speak enough of this content:
It stops me here; it is too much of joy.
And this, and this, the greatest discords be [*they kiss*
That e'er our hearts shall make!

IAGO O, you are well tuned now! But I'll set down the pegs that make this music, as honest as I am.

OTHELLO Come, let's to the castle.

News, friends: our wars are done; the Turks are drowned.
How does my old acquaintance of this isle?
Honey, you shall be well desired in Cyprus;
I have found great love amongst them. O my sweet,
I prattle out of fashion, and I dote
In mine own comfort. I prithee, good Iago,
Go to the bay, and disembark my coffers;
Bring thou the master to the citadel-
He is a good one, and his worthiness
Does challenge much respect. Come, Desdemona,
Once more well met at Cyprus.

[*all but Iago and Roderigo depart*

IAGO Do thou meet me presently at the harbour. Come hither. If thou be'st valiant – as they say base men being in love have then a nobility in their natures more than is native to them – list me. The lieutenant tonight watches on the court of guard. First, I must tell thee this: Desdemona is directly in love with him.

RODERIGO With him! Why, 'tis not possible.

IAGO Lay thy finger thus, and let thy soul be instructed. Mark me with what violence she first loved the Moor but for bragging and telling her fantastical lies. And will she love him still for prating? – Let not thy discreet heart think it. Her eye must be fed; and what delight shall she have to look on the devil? When the blood is made dull with the act of sport, there should be – again to inflame it and to give satiety a fresh appetite – loveliness in favour, sympathy in years, manners, and beauties; all which the Moor is defective in. Now, for want of these required conveniencies, her delicate tenderness will find itself abused, begin to heave the gorge, disrelish and abhor the Moor. Very nature will instruct her in it and compel her to some second choice. Now, sir, this granted – as it is a most pregnant and unforced position – who stands so eminent in the degree of this fortune as Cassio does? – A knave very voluble; no further conscionable than in putting on the mere form of civil and humane seeming, for the better compassing of his salt and most hidden loose affection. Why, none; why, none – a slipper and subtle knave; a finder-out of occasions; that has an eye can stamp and counterfeit advantages, though true advantage never present itself; a devilish knave! Besides, the knave is handsome, young, and hath all those requisites in him that folly and green minds look after; a pestilent complete knave; and the woman hath found him already.

RODERIGO I cannot believe that in her; she's full of most blest condition.

IAGO Blest fig's-end! The wine she drinks is made of grapes. If she had been blest, she would never have loved the Moor. Blest pudding! Didst thou not see her paddle with the palm of his hand? Didst not mark that?

RODERIGO Yes, that I did; but that was but courtesy.

IAGO Lechery, by this hand; an index and obscure prologue to the history of lust and foul thoughts. They met so near with their lips that their breaths embraced together – villanous thoughts, Roderigo! When these mutualities so marshal the way, hard at hand comes the master and main exercise, th'incorporate conclusion. Pish! But, sir, be you ruled by me. I have brought you from Venice. Watch you tonight; for the command, I'll lay't upon you. Cassio knows you not; I'll not be far from you. Do you find some occasion to anger Cassio, either by speaking too loud or tainting his discipline, or from what other course you please which the time shall more favourably minister.

RODERIGO Well.

IAGO Sir, he's rash and very sudden in choler, and haply may strike at you – provoke him that he may; for even out of that will I cause these of Cyprus to mutiny, whose qualification shall come into no true taste again but by the displanting of Cassio. So shall you have a shorter journey to your desires by the means I shall then have to prefer them, and the impediment most profitably removed, without the which there were no expectation of our prosperity.

RODERIGO I will do this, if you can bring it to any opportunity.

IAGO I warrant thee. Meet me by and by at the citadel. I must fetch his necessaries ashore. Farewell.

RODERIGO Adieu. [*goes*

IAGO That Cassio loves her, I do well believe't;
That she loves him, 'tis apt and of great credit.
The Moor, howbeit that I endure him not,
Is of a constant, loving, noble nature;
And I dare think he'll prove to Desdemona
A most dear husband. Now, I do love her too,
Not out of absolute lust – though peradventure
I stand accountant for as great a sin –
But partly led to diet my revenge
For that I do suspect the lusty Moor
Hath leaped into my seat, the thought whereof
Doth like a poisonous mineral gnaw my inwards;
And nothing can or shall content my soul
Till I am evened with him, wife for wife;
Or failing so, yet that I put the Moor
At least into a jealousy so strong
That judgment cannot cure. Which thing to do,
If this poor trash of Venice, whom I leash
For his quick hunting, stand the putting on,
I'll have our Michael Cassio on the hip,
Abuse him to the Moor in the rank garb –
For I fear Cassio with my night-cap too –
Make the Moor thank me, love me, and reward me,
For making him egregiously an ass,
And practising upon his peace and quiet
Even to madness. 'Tis here, but yet confused;
Knavery's plain face is never seen till used. [*goes*

SCENE 2

A street

Enter a Herald with a proclamation; people following

HERALD It is Othello's pleasure, our noble and valiant general, that, upon certain tidings now arrived importing the mere perdition of the Turkish fleet, every man put himself into triumph; some to dance, some to make bonfires, each man to what sport and revels his addiction leads him: for, besides these beneficial news, it is the celebration of his nuptial. So much was his pleasure should be proclaimed. All offices are open, and there is full liberty of feasting from this present hour of five till the bell have told eleven. Heaven bless the isle of Cyprus and our noble general Othello! [*he moves on*

SCENE 3

A hall in the citadel

Enter OTHELLO, DESDEMONA, CASSIO, *and Attendants*

OTHELLO Good Michael, look you to the guard tonight.
Let's teach ourselves that honourable stop,
Not to outsport discretion.

CASSIO Iago hath direction what to do;
But notwithstanding with my personal eye
Will I look to't.

OTHELLO Iago is most honest.
Michael, good night; tomorrow with your earliest
Let me have speech with you. Come, my dear love,
The purchase made, the fruits are to ensue;
That profit's yet to come 'tween me and you.
Good night.

[*Othello, Desdemona, and Attendants depart*

Enter IAGO

CASSIO Welcome, Iago; we must to the watch.

IAGO Not this hour, lieutenant; 'tis not yet ten o'clock. Our general cast us thus early for the love of his Desdemona; who let us not therefore blame: he hath not yet made wanton the night with her, and she is sport for Jove.

CASSIO She's a most exquisite lady.

IAGO And, I'll warrant her, full of game.

CASSIO Indeed she's a most fresh and delicate creature.

IAGO What an eye she has! Methinks it sounds a parley to provocation.

CASSIO An inviting eye; and yet methinks right modest.

IAGO And when she speaks, is it not an alarum to love?

CASSIO She is indeed perfection.

IAGO Well, happiness to their sheets! Come, lieutenant, I have a stoup of wine; and here without are a brace of Cyprus gallants that would fain have a measure to the health of black Othello.

CASSIO Not tonight, good Iago; I have very poor and unhappy brains for drinking. I could well wish courtesy would invent some other custom of entertainment.

IAGO O, they are our friends – but one cup; I'll drink for you.

CASSIO I have drunk but one cup tonight, and that was craftily qualified too, and behold what innovation it makes here. I am unfortunate in the infirmity and dare not task my weakness with any more.

IAGO What, man! 'Tis a night of revels; the gallants desire it.

CASSIO Where are they?

IAGO Here at the door; I pray you, call them in.

CASSIO I'll do't; but it dislikes me. [*goes*

IAGO If I can fasten but one cup upon him,
With that which he hath drunk tonight already,
He'll be as full of quarrel and offence
As my young mistress' dog. Now my sick fool Roderigo,
Whom love hath turned almost the wrong side out,
To Desdemona hath tonight caroused
Potations pottle-deep; and he's to watch.
Three else of Cyprus, noble swelling spirits,
That hold their honours in a wary distance,
The very elements of this warlike isle,

Have I tonight flustered with flowing cups;
And they watch too. Now, 'mongst this flock of drunkards,
Am I to put our Cassio in some action
That may offend the isle. But here they come;
If consequence do but approve my dream,
My boat sails freely, both with wind and stream.

Re-enter CASSIO; *with him* MONTANO *and Gentlemen; Servants following with wine*

CASSIO 'Fore God, they have given me a rouse already.

MONTANO Good faith, a little one; not past a pint, as I am a soldier.

IAGO Some wine, ho!
[*sings*] And let me the canakin clink, clink;
And let me the canakin clink;
A soldier's a man;
O, man's life's but a span;
Why, then, let a soldier drink.
Some wine, boys!

CASSIO 'Fore God, an excellent song.

IAGO I learned it in England, where indeed they are most potent in potting; your Dane, your German, and your swag-bellied Hollander – drink, ho! – Are nothing to your English.

CASSIO Is your Englishman so exquisite in his drinking?

IAGO Why, he drinks you with facility your Dane dead drunk; he sweats not to overthrow your Almain; he gives your Hollander a vomit ere the next pottle can be filled.

CASSIO To the health of our general!

MONTANO I am for it, lieutenant, and I'll do you justice.

IAGO O sweet England!
[*sings*] King Stephen was and-a worthy peer,
His breeches cost him but a crown;
He held them sixpence all too dear,
With that he called the tailor lown.

He was a wight of high renown,
And thou art but of low degree;
'Tis pride that pulls the country down;
Then take thy auld cloak about thee.

Some wine, ho!

CASSIO Why, this is a more exquisite song than the other.

IAGO Will you hear't again?

CASSIO No; for I hold him to be unworthy of his place that does those things. Well, God's above all; and there be souls must be saved, and there be souls must not be saved.

IAGO It's true, good lieutenant.

CASSIO For mine own part – no offence to the general, nor any man of quality – I hope to be saved.

IAGO And so do I too, lieutenant.

CASSIO Ay, but, by your leave, not before me; the lieutenant is to be saved before the ancient. Let's have no more of this; let's to our affairs. God forgive us our sins! Gentlemen, let's look to our business. Do not think, gentlemen, I am drunk; this is my ancient; this is my right hand, and this is my left hand. I am not drunk now: I can stand well enough, and I speak well enough.

ALL Excellent well.

CASSIO Why, very well then; you must not think then that I am drunk. [*goes out*

MONTANO To th'platform, masters; come, let's set the watch.

IAGO You see this fellow that is gone before:
He is a soldier fit to stand by Caesar
And give direction; and do but see his vice –
'Tis to his virtue a just equinox,
The one as long as th'other. 'Tis pity of him.
I fear the trust Othello puts him in,
On some odd time of his infirmity,
Will shake this island.

MONTANO But is he often thus?

IAGO 'Tis evermore the prologue to his sleep:
He'll watch the horologe a double set,
If drink rock not his cradle.

MONTANO It were well
The general were put in mind of it.
Perhaps he sees it not, or his good nature
Prizes the virtue that appears in Cassio,
And looks not on his evil: is not this true?

Enter RODERIGO

IAGO How, now, Roderigo!
I pray you, after the lieutenant; go. [*Roderigo goes*

MONTANO And 'tis great pity that the noble Moor
Should hazard such a place as his own second
With one of an ingraft infirmity:
It were an honest action to say
So to the Moor.

IAGO Not I, for this fair island:
I do love Cassio well, and would do much
To cure him of this evil. [*a cry within*, 'Help! Help!'
But hark! What noise?

Re-enter CASSIO, *pursuing* RODERIGO

CASSIO 'Zounds, you rogue, you rascal!

MONTANO What's the matter, lieutenant?

CASSIO A knave teach me my duty! I'll beat the knave
Into a twiggen bottle.

RODERIGO Beat me!

CASSIO Dost prate, rogue?
[*striking Roderigo*

MONTANO Nay, good lieutenant; pray sir, hold your hand.

CASSIO Let go, sir, or I'll knock you o'er the mazard.

MONTANO Come, come, you're drunk.

CASSIO Drunk! [*they fight*

IAGO Away, I say; go out and cry a mutiny. [*Roderigo goes*
[*aloud*] Nay, good lieutenant! God's will, gentlemen!
Help, ho! – lieutenant – sir – Montano – sir –
Help, masters! – Here's a goodly watch indeed!
[*a bell rings*
Who's that that rings the bell? – Diablo, ho!
The town will rise. God's will, lieutenant, hold;
You will be shamed for ever.

Re-enter OTHELLO *and Attendants*

OTHELLO What is the matter here?

MONTANO 'Zounds, I bleed still.
I am hurt to th'death. He dies. [*assailing Cassio again*

OTHELLO Hold, for your lives!

IAGO Hold, ho! Lieutenant – sir – Montano – gentlemen –

Have you forgot all sense of place and duty?
The general speaks to you; hold, hold, for shame!

OTHELLO Why, how now, ho! From whence ariseth this?
Are we turned Turks, and to ourselves do that
Which heaven hath forbid the Ottomites?
For Christian shame, put by this barbarous brawl.
He that stirs next to carve for his own rage
Holds his soul light; he dies upon his motion.
Silence that dreadful bell; it frights the isle
From her propriety. What is the matter, masters?
Honest Iago, that look'st dead with grieving,
Speak who began this; on thy love, I charge thee.

IAGO I do not know. Friends all but now, even now,
In quarter and in terms like bride and groom
Divesting them for bed; and then, but now,
As if some planet had unwitted men,
Swords out, and tilting one at other's breast,
In opposition bloody. I cannot speak
Any beginning to this peevish odds;
And would in action glorious I had lost
Those legs that brought me to a part of it!

OTHELLO How comes it, Michael, you are thus forgot?

CASSIO I pray you, pardon me; I cannot speak.

OTHELLO Worthy Montano, you were wont be civil;
The gravity and stillness of your youth
The world hath noted, and your name is great
In mouths of wisest censure: what's the matter
That you unlace your reputation thus,
And spend your rich opinion for the name
Of a night-brawler? Give me answer to it.

MONTANO Worthy Othello, I am hurt to danger;
Your officer, Iago, can inform you –
While I spare speech, which something now offends me –
Of all that I do know; nor know I aught
By me that's said or done amiss this night –
Unless self-charity be sometimes a vice,
And to defend ourselves it be a sin
When violence assails us.

OTHELLO Now, by heaven,
My blood begins my safer guides to rule,
And passion, having my best judgment collied,
Assays to lead the way. If I once stir,
Or do but lift this arm, the best of you
Shall sink in my rebuke. Give me to know
How this foul rout began, who set it on,
And he that is approved in this offence,
Though he had twinned with me, both at a birth,
Shall lose me. What! In a town of war,
Yet wild, the people's hearts brimful of fear,
To manage private and domestic quarrel,
In night, and on the court and guard of safety!
'Tis monstrous. Iago, who began't?

MONTANO If partially affined, or leagued in office,
Thou dost deliver more or less than truth,
Thou art no soldier.

IAGO Touch me not so near;
I had rather have this tongue cut from my mouth
Than it should do offence to Michael Cassio;
Yet, I persuade myself, to speak the truth
Shall nothing wrong him. This it is, general.
Montano and myself being in speech,
There comes a fellow crying out for help,
And Cassio following with determined sword
To execute upon him. Sir, this gentleman
Steps in to Cassio and entreats his pause;
Myself the crying fellow did pursue,
Lest by his clamour – as it so fell out –
The town might fall in fright; he, swift of foot,
Outran my purpose; and I returned the rather
For that I heard the clink and fall of swords,
And Cassio high in oath; which till tonight
I ne'er might say before. When I came back –
For this was brief – I found them close together
At blow and thrust; even as again they were
When you yourself did part them.
More of this matter can I not report;
But men are men; the best sometimes forget.

Though Cassio did some little wrong to him,
As men in rage strike those that wish them best,
Yet surely Cassio, I believe, received
From him that fled some strange indignity,
Which patience could not pass.

OTHELLO I know, Iago,
Thy honesty and love doth mince this matter,
Making it light to Cassio. Cassio, I love thee;
But never more be officer of mine.

Re-enter DESDEMONA, *attended*

Look if my gentle love be not raised up!
I'll make thee an example.

DESDEM. What's the matter?

OTHELLO All's well, dear sweeting; come away to bed.
Sir, for your hurts, myself will be your surgeon.

[*they lead Montano away*

Iago, look with care about the town,
And silence those whom this vile brawl distracted.
Come, Desdemona: 'tis the soldiers' life
To have their balmy slumbers waked with strife.

[*all but Iago and Cassio depart*

IAGO What, are you hurt, lieutenant?

CASSIO Ay, past all surgery.

IAGO Marry, heaven forbid!

CASSIO Reputation, reputation, reputation! O, I have lost my reputation! I have lost the immortal part of myself, and what remains is bestial. My reputation, Iago, my reputation!

IAGO As I am an honest man, I thought you had received some bodily wound; there is more sense in that than in reputation. Reputation is an idle and most false imposition; oft got without merit and lost without deserving. You have lost no reputation at all, unless you repute yourself such a loser. What, man! There are ways to recover the general again. You are but now cast in his mood, a punishment more in policy than in malice; even so as one would beat his offenceless dog to affright an imperious lion. Sue to him again, and he's yours.

CASSIO I will rather sue to be despised than to deceive so good a commander with so light, so drunken, and so indiscreet an officer. Drunk! And speak parrot! And squabble! Swagger! Swear! And discourse fustian with one's own shadow! O thou invisible spirit of wine, if thou hast no name to be known by, let us call thee devil!

IAGO What was he that you followed with your sword? What had he done to you?

CASSIO I know not.

IAGO Is't possible?

CASSIO I remember a mass of things, but nothing distinctly; a quarrel, but nothing wherefore. O, that men should put an enemy in their mouths to steal away their brains! That we should, with joy, pleasance, revel and applause, transform ourselves into beasts!

IAGO Why, but you are now well enough. How came you thus recovered?

CASSIO It hath pleased the devil drunkenness to give place to the devil wrath: one unperfectness shows me another, to make me frankly despise myself.

IAGO Come, you are too severe a moraller. As the time, the place, and the condition of this country stands, I could heartily wish this had not befallen; but since it is as it is, mend it for your own good.

CASSIO I will ask him for my place again; he shall tell me I am a drunkard! Had I as many mouths as Hydra, such an answer would stop them all. To be now a sensible man, by and by a fool, and presently a beast! O strange! Every inordinate cup is unblest, and the ingredience is a devil.

IAGO Come, come, wine is a good familiar creature, if it be well used; exclaim no more against it. And, good lieutenant, I think you think I love you.

CASSIO I have well approved it, sir. I drunk!

IAGO You or any man living may be drunk at a time. I'll tell you what you shall do. Our general's wife is now the general: I may say so in this respect, for that he hath devoted and given up himself to the contemplation, mark and denotement of her parts and graces. Confess yourself freely to her; importune her help to put you in your place again. She is of so free, so kind, so apt, so blessed a disposition, she holds it a vice in her goodness not to do more than she is requested. This broken joint between you and her husband entreat her to splinter; and, my fortunes against any lay worth naming, this crack of your love shall grow stronger than it was before.

CASSIO You advise me well.

IAGO I protest, in the sincerity of love and honest kindness.

CASSIO I think it freely; and betimes in the morning I will beseech the virtuous Desdemona to undertake for me. I am desperate of my fortunes if they check me here.

IAGO You are in the right. Good night, lieutenant; I must to the watch.

CASSIO Good night, honest Iago. [*goes*

IAGO And what's he then that says I play the villain,
When this advice I give is free and honest,
Probal to thinking, and indeed the course
To win the Moor again? For 'tis most easy
Th'inclining Desdemona to subdue
In any honest suit. She's framed as fruitful
As the free elements. And then for her
To win the Moor, were't to renounce his baptism,
All seals and symbols of redeemèd sin,
His soul is so enfettered to her love
That she may make, unmake, do what she list,
Even as her appetite shall play the god
With his weak function. How am I then a villain
To counsel Cassio to this parallel course,
Directly to his good? Divinity of hell!
When devils will the blackest sins put on,
They do suggest at first with heavenly shows,
As I do now; for while this honest fool
Plies Desdemona to repair his fortunes,
And she for him pleads strongly to the Moor,
I'll pour this pestilence into his ear,
That she repeals him for her body's lust;
And by how much she strives to do him good,
She shall undo her credit with the Moor.
So will I turn her virtue into pitch,
And out of her own goodness make the net

That shall enmesh them all.

Enter RODERIGO

How now, Roderigo!

RODERIGO I do follow here in the chase, not like a hound that hunts, but one that fills up the cry. My money is almost spent; I have been tonight exceedingly well cudgelled; and I think the issue will be, I shall have so much experience for my pains; and so, with no money at all and a little more wit, return again to Venice.

IAGO How poor are they that have not patience!
What wound did ever heal but by degrees?
Thou know'st we work by wit and not by witchcraft,
And wit depends on dilatory time.
Does't not go well? Cassio hath beaten thee,
And thou by that small hurt hast cashiered Cassio.
Though other things grow fair against the sun,
Yet fruits that blossom first will first be ripe.
Content thyself awhile. By th'mass, 'tis morning;
Pleasure and action make the hours seem short.
Retire thee; go where thou art billeted.
Away, I say; thou shalt know more hereafter.
Nay, get thee gone. [*Roderigo goes*
Two things are to be done:
My wife must move for Cassio to her mistress –
I'll set her on –
Myself the while to draw the Moor apart,
And bring him jump when he may Cassio find
Soliciting his wife. Ay, that's the way;
Dull not device by coldness and delay. [*goes*

ACT 3 SCENE 1

The citadel. Outside Othello's lodging

Enter CASSIO *and some Musicians*

CASSIO Masters, play here; I will content your pains; Something that's brief; and bid 'Good morrow, general'. [*music*

Enter Clown

CLOWN Why, masters, have your instruments been in Naples, that they speak i'th'nose thus?

1 MUSIC'N How, sir, how?

CLOWN Are these, I pray you, wind instruments?

1 MUSIC'N Ay, marry, are they, sir.

CLOWN O, thereby hangs a tail.

1 MUSIC'N Whereby hangs a tale, sir?

CLOWN Marry, sir, by many a wind instrument that I know. But, masters, here's money for you! And the general so likes your music, that he desires you, for love's sake, to make no more noise with it.

1 MUSIC'N Well, sir, we will not.

CLOWN If you have any music that may not be heard, to't again; but, as they say, to hear music the general does not greatly care.

1 MUSIC'N We have none such, sir.

CLOWN Then put up your pipes in your bag, for I'll away. Go; vanish into air; away! [*Musicians go*

CASSIO Dost thou hear, my honest friend?

CLOWN No, I hear not your honest friend; I hear you.

CASSIO Prithee, keep up thy quillets. There's a poor piece of gold for thee: if the gentlewoman that attends the general's wife be stirring, tell her there's one Cassio entreats her a little favour of speech. Wilt thou do this?

CLOWN She is stirring, sir; if she will stir hither, I shall seem to notify unto her.

CASSIO Do, good my friend. [*Clown goes*

Enter IAGO

In happy time, Iago.

IAGO You have not been abed then?

CASSIO Why, no; the day had broke before we parted.
I have made bold, Iago,
To send in to your wife: my suit to her
Is that she will to virtuous Desdemona
Procure me some access.

IAGO I'll send her to you presently;
And I'll devise a mean to draw the Moor
Out of the way, that your converse and business
May be more free.

CASSIO I humbly thank you for't. [*Iago goes*
I never knew
A Florentine more kind and honest.

Enter EMILIA

EMILIA Good morrow, good lieutenant: I am sorry
For your displeasure; but all will sure be well.
The general and his wife are talking of it,
And she speaks for you stoutly. The Moor replies
That he you hurt is of great fame in Cyprus
And great affinity, and that in wholesome wisdom
He might not but refuse you; but he protests he
loves you,
And needs no other suitor but his liking
To take the safest occasion by the front
To bring you in again.

CASSIO Yet, I beseech you,
If you think fit, or that it may be done,
Give me advantage of some brief discourse
With Desdemon alone.

EMILIA Pray you, come in;
I will bestow you where you shall have time
To speak your bosom freely.

CASSIO I am much bound to you.
[*they go*

SCENE 2

A room in the citadel

Enter OTHELLO, IAGO, *and Gentlemen*

OTHELLO These letters give, Iago, to the pilot,
And by him do my duties to the senate.
That done, I will be walking on the works;
Repair there to me.

IAGO Well, my good lord, I'll do't. [*goes*

OTHELLO This fortification, gentlemen, shall we see't?

GENT'MEN We'll wait upon your lordship. [*they go*

SCENE 3

Before the citadel

Enter DESDEMONA, CASSIO, *and* EMILIA

DESDEM. Be thou assured, good Cassio, I will do
All my abilities in thy behalf.

EMILIA Good madam, do; I warrant it grieves my husband
As if the case were his.

DESDEM. O, that's an honest fellow. Do not doubt, Cassio,
But I will have my lord and you again
As friendly as you were.

CASSIO Bounteous madam,
Whatever shall become of Michael Cassio,
He's never anything but your true servant.

DESDEM. I know't; I thank you. You do love my lord;
You have known him long; and be you well assured
He shall in strangeness stand no farther off
Than in a politic distance.

CASSIO Ay, but, lady,
That policy may either last so long,
Or feed upon such nice and waterish diet,
Or breed itself so out of circumstance,
That, I being absent, and my place supplied,

My general will forget my love and service.

DESDEM. Do not doubt that: before Emilia here
I give thee warrant of thy place. Assure thee,
If I do vow a friendship, I'll perform it
To the last article. My lord shall never rest:
I'll watch him tame, and talk him out of patience;
His bed shall seem a school, his board a shrift;
I'll intermingle everything he does
With Cassio's suit. Therefore be merry, Cassio;
For thy solicitor shall rather die
Than give thy cause away.

Enter OTHELLO *and* IAGO, *at a distance*

EMILIA Madam, here comes my lord.

CASSIO Madam, I'll take my leave.

DESDEM. Why, stay, and hear me speak.

CASSIO Madam, not now: I am very ill at ease,
Unfit for mine own purposes.

DESDEM. Well, do your discretion. [*Cassio goes*

IAGO Ha! I like not that.

OTHELLO What dost thou say?

IAGO Nothing, my lord; or if – I know not what.

OTHELLO Was not that Cassio parted from my wife?

IAGO Cassio, my lord! No, sure, I cannot think it,
That he would steal away so guilty-like,
Seeing you coming.

OTHELLO I do believe 'twas he.

DESDEM. How now, my lord!
I have been talking with a suitor here,
A man that languishes in your displeasure.

OTHELLO Who is't you mean?

DESDEM. Why, your lieutenant, Cassio. Good my lord,
If I have any grace or power to move you,
His present reconciliation take;
For if he be not one that truly loves you,
That errs in ignorance and not in cunning,
I have no judgment in an honest face.
I prithee, call him back.

OTHELLO Went he hence now?

DESDEM. Ay, sooth; so humbled,

That he hath left part of his grief with me
To suffer with him. Good love, call him back.

OTHELLO Not now, sweet Desdemon; some other time.

DESDEM. But shall't be shortly?

OTHELLO The sooner, sweet, for you.

DESDEM. Shall't be tonight at supper?

OTHELLO No, not tonight.

DESDEM. Tomorrow dinner then?

OTHELLO I shall not dine at home:
I meet the captains at the citadel.

DESDEM. Why then, tomorrow night; or Tuesday morn;
On Tuesday noon, or night; on Wednesday morn.
I prithee, name the time; but let it not
Exceed three days. In faith, he's penitent;
And yet his trespass, in our common reason –
Save that, they say, the wars must make example
Out of their best – is not almost a fault
T'incur a private check. When shall he come?
Tell me, Othello. I wonder in my soul
What you would ask me that I should deny,
Or stand so mammering on. What! Michael Cassio,
That came a-wooing with you, and so many a time,
When I have spoke of you dispraisingly,
Hath ta'en your part – to have so much to do
To bring him in! Trust me, I could do much –

OTHELLO Prithee, no more. Let him come when he will;
I will deny thee nothing.

DESDEM. Why, this is not a boon;
'Tis as I should entreat you wear your gloves,
Or feed on nourishing dishes, or keep you warm,
Or sue to you to do peculiar profit
To your own person. Nay, when I have a suit
Wherein I mean to touch your love indeed,
It shall be full of poise and difficult weight,
And fearful to be granted.

OTHELLO I will deny thee nothing.
Whereon, I do beseech thee, grant me this,
To leave me but a little to myself.

DESDEM. Shall I deny you? No; farewell, my lord.

OTHELLO Farewell, my Desdemona, I'll come straight.
DESDEM. Emilia, come. Be as your fancies teach you;
Whate'er you be, I am obedient.
[*Desdemona and Emilia go*
OTHELLO Excellent wretch! Perdition catch my soul
But I do love thee; and when I love thee not
Chaos is come again.
IAGO My noble lord –
OTHELLO What dost thou say, Iago?
IAGO Did Michael Cassio,
When you wooed my lady, know of your love?
OTHELLO He did, from first to last. Why dost thou ask?
IAGO But for a satisfaction of my thought;
No further harm.
OTHELLO Why of thy thought, Iago?
IAGO I did not think he had been acquainted with her.
OTHELLO O, yes, and went between us very oft.
IAGO Indeed!
OTHELLO Indeed? Ay, indeed. Discern'st thou aught in that?
Is he not honest?
IAGO Honest, my lord?
OTHELLO Honest? Ay, honest.
IAGO My lord, for aught I know.
OTHELLO What dost thou think?
IAGO Think, my lord?
OTHELLO Think, my lord! Alas, thou echo'st me,
As if there were some monster in thy thought
Too hideous to be shown. Thou dost mean something:
I heard thee say even now, thou likedst not that,
When Cassio left my wife. What didst not like?
And when I told thee he was of my counsel
In my whole course of wooing, thou criedst 'Indeed!'
And didst contract and purse thy brow together,
As if thou then hadst shut up in thy brain
Some horrible conceit. If thou dost love me,
Show me thy thought..
IAGO My lord, you know I love you.
OTHELLO I think thou dost;
And for I know thou'rt full of love, and honest,

And weigh'st thy words before thou giv'st them breath,
Therefore these stops of thine fright me the more:
For such things in a false disloyal knave
Are tricks of custom; but in a man that's just
They're close dilations, working from the heart
That passion cannot rule.

IAGO For Michael Cassio,
I dare be sworn I think that he is honest.

OTHELLO I think so too.

IAGO Men should be what they seem;
Or those that be not, would they might seem none!

OTHELLO Certain, men should be what they seem.

IAGO Why then, I think Cassio's an honest man.

OTHELLO Nay, yet there's more in this.
I prithee, speak to me as to thy thinkings,
As thou dost ruminate, and give thy worst of thought
The worst of words.

IAGO Good my lord, pardon me:
Though I am bound to every act of duty,
I am not bound to that all slaves are free to.
Utter my thoughts! Why, say they are vile and false –
As where's that palace whereinto foul things
Sometimes intrude not? Who has a breast so pure,
But some uncleanly apprehensions
Keep leets and law-days, and in session sit
With meditations lawful?

OTHELLO Thou dost conspire against thy friend, Iago,
If thou but think'st him wronged and mak'st his ear
A stranger to thy thoughts.

IAGO I do beseech you –
Though I perchance am vicious in my guess,
As, I confess, it is my nature's plague
To spy into abuses, and oft my jealousy
Shapes faults that are not – that your wisdom then,
From one that so imperfectly conceits,
Would take no notice, nor build yourself a trouble
Out of his scattering and unsure observance.
It were not for your quiet nor your good,
Nor for my manhood, honesty, or wisdom,

To let you know my thoughts.

OTHELLO What dost thou mean?

IAGO Good name in man and woman, dear my lord,
Is the immediate jewel of their souls:
Who steals my purse steals trash – 'tis something, nothing;
'Twas mine, 'tis his, and has been slave to thousands;
But he that filches from me my good name
Robs me of that which not enriches him
And makes me poor indeed.

OTHELLO I'll know thy thoughts!

IAGO You cannot, if my heart were in your hand;
Nor shall not, while 'tis in my custody.

OTHELLO Ha!

IAGO O, beware, my lord, of jealousy;
It is the green-eyed monster, which doth mock
The meat it feeds on: that cuckold lives in bliss
Who, certain of his fate, loves not his wronger;
But, O, what damnèd minutes tells he o'er
Who dotes, yet doubts, suspects, yet fondly loves!

OTHELLO O misery!

IAGO Poor and content is rich, and rich enough;
But riches fineless is as poor as winter
To him that ever fears he shall be poor.
Good heaven the souls of all my tribe defend
From jealousy!

OTHELLO Why, why is this?
Think'st thou I'd make a life of jealousy,
To follow still the changes of the moon
With fresh suspicions? No; to be once in doubt
Is once resolved. Exchange me for a goat,
When I shall turn the business of my soul
To such exsufflicate and blown surmise
Matching thy inference. 'Tis not to make me jealous
To say my wife is fair, loves company,
Is free of speech, sings, plays and dances well;
Where virtue is, these are more virtuous;
Nor from mine own weak merits will I draw
The smallest fear or doubt of her revolt;

For she had eyes and chose me. No, Iago:
I'll see before I doubt; when I doubt, prove;
And on the proof, there is no more but this,
Away at once with love or jealousy!

IAGO I am glad of it; for now I shall have reason
To show the love and duty that I bear you
With franker spirit. Therefore, as I am bound,
Receive it from me. I speak not yet of proof.
Look to your wife; observe her well with Cassio;
Wear your eye thus not jealous nor secure:
I would not have your free and noble nature
Out of self-bounty be abused. Look to't:
I know our country disposition well;
In Venice they do let heaven see the pranks
They dare not show their husbands; their best conscience
Is not to leave't undone, but keep't unknown.

OTHELLO Dost thou say so?

IAGO She did deceive her father, marrying you:
And when she seemed to shake and fear your looks,
She loved them most.

OTHELLO And so she did.

IAGO Why then,
She that so young could give out such a seeming,
To seel her father's eyes up close as oak,
He thought 'twas witchcraft – but I am much to blame;
I humbly do beseech you of your pardon
For too much loving you.

OTHELLO I am bound to thee for ever.

IAGO I see this hath a little dashed your spirits.

OTHELLO Not a jot, not a jot.

IAGO In faith, I fear it has.
I hope you will consider what is spoke
Comes from my love. But I do see you're moved.
I am to pray you not to strain my speech
To grosser issues nor to larger reach
Than to suspicion.

OTHELLO I will not.

IAGO Should you do so, my lord,
My speech should fall into such vile success

As my thoughts aimed not at. Cassio's my worthy
friend –
My lord, I see you're moved.

OTHELLO No, not much moved:
I do not think but Desdemona's honest.

IAGO Long live she so! And long live you to think so!

OTHELLO And yet, how nature erring from itself –

IAGO Ay, there's the point: as – to be bold with you –
Not to affect many proposèd matches
Of her own clime, complexion, and degree,
Whereto we see in all things nature tends –
Foh! One may smell, in such, a will most rank,
Foul disproportion, thoughts unnatural.
But pardon me: I do not in position
Distinctly speak of her; though I may fear
Her will, recoiling to her better judgment,
May fall to match you with her country forms,
And happily repent.

OTHELLO Farewell, farewell.
If more thou dost perceive, let me know more;
Set on thy wife to observe. Leave me, Iago.

IAGO [*going*] My lord, I take my leave.

OTHELLO Why did I marry? This honest creature doubtless
Sees and knows more, much more, than he unfolds.

IAGO [*returning*]
My lord, I would I might entreat your honour
To scan this thing no further. Leave it to time:
Although 'tis fit that Cassio have his place –
For sure he fills it up with great ability –
Yet if you please to hold him off awhile,
You shall by that perceive him and his means;
Note if your lady strain his entertainment
With any strong or vehement importunity –
Much will be seen in that. In the mean time,
Let me be thought too busy in my fears –
As worthy cause I have to fear I am –
And hold her free, I do beseech your honour.

OTHELLO Fear not my government.

IAGO I once more take my leave. [*goes*

OTHELLO This fellow's of exceeding honesty,
And knows all qualities, with a learnèd spirit,
Of human dealings. If I do prove her haggard,
Though that her jesses were my dear heart-strings,
I'd whistle her off and let her down the wind
To prey at fortune. Haply, for I am black
And have not those soft parts of conversation
That chamberers have, or for I am declined
Into the vale of years – yet that's not much –
She's gone; I am abused, and my relief
Must be to loathe her. O curse of marriage,
That we can call these delicate creatures ours,
And not their appetites! I had rather be a toad,
And live upon the vapour of a dungeon,
Than keep a corner in the thing I love
For others' uses. Yet, 'tis the plague of great ones;
Prerogatived are they less than the base;
'Tis destiny unshunnable, like death:
Even then this forkèd plague is fated to us
When we do quicken. Look where she comes:

Re-enter DESDEMONA *and* EMILIA

If she be false, O, then heaven mocks itself!
I'll not believe't.

DESDEM. How now, my dear Othello!
Your dinner, and the generous islanders
By you invited, do attend your presence.

OTHELLO I am to blame.

DESDEM. Why do you speak so faintly?
Are you not well?

OTHELLO I have a pain upon my forehead here.

DESDEM. Faith, that's with watching; 'twill away again:
Let me but bind it hard, within this hour
It will be well.

OTHELLO Your napkin is too little;
[*he puts the handkerchief from him; and she drops it*
Let it alone. Come, I'll go in with you.

DESDEM. I am very sorry that you are not well.
[*Othello and Desdemona go*

EMILIA I am glad I've found this napkin:
This was her first remembrance from the Moor;
My wayward husband hath a hundred times
Wooed me to steal it; but she so loves the token,
For he conjured her she should ever keep it,
That she reserves it evermore about her
To kiss and talk to. I'll have the work ta'en out,
And give't Iago. What he will do with it
Heaven knows, not I:
I nothing but to please his fantasy.

Re-enter IAGO

IAGO How now! What do you here alone?
EMILIA Do not you chide; I have a thing for you.
IAGO A thing, for me? It is a common thing –
EMILIA Ha!
IAGO To have a foolish wife.
EMILIA O, is that all? What will you give me now
For that same handkerchief?
IAGO What handkerchief?
EMILIA What handkerchief!
Why, that the Moor first gave to Desdemona;
That which so often you did bid me steal.
IAGO Hast stole it from her?
EMILIA No, faith; she let it drop by negligence,
And, to th'advantage, I being here took't up.
Look, here it is.
IAGO A good wench; give it me.
EMILIA What will you do with't, that you've been so earnest
To have me filch it?
IAGO [*snatching it*] Why, what's that to you?
EMILIA If't be not for some purpose of import,
Give't me again. Poor lady, she'll run mad
When she shall lack it.
IAGO Be not acknown on't; I have use for it.
Go, leave me. [*Emilia goes*
I will in Cassio's lodging lose this napkin,
And let him find it. Trifles light as air
Are to the jealous confirmations strong
As proofs of holy writ: this may do something.

The Moor already changes with my poison:
Dangerous conceits are in their natures poisons
Which at the first are scarce found to distaste
But, with a little act upon the blood,
Burn like the mines of sulphur.

Re-enter OTHELLO

I did say so:
Look where he comes! Not poppy, nor mandragora,
Nor all the drowsy syrups of the world,
Shall ever medicine thee to that sweet sleep
Which thou owedst yesterday.

OTHELLO Ha! Ha! False to me?

IAGO Why, how now, general! No more of that.

OTHELLO Avaunt! Be gone! Thou hast set me on the rack:
I swear 'tis better to be much abused
Than but to know't a little.

IAGO How now, my lord!

OTHELLO What sense had I of her stolen hours of lust?
I saw't not, thought it not, it harmed not me:
I slept the next night well, fed well, was merry;
I found not Cassio's kisses on her lips.
He that is robbed, not wanting what is stolen,
Let him not know't, and he's not robbed at all.

IAGO I am sorry to hear this.

OTHELLO I had been happy, if the general camp,
Pioneers and all, had tasted her sweet body,
So I had nothing known. O, now for ever
Farewell the tranquil mind! Farewell content!
Farewell the plumèd troops, and the big wars
That make ambition virtue – O, farewell!
Farewell the neighing steed and the shrill trump,
The spirit-stirring drum, th'ear-piercing fife,
The royal banner, and all quality,
Pride, pomp, and circumstance, of glorious war!
And, O you mortal engines, whose rude throats
Th'immortal Jove's dread clamours counterfeit,
Farewell! Othello's occupation's gone!

IAGO Is't possible, my lord?

OTHELLO Villain, be sure thou prove my love a whore;

Be sure of it; give me the ocular proof;
[*takes him by the throat*
Or, by the worth of mine eternal soul,
Thou hadst been better have been born a dog
Than answer my waked wrath!

IAGO Is't come to this?

OTHELLO Make me to see't; or, at the least, so prove it,
That the probation bear no hinge nor loop
To hang a doubt on; or woe upon thy life!

IAGO My noble lord –

OTHELLO If thou dost slander her and torture me,
Never pray more; abandon all remorse;
On horror's head horrors accumulate;
Do deeds to make heaven weep, all earth amazed;
For nothing canst thou to damnation add
Greater than that.

IAGO O grace! O heaven forgive me!
Are you a man? Have you a soul, or sense?
God bu'y you; take mine office. O wretched fool,
That liv'st to make thine honesty a vice!
O monstrous world! Take note, take note, O world,
To be direct and honest is not safe.
I thank you for this profit, and from hence
I'll love no friend sith love breeds such offence.

OTHELLO Nay, stay; thou shouldst be honest.

IAGO I should be wise; for honesty's a fool,
And loses that it works for.

OTHELLO By the world,
I think my wife be honest, and think she is not;
I think that thou art just, and think thou art not:
I'll have some proof. Her name, that was as fresh
As Dian's visage, is now begrimed and black
As mine own face. If there be cords, or knives,
Poison, or fire, or suffocating streams,
I'll not endure it. Would I were satisfied!

IAGO I see, sir, you are eaten up with passion:
I do repent me that I put it to you.
You would be satisfied?

OTHELLO Would! Nay, and will.

IAGO And may; but how? How satisfied, my lord?
Would you, the supervisor, grossly gape on –
Behold her topped?

OTHELLO Death and damnation! O!

IAGO It were a tedious difficulty, I think,
To bring them to that prospect: damn them then,
If ever mortal eyes do see them bolster
More than their own! What then? How then?
What shall I say? Where's satisfaction?
It is impossible you should see this,
Were they as prime as goats, as hot as monkeys,
As salt as wolves in pride, and fools as gross
As ignorance made drunk. But yet, I say,
If imputation and strong circumstance,
Which lead directly to the door of truth,
Will give you satisfaction, you might have't.

OTHELLO Give me a living reason she's disloyal.

IAGO I do not like the office;
But sith I am entered in this cause so far,
Pricked to't by foolish honesty and love,
I will go on. I lay with Cassio lately,
And being troubled with a raging tooth,
I could not sleep.
There are a kind of men so loose of soul,
That in their sleeps will mutter their affairs:
One of this kind is Cassio.
In sleep I heard him say 'Sweet Desdemona,
Let us be wary, let us hide our loves';
And then, sir, would he gripe and wring my hand,
Cry 'O sweet creature!' and then kiss me hard,
As if he plucked up kisses by the roots,
That grew upon my lips; then laid his leg
Over my thigh, and sighed, and kissed, and then
Cried 'Cursèd fate that gave thee to the Moor!'

OTHELLO O monstrous! Monstrous!

IAGO Nay, this was but his dream.

OTHELLO But this denoted a foregone conclusion:
'Tis a shrewd doubt, though it be but a dream.

IAGO And this may help to thicken other proofs

That do demonstrate thinly.
OTHELLO I'll tear her all to pieces.
IAGO Nay, but be wise: yet we see nothing done;
She may be honest yet. Tell me but this:
Have you not sometimes seen a handkerchief
Spotted with strawberries in your wife's hand?
OTHELLO I gave her such a one; 'twas my first gift.
IAGO I know not that; but such a handkerchief –
I am sure it was your wife's – did I today
See Cassio wipe his beard with.
OTHELLO If it be that –
IAGO If it be that, or any that was hers,
It speaks against her with the other proofs.
OTHELLO O, that the slave had forty thousand lives!
One is too poor, too weak for my revenge.
Now do I see 'tis true. Look: here, Iago,
All my fond love thus do I blow to heaven –
'Tis gone.
Arise, black vengeance, from thy hollow cell!
Yield up, O love, thy crown and hearted throne
To tyrannous hate! Swell, bosom, with thy fraught,
For 'tis of aspics' tongues!
IAGO Yet be content.
OTHELLO O, blood, blood, blood!
IAGO Patience, I say; your mind perhaps may change.
OTHELLO Never, Iago: like to the Pontic sea,
Whose icy current and compulsive course
Ne'er feels retiring ebb, but keeps due on
To the Propontic and the Hellespont;
Even so my bloody thoughts, with violent pace,
Shall ne'er look back, ne'er ebb to humble love,
Till that a capable and wide revenge
Swallow them up. Now, by yond marble heaven,
In the due reverence of a sacred vow [*kneels*
I here engage my words.
IAGO Do not rise yet. [*kneels*
Witness you ever-burning lights above,
You elements that clip us round about,
Witness that here Iago doth give up

The execution of his wit, hands, heart,
To wronged Othello's service! Let him command,
And to obey shall be without remorse,
What bloody business ever. [*they rise*

OTHELLO I greet thy love,
Not with vain thanks, but with acceptance bounteous,
And will upon the instant put thee to't:
Within these three days let me hear thee say
That Cassio's not alive.

IAGO My friend is dead;
'Tis done at your request. But let her live.

OTHELLO Damn her, lewd minx! O, damn her! damn her!
Come, go with me apart; I will withdraw,
To furnish me with some swift means of death
For the fair devil. Now art thou my lieutenant.

IAGO I am your own for ever. [*they go*

SCENE 4

The same

Enter DESDEMONA, EMILIA, *and Clown*

DESDEM. Do you know, sirrah, where Lieutenant Cassio lies?

CLOWN I dare not say he lies anywhere.

DESDEM. Why, man?

CLOWN He's a soldier; and for one to say a soldier lies, is stabbing.

DESDEM. Go to: where lodges he?

CLOWN To tell you where he lodges, is to tell you where I lie.

DESDEM. Can anything be made of this?

CLOWN I know not where he lodges; and for me to devise a lodging, and say he lies here or he lies there, were to lie in mine own throat.

DESDEM. Can you inquire him out, and be edified by report?

CLOWN I will catechize the world for him: that is, make questions and by them answer.

DESDEM. Seek him; bid him come hither. Tell him I have moved my lord on his behalf, and hope all will be well.

CLOWN To do this is within the compass of man's wit, and

therefore I will attempt the doing it. [*goes*

DESDEM. Where should I lose that handkerchief, Emilia?

EMILIA I know not, madam.

DESDEM. Believe me, I had rather lose my purse
Full of crusadoes; and but my noble Moor
Is true of mind and made of no such baseness
As jealous creatures are, it were enough
To put him to ill thinking.

EMILIA Is he not jealous?

DESDEM. Who, he! I think the sun where he was born
Drew all such humours from him.

EMILIA Look where he comes!

DESDEM. I will not leave him now till Cassio
Be called to him.

Enter OTHELLO

How is't with you, my lord?

OTHELLO Well, my good lady. [*aside*] O, hardness to dissemble!
How do you, Desdemona?

DESDEM. Well, my good lord.

OTHELLO Give me your hand: this hand is moist, my lady.

DESDEM. It yet hath felt no age nor known no sorrow.

OTHELLO This argues fruitfulness and liberal heart:
Hot, hot, and moist. This hand of yours requires
A sequester from liberty, fasting and prayer,
Much castigation, exercise devout;
For there's a young and sweating devil here
That commonly rebels. 'Tis a good hand,
A frank one.

DESDEM. You may, indeed, say so;
For 'twas that hand that gave away my heart.

OTHELLO A liberal hand: the hearts of old gave hands;
But our new heraldry is hands, not hearts.

DESDEM. I cannot speak of this. Come now, your promise.

OTHELLO What promise, chuck?

DESDEM. I have sent to bid Cassio come speak with you.

OTHELLO I have a salt and sorry rheum offends me;
Lend me thy handkerchief.

DESDEM. Here, my lord.

OTHELLO That which I gave you.

DESDEM. I have it not about me.
OTHELLO Not?
DESDEM. No, indeed, my lord.
OTHELLO That's a fault. That handkerchief
Did an Egyptian to my mother give;
She was a charmer, and could almost read
The thoughts of people: she told her, while she kept it
'Twould make her amiable and subdue my father
Entirely to her love; but if she lost it
Or made a gift of it, my father's eye
Should hold her loathèd and his spirits should hunt
After new fancies. She dying gave it me,
And bid me, when my fate would have me wive,
To give it her. I did so; and take heed on't:
Make it a darling like your precious eye;
To lose't or give't away were such perdition
As nothing else could match.
DESDEM. Is't possible?
OTHELLO 'Tis true. There's magic in the web of it:
A sibyl, that had numbered in the world
The sun to course two hundred compasses,
In her prophetic fury sewed the work;
The worms were hallowed that did breed the silk;
And it was dyed in mummy which the skilful
Conserved of maidens' hearts.
DESDEM. Indeed! Is't true?
OTHELLO Most veritable; therefore look to't well.
DESDEM. Then would to God that I had never seen't!
OTHELLO Ha! Wherefore?
DESDEM. Why do you speak so startingly and rash?
OTHELLO Is't lost? Is't gone? Speak, is it out o'th'way?
DESDEM. Heaven bless us!
OTHELLO Say you?
DESDEM. It is not lost; but what an if it were?
OTHELLO How!
DESDEM. I say it is not lost.
OTHELLO Fetch't; let me see't.
DESDEM. Why, so I can, sir, but I will not now.
This is a trick to put me from my suit:

Pray you, let Cassio be received again.

OTHELLO Fetch me the handkerchief: my mind misgives.

DESDEM. Come, come;
You'll never meet a more sufficient man.

OTHELLO The handkerchief!

DESDEM. I pray, talk me of Cassio.

OTHELLO The handkerchief!

DESDEM. A man that all his time
Hath founded his good fortunes on your love,
Shared dangers with you –

OTHELLO The handkerchief!

DESDEM. In sooth, you are to blame.

OTHELLO Away! [*he goes*

EMILIA Is not this man jealous?

DESDEM. I ne'er saw this before.
Sure there's some wonder in this handkerchief:
I am most unhappy in the loss of it.

EMILIA 'Tis not a year or two shows us a man:
They are all but stomachs and we all but food;
They eat us hungerly, and when they are full
They belch us. Look you, Cassio and my husband

Enter CASSIO *and* IAGO

IAGO There is no other way: 'tis she must do't;
And, lo, the happiness! Go and importune her.

DESDEM. How now, good Cassio! What's the news with you?

CASSIO Madam, my former suit: I do beseech you
That, by your virtuous means, I may again
Exist and be a member of his love
Whom I with all the office of my heart
Entirely honour. I would not be delayed:
If my offence be of such mortal kind
That nor my service past nor present sorrow,
Nor purposed merit in futurity,
Can ransom me into his love again,
But to know so must be my benefit;
So shall I clothe me in a forced content
And shut myself up in some other course
To fortune's alms.

DESDEM. Alas, thrice-gentle Cassio!

My advocation is not now in tune;
My lord is not my lord, nor should I know him
Were he in favour as in humour altered.
So help me every spirit sanctified,
As I have spoken for you all my best
And stood within the blank of his displeasure
For my free speech! You must awhile be patient:
What I can do I will; and more I will
Than for myself I dare – let that suffice you.

IAGO Is my lord angry?

EMILIA He went hence but now,
And certainly in strange unquietness.

IAGO Can he be angry? I have seen the cannon
When it hath blown his ranks into the air
And, like the devil, from his very arm
Puffed his own brother; and is he angry?
Something of moment then: I will go meet him;
There's matter in't indeed if he be angry.

DESDEM. I prithee, do so. [*Iago goes*
Something sure of state,
Either from Venice, or some unhatched practice
Made demonstrable here in Cyprus to him,
Hath puddled his clear spirit; and in such cases
Men's natures wrangle with inferior things,
Though great ones are their object. 'Tis even so;
For let our finger ache, and it indues
Our other healthful members to a sense
Of pain. Nay, we must think men are not gods,
Nor of them look for such observancy
As fits the bridal. Beshrew me much, Emilia,
I was, unhandsome warrior as I am,
Arraigning his unkindness with my soul;
But now I find I had suborned the witness,
And he's indicted falsely.

EMILIA Pray heaven it be state matters, as you think,
And no conception nor no jealous toy
Concerning you.

DESDEM. Alas the day, I never gave him cause!

EMILIA But jealous souls will not be answered so;

They are not ever jealous for the cause,
But jealous for they're jealous: 'tis a monster
Begot upon itself, born on itself.

DESDEM. Heaven keep that monster from Othello's mind!

EMILIA Lady, amen.

DESDEM. I will go seek him. Cassio, walk hereabout:
If I do find him fit, I'll move your suit,
And seek to effect it to my uttermost.

CASSIO I humbly thank your ladyship.

[*Desdemona and Emilia depart*

Enter BIANCA

BIANCA Save you, friend Cassio!

CASSIO What make you from home?
How is it with you, my most fair Bianca?
In faith, sweet love, I was coming to your house.

BIANCA And I was going to your lodging, Cassio.
What, keep a week away? Seven days and nights?
Eight score eight hours? And lovers' absent hours,
More tedious than the dial eight score times?
O weary reckoning!

CASSIO Pardon me, Bianca:
I have this while with leaden thoughts been pressed;
But I shall in a more continuate time
Strike off this score of absence. Sweet Bianca,

[*giving Desdemona's handkerchief*

Take me this work out.

BIANCA O Cassio, whence came this?
This is some token from a newer friend:
To the felt absence now I feel a cause;
Is't come to this? Well, well.

CASSIO Go to, woman!
Throw your vile guesses in the devil's teeth,
From whence you have them. You are jealous now
That this is from some mistress, some remembrance:
No, by my faith, Bianca.

BIANCA Why, whose is it?

CASSIO I know not neither. I found it in my chamber.
I like the work well. Ere it be demanded –
As like enough it will – I'd have it copied:

Take it, and do't; and leave me for this time.

BIANCA Leave you! Wherefore?

CASSIO I do attend here on the general;
And think it no addition, nor my wish,
To have him see me womaned.

BIANCA Why, I pray you?

CASSIO Not that I love you not.

BIANCA But that you do not love me.
I pray you, bring me on the way a little;
And say if I shall see you soon at night.

CASSIO 'Tis but a little way that I can bring you,
For I attend here; but I'll see you soon.

BIANCA 'Tis very good; I must be circumstanced. [*they go*

ACT 4 SCENE 1

The same

Enter OTHELLO *and* IAGO

IAGO Will you think so?
OTHELLO Think so, Iago!
IAGO What,
To kiss in private?
OTHELLO An unauthorized kiss.
IAGO Or to be naked with her friend in bed
An hour or more, not meaning any harm?
OTHELLO Naked in bed, Iago, and not mean harm!
It is hypocrisy against the devil:
They that mean virtuously and yet do so,
The devil their virtue tempts and they tempt heaven.
IAGO So they do nothing, 'tis a venial slip:
But if I give my wife a handkerchief –
OTHELLO What then?
IAGO Why, then, 'tis hers, my lord; and being hers,
She may, I think, bestow't on any man.
OTHELLO She is protectress of her honour too:
May she give that?
IAGO Her honour is an essence that's not seen;
They have it very oft that have it not:
But for the handkerchief –
OTHELLO By heaven, I would most gladly have forgot it.
Thou said'st – O, it comes o'er my memory,
As doth the raven o'er the infected house,
Boding to all – he had my handkerchief.
IAGO Ay, what of that?
OTHELLO That's not so good now.
IAGO What
If I had said I had seen him do you wrong?
Or heard him say – as knaves be such abroad,
Who having, by their own importunate suit,
Or voluntary dotage of some mistress,
Convincèd or supplied them, cannot choose

But they must blab –

OTHELLO Hath he said anything?

IAGO He hath, my lord; but, be you well assured,
No more than he'll unswear.

OTHELLO What hath he said?

IAGO Faith, that he did – I know not what he did.

OTHELLO What? What?

IAGO Lie –

OTHELLO With her?

IAGO With her, on her; what you will,

OTHELLO Lie with her! Lie on her! – We say lie on her, when they belie her. – Lie with her! 'Zounds, that's fulsome! Handkerchief – confessions – handkerchief! To confess and be hanged for his labour; first, to be, hanged; and then to confess. I tremble at it. Nature would not invest herself in such shadowing passion without some instruction. It is not words that shakes me thus. Pish! Noses, ears, and lips. Is't possible? – Confess? – Handkerchief? – O devil! [*falls in a trance*

IAGO Work on,
My medicine, work! Thus credulous fools are caught;
And many worthy and chaste dames even thus,
All guiltless, meet reproach. What, ho! My lord!
My lord, I say! Othello!

Enter CASSIO

How now, Cassio!

CASSIO What's the matter?

IAGO My lord is fallen into an epilepsy.
This is his second fit; he had one yesterday.

CASSIO Rub him about the temples.

IAGO No, forbear;
The lethargy must have his quiet course;
If not, he foams at mouth, and by and by
Breaks out to savage madness. Look, he stirs.
Do you withdraw yourself a little while.
He will recover straight; when he is gone,
I would on great occasion speak with you. [*Cassio goes*
How is it, general? Have you not hurt your head?

OTHELLO Dost thou mock me?

IAGO I mock you! No, by heaven.
Would you would bear your fortune like a man!

OTHELLO A hornèd man's a monster and a beast.

IAGO There's many a beast then in a populous city,
And many a civil monster.

OTHELLO Did he confess it?

IAGO Good sir, be a man:
Think every bearded fellow that's but yoked
May draw with you. There's millions now alive
That nightly lie in those unproper beds
Which they dare swear peculiar; your case is better.
O, 'tis the spite of hell, the fiend's arch-mock,
To lip a wanton in a secure couch,
And to suppose her chaste! No, let me know;
And knowing what I am, know what shall be.

OTHELLO O, thou art wise; 'tis certain.

IAGO Stand you awhile apart;
Confine yourself but in a patient list.
Whilst you were here o'erwhelmèd with your grief –
A passion most unsuiting such a man –
Cassio came hither; I shifted him away,
And laid good scuse upon your ecstasy;
Bade him anon return and speak with me;
The which he promised. Do but encave yourself,
And mark the fleers, the gibes, and notable scorns,
That dwell in every region of his face;
For I will make him tell the tale anew,
Where, how, how oft, how long ago and when
He hath and is again to cope your wife.
I say, but mark his gestures. Marry, patience;
Or I shall say you're all in all a spleen,
And nothing of a man.

OTHELLO Dost thou hear, Iago?
I will be found most cunning in my patience;
But – dost thou hear? – Most bloody.

IAGO That's not amiss;
But yet keep time in all. Will you withdraw?

[*Othello retires*

Now will I question Cassio of Bianca,
A hussy that by selling her desires
Buys herself bread and clothes: it is a creature
That dotes on Cassio; as 'tis the strumpet's plague
To beguile many and be beguiled by one.
He, when he hears of her, cannot refrain
From the excess of laughter. Here he comes.

Re-enter CASSIO

As he shall smile, Othello shall go mad;
And his unbookish jealousy must construe
Poor Cassio's smiles, gestures, and light behaviours,
Quite in the wrong. How do you now, lieutenant?

CASSIO The worser that you give me the addition
Whose want even kills me.

IAGO Ply Desdemona well, and you are sure on't.
Now, if this suit lay in Bianca's power,
How quickly should you speed!

CASSIO Alas, poor caitiff!

OTHELLO Look how he laughs already!

IAGO I never knew a woman love man so.

CASSIO Alas, poor rogue! I think, in faith, she loves me.

OTHELLO Now he denies it faintly, and laughs it out.

IAGO Do you hear, Cassio?

OTHELLO Now he importunes him to tell it o'er.
Go to; well said, well said.

IAGO She gives it out that you shall marry her.
Do you intend it?

CASSIO Ha, ha, ha!

OTHELLO Do you triumph, Roman? Do you triumph?

CASSIO I marry her! What, a customer! I prithee, bear some charity to my wit; do not think it so unwholesome. Ha, ha, ha!

OTHELLO So, so, so, so; they laugh that win.

IAGO Faith, the cry goes that you marry her.

CASSIO Prithee, say true.

IAGO I am a very villain else.

OTHELLO Have you scored me? Well.

CASSIO This is the monkey's own giving out: she is persuaded

I will marry her, out of her own love and flattery, not out of my promise.

OTHELLO Iago beckons me; now he begins the story.

CASSIO She was here even now; she haunts me in every place. I was the other day talking on the sea-bank with certain Venetians; and thither comes the bauble, and, by this hand, falls me thus about my neck –

OTHELLO Crying 'O dear Cassio!' As it were: his gesture imports it.

CASSIO So hangs, and lolls, and weeps upon me; so shakes, and pulls me: ha, ha, ha!

OTHELLO Now he tells how she plucked him to my chamber. O, I see that nose of yours, but not that dog I shall throw it to.

CASSIO Well, I must leave her company.

IAGO Before me! Look where she comes!

CASSIO 'Tis such another fitchew! Marry, a perfumed one!

Enter BIANCA

What do you mean by this haunting of me?

BIANCA Let the devil and his dam haunt you! What did you mean by that same handkerchief you gave me even now? I was a fine fool to take it. I must take out the work? A likely piece of work that you should find it in your chamber and not know who left it there! This is some minx's token, and I must take out the work? There; give it your hobby-horse. Wheresoever you had it, I'll take out no work on't.

CASSIO How now, my sweet Bianca! How now! How now!

OTHELLO By heaven, that should be my handkerchief!

BIANCA An you'll come to supper tonight, you may; an you will not, come when you are next prepared for. [*goes*

IAGO After her, after her.

CASSIO Faith, I must; she'll rail in the street else.

IAGO Will you sup there?

CASSIO Faith, I intend so.

IAGO Well, I may chance to see you; for I would very fain speak with you.

CASSIO Prithee, come; will you?

IAGO Go to; say no more. [*Cassio goes*

OTHELLO [*comes forward*] How shall I murder him, Iago?

IAGO Did you perceive how he laughed at his vice?

OTHELLO O Iago!

IAGO And did you see the handkerchief?

OTHELLO Was that mine?

IAGO Yours, by this hand – and to see how he prizes the foolish woman your wife! She gave it him, and he hath given it his whore.

OTHELLO I would have him nine years a-killing. A fine woman! A fair woman! A sweet woman!

IAGO Nay, you must forget that.

OTHELLO Ay, let her rot, and perish, and be damned tonight; for she shall not live. No, my heart is turned to stone: I strike it, and it hurts my hand. O, the world hath not a sweeter creature: she might lie by an emperor's side and command him tasks.

IAGO Nay, that's not your way.

OTHELLO Hang her! I do but say what she is: so delicate with her needle, an admirable musician – O, she will sing the savageness out of a bear – of so high and plenteous wit and invention –

IAGO She's the worse for all this.

OTHELLO O, a thousand, thousand times – and then, of so gentle a condition!

IAGO Ay, too gentle.

OTHELLO Nay, that's certain; but yet the pity of it, Iago! O Iago, the pity of it, Iago!

IAGO If you be so fond over her iniquity, give her patent to offend; for, if it touch not you, it comes near nobody.

OTHELLO I will chop her into messes – cuckold me!

IAGO O, 'tis foul in her.

OTHELLO With mine officer!

IAGO That's fouler.

OTHELLO Get me some poison, Iago – this night. I'll not expostulate with her, lest her body and beauty unprovide my mind again – this night, Iago.

IAGO Do it not with poison: strangle her in her bed, even the bed she hath contaminated.

OTHELLO Good, good: the justice of it pleases; very good.

IAGO And for Cassio, let me be his undertaker: you shall hear more by midnight.

OTHELLO Excellent good. [*a trumpet sounds*]
What trumpet is that same?

IAGO I warrant, something from Venice.

Enter LODOVICO, DESDEMONA, *and Attendants*

'Tis Lodovico!
This comes from the duke; and see, your wife is with him.

LODOVICO God save you, worthy general!

OTHELLO With all my heart, sir.

LODOVICO The duke and senators of Venice greet you.
[*gives him a letter*

OTHELLO I kiss the instrument of their pleasures.
[*opens and reads*

DESDEM. And what's the news, good cousin Lodovico?

IAGO I am very glad to see you, signior;
Welcome to Cyprus.

LODOVICO I thank you. How does Lieutenant Cassio?

IAGO Lives, sir.

DESDEM. Cousin, there's fallen between him and my lord
An unkind breach; but you shall make all well.

OTHELLO Are you sure of that?

DESDEM. My lord?

OTHELLO [*reads*] 'This fail you not to do, as you will – '

LODOVICO He did not call; he's busy in the paper.
Is there division 'twixt my lord and Cassio?

DESDEM. A most unhappy one; I would do much
T' atone them, for the love I bear to Cassio.

OTHELLO Fire and brimstone!

DESDEM. My lord?

OTHELLO Are you wise?

DESDEM. What, is he angry?

LODOVICO May be the letter moved him;
For, as I think, they do command him home,
Deputing Cassio in his government.

DESDEM. By my troth, I am glad on't.

OTHELLO Indeed!

DESDEM. My lord?

OTHELLO I am glad to see you mad.

DESDEM. Why, sweet Othello!

OTHELLO Devil! [*striking her*

DESDEM. I have not deserved this.

LODOVICO My lord, this would not be believed in Venice,
Though I should swear I saw't. 'Tis very much.
Make her amends; she weeps.

OTHELLO O devil, devil!
If that the earth could teem with woman's tears,
Each drop she falls would prove a crocodile.
Out of my sight!

DESDEM. I will not stay to offend you. [*going*

LODOVICO Truly, an obedient lady.
I do beseech your lordship, call her back.

OTHELLO Mistress!

DESDEM. My lord?

OTHELLO What would you with her, sir?

LODOVICO Who, I, my lord?

OTHELLO Ay; you did wish that I would make her turn.
Sir, she can turn and turn, and yet go on
And turn again; and she can weep, sir, weep;
And she's obedient, as you say, obedient,
Very obedient. Proceed you in your tears. –
Concerning this, sir, – O well-painted passion! –
I am commanded home. – Get you away;
I'll send for you anon. – Sir, I obey the mandate,
And will return to Venice. – Hence, avaunt! –
[*Desdemona goes*
Cassio shall have my place. And, sir, tonight,
I do entreat that we may sup together.
You are welcome, sir, to Cyprus. – Goats and monkeys!
[*he goes*

LODOVICO Is this the noble Moor whom our full senate
Call all in all sufficient? Is this the nature
Whom passion could not shake? Whose solid virtue
The shot of accident nor dart of chance
Could neither graze nor pierce?

IAGO He is much changed.

LODOVICO Are his wits safe? Is he not light of brain?

IAGO He's that he is. I may not breathe my censure
What he might be; if what he might he is not,

I would to heaven he were!

LODOVICO What, strike his wife!

IAGO Faith, that was not so well; yet would I knew
That stroke would prove the worst!

LODOVICO Is it his use?
Or did the letters work upon his blood,
And new-create this fault?

IAGO Alas, alas!
It is not honesty in me to speak
What I have, seen and known. You shall observe him,
And his own courses will denote him so
That I may save my speech; do but go after,
And mark how he continues.

LODOVICO I am sorry that I am deceived in him. [*they go*

SCENE 2

A room in the citadel

Enter OTHELLO *and* EMILIA

OTHELLO You have seen nothing, then?

EMILIA Nor ever heard, nor ever did suspect.

OTHELLO Yes, you have seen Cassio and she together.

EMILIA But then I saw no harm, and then I heard
Each syllable that breath made up between them.

OTHELLO What, did they never whisper?

EMILIA Never, my lord.

OTHELLO Nor send you out o'th'way?

EMILIA Never.

OTHELLO To fetch her fan, her gloves, her mask, nor nothing?

EMILIA Never, my lord.

OTHELLO That's strange.

EMILIA I durst, my lord, to wager she is honest,
Lay down my soul at stake. If you think other,
Remove your thought: it doth abuse your bosom.
If any wretch have put this in your head,
Let heaven requite it with the serpent's curse!
For if she be not honest, chaste, and true,

There's no man happy: the purest of their wives
Is foul as slander.

OTHELLO Bid her come hither; go. [*Emilia goes*
She says enough; yet she's a simple bawd
That cannot say as much. This is a subtle whore,
A closet lock and key of villainous secrets;
And yet she'll kneel and pray; I have seen her do't.

Enter DESDEMONA *with* EMILIA

DESDEM. My lord, what is your will?

OTHELLO Pray, chuck, come hither.

DESDEM. What is your pleasure?

OTHELLO Let me see your eyes;
Look in my face.

DESDEM. What horrible fancy's this?

OTHELLO [*to Emilia*] Some of your function, mistress:
Leave procreants alone and shut the door;
Cough, or cry hem, if anybody come –
Your mystery, your mystery; nay, dispatch.
[*Emilia goes out*

DESDEM. Upon my knees, what doth your speech import?
I understand a fury in your words,
But not the words.

OTHELLO Why, what art thou?

DESDEM. Your wife, my lord; your true and loyal wife.

OTHELLO Come, swear it, damn thyself;
Lest, being like one of heaven, the devils themselves
Should fear to seize thee. Therefore be double-damned:
Swear thou art honest.

DESDEM. Heaven doth truly know it.

OTHELLO Heaven truly knows that thou art false as hell.

DESDEM. To whom, my lord? With whom? How am I false?

OTHELLO Ah, Desdemon! Away! Away! Away!

DESDEM. Alas the heavy day! Why do you weep?
Am I the motive of these tears, my lord?
If haply you my father do suspect
An instrument of this your calling back,
Lay not your blame on me; if you have lost him,
Why, I have lost him too.

OTHELLO Had it pleased heaven

To try me with affliction; had they rained
All kind of sores and shames on my bare head,
Steeped me in poverty to the very lips,
Given to captivity me and my utmost hopes,
I should have found in some place of my soul
A drop of patience; but, alas, to make me
A fixèd figure for the time of scorn
To point his slow unmoving finger at!
Yet could I bear that too; well, very well;
But there, where I have garnered up my heart,
Where either I must live or bear no life,
The foundation from the which my current runs,
Or else dries up – to be discarded thence!
Or keep it as a cistern for foul toads
To knot and gender in! Turn thy complexion there,
Patience, thou young and rose-lipped cherubin,
Ay, there, look grim as hell!

DESDEM. I hope my noble lord esteems me honest.

OTHELLO O, ay; as summer flies are in the shambles,
That quicken even with blowing. O thou weed,
Who art so lovely fair and smell'st so sweet
That the sense aches at thee, would thou hadst ne'er been born!

DESDEM. Alas, what ignorant sin have I committed?

OTHELLO Was this fair paper, this most goodly book,
Made to write 'whore' upon? What committed!
Committed! O thou public commoner!
I should make very forges of my cheeks,
That would to cinders burn up modesty,
Did I but speak thy deeds. What committed!
Heaven stops the nose at it, and the moon winks;
The bawdy wind, that kisses all it meets,
Is hushed within the hollow mine of earth,
And will not hear it. What committed!
Impudent strumpet!

DESDEM. By heaven, you do me wrong.

OTHELLO Are not you a strumpet?

DESDEM. No, as I am a Christian.
If to preserve this vessel for my lord

From any other foul unlawful touch
Be not to be a strumpet, I am none.

OTHELLO What, not a whore?

DESDEM. No, as I shall be saved.

OTHELLO Is't possible?

DESDEM. O, heaven forgive us!

OTHELLO I cry you mercy then:
I took you for that cunning whore of Venice
That married with Othello.
[*raising his voice*] You, mistress,
That have the office opposite to Saint Peter,
And keep the gate of hell!

Re-enter EMILIA

You, you, ay, you.
We've done our course; there's money for your pains:
I pray you, turn the key, and keep our counsel. [*goes*

EMILIA Alas, what does this gentleman conceive?
How do you, madam? How do you, my good lady?

DESDEM. Faith, half asleep.

EMILIA Good madam, what's the matter with my lord?

DESDEM. With who?

EMILIA Why, with my lord, madam.

DESDEM. Who is thy lord?

EMILIA He that is yours, sweet lady.

DESDEM. I have none: do not talk to me, Emilia;
I cannot weep, nor answers have I none
But what should go by water. Prithee, tonight
Lay on my bed my wedding sheets – remember;
And call thy husband hither.

EMILIA Here's a change indeed! [*goes*

DESDEM. 'Tis meet I should be used so, very meet.
How have I been behaved, that he might stick
The small'st opinion on my least misuse?

Re-enter EMILIA *with* IAGO

IAGO What is your pleasure, madam? How is't with you?

DESDEM. I cannot tell. Those that do teach young babes
Do it with gentle means and easy tasks:
He might have chid me so; for, in good faith,

I am a child to chiding.
IAGO What's the matter, lady?
EMILIA Alas, Iago, my lord hath so bewhored her,
Thrown such despite and heavy terms upon her,
As true heart cannot bear.
DESDEM. Am I that name, Iago?
IAGO What name, fair lady?
DESDEM. Such as she said my lord did say I was.
EMILIA He called her whore: a beggar in his drink
Could not have laid such terms upon his callet.
IAGO Why did he so?
DESDEM. I do not know; I am sure I am none such.
IAGO Do not weep, do not weep. Alas the day!
EMILIA Hath she forsook so many noble matches,
Her father, and her country, and her friends,
To be called whore? Would it not make one weep?
DESDEM. It is my wretched fortune.
IAGO Beshrew him for't!
How comes this trick upon him?
DESDEM. Nay, heaven doth know.
EMILIA I will be hanged, if some eternal villain,
Some busy and insinuating rogue,
Some cogging, cozening slave, to get some office,
Have not devised this slander; I'll be hanged else.
IAGO Fie, there is no such man; it is impossible.
DESDEM. If any such there be, heaven pardon him!
EMILIA A halter pardon him! And hell gnaw his bones!
Why should he call her whore? Who keeps her company?
What place, what time, what form, what likelihood?
The Moor's abused by some most villainous knave,
Some base notorious knave, some scurvy fellow.
O heaven, that such companions thou'ldst unfold,
And put in every honest hand a whip
To lash the rascals naked through the world
Even from the east to th'west!
IAGO Speak within door.
EMILIA O, fie upon them! Some such squire he was
That turned your wit the seamy side without,

And made you to suspect me with the Moor.

IAGO You are a fool; go to.

DESDEM. Alas, Iago,
What shall I do to win my lord again?
Good friend, go to him; for, by this light of heaven,
I know not how I lost him. Here I kneel:
If e'er my will did trespass 'gainst his love
Either in discourse of thought or actual deed,
Or that mine eyes, mine ears, or any sense,
Delighted them in any other form,
Or that I do not yet, and ever did,
And ever will, though he do shake me off
To beggarly divorcement, love him dearly,
Comfort forswear me! Unkindness may do much;
And his unkindness may defeat my life,
But never taint my love. I cannot say 'whore':
It does abhor me now I speak the word;
To do the act that might the addition earn
Not the world's mass of vanity could make me.

IAGO I pray you, be content; 'tis but his humour:
The business of the state does him offence,
And he does chide with you.

DESDEM. If 'twere no other!

IAGO 'Tis but so, I warrant. [*trumpets sound*
Hark how these instruments summon to supper!
The messengers of Venice stay the meat:
Go in, and weep not; all things shall be well.
[*Desdemona and Emilia go*

Enter RODERIGO

How now, Roderigo!

RODERIGO I do not find that thou deal'st justly with me.

IAGO What in the contrary?

RODERIGO Every day thou daff'st me with some device, Iago; and rather, as it seems to me now, keep'st from me all conveniency than suppliest me with the least advantage of hope. I will indeed no longer endure it; nor am I yet persuaded to put up in peace what already I have foolishly suffered.

IAGO Will you hear me, Roderigo?

RODERIGO Faith, I have heard too much; for your words and performances are no kin together.

IAGO You charge me most unjustly.

RODERIGO With nought but truth. I have wasted myself out of my means. The jewels you have had from me to deliver to Desdemona would half have corrupted a votarist. You have told me she hath received them and returned me expectations and comforts of sudden respect and acquaintance; but I find none.

IAGO Well; go to; very well.

RODERIGO Very well! Go to! I cannot go to, man; nor 'tis not very well. By this hand, I think 'tis very scurvy, and begin to find myself fopped in it.

IAGO Very well.

RODERIGO I tell you 'tis not very well. I will make myself known to Desdemona. If she will return me my jewels, I will give over my suit and repent my unlawful solicitation; if not, assure yourself I will seek satisfaction of you.

IAGO You have said now.

RODERIGO Ay, and said nothing but what I protest intendment of doing.

IAGO Why, now I see there's mettle in thee; and even from this instant do build on thee a better opinion than ever before. Give me thy hand, Roderigo: thou hast taken against me a most just exception ; but yet, I protest, I have dealt most directly in thy affair.

RODERIGO It hath not appeared.

IAGO I grant indeed it hath not appeared, and your suspicion is not without wit and judgment. But, Roderigo, if thou hast that in thee indeed, which I have greater reason to believe now than ever – I mean purpose, courage, and valour – this night show it: if thou the next night following enjoy not Desdemona, take me from this world with treachery and devise engines for my life.

RODERIGO Well, what is it? Is it within reason and compass?

IAGO Sir, there is especial commission come from Venice to depute Cassio in Othello's place.

RODERIGO Is that true? Why then, Othello and Desdemona return again to Venice.

IAGO O, no; he goes into Mauritania, and takes away with him the fair Desdemona, unless his abode be lingered here by some accident: wherein none can be so determinate as the removing of Cassio.

RODERIGO How do you mean removing of him?

IAGO Why, by making him uncapable of Othello's place; knocking out his brains.

RODERIGO And that you would have me do?

IAGO Ay, if you dare do yourself a profit and a right. He sups tonight with a harlotry, and thither will I go to him: he knows not yet of his honourable fortune. If you will watch his going thence, which I will fashion to fall out between twelve and one, you may take him at your pleasure. I will be near to second your attempt, and he shall fall between us. Come, stand not amazed at it, but go along with me; I will show you such a necessity in his death that you shall think yourself bound to put it on him. It is now high supper-time, and the night grows to waste. About it.

RODERIGO I will hear further reason for this.

IAGO And you shall be satisfied. [*they go*

SCENE 3

Another room in the citadel

Enter OTHELLO, LODOVICO, DESDEMONA, EMILIA, *and Attendants*

LODOVICO I do beseech you, sir, trouble yourself no further.
OTHELLO O, pardon me; 'twill do me good to walk.
LODOVICO Madam, good night; I humbly thank your ladyship.
DESDEM. Your honour is most welcome.
OTHELLO Will you walk, sir?
O, Desdemona!
DESDEM. My lord?
OTHELLO Get you to bed on th'instant; I will be returned forthwith. Dismiss your attendant there: look't be done.
DESDEM. I will, my lord. [*Othello, Lodovico, and Attendants go*
EMILIA How goes it now? He looks gentler than he did.
DESDEM. He says he will return incontinent:

He hath commanded me to go to bed,
And bade me to dismiss you.

EMILIA Dismiss me!

DESDEM. It was his bidding; therefore, good Emilia,
Give me my nightly wearing, and adieu:
We must not now displease him.

EMILIA I would you had never seen him!

DESDEM. So would not I: my love doth so approve him,
That even his stubbornness, his checks, his frowns –
Prithee, unpin me – have grace and favour in them.

EMILIA I have laid those sheets you bade me on the bed.

DESDEM. All's one. Good faith, how foolish are our minds!
If I do die before thee, prithee, shroud me
In one of those same sheets.

EMILIA Come, come, you talk.

DESDEM. My mother had a maid called Barbara.
She was in love; and he she loved proved mad
And did forsake her. She had a song of 'willow' –
An old thing 'twas, but it expressed her fortune,
And she died singing it. That song tonight
Will not go from my mind. I have much to do
But to go hang my head all at one side
And sing it like poor Barbara. Prithee, dispatch.

EMILIA Shall I go fetch your night-gown?

DESDEM. No, unpin me here.
This Lodovico is a proper man.

EMILIA A very handsome man.

DESDEM. He speaks well.

EMILIA I know a lady in Venice would have walked barefoot to Palestine for a touch of his nether lip.

DESDEM. [*sings*] The poor soul sat sighing by a sycamore tree,
Sing all a green willow;
Her hand on her bosom, her head on her knee,
Sing willow, willow, willow:
The fresh streams ran by her, and murmured her moans;
Sing willow, willow, willow;
Her salt tears fell from her, and softened the stones –

Lay by these –
Sing willow, willow, willow;
Prithee, hie thee; he'll come anon –
Sing all a green willow must be my garland.
Let nobody blame him; his scorn I approve –
Nay, that's not next. Hark! Who is't that knocks?

EMILIA It's the wind.

DESDEM. [*sings*] I called my love false love; but what said he then?
Sing willow, willow, willow;
If I court moe women, you'll couch with moe men.
So, get thee gone; good night. Mine eyes do itch;
Does that bode weeping?

EMILIA 'Tis neither here nor there.

DESDEM. I have heard it said so. O, these men, these men!
Dost thou in conscience think – tell me, Emilia –
That there be women do abuse their husbands
In such gross kind?

EMILIA There be some such, no question.

DESDEM. Wouldst thou do such a deed for all the world?

EMILIA Why, would not you?

DESDEM. No, by this heavenly light!

EMILIA Nor I neither by this heavenly light: I might do't as well i'th'dark.

DESDEM. Wouldst thou do such a deed for all the world?

EMILIA The world's a huge thing: it is a great prize for a small vice.

DESDEM. In troth, I think thou wouldst not.

EMILIA In troth, I think I should; and undo't when I had done't. Marry, I would not do such a thing for a joint-ring, nor for measures of lawn, nor for gowns, petticoats, nor caps, nor any petty exhibition. But for all the whole world – ud's pity, who would not make her husband a cuckold to make him a monarch? I should venture purgatory for't.

DESDEM. Beshrew me, if I would do such a wrong for the whole world.

EMILIA Why, the wrong is but a wrong i'th'world; and having

the world for your labour, 'tis a wrong in your own world, and you might quickly make it right.

DESDEM. I do not think there is any such woman.

EMILIA Yes, a dozen; and as many to th'vantage as would store the world they played for.
But I do think it is their husbands' faults
If wives do fall. Say that they slack their duties
And pour our treasures into foreign laps,
Or else break out in peevish jealousies,
Throwing restraint upon us; or say they strike us,
Or scant our former having in despite –
Why, we have galls, and though we have some grace,
Yet have we some revenge. Let husbands know
Their wives have sense like them: they see, and smell,
And have their palates both for sweet and sour,
As husbands have. What is it that they do
When they change us for others? Is it sport?
I think it is. And doth affection breed it?
I think it doth. Is't frailty that thus errs?
It is so too. And have not we affections,
Desires for sport, and frailty, as men have?
Then let them use us well: else let them know,
The ills we do, their ills instruct us so.

DESDEM. Good night, good night. [*Emilia goes*
Heaven me such uses send,
Not to pick bad from bad, but by bad mend! [*goes*

ACT 5 SCENE I

A street

Enter IAGO *and* RODERIGO

IAGO Here, stand behind this bulk; straight will he come.
Wear thy good rapier bare, and put it home;
Quick, quick; fear nothing; I'll be at thy elbow.
It makes us, or it mars us; think on that,
And fix most firm thy resolution.

RODERIGO Be near at hand; I may miscarry in't.

IAGO Here, at thy hand. Be bold, and take thy stand. [*retires*

RODERIGO I have no great devotion to the deed;
And yet he hath given me satisfying reasons.
'Tis but a man gone. Forth, my sword: he dies.

IAGO I have rubbed this young quat almost to the sense,
And he grows angry. Now, whether he kill Cassio,
Or Cassio him, or each do kill the other,
Every way makes my gain: live Roderigo,
He calls me to a restitution large
Of gold and jewels that I bobbed from him,
As gifts to Desdemona –
It must not be; if Cassio do remain,
He hath a daily beauty in his life
That makes me ugly; and besides, the Moor
May unfold me to him – there stand I in much peril.
No, he must die. Be't so. I hear him coming.

Enter CASSIO

RODERIGO I know his gait; 'tis he. Villain, thou diest!
[*makes a pass at Cassio*

CASSIO That thrust had been mine enemy indeed,
But that my coat is better than thou think'st.
I will make proof of thine. [*draws, and wounds Roderigo*

RODERIGO O, I am slain!

[*Iago from behind strikes at Cassio's legs, and hurries off*

CASSIO I am maimed for ever. Help, ho! Murder! Murder!
[*falls*

Enter OTHELLO

OTHELLO The voice of Cassio: Iago keeps his word.
RODERIGO O, villain that I am!
OTHELLO It is even so.
CASSIO O, help, ho! Light! A surgeon!
OTHELLO 'Tis he. O brave Iago, honest and just,
That hast such noble sense of thy friend's wrong!
Thou teachest me: minion, your dear lies dead,
And your unblest fate hies. Strumpet, I come!
Forth of my heart, those charms, thine eyes, are blotted;
Thy bed lust-stained shall with lust's blood be spotted.
[*he goes*

Enter LODOVICO *and* GRATIANO

CASSIO What, ho! No watch? No passage? Murder! Murder!
GRATIANO 'Tis some mischance; the voice is very direful.
CASSIO O, help!
LODOVICO Hark!
RODERIGO O wretched villain!
LODOVICO Two or three groan. It is a heavy night;
These may be counterfeits: let's think't unsafe
To come in to the cry without more help.
[*they stand aside*
RODERIGO Nobody come? Then shall I bleed to death.
LODOVICO Hark!

Re-enter IAGO, *with a light*

GRATIANO Here's one comes in his shirt, with light and weapons.
IAGO Who's there? Whose noise is this that cries on murder?
LODOVICO We do not know.
IAGO Did not you hear a cry?
CASSIO Here, here! For heaven's sake, help me!
IAGO What's the matter?
GRATIANO This is Othello's ancient, as I take it.
LODOVICO The same indeed; a very valiant fellow.
IAGO What are you here that cry so grievously?
CASSIO Iago? O, I am spoiled, undone by villains!
Give me some help.
IAGO O me, lieutenant! What villains have done this?
CASSIO I think that one of them is hereabout,

And cannot make away.

IAGO O treacherous villains!
What are you there? [*spies Lodovico and Gratiano*
Come in and give some help.

RODERIGO O, help me here!

CASSIO That's one of them.

IAGO O murderous slave! O villain!
[*stabs Roderigo*

RODERIGO O damned Iago! O inhuman dog!

IAGO Kill men i'th'dark! Where be these bloody thieves?
How silent is this town! Ho! Murder! Murder!
[*Lodovico and Gratiano come forward*
What may you be? Are you of good or evil?

LODOVICO As you shall prove us, praise us.

IAGO Signior Lodovico?

LODOVICO He, sir.

IAGO I cry you mercy. Here's Cassio hurt by villains.

GRATIANO Cassio!

IAGO How is't, brother?

CASSIO My leg is cut in two.

IAGO Marry, heaven forbid!
Light, gentlemen: I'll bind it with my shirt.

Enter BIANCA

BIANCA What is the matter, ho? Who is't that cried?

IAGO Who is't that cried!

BIANCA O my dear Cassio!
My sweet Cassio! O Cassio, Cassio, Cassio!

IAGO O notable strumpet! Cassio, may you suspect
Who they should be that have thus mangled you?

CASSIO No.

GRATIANO I am sorry to find you thus: I have been to seek you.

IAGO Lend me a garter. So. O, for a chair,
To bear him easily hence!

BIANCA Alas, he faints! O Cassio, Cassio, Cassio!

IAGO Gentlemen all, I do suspect this trash
To be a party in this injury.
Patience awhile, good Cassio. Come, come;
Lend me a light. Know we this face or no?

Alas, my friend and my dear countryman
Roderigo? No – yes, sure; 'tis Roderigo.

GRATIANO What, of Venice?

IAGO Even he, sir. Did you know him?

GRATIANO Know him! Ay.

IAGO Signior Gratiano? I cry your gentle pardon:
These bloody accidents must excuse my manners,
That so neglected you.

GRATIANO I am glad to see you.

IAGO How do you, Cassio? O, a chair, a chair!

GRATIANO Roderigo!

IAGO He, he, 'tis he. [*a chair brought*] O, that's well said; the chair.
Some good man bear him carefully from hence;
I'll fetch the general's surgeon. [*to Bianca*] For you, mistress,
Save you your labour. He that lies slain here, Cassio,
Was my dear friend: what malice was between you?

CASSIO None in the world; nor do I know the man.

IAGO [*to Bianca*]
What, look you pale? O, bear him out o'th'air.
[*Cassio is borne in, and the body of Roderigo removed*
Stay you, good gentlemen. Look you pale, mistress?
Do you perceive the gastness of her eye?
Nay, if you stare, we shall hear more anon.
Behold her well; I pray you, look upon her:
Do you see, gentlemen? Nay, guiltiness will speak,
Though tongues were out of use.

Enter EMILIA

EMILIA 'Las, what's the matter? What's the matter, husband?

IAGO Cassio hath here been set on in the dark
By Roderigo, and fellows that are scaped:
He's almost slain, and Roderigo dead.

EMILIA Alas, good gentleman! Alas, good Cassio!

IAGO This is the fruits of whoring. Prithee, Emilia,
Go know of Cassio where he supped tonight.
What, do you shake at that?

BIANCA He supped at my house; but I therefore shake not.

IAGO O, did he so? I charge you, go with me.
EMILIA O, fie upon thee, strumpet!
BIANCA I am no strumpet; but of life as honest
As you that thus abuse me.
EMILIA As I! Foh! Fie upon thee!
IAGO Kind gentlemen, let's see poor Cassio dressed.
Come, mistress, you must tell's another tale.
Emilia, run you to the citadel,
And tell my lord and lady what hath happed.
Will you go on afore? [*aside*] This is the night
That either makes me or fordoes me quite. [*they go*

SCENE 2

A chamber in the citadel; Desdemona asleep in her bed

Enter OTHELLO *with a light; he locks the door*

OTHELLO It is the cause, it is the cause, my soul.
Let me not name it to you, you chaste stars!
It is the cause. Yet I'll not shed her blood,
Nor scar that whiter skin of hers than snow
And smooth as monumental alabaster –
Yet she must die, else she'll betray more men.
Put out the light, and then put out the light:
If I quench thee, thou flaming minister,
I can again thy former light restore
Should I repent me; but once put out thy light,
Thou cunning'st pattern of excelling nature,
I know not where is that Promethean heat
That can thy light relume. [*sets down the taper*
When I have plucked the rose,
I cannot give it vital growth again,
It needs must wither: I'll smell it on the tree. [*kisses her*
O balmy breath, that dost almost persuade
Justice to break her sword! One more, one more.
Be thus when thou art dead, and I will kill thee,
And love thee after. One more, and that's the last.
So sweet was ne'er so fatal. I must weep,

But they are cruel tears; this sorrow's heavenly:
It strikes where it doth love. She wakes.

DESDEM. Who's there? Othello?

OTHELLO Ay, Desdemona.

DESDEM. Will you come to bed, my lord?

OTHELLO Have you prayed tonight, Desdemona?

DESDEM. Ay, my lord.

OTHELLO If you bethink yourself of any crime
Unreconciled as yet to heaven and grace,
Solicit for it straight.

DESDEM. Alack, my lord, what may you mean by that?

OTHELLO Well, do it, and be brief; I will walk by:
I would not kill thy unpreparèd spirit;
No – heaven forfend! – I would not kill thy soul.

DESDEM. Talk you of killing?

OTHELLO Ay, I do.

DESDEM. Then heaven have mercy on me!

OTHELLO Amen, with all my heart!

DESDEM. If you say so, I hope you will not kill me.

OTHELLO Hum!

DESDEM. And yet I fear you; for you're fatal then
When your eyes roll so. Why I should fear I know not,
Since guiltiness I know not; but yet I feel I fear.

OTHELLO Think on thy sins.

DESDEM. They are loves I bear to you.

OTHELLO Ay, and for that thou diest.

DESDEM. That death's unnatural that kills for loving.
Alas, why gnaw you so your nether lip?
Some bloody passion shakes your very frame:
These are portents; but yet I hope, I hope,
They do not point on me.

OTHELLO Peace, and be still!

DESDEM. I will so. What's the matter?

OTHELLO That handkerchief which I so loved and gave thee,
Thou gav'st to Cassio.

DESDEM. No, by my life and soul!
Send for the man, and ask him.

OTHELLO Sweet soul, take heed,
Take heed of perjury: thou art on thy death-bed,

DESDEM. Ay, but not yet to die.
OTHELLO Yes, presently;
Therefore confess thee freely of thy sin;
For to deny each article with oath
Cannot remove nor choke the strong conception
That I do groan withal. Thou art to die.
DESDEM. O Lord have mercy on me!
OTHELLO I say, amen.
DESDEM. And have you mercy too! I never did
Offend you in my life; never loved Cassio
But with such general warranty of heaven
As I might love. I never gave him token.
OTHELLO By heaven, I saw my handkerchief in's hand.
O perjured woman! Thou dost stone my heart,
And mak'st me call what I intend to do
A murder, which I thought a sacrifice.
I saw the handkerchief.
DESDEM. He found it then;
I never gave it him. Send for him hither:
Let him confess a truth.
OTHELLO He hath confessed.
DESDEM. What, my lord?
OTHELLO That he hath used thee.
DESDEM. How? Unlawfully?
OTHELLO Ay.
DESDEM. He will not say so.
OTHELLO No, his mouth is stopped;
Honest Iago hath ta'en order for't.
DESDEM. O, my fear interprets! What, is he dead?
OTHELLO Had all his hairs been lives, my great revenge
Had stomach for them all.
DESDEM. Alas, he is betrayed, and I undone!
OTHELLO Out, strumpet! Weep'st thou for him to my face?
DESDEM. O, banish me, my lord, but kill me not!
OTHELLO Down, strumpet!
DESDEM. Kill me tomorrow; let me live tonight!
OTHELLO Nay, if you strive –
DESDEM. But half an hour!
OTHELLO Being done, there is no pause.

DESDEM. But while I say one prayer!

OTHELLO It is too late. [*he smothers her*

EMILIA [*at the door without*]
My lord, my lord! What, ho! My lord, my lord!

OTHELLO What noise is this? – Not dead? Not yet quite dead?
I that am cruel am yet merciful;
I would not have thee linger in thy pain.
So, so.

EMILIA [*without*] What, ho! My lord, my lord!

OTHELLO Who's there?

EMILIA [*without*]
O, good my lord, I'd speak a word with you!

OTHELLO Yes: 'tis Emilia. – By and by. – She's dead.
'Tis like she comes to speak of Cassio's death;
The noise was high. Ha! No more moving?
Still as the grave. Shall she come in? Were't good?
I think she stirs again. No. What's best to do?
If she come in, she'll sure speak to my wife –
My wife! My wife! What wife? I have no wife.
O, insupportable! O heavy hour!
Methinks it should be now a huge eclipse
Of sun and moon, and that th'affrighted globe
Should yawn at alteration.

EMILIA [*without*] I do beseech
That I may speak with you. O, good my lord!

OTHELLO I had forgot thee: O, come in, Emilia.
Soft; by and by. Let me the curtains draw.
Where art thou? [*unlocks the door*

Enter EMILIA

What's the matter with thee now?

EMILIA O, my good lord, yonder's foul murder done!

OTHELLO What, now?

EMILIA But now, my lord.

OTHELLO It is the very error of the moon;
She comes more nearer earth than she was wont
And makes men mad.

EMILIA Cassio, my lord, hath killed a young Venetian
Called Roderigo.

OTHELLO Roderigo killed!

And Cassio killed!

EMILIA No, Cassio is not killed.

OTHELLO Not Cassio killed! Then murder's out of tune,
And sweet revenge grows harsh.

DESDEM. O, falsely, falsely murdered!

EMILIA Alas, what cry is that?

OTHELLO That! What?

EMILIA Out, and alas! That was my lady's voice.
[*she draws back the curtain*
Help! Help, ho! Help! O lady, speak again!
Sweet Desdemona! O sweet mistress, speak!

DESDEM. A guiltless death I die.

EMILIA O, who hath done this deed?

DESDEM. Nobody: I myself. Farewell;
Commend me to my kind lord: O, farewell! [*dies*

OTHELLO Why, how should she be murdered?

EMILIA Alas, who knows?

OTHELLO You heard her say herself, it was not I.

EMILIA She said so: I must needs report the truth.

OTHELLO She's like a liar gone to burning hell:
'Twas I that killed her.

EMILIA O, the more angel she,
And you the blacker devil!

OTHELLO She turned to folly, and she was a whore.

EMILIA Thou dost belie her, and thou art a devil.

OTHELLO She was false as water.

EMILIA Thou art rash as fire to say
That she was false: O, she was heavenly true!

OTHELLO Cassio did top her: ask thy husband else;
O, I were damned beneath all depth in hell
But that I did proceed upon just grounds
To this extremity. Thy husband knew it all.

EMILIA My husband!

OTHELLO Thy husband.

EMILIA That she was false to wedlock?

OTHELLO Ay, with Cassio. Nay, had she been true,
If heaven would make me such another world
Of one entire and perfect chrysolite,
I'd not have sold her for it.

EMILIA My husband!
OTHELLO Ay, 'twas he that told he on her first;
An honest man he is, and hates the slime
That sticks on filthy deeds.
EMILIA My husband!
OTHELLO What needs this iterance, woman? I say thy husband.
EMILIA O mis'tress, villainy hath made mocks with love!
My husband say that she was false!
OTHELLO He, woman:
I say thy husband; dost understand the word?
My friend, thy husband, honest, honest Iago.
EMILIA If he say so, may his pernicious soul
Rot half a grain a day! He lies to th'heart.
She was too fond of her most filthy bargain.
OTHELLO Ha!
EMILIA Do thy worst:
This deed of thine is no more worthy heaven
Than thou wast worthy her.
OTHELLO Peace, you were best.
EMILIA Thou hast not half that power to do me harm
As I have to be hurt. O gull! O dolt!
As ignorant as dirt! Thou hast done a deed –
I care not for thy sword; I'll make thee known,
Though I lost twenty lives. Help! Help, ho! Help!
The Moor hath killed my mistress! Murder! Murder!

Enter MONTANO, GRATIANO, IAGO, *and others*

MONTANO What is the matter? How now, general!
EMILIA O, are you come, Iago? You have done well,
That men must lay their murders on your neck.
GRATIANO What is the matter?
EMILIA Disprove this villain, if thou be'st a man.
He says thou told'st him that his wife was false.
I know thou didst not, thou'rt not such a villain.
Speak, for my heart is full.
IAGO I told him what I thought, and told no more
Than what he found himself was apt and true.
EMILIA But did you ever tell him she was false?
IAGO I did.
EMILIA You told a lie, an odious, damnèd lie;

Upon my soul, a lie, a wicked lie!
She false with Cassio! Did you say with Cassio?

IAGO With Cassio, mistress. Go to, charm your tongue.

EMILIA I will not charm my tongue; I am bound to speak:
My mistress here lies murdered in her bed –

ALL O heavens forfend!

EMILIA And your reports have set the murder on.

OTHELLO Nay, stare not, masters: it is true indeed.

GRATIANO 'Tis a strange truth.

MONTANO O monstrous act!

EMILIA Villainy, villainy, villainy!
I think upon't; I think – I smell't: O villainy!
I thought so then; I'll kill myself for grief:
O villainy, villainy!

IAGO What, are you mad? I charge you, get you home.

EMILIA Good gentlemen, let me have leave to speak:
'Tis proper I obey him, but not now.
Perchance, Iago, I will ne'er go home.

OTHELLO O! O! O! [*falls on the bed*

EMILIA Nay, lay thee down and roar;
For thou hast killed the sweetest innocent
That e'er did lift up eye.

OTHELLO [*rising*] O, she was foul!
I scarce did know you, uncle. There lies your niece,
Whose breath indeed these hands have newly stopped.
I know this act shows horrible and grim.

GRATIANO Poor Desdemon! I am glad thy father's dead.
Thy match was mortal to him, and pure grief
Shore his old thread in twain. Did he live now,
This sight would make him do a desperate turn,
Yea, curse his better angel from his side,
And fall to reprobance.

OTHELLO 'Tis pitiful; but yet Iago knows
That she with Cassio hath the act of shame
A thousand times committed. Cassio confessed it;
And she did gratify his amorous works
With that recognizance and pledge of love
Which I first gave her – I saw it in his hand:
It was a handkerchief, an antique token

My father gave my mother.

EMILIA O God! O heavenly God!

IAGO 'Zounds! Hold your peace.

EMILIA 'Twill out, 'twill out. I peace!
No, I will speak as liberal as the north;
Let heaven and men and devils, let them all,
All, all, cry shame against me, yet I'll speak.

IAGO Be wise, and get you home.

EMILIA I will not.

[Iago offers to stab her

GRATIANO Fie!
Your sword upon a woman!

EMILIA O thou dull Moor! That handkerchief thou speak'st of
I found by fortune, and did give my husband;
For often with a solemn earnestness,
More than indeed belonged to such a trifle,
He begged of me to steal it.

IAGO Villainous whore!

EMILIA She give it Cassio! No, alas, I found it,
And I did give't my husband.

IAGO Filth, thou liest!

EMILIA By heaven, I do not, I do not, gentlemen.
O murderous coxcomb! What should such a fool
Do with so good a wife?

OTHELLO Are there no stones in heaven
But what serve for the thunder? Precious villain!

[he runs at Iago, but Montano disarms him; in the confusion, Iago stabs Emilia from behind and escapes

GRATIANO The woman falls; sure, he hath killed his wife.

EMILIA Ay, ay. O, lay me by my mistress' side.

GRATIANO He's gone, but his wife's killed.

MONTANO 'Tis a notorious villain. Take you this weapon,
Which I have here recovered from the Moor.
Come, guard the door without; let him not pass,
But kill him rather. I'll after that same villain,
For 'tis a damnèd slave. *[all but Othello and Emilia depart*

OTHELLO I am not valiant neither,
But every puny whipster gets my sword.
But why should honour outlive honesty?

Let it go all.

EMILIA What did thy song bode, lady?
Hark, canst thou hear me? I will play the swan,
And die in music. [*singing*] Willow, willow, willow.
Moor, she was chaste; she loved thee, cruel Moor;
So come my soul to bliss, as I speak true;
So speaking as I think, alas, I die. [*dies*

OTHELLO I have another weapon in this chamber:
It was a sword of Spain, the ice brook's temper –
O, here it is. Uncle, I must come forth.

GRATIANO [*at the door*] If thou attempt it, it will cost thee dear:
Thou hast no weapon, and perforce must suffer.

OTHELLO Look in upon me then, and speak with me,
Or, naked as I am, I will assault thee.

Re-enter GRATIANO

GRATIANO What is the matter?

OTHELLO Behold, I have a weapon:
A better never did itself sustain
Upon a soldier's thigh. I have seen the day
That with this little arm and this good sword
I have made my way through more impediments
Than twenty times your stop – but, O vain boast!
Who can control his fate? – 'Tis not so now.
Be not afraid, though you do see me weaponed:
Here is my journey's end, here is my butt
And very sea-mark of my utmost sail.
Do you go back dismayed? 'Tis a lost fear:
Man but a rush against Othello's breast,
And he retires. Where should Othello go?
Now, [*he turns to the bed*] how dost thou look now?
O ill-starred wench!
Pale as thy smock! When we shall meet at compt,
This look of thine will hurl my soul from heaven,
And fiends will snatch at it. Cold, cold, my girl!
Even like thy chastity.
O cursèd, cursèd slave! Whip me, ye devils,
From the possession of this heavenly sight!
Blow me about in winds! Roast me in sulphur!

Wash me in steep-down gulfs of liquid fire!
O Desdemon! Dead Desdemon! Dead! O! O!

Enter LODOVICO, MONTANO, CASSIO *carried in a chair, and Officers with* IAGO, *prisoner*

LODOVICO Where is this rash and most unfortunate man?
OTHELLO That's he that was Othello: here I am.
LODOVICO Where is that viper? Bring the villain forth.
OTHELLO I look down towards his feet: but that's a fable;
If that thou be'st a devil, I cannot kill thee.
[*wounds Iago*
LODOVICO Wrench his sword from him.
IAGO I bleed, sir, but not killed.
OTHELLO I am not sorry neither: I'd have thee live;
For, in my sense, 'tis happiness to die.
LODOVICO O thou Othello, that wert once so good,
Fallen in the practice of a damnèd slave,
What shall be said to thee?
OTHELLO Why, anything:
An honourable murderer, if you will;
For nought did I in hate, but all in honour.
LODOVICO This wretch hath part confessed his villainy.
Did you and he consent in Cassio's death?
OTHELLO Ay.
CASSIO Dear general, I never gave you cause.
OTHELLO I do believe it, and I ask your pardon.
Will you, I pray, demand that demi-devil
Why he hath thus ensnared my soul and body?
IAGO Demand me nothing: what you know, you know;
From this time forth I never will speak word.
LODOVICO What, not to pray?
GRATIANO Torments will ope your lips.
OTHELLO Well, thou dost best.
LODOVICO Sir, you shall understand what hath befallen,
Which, as I think, you know not. Here is a letter,
Found in the pocket of the slain Roderigo,
And here another: the one of them imports
The death of Cassio to be undertook
By Roderigo.

OTHELLO O villain!

CASSIO Most heathenish and most gross!

LODOVICO Now here's another discontented paper,
Found in his pocket too: and this, it seems,
Roderigo meant t'have sent this damnèd villain;
But that, belike, Iago in the nick
Came in and satisfied him.

OTHELLO O the pernicious caitiff!
How came you, Cassio, by that handkerchief
That was my wife's?

CASSIO I found it in my chamber:
And he himself confessed but even now
That there he dropped it for a special purpose
Which wrought to his desire.

OTHELLO O fool! Fool! Fool!

CASSIO There is besides, in Roderigo's letter,
How he upbraids Iago that he made him
Brave me upon the watch; whereon it came
That I was cast; and even but now he spake –
After long seeming dead – Iago hurt him,
Iago set him on.

LODOVICO You must forsake this room, and go with us;
Your power and your command is taken off,
And Cassio rules in Cyprus. For this slave,
If there be any cunning cruelty
That can torment him much and hold him long,
It shall be his. You shall close prisoner rest,
Till that the nature of your fault be known
To the Venetian state. Come, bring away.

OTHELLO Soft you; a word or two before you go.
I have done the state some service, and they know't,
No more of that. I pray you, in your letters,
When you shall these unlucky deeds relate,
Speak of me as I am; nothing extenuate,
Nor set down aught in malice. Then must you speak
Of one that loved not wisely but too well;
Of one not easily jealous but, being wrought,
Perplexed in the extreme; of one whose hand,
Like the base Indian, threw a pearl away

Richer than all his tribe; of one whose subdued eyes,
Albeit unusèd to the melting mood,
Drop tears as fast as the Arabian trees
Their medicinable gum – Set you down this;
And say besides, that in Aleppo once,
Where a malignant and a turbaned Turk
Beat a Venetian and traduced the state,
I took by th'throat the circumcisèd dog,
And smote him – thus. [*he stabs himself*

LODOVICO O bloody period!

GRATIANO All that's spoke is marred.

OTHELLO I kissed thee ere I killed thee: no way but this,
Killing myself, to die upon a kiss.
[*falls on the bed, and dies*

CASSIO This did I fear, but thought he had no weapon;
For he was great of heart.

LODOVICO [*to Iago*] O Spartan dog,
More fell than anguish, hunger, or the sea!
Look on the tragic loading of this bed –
This is thy work. The object poisons sight;
Let it be hid. [*they draw the curtains*] Gratiano, keep the house,
And seize upon the fortunes of the Moor,
For they succeed on you. To you, lord governor,
Remains the censure of this hellish villain,
The time, the place, the torture: O, enforce it!
Myself will straight aboard, and to the state
This heavy act with heavy heart relate. [*they go*

KING LEAR

INTRODUCTION

King Lear was first printed in 1608, and appeared in a substantially different version in 1623, probably representing the author's revisions of the original text. It uses a story known to Shakespeare from historical sources, especially from the *Chronicles* of Elizabethan historian Raphael Holinshed, the major source for the history plays and for *Macbeth*. It also reworks an existing anonymous play, *The True Chronicle History of King Leir*, but Shakespeare's manipulation of this familiar material produces his own highly original creation. The play's plot concerns Lear, old king of ancient Britain, who asks his three daughters how much they love him in order to divide up his kingdom between them. The two elder daughters, Goneril and Regan, satisfy their father's test through overstated and insincere protestations of affection. Only Cordelia, Lear's favourite, is unable to take part in this charade, and her angry father divides the land between his other daughters. Disgraced and disinherited, Cordelia is claimed as wife by the King of France, and leaves with her husband. Lear's faith in Goneril and Regan proves entirely misplaced, as they contrive to turn their father out of doors with only his Fool for company. In the madness and mental collapse which follows, Lear comes intermittently to realise his folly. Hearing of her father's situation, Cordelia arrives at Dover with a French army. In a subplot, the nobleman Gloucester's bastard son, Edmund, turns his father against his legitimate son, Edgar. Edgar dresses as a madman in order to stay close to his father, who has been tortured on the orders of Goneril and Regan and blinded. Both sisters are in love with Edmund, and in her passion, Goneril kills Regan and herself. Cordelia is hanged and Lear dies.

From this brief synopsis, it is clear that *King Lear* is a bleak story. Unlike versions of the Lear tale which allow a happy ending, Shakespeare's play is unremitting in its pessimism. Samuel Johnson was famously so upset by the death of Cordelia that he could not bear to reread the last scenes of the play, and many critics and readers since the eighteenth century have felt similarly devastated by *King Lear*'s desperate and desolate conclusion, in which the apocalypse of personal and political tragedy finishes with the banalities of Edgar's final words and the solemn tableau of the 'dead march'. The recognition scene between Cordelia and Lear which ought to set the play on the way to a resolution only ushers forth an ending – death – and in this cruel manipulation of expectations, Shakespeare is working against all the analogues from which the play is drawn. Lear's death, with the body of Cordelia in his arms, is agonisingly slow: like his remaining subjects, we want it to be over.

Perhaps it is this refusal to submit to fictitious comforts which makes the play so modern: it represents an existential view of a world in which no benevolent God or other agent will ensure that the good are rewarded and the bad punished, and there seems to be no mechanism to limit human cruelty and suffering. 'Humanity must perforce prey on itself,' says Albany, 'Like monsters of the deep' (4.2.49–50). While this may seem modern – parallels have been drawn with the plays of Samuel Beckett – *King Lear* is also the Shakespearean tragedy which comes closest to the art of the ancient Greek tragedians in its unflinching dissection of human torment. Alluding to this tragic model, Gloucester's attribution of a terrible arbitrary power to the gods, 'As flies to wanton boys are we to th' gods; They kill us for their sport' (4.1.36–37), seems to reduce human capacity for self-determination, but in the end humanity cannot duck responsibility. Gloucester's own belief in the gods is undermined by his speech renouncing the world (4.6.34–40): there are no gods, only mortals, the play seems to say, as Gloucester throws himself off an imaginary cliff produced through the theatrical trickery of the disguised Edgar. By contrast Edmund recalls Iago's belief in his own self-sufficiency and repudiates superstition, mocking the human tendency to 'admirable evasion' in 'mak[ing] guilty of our disasters the sun, the moon and stars' (1.2.114–23). Readings of the play which have attempted to salvage it as a Christian allegory seem wilfully inappropriate – the type of rationalisation that a character within the play might try to make of his predicament in the face of the crushing misery which is fundamentally inexplicable. While it does make use of biblical allusion and parallel – the story of Job, for example, or Cordelia as a Christ-like redemptive sacrifice – the play seems to pick up different ideologies, expressed at different moments and through different characters, in an attempt to explain human life, without fixing on any transcendent ideology, except perhaps a bitter stoicism. 'Nothing will come of nothing' (1.1.89), Lear tells Cordelia in the opening scene, and the play goes on to explore the implications of that nothingness in a senseless world without consolation.

King Lear approaches and constructs nothingness through its repeated motif of the loss of personal and social identity. Disguise is a physical symbol of these transformations, but whereas in Shakespeare's comedies, disguises are the means by which social and personal integration and identification are achieved, in *King Lear* these features work towards fragmentation and destruction. From the first scene in which Lear divests himself of kingship to Edgar's disguise as a madman, from the disinheriting of Cordelia to the blinding of Gloucester, the play systematically dismantles all the comforts of stable and continuous identity. Lear's bitter joking at his treatment in Goneril's court asks the question the play goes on to anatomise: 'Who is it that can tell me who I am?' (1.4.218). The play offers several answers but does not seem to endorse a single response. 'Royal Lear' and 'old man' (1.1.138, 145) Kent announces in the first scene; 'infirm and choleric' and one who 'hath ever but slenderly known himself' (1.1.289–95) is the judgment of Goneril and Regan; 'a poor, infirm, weak, and despised old man' (3.2.20), as Lear identifies himself. 'Lear's shadow', responds the Fool, representing the disintegration of Lear's substantive person as he is reduced to a pale imitation of his former self. 'Now thou art an O without a figure, [. . .] thou art nothing' (1.4.181–83) All the main characters undergo change, but none more so than Lear himself. In instigating the self-indulgent test in the first scene of the play, Lear begins a series of changes. While his first act in the play is willed and purposive, his subsequent behaviour is not so controlled, and he undergoes a shocking and irreversible personal collapse. Unaware that his whole identity is bound up with his position, after abdicating his authority and banishing his daughter he loses not only his kingdom but his reason and his very self. One way of making sense of this progression is to see in it an accompanying spiritual or mental transformation: by this logic, Lear loses material and social riches, but comes to a closer knowledge of a more fundamental truth. This, too, seems illusory. Lear's lessons are harsh ones, but they do him little good, and his self-knowledge at the end of the play is as partial and myopic as before, and as unable to stave off the inevitable destruction. He is by turns testy, misogynistic, clear-sighted and self-justificatory, and it is hard to make him an admirable or likeable character, although he has moments of extreme, even unbearable, pathos.

The play's dissection of reason and insanity is one of its most striking themes. Lear's madness, Edgar's disguise as a Bedlam beggar, and the gnomic wisdom of the Fool, coincide to offer an oblique commentary on the play world and propose alternative methods of understanding it. 'Folly' and its cognates 'fool' and 'foolishness' reverberate through the play, and this theme is often articulated and encapsulated by the character named for it. Court fools had a particular liberty in medieval and Renaissance society, and were privileged to speak wittily and critically of their masters: Goneril refers to 'your all-licensed fool' (1.4.189). Lear's Fool goads him unrelentingly for his folly in giving away the kingdom, but is also curiously tender in following his master through his deprivations. His is more a function than a character: it is significant that he has no name beyond that of his role. As the Fool disappears, Lear comes to recognise his own foolishness: 'I am a very foolish fond old man' (4.7.60); but this comes too late and ineffectually. All is foolish – in the sense of being meaningless – the play avers: 'When we are born, we cry that we are come To this great stage of fools' (4.6.182–83), a theatrical metaphor which amply expresses the emptiness of human existence. Associated with this grim insight is the play's thematisation of language. Cordelia's simple, catastrophic and proud refusal to engage in the linguistic inflation of her sisters' responses to Lear's test inaugurates a motif about true and false speech throughout the play. The truest speech turns out to be the most riddling or evasive, in the words of the Fool, or in Cordelia's aside telling the audience that her 'love's More ponderous than my tongue' (1.1.76–77). At the play's conclusion, Edgar urges the depleted cast to 'Speak what we feel, not what we ought to say' (5.3.324), as if genuine and unaffected speech can heal the play's pain. It was, however, exactly such speech, in the mouth of Cordelia at the beginning of the play, which set the tragic events in motion. In this recollection of its opening scene, the play's conclusion underlines *King Lear*'s refusal of the possibility of final reconciliation.

The scene: Britain

CHARACTERS IN THE PLAY

LEAR, *king of Britain*
KING OF FRANCE
DUKE OF BURGUNDY
DUKE OF CORNWALL, *husband to Regan*
DUKE OF ALBANY, *husband to Goneril*
EARL OF KENT
EARL OF GLOUCESTER
EDGAR, *son to Gloucester*
EDMUND, *bastard son to Gloucester*
CURAN, *a courtier*
OSWALD, *steward to Goneril*
OLD MAN, *tenant to Gloucester*
DOCTOR
FOOL

GONERIL, REGAN, CORDELIA — *daughters of Lear*

Gentleman, Herald, Captains, Knights of Lear's train, Messengers, Soldiers, Attendants, Servants

KING LEAR

ACT I SCENE I

The throne-room in King Lear's palace

'Enter KENT, GLOUCESTER, *and* EDMUND*'*

KENT I thought the king had more affected the Duke of Albany than Cornwall.

GLO'STER It did always seem so to us; but now, in the division of the kingdom, it appears not which of the dukes he values most, for equalities are so weighed that curiosity in neither can make choice of either's moiety.

KENT Is not this your son, my lord?

GLO'STER His breeding, sir, hath been at my charge. I have so often blushed to acknowledge him that now I am brazed to 't.

KENT I cannot conceive you.

GLO'STER Sir, this young fellow's mother could; whereupon she grew round-wombed, and had indeed, sir, a son for her cradle ere she had a husband for her bed. Do you smell a fault?

KENT I cannot wish the fault undone, the issue of it being so proper.

GLO'STER But I have a son, sir, by order of law, some year elder than this, who yet is no dearer in my account. Though this knave came something saucily to the world before he was sent for, yet was his mother fair; there was good sport at his making, and the whoreson must be acknowledged. Do you know this noble gentleman, Edmund?

EDMUND No, my lord.

GLO'STER My lord of Kent. Remember him hereafter as my honourable friend.

EDMUND My services to your lordship.

KENT I must love you, and sue to know you better.

EDMUND Sir, I shall study deserving.

GLO'STER He hath been out nine years, and away he shall again. [*A sennet sounded*] The king is coming.

'Enter one bearing a coronet.' 'Enter KING LEAR, CORNWALL, ALBANY, GONERIL, REGAN, CORDELIA, *and attendants'*

LEAR Attend the lords of France and Burgundy, Gloucester.

GLO'STER I shall, my liege. [*he goes out, attended by Edmund*

LEAR Meantime we shall express our darker purpose.
Give me the map there. Know that we have divided
In three our kingdom; and 'tis our fast intent
To shake all cares and business from our age,
Conferring them on younger strengths while we
Unburdened crawl toward death. Our son of Cornwall,
And you, our no less loving son of Albany,
We have this hour a constant will to publish
Our daughters' several dowers, that future strife
May be prevented now. The princes, France and Burgundy,
Great rivals in our youngest daughter's love,
Long in our court have made their amorous sojourn,
And here are to be answered. Tell me, my daughters
(Since now we will divest us both of rule,
Interest of territory, cares of state),
Which of you shall we say doth love us most,
That we our largest bounty may extend
Where nature doth with merit challenge. Goneril,
Our eldest-born, speak first.

GONERIL Sir, I love you more than word can wield the matter;
Dearer than eyesight, space and liberty;
Beyond what can be valued rich or rare;
No less than life with grace, health, beauty, honour;
As much as child e'er loved, or father found:
A love that makes breath poor, and speech unable.
Beyond all manner of 'so much' I love you.

CORDELIA What shall Cordelia speak? Love, and be silent.

LEAR [*showing the map*]
Of all these bounds, even from this line to this,
With shadowy forests and with champaigns riched,
With plenteous rivers and wide-skirted meads,
We make thee lady. To thine and Albany's issues
Be this perpetual. What says our second daughter,

Our dearest Regan, wife of Cornwall?

REGAN I am made of that self metal as my sister,
And prize me at her worth. In my true heart
I find she names my very deed of love
Only she comes too short, that I profess
Myself an enemy to all other joys
Which the most precious spirit of sense possesses,
And find I am alone felicitate
In your dear Highness' love.

CORDELIA Then poor Cordelia!
And yet not so, since I am sure my love's
More ponderous than my tongue.

LEAR To thee and thine, hereditary ever,
Remain this ample third of our fair kingdom,
No less in space, validity, and pleasure
Than that conferred on Goneril. Now, our joy,
Although our last and least, to whose young love
The vines of France and milk of Burgundy
Strive to be interessed, what can you say to draw
A third more opulent than your sisters? Speak.

CORDELIA Nothing, my lord.

LEAR Nothing?

CORDELIA Nothing.

LEAR Nothing will come of nothing; speak again.

CORDELIA Unhappy that I am, I cannot heave
My heart into my mouth. I love your Majesty
According to my bond, no more nor less.

LEAR How, how, Cordelia? Mend your speech a little,
Lest you may mar your fortunes.

CORDELIA Good my lord,
You have begot me, bred me, loved me. I
Return those duties back as are right fit,
Obey you, love you, and most honour you.
Why have my sisters husbands, if they say
They love you all? Haply, when I shall wed,
That lord whose hand must take my plight shall carry
Half my love with him, half my care and duty.
Sure I shall never marry like my sisters,
To love my father all.

LEAR But goes thy heart with this?

CORDELIA Ay, my good lord.

LEAR So young, and so untender?

CORDELIA So young, my lord, and true.

LEAR Let it be so; thy truth then be thy dower!
For, by the sacred radiance of the sun,
The mysteries of Hecate and the night,
By all the operation of the orbs
From whom we do exist and cease to be,
Here I disclaim all my paternal care,
Propinquity and property of blood,
And as a stranger to my heart and me
Hold thee from this for ever. The barbarous Scythian,
Or he that makes his generation messes
To gorge his appetite, shall to my bosom
Be as well neighboured, pitied, and relieved,
As thou my sometime daughter.

KENT Good my liege –

LEAR Peace, Kent!
Come not between the dragon and his wrath.
I loved her most, and thought to set my rest
On her kind nursery. [*to Cordelia*] Hence, and avoid my sight! –
So be my grave my peace as here I give
Her father's heart from her. Call France! Who stirs?
Call Burgundy! [*A courtier hurries forth*]
Cornwall and Albany,
With my two daughters' dowers digest the third;
Let pride, which she calls plainness, marry her.
I do invest you jointly with my power,
Pre-eminence, and all the large effects
That troop with majesty. Ourself, by monthly course,
With reservation of an hundred knights
By you to be sustained, shall our abode
Make with you by due turn. Only we shall retain
The name and all th' addition to a king: the sway,
Revenue, execution of the rest,
Belovèd sons, be yours; which to confirm,
This coronet part between you.

KENT Royal Lear,
Whom I have ever honoured as my king,
Loved as my father, as my master followed,
As my great patron thought on in my prayers –
LEAR The bow is bent and drawn; make from the shaft.
KENT Let it fall rather, though the fork invade
The region of my heart! Be Kent unmannerly
When Lear is mad. What wouldst thou do, old man?
Think'st thou that duty shall have dread to speak
When power to flattery bows? To plainness honour's bound
When majesty stoops to folly. Reserve thy state,
And in thy best consideration check
This hideous rashness. Answer my life my judgment,
Thy youngest daughter does not love thee least,
Nor are those empty-hearted whose low sounds
Reverb no hollowness.
LEAR Kent, on thy life, no more!
KENT My life I never held but as a pawn
To wage against thine enemies; ne'er feared to lose it,
Thy safety being motive.
LEAR Out of my sight!
KENT See better, Lear, and let me still remain
The true blank of thine eye.
LEAR Now by Apollo –
KENT Now by Apollo, king,
Thou swear'st thy gods in vain.
LEAR O vassal! miscreant!
[laying his hand on his sword
ALBANY, C'WALL Dear sir, forbear!
KENT Kill thy physician, and the fee bestow
Upon the foul disease. Revoke thy gift,
Or, whilst I can vent clamour from my throat,
I'll tell thee thou dost evil.
LEAR Hear me, recreant,
On thine allegiance, hear me!
That thou hast sought to make us break our vow –
Which we durst never yet – and with strained pride
To come betwixt our sentence and our power –

Which nor our nature nor our place can bear, –
Our potency made good, take thy reward.
Five days we do allot thee for provision
To shield thee from disasters of the world,
And on the sixth to turn thy hated back
Upon our kingdom. If, on the tenth day following,
Thy banished trunk be found in our dominions,
The moment is thy death. Away! By Jupiter,
This shall not be revoked.

KENT Fare thee well, king; sith thus thou wilt appear,
Freedom lives hence and banishment is here.
[*to Cordelia*]
The gods to their dear shelter take thee, maid,
That justly think'st and hast most rightly said.
[*to Goneril and Regan*]
And your large speeches may your deeds approve,
That good effects may spring from words of love.
Thus Kent, O princes, bids you all adieu;
He'll shape his old course in a country new. [*he goes*

'Flourish'. Re-enter GLOUCESTER, *with* FRANCE, BURGUNDY, *and attendants*

GLO'STER Here's France and Burgundy, my noble lord.

LEAR My lord of Burgundy,
We first address toward you, who with this king
Hath rivalled for our daughter. What in the least
Will you require in present dower with her,
Or cease your quest of love?

BURG'DY Most royal majesty,
I crave no more than hath your highness offered –
Nor will you tender less?

LEAR Right noble Burgundy,
When she was dear to us, we did hold her so;
But now her price is fall'n. Sir, there she stands.
If aught within that little seeming-substance,
Or all of it, with our displeasure pieced,
And nothing more, may fitly like your grace,
She's there, and she is yours.

BURG'DY I know no answer.

LEAR Will you, with those infirmities she owes,

Unfriended, new adopted to our hate,
Dowered with our curse and strangered with our oath,
Take her or leave her?

BURG'DY Pardon me, royal sir.
Election makes not up on such conditions.

LEAR Then leave her, sir; for, by the power that made me,
I tell you all her wealth. [*to France*] For you, great king,
I would not from your love make such a stray
To match you where I hate; therefore beseech you
T' avert your liking a more worthier way
Than on a wretch whom Nature is ashamed
Almost t' acknowledge hers.

FRANCE This is most strange,
That she whom even but now was your best object,
The argument of your praise, balm of your age,
The best, the dearest, should in this trice of time
Commit a thing so monstrous to dismantle
So many folds of favour. Sure her offence
Must be of such unnatural degree
That monsters it, or your fore-vouched affection
Fall into taint; which to believe of her
Must be a faith that reason without miracle
Should never plant in me.

CORDELIA I yet beseech your majesty –
If for I want that glib and oily art
To speak and purpose not, since what I well intend,
I'll do 't before I speak – that you make known
It is no vicious blot, murder or foulness,
No unchaste action or dishonoured step,
That hath deprived me of your grace and favour;
But even for want of that for which I am richer –
A still-soliciting eye, and such a tongue
That I am glad I have not, though not to have it
Hath lost me in your liking.

LEAR Better thou
Hadst not been born than not t' have pleased me better.

FRANCE Is it but this – a tardiness in nature
Which often leaves the history unspoke
That it intends? My lord of Burgundy,

What say you to the lady? Love's not love
When it is mingled with regards that stands
Aloof from th' entire point. Will you have her?
She is herself a dowry.

BURG'DY Royal king,
Give but that portion which yourself proposed,
And here I take Cordelia by the hand,
Duchess of Burgundy.

LEAR Nothing. I have sworn; I am firm.

BURG'DY I am sorry then you have so lost a father
That you must lose a husband.

CORDELIA Peace be with Burgundy!
Since that respect and fortunes are his love,
I shall not be his wife.

FRANCE Fairest Cordelia, that art most rich, being poor;
Most choice, forsaken; and most loved, despised;
Thee and thy virtues here I seize upon.
Be it lawful I take up what's cast away.
Gods, gods! 'Tis strange that from their cold'st neglect
My love should kindle to inflamed respect.
Thy dowerless daughter, king, thrown to my chance,
Is queen of us, of ours, and our fair France.
Not all the dukes of wat'rish Burgundy
Can buy this unprized precious maid of me.
Bid them farewell, Cordelia, though unkind;
Thou losest here, a better where to find.

LEAR Thou hast her, France; let her be thine, for we
Have no such daughter, nor shall ever see
That face of hers again. Therefore be gone
Without our grace, our love, our benison.
Come, noble Burgundy.

'Flourish'. LEAR, BURGUNDY, CORNWALL, ALBANY, GLOUCESTER, *and attendants depart*

FRANCE Bid farewell to your sisters.

CORDELIA The jewels of our father, with washed eyes
Cordelia leaves you. I know you what you are,
And like a sister am most loath to call
Your faults as they are named. Love well our father;
To your professèd bosoms I commit him:

But yet, alas, stood I within his grace,
I would prefer him to a better place.
So farewell to you both.

REGAN Prescribe not us our duty.

GONERIL Let your study
Be to content your lord, who hath received you
At Fortune's alms. You have obedience scanted,
And well are worth the want that you have wanted.

CORDELIA Time shall unfold what plighted cunning hides,
Who covert faults at last with shame derides.
Well may you prosper.

FRANCE Come, my fair Cordelia.

[he leads her away

GONERIL Sister, it is not little I have to say of what most nearly appertains to us both. I think our father will hence tonight.

REGAN That's most certain, and with you; next month with us.

GONERIL You see how full of changes his age is. The observation we have made of it hath not been little. He always loved our sister most, and with what poor judgment he hath now cast her off appears too grossly.

REGAN 'Tis the infirmity of his age; yet he hath ever but slenderly known himself.

GONERIL The best and soundest of his time hath been but rash; then must we look from his age to receive, not alone the imperfections of long-engraffed condition, but therewithal the unruly waywardness that infirm and choleric years bring with them.

REGAN Such unconstant starts are we like to have from him as this of Kent's banishment.

GONERIL There is further compliment of leave-taking between France and him. Pray you let us hit together. If our father carry authority with such disposition as he bears, this last surrender of his will but offend us.

REGAN We shall further think of it.

GONERIL We must do something, and i' th' heat.

[they go

SCENE 2

A room in the Earl of Gloucester's castle

Enter EDMUND, *with a letter*

EDMUND Thou, Nature, art my goddess; to thy law
My services are bound. Wherefore should I
Stand in the plague of custom, and permit
The curiosity of nations to deprive me,
For that I am some twelve or fourteen moonshines
Lag of a brother? Why bastard? wherefore base?
When my dimensions are as well compact,
My mind as generous, and my shape as true,
As honest madam's issue? Why brand they us
With base? With baseness? Bastardy? Base, base?
Who, in the lusty stealth of Nature, take
More composition and fierce quality
Than doth, within a dull, stale, tired bed,
Go to th' creating a whole tribe of fops
Got 'tween a sleep and wake? Well then,
Legitimate Edgar, I must have your land.
Our father's love is to the bastard Edmund
As to th' legitimate. Fine word, 'legitimate'!
Well, my legitimate, if this letter speed,
And my invention thrive, Edmund the base
Shall top th' legitimate. I grow, I prosper.
Now, gods, stand up for bastards!

'Enter GLOUCESTER*'*

GLO'STER Kent banished thus? And France in choler parted?
And the king gone tonight? Prescribed his power?
Confined to exhibition? All this done
Upon the gad? – Edmund, how now? What news?

EDMUND So please your lordship, none.
[*putting the letter in his pocket*

GLO'STER Why so earnestly seek you to put up that letter?

EDMUND I know no news, my lord.

GLO'STER What paper were you reading?

EDMUND Nothing, my lord.

GLO'STER No? What needed then that terrible dispatch of it into your pocket? The quality of nothing hath not such need to hide itself. Let's see. Come, if it be nothing, I shall not need spectacles.

EDMUND I beseech you, sir, pardon me. It is a letter from my brother that I have not all o'er-read; and for so much as I have perused, I find it not fit for your o'erlooking.

GLO'STER Give me the letter, sir.

EDMUND I shall offend either to detain or give it. The contents, as in part I understand them, are to blame.

GLO'STER Let's see, let's see.

EDMUND I hope, for my brother's justification, he wrote this but as an essay or taste of my virtue.

GLO'STER [*'reads'*] 'This policy and reverence of age makes the world bitter to the best of our times, keeps our fortunes from us till our oldness cannot relish them. I begin to find an idle and fond bondage in the oppression of aged tyranny, who sways, not as it hath power, but as it is suffered. Come to me, that of this I may speak more. If our father would sleep till I waked him, you should enjoy half his revenue for ever, and live the beloved of your brother. Edgar.'

Hum! Conspiracy? 'Sleep till I waked him, you should enjoy half his revenue.' My son Edgar! Had he a hand to write this? A heart and brain to breed it in? When came you to this? Who brought it?

EDMUND It was not brought me, my lord: there's the cunning of it. I found it thrown in at the casement of my closet.

GLO'STER You know the character to be your brother's?

EDMUND If the matter were good, my lord, I durst swear it were his; but, in respect of that, I would fain think it were not.

GLO'STER It is his.

EDMUND It is his hand, my lord; but I hope his heart is not in the contents.

GLO'STER Has he never before sounded you in this business?

EDMUND Never, my lord. But I have heard him oft maintain it to be fit that, sons at perfect age, and fathers declined, the father should be as ward to the son, and the son manage his revenue.

GLO'STER O villain, villain! His very opinion in the letter! Abhorred villain! Unnatural, detested, brutish villain! Worse than brutish! Go, sirrah, seek him. I'll apprehend him. Abominable villain! Where is he?

EDMUND I do not well know, my lord. If it shall please you to suspend your indignation against my brother till you can derive from him better testimony of his intent, you should run a certain course; where, if you violently proceed against hum, mistaking his purpose, it would make a great gap in your own honour, and shake in pieces the heart of his obedience. I dare pawn down my life for him that he hath writ this to feel my affection to your honour, and to no other pretence of danger.

GLO'STER Think you so?

EDMUND If your honour judge it meet, I will place you where you shall hear us confer of this and by an auricular assurance have your satisfaction, and that without any further delay than this very evening.

GLO'STER He cannot be such a monster!

EDMUND Nor is not, sure.

GLO'STER To his father, that so tenderly and entirely loves him! Heaven and earth! Edmund, seek him out; wind me into him, I pray you; frame the business after your own wisdom. I would unstate myself to be in a due resolution.

EDMUND I will seek him, sir, presently; convey the business as I shall find means, and acquaint you withal.

GLO'STER These late eclipses in the sun and moon portend no good to us. Though the wisdom of nature can reason it thus and thus, yet nature finds itself scourged by the sequent effects. Love cools, friendship falls off, brothers divide. In cities, mutinies; in countries, discord; in palaces, treason; and the bond cracked 'twixt son and father. This villain of mine comes under the prediction; there's son against father: the king falls from bias of nature; there's father against child. We have seen the best of our time. Machinations, hollowness, treachery, and all ruinous disorders follow us disquietly to our graves. Find out this villain, Edmund; it shall lose thee nothing; do it carefully. And the noble and true-hearted Kent banished; his offence, honesty! 'Tis strange. [*he goes*

EDMUND This is the excellent foppery of the world that when we are sick in fortune, often the surfeits of our own behaviour, we make guilty of our disasters the sun, the moon and stars; as if we were villains on necessity, fools by heavenly compulsion, knaves, thieves, and treachers by spherical predominance, drunkards, liars, and adulterers by an enforced obedience of planetary influence, and all that we are evil in by a divine thrusting on. An admirable evasion of whoremaster man, to lay his goatish disposition to the charge of a star! My father compounded with my mother under the Dragon's tail, and my nativity was under Ursa Major, so that it follows I am rough and lecherous. Fut, I should have been that I am, had the maidenliest star in the firmament twinkled on my bastardizing. Edgar –

'Enter EDGAR*'*

Pat! he comes, like the catastrophe of the old comedy. My cue is villainous melancholy, with a sigh like Tom o' Bedlam – O these eclipses do portend these divisions. [*humming sadly*] Fa, sol, la, me.

EDGAR How now, brother Edmund? What serious contemplation are you in?

EDMUND I am thinking, brother, of a prediction I read this other day, what should follow these eclipses.

EDGAR Do you busy yourself with that?

EDMUND I promise you, the effects he writes of succeed unhappily, as of unnaturalness between the child and the parent, death, dearth, dissolutions of ancient amities, divisions in state, menaces and maledictions against king and nobles, needless diffidences, banishment of friends, dissipation of cohorts, nuptial breaches, and I know not what.

EDGAR How long have you been a sectary astronomical?

EDMUND When saw you my father last?

EDGAR The night gone by.

EDMUND Spake you with him?

EDGAR Ay, two hours together.

EDMUND Parted you in good terms? Found you no displeasure in him, by word nor countenance?

EDGAR None at all.

EDMUND Bethink yourself wherein you may have offended him; and at my entreaty forbear his presence until some little time hath qualified the heat of his displeasure, which at this instant so rageth in him that with the mischief of your person it would scarcely allay.

EDGAR Some villain hath done me wrong.

EDMUND That's my fear. I pray you have a continent forbearance till the speed of his rage goes slower; and, as I say, retire with me to my lodging, from whence I will fitly bring you to hear my lord speak. Pray ye, go; there's my key. If you do stir abroad, go armed.

EDGAR Armed, brother?

EDMUND Brother, I advise you to the best. I am no honest man if there be any good meaning toward you. I have told you what I have seen and heard – but faintly, nothing like the image and horror of it. Pray you, away!

EDGAR Shall I hear from you anon?

EDMUND I do serve you in this business. [*Edgar goes*

A credulous father! And a brother noble,
Whose nature is so far from doing harms
That he suspects none; on whose foolish honesty
My practices ride easy! I see the business.
Let me, if not by birth, have lands by wit;
All with me's meet that I can fashion fit. [*he goes*

SCENE 3

A room in the Duke of Albany's palace

Enter GONERIL *and* OSWALD, *her steward*

GONERIL Did my father strike my gentleman for
chiding of his fool?

OSWALD Ay, madam.

GONERIL By day and night he wrongs me. Every hour
He flashes into one gross crime or other
That sets us all at odds. I'll not endure it.
His knights grow riotous, and himself upbraids us
On every trifle. When he returns from hunting
I will not speak with him: say I am sick.
If you come slack of former services,
You shall do well; the fault of it I'll answer.
[*horns heard*

OSWALD He's coming, madam; I hear him.

GONERIL Put on what weary negligence you please,
You and your fellows; I'd have it come to question.
If he distaste it, let him to my sister,
Whose mind and mine I know in that are one,
Not to be overruled. Idle old man,
That still would manage those authorities
That he hath given away! Now, by my life,
Old fools are babes again, and must be used
With checks as flatteries, when they are seen abused.
Remember what I have said.

OSWALD Well, madam.

GONERIL And let his knights have colder looks among you;
What grows of it, no matter. Advise your fellows so.
I would breed from hence occasions, and I shall,
That I may speak. I'll write straight to my sister
To hold my very course. Prepare for dinner.
[*they go*

SCENE 4

A hall in the same

'Enter KENT*' disguised*

KENT If but as well I other accents borrow,
That can my speech diffuse, my good intent
May carry through itself to that full issue
For which I razed my likeness. Now, banished Kent,
If thou canst serve where thou dost stand condemned,
So may it come thy master whom thou lov'st
Shall find thee full of labours.

Horns heard. LEAR *enters from hunting, with knights and attendants*

LEAR Let me not stay a jot for dinner; go get it ready. [*attendant goes out*] How now! What art thou?

KENT A man, sir.

LEAR What dost thou profess? What would'st thou with us?

KENT I do profess to be no less than I seem, to serve him truly that will put me in trust, to love him that is honest, to converse with him that is wise and says little, to fear judgment, to fight when I cannot choose, and to eat no fish.

LEAR What art thou?

KENT A very honest-hearted fellow, and as poor as the king.

LEAR If thou be'st as poor for a subject as he's for a king, thou art poor enough. What would'st thou?

KENT Service.

LEAR Who would'st thou serve?

KENT You.

LEAR Dost thou know me, fellow?

KENT No, sir; but you have that in your countenance which I would fain call master.

LEAR What's that?

KENT Authority.

LEAR What services canst thou do?

KENT I can keep honest counsel, ride, run, mar a curious tale in telling it, and deliver a plain message bluntly; that which ordinary men are fit for I am qualified in, and the best of me is diligence.

LEAR How old art thou?

KENT Not so young, sir, to love a woman for singing, nor so old to dote on her for anything. I have years on my back forty-eight.

LEAR Follow me; thou shalt serve me. If I like thee no worse after dinner I will not part from thee yet. Dinner, ho! Dinner! Where's my knave? My fool? Go you and call my fool hither. [*attendant goes out*

Enter OSWALD

You! You, sirrah! Where's my daughter?

OSWALD [*crossing the hall without pausing*] So please you –

[*goes out*

LEAR What says the fellow there? Call the clotpoll back! [*knight goes out*] Where's my fool? Ho! I think the world's asleep. [*knight returns*] How now? Where's that mongrel?

KNIGHT He says, my lord, your daughter is not well.

LEAR Why came not the slave back to me when I called him?

KNIGHT Sir, he answered me in the roundest manner he would not.

LEAR He would not?

KNIGHT My lord, I know not what the matter is, but to my judgment your highness is not entertained with that ceremonious affection as you were wont. There's a great abatement of kindness appears as well in the general dependants as in the duke himself also and your daughter.

LEAR Ha! Say'st thou so?

KNIGHT I beseech you pardon me, my lord, if I be mistaken, for my duty cannot be silent when I think your highness wronged.

LEAR Thou but remembrest me of mine own conception. I have perceived a most faint neglect of late, which I have rather blamed as mine own jealous curiosity than as a very pretence and purpose of unkindness; I will look further into't. But where's my fool? I have not seen him this two days.

KNIGHT Since my young lady's going into France, sir, the fool hath much pined away.

LEAR No more of that; I have noted it well. Go you and tell my daughter I would speak with her. [*Attendant goes out*] Go you, call hither my fool. [*Second attendant goes out*]

OSWALD *returns*

O you sir, you, come you hither, sir. Who am I, sir?

OSWALD My lady's father.

LEAR 'My lady's father', my lord's knave? You whoreson dog, you slave, you cur!

OSWALD I am none of these, my lord; I beseech your pardon.

LEAR Do you bandy looks with me, you rascal? [*strikes him*

OSWALD I'll not be strucken, my lord.

KENT Nor tripped neither, you base football player. [*tripping up his heels*

LEAR I thank thee, fellow. Thou serv'st me, and I'll love thee.

KENT Come, sir, arise, away! I'll teach you differences. Away, away! If you will measure your lubber's length again, tarry; but away! Go to; have you wisdom? [*Oswald goes*] So.

LEAR Now, my friendly knave, I thank thee. There's earnest of thy service. [*giving money*]

Enter FOOL

FOOL Let me hire him too. Here's my coxcomb. [*offers Kent his cap*

LEAR How now, my pretty knave? How dost thou?

FOOL Sirrah, you were best take my coxcomb.

KENT Why, fool?

FOOL Why? For taking one's part that's out of favour. Nay, an thou canst not smile as the wind sits, thou'lt catch cold shortly. There, take my coxcomb! Why, this fellow has banished two on's daughters, and did the third a blessing against his will. If thou follow him thou must needs wear my coxcomb. How now, nuncle? Would I had two coxcombs and two daughters!

LEAR Why, my boy?

FOOL If I gave them all my living, I'd keep my coxcombs myself. There's mine; beg another of thy daughters.

LEAR Take heed, sirrah – the whip.

FOOL Truth's a dog must to kennel; he must be whipped out, when the Lady's brach may stand by th' fire and stink.

LEAR A pestilent gall to me!

FOOL Sirrah, I'll teach thee a speech.

LEAR Do.

FOOL Mark it, nuncle!

Have more than thou showest,
Speak less than thou knowest,
Lend less than thou owest,
Ride more than thou goest,
Learn more than thou trowest,
Set less than thou throwest;
Leave thy drink and thy whore,
And keep in-a-door,
And thou shalt have more
Than two tens to a score.

KENT This is nothing, fool.

FOOL Then 'tis like the breath of an unfee'd lawyer – you gave me nothing for't. Can you make no use of nothing, nuncle?

LEAR Why, no, boy; nothing can be made out of nothing.

FOOL [*to Kent*] Prithee tell him, so much the rent of his land comes to. He will not believe a fool.

LEAR A bitter fool!

FOOL Dost thou know the difference, my boy, between a bitter fool and a sweet one?

LEAR No, lad; teach me.

FOOL That lord that counselled thee
To give away thy land,
Come place him here by me –
Do thou for him stand.
The sweet and bitter fool
Will presently appear:
The one in motley here, [*pointing to himself*
The other found out there! [*pointing to Lear*

LEAR Dost thou call me fool, boy?

FOOL All thy other titles thou hast given away; that thou wast born with.

KENT This is not altogether fool, my lord.

FOOL No, faith, lords and great men will not let me; if I had a monopoly out, they would have part on't: and ladies too, they will not let me have all the fool to myself; they'll be snatching. Nuncle, give me an egg, and I'll give thee two crowns.

LEAR What two crowns shall they be?

FOOL Why, after I have cut the egg i'th'middle and eat up the meat, the two crowns of the egg. When thou clovest thy crown i'th'middle and gav'st away both parts, thou bor'st thine ass on thy back o'er the dirt. Thou hadst little wit in thy bald crown when thou gav'st thy golden one away. If I speak like myself in this, let him be whipped that first finds it so.

[*singing*]

Fools had ne'er less grace in a year;
  For wise men are grown foppish,
And know not how their wits to wear,
  Their manners are so apish.

LEAR When were you wont to be so full of songs, sirrah?

FOOL I have used it, nuncle, e'er since thou mad'st thy daughters thy mothers – for when thou gav'st them the rod and putt'st down thine own breeches,

[*singing*]

Then they for sudden joy did weep,
  And I for sorrow sung,
That such a king should play bo-peep,
  And go the fools among.

Prithee, nuncle, keep a schoolmaster that can teach thy fool to lie: I would fain learn to lie.

LEAR An you lie, sirrah, we'll have you whipped.

FOOL I marvel what kin thou and thy daughters are: they'll have me whipped for speaking true, thou'lt have me whipped for lying; and sometimes I am whipped for holding my peace. I had rather be any kind o' thing than a fool: and yet I would not be thee, nuncle; thou hast pared thy wit o' both sides and left nothing i'th' middle. Here comes one o' the parings.

'*Enter* GONERIL'

LEAR How now, daughter? What makes that frontlet on? You are too much of late i'th'frown.

FOOL Thou wast a pretty fellow when thou hadst no need to care for her frowning; now thou art an O without a figure. I am better than thou art now; I am a fool, thou art nothing. [*to Goneril*] Yes, forsooth, I will hold my tongue; so your face bids me, though you say nothing.

Mum, mum:
He that keeps nor crust nor crumb,
Weary of all, shall want some.

[*pointing to Lear*] That's a shelled peascod.

GONERIL Not only, sir, this your all-licensed fool
But other of your insolent retinue
Do hourly carp and quarrel, breaking forth
In rank and not-to-be-endurèd riots.
I had thought, by making this well known unto you,
To have found a safe redress; but now grow fearful,
By what yourself too late have spoke and done,
That you protect this course, and put it on
By your allowance; which if you should, the fault
Would not scape censure, nor the redresses sleep
Which, in the tender of a wholesome weal,
Might in their working do you that offence,
Which else were shame, that then necessity
Will call discreet proceeding.

FOOL For you know, nuncle,
The hedge-sparrow fed the cuckoo so long
That it had it head bit off by it young.
So out went the candle, and we were left darkling.

LEAR Are you our daughter?

GONERIL I would you would make use of your good wisdom
(Whereof I know you are fraught) and put away
These dispositions which of late transport you
From what you rightly are.

FOOL May not an ass know when the cart draws the horse?
Whoop, Jug! I love thee.

LEAR Does any here know me? This is not Lear.
Does Lear walk thus, speak thus? Where are his eyes?
Either his notion weakens, his discernings

Are lethargied – Ha! Waking? 'Tis not so?
Who is it that can tell me who I am?

FOOL Lear's shadow!

LEAR I would learn that; for by the marks
Of sovereignty, knowledge, and reason,
I should be false persuaded I had daughters.

FOOL Which they will make an obedient father.

LEAR Your name, fair gentlewoman?

GONERIL This admiration, sir, is much o' th' savour
Of other your new pranks. I do beseech you
To understand my purposes aright.
As you are old and reverend, should be wise.
Here do you keep a hundred knights and squires –
Men so disordered, so debauched and bold,
That this our court, infected with their manners,
Shows like a riotous inn. Epicurism and lust
Makes it more like a tavern or a brothel
Than a graced palace. The shame itself doth speak
For instant remedy. Be then desired,
By her that else will take the thing she begs,
A little to disquantity your train;
And the remainders, that shall still depend,
To be such men as may besort your age
Which know themselves and you.

LEAR Darkness and devils!
Saddle my horses; call my train together!
Degenerate bastard, I'll not trouble thee;
Yet have I left a daughter.

GONERIL You strike my people, and your disordered rabble
Make servants of their betters.

'Enter ALBANY*'*

LEAR Woe that too late repents! – O, are you come?
Is it your will? Speak, sir! – Prepare my horses.
Ingratitude, thou marble-hearted fiend,
More hideous when thou show'st thee in a child
Than the sea-monster!

ALBANY Pray, sir, be patient.

LEAR [*to Goneril*] Detested kite, thou liest!

My train are men of choice and rarest parts,
That all particulars of duty know,
And in the most exact regard support
The worships of their name. O most small fault,
How ugly didst thou in Cordelia show,
Which, like an engine, wrenched my frame of nature
From the fixed place, drew from my heart all love,
And added to the gall. O Lear, Lear, Lear!
Beat at this gate that let thy folly in [*striking his head*
And thy dear judgment out! Go, go, my people.
[*knights and Kent go*

ALBANY My lord, I am guiltless, as I am ignorant
Of what hath moved you.

LEAR It may be so, my lord.
Hear, Nature; hear, dear goddess; hear!
Suspend thy purpose, if thou didst intend
To make this creature fruitful.
Into her womb convey sterility;
Dry up in her the organs of increase;
And from her derogate body never spring
A babe to honour her! If she must teem,
Create her child of spleen, that it may live
And be a thwart disnatured torment to her.
Let it stamp wrinkles in her brow of youth,
With cadent tears fret channels in her cheeks,
Turn all her mother's pains and benefits
To laughter and contempt, that she may feel
How sharper than a serpent's tooth it is
To have a thankless child! Away, away! [*he rushes forth*

ALBANY Now, gods that we adore, whereof comes this?

GONERIL Never afflict yourself to know more of it,
But let his disposition have that scope
As dotage gives it.

LEAR *returns distraught*

LEAR What, fifty of my followers at a clap?
Within a fortnight?

ALBANY What's the matter, sir?

LEAR I'll tell thee. [*to Goneril*] Life and death! I am ashamed
That thou hast power to shake my manhood thus;

That these hot tears, which break from me perforce,
Should make thee worth them. Blasts and fogs upon thee!
Th'untented woundings of a father's curse
Pierce every sense about thee! Old fond eyes,
Beweep this cause again, I'll pluck ye out,
And cast you, with the waters that you loose,
To temper clay. Yea, is't come to this?
Ha! Let it be so. I have another daughter,
Who I am sure is kind and comfortable.
When she shall hear this of thee, with her nails
She'll flay thy wolvish visage. Thou shalt find
That I'll resume the shape which thou dost think
I have cast off for ever. [*he goes*

GONERIL Do you mark that?

ALBANY I cannot be so partial, Goneril,
To the great love I bear you –

GONERIL Pray you, content. What, Oswald, ho!
[*to the Fool*]
You sir, more knave than fool, after your master!

FOOL Nuncle Lear, nuncle Lear! Tarry; take the fool with thee.
A fox, when one has caught her,
And such a daughter,
Should sure to the slaughter,
If my cap would buy a halter.
So the fool follows after. [*he runs off*

GONERIL This man hath had good counsel! A hundred knights?
'Tis politic and safe to let him keep
At point a hundred knights; yes, that on every dream,
Each buzz, each fancy, each complaint, dislike,
He may enguard his dotage with their powers,
And hold our lives in mercy. Oswald, I say!

ALBANY Well, you may fear too far.

GONERIL Safer than trust too far.
Let me still take away the harms I fear,
Not fear still to be taken. I know his heart.
What he hath uttered I have writ my sister.
If she sustain him and his hundred knights,

When I have showed th'unfitness –

Enter OSWALD

How now, Oswald?
What, have you writ that letter to my sister?

OSWALD Ay, madam.

GONERIL Take you some company, and away to horse!
Inform her full of my particular fear,
And thereto add such reasons of your own
As may compact it more. Get you gone,
And hasten your return. [*Oswald goes*]
No, no, my lord,
This milky gentleness and course of yours
Though I condemn not, yet, under pardon,
You are much more attaxed for want of wisdom
Than praised for harmful mildness.

ALBANY How far your eyes may pierce I cannot tell:
Striving to better, oft we mar what's well.

GONERIL Nay, then –

ALBANY Well, well; th'event. [*they go*

SCENE 5

Court before the same

Enter LEAR, KENT, *and* FOOL

LEAR Go you before to Cornwall with these letters. Acquaint my daughter no further with anything you know than comes from her demand out of the letter. If your diligence be not speedy, I shall be there afore you.

KENT I will not sleep, my lord, till I have delivered your letter. [*he goes*

FOOL If a man's brains were in's heels, were't not in danger of kibes?

LEAR Ay, boy.

FOOL Then I prithee be merry; thy wit shall not go slip-shod.

LEAR Ha, ha, ha!

FOOL Shalt see thy other daughter will use thee kindly; for, though she's as like this as a crab's like an apple, yet I can tell what I can tell.

LEAR What canst tell, boy?

FOOL She will taste as like this as a crab does to a crab. Thou canst tell why one's nose stands i'th'middle on's face?

LEAR No.

FOOL Why, to keep one's eyes of either side's nose, that what a man cannot smell out, he may spy into.

LEAR I did her wrong.

FOOL Canst tell how an oyster makes his shell?

LEAR No.

FOOL Nor I neither; but I can tell why a snail has a house.

LEAR Why?

FOOL Why, to put's head in; not to give it away to his daughters, and leave his horns without a case.

LEAR I will forget my nature. So kind a father! Be my horses ready?

FOOL Thy asses are gone about 'em. The reason why the seven stars are no moe than seven is a pretty reason.

LEAR Because they are not eight.

FOOL Yes, indeed; thou would'st make a good fool.

LEAR To take 't again perforce! Monster Ingratitude!

FOOL If thou wert my fool, nuncle, I'd have thee beaten for being old before thy time.

LEAR How's that?

FOOL Thou should'st not have been old till thou hadst been wise.

LEAR O let me not be mad, not mad, sweet heaven!
Keep me in temper; I would not be mad!

Enter Gentleman

How now! Are the horses ready?

GENT'MAN Ready, my lord.

LEAR Come, boy.

FOOL She that's a maid now, and laughs at my departure,
Shall not be a maid long, unless things be cut shorter.

[*they go*

ACT 2 SCENE 1

A court within the castle of the Earl of Gloucester

'Enter EDMUND *and* CURAN*', meeting*

EDMUND Save thee, Curan.

CURAN And you, sir. I have been with your father, and given him notice that the Duke of Cornwall and Regan his Duchess will be here with him this night.

EDMUND How comes that?

CURAN Nay, I know not. You have heard of the news abroad, I mean the whispered ones, for they are yet but ear-bussing arguments?

EDMUND Not I. Pray you, what are they?

CURAN Have you heard of no likely wars toward 'twixt the Dukes of Cornwall and Albany?

EDMUND Not a word.

CURAN You may do, then, in time. Fare you well, sir. [*he goes*

EDMUND The Duke be here tonight? The better! Best!
This weaves itself perforce into my business.
My father hath set guard to take my brother;
And I have one thing, of a queasy question,
Which I must act. Briefness and fortune, work!
Brother, a word! Descend! Brother, I say!

'Enter EDGAR*'*

My father watches: O sir, fly this place!
Intelligence is given where you are hid.
You have now the good advantage of the night.
Have you not spoken 'gainst the Duke of Cornwall?
He's coming hither, now i'th'night, i'th' haste,
And Regan with him. Have you nothing said
Upon his party 'gainst the Duke of Albany?
Advise yourself.

EDGAR I am sure on't, not a word.

EDMUND I hear my father coming. Pardon me,
In cunning I must draw my sword upon you.
Draw, seem to defend yourself; now quit you well. –

Yield! Come before my father. Light, ho! Here! –
Fly, brother. – Torches, torches! [*Edgar hastens away*
So; farewell.
Some blood drawn on me would beget opinion
Of my more fierce endeavour. [*wounds his arm*
I have seen drunkards
Do more than this in sport – Father, father!
Stop, stop! No help?

'Enter GLOUCESTER, *and servants with torches'*

GLO'STER Now, Edmund, where's the villain?

EDMUND Here stood he in the dark, his sharp sword out,
Mumbling of wicked charms, conjuring the moon
To stand auspicious mistress.

GLO'STER But where is he?

EDMUND Look, sir, I bleed.

GLO'STER Where is the villain, Edmund?

EDMUND Fled this way, sir, when by no means he could –

GLO'STER Pursue him, ho! Go after. [*Some servants go*
By no means what?

EDMUND Persuade me to the murder of your lordship.
But that I told him the revenging gods
'Gainst parricides did all the thunder bend,
Spoke with how manifold and strong a bond
The child was bound to th'father – sir, in fine,
Seeing how loathly opposite I stood
To his unnatural purpose, in fell motion
With his preparèd sword he charges home
My unprovided body, latched mine arm;
And when he saw my best alarumed spirits,
Bold in the quarrel's right, roused to th'encounter,
Or whether gasted by the noise I made,
Full suddenly he fled.

GLO'STER Let him fly far:
Not in this land shall he remain uncaught;
And found – dispatch. The noble Duke my master,
My worthy arch and patron, comes tonight.
By his authority I will proclaim it,
That he which finds him shall deserve our thanks,

Bringing the murderous coward to the stake;
He that conceals him, death.

EDMUND When I dissuaded him from his intent,
And found him pight to do it, with curst speech
I threatened to discover him. He replied,
'Thou unpossessing bastard, dost thou think,
If I would stand against thee, would the reposal
Of any trust, virtue, or worth in thee
Make thy words faithed? No. What I should deny,
(As this I would – ay, though thou didst produce
My very character) I'd turn it all
To thy suggestion, plot, and damnèd practice;
And thou must make a dullard of the world,
If they not thought the profits of my death
Were very pregnant and potential spurs
To make thee seek it.'

GLO'STER O strange and fastened villain!
Would he deny his letter, said he? I never got him.
[*a tucket heard*
Hark, the Duke's trumpet! I know not why he comes.
All ports I'll bar; the villain shall not scape;
The Duke must grant me that. Besides, his picture
I will send far and near, that all the kingdom
May have due note of him; and of my land,
Loyal and natural boy, I'll work the means
To make thee capable.

Enter CORNWALL, REGAN, *and attendants*

CORNWALL How now, my noble friend? Since I came hither,
Which I can call but now, I have heard strange news.

REGAN If it be true, all vengeance comes too short
Which can pursue th'offender. How dost, my lord?

GLO'STER O madam, my old heart is cracked, it's cracked.

REGAN What! Did my father's godson seek your life?
He whom my father named, your Edgar?

GLO'STER O lady, lady, shame would have it hid!

REGAN Was he not companion with the riotous knights
That tended upon my father?

GLO'STER I know not, madam. 'Tis too bad, too bad!

EDMUND Yes, madam; he was of that consort.
REGAN No marvel, then, though he were ill affected.
'Tis they have put him on the old man's death,
To have th'expense and waste of his revenues.
I have this present evening from my sister
Been well informed of them, and with such cautions
That, if they come to sojourn at my house,
I'll not be there.
CORNWALL Nor I, assure thee, Regan.
Edmund, I hear that you have shown your father
A childlike office.
EDMUND It was my duty, sir.
GLO'STER He did bewray his practice; and received
This hurt you see, striving to apprehend him.
CORNWALL Is he pursued?
GLO'STER Ay, my good lord.
CORNWALL If he be taken, he shall never more
Be feared of doing harm. Make your own purpose,
How in my strength you please. For you, Edmund,
Whose virtue and obedience doth this instant
So much commend itself, you shall be ours.
Natures of such deep trust we shall much need;
You we first seize on.
EDMUND I shall serve you, sir,
Truly, however else.
GLO'STER For him I thank your Grace.
CORNWALL You know not why we came to visit you?
REGAN Thus out of season, threading dark-eyed night:
Occasions, noble Gloucester, of some prize,
Wherein we must have use of your advice.
Our father he hath writ, so hath our sister,
Of differences, which I best thought it fit
To answer from our home. The several messengers
From hence attend dispatch. Our good old friend,
Lay comforts to your bosom, and bestow
Your needful counsel to our businesses,
Which craves the instant use.
GLO'STER I serve you, madam.
Your Graces are right welcome. [*'Flourish'. They go*

SCENE 2

Before Gloucester's castle

Enter KENT *and* OSWALD, *meeting*

OSWALD Good dawning to thee, friend. Art of this house?

KENT Ay.

OSWALD Where may we set our horses?

KENT I'th'mire.

OSWALD Prithee, if thou lov'st me, tell me.

KENT I love thee not.

OSWALD Why then, I care not for thee.

KENT If I had thee in Lipsbury Pinfold, I would make thee care for me.

OSWALD Why dost thou use me thus? I know thee not.

KENT Fellow, I know thee.

OSWALD What dost thou know me for?

KENT A knave, a rascal, an eater of broken meats; a base, proud, shallow, beggarly, three-suited, hundred-pound, filthy worsted-stocking knave; a lily-livered, action-taking, whoreson, glass-gazing, super-serviceable, finical rogue; one-trunk-inheriting slave; one that wouldst be a bawd in way of good service, and art nothing but the composition of a knave, beggar, coward, pandar, and the son and heir of a mongrel bitch: one whom I will beat into clamorous whining if thou deniest the least syllable of thy addition.

OSWALD Why, what a monstrous fellow art thou, thus to rail on one that is neither known of thee nor knows thee!

KENT What a brazen-faced varlet art thou, to deny thou knowest me! Is it two days since I tripped up thy heels and beat thee before the king? Draw, you rogue; for, though it be night, yet the moon shines. I'll make a sop o' th' moonshine of you, you whoreson cullionly barber-monger. Draw! [*drawing his sword*

OSWALD Away! I have nothing to do with thee.

KENT Draw, you rascal! You come with letters against the

king, and take Vanity the puppet's part against the royalty of her father. Draw, you rogue, or I'll so carbonado your shanks! Draw, you rascal! Come your ways!

OSWALD Help, ho! Murder! Help!

KENT Strike, you slave! Stand, rogue! Stand, you neat slave! Strike! [*beating him*

OSWALD Help, ho! Murder, murder!

Enter EDMUND *with his rapier drawn*

EDMUND How now? What's the matter? Part!

KENT With you, goodman boy, if you please! Come, I'll flesh ye; come on, young master!

Enter CORNWALL, REGAN, GLOUCESTER *and servants*

GLO'STER Weapons? Arms? What is the matter here?

CORNWALL Keep peace, upon your lives!
He dies that strikes again. What is the matter?

REGAN The messengers from our sister and the king!

CORNWALL What is your difference? Speak.

OSWALD I am scarce in breath, my lord.

KENT No marvel, you have so bestirred your valour. You cowardly rascal, Nature disclaims in thee; a tailor made thee.

CORNWALL Thou art a strange fellow; a tailor make a man?

KENT A tailor, sir. A stone-cutter or a painter could not have made him so ill, though they had been but two years o'th'trade.

CORNWALL Speak yet, how grew your quarrel?

OSWALD This ancient ruffian, sir, whose life I have spared
At suit of his grey beard –

KENT Thou whoreson zed, thou unnecessary letter! My lord, if you will give me leave, I will tread this unbolted villain into mortar and daub the wall of a jakes with him. Spare my grey beard, you wagtail?

CORNWALL Peace, sirrah!
You beastly knave, know you no reverence?

KENT Yes, sir; but anger hath a privilege.

CORNWALL Why art thou angry?

KENT That such a slave as this should wear a sword,
Who wears no honesty. Such smiling rogues as these,

Like rats, oft bite the holy cords atwain
Which are too intrince t'unloose: smooth every passion
That in the natures of their lords rebel,
Bring oil to fire, snow to the colder moods;
Renege, affirm, and turn their halcyon beaks
With every gale and vary of their masters,
Knowing nought (like dogs) but following.
A plague upon your epileptic visage!
Smile you my speeches, as I were a fool?
Goose, if I had you upon Sarum plain,
I'd drive ye cackling home to Camelot.

CORNWALL What, art thou mad, old fellow?

GLO'STER How fell you out? Say that.

KENT No contraries hold more antipathy
Than I and such a knave.

CORNWALL Why dost thou call him knave? What is his fault?

KENT His countenance likes me not.

CORNWALL No more perchance does mine, nor his, nor hers.

KENT Sirs, 'tis my occupation to be plain:
I have seen better faces in my time
Than stands on any shoulder that I see
Before me at this instant.

CORNWALL This is some fellow,
Who, having been praised for bluntness, doth affect
A saucy roughness, and constrains the garb
Quite from his nature. He cannot flatter, he!
An honest mind and plain, he must speak truth!
An they will take it, so; if not, he's plain.
These kind of knaves I know which in this plainness
Harbour more craft and more corrupter ends
Than twenty silly-ducking observants
That stretch their duties nicely.

KENT Sir, in good faith, in sincere verity,
Under th'allowance of your great aspect,
Whose influence, like the wreath of radiant fire
On flick'ring Phoebus' front –

CORNWALL What mean'st by this?

KENT To go out of my dialect, which you discommend so much. I know, sir, I am no flatterer. He that beguiled you in a plain accent was a plain knave, which for my part I will not be, though I should win your displeasure to entreat me to 't.

CORNWALL What was th'offence you gave him?

OSWALD I never gave him any.
It pleased the king his master very late
To strike at me upon his misconstruction,
When he, compact, and flattering his displeasure,
Tripped me behind: being down, insulted, railed
And put upon him such a deal of man
That worthied him, got praises of the king
For him attempting who was self-subdued,
And, in the fleshment of this dread exploit,
Drew on me here again.

KENT None of these rogues and cowards
But Ajax is their fool.

CORNWALL Fetch forth the stocks!
You stubborn ancient knave, you reverend braggart,
We'll teach you!

KENT Sir, I am too old to learn.
Call not your stocks for me; I serve the king,
On whose employment I was sent to you.
You shall do small respect, show too bold malice
Against the grace and person of my master,
Stocking his messenger.

CORNWALL Fetch forth the stocks!
As I have life and honour, there shall he sit till noon.

REGAN Till noon? Till night, my lord, and all night too.

KENT Why, madam, if I were your father's dog,
You should not use me so.

REGAN Sir, being his knave, I will.

CORNWALL This is a fellow of the self-same colour
Our sister speaks of. Come, bring away the stocks.
[*stocks brought out*

GLO'STER Let me beseech your Grace not to do so.
His fault is much, and the good king his master
Will check him for't. Your purposed low correction
Is such as basest and contemnèd'st wretches
For pilf'rings and most common trespasses

Are punished with. The king must take it ill
That he, so slightly valued in his messenger,
Should have him thus restrained.

CORNWALL I'll answer that.

REGAN My sister may receive it much more worse
To have her gentleman abused, assaulted,
For following her affairs. Put in his legs.
[*Kent is put in the stocks*
Come, my lord, away.
[*all go in except Gloucester and Kent*

GLO'STER I am sorry for thee, friend; 'tis the duke's pleasure,
Whose disposition, all the world well knows,
Will not be rubbed nor stopped. I'll entreat for thee.

KENT Pray do not, sir. I have watched, and travelled hard.
Some time I shall sleep out, the rest I'll whistle.
A good man's fortune may grow out at heels.
Give you good morrow!

GLO'STER The duke's to blame in this; 'twill be ill taken. [*he goes*

KENT Good king, that must approve the common saw,
Thou out of heaven's benediction com'st
To the warm sun!
Approach, thou beacon to this under globe,
That by thy comfortable beams I may
Peruse this letter. Nothing almost sees miracles
But misery. I know 'tis from Cordelia,
Who hath most fortunately been informed
Of my obscurèd course, and shall find time
From this enormous state, seeking to give
Losses their remedies. All weary and o'erwatched,
Take vantage, heavy eyes, not to behold
This shameful lodging.
Fortune, good night; smile once more; turn thy wheel.
[*sleeps*

SCENE 3

The open country

'Enter EDGAR*'*

EDGAR I heard myself proclaimed,
And by the happy hollow of a tree
Escaped the hunt. No port is free, no place
That guard and most unusual vigilance
Does not attend my taking. Whiles I may scape
I will preserve myself; and am bethought
To take the basest and most poorest shape
That ever penury in contempt of man
Brought near to beast. My face I'll grime with filth,
Blanket my loins, elf all my hairs in knots,
And with presented nakedness outface
The winds and persecutions of the sky.
The country gives me proof and precedent
Of Bedlam beggars who, with roaring voices,
Strike in their numbed and mortified bare arms
Pins, wooden pricks, nails, sprigs of rosemary;
And with this horrible object, from low farms,
Poor pelting villages, sheep-cotes, and mills,
Sometimes with lunatic bans, sometime with prayers,
Enforce their charity. 'Poor Turlygod, poor Tom!'
That's something yet! Edgar I nothing am. [*he goes*

SCENE 4

Before Gloucester's castle. Kent in the stocks

Enter LEAR, FOOL *and Gentleman*

LEAR 'Tis strange that they should so depart from home,
And not send back my messenger.

GENT'MAN As I learned,
The night before there was no purpose in them
Of this remove.

KENT Hail to thee, noble master!

LEAR Ha!
Mak'st thou this shame thy pastime?

KENT No, my lord.

FOOL Ha, ha! He wears cruel garters. Horses are tied by the heads, dogs and bears by th' neck, monkeys by th' loins, and men by th' legs. When a man's over-lusty at legs, then he wears wooden nether-stocks.

LEAR What's he that hath so much thy place mistook
To set thee here?

KENT – It is both he and she,
Your son and daughter.

LEAR No.

KENT Yes.

LEAR No, I say.

KENT I say yea.

LEAR No, no, they would not.

KENT Yes, yes, they have.

LEAR By Jupiter, I swear no!

KENT By Juno, I swear ay!

LEAR They durst not do 't,
They could not, would not do 't; 'tis worse than murder
To do upon respect such violent outrage.
Resolve me with all modest haste which way
Thou mightst deserve or they impose this usage,
Coming from us.

KENT My lord, when at their home
I did commend your Highness' letters to them,
Ere I was risen from the place that showed
My duty kneeling, came there a reeking post,
Stewed in his haste, half breathless, panting forth
From Goneril his mistress salutations;
Delivered letters, spite of intermission,
Which presently they read: on whose contents
They summoned up their meiny, straight took horse,
Commanded me to follow and attend
The leisure of their answer, gave me cold looks:
And meeting here the other messenger,
Whose welcome I perceived had poisoned mine –

Being the very fellow which of late
Displayed so saucily against your Highness –
Having more man than wit about me, drew.
He raised the house with loud and coward cries.
Your son and daughter found this trespass worth
The shame which here it suffers.

FOOL Winter's not gone yet if the wild geese fly that way.
Fathers that wear rags
Do make their children blind,
But fathers that bear bags
Shall see their children kind.
Fortune, that arrant whore,
Ne'er turns the key to th' poor.
But for all this thou shalt have as many dolours for thy daughters as thou canst tell in a year.

LEAR O how this mother swells up toward my heart!
Hysterica passio! Down, thou climbing sorrow;
Thy element's below. Where is this daughter?

KENT With the earl, sir, here within.

LEAR Follow me not; stay here. [*he goes in*

GENT Made you no more offence but what you speak of?

KENT None.
How chance the king comes with so small a number?

FOOL An thou hadst been set i'th'stocks for that question, thou'dst well deserved it.

KENT Why, fool?

FOOL We'll set thee to school to an ant, to teach thee there's no labouring i'th'winter. All that follow their noses are led by their eyes but blind men, and there's not a nose among twenty but can smell him that's stinking. Let go thy hold when a great wheel runs down a hill, lest it break thy neck with following; but the great one that goes upward, let him draw thee after. When a wise man gives thee better counsel, give me mine again. I would ha' none but knaves use it, since a fool gives it.
That sir which serves and seeks for gain
And follows but for form,
Will pack when it begins to rain
And leave thee in the storm.

But I will tarry; the Fool will stay
And let the wise man fly.
The knave turns fool that runs away;
The Fool no knave, perdy.

KENT Where learned you this, fool?

FOOL Not i'th'stocks, fool!

Re-enter LEAR *with* GLOUCESTER

LEAR Deny to speak with me? They are sick, they are weary,
They have travelled all the night? Mere fetches; ay,
The images of revolt and flying off.
Fetch me a better answer.

GLO'STER My dear lord,
You know the fiery quality of the duke,
How unremovable and fixed he is
In his own course.

LEAR Vengeance! plague! death! confusion!
Fiery? What quality? Why, Gloucester, Gloucester,
I'd speak with the Duke of Cornwall and his wife.

GLO'STER Well, my good lord, I have informed them so.

LEAR Informed them? Dost thou understand me, man?

GLO'STER Ay, my good lord.

LEAR The king would speak with Cornwall; the dear father
Would with his daughter speak, commands her service.
Are they informed of this? My breath and blood!
Fiery? The fiery duke? Tell the hot duke that –
No, but not yet; may be he is not well:
Infirmity doth still neglect all office
Whereto our health is bound. We are not ourselves
When nature, being oppressed, commands the mind
To suffer with the body. I'll forbear,
And am fall'n out with my more headier will
To take the indisposed and sickly fit
For the sound man. [*looking on Kent*]
Death on my state! Wherefore
Should he sit here? This act persuades me
That this remotion of the duke and her
Is practice only. Give me my servant forth.
Go tell the duke and 's wife I'd speak with them
Now, presently; bid them come forth and hear me,

Or at their chamber door I'll beat the drum
Till it cry sleep to death.

GLO'STER I would have all well betwixt you. [*goes*

LEAR O me, my heart! My rising heart! But down!

FOOL Cry to it, nuncle, as the cockney did to the eels when she put 'em i' th' paste alive. She knapped 'em o'th' coxcombs with a stick and cried 'Down, wantons, down!' 'Twas her brother that, in pure kindness to his horse, buttered his hay.

Re-enter GLOUCESTER, *with* CORNWALL, REGAN *and servants*

LEAR Good morrow to you both.

CORNWALL Hail to your Grace!
[*'Kent here set at liberty'*

REGAN I am glad to see your Highness.

LEAR Regan, I think you are. I know what reason
I have to think so; if thou shouldst not be glad,
I would divorce me from thy mother's tomb,
Sepulchring an adultress. [*to Kent*] O, are you free?
Some other time for that. – Beloved Regan,
Thy sister's naught. O Regan, she hath tied
Sharp-toothed unkindness, like a vulture, here.
[*points to his heart*
I can scarce speak to thee; thou'lt not believe
With how depraved a quality – O Regan!

REGAN I pray you, sir, take patience. I have hope
You less know how to value her desert
Than she to scant her duty.

LEAR Say? How is that?

REGAN I cannot think my sister in the least
Would fail her obligation. If, sir, perchance
She have restrained the riots of your followers,
'Tis on such ground, and to such wholesome end,
As clears her from all blame.

LEAR My curses on her!

REGAN O sir, you are old;
Nature in you stands on the very verge
Of his confine. You should be ruled and led
By some discretion that discerns your state
Better than you yourself. Therefore I pray you

That to our sister you do make return;
Say you have wronged her.

LEAR Ask her forgiveness?
Do you but mark how this becomes the house!
'Dear daughter, I confess that I am old: [*kneeling*
Age is unnecessary; on my knees I beg
That you'll vouchsafe me raiment, bed, and food!'

REGAN Good sir, no more; these are unsightly tricks.
Return you to my sister.

LEAR [*rising*] Never, Regan!
She hath abated me of half my train,
Looked black upon me, struck me with her tongue
Most serpent-like upon the very heart.
All the stored vengeances of heaven fall
On her ingrateful top. Strike her young bones,
You taking airs, with lameness!

CORNWALL Fie, sir, fie!

LEAR You nimble lightnings, dart your blinding flames
Into her scornful eyes! Infect her beauty,
You fen-sucked fogs, drawn by the pow'rful sun
To fall and blister her!

REGAN O the blest gods!
So will you wish on me when the rash mood –

LEAR No, Regan, thou shalt never have my curse.
Thy tender-hefted nature shall not give
Thee o'er to harshness. Her eyes are fierce; but thine
Do comfort and not burn. 'Tis not in thee
To grudge my pleasures, to cut off my train,
To bandy hasty words, to scant my sizes,
And in conclusion to oppose the bolt
Against my coming in. Thou better know'st
The offices of nature, bond of childhood,
Effects of courtesy, dues of gratitude:
Thy half o' th' kingdom hast thou not forgot,
Wherein I thee endowed.

REGAN Good sir, to th' purpose.

LEAR Who put my man i' th' stocks?
[*tucket heard*

CORNWALL What trumpet's that?

REGAN I know't – my sister's. This approves her letter,
That she would soon be here.

Enter OSWALD

Is your lady come?

LEAR This is a slave, whose easy-borrowed pride
Dwells in the sickly grace of her he follows.
Out, varlet, from my sight!

CORNWALL What means your Grace?

LEAR Who stocked my servant? Regan, I have good hope
Thou didst not know on't.

Enter GONERIL

Who comes here? O heavens,
If you do love old men, if your sweet sway
Allow obedience, if you yourselves are old,
Make it your cause; send down and take my part!
[*to Goneril*] Art not ashamed to look upon this beard?
O Regan! will you take her by the hand?

GONERIL Why not by th' hand, sir? How have I offended?
All's not offence that indiscretion finds
And dotage terms so.

LEAR O sides, you are too tough!
Will you yet hold? How came my man i' th' stocks?

CORNWALL I set him there, sir; but his own disorders
Deserved much less advancement.

LEAR You? Did you?

REGAN I pray you, father, being weak, seem so.
If, till the expiration of your month,
You will return and sojourn with my sister,
Dismissing half your train, come then to me.
I am now from home, and out of that provision
Which shall be needful for your entertainment.

LEAR Return to her? And fifty men dismissed?
No, rather I abjure all roofs, and choose
To wage against the enmity o'th'air,
To be a comrade with the wolf and owl –
Necessity's sharp pinch! Return with her?
Why, the hot-blooded France, that dowerless took
Our youngest born, I could as well be brought

To knee his throne and, squire-like, pension beg
To keep base life afoot. Return with her?
Persuade me rather to be slave and sumpter
To this detested groom. [*looking at Oswald*

GONERIL At your choice, sir.

LEAR I prithee, daughter, do not make me mad.
I will not trouble thee, my child; farewell:
We'll no more meet, no more see one another.
But yet thou art my flesh, my blood, my daughter –
Or rather a disease that's in my flesh,
Which I must needs call mine. Thou art a boil,
A plague-sore, or embossèd carbuncle
In my corrupted blood. But I'll not chide thee:
Let shame come when it will, I do not call it;
I do not bid the thunder-bearer shoot,
Nor tell tales of thee to high-judging Jove.
Mend when thou canst; be better at thy leisure:
I can be patient; I can stay with Regan,
I and my hundred knights.

REGAN Not altogether so.
I looked not for you yet, nor am provided
For your fit welcome. Give ear, sir, to my sister;
For those that mingle reason with your passion
Must be content to think you old, and so –
But she knows what she does.

LEAR Is this well spoken?

REGAN I dare avouch it, sir. What! Fifty followers?
Is it not well? What should you need of more?
Yea, or so many, sith that both charge and danger
Speak 'gainst so great a number? How in one house
Should many people, under two commands,
Hold amity? 'Tis hard, almost impossible.

GONERIL Why might not you, my lord, receive attendance
From those that she calls servants, or from mine?

REGAN Why not, my lord? If then they chanced to slack ye,
We could control them. If you will come to me
(For now I spy a danger), I entreat you
To bring but five and twenty: to no more
Will I give place or notice.

LEAR I gave you all –
REGAN And in good time you gave it.
LEAR Made you my guardians, my depositaries,
But kept a reservation to be followed
With such a number. What! Must I come to you
With five and twenty? Regan, said you so?
REGAN And speak 't again, my lord; no more with me.
LEAR Those wicked creatures yet do look well-favoured
When others are more wicked; not being the worst
Stands in some rank of praise.
[*to Goneril*] I'll go with thee.
Thy fifty yet doth double five and twenty,
And thou art twice her love.
GONERIL Hear me, my lord.
What need you five and twenty, ten, or five,
To follow in a house where twice so many
Have a command to tend you?
REGAN What need one?
LEAR O reason not the need! Our basest beggars
Are in the poorest things superfluous.
Allow not nature more than nature needs,
Man's life is cheap as beast's. Thou art a lady;
If only to go warm were gorgeous,
Why, nature needs not what thou gorgeous wear'st,
Which scarcely keeps thee warm. But for true need –
You heavens, give me patience – patience I need!
You see me here, you gods, a poor old man,
As full of grief as age, wretched in both.
If it be you that stirs these daughters' hearts
Against their father, fool me not so much
To bear it tamely; touch me with noble anger,
And let not women's weapons, water drops,
Stain my man's cheeks. No, you unnatural hags,
I will have such revenges on you both
That all the world shall – I will do such things –
What they are yet I know not, but they shall be
The terrors of the earth! You think I'll weep;
No, I'll not weep: [*storm heard approaching*
I have full cause of weeping, but this heart

Shall break into a hundred thousand flaws
Or ere I'll weep. O Fool, I shall go mad!
[*he goes forth, the* FOOL, GLOUCESTER, *and* KENT *following*

CORNWALL Let us withdraw; 'twill be a storm.

REGAN This house is little: the old man and's people
Cannot be well bestowed.

GONERIL 'Tis his own blame; hath put himself from rest,
And must needs taste his folly.

REGAN For his particular, I'll receive him gladly,
But not one follower.

GONERIL So am I purposed.
Where is my lord of Gloucester?

CORNWALL Followed the old man forth.
[*Gloucester re-enters*] He is returned.

GLO'STER The king is in high rage.

CORNWALL Whither is he going?

GLO'STER He calls to horse, but will I know not whither.

CORNWALL Tis best to give him way; he leads himself.

GONERIL My lord, entreat him by no means to stay.

GLO'STER Alack, the night comes on, and the bleak winds
Do sorely ruffle. For many miles about
There's scarce a bush.

REGAN O sir, to wilful men
The injuries that they themselves procure
Must be their schoolmasters. Shut up your doors;
He is attended with a desperate train,
And what they may incense him to, being apt
To have his ear abused, wisdom bids fear.

CORNWALL Shut up your doors, my lord; 'tis a wild night:
My Regan counsels well. Come out o' th' storm.
[*they go in*

ACT 3 SCENE 1

A heath

A storm with thunder and lightning.
Enter KENT *and a Gentleman meeting*

KENT Who's there besides foul weather?
GENT'MAN One minded like the weather, most unquietly.
KENT I know you. Where's the King?
GENT'MAN Contending with the fretful elements;
Bids the wind blow the earth into the sea,
Or swell the curlèd waters 'bove the main,
That things might change or cease; tears his white hair,
Which the impetuous blasts with eyeless rage
Catch in their fury and make nothing of;
Strives in his little world of man to out-storm
The to-and-fro-conflicting wind and rain.
This night, wherein the cub-drawn bear would couch,
The lion and the belly-pinchèd wolf
Keep their fur dry, unbonneted he runs,
And bids what will take all.
KENT But who is with him?
GENT'MAN None but the Fool, who labours to outjest
His heart-struck injuries.
KENT Sir, I do know you,
And dare upon the warrant of my note
Commend a dear thing to you. There is division,
Although as yet the face of it is covered
With mutual cunning, 'twixt Albany and Cornwall,
Who have – as who have not that their great stars
Throned and set high? – servants, who seem no less,
Which are to France the spies and speculations
Intelligent of our state. What hath been seen,
Either in snuffs and packings of the Dukes,
Or the hard rein which both of them hath borne
Against the old kind King; or something deeper
Whereof perchance these are but furnishings –
But true it is from France there comes a power

Into this scattered kingdom, who already,
Wise in our negligence, have secret feet
In some of our best ports and are at point
To show their open banner. Now to you:
If on my credit you dare build so far
To make your speed to Dover, you shall find
Some that will thank you, making just report
Of how unnatural and bemadding sorrow
The King hath cause to plain.
I am a gentleman of blood and breeding,
And from some knowledge and assurance offer
This office to you.

GENT'MAN I will talk further with you.

KENT No, do not.
For confirmation that I am much more
Than my out-wall, open this purse and take
What it contains. If you shall see Cordelia
(As fear not but you shall), show her this ring,
And she will tell you who your fellow is
That yet you do not know. Fie on this storm!
I will go seek the King.

GENT'MAN Give me your hand. Have you no more to say?

KENT Few words, but, to effect, more than all yet –
That when we have found the King (in which your pain
That way, I'll this) he that first lights on him
Holla the other. [*they go their separate ways*

SCENE 2

Another part of the heath

'Storm still.' Enter LEAR *and* FOOL

LEAR Blow, winds, and crack your cheeks! Rage! Blow!
You cataracts and hurricanoes, spout
Till you have drenched our steeples, drowned the cocks!
You sulph'rous and thought-executing fires,
Vaunt-couriers of oak-cleaving thunderbolts,
Singe my white head! And thou, all-shaking thunder,
Strike flat the thick rotundity o'th'world,

Crack Nature's moulds, all germens spill at once
That make ingrateful man!

FOOL O nuncle, court holy water in a dry house is better than this rain-water out o' door. Good nuncle, in; ask thy daughters blessing! Here's a night pities neither wise men nor fools.

LEAR Rumble thy bellyful! Spit, fire! spout, rain!
Nor rain, wind, thunder, fire are my daughters.
I tax not you, you elements, with unkindness:
I never gave you kingdom, called you children;
You owe me no subscription. Then let fall
Your horrible pleasure. Here I stand your slave,
A poor, infirm, weak, and despised old man
But yet I call you servile ministers,
That will with two pernicious daughters join
Your high-engendered battles 'gainst a head
So old and white as this. O, ho! 'Tis foul!

FOOL He that has a house to put's head in has a good head-piece.

The codpiece that will house
　Before the head has any,
The head and he shall louse:
　So beggars marry many.
The man that makes his toe
　What he his heart should make
Shall of a corn cry woe,
　And turn his sleep to wake.

For there was never yet fair woman but she made mouths in a glass.

Enter KENT

LEAR No, I will be the pattern of all patience;
I will say nothing.

KENT Who's there?

FOOL Marry, here's grace and a codpiece; that's a wise man and [*pointing at Lear*] a fool.

KENT Alas, sir, are you here? Things that love night
Love not such nights as these. The wrathful skies
Gallow the very wanderers of the dark

And make them keep their caves. Since I was man,
Such sheets of fire, such bursts of horrid thunder,
Such groans of roaring wind and rain, I never
Remember to have heard. Man's nature cannot carry
Th'affliction nor the fear.

LEAR
Let the great gods,
That keep this dreadful pudder o'er our heads,
Find out their enemies now. Tremble, thou wretch
That hast within thee undivulgèd crimes
Unwhipped of justice. Hide thee, thou bloody hand,
Thou perjured, and thou simular of virtue
That art incestuous. Caitiff, to pieces shake,
That under covert and convenient seeming
Hast practised on man's life. Close pent-up guilts,
Rive your concealing continents, and cry
These dreadful summoners grace. I am a man
More sinned against than sinning.

KENT
Alack, bare-headed?
Gracious my lord, hard by here is a hovel;
Some friendship will it lend you 'gainst the tempest:
Repose you there, while I to this hard house
(More harder than the stones whereof 'tis raised,
Which even but now, demanding after you,
Denied me to come in) return, and force
Their scanted courtesy.

LEAR
My wits begin to turn.
Come on, my boy. How dost, my boy? Art cold?
I am cold myself. Where is this straw, my fellow?
The art of our necessities is strange,
And can make vile things precious. Come, your hovel.
Poor fool and knave, I have one part in my heart
That's sorry yet for thee.

FOOL
[*sings*]
He that has and a little tiny wit –
With heigh-ho, the wind and the rain –
Must make content with his fortunes fit,
Though the rain it raineth every day.

LEAR
True, boy. Come, bring us to this hovel.
[*Lear and Kent go*

FOOL This is a brave night to cool a courtesan! I'll speak a prophecy ere I go:

When priests are more in word than matter;
When brewers mar their malt with water;
When nobles are their tailors' tutors;
No heretics burned, but wenches' suitors;
Then shall the realm of Albion
Come to great confusion.

When every case in law is right;
No squire in debt nor no poor knight;
When slanders do not live in tongues,
Nor cutpurses come not to throngs;
When usurers tell their gold i'th'field,
And bawds and whores do churches build;
Then comes the time, who lives to see 't,
That going shall be used with feet.

This prophecy Merlin shall make, for I live before his time. [*goes*

SCENE 3

A room in Gloucester's castle

'Enter GLOUCESTER *and* EDMUND, *with lights'*

GLO'STER Alack, alack, Edmund, I like not this unnatural dealing. When I desired their leave that I might pity him, they took from me the use of mine own house, charged me on pain of perpetual displeasure neither to speak of him, entreat for him, or any way sustain him.

EDMUND Most savage and unnatural!

GLO'STER Go to; say you nothing. There is division between the Dukes, and a worse matter than that. I have received a letter this night – 'tis dangerous to be spoken – I have locked the letter in my closet. These injuries the King now bears will be revenged home. There is part of a power already footed; we must incline to the King. I will look him and privily relieve him; go you and maintain talk with the Duke, that my charity be not of him perceived; if he ask for me, I am ill and gone to bed. If I die for it (as no less is threat'ned me), the King, my old master, must be relieved. There is strange things toward, Edmund; pray you be careful. [*he goes*

EDMUND This courtesy, forbid thee, shall the Duke
Instantly know, and of that letter too.
This seems a fair deserving, and must draw me
That which my father loses – no less than all.
The younger rises when the old doth fall.
[*he goes*

SCENE 4

The heath. Before a hovel. 'Storm still'

'Enter LEAR, KENT, *and* FOOL*'*

KENT Here is the place, my lord; good my lord, enter:
The tyranny of the open night's too rough
For nature to endure.

LEAR Let me alone.

KENT Good my lord, enter here.

LEAR Wilt break my heart?

KENT I had rather break mine own. Good my lord, enter.

LEAR Thou think'st 'tis much that this contentious storm
Invades us to the skin: so 'tis to thee;
But where the greater malady is fixed,
The lesser is scarce felt. Thou'dst shun a bear;
But if thy flight lay toward the roaring sea,
Thou'dst meet the bear i'th'mouth. When the mind's free,
The body's delicate; this tempest in my mind
Doth from my senses take all feeling else
Save what beats there – filial ingratitude!
Is it not as this mouth should tear this hand
For lifting food to 't? But I will punish home.
No, I will weep no more. In such a night
To shut me out? Pour on; I will endure.
In such a night as this? O Regan, Goneril!

Your old kind father whose frank heart gave all!
O, that way madness lies; let me shun that!
No more of that.

KENT Good my lord, enter here.

LEAR Prithee go in thyself, seek thine own ease;
This tempest will not give me leave to ponder
On things would hurt me more. But I'll go in.
[*to the Fool*] In, boy, go first. You houseless poverty –
Nay, get thee in; I'll pray, and then I'll sleep.
[*Fool goes in*
Poor naked wretches, whereso'er you are,
That bide the pelting of this pitiless storm,
How shall your houseless heads and unfed sides,
Your looped and windowed raggedness, defend you
From seasons such as these? O, I have ta'en
Too little care of this! Take physic, pomp;
Expose thyself to feel what wretches feel,
That thou mayst shake the superflux to them
And show the heavens more just.

EDGAR [*within*] Fathom and half, fathom and half! Poor Tom!
[*the Fool runs out from the hovel*

FOOL Come not in here, nuncle, here's a spirit. Help me, help me!

KENT Give me thy hand. Who's there?

FOOL A spirit, a spirit! He says his name's poor Tom.

KENT What art thou that dost grumble there i'th'straw?
Come forth!

Enter EDGAR, *disguised as a madman, from the hovel*

EDGAR Away! The foul fiend follows me!
Through the sharp hawthorn blow the cold winds.
Humh! Go to thy bed and warm thee.

LEAR Didst thou give all to thy daughters? And art thou come to this?

EDGAR Who gives anything to poor Tom? Whom the foul fiend hath led through fire and through flame, through ford and whirlpool, o'er bog and quagmire; that hath laid knives under his pillow, and halters in his pew; set ratsbane by his porridge; made him proud of heart, to ride on a bay trotting horse over four-inched bridges, to course his own shadow for a traitor. Bless thy five wits! Tom's a-cold. O, do de, do de, do de. Bless thee from whirlwinds, star-blasting, and taking! Do poor Tom some charity, whom the foul fiend vexes. There could I have him now – and there – and there again – and there! [*'storm still'*

LEAR What, has his daughters brought him to this pass?
Couldst thou save nothing? Wouldst thou give 'em all?

FOOL Nay, he reserved a blanket; else we had been all shamed.

LEAR Now all the plagues that in the pendulous air
Hang fated o'er men's faults light on thy daughters!

KENT He hath no daughters, sir.

LEAR Death, traitor! Nothing could have subdued nature
To such a lowness but his unkind daughters.
Is it the fashion that discarded fathers
Should have thus little mercy on their flesh?
Judicious punishment! 'Twas this flesh begot
Those pelican daughters.

EDGAR Pillicock sat on Pillicock Hill.
Alow! alow, loo, loo!

FOOL This cold night will turn us all to fools and madmen.

EDGAR Take heed o'th'foul fiend. Obey thy parents, keep thy word justly, swear not, commit not with man's sworn spouse, set not thy sweet heart on proud array. Tom's a-cold.

LEAR What hast thou been?

EDGAR A servingman, proud in heart and mind; that curled my hair, wore gloves in my cap; served the lust of my mistress' heart, and did the act of darkness with her; swore as many oaths as I spake words and broke them in the sweet face of heaven – one that slept in the contriving of lust, and waked to do it. Wine loved I deeply, dice dearly; and in woman out-paramoured the Turk. False of heart, light of ear, bloody of hand; hog in sloth, fox in stealth, wolf in greediness, dog in madness, lion in prey. Let not the creaking of shoes nor the rustling of silks betray thy poor heart to woman. Keep thy foot out of brothels, thy hand out of plackets, thy pen from lenders' books, and defy the foul fiend.

Still through the hawthorn blows the cold wind,
Says suum, mun, hey nonny nonny.
Dolphin my boy, boy! – sessa! let him trot by.

[*'storm still'*

LEAR Thou wert better in a grave than to answer with thy uncovered body this extremity of the skies. Is man no more than this? Consider him well. Thou ow'st the worm no silk, the beast no hide, the sheep no wool, the cat no perfume. Ha! Here's three on's are sophisticated: thou art the thing itself. Unaccommodated man is no more but such a poor, bare, forked animal as thou art. Off, off, you lendings! Come, unbutton here!

[*strives to tear off his clothes*

FOOL Prithee, nuncle, be contented; 'tis a naughty night to swim in!

Sees GLOUCESTER *approaching 'with a torch'*

Now a little fire in a wild field were like an old lecher's heart – small spark, all the rest on's body cold. Look, here comes a walking fire.

EDGAR This is the foul Flibbertigibbet. He begins at curfew, and walks till first cock. He gives the web and the pin, squinies the eye, and makes the harelip; mildews the white wheat, and hurts the poor creature of earth.

S'Withold footed thrice the 'old:
He met the nightmare and her ninefold:
Bid her alight
And her troth plight –
And aroint thee, witch, aroint thee!

KENT How fares your grace?

LEAR What's he?

KENT Who's there? What is't you seek?

GLO'STER What are you there? Your names?

EDGAR Poor Tom, that eats the swimming frog, the toad, the tadpole, the wall-newt and the water; that in the fury of his heart, when the foul fiend rages, eats cow-dung for sallets, swallows the old rat and the ditch-dog, drinks the green mantle of the standing pool; who is whipped from tithing to tithing, and stock-punished and imprisoned; who hath had three suits to his back, six shirts to his body,

Horse to ride, and weapon to wear;
But mice and rats and such small deer
Have been Tom's food for seven long year.

Beware my follower. Peace, Smulkin; peace, thou fiend!

GLO'STER What, hath your Grace no better company?

EDGAR The Prince of Darkness is a gentleman! Modo he's called, and Mahu.

GLO'STER Our flesh and blood, my lord, is grown so vile,
That it doth hate what gets it.

EDGAR Poor Tom's a-cold.

GLO'STER Go in with me; my duty cannot suffer
T' obey in all your daughters' hard commands.
Though their injunction be to bar my doors
And let this tyrannous night take hold upon you,
Yet have I ventured to come seek you out
And bring you where both fire and food is ready.

LEAR First let me talk with this philosopher.
What is the cause of thunder?

KENT Good my lord, take his offer; go into th' house.

LEAR I'll talk a word with this same learned Theban.
What is your study?

EDGAR How to prevent the fiend and to kill vermin.

LEAR Let me ask you one word in private.

KENT Importune him once more to go, my lord;
His wits begin t' unsettle. [*'storm still'*

GLO'STER Canst thou blame him?
His daughters seek his death. Ah, that good Kent!
He said it would be thus, poor banished man!
Thou sayest the King grows mad; I'll tell thee, friend,
I am almost mad myself. I had a son,
Now outlawed from my blood: he sought my life
But lately, very late: I loved him, friend,
No father his son dearer: true to tell thee,
The grief hath crazed my wits. What a night's this!
I do beseech your Grace –

LEAR O cry you mercy, sir.
Noble philosopher, your company.

EDGAR Tom's a-cold.

GLO'STER In, fellow, there, into th' hovel; keep thee warm.

LEAR Come, let's in all.

KENT This way, my lord.

LEAR With him;
I will keep still with my philosopher.

KENT Good my lord, soothe him; let him take the fellow.

GLO'STER Take him you on.

KENT Sirrah, come on; go along with us.

LEAR Come, good Athenian.

GLO'STER No words, no words; hush!

EDGAR Child Roland to the dark tower came.
His word was still 'Fie, foh, and fum.
I smell the blood of a British man.' [*they go*

SCENE 5

A room in Gloucester's castle

'*Enter* CORNWALL *and* EDMUND'

CORNWALL I will have my revenge ere I depart his house.

EDMUND How, my lord, I may be censured, that nature thus gives way to loyalty, something fears me to think of.

CORNWALL I now perceive it was not altogether your brother's evil disposition made him seek his death; but a provoking merit, set awork by a reproveable badness in himself.

EDMUND How malicious is my fortune, that I must repent to be just! This is the letter he spoke of, which approves him an intelligent party to the advantages of France. O heavens! That this treason were not – or not I the detector!

CORNWALL Go with me to the Duchess.

EDMUND If the matter of this paper be certain, you have mighty business in hand.

CORNWALL True or false, it hath made thee Earl of Gloucester. Seek out where thy father is, that he may be ready for our apprehension.

EDMUND [*aside*] If I find him comforting the King, it will stuff his suspicion more fully. [*to Cornwall*] I will persever in my course of loyalty, though the conflict be sore between that and my blood.

CORNWALL I will lay trust upon thee; and thou shalt find a dearer father in my love. [*they leave*

SCENE 6

A room in a farmhouse adjoining Gloucester's castle

Enter GLOUCESTER *and* KENT

GLO'STER Here is better than the open air; take it thankfully. I will piece out the comfort with what addition I can: I will not be long from you.

KENT All the power of his wits have given way to his impatience. The gods reward your kindness!

[*Gloucester goes out*

Enter LEAR, EDGAR, *and* FOOL

EDGAR Frateretto calls me, and tells me Nero is an angler in the lake of darkness. Pray, innocent, and beware the foul fiend.

FOOL Prithee, nuncle, tell me whether a madman be a gentleman or a yeoman.

LEAR A king, a king!

FOOL No, he's a yeoman that has a gentleman to his son; for he's a mad yeoman that sees his son a gentleman before him.

LEAR To have a thousand with red burning spits
Come hizzing in upon 'em!

EDGAR The foul fiend bites my back.

FOOL He's mad that trusts in the tameness of a wolf, a horse's health, a boy's love, or a whore's oath.

LEAR It shall be done; I will arraign them straight.
[*to Edgar*] Come sit thou here, most learned justicer;
[*to the Fool*]
Thou sapient sir, sit here. Now, you she-foxes –

EDGAR Look where he stands and glares! Want'st thou eyes at trial, madam?

[*sings*] Come o'er the burn, Bessy, to me.

FOOL [*sings*] Her boat hath a leak,
And she must not speak
Why she dares not come over to thee.

EDGAR The foul fiend haunts poor Tom in the voice of a nightingale. Hoppedance cries in Tom's belly for two white herring. Croak not, black angel; I have no food for thee.

KENT How do you, sir? Stand you not so amazed.
Will you lie down and rest upon the cushions?

LEAR I'll see their trial first. Bring in their evidence.
[*to Edgar*] Thou robèd man of justice, take thy place;
[*to the Fool*] And thou, his yokefellow of equity,
Bench by his side.
[*to Kent*] You are o'th'commission;
Sit you too.

EDGAR Let us deal justly.
Sleepest or wakest thou, jolly shepherd?
Thy sheep be in the corn;
And for one blast of thy minikin mouth
Thy sheep shall take no harm.
Purr the cat is gray.

LEAR Arraign her first; 'tis Goneril. I here take my oath before this honourable assembly, she kicked the poor king, her father.

FOOL Come hither, mistress; is your name Goneril?

LEAR She cannot deny it.

FOOL Cry you mercy, I took you for a joined-stool.

LEAR Ant here's another, whose warped looks proclaim
What stone her heart is made on. Stop her there!
Arms, arms, sword, fire! Corruption in the place!
False justicer, why hast thou let her scape?

EDGAR Bless thy five wits!

KENT O pity! Sir, where is the patience now
That you so oft have boasted to retain?

EDGAR My tears begin to take his part so much
They mar my counterfeiting.

LEAR The little dogs and all,
Tray, Blanche, and Sweetheart; see, they bark at me.

EDGAR Tom will throw his head at them. Avaunt, you curs!

Be thy mouth or black or white,
Tooth that poisons if it bite;
Mastiff, greyhound, mongrel grim,
Hound or spaniel, brach or lym,
Or bobtail tyke or trundle-tail,
Tom will make him weep and wail;
For, with throwing thus my head,
Dogs leaped the hatch, and all are fled.

Do, de, de, de. Sessa! Come, march to wakes and fairs and market towns. Poor Tom, thy horn is dry.

LEAR Then let them anatomize Regan; see what breeds about her heart. Is there any cause in nature that make these hard hearts? [*to Edgar*] You, sir, I entertain for one of my hundred; only I do not like the fashion of your garments. You will say they are Persian; but let them be changed.

KENT Now good my lord, lie here and rest awhile.

LEAR Make no noise, make no noise; draw the curtains. So, so; we'll go to supper i'th'morning.

FOOL And I'll go to bed at noon.

Enter GLOUCESTER

GLO'STER Come hither, friend. Where is the King my master?

KENT Here, sir: but trouble him not; his wits are gone.

GLO'STER Good friend, I prithee take him in thy arms.
I have o'erheard a plot of death upon him.
There is a litter ready; lay him in't,
And drive toward Dover, friend, where thou shalt meet
Both welcome and protection. Take up thy master;
If thou should'st dally half an hour, his life,
With thine, and all that offer to defend him,
Stand in assurèd loss. Take up, take up
And follow me, that will to some provision
Give thee quick conduct.

KENT Oppressèd nature sleeps.
This rest might yet have balmed thy broken sinews,
Which, if convenience will not allow,
Stand in hard cure.
[*to the Fool*] Come, help to bear thy master;

Thou must not stay behind.

GLO'STER Come, come, away!

[Gloucester, Kent and the Fool leave, carrying Lear

EDGAR When we our betters see bearing our woes,
We scarcely think our miseries our foes.
Who alone suffers, suffers most i'th'mind,
Leaving free things and happy shows behind.
But then the mind much sufferance doth o'erskip
When grief hath mates, and bearing fellowship.
Haw light and portable my pain seems now,
When that which makes me bend makes the King bow.
He childed as I fathered! Tom, away!
Mark the high noises, and thyself bewray
When false opinion, whose wrong thoughts defile thee,
In thy just proof repeals and reconciles thee.
What will hap more tonight, safe scape the King!
Lurk, lurk. *[he goes*

SCENE 7

A room in Gloucester's castle

Enter CORNWALL, REGAN, GONERIL, EDMUND, *and Servants*

CORNWALL *[to Goneril]* Post speedily to my lord your husband; show him this letter: the army of France is landed. Seek out the traitor Gloucester.

REGAN Hang him instantly.

GONERIL Pluck out his eyes.

CORNWALL Leave him to my displeasure. Edmund, keep you our sister company. The revenges we are bound to take upon your traitorous father are not fit for your beholding. Advise the Duke, where you are going, to a most festinate preparation: we are bound to the like. Our posts shall be swift and intelligent betwixt us. Farewell, dear sister; farewell, my Lord of Gloucester.

Enter OSWALD

How now? Where's the King?

OSWALD My Lord of Gloucester hath conveyed him hence.

Some five or six and thirty of his knights,
Hot questrists after him, met him at gate,
Who, with some other of the lord's dependants,
Are gone with him toward Dover, where they boast
To have well-armèd friends.

CORNWALL Get horses for your mistress.

GONERIL Farewell, sweet lord, and sister.

CORNWALL Edmund, farewell. *[Goneril, Edmund and Oswald go*
Go seek the traitor Gloucester;
Pinion him like a thief, bring him before us.
[Servants go
Though well we may not pass upon his life
Without the form of justice, yet our power
Shall do a court'sy to our wrath, which men
May blame, but not control.

Re-enter Servants, with GLOUCESTER *prisoner*

Who's there? The traitor?

REGAN Ingrateful fox! 'tis he.

CORNWALL Bind fast his corky arms.

GLO'STER What means your Graces? Good my friends, consider
You are my guests. Do me no foul play, friends.

CORNWALL Bind him, I say. *[Servants bind him*

REGAN Hard, hard. O filthy traitor!

GLO'STER Unmerciful lady as you are, I'm none.

CORNWALL To this chair bind him. Villain, thou shalt find –
[Regan plucks his beard

GLO'STER By the kind gods, 'tis most ignobly done
To pluck me by the beard.

REGAN So white, and such a traitor?

GLO'STER Naughty lady,
These hairs which thou dost ravish from my chin
Will quicken and accuse thee. I am your host:
With robbers' hands my hospitable favours
You should not ruffle thus. What will you do?

CORNWALL Come, sir. What letters had you late from France?

REGAN Be simple-answered, for we know the truth.

CORNWALL And what confederacy have you with the traitors
Late footed in the kingdom?

REGAN To whose hands

You have sent the lunatic king. Speak.

GLO'STER I have a letter, guessingly set down,
Which came from one that's of a neutral heart,
And not from one opposed.

CORNWALL Cunning.

REGAN And false.

CORNWALL Where hast thou sent the King?

GLO'STER To Dover.

REGAN Wherefore to Dover? Wast thou not charged at peril –

CORNWALL Wherefore to Dover? Let him answer that.

GLO'STER I am tied to th' stake, and I must stand the course.

REGAN Wherefore to Dover?

GLO'STER Because I would not see thy cruel nails
Pluck out his poor old eyes, nor thy fierce sister
In his anointed flesh rash boarish fangs.
The sea, with such a storm as his loved head
In hell-black night endured, would have buoyed up,
And quenched the stellèd fires;
Yet, poor old heart, he holp the heavens to rain.
If wolves had at thy gate howled that dearn time,
Thou should'st have said 'Good porter, turn the key'.
All cruels else subscribe: but I shall see
The wingèd Vengeance overtake such children.

CORNWALL See 't shalt thou never. Fellows, hold the chair.
Upon these eyes of thine I'll set my foot.

GLO'STER He that will think to live till he be old,
Give me some help. O cruel! O you gods!

REGAN One side will mock another. Th'other too!

CORNWALL If you see vengeance –

I SERVANT Hold your hand, my lord!
I have served you ever since I was a child,
But better service have I never done you
Than now to bid you hold.

REGAN How, now, you dog?

I SERVANT If you did wear a beard upon your chin,
I'd shake it on this quarrel.

REGAN What do you mean?

CORNWALL My villain? [*he unsheathes his sword*

I SERVANT Nay, then, come on, and take the chance of anger.

REGAN [*to another Servant*] Give me thy sword. A peasant stand up thus?
[*'she takes a sword and runs at him behind'*

I SERVANT O, I am slain! My lord, you have one eye left
To see some mischief on him. O! [*he dies*

CORNWALL Lest it see more, prevent it. Out, vile jelly!
Where is thy lustre now?

GLO'STER All dark and comfortless! Where's my son Edmund?
Edmund, enkindle all the sparks of nature
To quit this horrid act.

REGAN Out, treacherous villain!
Thou call'st on him that hates thee. It was he
That made the overture of thy treasons to us,
Who is too good to pity thee.

GLO'STER O, my follies! Then Edgar was abused.
Kind gods, forgive me that, and prosper him!

REGAN Go thrust him out at gates, and let him smell
His way to Dover. [*they lead him out*
How is 't, my lord? How look you?

CORNWALL I have received a hurt. Follow me, lady.
Turn out that eyeless villain. Throw this slave
Upon the dunghill. Regan, I bleed apace.
Untimely comes this hurt. Give me your arm.
[*he goes in, supported by Regan*

2 SERVANT I'll never care what wickedness I do,
If this man come to good.

3 SERVANT If she live long,
And in the end meet the old course of death,
Women will all turn monsters.

2 SERVANT Let's follow the old earl, and get the bedlam
To lead him where he would; his roguish madness
Allows itself to anything.

3 SERVANT Go thou; I'll fetch some flax and whites of eggs
To apply to his bleeding face. Now heaven help him!
[*they go*

ACT 4 SCENE I

The heath

'Enter EDGAR*'*

EDGAR
Yet better thus, and known to be contemned,
Than still contemned and flattered. To be worst,
The lowest and most dejected thing of Fortune,
Stands still in esperance, lives not in fear.
The lamentable change is from the best;
The worst returns to laughter. Welcome, then,
Thou unsubstantial air that I embrace:
The wretch that thou hast blown unto the worst
Owes nothing to thy blasts.

'Enter GLOUCESTER, *led by an* OLD MAN*'*

But who comes here?
My father, poorly eyed! World, world, O world!
But that thy strange mutations make us hate thee,
Life would not yield to age.

OLD MAN
O my good lord,
I have been your tenant, and your father's tenant,
These fourscore years.

GLO'STER
Away, get thee away! Good friend, be gone:
Thy comforts can do me no good at all;
Thee they may hurt.

OLD MAN
You cannot see your way.

GLO'STER
I have no way, and therefore want no eyes;
I stumbled when I saw. Full oft 'tis seen
Our means secure us, and our mere defects
Prove our commodities. O dear son Edgar,
The food of thy abusèd father's wrath!
Might I but live to see thee in my touch,
I'd say I had eyes again

OLD MAN
How now? Who's there?

EDGAR
O gods! Who is't can say 'I am at the worst'?
I am worse than e'er I was.

OLD MAN
'Tis poor mad Tom.

EDGAR And worse I may be yet: the worst is not
So long as we can say 'This is the worst'.
OLD MAN Fellow, where goest?
GLO'STER Is it a beggar-man?
OLD MAN Madman, and beggar too.
GLO'STER He has some reason, else he could not beg.
I' th' last night's storm I such a fellow saw,
Which made me think a man a worm. My son
Came then into my mind, and yet my mind
Was then scarce friends with him: I have heard more since.
As flies to wanton boys are we to th' gods;
They kill us for their sport.
EDGAR How should this be?
Bad is the trade that must play fool to sorrow,
Ang'ring itself and others. – Bless thee, master!
GLO'STER Is that the naked fellow?
OLD MAN Ay, my lord.
GLO'STER Then prithee get thee away. If, for my sake,
Thou wilt o'ertake us hence a mile or twain
I' th' way toward Dover, do it for ancient love;
And bring some covering for this naked soul
Which I'll entreat to lead me.
OLD MAN Alack, sir, he is mad!
GLO'STER 'Tis the time's plague when madmen lead the blind.
Do as I bid thee; or rather do thy pleasure:
Above the rest, be gone.
OLD MAN I'll bring him the best 'parel that I have,
Come on't what will. [*he goes*
GLO'STER Sirrah, naked fellow!
EDGAR Poor Tom's a-cold. [*aside*] I cannot daub it further.
GLO'STER Come hither, fellow.
EDGAR And yet I must. Bless thy sweet eyes, they bleed!
GLO'STER Know'st thou the way to Dover?
EDGAR Both stile and gate, horseway and footpath. Poor Tom hath been scared out of his good wits. Bless thee, good man's son, from the foul fiend! Five fiends have been in poor Tom at once: as Obidicut, of lust; Hobbididence, prince of darkness; Mahu, of stealing; Modo, of murder;

Flibbertigibbet, of mocking and mowing, who since possesses chambermaids and waiting-women. So, bless thee, master!

GLO'STER Here, take this purse, thou whom the heavens' plagues
Have humbled to all strokes: that I am wretched
Makes thee the happier; Heavens, deal so still!
Let the superfluous and lust-dieted man,
That slaves your ordinance, that will not see
Because he does not feel, feel your power quickly;
So distribution should undo excess,
And each man have enough. Dost thou know Dover?

EDGAR Ay, master.

GLO'STER There is a cliff, whose high and bending head
Looks fearfully in the confinèd deep.
Bring me but to the very brim of it,
And I'll repair the misery thou dost bear
With something rich about me. From that place
I shall no leading need.

EDGAR Give me thy arm;
Poor Tom shall lead thee. [*they go*

SCENE 2

Before the Duke of Albany's palace

Enter GONERIL *and* EDMUND

GONERIL Welcome, my lord. I marvel our mild husband
Not met us on the way.

Enter OSWALD

Now, where's your master?

OSWALD Madam, within; but never man so changed.
I told him of the army that was landed;
He smiled at it: I told him you were coming;
His answer was, 'The worse'. Of Gloucester's treachery
And of the loyal service of his son
When I informed him, then he called me sot
And told me I had turned the wrong side out.
What most he should dislike seems pleasant to him;

What like, offensive.

GONERIL [*to Edmund*] Then shall you go no further.
It is the cowish terror of his spirit,
That dares not undertake; he'll not feel wrongs
Which tie him to an answer. Our wishes on the way
May prove effects. Back, Edmund, to my brother;
Hasten his musters and conduct his powers:
I must change arms at home and give the distaff
Into my husband's hands. This trusty servant
Shall pass between us: ere long you are like to hear
(If you dare venture in your own behalf)
A mistress's command. Wear this. [*giving a favour*]
Spare speech;
Decline your head: this kiss, if it durst speak,
Would stretch thy spirits up into the air.
Conceive, and fare thee well.

EDMUND Yours in the ranks of death!

GONERIL My most dear Gloucester!
[*Edmund goes*
O, the difference of man and man!
To thee a woman's services are due;
A fool usurps my bed.

OSWALD Madam, here comes my lord.
[*he goes*

'*Enter* ALBANY'

GONERIL I have been worth the whistling.

ALBANY O Goneril,
You are not worth the dust which the rude wind
Blows in your face! I fear your disposition.
That nature which contemns it origin
Cannot be bordered certain in itself.
She that herself will sliver and disbranch
From her material sap, perforce must wither
And come to deadly use.

GONERIL No more! The text is foolish.

ALBANY Wisdom and goodness to the vile seem vile;
Filths savour but themselves. What have you done?
Tigers, not daughters, what have you performed?

A father, and a gracious agèd man,
Whose reverence even the head-lugged bear would lick,
Most barbarous, most degenerate, have you madded.
Could my good brother suffer you to do it?
A man, a prince, by him so benefited!
If that the heavens do not their visible spirits
Send quickly down to tame these vile offences,
It will come
Humanity must perforce prey on itself
Like monsters of the deep.

GONERIL Milk-livered man!
That bear'st a cheek for blows, a head for wrongs:
Who hast not in thy brows an eye discerning
Thine honour from thy suffering; that not know'st
Fools do those villains pity who are punished
Ere they have done their mischief. Where's thy drum?
France spreads his banners in our noiseless land,
With plumèd helm thy state begins to threat,
Whilst thou, a moral fool, sits still and cries
'Alack, why does he so?'

ALBANY See thyself, devil!
Proper deformity shows not in the fiend
So horrid as in woman.

GONERIL O vain fool!

ALBANY Thou changèd and self-covered thing, for shame
Bemonster not thy feature! Were't my fitness
To let these hands obey my blood,
They are apt enough to dislocate and tear
Thy flesh and bones: howe'er thou art a fiend,
A woman's shape doth shield thee.

GONERIL Marry, your manhood! Mew!

'Enter a Messenger'

ALBANY What news?

MESSENGER O, my good lord, the Duke of Cornwall's dead,
Slain by his servant, going to put out
The other eye of Gloucester.

ALBANY Gloucester's eyes!

MESSENGER A servant that he bred, thrilled with remorse,

Opposed against the act, bending his sword
To his great master; who, thereat enraged,
Flew on him, and amongst them felled him dead;
But not without that harmful stroke which since
Hath plucked him after.

ALBANY This shows you are above,
You justicers, that these our nether crimes
So speedily can venge! But, O poor Gloucester!
Lost he his other eye?

MESSENGER Both, both, my lord.
This letter, madam, craves a speedy answer;
'Tis from your sister. *[presents a letter*

GONERIL One way I like this well;
But being widow, and my Gloucester with her,
May all the building in my fancy pluck
Upon my hateful life. Another way
The news is not so tart. – I'll read, and answer.
[she goes out

ALBANY Where was his son when they did take his eyes?

MESSENGER Come with my lady hither.

ALBANY He is not here.

MESSENGER No, my good lord; I met him back again.

ALBANY Knows he the wickedness?

MESSENGER Ay, my good lord; 'twas he informed against him,
And quit the house on purpose, that their punishment
Might have the freer course.

ALBANY Gloucester, I live
To thank thee for the love thou show'dst the King,
And to revenge thine eyes. Come hither, friend;
Tell me what more thou know'st. *[they go*

SCENE 3

The French camp near Dover

'Enter KENT *and a Gentleman'*

KENT Why the King of France is so suddenly gone back know you no reason?

GENT'MAN Something he left imperfect in the state, which since his coming forth is thought of, which imports to the kingdom so much fear and danger that his personal return was most required and necessary.

KENT Who hath he left behind him general?

GENT'MAN The Marshal of France, Monsieur La Far.

KENT Did your letters pierce the queen to any demonstration of grief?

GENT'MAN Ay, sir; she took them, read them in my presence,
And now and then an ample tear trilled down
Her delicate cheek. It seemed she was a queen
Over her passion, who, most rebel-like,
Sought to be king o'er her.

KENT O, then it moved her.

GENT'MAN Not to a rage; patience and sorrow strove
Who should express her goodliest. You have seen
Sunshine and rain at once; her smiles and tears
Were like, a better way: those happy smilets
That played on her ripe lip seemed not to know
What guests were in her eyes, which parted thence
As pearls from diamonds dropped. In brief,
Sorrow would be a rarity most beloved
If all could so become it.

KENT Made she no verbal question?

GENT'MAN Faith, once or twice she heaved the name of 'father'
Pantingly forth, as if it pressed her heart;
Cried 'Sisters, sisters! Shame of ladies! Sisters!
Kent! Father! Sisters! What, i'th'storm? i'th'night?
Let pity not believe it!' There she shook
The holy water from her heavenly eyes
That clamour moistened; then away she started

To deal with grief alone.

KENT It is the stars,
The stars above us, govern our conditions;
Else one self mate and make could not beget
Such different issues. You spoke not with her since?

GENT'MAN No.

KENT Was this before the King returned?

GENT'MAN No, since.

KENT Well, sir, the poor distressèd Lear's i'th'town,
Who sometime, in his better tune, remembers
What we are come about, and by no means
Will yield to see his daughter.

GENT'MAN Why, good sir?

KENT A sovereign shame so elbows him: his own unkindness,
That stripped her from his benediction, turned her
To foreign casualties, gave her dear rights
To his dog-hearted daughters – these things sting
His mind so venomously that burning shame
Detains him from Cordelia.

GENT'MAN Alack, poor gentleman!

KENT Of Albany's and Cornwall's powers you heard not?

GENT'MAN 'Tis so, they are afoot.

KENT Well, sir, I'll bring you to our master Lear
And leave you to attend him. Some dear cause
Will in concealment wrap me up awhile;
When I am known aright, you shall not grieve
Lending me this acquaintance. I pray you go
Along with me. [*they go*

SCENE 4

The same

Enter, with drum and colours, CORDELIA, *Doctor, and Soldiers*

CORDELIA Alack, 'tis he! Why, he was met even now
As mad as the vexed sea, singing aloud,
Crowned with rank fumiter and furrow-weeds,
With hardocks, hemlock, nettles, cuckoo-flowers,
Darnel, and all the idle weeds that grow
In our sustaining corn. A century send forth;
Search every acre in the high-grown field,
And bring him to our eye. [*an Officer goes*
What can man's wisdom
In the restoring his bereavèd sense?
He that helps him take all my outward worth.

DOCTOR There is means, madam.
Our foster-nurse of nature is repose,
The which he lacks. That to provoke in him
Are many simples operative, whose power
Will close the eye of anguish.

CORDELIA All blest secrets,
All you unpublished virtues of the earth,
Spring with my tears! Be aidant and remediate
In the good man's distress! – Seek, seek for him,
Lest his ungoverned rage dissolve the life
That wants the means to lead it.

Enter Messenger

MESSENGER News, madam!
The British powers are marching hitherward.

CORDELIA 'Tis known before; our preparation stands
In expectation of them. O dear father,
It is thy business that I go about!
Therefore great France
My mourning and importuned tears hath pitied.
No blown ambition doth our arms incite,
But love, dear love, and our aged father's right.
Soon may I hear and see him! [*they go*

SCENE 5

Gloucester's castle

Enter REGAN *and* OSWALD

REGAN But are my brother's powers set forth?
OSWALD Ay, madam.
REGAN Himself in person there?
OSWALD Madam, with much ado.
Your sister is the better soldier.
REGAN Lord Edmund spake not with your lord at home?
OSWALD No, madam.
REGAN What might import my sister's letter to him?
OSWALD I know not, lady.
REGAN Faith, he is posted hence on serious matter.
It was great ignorance, Gloucester's eyes being out,
To let him live: where he arrives he moves
All hearts against us. Edmund, I think, is gone,
In pity of his misery, to dispatch
His nighted life; moreover, to descry
The strength o'th'enemy.
OSWALD I must needs after him, madam, with my letter.
REGAN Our troops set forth tomorrow. Stay with us;
The ways are dangerous.
OSWALD I may not, madam;
My lady charged my duty in this business.
REGAN Why should she write to Edmund? Might not you
Transport her purposes by word? Belike,
Some things, I know not what. I'll love thee much –
Let me unseal the letter.
OSWALD Madam, I had rather –
REGAN I know your lady does not love her husband;
I am sure of that: and at her late being here
She gave strange oeillades and most speaking looks
To noble Edmund. I know you are of her bosom.
OSWALD I, madam!
REGAN I speak in understanding: you are: I know't;
Therefore I do advise you take this note.

My lord is dead; Edmund and I have talked,
And more convenient is he for my hand
Than for your lady's. You may gather more.
If you do find him, pray you give him this;
And when your mistress hears thus much from you,
I pray desire her call her wisdom to her.
So fare you well.
If you do chance to hear of that blind traitor,
Preferment falls on him that cuts him off.

OSWALD Would I could meet him, madam! I should show
What party I do follow.

REGAN Fare thee well. [*they go*

SCENE 6

The country near Dover

'Enter GLOUCESTER, *and* EDGAR*' dressed like a peasant*

GLO'STER When shall I come to th' top of that same hill?

EDGAR You do climb up it now; look how we labour.

GLO'STER Methinks the ground is even.

EDGAR Horrible steep.
Hark, do you hear the sea?

GLO'STER No, truly.

EDGAR Why, then your other senses grow imperfect
By your eyes' anguish.

GLO'STER So may it be indeed.
Methinks thy voice is altered, and thou speak'st
In better phrase and matter than thou didst.

EDGAR You're much deceived: in nothing am I changed
But in my garments.

GLO'STER Methinks you're better spoken.

EDGAR Come on, sir, here's the place: stand still; how fearful
And dizzy 'tis to cast one's eyes so low!
The crows and choughs that wing the midway air
Show scarce so gross as beetles. Half way down
Hangs one that gathers samphire – dreadful trade!
Methinks he seems no bigger than his head.
The fishermen that walk upon the beach

Appear like mice: and yond tall anchoring bark
Diminished to her cock; her cock a buoy
Almost too small for sight. The murmuring surge,
That on th'unnumbered idle pebble chafes,
Cannot be heard so high. I'll look no more,
Lest my brain turn and the deficient sight
Topple down headlong.

GLO'STER Set me where you stand.

EDGAR Give me your hand. You are now within a foot
Of th'extreme verge. For all beneath the moon
Would I not leap upright.

GLO'STER Let go my hand.
Here, friend, 's another purse, in it a jewel
Well worth a poor man's taking. Fairies and gods
Prosper it with thee! Go thou further off:
Bid me farewell, and let me hear thee going.

EDGAR Now fare ye well, good sir.

GLO'STER With all my heart!

EDGAR Why I do trifle thus with his despair
Is done to cure it.

GLO'STER O you mighty gods! [*'he kneels'*
This world I do renounce, and in your sights
Shake patiently my great affliction off.
If I could bear it longer, and not fall
To quarrel with your great opposeless wills,
My snuff and loathèd part of nature should
Burn itself out. If Edgar live, O bless him!
Now, fellow, fare thee well.

EDGAR Gone, sir; farewell!
[*Gloucester falls forward, and swoons*
And yet I know not how conceit may rob
The treasury of life when life itself
Yields to the theft. Had he been where he thought,
By this had thought been past. [*aloud*] Alive, or dead?
Ho, you sir! Friend! Hear you, sir! Speak!
[*aside*] Thus might he pass indeed: yet he revives.
[*aloud*] What are you, sir?

GLO'STER Away, and let me die.

EDGAR Hadst thou been aught but gossamer, feathers, air,

(So many fathom down precipitating),
Thou'dst shivered like an egg: but thou dost breathe,
Hast heavy substance, bleed'st not, speak'st, art sound.
Ten masts at each make not the altitude
Which thou hast perpendicularly fell:
Thy life's a miracle. Speak yet again.

GLO'STER But have I fall'n, or no?

EDGAR From the dread summit of this chalky bourn.
Look up a-height; the shrill-gorged lark so far
Cannot be seen, or heard. Do but look up.

GLO'STER Alack, I have no eyes.
Is wretchedness deprived that benefit
To end itself by death? 'Twas yet some comfort
When misery could beguile the tyrant's rage
And frustrate his proud will.

EDGAR Give me your arm.
Up; so. How is't? Feel you your legs? You stand.

GLO'STER Too well, too well.

EDGAR This is above all strangeness.
Upon the crown o'th'cliff what thing was that
Which parted from you?

GLO'STER A poor unfortunate beggar.

EDGAR As I stood here below methought his eyes
Were two full moons; he had a thousand noses,
Horns whelked and waved like the enridgèd sea.
It was some fiend. Therefore, thou happy father,
Think that the clearest gods, who make them honours
Of men's impossibilities, have preserved thee.

GLO'STER I do remember now. Henceforth I'll bear
Affliction till it do cry out itself
'Enough, enough', and die. That thing you speak of,
I took it for a man. Often 'twould say
'The fiend, the fiend', – he led me to that place.

EDGAR Bear free and patient thoughts.

Enter LEAR, *crowned with wild flowers and nettles*

But who comes here?
The safer sense will ne'er accommodate
His master thus.

LEAR No, they cannot touch me for coining; I am the king himself.

EDGAR O thou side-piercing sight!

LEAR Nature's above art in that respect. There's your press-money. That fellow handles his bow like a crow-keeper: draw me a clothier's yard. Look, look, a mouse! Peace, peace; this piece of toasted cheese will do't. There' my gauntlet; I'll prove it on a giant. Bring up the brown bills. O, well flown, bird; i'th' clout, i'th' clout: hewgh! Give the word.

EDGAR Sweet marjoram.

LEAR Pass.

GLO'STER I know that voice.

LEAR Ha! Goneril with a white beard? They flattered me like a dog, and told me I had the white hairs in my beard ere the black ones were there. To say 'ay' and 'no' to everything that I said! 'Ay', and 'no' too, was no good divinity. When the rain came to wet me once and the wind to make me chatter, when the thunder would not peace at my bidding, there I found 'em, there I smelt 'em out! Go to, they are not men o' their words: they told me I was everything; 'tis a lie – I am not ague-proof.

GLO'STER The trick of that voice I do well remember:
Is't not the King?

LEAR [*touching his crown*] Ay, every inch a king!
When I do stare, see how the subject quakes.
I pardon that man's life. What was thy cause?
Adultery?
Thou shalt not die. Die for adultery? No!
The wren goes to 't, and the small gilded fly
Does lecher in my sight.
Let copulation thrive: for Gloucester's bastard son
Was kinder to his father than my daughters
Got 'tween the lawful sheets.
To 't, luxury, pell-mell! For I lack soldiers.
Behold yond simp'ring dame
Whose face between her forks presages snow,
That minces virtue and does shake the head

To hear of pleasure's name;
The fitchew nor the soiled horse goes to 't
With a more riotous appetite.
Down from the waist they are centaurs,
Though women all above.
But to the girdle do the gods inherit,
Beneath is all the fiend's.
There's hell, there's darkness, there is the sulphurous pit;
Burning, scalding, stench, consumption: fie, fie, fie,
pah, pah!
Give me an ounce of civet; good apothecary, sweeten my imagination: there's money for thee.

GLO'STER O, let me kiss that hand!

LEAR Let me wipe it first; it smells of mortality.

GLO'STER O ruined piece of Nature! This great world
Shall so wear out to naught. Dost thou know me?

LEAR I remember thine eyes well enough. Dost thou squiny at me?
No, do thy worst, blind Cupid; I'll not love.
Read thou this challenge; mark but the penning of it.

GLO'STER Were all thy letters suns, I could not see.

EDGAR I would not take this from report. It is,
And my heart breaks at it.

LEAR Read.

GLO'STER What! With the case of eyes?

LEAR O ho, are you there with me? No eyes in your head, nor no money in your purse? Your eyes are in a heavy case, your purse in a light; yet you see how this world goes.

GLO'STER I see it feelingly.

LEAR What! Art mad? A man may see how this world goes with no eyes. Look with thine ears: see how yond justice rails upon yond simple thief. Hark in thine ear: change places and, handy-dandy, which is the justice, which is the thief? Thou hast seen a farmer's dog bark at a beggar?

GLO'STER Ay, sir.

LEAR And the creature run from the cur? There thou mightst behold the great image of authority – a dog's obeyed in office.

Thou rascal beadle, hold thy bloody hand!
Why dost thou lash that whore? Strip thy own back;
Thou hotly lusts to use her in that kind
For which thou whipp'st her. The usurer hangs the
cozener.
Through tattered clothes great vices do appear;
Robes and furred gowns hide all. Plate sin with gold,
And the strong lance of justice hurtless breaks:
Arm it in rags, a pigmy's straw does pierce it.
None does offend, none, I say none. I'll able 'em;
Take that of me, my friend, who have the power
To seal th'accuser's lips. Get thee glass eyes
And, like a scurvy politician, seem
To see the things thou dost not. Now, now, now, now!
Pull off my boots: harder, harder! So.

EDGAR O, matter and impertinency mixed!
Reason in madness!

LEAR If thou wilt weep my fortunes, take my eyes.
I know thee well enough; thy name is Gloucester.
Thou must be patient. We came crying hither;
Thou know'st the first time that we smell the air
We wawl and cry. I will preach to thee: mark!

GLO'STER Alack, alack the day!

LEAR When we are born, we cry that we are come
To this great stage of fools. This' a good block!
[*taking off the crown*
It were a delicate stratagem to shoe
A troop of horse with felt: I'll put't in proof,
And when I have stol'n upon these son-in-laws,
Then kill, kill, kill, kill, kill, kill!

'Enter a Gentleman' with attendants

GENT'MAN O, here he is: lay hand upon him. Sir,
Your most dear daughter –

LEAR No rescue? What, a prisoner? I am even
The natural fool of Fortune. Use me well;
You shall have ransom. Let me have surgeons;
I am cut to th'brains.

GENT'MAN You shall have anything.

LEAR No seconds? All myself?
Why, this would make a man a man of salt,
To use his eyes for garden water-pots,
Ay, and laying autumn's dust. I will die bravely,
Like a smug bridegroom. What! I will be jovial.
Come, come, I am a king, masters, know you that?

GENT'MAN You are a royal one, and we obey you.

LEAR Then there's life in't. Come, an you get it you shall get it by running. Sa, sa, sa, sa.

[he runs away; attendants follow

GENT'MAN A sight most pitiful in the meanest wretch,
Past speaking of in a king! Thou hast one daughter
Who redeems nature from the general curse
Which twain have brought her to.

EDGAR Hail, gentle sir!

GENT'MAN Sir, speed you. What's your will?

EDGAR Do you hear aught, sir, of a battle toward?

GENT'MAN Most sure, and vulgar: everyone hears that,
Which can distinguish sound.

EDGAR But, by your favour,
How near's the other army?

GENT'MAN Near, and on speedy foot: the main descry
Stands on the hourly thought.

EDGAR I thank you, sir: that's all.

GENT'MAN Though that the queen on special cause is here,
Her army is moved on.

EDGAR I thank you, sir.

[Gentleman goes

GLO'STER You ever-gentle gods, take my breath from me;
Let not my worser spirit tempt me again
To die before you please!

EDGAR Well pray you, father.

GLO'STER Now, good sir, what are you?

EDGAR A most poor man, made tame to Fortune's blows,
Who, by the art of known and feeling sorrows,
Am pregnant to good pity. Give me your hand;
I'll lead you to some biding.

GLO'STER Hearty thanks:
The bounty and the benison of Heaven

To boot, and boot!

Enter OSWALD

OSWALD A proclaimed prize! Most happy!
That eyeless head of thine was first framed flesh
To raise my fortunes. Thou old unhappy traitor,
Briefly thyself remember; the sword is out
That must destroy thee.

GLO'STER Now let thy friendly hand
Put strength enough to't. [*Edgar interposes*

OSWALD Wherefore, bold peasant,
Dar'st thou support a published traitor? Hence,
Lest that th'infection of his fortune take
Like hold on thee. Let go his arm.

EDGAR Chill not let go, zir, without vurther cagion.

OSWALD Let go, slave, or thou diest.

EDGAR Good gentleman, go your gate, and let poor voke pass. An 'chud ha' bin zwaggered out of my life, 'twould not ha' bin zo long as 'tis by a vortnight. Nay, come not near th'old man; keep out, che vor' ye, or Ice try whither your costard or my ballow be the harder. Chill be plain with you.

OSWALD Out, dunghill! [*'they fight'*

EDGAR Chill pick your teeth, zir. Come; no matter vor your foins. [*Oswald falls*

OSWALD Slave, thou hast slain me. Villain, take my purse:
If ever thou wilt thrive, bury my body,
And give the letters which thou find'st about me
To Edmund, Earl of Gloucester; seek him out
Upon the British party. O, untimely death! Death!
[*'he dies'*

EDGAR I know thee well – a serviceable villain,
As duteous to the vices of thy mistress
As badness would desire.

GLO'STER What, is he dead?

EDGAR Sit you down, father; rest you.
Let's see these pockets; the letters that he speaks of
May be my friends. He's dead; I am only sorry
He had no other deathsman. Let us see.
Leave, gentle wax; and, manners, blame us not:

To know our enemies' minds we rip their hearts;
Their papers is more lawful. [*'reads the letter'*

Let our reciprocal vows be rememb'red. You have many opportunities to cut him off: if your will want not, time and place will be fruitfully offered. There is nothing done if he return the conqueror: then am I the prisoner, and his bed my gaol; from the loathed warmth wherof deliver me, and supply the place for your labour.

Your (wife, so I would say) affectionate servant,
Goneril.

O indistinguished space of woman's will!
A plot upon her virtuous husband's life,
And the exchange my brother! Here in the sands
Thee I'll rake up, thou post unsanctified
Of murderous lechers; and in the mature time
With this ungracious paper strike the sight
Of the death-practised Duke. For him 'tis well
That of thy death and business I can tell.

GLO'STER The King is mad; how stiff is my vile sense
That I stand up and have ingenious feeling
Of my huge sorrows! Better I were distract:
So should my thoughts be severed from my griefs,
And woes by wrong imaginations lose
The knowledge of themselves. [*'drum afar off'*

EDGAR Give me your hand:
Far off methinks I hear the beaten drum.
Come, father, I'll bestow you with a friend. [*they go*

SCENE 7

A tent in the French camp

Enter CORDELIA, KENT, DOCTOR *and Gentleman*

CORDELIA O thou good Kent, how shall I live and work
To match thy goodness? My life will be too short,
And every measure fail me.
KENT To be acknowledged, madam, is o'er-paid.
All my reports go with the modest truth;
Nor more, nor clipped, but so.
CORDELIA Be better suited:
These weeds are memories of those worser hours;
I prithee put them off.
KENT Pardon, dear madam;
Yet to be known shortens my made intent.
My boon I make it that you know me not
Till time, and I, think meet.
CORDELIA Then be't so, my good lord.
[*to the Doctor*] How does the King?
DOCTOR Madam, sleeps still.
CORDELIA O you kind gods,
Cure this great breach in his abusèd nature!
Th'untuned and jarring senses, O, wind up
Of this child-changèd father!
DOCTOR So please your Majesty
That we may wake the king? He hath slept long.
CORDELIA Be governed by your knowledge, and proceed
I'th'sway of your own will. Is he arrayed?
GENT'MAN Ay, madam: in the heaviness of sleep
We put fresh garments on him.
DOCTOR Be by, good madam, when we do awake him;
I doubt not of his temperance.
CORDELIA Very well.

'Enter LEAR *asleep in a chair carried by servants',*
clad in his royal robes. Soft music

DOCTOR Please you draw near. Louder the music there!
CORDELIA O my dear father, restoration hang

Thy medicine on my lips, and let this kiss
Repair those violent harms that my two sisters
Have in thy reverence made!

KENT Kind and dear princess!

CORDELIA Had you not been their father, these white flakes
Did challenge pity of them. Was this a face
To be opposed against the warring winds?
To stand against the deep dread-bolted thunder
In the most terrible and nimble stroke
Of quick cross lightning? To watch – poor perdu! –
With this thin helm? Mine enemy's dog,
Though he had bit me, should have stood that night
Against my fire; and wast thou fain, poor father,
To hovel thee with swine and rogues forlorn,
In short and musty straw? Alack, alack!
'Tis wonder that thy life and wits at once
Had not concluded all. He wakes; speak to him.

DOCTOR Madam, do you; 'tis fittest.

CORDELIA How does my royal lord? How fares your Majesty?

LEAR You do me wrong to take me out o'th'grave:
Thou art a soul in bliss; but I am bound
Upon a wheel of fire, that mine own tears
Do scald like molten lead.

CORDELIA Sir, do you know me?

LEAR You are a spirit, I know; when did you die?

CORDELIA Still, still, far wide!

DOCTOR He's scarce awake; let him alone awhile.

LEAR Where have I been? Where am I? Fair daylight?
I am mightily abused; I should e'en die with pity
To see another thus. I know not what to say.
I will not swear these are my hands: let's see;
I feel this pin prick. Would I were assured
Of my condition!

CORDELIA [*kneels*] O, look upon me, sir,
And hold your hand in benediction o'er me;
No, sir, you must not kneel. [*seeing him about to rise*

LEAR Pray do not mock me;
I am a very foolish fond old man,
Fourscore and upward, not an hour more nor less;

And, to deal plainly,
I fear I am not in my perfect mind.
Methinks I should know you, and know this man,
Yet I am doubtful: for I am mainly ignorant
What place this is; and all the skill I have
Remembers not these garments, nor I know not
Where I did lodge last night. Do not laugh at me,
For (as I am a man) I think this lady
To be my child Cordelia.

CORDELIA And so I am: I am!

LEAR Be your tears wet? Yes, faith: I pray weep not.
If you have poison for me, I will drink it:
I know you do not love me, for your sisters
Have (as I do remember) done me wrong;
You have some cause; they have not.

CORDELIA No cause, no cause.

LEAR Am I in France?

KENT In your own kingdom, sir.

LEAR Do not abuse me.

DOCTOR Be comforted, good madam: the great rage,
You see, is killed in him; and yet it is danger
To make him even o'er the time he has lost.
Desire him to go in; trouble him no more
Till further settling.

CORDELIA Will't please your Highness walk?

LEAR You must bear with me. Pray you now, forget and forgive; I am old and foolish. [*all go but Kent and Gentleman*

GENT'MAN Holds it true, sir, that the Duke of Cornwall was so slain?

KENT Most certain, sir.

GENT'MAN Who is conductor of his people?

KENT As 'tis said, the bastard son of Gloucester.

GENT'MAN They say Edgar, his banished son, is with the Earl of Kent in Germany.

KENT Report is changeable. 'Tis time to look about; the powers of the kingdom approach apace.

GENT'MAN The arbitrement is like to be bloody. Fare you well, sir. [*goes*

KENT My point and period will be throughly wrought,
Or well or ill, as this day's battle's fought. [*goes*

ACT 5 SCENE 1

The British camp near Dover

'Enter, with drum and colours, EDMUND, REGAN, *officers, and soldiers'*

EDMUND Know of the Duke if his last purpose hold,
Or whether since he is advised by aught
To change the course; he's full of alteration
And self-reproving; bring his constant pleasure.
[to an officer, who goes out

REGAN Our sister's man is certainly miscarried.

EDMUND 'Tis to be doubted, madam.

REGAN Now, sweet lord,
You know the goodness I intend upon you.
Tell me – but truly – but then speak the truth –
Do you not love my sister?

EDMUND In honoured love.

REGAN But have you never found my brother's way
To the forfended place?

EDMUND That thought abuses you.

REGAN I am doubtful that you have been conjunct
And bosomed with her, as far as we call hers.

EDMUND No, by mine honour, madam.

REGAN I never shall endure her: dear my lord,
Be not familiar with her.

EDMUND Fear me not.
She and the Duke her husband!

'Enter, with drum and colours, ALBANY, GONERIL, *soldiers'*

GONERIL I had rather lose the battle than that sister
Should loosen him and me.

ALBANY Our very loving sister, well be-met.
Sir, this I hear: the King is come to his daughter,
With others whom the rigour of our state
Forced to cry out. Where I could not be honest,
I never yet was valiant: for this business,
It touches us as France invades our land,
Not bolds the King, with others whom, I fear,

Most just and heavy causes make oppose.

EDMUND Sir, you speak nobly.

REGAN Why is this reasoned?

GONERIL Combine together 'gainst the enemy;
For these domestic and particular broils
Are not the question here.

ALBANY Let's then determine
With th'ancient of war on our proceeding.

EDMUND I shall attend you presently at your tent.

REGAN Sister, you'll go with us?

GONERIL No.

REGAN Tis most convenient; pray go with us.

GONERIL O ho, I know the riddle. – I will go.

As they are going out, enter EDGAR *disguised*

EDGAR If e'er your Grace had speech with man so poor,
Hear me one word.

ALBANY I'll overtake you.
[*all but Albany and Edgar depart*
Speak.

EDGAR Before you fight the battle, ope this letter.
If you have victory, let the trumpet sound
For him that brought it: wretched though I seem,
I can produce a champion that will prove
What is avouchèd there. If you miscarry,
Your business of the world hath so an end,
And machination ceases. Fortune love you!

ALBANY Stay till I have read the letter.

EDGAR I was forbid it.
When time shall serve, let but the herald cry,
And I'll appear again.

ALBANY Why, fare thee well;
I will o'erlook thy paper. [*Edgar goes*

EDMUND *returns*

EDMUND The enemy's in view; draw up your powers.
Here is the guess of their true strength and forces,
By diligent discovery; but your haste
Is now urged on you.

ALBANY We will greet the time. [*he goes*

EDMUND To both these sisters have I sworn my love;
Each jealous of the other, as the stung
Are of the adder. Which of them shall I take?
Both? One? Or neither? Neither can be enjoyed
If both remain alive: to take the widow
Exasperates, makes mad her sister Goneril;
And hardly shall I carry out my side,
Her husband being alive. Now then, we'll use
His countenance for the battle, which being done,
Let her who would be rid of him devise
His speedy taking off. As for the mercy
Which he intends to Lear and to Cordelia,
The battle done, and they within our power,
Shall never see his pardon: for my state
Stands on me to defend, not to debate. [*he goes*

SCENE 2

A field between the two camps

'Alarum'. Enter the French army, CORDELIA *leading* LEAR *by the hand, and pass by*

'Enter EDGAR *and* GLOUCESTER*'*

EDGAR Here, father, take the shadow of this tree
For your good host. Pray that the right may thrive.
If ever I return to you again,
I'll bring you comfort.

GLO'STER Grace go with you, sir! [*Edgar goes*

'Alarum' heard from the battlefield hard by, and later a 'retreat'

Enter EDGAR

EDGAR Away, old man; give me thy hand, away!
King Lear hath lost, he and his daughter ta'en.
Give me thy hand; come on!

GLO'STER No further, sir; a man may rot even here.

EDGAR What, in ill thoughts again? Men must endure
Their going hence, even as their coming hither;
Ripeness is all. Come on.

GLO'STER And that's true too. [*they go*

SCENE 3

The British camp near Dover

'Enter in conquest with drum and colours, EDMUND; LEAR *and* CORDELIA *as prisoners; soldiers, Captain*

EDMUND Some officers take them away: good guard,
Until their greater pleasures first be known
That are to censure them.

CORDELIA We are not the first
Who with best meaning have incurred the worst.
For thee, oppressèd King, I am cast down;
Myself could else out-frown false Fortune's frown.
Shall we not see these daughters and these sisters?

LEAR No, no, no, no! Come, let's away to prison:
We two alone will sing like birds i'th'cage;
When thou dost ask me blessing, I'll kneel down
And ask of thee forgiveness. So we'll live,
And pray, and sing, and tell old tales, and laugh
At gilded butterflies, and hear poor rogues
Talk of court news; and we'll talk with them too –
Who loses and who wins, who's in, who's out –
And take upon 's the mystery of things,
As if we were God's spies; and we'll wear out,
In a walled prison, packs and sects of great ones
That ebb and flow by th'moon.

EDMUND Take them away.

LEAR Upon such sacrifices, my Cordelia,
The gods themselves throw incense. Have I caught thee?
He that parts us shall bring a brand from heaven
And fire us hence like foxes. Wipe thine eyes;
The good-years shall devour them, flesh and fell,
Ere they shall make us weep! We'll see 'em starved first.
Come. [*Lear and Cordelia are led away under guard*

EDMUND Come hither, captain; hark.
Take thou this note;
[*giving a paper*] go follow them to prison.
One step I have advanced thee; if thou dost

As this instructs thee, thou dost make thy way
To noble fortunes. Know thou this, that men
Are as the time is: to be tender-minded
Does not become a sword: thy great employment
Will not bear question; either say thou'lt do't,
Or thrive by other means.

CAPTAIN I'll do't, my lord.

EDMUND About it; and write happy when thou'st done.
Mark – I say instantly; and carry it so
As I have set it down.

CAPTAIN I cannot draw a cart, nor eat dried oats;
If it be man's work I'll do't. *[he goes*

'Flourish. Enter ALBANY, GONERIL, REGAN, *Soldiers'*

ALBANY Sir, you have showed today your valiant strain,
And Fortune led you well. You have the captives
Who were the opposites of this day's strife:
I do require them of you, so to use them
As we shall find their merits and our safety
May equally determine.

EDMUND Sir, I thought it fit
To send the old and miserable King
To some retention and appointed guard;
Whose age had charms in it, whose title more,
To pluck the common bosom on his side
And turn our impressed lances in our eyes
Which do command them. With him I sent the Queen,
My reason all the same; and they are ready
Tomorrow, or at further space, t'appear
Where you shall hold your session. At this time
We sweat and bleed: the friend hath lost his friend;
And the best quarrels, in the heat, are cursed
By those that feel their sharpness.
The question of Cordelia and her father
Requires a fitter place.

ALBANY Sir, by your patience,
I hold you but a subject of this war,
Not as a brother.

REGAN That's as we list to grace him.

Methinks our pleasure might have been demanded
Ere you had spoke so far. He led our powers,
Bore the commission of my place and person
The which immediacy may well stand up
And call itself your brother.

GONERIL Not so hot!
In his own grace he doth exalt himself
More than in your addition.

REGAN In my rights
By me invested, he compeers the best.

ALBANY That were the most if he should husband you.

REGAN Jesters do oft prove prophets.

GONERIL Holla, holla!
That eye that told you so looked but asquint.

REGAN Lady, I am not well, else I should answer
From a full-flowing stomach. General,
Take thou my soldiers, prisoners, patrimony:
Dispose of them, of me; the walls are thine.
Witness the world that I create thee here
My lord and master.

GONERIL Mean you to enjoy him?

ALBANY The let-alone lies not in your good will.

EDMUND Nor in thine, lord.

ALBANY Half-blooded fellow, yes.

REGAN [*to Edmund*]
Let the drum strike; and prove my title thine.

ALBANY Stay yet; hear reason. Edmund, I arrest thee
On capital treason, and, in thy attaint,
[*pointing to Goneril*
This gilded serpent. For your claim, fair sister,
I bar it in the interest of my wife;
'Tis she is sub-contracted to this lord,
And I, her husband, contradict your banns.
If you will marry, make your loves to me;
My lady is bespoke.

GONERIL An interlude!

ALBANY Thou art armed, Gloucester: let the trumpet sound;
If none appear to prove upon thy person
Thy heinous, manifest, and many treasons,

There is my pledge! [*throwing down a glove*
I'll make it on thy heart,
Ere I taste bread, thou art in nothing less
Than I have here proclaimed thee.

REGAN Sick, O sick!

(GONERIL If not, I'll ne'er trust medicine.

EDMUND There's my exchange! [*throwing down a glove*
What in the world he is
That names me traitor, villain-like he lies.
Call by the trumpet; he that dares approach,
On him, on you – who not? – I will maintain
My truth and honour firmly.

ALBANY A herald, ho!

EDMUND A herald, ho, a herald!

ALBANY Trust to thy single virtue; for the soldiers,
All levied in my name, have in my name
Took their discharge.

REGAN My sickness grows upon me.

ALBANY She is not well; convey her to my tent.
[*Regan is led away*

Enter a HERALD

Come hither, herald – Let the trumpet sound –
And read out this. [*a trumpet sounds*

HERALD [*reads*] If any man of quality or degree within the lists of the army will maintain upon Edmund, supposed Earl of Gloucester, that he is a manifold traitor, let him appear by the third sound of the trumpet. He is bold in his defence. [*'first trumpet'*
Again! [*'second trumpet'*
Again! [*'third trumpet'*

An answering trumpet is heard. Enter EDGAR, *in armour*

ALBANY Ask him his purposes – why he appears
Upon this call o'th'trumpet.

HERALD What are you?
Your name, your quality, and why you answer
This present summons?

EDGAR Know my name is lost;
By treason's tooth bare-gnawn and canker-bit:

Yet am I noble as the adversary
I come to cope.

ALBANY Which is that adversary?

EDGAR What's he that speaks for Edmund, Earl of Gloucester?

EDMUND Himself: what say'st thou to him?

EDGAR Draw thy sword,
That, if my speech offend a noble heart,
Thy arm may do thee justice; here is mine:
Behold, it is the privilege of mine honours,
My oath, and my profession. I protest,
Maugre thy strength, place, youth, and eminence,
Despite thy victor-sword and fire-new fortune,
Thy valour and thy heart, thou art a traitor,
False to thy gods, thy brother, and thy father,
Conspirant 'gainst this high illustrious prince,
And, from th'extremest upward of thy head
To the descent and dust below thy foot,
A most toad-spotted traitor. Say thou no,
This sword, this arm, and my best spirits are bent
To prove upon thy heart, whereto I speak,
Thou liest.

EDMUND In wisdom I should ask thy name;
But since thy outside looks so fair and warlike,
And that thy tongue some say of breeding breathes,
What safe and nicely I might well delay
By rule of knighthood, I disdain and spurn.
Back do I toss these treasons to thy head,
With the hell-hated lie o'erwhelm thy heart,
Which, for they yet glance by and scarcely bruise,
This sword of mine shall give them instant way
Where they shall rest for ever. Trumpets, speak!

'Alarums'. They fight. Edmund falls

ALBANY Save him, save him!

GONERIL This is practice, Gloucester:
By th' law of war thou wast not bound to answer
An unknown opposite: thou art not vanquished,
But cozened and beguiled.

ALBANY Shut your mouth, dame,

Or with this paper shall I stop it. –
[*to Edgar*] Hold, sir –
[*showing Goneril her name on the letter*
Thou worse than any name, read thine own evil.
No tearing, lady! I perceive you know it.

GONERIL Say if I do – the laws are mine, not thine;
Who can arraign me for't?

ALBANY Most monstrous! O!
Know'st thou this paper?

GONERIL Ask me not what I know. [*goes*

ALBANY Go after her: she's desperate; govern her. [*officer goes*

EDMUND What you have charged me with, that have I done,
And more, much more; the time will bring it out:
'Tis past, and so am I. But what art thou
That hast this fortune on me? If thou'rt noble,
I do forgive thee.

EDGAR Let's exchange charity.
I am no less in blood than thou art, Edmund;
If more, the more thou'st wronged me.
My name is Edgar, and thy father's son.
The gods are just, and of our pleasant vices
Make instruments to plague us:
The dark and vicious place where thee he got
Cost him his eyes.

EDMUND Thou'st spoken right, 'tis true.
The wheel is come full circle; I am here.

ALBANY [*to Edgar*] Methought thy very gait did prophesy
A royal nobleness: I must embrace thee;
Let sorrow split my heart if ever I
Did hate thee or thy father.

EDGAR Worthy prince, I know't.

ALBANY Where have you hid yourself?
How have you known the miseries of your father?

EDGAR By nursing them, my lord. List a brief tale;
And when 'tis told, O that my heart would burst!
The bloody proclamation to escape
That followed me so near (O, our life's sweetness!
That we the pain of death would hourly die,
Rather than die at once!) taught me to shift

Into a madman's rags, t'assume a semblance
That very dogs disdained: and in this habit
Met I my father with his bleeding rings,
Their precious stones new lost; became his guide,
Led him, begged for him, saved him from despair;
Never (O fault!) revealed myself unto him
Until some half hour past, when I was armed.
Not sure, though hoping, of this good success,
I asked his blessing, and from first to last
Told him our pilgrimage. But his flawed heart
(Alack, too weak the conflict to support)
'Twixt two extremes of passion, joy and grief,
Burst smilingly.

EDMUND This speech of yours hath moved me,
And shall perchance do good: but speak you on;
You look as you had something more to say.

ALBANY If there be more, more woeful, hold it in,
For I am almost ready to dissolve,
Hearing of this.

EDGAR This would have seemed a period
To such as love not sorrow; but another,
To amplify too much, would make much more,
And top extremity. Whilst I
Was big in clamour, came there in a man,
Who, having seen me in my worst estate,
Shunned my abhorred society; but then, finding
Who 'twas that so endured, with his strong arms
He fastened on my neck and bellowed out
As he'd burst heaven: threw him on my father;
Told the most piteous tale of Lear and him
That ever ear received, which in recounting
His grief grew puissant and the strings of life
Began to crack: twice then the trumpets sounded,
And there I left him tranced.

ALBANY But who was this?

EDGAR Kent, sir, the banished Kent, who in disguise
Followed his enemy king and did him service
Improper for a slave.

'Enter a Gentleman', 'with a bloody knife'

GENT'MAN Help, help! O help!

EDGAR What kind of help?

ALBANY Speak, man!

EDGAR What means this bloody knife?

GENT'MAN 'Tis hot, it smokes;
It came even from the heart of – O, she's dead!

ALBANY Who dead? Speak, man!

GENT'MAN Your lady, sir, your lady: and her sister
By her is poisoned; she confesses it.

EDMUND I was contracted to them both; all three
Now marry in an instant.

EDGAR Here comes Kent.

Enter KENT

ALBANY Produce the bodies, be they alive or dead.
[*Gentleman goes*
This judgment of the heavens, that makes us tremble,
Touches us not with pity. [*notices Kent*] O, is this he?
The time will not allow the compliment
Which very manners urges.

KENT I am come
To bid my king and master aye good night.
Is he not here?

ALBANY Great thing of us forgot!
Speak, Edmund; where's the king? And where's Cordelia?
[*'The bodies of Goneril and Regan are brought in'*
See'st thou this object, Kent?

KENT Alack, why thus?

EDMUND Yet Edmund was beloved:
The one the other poisoned for my sake,
And after slew herself.

ALBANY Even so. Cover their faces.

EDMUND I pant for life. Some good I mean to do,
Despite of mine own nature. Quickly send
(Be brief in it) to th' castle, for my writ
Is on the life of Lear and on Cordelia.
Nay, send in time!

ALBANY Run, run, O run!

EDGAR To who, my lord? – Who has the office? Send
Thy token of reprieve.

EDMUND Well thought on. Take my sword,
Give it to the captain.

ALBANY Haste thee, for thy life!
[Edgar hurries forth

EDMUND He hath commission from thy wife and me
To hang Cordelia in the prison and
To lay the blame upon her own despair,
That she fordid herself.

ALBANY The gods defend her!
Bear him hence awhile. *[Edmund is borne off*

'Enter LEAR *with* CORDELIA *in his arms',* EDGAR, *Captain, and others following*

LEAR Howl, howl, howl! O, you are men of stones!
Had I your tongues and eyes, I'd use them so
That heaven's vault should crack! She's gone for ever.
I know when one is dead, and when one lives;
She's dead as earth. Lend me a looking-glass;
If that her breath will mist or stain the stone,
Why, then she lives.

KENT Is this the promised end?

EDGAR Or image of that horror.

ALBANY Fall and cease!

LEAR This feather stirs – she lives! If it be so,
It is a chance which does redeem all sorrows
That ever I have felt.

KENT [*kneeling*] O my good master!

LEAR Prithee away!

EDGAR 'Tis noble Kent, your friend.

LEAR A plague upon you, murderers, traitors all!
I might have saved her; now she's gone for ever!
Cordelia, Cordelia, stay a little – Ha?
What is't thou say'st? – Her voice was ever soft,
Gentle and low, an excellent thing in woman –
I killed the slave that was a-hanging thee.

OFFICER 'Tis true, my lords, he did.

LEAR Did I not, fellow?

I have seen the day, with my good biting falchion
I would have made them skip: I am old now,
And these same crosses spoil me. Who are you?
Mine eyes are not o' th' best; I'll tell you straight.

KENT If Fortune brag of two she loved and hated,
One of them we behold.

LEAR This is a dull sight. Are you not Kent?

KENT The same
Your servant Kent. Where is your servant Caius?

LEAR He's a good fellow, I can tell you that;
He'll strike, and quickly too. He's dead and rotten.

KENT No, my good lord; I am the very man –

LEAR I'll see that straight.

KENT That from your first of difference and decay
Have followed your sad steps –

LEAR You are welcome hither.

KENT Nor no man else. All's cheerless, dark, and deadly.
Your eldest daughters have fordone themselves,
And desperately are dead.

LEAR Ay, so I think.

ALBANY He knows not what he says, and vain is it
That we present us to him.

EDGAR Very bootless.

'Enter Captain'

CAPTAIN Edmund is dead, my lord.

ALBANY That's but a trifle here.
You lords and noble friends, know our intent:
What comfort to this great decay may come
Shall be applied. For us, we will resign,
During the life of this old majesty,
To him our absolute power;
[*to Edgar and Kent*] to you your rights,
With boot and such addition as your honours
Have more than merited. All friends shall taste
The wages of their virtue, and all foes
The cup of their deservings. O see, see!

LEAR And my poor fool is hanged! No, no, no life!
Why should a dog, a horse, a rat have life,

And thou no breath at all? Thou'lt come no more,
Never, never, never, never, never!
Pray you, undo this button. Thank you, sir.
Do you see this? Look on her! Look – her lips!
Look there, look there!

EDGAR He faints! My lord, my lord!

KENT Break, heart! I prithee break.

EDGAR Look up, my lord.

KENT Vex not his ghost: O, let him pass; he hates him,
That would upon the rack of this tough world
Stretch him out longer. [*Lear dies*

EDGAR He is gone indeed.

KENT The wonder is he hath endured so long;
He but usurped his life.

ALBANY Bear them from hence. Our present business
Is general woe.
[*to Kent and Edgar*] Friends of my soul, you twain
Rule in this realm, and the gored state sustain.

KENT I have a journey, sir, shortly to go:
My master calls me; I must not say no.

EDGAR The weight of this sad time we must obey;
Speak what we feel, not what we ought to say.
The oldest hath borne most: we that are young
Shall never see so much, nor live so long.

[*The bodies are borne out, all follow with 'a death march'*

MACBETH

INTRODUCTION

Macbeth is a dark thriller of a play, considerably shorter than the other four tragedies in this volume. Its highly compressed and bloody story is derived from historical sources, particularly Holinshed's *Chronicles of Scotland*, and it was written in 1606. In its treatment of Scottish history, the play is often seen to address the interests of James I, who gave his patronage to Shakespeare's company in 1603. James traced his ancestry from Banquo, and was well known to be interested in witchcraft, and *Macbeth* is a document of the relationship between the king and his players. In the play, Macbeth is a Scottish lord highly regarded for his valour in his country's wars. With his friend Banquo, he meets three witches who prophesy that he will become king, and that Banquo's children shall be kings. Macbeth and his wife kill the king, Duncan, and Macbeth becomes king. To safeguard his position of power, he arranges for Banquo to be killed, although Fleance, Banquo's son, escapes. Other murders are also ordered by the desperate yet haunted Macbeth. In England, forces loyal to Duncan's sons gather. Meeting the witches again, Macbeth feels reassured by their forecast, but their riddling prophecies have misled him. Lady Macbeth commits suicide, and in the battle Macbeth is killed by Macduff, whose wife and children the king has murdered. Duncan's heir Malcolm is crowned king of Scotland.

Macbeth is a tragedy preoccupied with the nature of what is manly. Lady Macbeth taunts her husband with 'When you durst do it, then you were a man' in response to his 'I dare do all that may become a man; Who dares do more is none.' (1.7.46–49) Physical prowess and moral scruple are in conflict as alternative indices of masculinity. The two murderers summoned by Macbeth to dispatch Banquo call themselves men, but Macbeth describes them as men only in so much as 'hounds and greyhounds, mongrels, spaniels, curs, Shoughs, water-rugs, and demi-wolves' (3.1.92–93) are all dogs. Lady Macbeth asks 'Are you a man?' (3.4.58) when it seems her husband has lost his wits in the banquet, and Macbeth uses the same formulation when the ghost of Banquo disappears from his sight: 'I am a man again' (3.4.108). Malcolm urges Macduff to 'Dispute it like a man', when he hears of the slaughter of his family, but Macduff's response is to propose manliness as the fusing of the physical and emotional: 'I shall do so; But I must also feel it as a man' (4.3.220–21). Manliness is sometimes synonymous with humanity, sometimes with extreme brutality, in a conflict of meanings which represent, in miniature, the complex value-systems of the warlike society of Macbeth's Scotland.

The play is also concerned with women's role in men's lives. From the destructive prophecies of the witches and their bubbling cauldron which parodies natural reproduction in its catalogue of ingredients (Orson Welles' 1946 film of the play develops this suggestion in opening with the witches and the cauldron, from which they shape an effigy of Macbeth in a grotesque birth-ritual), to Lady Macbeth's denial of her femininity, the female is presented as monstrous and dangerous. Lady Macbeth calls on spirits to 'unsex' her (1.5.40) and to take away her maternal qualities: 'Come to my woman's breasts And take my milk for gall' (1.5.46–47). Berating Macbeth for his cowardice, she declares: 'I have given suck, and know How tender 'tis to love the babe that milks me' (1.7.54–55), but this child and the brightly chattering son of Macduff are evoked only in order to be murdered, either symbolically by Lady Macbeth who promises herself willing to 'dash[. . .] the brains out', or actually in the case of young Macduff. The play does not mention any children of the Macbeth line – the child to whom Lady Macbeth says she gave suck is never mentioned again – and this absence reinforces the unnatural sterility of his quest for power. It is Banquo who will found a dynasty, the witches prophesy, whereas Macbeth's is a 'fruitless crown' and 'barren sceptre' (3.1.60–61). Children play an important symbolic role in the play: the witches produce the apparitions of a 'bloody child' and a child-king; Macbeth describes his infirmity as 'the baby of a girl' (3.4.106); Hecate describes him as the witches' 'wayward son' (3.5.11), and even Lady Macbeth describes her husband as unweaned from goodness: 'too full o' th' milk of human kindness' (1.5.16). The play's concern with succession and royal dynasties is partly a feature of the circumstances of its original presentation. As the eighth generation of Banquo's line, James I was implied as the latest in the 'show of eight kings' (stage direction following 4.1.111) shown to Macbeth by the witches. (Part of the play's anxieties about motherhood may also refer to James' own mother, Mary Queen of Scots, who was executed by Elizabeth I and was thus an unsuitable connection for the new king and one whose influence was to be mistrusted and minimised). Given the play's apprehensive representation of women, therefore, it is entirely appropriate that Macbeth's nemesis should take the form of Macduff. Macduff's invincibility is signalled by the circumstances of his birth: the witches' prophecy that 'none of woman born Shall harm Macbeth' (4.1.80–81) is revealed, via the expedient of Macduff's birth by caesarian section 'from his mother's womb Untimely ripped', to be misleading. Macduff alone seems to have bypassed the inevitable vulnerability of men to women and to have rendered himself immune to women's influence.

Unlike the other tragic characters, Macbeth's crimes are all too obvious. He murders Duncan and causes many others to be murdered. *Macbeth* is not particularly concerned with the events which lead up to the crime, not over-interested in motive or explanation as, say *Othello* or *Hamlet* might be seen to be, but rather with observing and diagnosing the psychological effects of crime on the criminal. It might be assumed, then, that his characterisation offers a kind of moral clarity absent from the other plays. This is not so, however. In his soliloquies, Macbeth represents himself as a divided and increasingly tortured personality. He recognises his own flaw – his 'vaulting ambition, which o'erleaps itself' (1.7.27) – and when the witches' reassurances are revealed to be worthless, he resolves to fight on, in a reversion to the kind of valour which marked the admiring reports about him in the second scene of the play. Indeed, like the Thane of Cawdor whose title he gathers up as the first step towards greatness, it could be said of Macbeth that 'nothing in his life Became him like the leaving it' (1.4.7–8). The extent to which Macbeth is entirely culpable for his crimes is also arguable. The role of the witches in fanning his ambitious desires may be interpreted either as decisive or reflective. Do they control him as their puppet, encouraging him to kill Duncan and seize the crown? Or do they represent his hidden desires for power? If the former, their supernatural intervention may discharge Macbeth of some of the responsibility for the play's carnage; if the latter, they can be seen to make the play into a darker and more unsettling exploration of the psyche. If the witches are external agents, the fact that they do not reappear may be problematic – they are still roaming the blasted heath with apparently malevolent intent. If they are manifestations of Macbeth's own wishes, it is interesting that Banquo also sees them. In Holinshed's *Chronicles*, Shakespeare's major source for the play, Macbeth and Banquo are partners in crime. Macbeth's individual crimes also need to be seen in the context of a bloody and violent society, which valorises and rewards bloodthirsty brutality. Macbeth's first honour is given him by the king in recognition of his exploits, when his sword 'Smoked with bloody execution' and, without any ceremony, he 'unseamed [Macdonwald] from the nave to the chops' (1.2.18, 22). It is arguable that Macbeth's subsequent promotions are achieved through that same murderous instinct.

The language of the play is preoccupied with images of darkness. Actual darkness cloaks the murder of Duncan, metaphorical darkness spurs the deed. Lady Macbeth invokes 'thick night' and the 'dunnest smoke of hell' to shield her actions from view of heaven. Ironically, it is night-time when the true inescapability of what she has done is revealed; in her sleep-walking, the embodiment of Macbeth's murder of sleep (2.2.36), night becomes the theatre of the conscience, in which she can gain no forgetful peace. Macbeth reiterates this invocation, calling on 'seeling night' whose 'black agents' will undertake his work (3.2.46–53). It is night when Macbeth and Banquo meet in 2.1, and again when Banquo is murdered. Macbeth ponders on this hour when 'o'er the one half-world Nature seems dead and wicked dreams abuse The curtained sleep' (2.1.49–51). After the Macbeths' regicide, Ross describes an unnaturally dark day when 'dark night strangles the travelling lamp' and 'darkness does the face of earth entomb'

(2.4.7–9). Darkness represents the moral turmoil of the play-world and the predominance of evil; and thus when Siward tells Malcolm in the battle that 'the day almost itself professes yours' (5.7.27), the phrase is more than military convention. Malcolm's forces have been fighting for the day as well as during it, and their triumph represents a new dawn after a nightmarish darkness.

The Scene: Scotland and (in 4.3) England

CHARACTERS IN THE PLAY

DUNCAN, *King of Scotland*
MALCOLM } *his sons*
DONALBAIN } *his sons*
MACBETH, *at first a general, later King of Scotland*
BANQUO, *a general*
MACDUFF } *noblemen of Scotland*
LENNOX
ROSS
MENTEITH
ANGUS
CAITHNESS
FLEANCE, *son to Banquo*
SIWARD, *Earl of Northumberland, general of the English forces*
YOUNG SIWARD, *his son*
SETON, *armour-bearer to Macbeth*
A Boy, son to Macduff
A Captain
A Porter
An Old Man
An English Doctor
A Scotch Doctor
Three Murderers

LADY MACBETH
LADY MACDUFF
A Gentlewoman attending on Lady Macbeth
The Weird Sisters
HECATE
Apparitions

Lords, Gentlemen, Officers, Soldiers, Attendants, and Messengers

MACBETH

ACT I SCENE I

'Thunder and lightning. Enter three Witches'

I WITCH When shall we three meet again
In thunder, lightning, or in rain?
2 WITCH When the hurlyburly's done,
When the battle's lost and won.
3 WITCH That will be ere the set of sun.
I WITCH Where the place?
2 WITCH Upon the heath.
3 WITCH There to meet with Macbeth.
I WITCH I come, Graymalkin!
2 WITCH Paddock calls.
3 WITCH Anon!
ALL Fair is foul, and foul is fair:
Hover through the fog and filthy air.
[*they vanish in mist*

SCENE 2

A camp

'Alarum'. 'Enter King' DUNCAN, *'*MALCOLM, DONALBAIN, LENNOX, *with attendants, meeting a bleeding Captain'*

DUNCAN What bloody man is that? He can report,
As seemeth by his plight, of the revolt
The newest state.
MALCOLM This is the sergeant,
Who like a good and hardy soldier fought
'Gainst my captivity. Hail, brave friend!
Say to the king the knowledge of the broil
As thou didst leave it.
CAPTAIN Doubtful it stood,
As two spent swimmers that do cling together
And choke their art. The merciless Macdonwald
(Worthy to be a rebel, for to that

The multiplying villainies of nature
Do swarm upon him) from the Western Isles
Of kerns and gallowglasses is supplied,
And Fortune, on his damnèd quarrel smiling,
Showed like a rebel's whore: but all's too weak:
For brave Macbeth (well he deserves that name)
Disdaining fortune, with his brandished steel,
Which smoked with bloody execution,
Like Valour's minion carvèd out his passage,
Till he faced the slave;
Which ne'er shook hands, nor bade farewell to him,
Till he unseamed him from the nave to th' chops,
And fixed his head upon our battlements.

DUNCAN O, valiant cousin! Worthy gentleman!

CAPTAIN As whence the sun 'gins his reflection
Shipwracking storms and direful thunders break;
So from that spring whence comfort seemed to come
Discomfort swells: mark, king of Scotland, mark!
No sooner justice had, with valour armed,
Compelled these skipping kerns to trust their heels,
But the Norweyan lord, surveying vantage,
With furbished arms and new supplies of men,
Began a fresh assault.

DUNCAN: Dismayed not this
Our captains, Macbeth and Banquo?

CAPTAIN Yes;
As sparrows, eagles; or the hare, the lion.
If I say sooth, I must report they were
As cannons overcharged with double cracks;
So they
Doubly redoubled strokes upon the foe:
Except they meant to bathe in reeking wounds,
Or memorize another Golgotha,
I cannot tell:
But I am faint, my gashes cry for help.

DUNCAN So well thy words become thee as thy wounds,
They smack of honour both. Go get him surgeons.
[*attendants help him thence*
Who comes here?

'Enter Ross and Angus'

MALCOLM The worthy thane of Ross.

LENNOX What a haste looks through his eyes! So should he look
That seems to speak things strange.

ROSS God save the king!

DUNCAN Whence cam'st thou, worthy thane?

ROSS From Fife, great king,
Where the Norweyan banners flout the sky,
And fan our people cold.
Norway himself, with terrible numbers,
Assisted by that most disloyal traitor
The thane of Cawdor, began a dismal conflict,
Till that Bellona's bridegroom, lapped in proof,
Confronted him with self-comparisons,
Point against point, rebellious arm 'gainst arm,
Curbing his lavish spirit: and, to conclude,
The victory fell on us.

DUNCAN Great happiness!

ROSS That now
Sweno, the Norways' king, craves composition;
Nor would we deign him burial of his men
Till he disbursèd, at Saint Colme's Inch,
Ten thousand dollars to our general use.

DUNCAN No more that thane of Cawdor shall deceive
Our bosom interest: go pronounce his present death,
And with his former title greet Macbeth.

ROSS I'll see it done.

DUNCAN What he hath lost, noble Macbeth hath won.

[*they go*

SCENE 3

A barren heath

'Thunder. Enter the three Witches'

I WITCH Where hast thou been, sister?
2 WITCH Killing swine.
3 WITCH Sister, where thou?
I WITCH A sailor's wife had chestnuts in her lap,
And munched, and munched, and munched: 'Give me', quoth I.
'Aroint thee, witch!' the rump-fed ronyon cries.
Her husband's to Aleppo gone, master o'th' Tiger:
But in a sieve I'll thither sail,
And, like a rat without a tail,
I'll do, I'll do, and I'll do.
2 WITCH I'll give thee a wind.
I WITCH Th'art kind.
3 WITCH And I another.
I WITCH I myself have all the other,
And the very ports they blow,
All the quarters that they know
I'th' shipman's card.
I will drain him dry as hay:
Sleep shall, neither night nor day
Hang upon his pent-house lid;
He shall live a man forbid:
Weary sev'nights nine times nine
Shall he dwindle, peak, and pine:
Though his bark cannot be lost,
Yet it shall be tempest-tost.
Look what I have.
2 WITCH Show me, show me.
I WITCH Here I have a pilot's thumb,
Wrecked as homeward he did come. [*'drum within'*
3 WITCH A drum, a drum!
Macbeth doth come.

They dance in a ring, whirling faster and faster

ALL The Weïrd Sisters, hand in hand,
Posters of the sea and land,
Thus do go, about, about,
Thrice to thine, and thrice to mine,
And thrice again, to make up nine.
Peace! the charm's wound up.
[*they stop suddenly, and a mist hides them*

'Enter MACBETH *and* BANQUO*'*

MACBETH So foul and fair a day I have not seen.
BANQUO How far is't called to Forres? [*the mist thins*
What are these,
So withered, and so wild in their attire,
That look not like th'inhabitants o'th'earth,
And yet are on't? Live you? Or are you aught
That man may question? You seem to understand me,
By each at once her choppy finger laying
Upon her skinny lips: you should be women,
And yet your beards forbid me to interpret
That you are so.
MACBETH Speak, if you can: what are you?
1 WITCH All hail, Macbeth! Hail to thee, thane of Glamis!
2 WITCH All hail, Macbeth! Hail to thee, thane of Cawdor!
3 WITCH All hail, Macbeth! That shalt be king hereafter.
BANQUO Good sir, why do you start, and seem to fear
Things that do sound so fair? I'th' name of truth,
Are ye fantastical, or that indeed
Which outwardly ye show? My noble partner
You greet with present grace and great prediction
Of noble having and of royal hope,
That he seems rapt withal: to me you speak not.
If you can look into the seeds of time,
And say which grain will grow and which will not,
Speak then to me, who neither beg nor fear
Your favours nor your hate.
1 WITCH Hail!
2 WITCH Hail!
3 WITCH Hail!

1 WITCH Lesser than Macbeth, and greater.
2 WITCH Not so happy, yet much happier.
3 WITCH Thou shalt get kings, though thou be none:
So all hail, Macbeth and Banquo!
1 WITCH Banquo and Macbeth, all hail! [*the mist thickens*
MACBETH Stay, you imperfect speakers, tell me more
By Sinel's death I know I am thane of Glamis,
But how of Cawdor? The thane of Cawdor lives
A prosperous gentleman; and to be king
Stands not within the prospect of belief,
No more than to be Cawdor. Say from whence
You owe this strange intelligence, or why
Upon this blasted heath you stop our way
With such prophetic greeting. Speak, I charge you.
[*they disappear*
BANQUO The earth hath bubbles, as the water has,
And these are of them: whither are they vanished?
MACBETH Into the air; and what seemed corporal, melted,
As breath into the wind. Would they had stayed!
BANQUO Were such things here as we do speak about?
Or have we eaten on the insane root
That takes the reason prisoner?
MACBETH Your children shall be kings.
BANQUO You shall be king.
MACBETH And thane of Cawdor too: Went it not so?
BANQUO To th' selfsame tune and words. Who's here?

'Enter ROSS *and* ANGUS*'*

ROSS The king hath happily received, Macbeth,
The news of thy success: and when he reads
Thy personal venture in the rebels' fight,
His wonders and his praises do contend
Which should be thine or his: silenced with that,
In viewing o'er the rest o'th' self-same day,
He finds thee in the stout Norweyan ranks,
Nothing afeard of what thyself didst make
Strange images of death. As thick as hail
Came post with post, and every one did bear
Thy praises in his kingdom's great defence,

And poured them down before him.

ANGUS We are sent
To give thee from our royal master thanks,
Only to herald thee into his sight,
Not pay thee.

ROSS And for an earnest of a greater honour,
He bade me, from him, call thee thane of Cawdor:
In which addition, hail, most worthy thane,
For it is thine.

BANQUO What, can the devil speak true?

MACBETH The thane of Cawdor lives: why do you dress me
In borrowed robes?

ANGUS Who was the thane lives yet,
But under heavy judgment bears that life
Which he deserves to lose. Whether he was combined
With those of Norway, or did line the rebel
With hidden help and vantage, or that with both
He laboured in his country's wreck, I know not;
But treasons capital, confessed, and proved,
Have overthrown him.

MACBETH Glamis, and thane of Cawdor:
The greatest is behind. [*aloud*] Thanks for your pains –
[*aside to Banquo*]
Do you not hope your children shall be kings,
When those that gave the thane of Cawdor to me
Promised no less to them?

BANQUO That, trusted home,
Might yet enkindle you unto the crown,
Besides the thane of Cawdor. But 'tis strange:
And oftentimes, to win us to our harm,
The instruments of darkness tell us truths,
Win us with honest trifles, to betray's
In deepest consequence.
Cousins, a word, I pray you.
[*to Ross and Angus, who move towards him*

MACBETH Two truths are told,
As happy prologues to the swelling act
Of the imperial theme. [*aloud*] I thank you, gentlemen.
[*aside*] This supernatural soliciting

Cannot be ill; cannot be good. If ill,
Why hath it given me earnest of success,
Commencing in a truth? I am thane of Cawdor.
If good, why do I yield to that suggestion
Whose horrid image doth unfix my hair,
And make my seated heart knock at my ribs,
Against the use of nature? Present fears
Are less than horrible imaginings:
My thought, whose murder yet is but fantastical,
Shakes so my single state of man that function
Is smothered in surmise, and nothing is
But what is not.

BANQUO Look how our partner's rapt.

MACBETH If chance will have me king, why, chance may crown me,
Without my stir.

BANQUO New honours come upon him,
Like our strange garments, cleave not to their mould
But with the aid of use.

MACBETH Come what come may,
Time and the hour runs through the roughest day.

BANQUO Worthy Macbeth, we stay upon your leisure.

MACBETH Give me your favour: my dull brain was wrought
With things forgotten. Kind gentlemen, your pains
Are registered where every day I turn
The leaf to read them. Let us toward the king.
[*aside to Banquo*
Think upon what hath chanced; and at more time,
The interim having weighed it, let us speak
Our free hearts each to other.

BANQUO Very gladly,

MACBETH Till then, enough – Come, friends.
[*they go forward*

SCENE 4

Forres. A room in the Palace

'Flourish. Enter King' DUNCAN, *'*MALCOLM, DONALBAIN, LENNOX, *and Attendants'*

DUNCAN Is execution done on Cawdor? Are not
Those in commission yet returned?

MALCOLM My liege,
They are not yet come back. But I have spoke
With one that saw him die: who did report
That very frankly he confessed his treasons,
Implored your highness' pardon, and set forth
A deep repentance: nothing in his life
Became him like the leaving it; he died
As one that had been studied in his death,
To throw away the dearest thing he owed
As 'twere a careless trifle.

DUNCAN There's no art
To find the mind's construction in the face:
He was a gentleman on whom I built
An absolute trust.

'Enter MALCOLM, BANQUO, ROSS, *and* ANGUS*'*

O worthiest cousin!
The sin of my ingratitude even now
Was heavy on me. Thou art so far before,
That swiftest wing of recompense is slow
To overtake thee. Would thou hadst less deserved,
That the proportion both of thanks and payment
Might have been mine! Only I have left to say,
More is thy due than more than all can pay.

MACBETH The service and the loyalty I owe,
In doing it, pays itself. Your highness' part
Is to receive our duties: and our duties
Are to your throne and state children and servants,
Which do but what they should, by doing everything
Safe toward your love and honour.

DUNCAN Welcome hither:
I have begun to plant thee, and will labour
To make thee full of growing. Noble Banquo,
That hast no less deserved, nor must be known
No less to have done so: let me infold thee,
And hold thee to my heart.

BANQUO There if I grow,
The harvest is your own.

DUNCAN My plenteous joys,
Wanton in fulness, seek to hide themselves
In drops of sorrow. Sons, kinsmen, thanes,
And you whose places are the nearest, know,
We will establish our estate upon
Our eldest, Malcolm, whom we name hereafter
The Prince of Cumberland: which honour must
Not unaccompanied invest him only,
But signs of nobleness, like stars, shall shine
On all deservers. From hence to Inverness,
And bind us further to you.

MACBETH The rest is labour, which is not used for you:
I'll be myself the harbinger, and make joyful
The hearing of my wife with your approach;
So humbly take my leave.

DUNCAN My worthy Cawdor!

MACBETH The Prince of Cumberland! That is a step
On which I must fall down, or else o'er-leap,
For in my way it lies. Stars, hide your fires!
Let not light see my black and deep desires:
The eye wink at the hand; yet let that be
Which the eye fears, when it is done, to see. [*he goes*

DUNCAN True, worthy Banquo; he is full so valiant,
And in his commendations I am fed;
It is a banquet to me. Let's after him,
Whose care is gone before to bid us welcome:
It is a peerless kinsman. [*'Flourish'. They go*

SCENE 5

Inverness. Before Macbeth's castle

'Enter MACBETH'S *wife alone, with a letter'*

LADY M. [*reads*] 'They met me in the day of success; and I have learned by the perfect'st report, they have more in them than mortal knowledge. When I burned in desire to question them further, they made themselves air, into which they vanished. Whiles I stood rapt in the wonder of it, came missives from the king, who all- hailed me, 'Thane of Cawdor', by which title, before, these Weird Sisters saluted me, and referred me to the coming on of time, with 'Hail, king that shalt be!' This have I thought good to deliver thee (my dearest partner of greatness) that thou mightst not lose the dues of rejoicing, by being ignorant of what greatness is promised thee. Lay it to thy heart, and farewell.'

Glamis thou art, and Cawdor, and shalt be
What thou art promised: yet do I fear thy nature,
It is too full o'th' milk of human kindness
To catch the nearest way: thou wouldst be great,
Art not without ambition, but without
The illness should attend it: what thou wouldst highly,
That wouldst thou holily; wouldst not play false,
And yet wouldst wrongly win: thou'ldst have,
great Glamis,
That which cries 'Thus thou must do', if thou have it,
And that which rather thou dost fear to do
Than wishest should be undone. Hie thee hither,
That I may pour my spirits in thine ear,
And chastise with the valour of my tongue
All that impedes thee from the golden round,
Which fate and metaphysical aid doth seem
To have thee crowned withal.

An attendant enters

What is your tidings?

ATTEN'T The king comes here tonight.

LADY M. Thou'rt mad to say it!
Is not thy master with him? Who, were't so,
Would have informed for preparation.

ATTEN'T So please you, it is true: our thane is coming:
One of my fellows had the speed of him;
Who, almost dead for breath, had scarcely more
Than would make up his message.

LADY M. Give him tending,
He brings great news. [*attendant goes*] The raven himself is hoarse
That croaks the fatal entrance of Duncan
Under my battlements. Come, you spirits
That tend on mortal thoughts, unsex me here,
And fill me, from the crown to the toe, top-full
Of direst cruelty! Make thick my blood,
Stop up th'access and passage to remorse,
That no compunctious visitings of nature
Shake my fell purpose, nor keep peace between
Th'effect and it! Come to my woman's breasts,
And take my milk for gall, you murd'ring ministers,
Wherever in your sightless substances
You wait on nature's mischief! Come, thick night,
And pall thee in the dunnest smoke of hell,
That my keen knife see not the wound it makes,
Nor heaven peep through the blanket of the dark,
To cry 'Hold, hold!'

'*Enter* MACBETH'

Great Glamis! Worthy Cawdor!
Greater than both, by the all-hail hereafter!
Thy letters have transported me beyond
This ignorant present, and I feel now
The future in the instant.

MACBETH My dearest love,
Duncan comes here tonight.

LADY M. And when goes hence?

MACBETH Tomorrow, as he purposes.

LADY M. O, never

Shall sun that morrow see!
Your face, my thane, is as a book, where men
May read strange matters. To beguile the time,
Look like the time, bear welcome in your eye,
Your hand, your tongue: look like th'innocent flower,
But be the serpent under't. He that's coming
Must be provided for: and you shall put
This night's great business into my dispatch,
Which shall to all our nights and days to come
Give solely sovereign sway and masterdom.

MACBETH We will speak further.

LADY M. Only look up clear.
To alter favour ever is to fear:
Leave all the rest to me. [*they go within*

SCENE 6

'Hautboys'. 'Enter King' DUNCAN, *'*MALCOLM, DONALBAIN, BANQUO, LENNOX, MACDUFF, ROSS, ANGUS, *and attendants'*

DUNCAN This castle hath a pleasant seat; the air
Nimbly and sweetly recommends itself
Unto our gentle senses.

BANQUO This guest of summer,
The temple-haunting martlet, does approve,
By his loved mansionry, that the heaven's breath
Smells wooingly here: no jutty, frieze,
Buttress, nor coign of vantage, but this bird
Hath made his pendent bed and procreant cradle:
Where they most breed and haunt, I have observed
The air is delicate.

'Enter LADY*'* MACBETH

DUNCAN See, see! our honoured hostess!
The love that follows us sometime is our trouble,
Which still we thank as love. Herein I teach you
How you shall bid God 'ield us for your pains,
And thank us for your trouble.

LADY M. All our service
In every point twice done, and then done double,

Were poor and single business to contend
Against those honours deep and broad, wherewith
Your majesty loads our house: for those of old,
And the late dignities heaped up to them,
We rest your hermits.

DUNCAN Where's the thane of Cawdor?
We coursed him at the heels, and had a purpose
To be his purveyor: but he rides well,
And his great love (sharp as his spur) hath holp him
To his home before us. Fair and noble hostess,
We are your guest tonight.

LADY M. Your servants ever
Have theirs, themselves, and what is theirs, in compt,
To make their audit at your highness' pleasure,
Still to return your own.

DUNCAN Give me your hand:
Conduct me to mine host; we love him highly,
And shall continue our graces towards him.
By your leave, hostess. [*he conducts her into the castle*

ACT I SCENE 7

A court in Macbeth's castle, open to the sky, with doors to the rear, one on the left the main gate or south entry, one on the right leading to rooms within, and between them a covered recess running back, beneath a gallery, to a third door, through which when ajar may be seen a flight of stairs to an upper chamber. A bench with a table before it against a side wall.

'Hautboys. Torches. Enter a sewer' directing 'divers servants' who pass 'with dishes and service' across the court. As they come through the door on the right a sound of feasting is heard within. 'Then enter MACBETH*' from the same door*

MACBETH If it were done, when 'tis done, then 'twere well
It were done quickly: if th'assassination
Could trammel up the consequence, and catch,
With his surcease, success; that but this blow
Might be the be-all and the end-all – here,
But here, upon this bank and shoal of time,
We'ld jump the life to come. But in these cases

We still have judgment here – that we but teach
Bloody instructions, which being taught return
To plague th'inventor: this even-handed justice
Commends th'ingredience of our poisoned chalice
To our own lips. He's here in double trust:
First, as I am his kinsman and his subject,
Strong both against the deed; then, as his host,
Who should against his murderer shut the door,
Not bear the knife myself. Besides, this Duncan
Hath borne his faculties so meek, hath been
So clear in his great office, that his virtues
Will plead like angels, trumpet-tongued, against
The deep damnation of his taking-off
And pity, like a naked new-born babe,
Striding the blast, or Heaven's cherubin, horsed
Upon the sightless couriers of the air,
Shall blow the horrid deed in every eye,
That tears shall drown the wind. I have no spur
To prick the sides of my intent, but only
Vaulting ambition, which o'erleaps itself,
And falls on th'other –

'*Enter* LADY' MACBETH

How now, what news?

LADY M. He has almost supped: why have you left the chamber?

MACBETH Hath he asked for me?

LADY M. Know you not he has?

MACBETH We will proceed no further in this business:
He hath honoured me of late, and I have bought
Golden opinions from all sorts of people,
Which would be worn now in their newest gloss,
Not cast aside so soon.

LADY M. Was the hope drunk
Wherein you dressed yourself? Hath it slept since?
And wakes it now, to look so green and pale
At what it did so freely? From this time
Such I account thy love. Art thou afeard
To be the same in thine own act and valour
As thou art in desire? Wouldst thou have that
Which thou esteem'st the ornament of life,

And live a coward in thine own esteem,
Letting 'I dare not' wait upon 'I would',
Like the poor cat i'th'adage?

MACBETH Prithee, peace:
I dare do all that may become a man;
Who dares do more, is none.

LADY M. What beast was't then
That made you break this enterprise to me?
When you durst do it, then you were a man;
And, to be more than what you were, you would
Be so much more the man. Nor time nor place
Did then adhere, and yet you would make both:
They have made themselves, and that their fitness now
Does unmake you. I have given suck, and know
How tender 'tis to love the babe that milks me –
I would, while it was smiling in my face,
Have plucked my nipple from his boneless gums,
And dashed the brains out, had I so sworn as you
Have done to this.

MACBETH If we should fail?

LADY M. We fail?
But screw your courage to the sticking place,
And we'll not fail. When Duncan is asleep
(Whereto the rather shall his day's hard journey
Soundly invite him) his two chamberlains
Will I with wine and wassail so convince,
That memory, the warder of the brain,
Shall be a fume, and the receipt of reason
A limbec only: when in swinish sleep
Their drenchèd natures lie as in a death,
What cannot you and I perform upon
Th'unguarded Duncan? What not put upon
His spongy officers, who shall bear the guilt
Of our great quell?

MACBETH Bring forth men-children only!
For thy undaunted mettle should compose
Nothing but males. Will it not be received,
When we have marked with blood those sleepy two
Of his own chamber, and used their very daggers,

That they have done't?

LADY M. Who dares receive it other,
As we shall make our griefs and clamour roar
Upon his death?

MACBETH I am settled, and bend up
Each corporal agent to this terrible feat.
Away, and mock the time with fairest show:
False face must hide what the false heart doth know.

[they return to the chamber

ACT 2 SCENE 1

The same, one or two hours later. 'Enter' from the back 'BANQUO, and FLEANCE with a torch before him'. They come forward, leaving the door open behind them

BANQUO How goes the night, boy?
FLEANCE [*gazing at the sky*] The moon is down; I have not heard the clock.
BANQUO And she goes down at twelve.
FLEANCE I take't, 'tis later, sir.
BANQUO Hold, take my sword. There's husbandry in heaven,
Their candles are all out. [*unclasps his belt with its dagger*
Take thee that too.
A heavy summons lies like lead upon me,
And yet I would not sleep. Merciful powers,
Restrain in me the cursèd thoughts that nature
Gives way to in repose! [*he starts*] Give me my sword,

'Enter' (from the right) 'MACBETH, and a servant, with a torch'

Who's there?
MACBETH A friend.
BANQUO What, sir, not yet at rest? The king's a-bed.
He hath been in unusual pleasure, and
Sent forth great largess to your offices.
This diamond he greets your wife withal,
By the name of most kind hostess; and shut up
In measureless content.
MACBETH Being unprepared,
Our will became the servant to defect,
Which else should free have wrought.
BANQUO All's well.
I dreamt last night of the three Weird Sisters
To you they have showed some truth.
MACBETH I think not of them:
Yet, when we can entreat an hour to serve,
We would spend it in some words upon that business,
If you would grant the time.
BANQUO At your kind'st leisure.

MACBETH If you shall cleave to my consent, when 'tis,
It shall make honour for you.

BANQUO So I lose none
In seeking to augment it, but still keep
My bosom franchised and allegiance clear,
I shall be counselled.

MACBETH Good repose the while!

BANQUO Thanks, sir: the like to you!

[Banquo and Fleance go to their chamber

MACBETH Go bid thy mistress, when my drink is ready,
She strike upon the bell. Get thee to bed.

[the servant goes; he sits at the table

Is this a dagger which I see before me,
The handle toward my hand? Come, let me clutch thee:
I have thee not, and yet I see thee still.
Art thou not, fatal vision, sensible
To feeling as to sight? Or art thou but
A dagger of the mind, a false creation,
Proceeding from the heat-oppressèd brain?
I see thee yet, in form as palpable
As this which now I draw.
Thou marshall'st me the way that I was going,
And such an instrument I was to use! *[he rises*
Mine eyes are made the fools o'th'other senses,
Or else worth all the rest: I see thee still;
And on thy blade and dudgeon gouts of blood,
Which was not so before. There's no such thing:
It is the bloody business which informs
Thus to mine eyes. Now o'er the one half-world
Nature seems dead, and wicked dreams abuse
The curtained sleep; Witchcraft celebrates
Pale Hecate's off'rings; and withered Murder,
Alarumed by his sentinel, the wolf,
Whose howl's his watch, thus with his stealthy pace,
With Tarquin's ravishing strides, towards his design
Moves like a ghost. Thou sure and firm-set earth,
Hear not my steps, which way they walk, for fear
Thy very stones prate of my whereabout,

And take the present horror from the time,
Which now suits with it. Whiles I threat, he lives:
Words to the heat of deeds too cold breath gives.
[*'a bell rings'*
I go, and it is done: the bell invites me.
Hear it not, Duncan, for it is a knell
That summons thee to heaven, or to hell.
[*he steals out by the open door at back, and step by step climbs the stair. A pause*

SCENE 2

LADY MACBETH *enters from the right, with a cup in her hand*

LADY M. That which hath made them drunk hath made me bold:
What hath quenched them hath given me fire.
[*she pauses*] Hark! Peace:
It was the owl that shrieked, the fatal bellman,
Which gives the stern'st good-night. He is about it:
The doors are open; and the surfeited grooms
Do mock their charge with snores: I have drugged their possets,
That death and nature do contend about them,
Whether they live or die.

MACBETH [*within*] Who's there? What, ho!

LADY M. Alack! I am afraid they have awaked,
And 'tis not done: th'attempt and not the deed
Confounds us. Hark! I laid their daggers ready,
He could not miss 'em. Had he not resembled
My father as he slept, I had done't.

She turns as if making towards the stair, to find MACBETH *standing in the door, his arms bathed in blood and with two daggers clasped in his left hand. He totters forward*

My husband !

MACBETH [*whispers*] I have done the deed. Didst thou not hear a noise?

LADY M. I heard the owl scream, and the crickets cry.
Did not you speak?

MACBETH When?

LADY M. Now.

MACBETH As I descended?

LADY M. Ay.

MACBETH Hark! *[they listen*
Who lies i'th' second chamber?

LADY M. Donalbain.

MACBETH This is a sorry sight.
[stretching forth his right hand

LADY M. A foolish thought, to say a sorry sight.

MACBETH There's one did laugh in's sleep, and one cried 'Murder!'
That they did wake each other: I stood and heard them:
But they did say their prayers, and addressed them
Again to sleep.

LADY M. There are two lodged together.

MACBETH One cried 'God bless us!' and 'Amen' the other,
As they had seen me with these hangman's hands:
List'ning their fear, I could not say 'Amen',
When they did say 'God bless us'.

LADY M. Consider it not so deeply.

MACBETH But wherefore could not I pronounce 'Amen'?
I had most need of blessing, and 'Amen'
Stuck in my throat.

LADY M. These deeds must not be thought
After these ways; so, it will make us mad.

MACBETH Methought I heard a voice cry 'Sleep no more!
Macbeth does murder sleep' – the innocent sleep,
Sleep that knits up the ravelled sleave of care,
The death of each day's life, sore labour's bath,
Balm of hurt minds, great Nature's second course,
Chief nourisher in life's feast, –

LADY M. What do you mean?

MACBETH Still it cried 'Sleep no more!' to all the house:
'Glamis hath murdered sleep, and therefore Cawdor
Shall sleep no more: Macbeth shall sleep no more!'

LADY M. Who was it that thus cried? Why, worthy thane,
You do unbend your noble strength, to think
So brainsickly of things. Go get some water,
And wash this filthy witness from your hand.
Why did you bring these daggers from the place?

They must lie there: go carry them, and smear
The sleepy grooms with blood.

MACBETH I'll go no more:
am afraid to think what I have done;
Look on't again I dare not.

LADY M. Infirm of purpose!
Give me the daggers: the sleeping and the dead
Are but as pictures: 'tis the eye of childhood
That fears a painted devil. If he do bleed,
I'll gild the faces of the grooms withal,
For it must seem their guilt.
[*she goes up. A knocking heard*

MACBETH Whence is that knocking?
How is't with me, when every noise appals me?
What hands are here? Ha! They pluck out mine eyes!
Will all great Neptune's ocean wash this blood
Clean from my hand? No; this my hand will rather
The multitudinous seas incarnadine,
Making the green one red.

LADY MACBETH *returns, closing the inner door*

LADY M. My hands are of your colour; but I shame
To wear a heart so white. [*knocking*] I hear a knocking
At the south entry: retire we to our chamber:
A little water clears us of this deed:
How easy is it then! Your constancy
Hath left you unattended. [*knocking*]
Hark! More knocking.
Get on your nightgown, lest occasion call us
And show us to be watchers: be not lost
So poorly in your thoughts.

MACBETH To know my deed, 'twere best not know myself.
[*knocking*
Wake Duncan with thy knocking! I would thou couldst!
[*they go in*

SCENE 3

The knocking grows yet louder; a drunken Porter enters the court

PORTER Here's a knocking indeed! If a man were porter of hell-gate, he should have old turning the key. [*knocking*] Knock, knock, knock! Who's there, i'th' name of Beelzebub? Here's a farmer, that hanged himself on th'expectation of plenty: come in, time-server; have napkins enow about you, here you'll sweat for't. [*knocking*] Knock, knock! Who's there, in th'other devil's name? Faith, here's an equivocator, that could swear in both the scales against either scale, who committed treason enough for God's sake, yet could not equivocate to heaven: O, come in, equivocator. [*knocking*] Knock, knock, knock! Who's there? Faith, here's an English tailor come hither, for stealing out of a French hose: come in, tailor, here you may roast your goose. [*knocking*] Knock, knock! Never at quiet! What are you? But this place is too cold for hell. I'll devil-porter it no further: I had thought to have let in some of all professions, that go the primrose way to th'everlasting bonfire. [*knocking*] Anon, anon! I pray you, remember the porter. [*opens the gate*

'Enter MACDUFF *and* LENNOX*'*

MACDUFF Was it so late, friend, ere you went to bed, that you do lie so late?

PORTER Faith, sir, we were carousing till the second cock: and drink, sir, is a great provoker of three things.

MACDUFF What three things does drink especially provoke?

PORTER Marry, sir, nose-painting, sleep, and urine. Lechery, sir, it provokes and unprovokes: it provokes the desire, but it takes away the performance. Therefore, much drink may be said to be an equivocator with lechery: it makes him, and it mars him; it sets him on, and it takes him off; it persuades him, and disheartens him; makes him stand to, and not stand to: in conclusion, equivocates him in a sleep, and giving him the lie, leaves him.

MACDUFF I believe drink gave thee the lie last night.

PORTER That it did, sir, i'the very throat on me: but I requited him for his lie, and, I think, being too strong for him, though he took up my legs sometime, yet I made a shift to cast him.

MACDUFF Is thy master stirring?

MACBETH returns, in a dressing gown

Our knocking has awaked him; here he comes.

LENNOX Good-morrow, noble sir.

MACBETH Good-morrow, both.

MACDUFF Is the king stirring, worthy thane?

MACBETH Not yet.

MACDUFF He did command me to call timely on him;
I have almost slipped the hour.

MACBETH I'll bring you to him.

[they move towards the inner door

MACDUFF I know this is a joyful trouble to you;
But yet 'tis one.

MACBETH The labour we delight in physics pain.
This is the door. *[he points*

MACDUFF I'll make so bold to call,
For 'tis my limited service. *[he goes in*

LENNOX Goes the king hence today?

MACBETH He does: he did appoint so.

LENNOX The night has been unruly: where we lay,
Our chimneys were blown down, and, as they say,
Lamentings heard i'th'air, strange screams of death,
And prophesying with accents terrible
Of dire combustion and confused events
New hatched to th' woeful time. The obscure bird
Clamoured the livelong night: some say, the earth
Was feverous and did shake.

MACBETH 'Twas a rough night.

LENNOX My young remembrance cannot parallel
A fellow to it.

MACDUFF returns

MACDUFF O horror! horror! horror! Tongue, nor heart,
Cannot conceive nor name thee!

MACBETH, LENNOX What's the matter?
MACDUFF Confusion now hath made his masterpiece!
Most sacrilegious murder hath broke ope
The Lord's anointed temple, and stole thence
The life o'th' building.
MACBETH What is't you say? The life?
LENNOX Mean you his majesty?
MACDUFF Approach the chamber, and destroy your sight
With a new Gorgon: do not bid me speak;
See, and then speak yourselves. [*Macbeth and Lennox go*
Awake! awake!
Ring the alarum bell! Murder and treason!
Banquo and Donalbain! Malcolm, awake!
Shake off this downy sleep, death's counterfeit,
And look on death itself! Up, up, and see
The great doom's image! Malcolm! Banquo!
As from your graves rise up, and walk like sprites,
To countenance this horror! [*'bell rings'*

'Enter LADY*'* MACBETH *in a dressing gown*

LADY M. What's the business,
That such a hideous trumpet calls to parley
The sleepers of the house? Speak, speak!
MACDUFF O, gentle lady,
'Tis not for you to hear what I can speak:
The repetition, in a woman's ear,
Would murder as it fell.

'Enter BANQUO*' half-clad*

O Banquo! Banquo!
Our royal master's murdered!
LADY M. Woe, alas!
What, in our house!
BANQUO Too cruel, anywhere.
Dear Duff, I prithee, contradict thyself,
And say it is not so.

MACBETH *and* LENNOX *return*

MACBETH Had I but died an hour before this chance,
I had lived a blessèd time; for from this instant
There's nothing serious in mortality:

All is but toys: renown and grace is dead,
The wine of life is drawn, and the mere lees
Is left this vault to brag of.

MALCOLM *and* DONALBAIN *come in haste through the door on the right*

DONALB'N: What is amiss?
MACBETH You are, and do not know't:
The spring, the head, the fountain of your blood
Is stopped – the very source of it is stopped.
MACDUFF Your royal father's murdered.
MALCOLM O, by whom?
LENNOX Those of his chamber, as it seemed, had done't:
Their hands and faces were all badged with blood,
So were their daggers, which unwiped we found
Upon their pillows:
They stared and were distracted, no man's life
Was to be trusted with them.
MACBETH O, yet I do repent me of my fury,
That I did kill them.
MACDUFF Wherefore did you so?
MACBETH Who can be wise, amazed, temp'rate and furious,
Loyal and neutral, in a moment? No man:
Th'expedition of my violent love
Outrun the pauser, reason. Here lay Duncan,
His silver skin laced with his golden blood,
And his gashed stabs looked like a breach in nature
For ruin's wasteful entrance: there, the murderers,
Steeped in the colours of their trade, their daggers
Unmannerly breeched with gore: who could refrain,
That had a heart to love, and in that heart
Courage to make's love known?
LADY M. [*seeming to faint*] Help me hence, ho!

MACBETH *goes to her*

MACDUFF Look to the lady.
MALCOLM Why do we hold our tongues,
That most may claim this argument for ours?
DONALB'N What should be spoken here, where our fate,
Hid in an auger-hole, may rush and seize us?

Let's away.
Our tears are not yet brewed.

MALCOLM Nor our strong sorrow
Upon the foot of motion. *[enter waiting-women*

BANQUO *[directs them]* Look to the lady. *[they lead her forth*
And when we have our naked frailties hid,
That suffer in exposure, let us meet,
And question this most bloody piece of work,
To know it further. Fears and scruples shake us:
In the great hand of God I stand, and thence
Against the undivulged pretence I fight
Of treasonous malice.

MACDUFF And so do I.

ALL So all.

MACBETH Let's briefly put on manly readiness.
And meet i'th'hall together.

ALL Well contented.
[all go in but Malcolm and Donalbain

MALCOLM What will you do? Let's not consort with them:
To show an unfelt sorrow is an office
Which the false man does easy. I'll to England.

DONALB'N To Ireland, I: our separated fortune
Shall keep us both the safer: where we are
There's daggers in men's smiles: the near in blood,
The nearer bloody.

MALCOLM This murderous shaft that's shot
Hath not yet lighted, and our safest way
Is to avoid the aim. Therefore to horse,
And let us not be dainty of leave-taking,
But shift away: there's warrant in that theft
Which steals itself when there's no mercy left.
[they go

SCENE 4

Before Macbeth's castle. A day strangely dark

'Enter ROSS *with an Old Man'*

OLD MAN Threescore and ten I can remember well,
Within the volume of which time I have seen
Hours dreadful and things strange; but this sore night
Hath trifled former knowings.

ROSS [*looks up*] Ha, good father,
Thou seest the heavens, as troubled with man's act,
Threatens his bloody stage: by th' clock 'tis day,
And yet dark night strangles the travelling lamp:
Is't night's predominance, or the day's shame,
That darkness does the face of earth entomb,
When living light should kiss it?

OLD MAN 'Tis unnatural,
Even like the deed that's done. On Tuesday last
A falcon towering in her pride of place
Was by a mousing owl hawked at and killed.

ROSS And Duncan's horses – a thing most strange and certain –
Beauteous and swift, the minions of their race,
Turned wild in nature, broke their stalls, flung out,
Contending 'gainst obedience, as they would make
War with mankind.

OLD MAN 'Tis said they eat each other.

ROSS They did so, to th'amazement of mine eyes,
That looked upon't.

MACDUFF *comes from the Castle*

Here comes the good Macduff.
How goes the world, sir, now?

MACDUFF [*points at the sky*] Why, see you not?

ROSS Is't known who did this more than bloody deed?

MACDUFF Those that Macbeth hath slain.

ROSS Alas, the day!
What good could they pretend?

MACDUFF They were suborned.
Malcolm and Donalbain, the king's two sons,
Are stol'n away and fled, which puts upon them
Suspicion of the deed.

ROSS 'Gainst nature still!
Thriftless ambition, that wilt ravin up
Thine own life's means! Then 'tis most like
The sovereignty will fall upon Macbeth.

MACDUFF He is already named, and gone to Scone
To be invested.

ROSS Where is Duncan's body?

MACDUFF Carried to Colme kill,
The sacred storehouse of his predecessors,
And guardian of their bones.

ROSS Will you to Scone?

MACDUFF No cousin, I'll to Fife.

ROSS Well, I will thither.

MACDUFF Well, may you see things well done there: adieu!
Lest our old robes sit easier than our new!

ROSS Farewell, father.

OLD MAN God's benison go with you, and with those
That would make good of bad and friends of foes!

[*they go*

[*Some weeks pass*]

ACT 3 SCENE 1

An audience chamber in the palace at Forres

BANQUO *enters*

BANQUO Thou hast it now, King, Cawdor, Glamis, all,
As the weird women promised, and I fear
Thou play'dst most foully for't: yet it was said
It should not stand in thy posterity,
But that myself should be the root and father
Of many kings. If there come truth from them –
As upon thee, Macbeth, their speeches shine –
Why, by the verities on thee made good,
May they not be my oracles as well,
And set me up in hope? But hush, no more.

'Sennet sounded. Enter MACBETH, *as King,* LADY' MACBETH, *as Queen,* 'LENNOX, ROSS, *Lords and attendants'*

MACBETH Here's our chief guest.
LADY M. If he had been forgotten,
It had been as a gap in our great feast,
And all-thing unbecoming.
MACBETH Tonight we hold a solemn supper, sir,
And I'll request your presence.
BANQUO Let your highness
Command upon me, to the which my duties
Are with a most indissoluble tie
For ever knit.
MACBETH Ride you this afternoon?
BANQUO Ay, my good lord.
MACBETH We should have else desired your good advice
(Which still hath been both grave and prosperous)
In this day's council; but we'll take tomorrow.
Is't far you ride?
BANQUO As far, my lord, as will fill up the time
'Twixt this and supper. Go not my horse the better,

I must become a borrower of the night
For a dark hour or twain.

MACBETH Fail not our feast.

BANQUO My lord, I will not.

MACBETH We hear our bloody cousins are bestowed
In England and in Ireland, not confessing
Their cruel parricide, filling their hearers
With strange invention: but of that tomorrow,
When therewithal we shall have cause of state
Craving us jointly. Hie you to horse: adieu,
Till you return at night. Goes Fleance with you?

BANQUO Ay, my good lord: our time does call upon's.

MACBETH I wish your horses swift and sure of foot;
And so I do commend you to their backs.
Farewell. [*Banquo goes*
Let every man be master of his time
Till seven at night; to make society
The sweeter welcome, we will keep ourself
Till supper-time alone: while then, God be with you!
[*all depart but Macbeth and a servant*
Sirrah, a word with you: attend those men
Our pleasure?

ATTEND'T They are, my lord, without the palace gate.

MACBETH Bring them before us. [*the servant goes*
To be thus is nothing,
But to be safely thus: our fears in Banquo
Stick deep, and in his royalty of nature
Reigns that which would be feared. 'Tis much he dares,
And, to that dauntless temper of his mind,
He hath a wisdom that doth guide his valour
To act in safety. There is none but he
Whose being I do fear: and under him
My Genius is rebuked, as it is said
Mark Antony's was by Caesar. He chid the Sisters,
When first they put the name of king upon me,
And bade them speak to him; then prophet-like
They hailed him father to a line of kings:
Upon my head they placed a fruitless crown,

And put a barren sceptre in my gripe,
Thence to be wrenched with an unlineal hand,
No son of mine succeeding. If't be so,
For Banquo's issue have I filed my mind,
For them the gracious Duncan have I murdered,
Put rancours in the vessel of my peace
Only for them, and mine eternal jewel
Given to the common enemy of man,
To make them kings, the seed of Banquo kings!
Rather than so, come Fate into the list,
And champion me to th'utterance. Who's there?

The servant returns 'with two murderers'

Now go to the door, and stay there till we call.
[*servant goes out*
Was it not yesterday we spoke together?

I MURD'R It was, so please your highness.

MACBETH Well then, now
Have you considered of my speeches? Know
That it was he in the times past which held you
So under fortune, which you thought had been
Our innocent self: this I made good to you
In our last conference; passed in probation with you,
How you were borne in hand, how crossed, the instruments,
Who wrought with them, and all things else that might
To half a soul and to a notion crazed
Say 'Thus did Banquo'.

I MURD'R You made it known to us.

MACBETH I did so; and went further, which is now
Our point of second meeting. Do you find
Your patience so predominant in your nature,
That you can let this go? Are you so gospelled,
To pray for this good man, and for his issue,
Whose heavy hand hath bowed you to the grave
And beggared yours for ever?

I MURD'R We are men, my liege.

MACBETH Ay, in the catalogue ye go for men,
As hounds and greyhounds, mongrels, spaniels, curs,

Shoughs, water-rugs, and demi-wolves, are clept
All by the name of dogs: the valued file
Distinguishes the swift, the slow, the subtle,
The housekeeper, the hunter, every one
According to the gift which bounteous nature
Hath in him closed, whereby he does receive
Particular addition, from the bill
That writes them all alike: and so of men.
Now, if you have a station in the file,
Not i'th' worst rank of manhood, say't,
And I will put that business in your bosoms,
Whose execution takes your enemy off,
Grapples you to the heart and love of us,
Who wear our health but sickly in his life
Which in his death were perfect.

2 MURD'R I am one, my liege,
Whom the vile blows and buffets of the world
Hath so incensed that I am reckless what
I do to spite the world.

1 MURD'R And I another
So weary with disasters, tugged with fortune,
That I would set my life on any chance,
To mend it, or be rid on't.

MACBETH Both of you
Know Banquo was your enemy.

BOTH MURD'RS: True, my lord.

MACBETH So is he mine: and in such bloody distance
That every minute of his being thrusts
Against my near'st of life: and though I could
With barefaced power sweep him from my sight
And bid my will avouch it, yet I must not,
For certain friends that are both his and mine,
Whose loves I may not drop, but wail his fall
Who I myself struck down: and thence it is
That I to your assistance do make love,
Masking the business from the common eye,
For sundry weighty reasons.

2 MURD'R We shall, my lord,
Perform what you command us.

I MURD'R Though our lives –

MACBETH Your spirits shine through you. Within this hour at most
I will advise you where to plant yourselves,
Acquaint you with the perfect spy o'th' time,
The moment on't, for't must be done tonight,
And something from the palace; always thought
That I require a clearness: and with him –
To leave no rubs nor botches in the work –
Fleance his son, that keeps him company,
Whose absence is no less material to me
Than is his father's, must embrace the fate
Of that dark hour. Resolve yourselves apart;
I'll come to you anon.

BOTH MURD'RS: We are resolved, my lord.

MACBETH I'll call upon you straight; abide within. [*they go*
It is concluded: Banquo, thy soul's flight,
If it find heaven, must find it out tonight.
[*he leaves by another door*

SCENE 2

LADY MACBETH *enters with a servant*

LADY M. Is Banquo gone from court?

SERVANT Ay, madam, but returns again tonight.

LADY M. Say to the king, I would attend his leisure
For a few words.

SERVANT Madam, I will. [*he goes*

LADY M. Nought's had, all's spent,
Where our desire is got without content;
'Tis safer to be that which we destroy
Than by destruction dwell in doubtful joy.

MACBETH *enters lost in thought*

How now, my lord! why do you keep alone,
Of sorriest fancies your companions making,
Using those thoughts which should indeed have died
With them they think on? Things without all remedy
Should be without regard: what's done, is done.

MACBETH We have scorched the snake, not killed it:
She'll close and be herself, whilst our poor malice
Remains in danger of her former tooth.
But let the frame of things disjoint, both the worlds suffer,
Ere we will eat our meal in fear, and sleep
In the affliction of these terrible dreams
That shake us nightly: better be with the dead,
Whom we, to gain our peace, have sent to peace,
Than on the torture of the mind to lie
In restless ecstasy. Duncan is in his grave;
After life's fitful fever he sleeps well;
Treason has done his worst: nor steel, nor poison,
Malice domestic, foreign levy, nothing,
Can touch him further.

LADY M. Come on;
Gentle my lord, sleek o'er your rugged looks,
Be bright and jovial among your guests tonight.

MACBETH So shall I, love, and so I pray be you:
Let your remembrance apply to Banquo;
Present him eminence, both with eye and tongue:
Unsafe the while, that we
Must lave our honours in these flattering streams,
And make our faces vizards to our hearts,
Disguising what they are.

LADY M. You must leave this.

MACBETH O, full of scorpions is my mind, dear wife!
Thou know'st that Banquo and his Fleance lives.

LADY M. But in them nature's copy's not eterne.

MACBETH There's comfort yet, they are assailable,
Then be thou jocund: ere the bat hath flown
His cloistered flight, ere to black Hecate's summons
The shard-borne beetle with his drowsy hums
Hath rung night's yawning peal, there shall be done
A deed of dreadful note.

LADY M. What's to be done?

MACBETH Be innocent of the knowledge, dearest chuck,
Till thou applaud the deed. Come, seeling night,
Scarf up the tender eye of pitiful day,

And with thy bloody and invisible hand
Cancel and tear to pieces that great bond
Which keeps me paled! Light thickens, and the crow
Makes wing to th' rooky wood:
Good things of day begin to droop and drowse,
Whiles night's black agents to their preys do rouse.
Thou marvell'st at my words: but hold thee still;
Things bad begun make strong themselves by ill:
So, prithee, go with me. [*they go*

SCENE 3

A steep lane leading through a wood to gates of the royal park, some way from the palace. The two murderers come up, with a third

1 MURD'R But who did bid thee join with us?
3 MURD'R Macbeth.
2 MURD'R He needs not our mistrust, since he delivers
Our offices and what we have to do,
To the direction just.
1 MURD'R Then stand with us.
The west yet glimmers with some streaks of day:
Now spurs the lated traveller apace
To gain the timely inn, and near approaches
The subject of our watch.
3 MURD'R Hark! I hear horses.
BANQUO [*at a distance*]
Give us a light there, ho!
2 MURD'R Then 'tis he; the rest
That are within the note of expectation
Already are i'th' court.
1 MURD'R His horses go about.
3 MURD'R Almost a mile: but he does usually –
So all men do – from hence to th' palace gate
Make it their walk.

'BANQUO *and* FLEANCE *with a torch' are seen coming up the lane*

2 MURD'R A light, a light!
3 MURD'R 'Tis he.

I MURD'R Stand to't.

BANQUO It will be rain tonight.

I MURD'R Let it come down.

[*1 Murderer strikes out the torch; the others set upon Banquo*

BANQUO O, treachery! Fly, good Fleance, fly, fly, fly!
Thou mayst revenge. O slave!

[*he dies; Fleance escapes*

3 MURD'R Who did strike out the light?

I MURD'R Was't not the way?

3 MURD'R There's but one down; the son is fled.

2 MURD'R We have lost
Best half of our affair.

I MURD'R Well, let's away, and say how much is done.

[*they go*

SCENE 4

The hall of the palace. At the upper end a dais with doors to left and right, between which are two thrones and a table before them, while a longer table, at right angles, extends down the room

A 'banquet prepared. Enter MACBETH, LADY' MACBETH, 'ROSS, LENNOX, *Lords, and attendants'*

MACBETH You know your own degrees, sit down: at first
And last, the hearty welcome.

LORDS Thanks to your majesty.

Macbeth leads Lady Macbeth to the dais; the Lords sit on either side of the long table, leaving an empty stool at the head

MACBETH Ourself will mingle with society,
And play the humble host:

[*Lady Macbeth ascends to her throne*

Our hostess keeps her state, but in best time
We will require her welcome.

LADY M. Pronounce it for me, sir, to all our friends,
For my heart speaks they are welcome.

As Macbeth passes by the door on the left 1 Murderer appears there. The Lords rise and bow to Lady Macbeth

MACBETH See, they encounter thee with their hearts' thanks.

Both sides are even: here I'll sit i'th' midst.
[point to the empty stool
Be large in mirth, anon we'll drink a measure
The table round.
[*turns to the door*] There's blood upon thy face.

MURD'R 'Tis Banquo's then.

MACBETH 'Tis better thee without than he within.
Is he dispatched?

MURD'R My lord, his throat is cut, that I did for him.

MACBETH Thou art the best o'th' cut-throats! Yet he's good
That did the like for Fleance: if thou didst it,
Thou art the nonpareil.

MURD'R Most royal sir,
Fleance is 'scaped.

MACBETH Then comes my fit again: I had else been perfect;
Whole as the marble, founded as the rock,
As broad and general as the casing air:
But now I am cabined, cribbed, confined, bound in
To saucy doubts and fears. But Banquo's safe?

MURD'R Ay, my good lord: safe in a ditch he bides,
With twenty trenchèd gashes on his head;
The least a death to nature.

MACBETH Thanks for that:
There the grown serpent lies; the worm that's fled
Hath nature that in time will venom breed,
No teeth for th' present. Get thee gone; tomorrow
We'll hear ourselves again. *[Murderer goes*

LADY M. My royal lord,
You do not give the cheer. The feast is sold
That is not often vouched, while 'tis a-making,
'Tis given with welcome: to feed were best at home;
From thence the sauce to meat is ceremony;
Meeting were bare without it.

['The Ghost of Banquo' appears, 'and sits in Macbeth's place'

MACBETH Sweet remembrancer!
Now good digestion wait on appetite,
And health on both!

LENNOX May't please your highness sit?

MACBETH Here had we now our country's honour roofed,
Were the graced person of our Banquo present;
Who may I rather challenge for unkindness
Than pity for mischance!

ROSS His absence, sir,
Lays blame upon his promise. Please't your highness
To grace us with your royal company?

MACBETH The table's full.

LENNOX Here is a place reserved, sir.

MACBETH Where?

LENNOX Here, my good lord. What is't that moves your highness?

MACBETH Which of you have done this?

LORDS What, my good lord?

MACBETH Thou canst not say I did it: never shake
Thy gory locks at me. [*Lady Macbeth rises*

ROSS Gentlemen, rise, his highness is not well.

LADY M. [*coming down*] Sit, worthy friends: my lord is often thus,
And hath been from his youth: pray you, keep seat,
The fit is momentary, upon a thought
He will again be well: if much you note him,
You shall offend him and extend his passion:
Feed, and regard him not. [*aside*] Are you a man?

MACBETH Ay, and a bold one, that dare look on that
Which might appal the devil.

LADY M. O proper stuff!
This is the very painting of your fear:
This is the air-drawn dagger which, you said,
Led you to Duncan. O, these flaws and starts
(Impostors to true fear) would well become
A woman's story at a winter's fire,
Authorized by her grandam. Shame itself!
Why do you make such faces? When all's done,
You look but on a stool.

MACBETH Prithee, see there! Behold! Look! Lo! How say you?
Why what care I? If thou canst nod, speak too.
If charnel-houses and our graves must send
Those that we bury back, our monuments
Shall be the maws of kites. [*the Ghost vanishes*

LADY M. What! Quite unmanned in folly?

MACBETH If I stand here, I saw him.

LADY M. Fie, for shame!

MACBETH [*paces to and fro*]
Blood hath been shed ere now, i'th'olden time,
Ere humane statute purged the gentle weal;
Ay, and since too, murders have been performed
Too terrible for the ear: the time has been,
That, when the brains were out, the man would die,
And there an end: but now they rise again,
With twenty mortal murders on their crowns,
And push us from our stools. This is more strange
Than such a murder is.

LADY M. [*touches his arm*] My worthy lord,
Your noble friends do lack you.

MACBETH I do forget.
Do not muse at me, my most worthy friends;
I have a strange infirmity, which is nothing
To those that know me. Come, love and health to all;
Then I'll sit down. Give me some wine, fill full.
[*as he raises his cup, the Ghost reappears in the seat behind him*]
I drink to th' general joy o'th' whole table,
And to our dear friend Banquo, whom we miss;
Would he were here! To all, and him we thirst,
And all to all!

LORDS [*drinking*]. Our duties, and the pledge.

MACBETH [*turns to his seat*] Avaunt, and quit my sight! Let the earth hide thee!

[*drops the cup*]

Thy bones are marrowless, thy blood is cold;
Thou hast no speculation in those eyes
Which thou dost glare with!

LADY M. Think of this, good peers,
But as a thing of custom: 'tis no other;
Only it spoils the pleasure of the time.

MACBETH What man dare, I dare:
Approach thou like the ruggèd Russian bear,
The armed rhinoceros, or th'Hyrcan tiger,

Take any shape but that, and my firm nerves
Shall never tremble: or be alive again,
And dare me to the desert with thy sword;
If trembling I inhabit then, protest me
The baby of a girl. Hence, horrible shadow!
Unreal mock'ry, hence! [*the Ghost vanishes*
Why, so; being gone,
I am a man again. Pray you, sit still.

LADY M. You have displaced the mirth, broke the good meeting,
With most admired disorder.

MACBETH Can such things be,
And overcome us like a summer's cloud,
Without our special wonder? You make me strange
Even to the disposition that I owe,
When now I think you can behold such sights,
And keep the natural ruby of your cheeks,
When mine is blanched with fear.

ROSS What sights, my lord?

LADY M. I pray you, speak not; he grows worse and worse;
Question enrages him: at once, good night.
Stand not upon the order of your going, [*they rise*
But go at once.

LENNOX Good night, and better health
Attend his majesty!

LADY M. A kind good night to all! [*they leave*

MACBETH It will have blood; they say, blood will have blood:
Stones have been known to move and trees to speak;
Augures and understood relations have
By maggot-pies and choughs and rooks brought forth
The secret'st man of blood. What is the night?

LADY M. Almost at odds with morning, which is which.

MACBETH How say'st thou, that Macduff denies his person
At our great bidding?

LADY M. Did you send to him, sir?

MACBETH I hear it by the way; but I will send:
There's not a one of them but in his house
I keep a servant fee'd. I will tomorrow
(And betimes I will) to the Weird Sisters:
More shall they speak; for now I am bent to know,

By the worst means, the worst. For mine own good
All causes shall give way: I am in blood
Stepped in so far that, should I wade no more,
Returning were as tedious as go o'er:
Strange things I have in head that will to hand,
Which must be acted ere they may be scanned.

LADY M. You lack the season of all natures, sleep.

MACBETH Come, we'll to sleep. My strange and self-abuse
Is the initiate fear that wants hard use:
We are yet but young in deed. [*they go*

SCENE 5

A heath

'*Thunder. Enter the three Witches*', *meeting* HECATE

I WITCH Why, how now, Hecat, you look angerly.

HECATE Have I not reason, beldams as you are,
Saucy and overbold? How did you dare
To trade and traffic with Macbeth
In riddles and affairs of death;
And I, the mistress of your charms,
The close contriver of all harms,
Was never called to bear my part,
Or show the glory of our art?
And, which is worse, all you have done
Hath been but for a wayward son,
Spiteful and wrathful, who (as others do)
Loves for his own ends, not for you.
But make amends now: get you gone,
And at the pit of Acheron
Meet me i'th' morning: thither he
Will come to know his destiny.
Your vessels and your spells provide,
Your charms and everything beside.
I am for th'air; this night I'll spend
Unto a dismal and a fatal end.
Great business must be wrought ere noon:
Upon the corner of the moon

There hangs a vap'rous drop profound;
I'll catch it ere it come to ground:
And that distilled by magic sleights
Shall raise such artificial sprites
As by the strength of their illusion
Shall draw him on to his confusion.
He shall spurn fate, scorn death, and bear
His hopes 'bove wisdom, grace, and fear:
And you all know security
Is mortals' chiefest enemy.

'Music and a song': 'Come away, come away', etc.
A cloud descends

Hark, I am called: my little spirit, see,
Sits in a foggy cloud, and stays for me.
[she flies away on the cloud

I WITCH Come, let's make haste; she'll soon be back again.
[they vanish

SCENE 6

A castle in Scotland

'Enter LENNOX *and another Lord'*

LENNOX My former speeches have but hit your thoughts,
Which can interpret farther: only I say
Things have been strangely borne. The gracious Duncan
Was pitied of Macbeth: marry, he was dead:
And the right valiant Banquo walked too late –
Whom you may say (if't please you) Fleance killed,
For Fleance fled: men must not walk too late.
Who cannot want the thought, how monstrous
It was for Malcolm and for Donalbain
To kill their gracious father? Damnèd fact!
How it did grieve Macbeth! Did he not straight,
In pious rage, the two delinquents tear,
That were the slaves of drink and thralls of sleep?
Was not that nobly done? Ay, and wisely too;
For 'twould have angered any heart alive

To hear the men deny't. So that, I say,
He has borne all things well: and I do think
That, had he Duncan's sons under his key
(As, an't please heaven, he shall not) they should find
What 'twere to kill a father; so should Fleance.
But, peace! For from broad words, and 'cause he failed
His presence at the tyrant's feast, I hear,
Macduff lives in disgrace. Sir, can you tell
Where he bestows himself?

LORD The son of Duncan
(From whom this tyrant holds the due of birth)
Lives in the English court, and is received
Of the most pious Edward with such grace
That the malevolence of fortune nothing
Takes from his high respect. Thither Macduff
Is gone to pray the holy king, upon his aid
To wake Northumberland and warlike Siward,
That by the help of these (with Him above
To ratify the work) we may again
Give to our tables meat, sleep to our nights;
Free from our feasts and banquets bloody knives;
Do faithful homage and receive free honours:
All which we pine for now. And this report
Hath so exasperate the king that he
Prepares for some attempt of war.

LENNOX Sent he to Macduff?

LORD He did: and with an absolute 'Sir, not I',
The cloudy messenger turns me his back,
And hums, as who should say, 'You'll rue the time
That clogs me with this answer.'

LENNOX And that well might
Advise him to a caution, t'hold what distance
His wisdom can provide. Some holy angel
Fly to the court of England and unfold
His message ere he come, that a swift blessing
May soon return to this our suffering country
Under a hand accursed!

LORD I'll send my prayers with him.
[*they go*

ACT 4 SCENE I

A cavern and in the midst a fiery pit with a boiling cauldron above it. 'Thunder', as the Weird Sisters rise, one after the other, from the flames

I WITCH Thrice the brinded cat hath mewed.
2 WITCH Thrice and once the hedge-pig whined.
3 WITCH Harpier cries: 'Tis time, 'tis time.
I WITCH Round about the cauldron go:
In the poisoned entrails throw. [*they move leftwards about it*
Toad, that under cold stone
Days and nights has thirty-one
Sweltered venom sleeping got,
Boil thou first i'th' charmèd pot!
ALL Double, double toil and trouble;
Fire burn and cauldron bubble. [*they stir the cauldron*
2 WITCH Fillet of a fenny snake,
In the cauldron boil and bake:
Eye of newt and toe of frog,
Wool of bat and tongue of dog,
Adder's fork and blind-worm's sting,
Lizard's leg and howlet's wing,
For a charm of powerful trouble,
Like a hell-broth boil and bubble.
ALL Double, double toil and trouble;
Fire burn and cauldron bubble. [*they stir*
3 WITCH Scale of dragon, tooth of wolf,
Witch's mummy, maw and gulf
Of the ravined salt-sea shark,
Root of hemlock digged i'th' dark,
Liver of blaspheming Jew,
Gall of goat and slips of yew
Slivered in the moon's eclipse,
Nose of Turk and Tartar's lips,
Finger of birth-strangled babe
Ditch-delivered by a drab,
Make the gruel thick and slab:
Add thereto a tiger's chaudron,

For th'ingredience of our cauldron.

ALL Double, double toil and trouble;
Fire burn and cauldron bubble. [*they stir*

2 WITCH Cool it with a baboon's blood,
Then the charm is firm and good.

'Enter HECATE *and the other three Witches'*

HECATE O, well done! I commend your pains,
And everyone shall share i'th' gains:
And now about the cauldron sing,
Like elves and fairies in a ring,
Enchanting all that you put in.

'Music and song: Black spirits, etc.' Hecate goes

2 WITCH By the pricking of my thumbs,
Something wicked this way comes;
Open, locks,
Whoever knocks!

A door flies open, showing MACBETH *without*

MACBETH [*enters*] How now, you secret, black, and midnight hags!
What is't you do?

ALL A deed without a name.

MACBETH I conjure you, by that which you profess
(Howe'er you come to know it), answer me:
Though you untie the winds and let them fight
Against the churches; though the yesty waves
Confound and swallow navigation up;
Though bladed corn be lodged and trees blown down;
Though castles topple on their warders' heads;
Though palaces and pyramids do slope
Their heads to their foundations; though the treasure
Of Nature's germens tumble all together,
Even till destruction sicken; answer me
To what I ask you.

I WITCH Speak.

2 WITCH Demand.

3 WITCH We'll answer.

I WITCH Say if th'hadst rather hear it from our mouths,
Or from our masters.

MACBETH Call 'em, let me see 'em!

I WITCH Pour in sow's blood, that hath eaten
Her nine farrow; grease that's sweaten
From the murderer's gibbet throw
Into the flame.

ALL Come, high or low;
Thyself and office deftly show.

'Thunder. First Apparition, an armed head' like Macbeth's, rises from the cauldron

MACBETH Tell me, thou unknown power –

I WITCH He knows thy thought:
Hear his speech, but say thou nought.

I APPAR'N Macbeth! Macbeth! Macbeth! beware Macduff,
Beware the thane of Fife. Dismiss me. Enough.
[*'descends'*

MACBETH Whate'er thou art, for thy good caution thanks;
Thou hast harped my fear aright. But one word more –

I WITCH He will not be commanded: here's another,
More potent than the first.

'Thunder. Second Apparition, a bloody child'

2 APPAR'N Macbeth! Macbeth! Macbeth!

MACBETH Had I three ears, I'd hear thee.

2 APPAR'N Be bloody, bold, and resolute: laugh to scorn
The power of man; for none of woman born
Shall harm Macbeth. [*'descends'*

MACBETH Then live, Macduff: what need I fear of thee?
But yet I'll make assurance double sure,
And take a bond of fate: thou shalt not live,
That I may tell pale-hearted fear it lies,
And sleep in spite of thunder.

'Thunder. Third Apparition, a child crowned, with a tree in his hand'

What is this,
That rises like the issue of a king,
And wears upon his baby-brow the round
And top of sovereignty?

ALL Listen, but speak not to't.

3 APPAR'N Be lion-mettled, proud, and take no care
Who chafes, who frets, or where conspirers are:
Macbeth shall never vanquished be until

Great Birnam wood to high Dunsinane hill
Shall come against him. [*'descends'*

MACBETH That will never be;
Who can impress the forest, bid the tree
Unfix his earth-bound root? Sweet bodements! Good.
Rebellious dead, rise never, till the wood
Of Birnam rise, and our high-placed Macbeth
Shall live the lease of nature, pay his breath
To time and mortal custom. Yet my heart
Throbs to know one thing; tell me, if your art
Can tell so much: shall Banquo's issue ever
Reign in this kingdom?

ALL Seek to know no more.

MACBETH I will be satisfied: deny me this,
And an eternal curse fall on you! Let me know.

'Hautboys' play as the cauldron descends

Why sinks that cauldron? And what noise is this?

I WITCH Show!

2 WITCH Show!

3 WITCH Show!

ALL Show his eyes, and grieve his heart;
Come like shadows, so depart.

'A show of eight kings', who pass one by one across the back of the cavern as Macbeth speaks, the 'last with a glass in his hand'; Banquo's Ghost following

MACBETH Thou art too like the spirit of Banquo: down!
Thy crown does sear mine eyeballs. And thy hair,
Thou other gold-bound brow, is like the first.
A third is like the former. Filthy hags!
Why do you show me this? – A fourth? Start, eyes!
What, will the line stretch out to th' crack of doom,
Another yet? A seventh? I'll see no more:
And yet the eighth appears, who bears a glass
Which shows me many more; and some I see
That two-fold balls and treble sceptres carry.
Horrible sight. Now I see 'tis true,
For the blood-boltered Banquo smiles upon me,
And points at them for his. What, is this so?

I WITCH Ay, sir, all this is so. But why
Stands Macbeth thus amazedly?
Come, sisters, cheer we up his sprites,
And show the best of our delights.
I'll charm the air to give a sound,
While you perform your antic round:
That this great king may kindly say
Our duties did his welcome pay.

'Music. The Witches dance, and vanish'

MACBETH Where are they? Gone? Let this pernicious hour
Stand aye accursèd in the calendar
Come in, without there!

'Enter LENNOX*'*

LENNOX What's your grace's will?
MACBETH Saw you the Weird Sisters?
LENNOX No, my lord.
MACBETH Came they not by you?
LENNOX No indeed, my lord.
MACBETH Infected be the air whereon they ride,
And damned all those that trust them! I did hear
The galloping of horse. Who was't came by?
LENNOX 'Tis two or three, my lord, that bring you word
Macduff is fled to England.
MACBETH Fled to England!
LENNOX Ay, my good lord.
MACBETH Time, thou anticipat'st my dread exploits:
The flighty purpose never is o'ertook
Unless the deed go with it. From this moment
The very firstlings of my heart shall be
The firstlings of my hand. And even now
To crown my thoughts with acts, be it thought and done:
The castle of Macduff I will surprise,
Seize upon Fife, give to th'edge o'th' sword
His wife, his babes, and all unfortunate souls
That trace him in his line. No boasting like a fool;
This deed I'll do before this purpose cool.
But no more sights! [*aloud*] Where are these gentlemen?
Come, bring me where they are. [*they go*

SCENE 2

Fife. Macduff's castle

'Enter MACDUFF*'s Wife, her Son, and* ROSS*'*

L. M'DUFF What had he done, to make him fly the land?

ROSS You must have patience, madam.

L. M'DUFF He had none:
His flight was madness: when our actions do not,
Our fears do make us traitors.

ROSS You know not
Whether it was his wisdom or his fear.

L. M'DUFF Wisdom! To leave his wife, to leave his babes,
His mansion and his titles, in a place
From whence himself does fly? He loves us not;
He wants the natural touch: for the poor wren,
The most diminutive of birds, will fight,
Her young ones in her nest, against the owl.
All is the fear and nothing is the love;
As little is the wisdom, where the flight
So runs against all reason.

ROSS My dearest coz,
I pray you, school yourself. But, for your husband,
He is noble, wise, judicious, and best knows
The fits o'th' season. I dare not speak much further,
But cruel are the times, when we are traitors
And do not know ourselves; when we hold rumour
From what we fear, yet know not what we fear,
But float upon a wild and violent sea,
Each way and none. I take my leave of you:
Shall not be long but I'll be here again:
Things at the worst will cease, or else climb upward
To what they were before. My pretty cousin,
Blessing upon you!

L. M'DUFF Fathered he is, and yet he's fatherless.

ROSS I am so much a fool, should I stay longer
It would be my disgrace and your discomfort.
I take my leave at once. [*he hurries forth*

L. M'DUFF Sirrah, your father's dead,
And what will you do now? How will you live?

SON As birds do, mother.

L. M'DUFF What, with worms and flies?

SON With what I get, I mean, and so do they.

L. M'DUFF Poor bird! Thou'ldst never fear the net nor lime,
The pitfall nor the gin.

SON Why should I, mother? Poor birds they are not set for.
My father is not dead, for all your saying.

L. M'DUFF Yes, he is dead: how wilt thou do for a father?

SON Nay, how will you do for a husband?

L. M'DUFF Why, I can buy me twenty at any market.

SON Then you'll buy'em to sell again.

L. M'DUFF Thou speak'st with all thy wit, and yet i faith
With wit enough for thee.

SON Was my father a traitor, mother?

L. M'DUFF Ay, that he was.

SON What is a traitor?

L. M'DUFF Why, one that swears and lies.

SON And be all traitors that do so?

L. M'DUFF Every one that does so is a traitor, and must be hanged.

SON And must they all be hanged that swear and lie?

L. M'DUFF Every one.

SON Who must hang them?

L. M'DUFF Why, the honest men.

SON Then the liars and swearers are fools; for there are liars and swearers enow to beat the honest men and hang up them.

L. M'DUFF Now God help thee, poor monkey! But how wilt thou do for a father?

SON If he were dead, you'ld weep for him: if you would not, it were a good sign that I should quickly have a new father.

L. M'DUFF Poor prattler, how thou talk'st!

'Enter a MESSENGER*'*

MESSENGER Bless you, fair dame! I am not to you known,
Though in your state of honour I am perfect
I doubt some danger does approach you nearly.
If you will take a homely man's advice,

Be not found here; hence, with your little ones.
To fright you thus, methinks I am too savage;
To do worse to you were fell cruelty,
Which is too nigh your person. Heaven preserve you!
I dare abide no longer. [*he goes*

L. M'DUFF Whither should I fly?
I have done no harm. But I remember now
I am in this earthly world; where to do harm
Is often laudable, to do good sometime
Accounted dangerous folly: why then, alas,
Do I put up that womanly defence,
To say I have done no harm?

'Enter MURDERERS*'*

What are these faces?

I MURD'R Where is your husband?

L. M'DUFF I hope in no place so unsanctified
Where such as thou mayst find him.

I MURD'R He's a traitor.

SON Thou liest, thou shag-haired villain.

I MURD'R What, you egg! [*stabs him*
Young fry of treachery!

SON He has killed me, mother:
Run away, I pray you. [*dies*

[*Lady Macduff hurries forth 'crying murder', pursued by the Murderers*

SCENE 3

England. Before the palace of King Edward the Confessor.

MALCOLM *and* MACDUFF *come forth*

MALCOLM Let us seek out some desolate shade, and there
Weep our sad bosoms empty.

MACDUFF Let us rather
Hold fast the mortal sword, and like good men
Bestride our down-fall'n birthdom: each new morn
New widows howl, new orphans cry, new sorrows
Strike heaven on the face, that it resounds
As if it felt with Scotland and yelled out

Like syllable of dolour.

MALCOLM What I believe, I'll wail;
What know, believe; and what I can redress,
As I shall find the time to friend, I will.
What you have spoke, it may be so perchance.
This tyrant, whose sole name blisters our tongues,
Was once thought honest: you have loved him well;
He hath not touched you yet. I am young, but something
You may deserve of him through me; and wisdom
To offer up a weak, poor, innocent lamb,
T'appease an angry god.

MACDUFF I am not treacherous.

MALCOLM But Macbeth is.
A good and virtuous nature may recoil
In an imperial charge. But I shall crave your pardon;
That which you are, my thoughts cannot transpose:
Angels are bright still, though the brightest fell:
Though all things foul would wear the brows of grace,
Yet grace must still look so.

MACDUFF I have lost my hopes.

MALCOLM Perchance even there where I did find my doubts.
Why in that rawness left you wife and child,
Those precious motives, those strong knots of love,
Without leave-taking? I pray you,
Let not my jealousies be your dishonours,
But mine own safeties: you may be rightly just,
Whatever I shall think.

MACDUFF Bleed, bleed, poor country!
Great tyranny, lay thou thy basis sure,
For goodness dares not check thee: wear thou thy wrongs,
The title is affeered! Fare thee well, lord:
I would not be the villain that thou think'st
For the whole space that's in the tyrant's grasp,
And the rich East to boot.

MALCOLM Be not offended:
I speak not as in absolute fear of you:
I think our country sinks beneath the yoke,
It weeps, it bleeds, and each new day a gash

Is added to her wounds. I think withal
There would be hands uplifted in my right;
And here from gracious England have I offer
Of goodly thousands. But for all this,
When I shall tread upon the tyrant's head,
Or wear it on my sword, yet my poor country
Shall have more vices that it had before,
More suffer and more sundry ways than ever,
By him that shall succeed.

MACDUFF What should he be?

MALCOLM It is myself I mean: in whom I know
All the particulars of vice so grafted
That, when they shall be opened, black Macbeth
Will seem as pure as snow, and the poor state
Esteem him as a lamb, being compared
With my confineless harms.

MACDUFF Not in the legions
Of horrid hell can come a devil more damned
In evils to top Macbeth.

MALCOLM I grant him bloody,
Luxurious, avaricious, false, deceitful,
Sudden, malicious, smacking of every sin
That has a name: but there's no bottom, none,
In my voluptuousness: your wives, your daughters,
Your matrons and your maids, could not fill up
The cistern of my lust, and my desire
All continent impediments would o'erbear
That did oppose my will. Better Macbeth,
Than such an one to reign.

MACDUFF Boundless intemperance
In nature is a tyranny; it hath been
Th'untimely emptying of the happy throne,
And fall of many kings. But fear not yet
To take upon you what is yours: you may
Convey your pleasures in a spacious plenty,
And yet seem cold, the time you may so hoodwink:
We have willing dames enough; there cannot be
That vulture in you, to devour so many
As will to greatness dedicate themselves,

Finding it so inclined.
MALCOLM With this there grows
In my most ill-composed affection such
A stanchless avarice that, were I king,
I should cut off the nobles for their lands,
Desire his jewels and this other's house,
And my more-having would be as a sauce
To make me hunger more, that I should forge
Quarrels unjust against the good and loyal,
Destroying them for wealth.
MACDUFF This avarice
Sticks deeper; grows with more pernicious root
Than summer-seeming lust: and it hath been
The sword of our slain kings: yet do not fear;
Scotland hath foisons to fill up your will
Of your mere own. All these are portable,
With other graces weighed.
MALCOLM But I have none. The king-becoming graces,
As justice, verity, temp'rance, stableness,
Bounty, perseverance, mercy, lowliness,
Devotion, patience, courage, fortitude,
I have no relish of them, but abound
In the division of each several crime,
Acting it many ways. Nay, had I power, I should
Pour the sweet milk of concord into hell,
Uproot the universal peace, confound
All unity on earth.
MACDUFF O Scotland! Scotland!
MALCOLM If such a one be fit to govern, speak:
I am as I have spoken.
MACDUFF Fit to govern!
No, not to live. O nation miserable!
With an untitled tyrant bloody-sceptred,
When shalt thou see thy wholesome days again,
Since that the truest issue of thy throne
By his own interdiction stands accurst,
And does blaspheme his breed? Thy royal father
Was a most sainted king; the queen that bore thee
Oft'ner upon her knees than on her feet,

Died every day she lived. Fare thee well!
These evils thou repeat'st upon thyself
Hath banished me from Scotland. O my breast,
Thy hope ends here!

MALCOLM Macduff, this noble passion,
Child of integrity, hath from my soul
Wiped the black scruples, reconciled my thoughts
To thy good truth and honour. Devilish Macbeth
By many of these trains hath sought to win me
Into his power: and modest wisdom plucks me
From over-credulous haste: but God above
Deal between thee and me! for even now
I put myself to thy direction, and
Unspeak mine own detraction; here abjure
The taints and blames I laid upon myself,
For strangers to my nature. I am yet
Unknown to woman, never was forsworn,
Scarcely have coveted what was mine own,
At no time broke my faith, would not betray
The devil to his fellow, and delight
No less in truth than life: my first false speaking
Was this upon myself: what I am truly
Is thine and my poor country's to command:
Whither indeed, before thy here-approach,
Old Siward, with ten thousand warlike men,
Already at a point, was setting forth:
Now we'll together, and the chance of goodness
Be like our warranted quarrel! Why are you silent?

MACDUFF Such welcome and unwelcome things at once
'Tis hard to reconcile.

'A Doctor' comes from the palace

MALCOLM Well, more anon. Comes the king forth, I pray you?

DOCTOR Ay, sir: there are a crew of wretched souls
That stay his cure: their malady convinces
The great assay of art; but at his touch,
Such sanctity hath heaven given his hand,
They presently amend.

MALCOLM I thank you, doctor. [*the Doctor goes*

MACDUFF What's the disease he means?

MALCOLM 'Tis called the evil:
A most miraculous work in this good king,
Which often, since my here-remain in England,
I have seen him do. How he solicits heaven,
Himself best knows: but strangely-visited people,
All swoln and ulcerous, pitiful to the eye,
The mere despair of surgery, he cures,
Hanging a golden stamp about their necks,
Put on with holy prayers: and 'tis spoken,
To the succeeding royalty he leaves
The healing benediction. With this strange virtue
He hath a heavenly gift of prophecy,
And sundry blessings hang about his throne
That speak him full of grace.

ROSS *approaches*

MACDUFF See who comes here.
MALCOLM My countryman; but yet I know him not.
MACDUFF My ever gentle cousin, welcome hither.
MALCOLM I know him now: good God, betimes remove
The means that makes us strangers!
ROSS Sir, amen.
MACDUFF Stands Scotland where it did?
ROSS Alas, poor country,
Almost afraid to know itself! It cannot
Be called our mother, but our grave; where nothing,
But who knows nothing, is once seen to smile;
Where sighs and groans and shrieks that rend the air,
Are made, not marked; where violent sorrow seems
A modern ecstasy: the dead man's knell
Is there scarce asked for who, and good men's lives
Expire before the flowers in their caps,
Dying or ere they sicken.
MACDUFF O, relation
Too nice, and yet too true!
MALCOLM What's the newest grief?
ROSS That of an hour's age doth hiss the speaker;
Each minute teems a new one.
MACDUFF How does my wife?
ROSS Why, well.

MACDUFF And all my children?
ROSS Well too.
MACDUFF The tyrant has not battered at their peace?
ROSS No, they were well at peace, when I did leave 'em.
MACDUFF Be not a niggard of your speech: how goes't?
ROSS When I came hither to transport the tidings
Which I have heavily borne, there ran a rumour
Of many worthy fellows that were out;
Which was to my belief witnessed the rather,
For that I saw the tyrant's power a-foot.
Now is the time of help: your eye in Scotland
Would create soldiers, make our women fight,
To doff their dire distresses.
MALCOLM Be't their comfort
We are coming thither: gracious England hath
Lent us good Siward and ten thousand men;
An older and a better soldier none
That Christendom gives out.
ROSS Would I could answer
This comfort with the like! But I have words,
That would be howled out in the desert air,
Where hearing should not latch them.
MACDUFF What concern they?
The general cause? Or is it a fee-grief
Due to some single breast?
ROSS No mind that's honest
But in it shares some woe, though the main part
Pertains to you alone.
MACDUFF If it be mine,
Keep it not from me, quickly let me have it.
ROSS Let not your ears despise my tongue for ever,
Which shall possess them with the heaviest sound
That ever yet they heard.
MACDUFF Humh! I guess at it.
ROSS Your castle is surprised; your wife and babes
Savagely slaughtered: to relate the manner,
Were, on the quarry of these murdered deer,
To add the death of you.
MALCOLM Merciful heaven!

What, man! Ne'er pull your hat upon your brows;
Give sorrow words: the grief that does not speak
Whispers the o'er-fraught heart and bids it break.

MACDUFF My children too?

ROSS Wife, children, servants, all
That could be found.

MACDUFF And I must be from thence!
My wife killed too?

ROSS I have said.

MALCOLM Be comforted:
Let's make us med'cines of our great revenge,
To cure this deadly grief.

MACDUFF He has no children. All my pretty ones?
Did you say all? O, hell-kite! All?
What, all my pretty chickens and their dam
At one fell swoop?

MALCOLM Dispute it like a man.

MACDUFF I shall do so;
But I must also feel it as a man:
I cannot but remember such things were,
That were most precious to me. Did heaven look on,
And would not take their part? Sinful Macduff,
They were all struck for thee! Naught that I am,
Not for their own demerits, but for mine,
Fell slaughter on their souls: heaven rest them now!

MALCOLM Be this the whetstone of your sword: let grief
Convert to anger; blunt not the heart, enrage it.

MACDUFF O, I could play the woman with mine eyes,
And braggart with my tongue! But, gentle heavens,
Cut short all intermission; front to front
Bring thou this fiend of Scotland and myself;
Within my sword's length set him; if he 'scape,
Heaven forgive him too!

MALCOLM This tune goes manly.
Come, go we to the king, our power is ready,
Our lack is nothing but our leave. Macbeth
Is ripe for shaking, and the powers above
Put on their instruments. Receive what cheer you may;
The night is long that never finds the day. [*they go*

ACT 5 SCENE 1

Dunsinane. A room in the castle. 'Enter a Doctor of Physic, and a Waiting Gentlewoman'

DOCTOR I have two nights watched with you, but can perceive no truth in your report. When was it she last walked?

G'WOMAN Since his majesty went into the field, I have seen her rise from her bed, throw her night-gown upon her, unlock her closet, take forth paper, fold it, write upon't, read it, afterwards seal it, and again return to bed; yet all this while in a most fast sleep.

DOCTOR A great perturbation in nature, to receive at once the benefit of sleep and do the effects of watching! In this slumbry agitation, besides her walking and other actual performances, what, at any time, have you heard her say?

G'WOMAN That, sir, which I will not report after her.

DOCTOR You may to me, and 'tis most meet you should.

G'WOMAN Neither to you nor anyone, having no witness to confirm my speech.

'Enter LADY*'* MACBETH, *'with a taper'*

Lo you, here she comes! This is her very guise, and upon my life fast asleep. Observe her, stand close.

DOCTOR How came she by that light?

G'WOMAN Why, it stood by her: she has light by her continually, 'tis her command.

DOCTOR You see, her eyes are open.

G'WOMAN Ay, but their sense are shut.

DOCTOR What is it she does now? Look, how she rubs her hands.

G'WOMAN It is an accustomed action with her, to seem thus washing her hands: I have known her continue in this a quarter of an hour.

LADY M. Yet here's a spot.

DOCTOR Hark, she speaks! I will set down what comes from her, to satisfy my remembrance the more strongly.

LADY M. Out, damnèd spot! Out, I say! One: two: why, then 'tis time to do't. Hell is murky! Fie, my lord, fie! A soldier, and afeard? What need we fear who knows it, when none can call our power to accompt? Yet who would have thought the old man to have had so much blood in him?

DOCTOR Do you mark that?

LADY M. The thane of Fife had a wife; where is she now? What, will these hands ne'er be clean? No more o'that, my lord, no more o'that: you mar all with this starting.

DOCTOR Go to, go to; you have known what you should not.

G'WOMAN She has spoke what she should not, I am sure of that: heaven knows what she has known.

LADY M. Here's the smell of the blood still: all the perfumes of Arabia will not sweeten this little hand. Oh! oh! oh!

DOCTOR What a sigh is there! The heart is sorely charged.

G'WOMAN I would not have such a heart in my bosom, for the dignity of the whole body.

DOCTOR Well, well, well, –

G'WOMAN Pray God it be, sir.

DOCTOR This disease is beyond my practice: yet I have known those which have walked in their sleep who have died holily in their beds.

LADY M. Wash your hands, put on your night-gown, look not so pale: I tell you yet again, Banquo's buried; he cannot come out on's grave.

DOCTOR Even so?

LADY M. To bed, to bed: there's knocking at the gate: come, come, come, come, give me your hand: what's done, cannot be undone: to bed, to bed, to bed. [*she goes out*

DOCTOR Will she go now to bed?

G'WOMAN Directly.

DOCTOR Foul whisp'rings are abroad: unnatural deeds
Do breed unnatural troubles: infected minds
To their deaf pillows will discharge their secrets:
More needs she the divine than the physician:
God, God forgive us all! Look after her,
Remove from her the means of all annoyance,
And still keep eyes upon her. So, good night:
My mind she has mated and amazed my sight:
I think, but dare not speak.

G'WOMAN Good night, good doctor.

[*they go*

SCENE 2

The country near Dunsinane. 'Drum and Colours. Enter MENTEITH, CAITHNESS, ANGUS, LENNOX, *Soldiers'*

MENTEITH The English power is near, led on by Malcolm,
His uncle Siward and the good Macduff.
Revenges burn in them: for their dear causes
Would to the bleeding and the grim alarm
Excite the mortified man.

ANGUS Near Birnam wood
Shall we well meet them, that way are they coming.

CAITHNESS Who knows if Donalbain be with his brother?

LENNOX For certain, sir, he is not: I have a file
Of all the gentry: there is Siward's son,
And many unrough youths, that even now
Protest their first of manhood.

MENTEITH What does the tyrant?

CAITHNESS Great Dunsinane he strongly fortifies:
Some say he's mad; others, that lesser hate him,
Do call it valiant fury: but, for certain,
He cannot buckle his distempered cause
Within the belt of rule.

ANGUS Now does he feel
His secret murders sticking on his hands;
Now minutely revolts upbraid his faith-breach;
Those he commands move only in command,
Nothing in love: now does he feel his title
Hang loose about him, like a giant's robe
Upon a dwarfish thief.

MENTEITH Who then shall blame
His pestered senses to recoil and start,
When all that is within him does condemn
Itself for being there?

CAITHNESS Well, march we on,
To give obedience where 'tis truly owed:
Meet we the med'cine of the sickly weal,
And with him pour we, in our country's purge,

Each drop of us.

LENNOX Or so much as it needs
To dew the sovereign flower and drown the weeds.
Make we our march towards Birnam.

[*'exeunt, marching'*

SCENE 3

Dunsinane. A court in the castle. 'Enter MACBETH, *Doctor, and Attendants'*

MACBETH Bring me no more reports, let them fly all:
Till Birnam wood remove to Dunsinane
I cannot taint with fear. What's the boy Malcolm?
Was he not born of woman? The spirits that know
All mortal consequence have pronounced me thus:
'Fear not, Macbeth, no man that's born of woman
Shall e'er have power upon thee'. Then fly, false thanes,
And mingle with the English epicures:
The mind I sway by and the heart I bear
Shall never sag with doubt nor shake with fear.

A 'servant' enters

The devil damn thee black, thou cream-faced loon!
Where got'st thou that goose look?

SERVANT There is ten thousand –

MACBETH Geese, villain?

SERVANT Soldiers, sir.

MACBETH Go prick thy face and over-red thy fear,
Thou lily-livered boy. What soldiers, patch?
Death of thy soul! Those linen cheeks of thine
Are counsellors to fear. What soldiers, whey-face?

SERVANT The English force, so please you.

MACBETH Take thy face hence. [*servant goes*
Seton! [*brooding*] I am sick at heart,
When I behold – Seton, I say! – This push
Will cheer me ever, or disseat me now.
I have lived long enough: my way of life
Is fall'n into the sere, the yellow leaf,

And that which should accompany old age,
As honour, love, obedience, troops of friends,
I must not look to have; but, in their stead,
Curses, not loud but deep, mouth-honour, breath
Which the poor heart would fain deny and dare not.
Seton!

SETON *enters*

SETON What's your gracious pleasure?
MACBETH What news more?
SETON All is confirmed, my lord, which was reported.
MACBETH I'll fight, till from my bones my flesh be hacked.
Give me my armour.
SETON 'Tis not needed yet.
MACBETH I'll put it on.
Send out moe horses, skirr the country round,
Hang those that talk of fear. Give me mine armour.
[Seton goes to fetch it
How does your patient, doctor?
DOCTOR Not so sick, my lord,
As she is troubled with thick-coming fancies,
That keep her from her rest.
MACBETH Cure her of that:
Canst thou not minister to a mind diseased,
Pluck from the memory a rooted sorrow,
Raze out the written troubles of the brain,
And with some sweet oblivious antidote
Cleanse the stuffed bosom of that perilous stuff
Which weighs upon the heart?
DOCTOR Therein the patient
Must minister to himself.

Seton returns with armour and an armourer, who presently begins to equip Macbeth

MACBETH Throw physic to the dogs, I'll none of it.
Come, put mine armour on; give me my staff;
Seton, send out; doctor, the thanes fly from me;
Come, sir, dispatch. – If thou couldst, doctor, cast
The water of my land, find her disease,
And purge it to a sound and pristine health,

I would applaud thee to the very echo,
That should applaud again. – Pull't off, I say. –
What rhubarb, senna, or what purgative drug,
Would scour these English hence? Hear'st thou of them?

DOCTOR Ay, my good lord; your royal preparation
Makes us hear something.

MACBETH Bring it after me.
I will not be afraid of death and bane
Till Birnam forest come to Dunsinane.
[he goes; Seton follows with armourer

DOCTOR Were I from Dunsinane away and clear,
Profit again should hardly draw me here. *[he goes*

SCENE 4

Country near Birnam. 'Drum and Colours. Enter MALCOLM, SIWARD, MACDUFF, SIWARD'S *Son,* MENTEITH, CAITHNESS, ANGUS', LENNOX, ROSS, *'and Soldiers, marching'*

MALCOLM Cousins, I hope, the days are near at hand
That chambers will be safe.

MENTEITH We doubt it nothing.

SIWARD What wood is this before us?

MENTEITH The wood of Birnam.

MALCOLM Let every soldier hew him down a bough,
And bear't before him: thereby shall we shadow
The numbers of our host, and make discovery
Err in report of us.

SOLDIER It shall be done.

SIWARD We learn no other but the confident tyrant
Keeps still in Dunsinane, and will endure
Our setting down before't.

MALCOLM 'Tis his main hope:
For where there is advantage to be gone,
Both more and less have given him the revolt,
And none serve with him but constrainèd things
Whose hearts are absent too.

MACDUFF Let our just censures
Attend the true event, and put we on

Industrious soldiership.

SIWARD The time approaches,
That will with due decision make us know
What we shall say we have and what we owe.
Thoughts speculative their unsure hopes relate,
But certain issue strokes must arbitrate:
Towards which advance the war. [*'exeunt marching'*

SCENE 5

Dunsinane. The court of the castle as before. 'Enter MACBETH, SETON, *and Soldiers with Drum and Colours'*

MACBETH Hang out our banners on the outward walls;
The cry is still 'They come': our castle's strength
Will laugh a siege to scorn: here let them lie
Till famine and the ague eat them up:
Were they not forced with those that should be ours,
We might have met them dareful, beard to beard,
And beat them backward home. [*'a cry within of women'*
What is that noise?

SETON It is the cry of women, my good lord. [*goes*

MACBETH I have almost forgot the taste of fears:
The time has been, my senses would have cooled
To hear a night-shriek, and my fell of hair
Would at a dismal treatise rouse and stir
As life were in't: I have supped full with horrors;
Direness, familiar to my slaughterous thoughts,
Cannot once start me.

SETON *returns*

Wherefore was that cry?

SETON The queen, my lord, is dead.

MACBETH She should have died hereafter;
There would have been a time for such a word.
Tomorrow, and tomorrow, and tomorrow,
Creeps in this petty pace from day to day,
To the last syllable of recorded time;
And all our yesterdays have lighted fools
The way to dusty death. Out, out, brief candle!

Life's but a walking shadow, a poor player
That struts and frets his hour upon the stage,
And then is heard no more: it is a tale
Told by an idiot, full of sound and fury,
Signifying nothing.

'Enter a messenger'

Thou com'st to use thy tongue; thy story quickly.

MESSENGER Gracious my lord,
I should report that which I say I saw,
But know not how to do't.

MACBETH Well, say, sir.

MESSENGER As I did stand my watch upon the hill,
I looked toward Birnam, and anon methought
The wood began to move.

MACBETH Liar and slave!

MESSENGER Let me endure your wrath, if't be not so:
Within this three mile may you see it coming.
I say, a moving grove.

MACBETH If thou speak'st false,
Upon the next tree shalt thou hang alive,
Till famine cling thee: if thy speech be sooth,
I care not if thou dost for me as much.
I pall in resolution, and begin
To doubt th'equivocation of the fiend
That lies like truth: 'Fear not, till Birnam wood
Do come to Dunsinane'; and now a wood
Comes toward Dunsinane. Arm, arm, and out!
If this which he avouches does appear,
There is nor flying hence nor tarrying here.
I 'gin to be aweary of the sun,
And wish th'estate o'th' world were now undone.
Ring the alarum bell! Blow, wind! Come, wrack!
At least we'll die with harness on our back.

[*they hurry forth*

SCENE 6

Dunsinane. Before the castle gate. 'Drum and Colours. Enter MALCOLM, SIWARD, MACDUFF, *and their army, with boughs'*

MALCOLM Now near enough: your leavy screens throw down,
And show like those you are. You, worthy uncle,
Shall with my cousin your right noble son
Lead our first battle: worthy Macduff and we
Shall take upon's what else remains to do,
According to our order.

SIWARD Fare you well.
Do we but find the tyrant's power tonight,
Let us be beaten, if we cannot fight.

MACDUFF Make all our trumpets speak; give them all breath,
Those clamorous harbingers of blood and death.

They go forward, their trumpets sounding.

SCENE 7

MACBETH *comes from the castle*

MACBETH They have tied me to a stake; I cannot fly,
But bear-like I must fight the course. What's he
That was not born of woman? Such a one
Am I to fear, or none.

Young SIWARD *comes up*

YOUNG S. What is thy name?

MACBETH Thou'lt be afraid to hear it.

YOUNG S. No; though thou call'st thyself a hotter name
Than any is in hell.

MACBETH My name's Macbeth.

YOUNG S. The devil himself could not pronounce a title
More hateful to mine ear.

MACBETH No, nor more fearful.

YOUNG S. Thou liest, abhorrèd tyrant, with my sword

I'll prove the lie thou speak'st.

[*they 'fight, and young Siward' is 'slain'*

MACBETH Thou wast born of woman.
But swords I smile at, weapons laugh to scorn,
Brandished by man that's of a woman born.

He passes on and presently a sound of more fighting is heard. MACDUFF *comes up*

MACDUFF That way the noise is. Tyrant, show thy face!
If thou beest slain and with no stroke of mine,
My wife and children's ghosts will haunt me still.
I cannot strike at wretched kerns, whose arms
Are hired to bear their staves; either thou, Macbeth,
Or else my sword with an unbattered edge
I sheathe again undeeded. There thou shouldst be;
By this great clatter, one of greatest note
Seems bruited. Let me find him, fortune!
And more I beg not. [*he follows Macbeth. 'Alarums'*

MALCOLM *and* SIWARD *come up*

SIWARD This way, my lord; the castle's gently rendered:
The tyrant's people on both sides do fight,
The noble thanes do bravely in the war,
The day almost itself professes yours,
And little is to do.

MALCOLM We have met with foes
That strike beside us.

SIWARD Enter, sir, the castle.

[*they pass in at the gate. 'Alarum'*

SCENE 8

MACBETH *returns*

MACBETH Why should I play the Roman fool, and die
On mine own sword? Whiles I see lives, the gashes
Do better upon them.

MACDUFF *returns, following him*

MACDUFF Turn, hell-hound, turn.

MACBETH Of all men else I have avoided thee:
But get thee back, my soul is too much charged
With blood of thine already.

MACDUFF I have no words:
My voice is in my sword, thou bloodier villain
Than terms can give thee out! *[they 'fight'. 'Alarum'*

MACBETH Thou losest labour.
As easy mayst thou the intrenchant air
With thy keen sword impress as make me bleed:
Let fall thy blade on vulnerable crests,
I bear a charmèd life, which must not yield
To one of woman born.

MACDUFF Despair thy charm,
And let the angel whom thou still hast served
Tell thee, Macduff was from his mother's womb
Untimely ripped.

MACBETH Accursèd be that tongue that tells me so,
For it hath cowed my better part of man!
And be these juggling fiends no more believed,
That palter with us in a double sense,
That keep the word of promise to our ear,
And break it to our hope. I'll not fight with thee.

MACDUFF Then yield thee, coward,
And live to be the show and gaze o'th' time.
We'll have thee, as our rarer monsters are,
Painted upon a pole, and underwrit,
'Here may you see the tyrant'.

MACBETH I will not yield,
To kiss the ground before young Malcolm's feet,
And to be baited with the rabble's curse.
Though Birnam wood be come to Dunsinane,
And thou opposed, being of no woman born,
Yet I will try the last. Before my body
I throw my warlike shield: lay on, Macduff,
And damned be him that first cries 'Hold, enough'.

[they fight to and fro beneath the castle wall,
until at length 'Macbeth' is 'slain'

SCENE 9

Within the castle

'Retreat and flourish. Enter, with Drum and Colours, MALCOLM, SIWARD, ROSS, *Thanes and Soldiers'*

MALCOLM I would the friends we miss were safe arrived.
SIWARD Some must go off: and yet, by these I see,
So great a day as this is cheaply bought.
MALCOLM Macduff is missing, and your noble son.
ROSS Your son, my lord, has paid a soldier's debt:
He only lived but till he was a man,
The which no sooner had his prowess confirmed
In the unshrinking station where he fought,
But like a man he died.
SIWARD Then he is dead?
ROSS Ay, and brought off the field: your cause of sorrow
Must not be measured by his worth, for then
It hath no end.
SIWARD Had he his hurts before?
ROSS Ay, on the front.
SIWARD Why then, God's soldier be he!
Had I as many sons as I have hairs,
I would not wish them to a fairer death:
And so his knell is knolled.
MALCOLM He's worth more sorrow,
And that I'll spend for him.
SIWARD He's worth no more.
They say he parted well and paid his score:
And so God be with him! Here comes newer comfort.

'Enter MACDUFF, *with Macbeth's head' on a pole*

MACDUFF Hail, king! For so thou art. Behold, where stands
Th'usurper's cursèd head: the time is free:
I see thee compassed with thy kingdom's pearl,
That speak my salutation in their minds;
Whose voices I desire aloud with mine:

Hail, king of Scotland!

ALL Hail, king of Scotland! [*'flourish'*

MALCOLM We shall not spend a large expense of time
Before we reckon with your several loves,
And make us even with you. My thanes and kinsmen,
Henceforth be earls, the first that ever Scotland
In such an honour named. What's more to do,
Which would be planted newly with the time,
As calling home our exiled friends abroad
That fled the snares of watchful tyranny,
Producing forth the cruel ministers
Of this dead butcher and his fiend-like queen,
Who, as 'tis thought, by self and violent hands
Took off her life; this, and what needful else
That calls upon us, by the grace of Grace
We will perform in measure, time, and place:
So thanks to all at once, and to each one,
Whom we invite to see us crowned at Scone.

[*'flourish'. They march away*